THE OU
HEBRIDES

From the lone shieling of the misty island
Mountains divide us, and the waste of seas
Yet still the blood is strong, the heart is Highland,
And we in dreams behold the Hebrides

c.1829, Anon.

Rab Anderson,
Kevin Howett & Colin Moody

SCOTTISH MOUNTAINEERING CLUB
CLIMBERS' GUIDE

Published in Great Britain by The Scottish Mountaineering Trust, 2018

ISBN 978-1-907233-18-0
A catalogue record for this book is available from the British Library

Front Cover: The Scoop, E7 6b, Sròn Uladail, Harris, climber Tony Stone (photo Iain Small)
Inside Rear Cover: Deepest Blue, E2 5c, Creag Liam, Lewis, climber Mike Hutton (Mike Hutton Collection)

Route descriptions of climbs in this guide, together with their grades and any references to in situ or natural protection are made in good faith, based on past or first ascent descriptions, checked and substantiated where possible by the authors.

However, climbs lose holds and are altered by rockfall, the sea and the elements. Rock can become dirty and loose, and any in situ protection or abseil equipment deteriorates. Even minor alterations can have a dramatic effect on a climb's grade or seriousness. Therefore, it is essential that climbers judge the condition of any route for themselves, before they start climbing.

The authors, editors, friends and assistants involved in the publication of this guide, the Scottish Mountaineering Club, the Scottish Mountaineering Trust and Scottish Mountaineering Trust (Publications) Ltd, can therefore accept no liability whatever for damage to property, nor for personal injury or death, arising directly or indirectly from the use of this publication.

Production: Scottish Mountaineering Trust (Publications) Ltd
Layouts & typesetting: Rob Lovell
Series Editor: Brian Davison
Diagram and map graphics: Tom Prentice, Rab Anderson, Benard Newman & Noel Williams
Printed & bound by Latitude Press Limited
Maps are derived from Ordnance Survey OpenData™
© Crown copyright and database right 2018
Geological Map of the Outer Hebrides illustration by Craig Ellery in The Outer Hebrides: a landscape fashioned by geology; Goodenough, Kathryn. (BGS) Merritt, Jon W (BGS), McKirdy, Alan Peter. - Perth: Scottish Natural Heritage (SNH), 2011

Distributed by Cordee, 11 Jacknell Road, Dodwells Industrial Estate, Hinkley, LE10 3BS
(t) 01455 61185 (e) sales@cordee.co.uk (w) www.cordee.co.uk

For details of other SMC guidebooks see p480
www.smc.org.uk/publications

Lying in the Atlantic to the west of mainland Scotland, the Outer Hebrides form the largest single chain of Scottish Islands, extending southwards for some 200km (130miles) from a line almost level with the north-western tip of the mainland. Also known as the Western Isles, the group is sometimes referred to as the Long Isle and makes up the Comhairle nan Eilean Siar local authority area.

The Isle of Lewis and the Isle of Harris form the northern half of this chain and despite their names they are in fact one island separated by a 10km wide neck of land. Extending southwards from Harris are the Uists, which are made up of five main islands. In the north is Berneray, from where a ferry crosses to Harris, and this is linked to North Uist by a causeway which is in turn linked to Benbecula by a causeway over Grimsay. Causeways also link Benbecula to South Uist and South Uist to Eriskay, from where a ferry provides the link to Barra.

Finally, the tail of this long chain of islands is formed by Barra and a group known as the Bishop's Isles. Barra is the principal island in this group and a causeway links it to neighbouring Vatersay. South of these lie the uninhabited Isles of Sandray, Pabbay, Mingulay and then the last island in the chain, Berneray with its lonely lighthouse.

Out west from Harris and thrusting up from the ocean floor on the edge of the continental shelf are the remote and mystical islands of the St Kilda archipelago. These magnificent islands rise over 300m above the sea and are often visible from the Outer Hebrides despite the fact that they lie some 60km away.

There is much to interest the climber in the Outer Hebrides albeit that the best bits pretty much lie at opposite ends of the island chain. Lewis is principally known for its sea-cliff climbing, although a small range of hills in the Uig area does provide some inland cliffs including one of the UK's major mountain crags. This choice of climbing on the sea-cliffs or in the hills, whilst being close to superb beaches with the relative proximity of other activities and comforts, can make for a somewhat more relaxed holiday atmosphere.

Harris is a lovely place with some fine beaches and although there is no notable sea-cliff climbing, there is a fine range of hills which includes another of the country's major cliffs, along with a number of other crags on which to potter and explore.

The full length of the Atlantic side of the Uists is almost one long beach and whilst it is a special place, there is little for the climber there. However, the eastern side of these islands is formed by a range of hills and it is in these and on the coastline beneath them that there is some climbing and possibly more to be revealed. This is certainly a place to be explored by anyone with a sense of adventure.

Barra is a beautiful little island and whilst it is generally used as a stopover by climbers heading for the islands to its south, some good climbing areas have been developed. At the opposite end of the spectrum, and for those seeking total remoteness, there is the solitude and seclusion offered by the world class sea-cliff climbing on the uninhabited islands to the south of Barra, principally on Mingulay and Pabbay. Here there are no comforts other than those that are carried by boat.

Even on the habited islands there is a distinct feeling of getting away from everything. The smell of burning peat, the old houses and shielings, the ancient and mystical standing stones and the long-grassed-over remains of lazy beds paint a picture of a bygone civilisation. The islands of the Outer Hebrides have their own special charm and leave a lasting impression on all who visit. A trip out here is an adventure which allows one to sense the elements.

Rab Anderson
Co-ordinating author

A great many people have helped bring this guidebook to fruition, too many to mention, though some specific thanks are due to people whom without which the guide simply would not have been possible. Firstly, Rab would like to thank Chris Anderson, and Mark Garthwaite for sharing his obsession for Lewis. Colin's specific thanks go to Cynthia Grindley and Pete Whillance. Kevin's thanks go to Graham Little for opening climbers' eyes to the Bishop's Isles and to his sons Rory and Niall for sharing the adventures from an early age. Thanks also to Jonathan Grant and Susan Bain of the National Trust for Scotland, and Francis (the Boatman) and Becca Gillies for getting people to the islands safely. Finally, Kevin would like to dedicate his section to the late Mingulayan John Allan McNeil whose boat exploits were often a bit 'on the edge' and Alan (Yag) McSherry whose smile was taken too early.

Thanks to Rob Lovell (Publications Manager) for taking on this immense project as his first job for the SMC and to Tom Prentice for his expert guidance and work in preparing images for the diagrams, many of which were complex stitches. Thanks also to Grahame Nicoll, Bernard Newman, Noel Williams and Susan Jensen who have been instrumental during production and proofing.

Others who have provided valuable information include Crispin Waddy, Donie O'Sullivan, Chris Plant, Dave MacLeod, Dave (Cubby) Cuthbertson, Steve Crowe, Robert Durran, Neil Morrison, Wilson Moir, Paul Allen, Mark Atkins, Adam Ellwood, Julian Lines, Ron Kenyon, Steve Grey and friends, Cam Forrest, Ian Taylor, Mike Hutton, Mick Tighe, Keith Archer, Ross Jones, Grahame Nicoll, John MacKenzie, Dave McGimpsey, Tony Stone, Neil Morbey, Tim Catterall, Brian Hall, Grant Farquhar, Leanne Callaghan, Greg Boswell, John Spencer, Ralf Gantzhorn, Rob Woodall, Ruairidh Mackenzie, Alasdair Fulton, Adam Ellwood and Ferdia Earle. Finally, thanks to photographic contributors, who have helped make this guide something we are proud of, and that we hope you enjoy.

Rab Anderson, Kevin Howett and Colin Moody, August 2018

Sea Pink (E3, p86) Eilean Geo, Lewis
Andy Turner (photo Mike Hutton)

Environment

Access

Part 1 of the Land Reform (Scotland) Act 2003 gives you the right to be on most land and inland water for recreation, providing you act responsibly. This includes climbing, hillwalking, cycling and wild camping. These access rights and responsibilities are explained in the Scottish Outdoor Access Code <**www.outdooraccess-scotland.com**>. The key elements are:

- Take personal responsibility for your own actions and act safely.
- Respect people's privacy and peace of mind.
- Help land managers and others to work safely and effectively.
- Care for the environment and take your litter home.
- Keep your dog under proper control.
- Take extra care if you're organising an event or running a business.

Stalking, Shooting & Lambing

The stag stalking season is from 1st July to 20th October, although few estates start at the beginning of the season. Hinds continue to be culled until 15th February. There is no stalking on Sundays, although requests to avoid disturbing deer and taking alternative routes may still be made.

It is important to avoid disturbing sheep during the lambing season from March and May. Dogs should be kept on a lead near livestock throughout the year.

Conservation, Fauna & Flora

The islands are special places - environmentally, archaeologically and aesthetically. Do all you can to keep them that way and help maintain access. St Kilda, Mingulay, Pabbay and Berneray are owned by the National Trust for Scotland and are designated as Special Protection Areas under EU Law. There are colonies of sea birds on the cliffs and ground nesting birds elsewhere. Take great care and limit disturbance during nesting periods, particularly April to July. Mingulay is birdier than Pabbay and on the hillsides bonxies (great skuas) protect their territory by diving at intruders. There are other aggressive sea birds, so here and on Lewis, always be wary of an attack, particularly when standing at the edge of a cliff! Fortunately, few of the sea-cliffs of interest to the climber are badly affected by birds since there are enough other cliffs with broken ledges and grass for them to occupy.

Some of the rarer S1 species such as white-tailed (sea) eagle, golden eagle and peregrine falcon can be found on inland crags.

Willful disturbance of nesting birds is a criminal offence and if convicted, there is a fine of up to £5000 and confiscation of climbing equipment, and perhaps even the vehicle.

Mountaineering Scotland (see below) provide a useful Guide for Climbers on nesting birds, and this document can be obtained through their website. It is the respons-

Bonxie (photo Tim Catterall)

ibility of the individual to ascertain what birds might be encountered, as well as where there might be voluntary restrictions, and to obtain advice as to whether their presence might disturb nesting birds. One particularly relevant site in this guide is the golden eagle that nests on Sròn Uladail in Harris.

Keep an eye on the sea for whales, sharks, dolphins and porpoise. Information on these and recordings of sightings can be made to the Sea Watch Foundation.

Fish are plentiful, so take a rod, which is useful to stock the larder, especially on the uninhabited islands. This can also keep you occupied when the weather is poor! Fishing in the sea is free of charge, however, a permit, or at least the permission of the landowner or crofter, may be required for the hill lochs (for brown trout) although such fishing appears to be free on Lewis. Fishing for salmon and sea trout on rivers and lochs requires a permit.

When cleaning routes take care, some of the flora may be rare. The machair (a Gaelic word meaning fertile low lying grassy plain) is the land behind the coast and its beaches. These areas are renowned for their grasses and wildflowers, as well as the insects and wildlife that make the machair their home. It is a rare habitat, so due care and attention should be paid to help protect it, especially when taking vehicles to these areas.

Camping, Litter & Pollution

Responsible wild camping is permitted under the access legislation. Avoid camping near houses or in cultivated fields. Do not cause pollution, take a shovel and bury human waste carefully out of sight and far away from any habitation or watercourse. Do not burying rubbish, as this will also pollute the environment. There are ruined buildings on some of the islands; do not camp in these and do not disturb, or dismantle them to help secure tents and make fire surrounds. Take everything home that you brought and dispose of it properly. Leave as little trace of your stay as possible.

Vehicles

Many roads on the islands are single track; be courteous to other drivers and do not impede following traffic - passing places are not just there to allow oncoming traffic to get by. When parking, avoid obstructing passing places and any entrances to houses or fields.

A number of the parking areas in this guide are near peoples homes so due care and attention should be paid in order to respect their privacy. Avoid driving along any private roads without permission. Keep an eye out for the livestock, which wander at will!

Bothies

The Mountain Bothies Association only has one bothy in the Outer Hebrides and this is on South Uist; check <**www.mountainbothies.org.uk**>.

Mountaineering Scotland

Mountaineering Scotland is the representative body for climbers and walkers in Scotland. One of its primary concerns is the continued free access to the hills and crags. Information about bird restrictions, stalking and general access issues can be obtained from that organisation. Should you encounter problems regarding access you should contact Mountaineering Scotland (The Old Granary, West Mill Street, Perth PH1 5QP). **Tel: 01738 638 227**. Email: <**info@mountaineering-scotland.org.uk**> Web: <**www.mountaineering-scotland.org.uk**>.

Safety & Miscellaneous Notes

Participation

Climbing and mountaineering are activities with a danger of personal injury or death. Participants in these activities should be aware of and accept these risks and be responsible for their own actions and involvement.

The same applies to use of any in-situ protection or abseil anchors. It is up to the individual to assess the potential reliability of any in-situ gear. The rock should be treated with caution, especially when much of it is subjected to the worst that the Atlantic Ocean can throw at it.

You are responsible for your own actions and should not hold landowners liable for an accident, even if it happens while climbing over a fence or dyke.

It should be noted that due to the relative remoteness of the islands and the cost involved in getting there, visits by climbers are generally infrequent. This means that a great number of the climbs will have received very few ascents and in many cases there are no known repeats. Information cannot be guaranteed to be correct and grades will vary. Gone are the days when an author can be expected to climb all of the routes in a guidebook, particularly when it is to a far flung place such as the Outer Hebrides, so this should be borne in mind when venturing onto the rock. Any information on the climbing, such as new routes, grades, stars, length, errors, etc. should be sent to the Scottish Mountaineering Club, details at <**www.smc.org.uk**>.

Sea-Cliff & Mountain Rescue

Phone (999), or where there is no signal, drop in to the nearest house and ask them to do so. Depending on the location, Mountain Rescue or Coastguard may be called out. Give concise information about the location and if on a sea-cliff also provide details on the sea state and tide. Remember, the emergency services and indeed many locals might not know the climbers' names of the cliffs, so give them as much information as possible, including the grid reference so that they can locate the casualty. In case the rescue organisation has the guidebook, also give them the relevant guidebook details, cliff and climb name, etc. Also provide details of the injuries to the casualty and any assistance available at the accident site. If the casualty has to be left, attempt to leave them in as safe a place as possible, as warm and sheltered as you can, and mark the location.

Mobile Phones & WiFi

Mobile phones and GPS can help in communications and locating your position, but mobiles do not work in many places, particularly in parts of the Outer Hebrides. Both also rely on batteries and electronics that can fail or be damaged. The introduction to the Lewis section gives details on where mobile reception can be obtained on Lewis and Harris. The seriousness of the remote situation on the Barra Isles and some other uninhabited islands should not be underestimated and consideration should be given to a means of communication other than mobile phones such as satellite phone, or marine band VHF, or at the very least, some flares. The boatman may arrange for the loan of a VHF set for a fee.

Despite pledges from the Scottish government, the mobile and WiFi network in the Outer Hebrides is not up to the standard elsewhere.

Tides & Sea State

The sea in the Outer Hebrides should be treated with respect. In the introduction to each sea-cliff, information has been given as to whether a cliff is tidal or non-tidal. However, this does not mean that a particular cliff will be free of water at low tide. There is a big difference in the sea state between somewhere like Reiff on the mainland and the Outer Hebrides, where cliffs face full on into the Atlantic. The islands are exposed to the full effect of frontal systems which track across the ocean and the sea can change rapidly. The tidal nature of a cliff should only be treated as a rough indication to assist with route selection. It is not unusual to climb at high tide one day with the sea lapping gently at your feet, and find the next day that the tide is out yet waves are breaking halfway up the cliff. It is up to each individual to assess sea state and tide before committing to a climb.

It is recommended that some means of escape be left in place when accessing the base of most cliffs, such as an abseil rope and ascenders. Not only can the sea enforce escape but the weather can too, since it can turn from bright sunshine to pouring rain in an instant. The rock, especially low down and where it is black in colour, can become incredibly greasy, which is not much use if you are stranded at the foot of a cliff with no means of escape and an incoming tide. You have been warned!

A bit of weather watching, knowledge of the tide

times and some shrewd judgment goes a long way towards making a successful day's climbing.

One useful source for the Tide Tables is the Climbers Club Website <**www.climbers-club.co.uk**> (look for Carloway). Details of the tides are also printed in the local papers and there is limited information in some Scottish nationals. The BBC's weather website has more comprehensive Tide Tables (the UK Hydrographic Office's 'Admiralty Easy Tide') and other useful information, as does the Met Office; see below.

Weather

Contrary to popular belief, the Scottish climate, unpredictable at the best of times, is actually often better than you might think. It is often a matter of knowing where to go and when. The climate in the Outer Hebrides is generally mild but nearly always with a fresh to strong breeze. Although this makes it cooler, it helps dry things off and is good for keeping the midge at bay. The weather passes over quickly and it is not uncommon to be sat in drizzle and sea mist until 5pm to then suddenly have the sun come through and be climbing until late into the evening on warm, sunny rock. Be prepared to capitalise even when all appears lost!

The only thing that could be said about predicting the weather is that it has been found that when high pressure sits over England and the south of Scotland, poorer weather often whips around the top of the high pressure area and produces unstable weather in the Outer Hebrides, particularly at the northern end of the island chain. However, when the weather has been poor to the south it has generally been good in the Outer Hebrides - rain-affected play at Wimbledon can mean sun on rock here! In years when the jet stream has slipped south, north-easterlies have tended to influence the weather and although these make it unseasonably cold in areas exposed to the wind, once on the cliffs on the west side of the islands it is sheltered and out the wind, with slack seas.

Forecasts

Internet & mobile: Given that the majority of the climbing is on sea-cliffs on the Atlantic seaboard, weather forecasts are particularly important. You can search for local forecasts on various Hebridean localities (have a map to hand and simply enter an island name or one of a number of hamlets and towns). A number are available (the are many others) as follows:
<**www.metoffice.gov.uk**> Good zoomable observations and forecast charts; Marine Forecast; Tide Times.
<**www.bbc.co.uk/weather**> Updated UK video forecast, and if you search for a Scottish destination's weather it will give the Scotland-specific BBC weather video. There is also a Coast and Sea section which covers Coastal Forecast (Ardnamurchan Point to Cape Wrath); Tide Tables (UK Hydrographic Office 'Admiralty Easy Tide'); Inshore Waters (Ardnamurchan Point to Cape Wrath including the Outer Hebrides) and the Shipping Forecast (Hebrides, as well as Rockall, Bailey, SE Iceland and Faeroes to see what's happening further out).
<**www.surf-forecast.com**> - Scotland Outer Hebrides – various locations
<**www.mwis.org.uk**> good Synoptic Charts although the mountain forecasts are not much use for The Hebrides.
TV: The BBC probably offers the better and more detailed forecast; if required, those with access to regional variations should be able to pick up the Scottish forecast.
Radio: Radio 4 gives the most concise forecasts, although often lacking detail for Scotland. Radio Scotland forecasts are good. A good combination is the Shipping Forecast on Radio 4 (17.54 pm) followed by the weather forecast (17.57 pm) with other details (both also available online). A Radio Scotland forecast then follows (17.58pm), but usually doesn't overlap. An Outdoor Conditions forecast (18:25 Monday-Friday, and on Saturday and Sunday during the 07:00 and 19:00 bulletins) on Radio Scotland with another weather forecast (20.58pm).

Midges, Clegs, Deer Ked & Ticks

Biting insects such as midges, clegs and deer ked can make life unpleasant at times. The milder island climate means that midges can be plentiful, especially inland and in sheltered spots. One consolation is that the Outer Hebrides are exposed to the wind which helps to combat these things, especially on the sea-cliffs where it is very rare to be troubled by them. It does happen though, so be prepared.

Ticks however can carry Lyme disease, and incidents appear to be increasing, so it is worth reading up on them. Mountaineering Scotland, the BMC and Lyme Disease Action UK all have relevant information.

Prophecy of Drowning (E2, p339), The Great Arch, Pabbay
Katy Whittaker & Jo Stadden (photo Rob Greenwood)

Getting There & Travel

This is an island guide, so a trip by sea or by air is required to get to there. Caledonian MacBrayne <**www.calmac.co.uk**> (0800 0665000) run the following car and passenger ferry services:

- Oban to Castlebay (Barra)
- Castlebay (Barra) to Eriskay (linked to South Uist by a causeway)
- Mallaig to Lochboisdale (South Uist)
- Uig (Skye) to Lochmaddy (North Uist)
- Berneray (North Uist) to Leverburgh (Harris)
- Uig (Skye) to Tarbert (Harris)
- Ullapool to Stornoway (Lewis)

There are further brief details under the start of each particular island section. In addition to the standard single crossings and returns there are Hopscotch tickets that allow one to visit a number of islands. Ferry times are important to the climber, as are drive times; from central Scotland and places south, Ullapool is a shorter and easier drive than Uig (Skye) but the ferry is more expensive. A bit of a logistics exercise is likely to be required, especially when one adds the journey time on the other side to get to one's destination, such as the hour or so from Stornoway (Lewis) to the Uig sea cliffs and slightly longer from Tarbert (Harris). Take note that there are check-in times, especially for vehicles. There are also variations between summer and winter timetables, so make sure that you look at the correct one for the time of your trip. Also note that as a foot passenger Cal Mac will only allow one trip onto the boat with all you can carry!

For the uninhabited islands where there is no regular boat crossing, then the information on how to get to that island is covered in the introductory sections for those islands.

There are airports on Barra, Benbecula and Lewis (Stornoway). Loganair fly to all three and Flybe through their partnership with Eastern Airways fly to Stornoway.

There are good bus services and a number of car hire companies.

Comhairle nan Eilean Siar (Western Isles Council) <**www.cne-siar.gov.uk**> has bus timetables and travel information as does Visit Outer Hebrides <**www.visitouterhebrides**>.

Technical Notes

Rock Climbing Grades

Traditional Climbs: The grading system ranges from Easy, Moderate (M), Difficult (D), Very Difficult (VD), Severe (S), Hard Severe (HS), Very Severe (VS), Hard Very Severe (HVS) to Extremely Severe. The Extremely Severe grade has been subdivided into E1, E2, E3, E4, E5, E6, E7 and E8 and so on.

Technical grades are given for routes of S and above where known. Within each E grade, routes with a technical grade at the lower end of the range will be sustained or poorly protected, while those with grades at the upper end are likely to have a shorter and generally well protected crux. Many routes will not have had repeats so grades should be viewed with some subjectivity. If any of the older routes (most likely pre 1970s), in particular those in the mountains, have a VS grade against them and no technical grade, they could encompass anything from VS to E2.

Sport Routes: The area covered by this guide has no sports routes. However, for those who are familiar with these grades, as a rough guide F5 would be in the VS to HVS range and could be 4c to 5b. F6a is approximately E1 and could be 5a to 5c. F6b is approximately E2 and could be 5b to 6a. F6c climbs would be in E3 and E4 range and could be 5c to 6a. F7a would be in the E4 and E5 range and could be 6a to 6b. Higher up the situation becomes more complex, but if you climb at that grade you should know the score!

Deep Water Soloing (DWS)

Much of the climbing in this guide is on sea-cliffs and there are now a number of (DWS) climbs. All soloing exposes the climber to an above average risk and soloing above the sea should not be thought of as less risky than soloing above land. The impact on the body when hitting the water can be severe, especially in an uncontrolled fall, and even a slight winding could have fatal consequences. In a remote situation such as the Outer Hebrides with the unpredictable nature of the Atlantic, both the situation and the consequences should be fully considered. Deep Water Soloing out here should be practiced when the sea is calm and by experienced climbers who are also strong swimmers. A brief explanation of the grading system developed in the south of England is given.

XS – to signify the seriousness of (DWS) the old XS, or extremely severe grade has been used followed by the UK technical grade followed by an (S) grade (see below). The use of XXS is obvious! Some routes above water that have been led normally and subsequently soloed will have the normal grade given first. The use of XS with a low technical grade, such as 4b, means that if the route were able to be climbed normally it would only be graded S or VS.

S0 These are essentially safe above mid-tide with the crux up to 9m up.

S1 The water depth needs to be checked. Alternatively the route may have a high crux.

S2 These might require a jump (rather than a fall) to reach the deepest water, the crux is often high up.

S3 A connoisseur's route; needs prior risk assessing, mandatory spring tides and good techniques for falling into shallow water. The crux is often high up.

Bouldering

This is not a bouldering guide. However, a brief summary of the bouldering in Lewis & Harris is given on p245, and for Barra on p265. There are a growing number of descriptions for bouldering on the internet and other publishers produce bouldering guides which may cover some of the areas in this guide.

Winter Climbing

The focus of this guide is on rock climbing. There are few winter climbs in the Outer Hebrides and whilst they have been described there are no accompanying technical notes; these can be found in the SMC guides to the mountain areas where winter climbing takes place.

Pegs and Bolts

Scotland has a tradition of climbs with leader-placed protection. Placing pegs is considered unacceptable in summer rock due to improved equipment and the option of move rehearsal as an alternative to hammered protection. Some older climbs may have peg runners but their condition is likely to be poor and the difficulty in passing them perhaps harder than the grade given. Bolts are considered unacceptable on mountain cliffs and on sea-cliffs. There are a few places on Lewis where stakes are perhaps required (notably the grassy flat top of the cliffs at the Butt of Lewis); first ascensionists should remove these afterwards but note their use in descriptions.

Ropes

Pitch lengths are generally rounded-up to the nearest 5m. While 50m ropes would suffice in most cases, 60m ropes are now standard and recommended. It is worth noting that longer ropes, or ropes left at the top of some of the sea-cliffs, may be required to reach suitable belays.

Low stretch (static) ropes and rope protectors are useful for abseil descents. On Lewis, 60m abseil ropes (or 50m with short rope extensions) are generally fine for the sea-cliffs but on Mingulay and Pabbay, 100m ropes (and in a few cases, even longer) and rope-protectors are are essential.

Consider leaving a pair of ascenders on the end of the abseil rope, preferably in a rope bag, just in case - the weather and the sea state can change rapidly.

Brief Gaelic Glossary

Geòdha – inlet, chasm, zawn. Shortened to geo as a climbers' term.
Aird – major point or headland.
Rubha – promontory or headland
Traigh – the shore (beach)
Druim – ridge
Bagh - bay

Approach Information

Directions: This means the road directions to a particular area or cliff and its associated parking.

Approach: This means the approach on foot, either to the base of an inland cliff, or to the top of a sea-cliff.

Descent: As well as relating to the means of descending from the top of an inland or mountain cliff, this also relates to the means of accessing the base of a sea-cliff, either by abseil, or by scrambling in.

Left and Right

The terms generally refer to a climber facing the cliff. However, given the more complex nature of locating routes and accessing them on sea-cliffs, a compass direction and the words landward, or seaward, or facing out and facing in may also be used. Fore example, when describing abseils 'looking out' may be used for the location, and 'facing in' once on the abseils.

Routes are generally described from left to right and this should be assumed in most cases. The text will only mention the direction from which routes are described when it is from right to left.

Diagrams

If a route has been numbered, this indicates that there is a diagram depicting the cliff, which will be found close to the relevant text. The numbers of the climbs in the text correspond to the numbers on the diagrams although some numbered climbs might not actually be shown.

Maps, Grid References & Guidebooks

OS Explorer maps are perhaps best, especially for the sea-cliffs and their approaches. OS 1:25 000 Explorer Sheets 452, 453, 454, 455, 456, 457, 458, 459, 460 and OS 1:50,000 Landranger Sheets 8, 13, 14 18 22 and 31 cover the Outer Hebrides.

Grid references are a mix between 8 and 6 figure depending on the location being described.

Hamish Haswell-Smith's book The Scottish Islands makes interesting reading for anyone interested in the islands. For non-climbing days, there are a number of walking guidebooks available locally and on the internet.

Place Names

It is worth noting that there is some confusion in the spelling and pronunciation between the original Norse names, the Gaelic names and the anglicised versions of both. The Ordnance Survey has attempted to resolve this in some way with the results that their maps don't necessarily match with the names in use. A prime example being on Lewis where the hamlet name Mangersta/ Mangarstadh appears on maps and Mangurstadh is on the road sign, with the added confusion of the headland name on the map being Àird Mhòr Mhangarstaidh.

Recommended Routes

A star system has been used to denote quality. Routes with no stars may not necessarily be poor since information may be lacking. Some routes may not have been starred on purpose, or there may not have been any repeats to confirm the starring. Stars should therefore be considered as a rough guide and used with some subjectivity. It is fair to assume though that the higher starred routes are likely to be good, even if not quite as good as originally thought!

*	Good climbing, but the route may lack line, situation or balance.
**	A good route but lacking one or more of the features that make it a climb of the highest quality.
***	A route of the highest quality, combining superb climbing with line, character and situation.
****	The best climbs of their class in Scotland.

THE STORY IN THE ROCKS

The rocks of the Outer Hebrides are among the oldest in Europe and have an extremely complex history. They have been involved in a number of mountain building events and so have been buried and heated deep within the Earth's crust on more than one occasion. This caused them to change into a complex series of metamorphic rocks which are generally referred to as Lewisian Gneiss. They are named after the Isle of Lewis but also form all of Barra, the Uists and Harris as well.

Although the same rocks also occur in the north-western part of the Scottish mainland, the rocks in the Outer Hebrides have more in common with the rocks of Greenland (to which Scotland was once joined) than they do with much of the rest of Britain.

Most of the gneisses originated as molten material which cooled and crystallised to form igneous rocks around 3000 million years ago. The magma was generally rich in silica and cooled to form a rock called granite. Some magma, however, had a more 'basic' composition and cooled to form a darker igneous rock called gabbro. Associated with these igneous rocks there were also much lesser amounts of sedimentary rocks such as limestone and mudstone.

Great complexity

When all these rocks were subsequently metamorphosed they lost their original character. The granites changed to banded gneisses with alternating pale and dark bands a few centimetres thick. The gabbros changed to dark-coloured metamorphic rocks such as amphibolite and the sedimentary rocks changed to garnet schists and marble.

Then around 2200 million years ago the Earth's crust came under tension and numerous large vertical fissures developed. Magma with the chemical composition of gabbro was intruded into these fissures and crystallised to form narrow sheets called dykes.

After the injection of these dykes there were further igneous intrusions of gabbro as well as intrusions of an unusual rock called anorthosite (a pale rock consisting almost entirely of the mineral feldspar), which occurs in south Harris and the northern tip of Lewis.

Granite Veins

During the major Laxfordian mountain building event which followed, the rocks were again deformed and heated.

Then about 1700 million years ago, particularly in western Lewis and South Harris, numerous veins of pink granite were intruded into the bedrock. The rocks became so hot that many of the existing rocks were on the point of melting and when they did eventually cool again they formed a new rock called migmatite.

Also intruded at about this time – shortly after the granite veins – were conspicuous veins of a coarse-grained igneous rock called pegmatite. This rock contains large crystals of quartz and feldspar with lesser amounts of mica and is generally a paler colour than the granite veins.

Prolonged erosion

Much of the remaining history of Lewis involves a very prolonged period of erosion. Large quantities of rock were removed to reveal rocks which had previously been deeply buried. A major fault zone developed on the eastern side of the Outer Hebrides and the rocks there were disrupted by complex movements which took place over the next 700 million years.

By about 400 million years ago the various blocks of crust (called terranes) that form Scotland had finally moved together. By 250 million years ago Scotland lay in the centre of a Supercontinent called Pangea.

Sedimentary rocks

In the Stornoway area during the Permian-Triassic (about 250 million years ago) numerous layers of sediment were deposited as overlapping alluvial fans. Over time these formed sedimentary rocks called conglomerates with lesser amounts of sandstones and mudstones. The beds are devoid of fossils.

Thick deposits of Jurassic age were laid down shortly after this in the Minch basin which developed in the sea to the east of Lewis.

More igneous activity

The next major event occurred about 55 million years ago when Greenland and Europe started to rift apart as the North Atlantic Ocean began to form. There was much igneous activity along the west coast of Scotland at this time. Large volcanic centres were formed on Skye, Rum, Ardnumurchan and Mull. It was also during this time that the igneous rocks of St Kilda were formed, as well as the Shiant Isles.

The only rocks of this age found on Lewis and Harris are narrow dykes running generally in a NNW–SSE direction which are thought to have been associated with the volcanic centre on Skye. They tend to weather to a brown colour and on the coast often prove softer than the bedrock. Similar dykes associated with the Mull igneous centre occur in South Uist. An unusual dyke with a much younger age (45 million years ago) also occurs by Loch Roag. This suggests that, during the opening of the North Atlantic, igneous activity in north-west Scotland extended over a period of some 10 million years.

Final sculpting by ice

The Earth has been completely free of ice for much of its history but at widely spaced intervals it has experienced Ice Ages. It was completely free of ice some 50 million years ago, but, as the climate began to cool, ice started to build up initially on Antarctica and later on Greenland. Eventually when it became significantly colder about 2 million years ago ice began to spread down into northern latitudes and the most recent Ice Age proper began. The climate did not stay cold permanently, but instead fluctuated several times between glacial and warmer interglacial conditions.

When glacial conditions were at their maximum, the whole of Scotland was covered by an ice sheet which spread as far south as London. During the most recent glacial maximum (28,000 years ago) a large ice sheet again covered Scotland, but the ice was not as thick as previously. Some of the highest summits protruded above the ice as features called nunataks. A separate dome of ice built up over the Outer Hebrides and this merged with ice spreading west from the mainland.

Much moraine and fluvio-glacial material can be seen in the area around Uig. A broad ridge of fluvio-glacial material south of Uig Lodge has been interpreted as a kame – debris deposited by meltwater flowing from a glacier.

One of the most conspicuous glacial features in the Uig area is Gleann Bhaltois. This prominent channel is thought to have been eroded by a large volume of meltwater which flowed from west to east, probably underneath the ice initially. Sea level would have been much lower at that time because of all the ice tied up on the land. It is difficult to reconcile the direction of meltwater flow in Gleann Bhaltois with the position of the ice sheet, and further research is needed to unravel the details of how this feature was formed.

After the ice

In many places on the western seaboard of the Outer Hebrides, notably on the Uists, the landscape is characterised by coastal dunes backed by flat grasslands. This delightful sandy terrain is known as machair and in the spring it develops a colourful display of flowers. The sand is largely made up of shell fragments which were broken up by wave action during storms and blown inland by the wind.

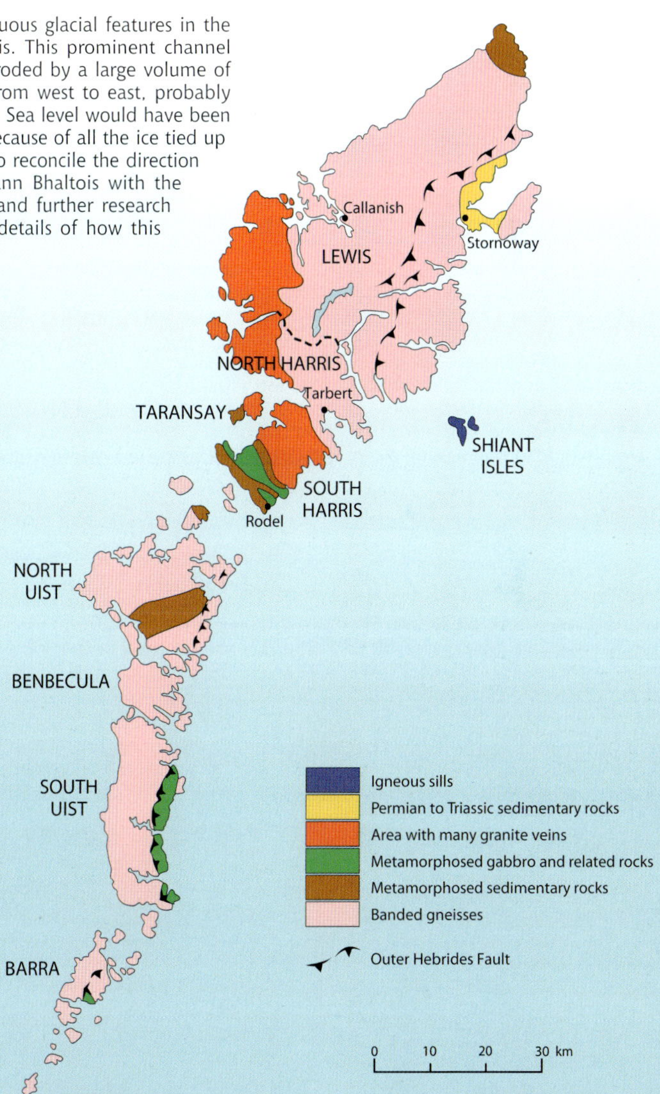

ISLE OF LEWIS (EILEAN LEODHAIS)

www.visitouterhebrides.co.uk
www.isle-of-lewis.com

As well as being the most northerly in the chain of island that makes up the Outer Hebrides, or Western Isles, the Isle of Lewis is also the largest. Lewis and Harris are in fact one island with a geographical boundary formed by a neck of land some 10km wide between the fjord-like sea lochs of Loch Rèasort in the west and Loch Seaforth in the east. Loch Rèasort also effectively splits the principal hills of North Harris from the Uig Hills of Lewis. There is only one road through this neck of land, the A859, and this provides the access route for climbers wishing to travel between Lewis and Harris.

Stornoway (Steòrnabhagh) is the principal town and ferry port on Lewis and is located on the east side of the island. Nearly all of the climbing on Lewis is on the west side of the island, on sea-cliffs and in the Uig Hills. Outwith the Uig Hills there are very few inland crags. Almost all of the habitation is around the coastal fringes in ribbon settlements and crofting communities. The central part of the island is either peat bog, or water in the form of countless lochans. Two major roads, the A857 and the A858 provide a link between the east and west side of the island. Another road, the Pentland Road (Rathaid a' Phentland) cuts across the island but this is a single track road with passing places. Although superseded by the A858, the Pentland Road is still used and should be travelled at least once by anyone keen to explore the island.

The climbing on Lewis has been split into two principal sections: firstly the Lewis Sea-Cliffs & Outcrops then a separate section of climbing in the Uig Hills.

Maps: Lewis and Harris are covered by OS 1:25000 Explorer Series Sheets 455, 456, 457, 458, 459 and 460 and OS 1:50000 Landranger Series Sheets 8, 13, 14 & 18.

Ferries: Lewis and Harris can be reached by Caledonian Macbrayne vehicle and passenger ferry service <**www.calmac.co.uk**> (0800 0665000): Ullapool to Stornoway (Lewis); Uig (Skye) to Tarbert (Harris) and Berneray (North Uist) to Leverburgh (Harris).

Mainland buses: City Link buses connect with the ferries at Ullapool and Uig (Skye).

Flights: Loganair (Scotland's Airline) fly to Stornoway on Lewis and Benbecula in The Uists (as well as Barra) <**www.loganair.co.uk**>. Flybe/Eastern Airways fly to Stornoway<**www.flybe.com**> and <**www.easternairways.com**>

On island Transport: There are car hire companies and the bus service is good. Comhairle nan Eilean Siar (Western Isles Council) <**www.cne-siar.gov.uk**> has bus timetables and travel information as does Visit Outer Hebrides <**www.visitouterhebrides.co.uk**>.

Drive times: Between the island ferry ports of Stornoway and Tarbert it is 36 miles (58km); about a 50min drive. Between Tarbert and Leverburgh it is 20 miles (32km, 30min). Between Stornoway and Timsgarry in the Uig Sea-Cliffs area it is 34 miles (54km, 50min), and between Tarbert and Timsgarry it is 55 miles (88km) and about a 1h 15min drive.

Amenities: The only two major supermarkets on the island are located in Stornoway. There is a Tesco opposite the entrance to the ferry terminal and a Co-op on the way out of town, on the opposite side of the road from a petrol station. If travelling north from Tarbert on Harris to the west side of Lewis, Stornoway is only some 10min drive out of the way. On the mainland, Ullapool has a Tesco and on Skye, Portree has a large Co-op on the road out to the ferry at Uig.

On Lewis itself, there are small shops and the odd petrol station in various places. More specifically at Timsgarry (Timsgearraidh) in Uig there is a Community Shop, which is licensed, together with post office, petrol station and laundry. The shop is regularly stocked and will take orders; it also has a small cafe and an internet connection. At Loch Croistean (passed on the way into the Uig area) there is a lovely cafe and restaurant in the old school building. Baile-na-Cille overlooking the bay at Uig does food and also has accommodation. A restaurant is apparently being built near the shop at Timsgarry, so keep an eye out for this. The local Community Centre has a small cafe and other amenities such as an internet area, a gym and a local history museum, whilst out at Àird Uig there is The Edge Cafe (open Sundays). The Scallop Shack at Miavaig harbour has fresh scallops for the pan whilst Uig Lodge smoke their own salmon and then there is the Abhainn Dearg Distillery – what more, happy campers! Apart from The Edge Cafe little if anything opens on a Sunday, although this is gradually changing, so make sure that you are well stocked with life's essentials to see you through the weekend.

Climbing Walls: There is a climbing wall at the Lewis Sports Centre in Stornoway.

Accommodation: Although there are numerous places to camp rough it is perhaps better for both yourself and the environment to use one of the recognised sites. There are two favoured camp sites for climbers.

One is in a beautiful location at the lovely beach of Tràigh Uige **(NB 049 329)** and has good toilet and shower facilities.

The other site is at Reef (Riof), close to Valtos (Bhaltos), and also has good toilet and shower facilities. The site overlooks the splendid beach at Tràigh na Beirigh **(NB 101 359)** close to a small crag and bouldering. The top of the Acha Mòr antenna can just be seen from the seaward side of the site, so the mobile signal should be okay, although getting an internet connection might not be!

There are various holiday cottages but these generally have to be booked well in advance, unless fortunate enough to find one with the odd spare week, or a cancellation. There are some B&Bs, information on which can be obtained from the Tourist Information Office in Stornoway (01851 703088) or online <**www.visitouterhebrides.co.uk**>, or locally at the Timsgarry shop.

Mobile Phones: Whilst there are some who might be happy to escape from mobile phones, there is no doubt that out here they are of benefit. Not just in case of emergency but also for those all-important weather and wind forecasts, as well as tidal information. Caledonian MacBrayne also send notification texts for cancelled or interrupted ferry sailings due to adverse weather, which does happen.

Reception in the mountain areas of Lewis and Harris is, as usual in such areaa is pretty much limited to the summits. Parts of Creag Dubh Dìobadail are not far off line-of-sight to the main Achamore antennas (Vodafone, Orange/EE, O2 and Three) on Eitseal **(NB 305 304)** by the tall transmission mast in the centre of Lewis. Sròn Uladail has no reception, although the top of the hill might be able to pick up the Achamore antennas on Lewis. Creag Mò should pick up the Vodafone antenna by the road on the hillside opposite and the Ath Linne antenna (O2) above Loch Seaforth.

The tops of most of the sea-cliffs on Lewis should have coverage as follows:

Uig - Limited to the antenna on Forsnabhal (Orange/EE), the small but prominent hill on the Àird Uig peninsula. However, there are a few windows where certainly Vodafone, possibly O2 and Three signals can be picked up from the Achamore antennas. One is from the road below the minor highpoint, before it rounds the corner to descend to the parking area at the road end on the Àird Mhòr Mhangarstaidh headland. Another is at the highpoint of the road over to Valtos on the way to the campsite at Reef, where the Achamore antenna signal can also be picked up. Another is on top of Forsnabhal, the hill above the Àird Uig road, with the Orange/antenna on it; there is road access but a walk up the steps is required to get line of sight from the summit.

Great Bernera – The sea-cliffs on the west side should pick up the Forsnabhal antenna (Orange/EE) and from the top of the slope above the crags, the Achamore (Vodafone, O2 and Three), Breasclete (O2 and Vodafone) and Carloway (Orange/EE) antennas should be picked up.

Garenin, Dalbeg, Shawbost and Bragar – The sea-cliffs here should all pick up the Beinn na Cloich **(NB 247 447)** antenna (O2 and Vodafone); Bragar certainly has Vodafone reception. The Forsnabhal, Carloway, Bragar and Barvas antennas (Orange/EE) should all be picked up.

Butt of Lewis - The sea-cliffs should pick up the Airigh na Gaoithe **(NB 533 604)** antennas (Vodafone and Orange/EE) above Ness, as well as the Borve/Gabhsann antenna (Vodafone and Orange/EE) and (O2) on Tom a' Mhile **(NB 441 574)**.

The list is not exhaustive and there are various other antennae dotted elsewhere about Lewis and Harris, so there should be reception for various networks here and there when travelling. Stornoway and Tarbert should have full coverage. See <**https://checker.ofcom.org.uk/mobile-coverage**> or keyword search 'sitefinder for mobile phone masts'.

The Flannan Isles
(photo Rab Anderson)

Lewis Sea-Cliffs and Outcrops

Maps p19 & p20

The coastline around the Isle of Lewis has been shaped over millions of years by nature and the elements, providing a wonderful and adventurous playground for the climber to explore. Not all of this wild, remote and rugged coastline is suitable for the climber, and interspersed with the good rock there are large stretches of poor cliff. Regulars who visit the cliffs will also notice the periodic changes where the forces of nature have taken their toll on the coast, even on the areas of good cliff. In the few years prior to the publication of this guide the rate of change has been more notable than in the twenty years beforehand. The severity of the winter gales and the mountainous seas they create appear to have increased, effecting changes both major and minor; the climber needs to be aware that what may have been there one year may not be there the next! Nonetheless, it is these processes that make the coastline what it is and the resultant rock architecture and the surrounding landscape is impressive. Deep geòdhas (geos in climber-speak) bite into a coastline of cliffs, skerries, sea stacks and natural arches, interspersed with rocky bays and fabulous sandy beaches backed by vibrant fields full of wild flowers - the beautiful machair. It is a mesmerising place of perpetual motion, from the windblown flowers and grasses to the shifting sky, the crashing sea and the whirling birds.

The rock itself is Lewisian Banded Gneiss, some of the oldest on the planet. Like the sea and the weather, the rock too continually changes its appearance; sometimes rough and colourful, at other times smooth and jet black. Colourful intrusions of pegmatite, quartz and amphibolite criss-cross the cliffs and when the light plays across them it's as if they have been painted. Where the rock is solid it is as good as it gets anywhere and arguably one of the most enjoyable to climb on.

The climbing too is continually varied, on all types of features and angles of rock, covering a broad grade spectrum. The cliffs are not particularly big but the varied nature of gneiss enables a lot of moves to be packed in, which when combined with the setting means that climbs tend to punch above their weight. And just for good measure, the full force of the Atlantic incessantly throws itself at the rock beneath one's feet.

Development since the 1996 guide has been substantial and there is now much to go at as the area sees more visitors keen to explore and experience what this outpost on the edge of the UK has to offer. Nearly all of the climbing is on the Atlantic, or west side of Lewis and despite the closeness of the local settlements and the comforts of modern life, there is a distinct feeling of being away from it all.

Layout: The Lewis Sea-Cliffs are described from the south running clockwise, or northwards, around the island starting with the Uig Sea-Cliffs. The coastline is divided into the following main areas: Uig Sea-Cliffs; Great Bernera and The Bernera Islands (the information

The Callanish Stones
(photo Rab Anderson)

for these islands being on the SMC website); Garenin; Dalbeg; Shawbost and Bragar; Ness then finally The East Coast.

Conditions: It is worth noting that the proximity of the hills to the Uig Sea-Cliffs can affect the weather in that area and there are times when the weather is poor here whilst further north it can be fine. The opposite can be true of course! Sea mist can occur, particularly in the mornings, especially in the southern part of the Uig area from Mangersta southwards. In these conditions the cliffs on the north side of Uig sands can be clear, as indeed can any of the cliffs further north.

There are days when the drizzle and the sea mist can make it seem like the world is about to end. However, keep the faith and be prepared to capitalise, for things often clear later in the day and due to their westerly aspect the crags dry rapidly. In the summer one can easily climb up to 11pm. A reasonable rule of thumb is that if the road is dry then there is a good chance of dry rock. If a big sea has been running there will also be greasiness from salt and sea spray to contend with, which also usually dries later in the day, if and when the sun gets to it.

Predicting the weather out here is not that simple and it does change rapidly; Lewis is called the windy isle for a reason! Facing onto the Atlantic, the cliffs on the west side of Lewis are exposed to the results of the low pressure areas and their associated frontal systems which the jet stream pulls across the top of the UK. These can hit the coast hard, to such an extent that even in summer in good weather, if the wind gets up the sea state can change rapidly to create a big swell which can swamp the crags. See p9 & p10 for more Tide and Sea-state and Weather information.

St Kilda lies some 60 miles (96km) to the south-west of the Uig area and although a distant speck on the horizon, if it can be seen then the weather is considered settled. The Flannan Isles lie some 20 miles (32km) west from Uig and are easily seen; if they disappear then poor weather or a squall could be expected.

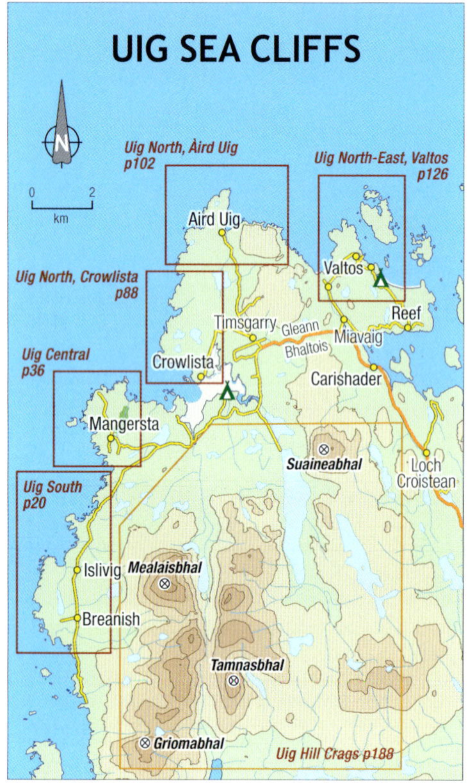

Uig Sea-Cliffs

Maps p19 & above

Uig is undoubtedly the jewel in the crown of Lewis, containing the best scenery and the bulk of the sea-cliff climbing, the major hills and their cliffs. Wonderful rock architecture and fabulous beaches are set amidst a rugged and superbly scenic Atlantic coastline, backed by fine hills and idyllic little lochans. For this reason many people base themselves here.

Layout: The Uig Sea-Cliffs are split into the following five main sections, running from south to north: A. Uig South (Breanish); B. Uig Central (Mhangarstaidh); C. Uig North (Crowlista), D. Uig North (Àird Uig); then E. Uig North-East (Valtos).

Directions: Turn off the main A858 between Stornoway and Callanish onto the B8011 at Garynahine (Gearraidh na h-Aibhne) and follow this road past the turn off to Great Bernera, dropping down around the head of Loch Ròg where Sròn Uladail in Harris presents a striking silhouette ahead. Continue along Loch Ròg to Carishader (Cairisiader), then past the harbour at Miavaig (Miabhaig) and on up the fine subglacial meltwater channel of Gleann Bhaltois to Uig. At Miavaig at the entrance to Gleann Bhaltois a turn off leads to Valtos (Bhaltos) and Reef (Riof), with one of the campsites. At the top of the meltwater channel, a turn off leads north to Àird Uig and the climbing areas there; whilst south leads past the shop at Timsgarry (Timsgearraidh) to a turn off leading to the magnificent sands at Tràigh Uige and the campsite there. A little further south along the road is the turn off to Mangersta (Mangurstadh) and the Àird Mhòr Mhangarstaidh headland. The road then continues south past the beach at Tràigh Mhangarstaidh, then through Islivig (Islibhig) to Breanish (Breanais) where it ends 3km further on.

UIG SOUTH

Map left & opposite

This is the southernmost section of the Lewis sea-cliffs, covering the stretch of coast running northwards from the road-end beyond Breanish to the beach at Tràigh Mhangarstaidh. It starts with a minor cliff further south down the coast at Àird Ghriamanais opposite the island of Eilean Mhealasta, extending past the headlands of Àird Bhreinis, Àird Feinis, Rubha an Taroin and Seilebhig Point.

ÀIRD GHRIAMANAIS

Geòdha na Traghad

(NA 9944 2131)

On the north side of the small headland of Àird Ghriamanais, short crags rise in a bay above a lovely small beach just north of the burn draining from Gleann Modaill, about 1hr 30min walk from the road-end beyond Breanish. The rock quality is variable. **Obskua**, 12m S 4a (D.Collier, J.Hartley, 28 May 1997), ascends a thin quartzy flake to the left of an overhanging arete, reached by a scramble from the north. The walk along the coast and the setting are pleasant but the cliff is perhaps only of interest on a day when climbing is not the main objective.

ÀIRD BHREINIS

Map opposite

Lying to the west of Islivig, this headland contains six named geos. It is a complex area and although there is a fair amount of rock it is quite bitty. However, the coastal scenery is interesting and for those with a sense of adventure it is worth exploring.

The northern end of the headland contains a useful landmark in the form of the small Loch nam Faoileag, which is set back from the bay of Camus Islibhig to the north. Dubh Sgeir, Staca Leathann and a series of other small stacks and skerries sit off the north-western end of this stretch of coast. Opposite these and heading south are firstly Geòdha Caol, then Geòdha Dubh which lies due west from the northern tip of Loch nam Faoileag. Continuing south, a fence runs from the lochan to Geòdh' a' Gharaidh, into which you can walk down. There are some recent climbs here but details have not been submitted for inclusion in this guide. When availale these will appear online (<**www.smc.org.uk**>).

The next geo south, Geòdha Cam, can also be walked into and it has a slabby south-east facing slab. Immediately south again is another, bigger geo which lies just north of a cairn on the skyline. This is Geòdh' an Taghain, a narrow geo some 150m long and 25m high, where there are a number of routes. The slim promontory between these two geos is Rubha Bàn.

The skyline cairn to the south of Geòdh' an Taghain marks the impressive, large and deep Seilearo blow hole. The seaward entrance to the blowhole is formed by Geòdha Dubh Seilearo.

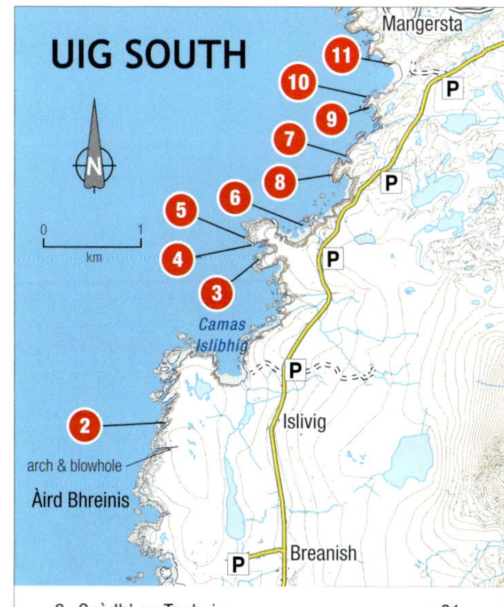

Geòdh' an Taghain

(NA 9812 2751) Tidal SE facing Diagram p22

This is first geo to the north of the Seilearo blowhole. A recognisable feature on top of the south-east facing wall is a large, angular white boulder out towards the seaward end of the Rubha Bàn promontory. The initial section of the geo is non-tidal and the floor can be gained by walking down through boulders into it. Unfortunately, despite being sunny, sheltered and appearing to be one continuous wall of good-looking rock, much of the easily accessible section is composed of pink quartz-like feldspar which is pretty loose and disappointing. However, the rock improves towards the seaward end in the vicinity of the large cliff-top boulder and this is where all but one of the climbs lie. Routes are described left to right from the seaward tip of the promontory.

Directions: Follow the road south and park off the road before the first house at the northern end of Islivig. Alternatively, continue to Breanish and turn right to park in the vicinity of the turning circle at the road-end.

Approach: From Islivig, follow a track down the side of the first croft to the bay and cross the burn by a bridge. Gain the northern tip of Loch nam Faoileag then the coast beyond. Continue south past the fence running into Geòdh' a' Gharaidh, then pass Geòdha Cam to reach Geòdh' an Taghain (1.5km, 20min).
From Breanish, follow the track through the wall and go up right to a cairn then head for a tall cairn on the far side of the bay over to the right. Now head for another tall cairn passing the Seilearo blowhole (2km, 30min).

Descent: For the first routes, abseil down Taghain Corner from cracks on top of the promontory step.

The first section lies beyond a step up on the promontory, some 20m to the west of the angular cliff-top boulder. At the seaward end a large mid-height platform ledge extends around the promontory tip. This initial section is defined on the right by the corner-crack of Taghain Corner which arrives on top of the cliff at the step up. To the right of the corner there is a deep recess. A good tidal ledge runs beneath this section and the first four climbs start here.

1 Goose Step 25m HVS 5a *
R.Anderson, C.Anderson, 10 Jul 2013
Start at the left end of the tidal ledge. Cracks up the left side of the wall lead to the edge of the mid-height platform. Continue up a thin layback crack-groove to a ledge then move up right onto the arete to finish.

2 Force of Nature 25m HVS 5a **
R.Anderson, C.Anderson, 10 Jul 2013
Start at the same place as Goose Step. Climb to a ledge in a groove and continue over the left side of a small roof into a corner beneath a large block roof. Go left around the block, step right onto it and climb to the top.

3 Taghain Corner 25m HVS 4c *
R.Anderson, C.Anderson, 10 Jul 2013
From the ledge at the base of the wall, climb up and right to a large ledge (non-tidal start) then climb the corner-crack.

4 Another Crack 25m E2 5c *
R.Anderson, C.Anderson, 10 Jul 2017
Start at the foot of the deep recess. Climb up and left to the ledge below Taghain Corner then climb the crack in the headwall above, pulling out right to finish up the edge.

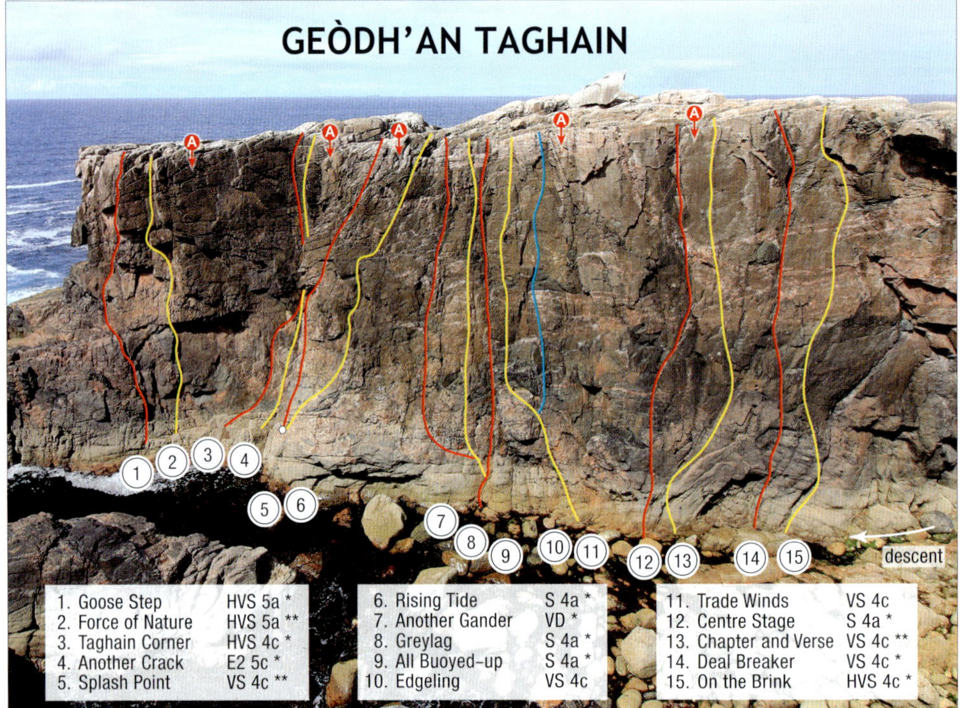

To the right of the deep recess the wall steps out and is slabbier in nature.

Descent: Abseil to small ledges; wires under the seaward side of the large boulder provide the anchors and the rope needs to be taken diagonally across to the edge. For the first two climbs near the left edge, either take a more diagonal line, or use the Taghain Corner abseil anchors.

5 Splash Point 25m VS 4c **
R.Anderson, C.Anderson, 10 Jul 2013
Belay on a small ledge below pink rock forming the left edge of this section of wall. Climb the edge overlooking the deep recess to the right of Taghain Corner to a small roof. Reach over then step right and climb to the top.

6 Rising Tide 25m S 4a *
R.Anderson, C.Anderson, 10 Jul 2013
Start at the same point as Splash point then go up and right to climb a short groove and continue to the top.

The next three climbs start from a belay on a small tidal ledge (there are higher ledges) at the base of the corner-crack defining the landward end of this section of wall. The base of the corner can be gained at low tide from the floor of the geo.

7 Another Gander 25m VD *
R.Anderson, C.Anderson, 10 Jul 2013
From the left end of the ledge, climb onto then up the centre of the slab.

8 Greylag 25m S 4a *
R.Anderson, C.Anderson, 10 Jul 2013
Move up off the right end of the ledge and follow a thin crack just to the left of the corner-crack.

9 All Buoyed-up 25m S 4a *
R.Anderson, C.Anderson, 10 Jul 2013
The corner-crack; the base contains around several jammed buoys.

The next section of wall continues rightwards from the corner crack of All Buoyed-up. There is a small roofed recess at the base of the wall.

Descent: From the floor of the geo when the tide is out, or by abseil off a small flat block on the landward side of the large boulder.

10 Edgeling 25m VS 4c *
R.Anderson, C.Anderson, 10 Jul 2017
To the left of the small roofed recess, climb up and left to ledges on the edge overlooking All Buoyed-up. Continue close to the edge past a pocket to gain the top.

11 Trade Winds 25m VS 4c
R.Anderson, C.Anderson, 10 Jul 2017
Follow Edgeling to the ledges then weave up the wall to the right, keeping clear of the leaning groove to the right which appears to be lined with stacked blocks.

12 Centre Stage 25m S 4a *
R.Anderson, C.Anderson, 10 Jul 2017
Start to the left of the small roofed recess then go up left to a ledge and climb the central groove. The line to the left needs to have the loose flakes at the top removed.

13 Chapter and Verse 25m VS 4c **
R.Anderson, C.Anderson, 10 Jul 2017
Climb the left side of the small roofed recess and continue to a finish up the thin crack.

14 Deal Breaker 25m VS 4c *
R.Anderson, C.Anderson, 10 Jul 2017
Climb the right side of the roofed recess and continue by cracks and a shallow groove to finish through a small recess.

15 On the Brink 25m HVS 4c *
R.Anderson, C.Anderson, 10 Jul 2017
Go up the slanting crack right of Deal Breaker a short way, step left then climb black rock. Continue slightly right up pink rock to a shallow groove and go awkwardly up left around two small roofs to finish up a corner-groove.

16 Disappointment Arete 25m HVS 4c
R.Anderson, C.Anderson, 14 Jul 1998
This is on the first section of the non-tidal landward wall, which ends at an arete where the wall steps back. Climb the arete on its right side; poor with dodgy rock.

ÀIRD FEINIS

Map p21

This is the prominent, flat-topped headland seen when travelling along the road between Mangersta and Islivig to the south. It is worth a stroll around in its own right for the view north across the bay of stacks and pinnacles to the cliffs on the Àird Mhòr Mhangarstaidh headland, and to visit the lovely wave-washed platform on the north-west side which slopes into the sea.

Directions: Follow the road south past first the turn off signed to Mangurstadh then the parking for the beach. Just after a narrow walled in section of the road, there are some buildings up on the left (the remnants of a former radar station) and a cattle grid, at which point the Àird Feinis headland and its prominent cairn come into view. A few hundred metres further on, park off the road on the left on the grass, directly opposite the cairn.

The north-eastern aspect is seen from the road and overlooks a photogenic bay of stacks and pinnacles. There are some big cliffs here but they are dank, vegetated and birdy. The north-west side is composed of compact easy-angled slabs which slope gently into the sea. A large boulder is located on these slabs and provides some pleasant boulder problems with a fine backdrop. The western aspect throws out three subsidiary headlands, or promontories, two of which provide good climbing.

The southernmost promontory is the closest to the road and is Rubha Sith, on the north side of which is the Searraich Wall at the entrance to Geòdha an t-Searraich. The central promontory is formed by the narrow sharp-edged ridge of Rubha Loisgte which separates Geòdha an t-Searraich from Geòdha Dubh and the northernmost promontory of Àird Point which also contains the minor Green Geòdha.

Approach: A walk across flat ground gains a fence across the headland. For the Searraich Wall, just before reaching the fence, go left and walk out along the Rubha Sith promontory, descending towards the tip. For Àird Point and Green Geòdha, cross the fence via the stile and head past the cairn onto the washed slabs on the western side, dropping gently south-west (left) to the tip where a slight rise indicates the top of Àird Point.

Rubha Sith

Searraich Wall

(NA 9923 2905) Non-tidal NW facing Map p21

Located on the north side of the Rubha Sith promontory, this fairly extensive cliff sits at the entrance to Geòdha an t-Searraich, between it and the wide Toirisgeo to the south. It was originally called the Biorach Wall when the OS named the stac out in front as Staca Biorach. However, subsequent maps gave this name to the stac in Toirisgeo to the south, so the name was changed.

The wall can be viewed from directly opposite at Àird Point, where it appears as a long, black wall running the length of the promontory. At the far left end, closest to the back of the geo, there is an area of cracks above a roof, then a slabby cracked section; the Cracked Slabs Area. Next is a recessed, slabby section; the Recessed Slabs Area on whose right side is Slabby Buttress. The final section is an area of cracks, grooves and aretes whose most identifiable feature is a deep, dark V-slot: The V-Zone. A squat, crenellated sea-stack sits just out in front of the cliff and tends to break up some of the Atlantic rollers.

The sections of cliff and the climbs are described left to right running out to the seaward end.

Cracked Slabs Area

Diagram p24

The first routes are at the left-hand side on an area of slabs which are seamed with cracks and abound with holds. Around the high tide mark at the left end of this area there is a large ledge just left of a roof.

Descent: Abseil down the centre of the slabs heading leftwards to a gain a small ledge just below the roof and head leftwards to the large pedestal ledge. A possible descent on foot could be made down the corner on the right side of this section, which is the left-bounding corner of the Recessed Slabs Area.

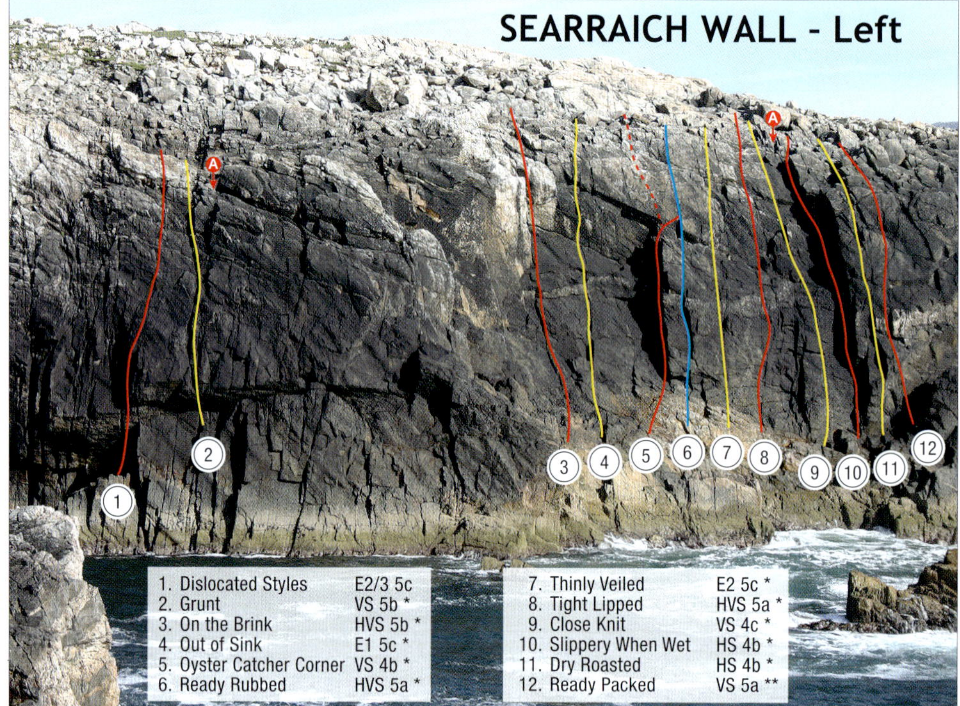

1 Dislocated Styles 30m E2/3 5c
R.Anderson, C.Anderson, 21 Jul 2001
From the pedestal ledge, climb up right to the roof and pull round its left side into a crack. Move up, then out right onto the edge and finish easily.

2 Grunt 30m VS 5b *
R.Anderson, C.Anderson, 21 Jul 2001
From the small ledge to the right of the pedestal ledge, climb the crack through the roof and up easier slabs.

Recessed Slabs Area

This is the central recessed area of black slabs. Corners bound this area on either side and a ledge system runs along its base. A central left-facing corner effectively splits this area into two sections. The climbs are generally short and ease with height; the rock is good.

Descent: Defining the right or seaward side of this area is a slabby corner; abseil down this from a large boulder 5m back from its top, it is also possible to scramble in down the left side.

3 On the Brink 20m HVS 5b *
R.Anderson, C.Anderson, 12 Jul 2012
At the left side of this recessed section, climb an obvious crack then an interesting white corner.

4 Out of Sink 20m E1 5c *
R.Anderson, C.Anderson, 12 Jul 2012
In the centre of this section climb a crack to a difficult finish up the crack in the headwall; lovely crux moves but a bit unbalanced in grade.

5 Oyster Catcher Corner 25m VS 4b *
R.Anderson, C.Anderson, 12 Jul 2012
The central left-facing corner. Either finish up the crack in the upper slab as for Ready Rubbed, or step left and climb the slab above the corner (5a).

6 Ready Rubbed 25m HVS 5a *
R.Anderson, C.Anderson, 14 Jul 2002
The groove just right of the arete forming the central corner; finish up a thin crack in the upper slab.

7 Thinly Veiled 25m E2 5c *
R.Anderson, C.Anderson, 12 Jul 2012
The hairline crack just right of Ready Rubbed.

8 Tight Lipped 25m HVS 5a *
R.Anderson, C.Anderson, 14 Jul 2002
The thin crack in the middle of this slab.

9 Close Knit 25m VS 4c *
R.Anderson, C.Anderson, 14 Jul 2002
The crack 3m to the left of the slabby corner at the right side of the slabs.

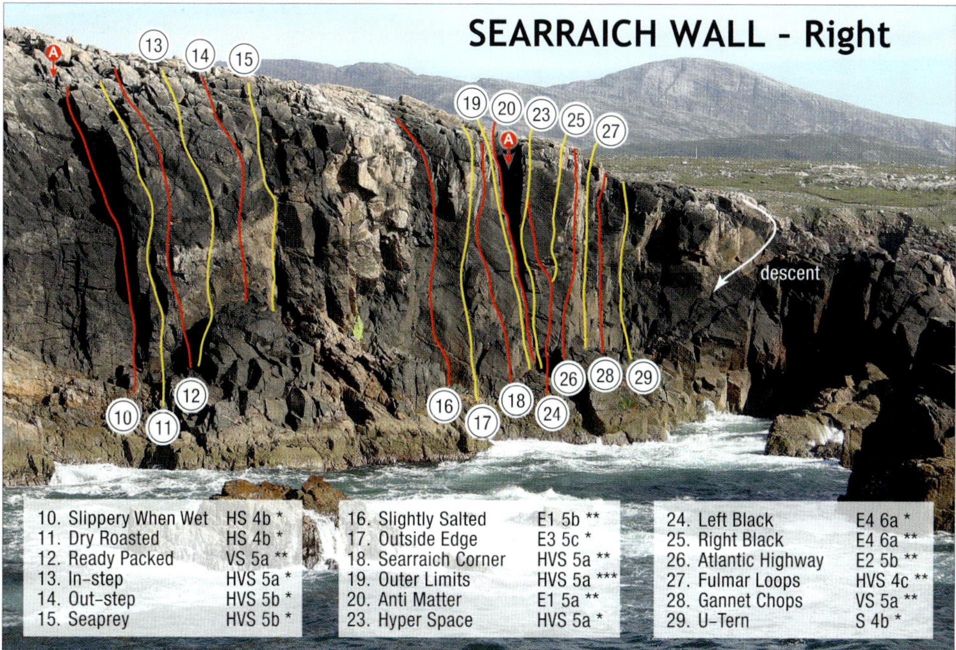

10 Slippery When Wet 25m HS 4b *
R.Anderson, C.Anderson, 12 Jul 2012
The corner which defines the right side of the Recessed Slabs.

Slabby Buttress

This small buttress is bounded on its left by the corner of Slippery When Wet, which defines the right side of the Recessed Slabs, and on its right by a steep corner, to the right of which is a tidal rift before the final area of cliff. At the base of the buttress there is a sheltered trough well above the sea.

Descent: By abseil, as for the Recessed Slabs Area from the large boulder above Slippery When Wet, or down the buttress itself from boulders further west.

11 Dry Roasted 20m HS 4b *
R.Anderson, C.Anderson, 18 Jul 2001
From the base of the corner of Slippery When Wet, step right and climb the rib to the top.

12 Ready Packed 20m VS 5a **
R.Anderson, C.Anderson, 14 Jul 2002
A parallel line to Dry Roasted, starting just up to the right. Climb a short wall then go directly up quartzy rock to finish up the ensuing slabs.

13 In-step 20m HVS 5a *
R.Anderson, C.Anderson, 13 Jul 2002
Start in the centre of the buttress at the highest point of the trough and climb short steep, stepped walls to gain a crack-line; follow this to the top.

14 Out-step 20m HVS 5b *
R.Anderson, C.Anderson, 13 Jul 2002
Immediately right of In-step, climb stepped walls to an obvious right-angled groove in the right side of a block like overlap. Enter the groove and continue to the top. It is possible to start up Out-step and go left to finish up In-step at about VS 4b.

15 Seaprey 25m HVS 5b *
R.Anderson, C.Anderson, 13 Jul 2002
Start beneath the right-bounding arete of the buttress at the lowest point of the trough. Climb a groove in the arete and move up until forced steeply up right into the corner, which is followed to the top.

The V-Zone

The steeper area of grooves and aretes on the right side of the promontory just before it ends at the seaward tip. A deep, full height V-slot is located towards the centre of this section. Fine rock and good ledges above the high tide mark make this a useful venue.

Descent: Abseil down the left wall of the V-slot. It is possible to scramble in down the right (seaward) end of the cliff.

16 Slightly Salted 20m E1 5b **
R.Anderson. C.Anderson, 18 Jul 2001
This lies at the left end of this section, to the right of a tidal rift, on the other side of which is Slabby Buttress. Around the edge to the left of Searraich Corner, climb a slanting, sharp crack leading to a finish up a short corner.

17 Outside Edge 15m E3 5c *
R.Anderson, C.Anderson, 12 Aug 2006
The arete left of Searraich Corner; started on the right.

18 Searraich Corner 20m HVS 5a **
R.Anderson. C.Anderson, 18 Jul 2001
The leaning black corner left of the V-slot. There has been some wave damage at the start and it is not sure how this has affected the route.

19 Outer Limits 20m HVS 5a ***
R.Anderson. C.Anderson, 18 Jul 2001
The crack in the right side of the left arete of the V-slot; a bold start gives the crux.

20 Anti Matter 20m E1 5a **
R.Anderson, C.Anderson, 19 Jul 2001
The crack-line running up the left wall at the entrance to the V-slot has some quite bold climbing.

21 Black Hole 20m E1 5a *
R.Anderson, C.Anderson, 19 Jul 2001
Move up into the V-slot and climb the black seams up the left wall.

22 The Singularity 20m VS 5a *
R.Anderson, C.Anderson, 19 Jul 2001
The V-slot via the left-hand fork.

23 Hyper Space 20m HVS 5a *
R.Anderson, C.Anderson, 19 Jul 2001
At the entrance to the V-slot, bridge up, then transfer to cracks in the right arete and climb these until it is possible to swing around onto the frontal edge, up which a finish is made.

24 Left Black 20m E4 6a *
R.Anderson, 19 Jul 2001
The roof and black wall right of the entrance to the V-slot. Climb to the centre of the roof and place wires in a thin crack. Move left beneath the roof and reach up to holds on the left edge (RP1). A difficult stretch gains small holds in the horizontal break and gear. Climb the left arete to the top.

25 Right Black 20m E4 6a **
R.Anderson, 19 Jul 2001
Climb to the centre of the roof and place wires in a thin crack. Pull up past these to a hold at the end of the horizontal break and move up onto the right arete. Continue up this and finish more centrally.

26 Atlantic Highway 20m E2 5b **
R.Anderson, C.Anderson, 18 Jul 2001
The outer arete to the right of the V-slot, the first half climbed on the left side the remainder on the right. A fine little route that packs a lot in.

27 Fulmar Loops 20m HVS 4c **
R.Anderson, C.Anderson, 18 Jul 2001
Just to the right of the arete is a wide, recessed groove line with seamed rock. Climb the right side and finish more directly.

28 Gannet Chops 20m VS 5a **
R.Anderson, C.Anderson, 19 Jul 2001
Just right of Fulmar Loops, climb the corner-groove line with a white quartzy left wall to finish directly up cracks.

29 U-Tern 20m S 4b *
R.Anderson, C.Anderson, 19 Jul 2001
The black, stepped corner-groove line just right of Gannet Chops.

Outer Limits (HVS) Claire McElwain (photo Steve Grey)

Green Geòdha

(NA 9917 2923) Non-tidal SW facing Map p21

Immediately south of Àird Point is a small, narrow geo at the entrance to Geòdha Dubh. When viewed from directly opposite, on the platform just before the slabby descent to Àird Point, the most obvious line is a long left-slanting corner-crack on greenish coloured rock.

Descent: Either scramble in, or abseil in just left of the corner-crack.

Greenstone Cowboy 15m E2 5b
R.Anderson, C.Anderson, 14 Jul 2001
The left-slanting corner-crack.

Greensleeves 15m VS 4b *
R.Anderson, C.Anderson, 14 Jul 2001
The slabby, stepped rib left of the crack. There is no gear until just below the top, but the climbing is easy and the rock good.

Over the back from here to the south-east is a wall facing the Searraich Wall, which forms a gigantic overlapped slab. At low tide this can be approached easily from the bay; otherwise a 35m traverse out to the slab is needed.

Route Major 60m S
J.R.Mackenzie, A.MacDonald, A.MacDonald, 17 Aug 1971
Start beneath the left-hand corner and go up a slab to step left into a corner. Climb a chimney and belay in a recess. Surmount the overlap above then go easily left and up a steep corner on big loose holds. Traverse right to the centre of the slabs to follow fault-lines to finish.

Àird Point

(NA 9913 2926) Tidal W facing Map p21

Located just to the north of the entrance to Green Geòdha this good cliff is close to the western tip of the Àird Feinis headland. Although the crag looks small the routes pack a punch and have a surprisingly big feel to them. The rock is steep and perfect; no doubt due to the continual battering it takes from the sea as indicated by the very active blowhole in the narrow rift just to the west.

Descent: The base of the crag can be reached by scrambling down its southern side. Although easy it is perhaps advisable to leave a rope down the final slab to the foot of the crag in case the rock gets soaked. At low tide in calm seas it is possible to reach all the routes from here. At other times only two are accessible and then sometimes only just! The left-hand route on the wall can be reached by scrambling, or abseiling down a long sloping V shaped groove on the north then down a short step to a large plinth. This is not a place to be in rough seas and even in moderate conditions, a tied-down belayer wearing waterproofs may be required, especially for the aptly named Wave Dancing.

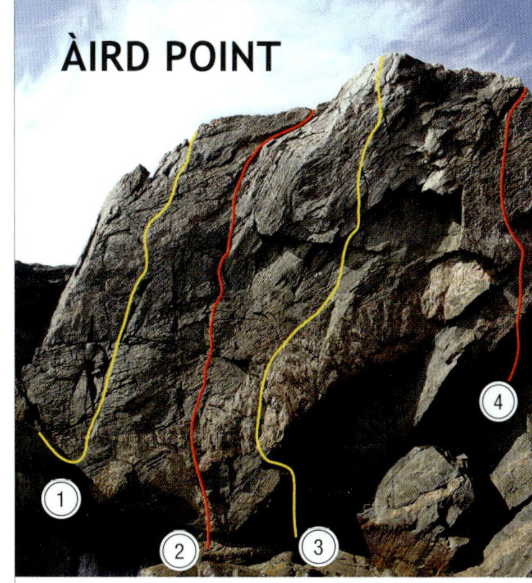

1. Tidal Rave E4 6a **
2. Wave Dancing E4 6a ***
3. Top Tackle Tips E6 6a ***
4. Spicy Wall E7 6c *

1 Tidal Rave 20m E4 6a **
R.Anderson, C.Anderson, 14 Jul 2001
The left-hand route. From the raised plinth at the left side of the wall, descend a short way to a small ledge just above the high tide mark. Step into a crack-line and climb this to a break, then go steeply up right to where it fades at an obvious hold. Pull through the quartzy section and finish directly. There is a good link from this route into the top of Wave Dancing (E4 5c, I.Taylor, T.Fryer, Apr 2008).

2 Wave Dancing 25m E4 6a ***
R.Anderson, C.Anderson, D.Cuthbertson, 17 Jul 2001
A brilliant route up the crack-line and slight depression in the centre of the wall. A handrail to the right of the line enables a side runner of sorts to be placed in the flake-crack of Top Tackle Tips - more to stop one rolling off into the sea than hitting the ground. From a jug in the middle of the wall, boulder directly up pink quartzy rock to a horizontal break. Forge up the middle of the wall through a pink vein and continue in the same line to the top.

3 Top Tackle Tips 25m E6 6a ***
D Cuthbertson, R.Anderson, 17 Jul 2001
A stunning route up the right side of the wall. Just right of Wave Dancing is an obvious jutting pedestal hold. Hand-traverse the hold, swing into a quartzy crack and follow this up then slightly right to a footledge. Move up to the overlap and downward-pointing tooth of rock. Launch up the wall and move up then out left just below the top.

Wave Dancing (E4) Rab Anderson
(photo Cubby Images)

4 Spicy Wall 10m E7 6c *
D.MacLeod, N.Berry, May 2014
Start at the right end of the crag at a smooth undercut wall. Move up underneath the overhang on large jugs to arrange protection on the right. Pull through the overhang leftwards with difficulty to a break (crucial cam slot on the left). Press on directly up the centre of the smooth wall with further tricky climbing to eventually gain good holds just below the top in a diagonal crack.

Crois Geòdha & Geòdha an Fhithich

(NA 997 294) Map p21

This is the large photogenic bay to the north-east of the Àird Feinis headland, between it the Rubh' an Taroin headland. It contains a number of sgeirs, stacks and pinnacles, well viewed from the walk out to Àird Feinis. The obvious, pointed stack has apparently been climbed. The boulder beach can be reached by carefully descending steep grassy slopes on the Àird Feinis side.

MULLACH AN TAROIN

Map p21

This small highpoint lies between the Tràigh Mhangarstaidh beach and the Àird Feinis headland to the south. It forms a low ridge line, on the seaward side of which lie the small Rubha an Taroin headland and Geòdha an Taroin. There is some good climbing out here but the headland catches the waves and many of the climbs require calm sea conditions.

Directions: Follow the road past the parking for the Tràigh Mhangarstaidh beach. The road briefly widens and narrows again, then drops into a shallow valley before heading uphill. Park here in a good three-car parking place on the left (south-east) at the lowest point of the road **(NB 006 298)**. When continuing south on the road up the hill, a seamed red slab on the south side of the Rubha an Taroin headland comes into view just beyond the low ridge line of Mullach an Taroin.

Approach: From the parking place, cross some flat ground then head up and over the low ridge line of Mullach an Taroin, dropping down to reach the first geo, then the headland beyond.

Geòdha an Taroin (Taron Meallach)

(NB 001 300) Map p21

Located to the north of the Rubha an Taroin headland, this geo contains three walls. The south side is formed by the dark north-facing wall of the actual headland, Taroin Head, which is clearly seen on the approach; the feature stands out when seen on looking south from the road out to Àird Mhòr Mhangarstaidh. The landward, or east side, is a hidden wall facing out to sea (the North-West Wall) whilst the north side of the geo is formed by the fine and sunny South-West Wall, the top of which is reached first on the approach

South-West Wall

(NB 0020 3003) Partially Tidal SW facing Diagrams p30 & p31

This lovely wall sits above a sloping shelf, which is only tidal towards the landward end of the geo. Be warned: if a big swell is running waves do break halfway up the crag! The wall can be viewed from the opposite side of the geo where a series of grooves and roofs are crossed by distinctive full-height quartzy bands. The cliff decreases in height towards the seaward end where it slabs off. A largish boulder sits on the top just back from the edge.

Descent: The shelf beneath the main wall can be easily reached by following the edge of the slabs at the northern seaward end then scrambling down a short step and a crack in a slab to traverse southwards into the geo. Another option is to abseil in from one of the boulders on the top.

1 The Dividing Line 30m E3 5c **
R.Anderson, C.Anderson, 18 Jul 2013
This lies beneath the slabs at the far left end of the crag, on the shorter west-facing wall. Climb up (Friend 4) and right along the obvious line where the black rock joins the quartz. Continue up a steep crack and finish up the easy slab.

2 Moac Wall 30m E1 5b ****
M.Tighe, B.Newton, D.Kirtley, J.Pollard, 9 Jun 1974
Another of the area's classics. Start towards the left side of the wall, between a cave-like recess with a huge right-slanting pegmatite vein coming out of its top and a square-cut niche on the right. Climb a cracked wall to the left end of an overlap then trend left up cracks which lead through the huge vein to the left of a smooth quartz-like shield. Climb up and right above the shield to a steep finish.
Variation: **2a Moac Wall Original**
Continues the left trend, following cracks across a small overlap; not quite as good.

3 Twelve Years On 30m E2 5b ***
M.Tighe, I.Donaldson, J.Mathieson, Jun 1986
This takes the groove and crack-line that rise above the square-cut niche. Start as for Moac Wall and climb the cracked wall to the left end of the overlap, then go up right beneath this. The bulging crack leads to an easier finish.

4 Less Awkward than The Principle 30m E3 6a ***
D.Etherington, G.Reid, May 1998
Just to the right of the square-cut niche at the start of Twelve Years On is a roofed recess with a crack out its top. Climb out of the left-hand side of this recess by the steep roof crack. Follow the crack up and leftwards to the edge overlooking Twelve Years On then move up and right into

the obvious sharp edged V-groove; climb this with great interest to a finish up Twelve Years On.

5 Achevalier 30m E3 5c **
R.Anderson, C.Anderson, 4 Jul 1997
This takes the obvious deep groove system to the right of Less Awkward Than the Principal and starts at the right side of the roofed recess of that route, just left of a prominent patch of seaweed. Make bouldery moves up the right side of the recess to gain a sloping ledge. Continue directly up the awkward narrow, capped groove into the prominent, deep V-groove above, then on up the left-slanting line.

6 Slotted-in 30m E2 5c **
R.Anderson, C.Anderson, 23 Jul 2014
Immediately to the right of Achevalier is a parallel running, left-slanting stepped groove. Start as for Achevalier and climb to the sloping ledge then swing right and go up onto another sloping ledge. Climb the left-slanting stepped groove via an awkward flared slot.

7 Neighbourhood Watch 30m E3 5c ***
I.Taylor, T.Fryer, 3 Jul 2011
Start at the next groove along, at the right side of an obvious wide pink intrusion which runs up the full height of the cliff. Climb the left-hand side of the groove to a pink and yellow quartzy ledge on the intrusion. Continue directly up through the bulge above and follow a superb grey ramp-line up and left.

8 Fulminate 30m E4 6a *
P.Thorburn, B.Fyffe, Jun 2005
This climbs the right side of the wide pink intrusion. Start as for Neighbourhood Watch and climb to the ledge on the pink intrusion. Step right onto the projecting ledge in the black wall and continue steeply up rightwards to easier ground.

9 Death Rattle 30m E3 6a *
M.Garthwaite, R.Anderson, 13 Jul 2013
This starts up the obvious crack-line immediately to the right of Fulminate, and is the line that route climbs into at the top. Climb up and right into the crack-line and climb it to a wide crack at the steepening. The continuation to Fulminate has suspect rock. Instead, traverse right to the edge then make trying moves up and right to a ledge. Step left and climb a quartzy crack-line to gain the top.

The following routes are on the landward end. The first two are above water when the tide is in. The first climb takes a huge groove which lies to the right of a massive and distinctive quartzy V-shape. Two smooth egg-shaped boulders on the cliff-top above the groove which provide useful abseil anchors.

10 Copper Koala 25m E1 5b (S3) ***
J.Lines, 16 Jun 2007
The huge groove has great climbing and is possibly easy for the grade. Take a belay on a small ledge just above the high water mark and follow the groove with increasing difficulty to pull out right at the top.

11 Frozen smoke 25m XS 5c (S1/S3) **
J.Lines (DWS), 15 Jun 2007
Just to the right of Copper Koala is a tight, hanging groove, follow this awkwardly (crux) to an amazing suspended prow above the water. Gain this immediately and climb direct to a large ledge (S1). Continue carefully up the easier and slightly loose back wall (S3).

The final section of wall to the right lies above a good tidal ledge. A block above this section of wall provides an abseil point, down the wall to the right of a huge, leaning stepped corner.

12 Daddy Longlegs 25m E3 5c **
M.Garthwaite, R.Anderson, 13 Jul 2013
The huge, leaning stepped corner is climbed with great positions and much technical interest.

Moac Wall (E1) Shauna Clarke
(photo Robert Durran)

North-West Wall

(NB 0015 2992) Non-tidal NW facing

This is the hidden wall that faces out to sea, just beyond the narrow neck leading out to the headland. It is best seen from the top of Taroin Head, on the headland opposite. An obvious crack-line runs up a depression in the centre of the wall and a wedge shaped piece of rock sits at its base.

Descent: Abseil from a threaded boulder on the cliff-top.

Wedge on a Ledge 30m E2 6a
B.Fyffe, P.Thorburn, Jun 2005
Climb a thin crack above the apex of the wedge to ledges (crux). Continue up the wall to the left of the wide cracked fault.

Mullach Crack 35m HVS 4c
R.Anderson, M.Garthwaite, 24 Jul 2005
The obvious wide cracked fault towards the right side of the wall, gained by climbing up and left to it from a belay in the V to the right of the wedge.

Taroin Head

(NB 0011 2995) Tidal NE facing

Forming the south side at the entrance to the geo, this is the big dark, north-facing wall. A prominent boulder sits on the edge.

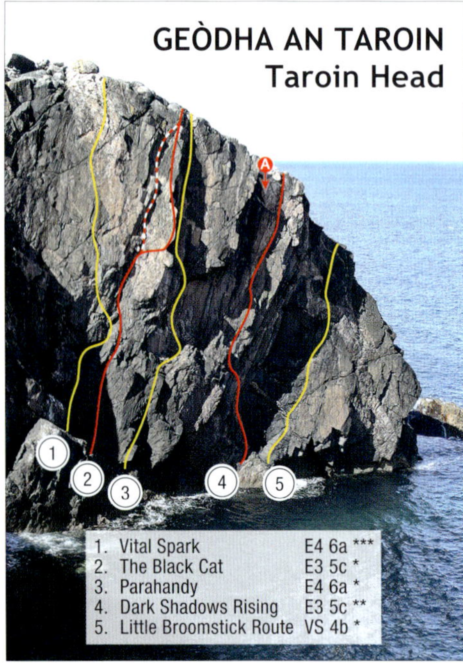

Descent: Abseil from the boulder on the top, down the face to good ledges, which form a ramp running into the sea. There is a slime streak on the wall at the ledge.

1 Vital Spark 35m E4 6a ***
P.Thorburn, B.Fyffe, Jun 2005
Climbs the wall at its highest point, starting on the ramp just left of the slime streak. Climb to a roof, then traverse right into the groove of The Black Cat and climb this to stand on a flake. Climb slightly left and up to the first diagonal break. Boldly climb the wall just left of the pink intrusion to a second diagonal break then continue more easily, being wary of the odd loose hold.

2 The Black Cat 35m E3 5c *
B.Fyffe, P.Thorburn, Jun 2005
A line based on the groove just to the right of the previous route. Climb a short wall just to the right of the slime streak, then trend up and left into a shallow groove. Climb this to the first hollow blocks. Move rightwards to gain a notch on the arete then continue up the left side of the arete past another notch to the top. Gained up the Vital Spark, the groove can be climbed directly on suspect rock at E4 5c (M.Garthwaite, R.Anderson, 24 Jul 2005).

3 Parahandy 35m E4 6a *
P.Thorburn, B.Fyffe, Jun 2005
The hanging corner system in the centre of the cliff. Start at the seaward end of the ramp. Climb rightward-leaning black grooves to ledges (possible belay and higher start). Climb a flake, step left, then pull over the roof into the corner system and continue more easily up this.

4 Dark Shadows Rising 30m E3 5c **
P.Thorburn, B.Fyffe, Jun 2005
To the right, past a blank corner system, is a right-slanting intrusion. Abseil to small ledges near the base of the next corner system to the right. Follow a short crack into the corner. Pull left onto the wall above then follow a pink band and exit by a large block on the arete.

5 Little Broomstick Route 20m VS 4b *
B.Fyffe, P.Thorburn, Jun 2005
This takes the wall to the right of the right-hand corner system. Start as for Dark Shadows Rising then climb rightwards up a small ramp and go straight up the wall above on good holds.

Rubh' an Taroin

(NB 001 299) Map p21

Beyond Taroin Head the rocks turn to face west and there are a number of climbs. It is possible to scramble down easy-angled rock forming the edge of Taroin Head to get close to the sea. This easy-angled descent overlooks a shallow bay with a viciously overhung wall on its south side.

Shallow Bay

(NB 0009 2999) Tidal SW facing

The shallow bay below the northern tip of the headland contains four routes on its north side; a prominent block on the cliff edge is an identifiable feature.

Descent: By abseil.

Sea Storm VS
M.Tighe, B.Newton and Party, Jun 1987
This is located towards the left side of the wall.

Ken's Dilemma E1
M.Tighe, B.Newton and Party, Jun 1987
This is left of centre on the wall.

Red Ramp VD
M.Tighe, B.Newton and Party, Jun 1987
The next route to the right.

Bay Back Crack S
M.Tighe, B.Newton and Party, Jun 1987
This lies in the back of the bay.

Moving south again there is a huge boulder on the cliff-top with a platform in front of it, where the two obvious Taroin Chimneys exit. Immediately south of this area is the South-West Bay then a sea cave with an awesomely steep west-facing wall that forms the tip of the headland. Around the tip is the South-East Face and the big red slab seen from the road.

Taroin Chimneys Area

(NB 0003 2985) Tidal W facing

The wall running southwards in the centre of the west facing side of the headland has two obvious chimneys located in its centre, exiting beside a huge boulder on the cliff edge. A golden wall of perfect rock lies left of the chimneys; routes are described left to right from here.

Approach: Walk southwards along the boulder strewn ridge of the headland and cut down westwards towards the sea, then scramble down to the huge boulder.

Descent: From a thread on a boulder that is wedged under the south-west corner of the huge boulder, abseil down the side of the wide crack of Ruby Crack.

The Taroin Chimneys are to the left and the routes are described from left to right starting to the left of these.

Golden Promise 20m E2 5c **
R.Anderson, M.Garthwaite, 23 Jul 2005
Climb the obvious slabby groove in the wall left of Left-hand Taroin Chimney to a steepening; step right, then climb to a projecting hold and continue directly to the top.

Wibble Wobble 20m E3 5c **
Climb a hairline crack up the slim groove just right of Golden Promise, move up left towards the projection on this route, then go back right and climb directly to the top.

Left-hand Taroin Chimney 20m VS
M.Tighe, B.Newton and Party, Jun 1987
Compact rock and poorly protected.

Right-hand Taroin Chimney 25m VS
M.Tighe, B.Newton and Party, Jun 1987
Also compact rock and also poorly protected.

Ocean Boulevard 25m E2 5c ***
R.Anderson, M.Garthwaite, 24 Jul 2005
Climb the line of shallow grooves in the centre of the buttress just right of the right-hand chimney and continue directly up short stepped corners all the way to the top.

Gurning Groove 25m E5 6a **
M.Garthwaite, R.Anderson, 25 Jul 2005
The flying groove and recessed slab running up the right side of the buttress just right of Ocean Boulevard. Climb the groove to the slab, move left beneath the roof, step down and across left then go up to finish.

Gurning Groove (E5) Mark Garthwaite (photo Rab Anderson)

Ruby Crack 20m VD **
R.Anderson, M.Garthwaite, 23 Jul 2005
The pleasant wide crack that leads directly to the abseil boulder.

To the right, at the end of the bay, is a short wall of fine compact rock, with two crack-lines running up it.

Breaking Down 15m VS 4b *
R.Anderson, M.Garthwaite, 23 Jul 2005
The left-hand crack.

Cracking Up 15m HVS 4c **
M.Garthwaite, R.Anderson, 23 Jul 2005
The right-hand crack.

South West Bay

(NB 0003 2982) Tidal W facing

Abutting the Taroin Chimneys Area is another shallow bay just before the impressive overhung wall in the bay that forms the southern extremity of the headland. The rock is excellent.

Descent: Abseil down grooves in the centre of the bay.

Ribbed for Pleasure 20m VS 4b **
R.Anderson, J.Newman, B.Newman, 24 Jul 2005
The crack up the narrow rib in the centre of the bay, just left of the abseil groove.

Extra Sure (VS) Mark Garthwaite & Jan Newman (photo Rab Anderson)

Extra Sure 20m VS 4c **
M.Garthwaite, R.Anderson, B.Newman, J.Newman, Jul 2005
The fine steep crack in the grey wall on the right side of the bay, right of the abseil groove.

South-East Face

(NB 0005 2978) Tidal SE facing

To the right of the southernmost tip, the south-east side of the headland overlooks a bay and faces the road. There is one route near the tip, a right-facing black corner-groove cutting through a bulge just left of a deep, recessed chimney before an area of easy-angled, seamed red slabs.

Descent: Scramble down an easy-angled blocky groove to the southern tip, then make a short abseil to a wave washed platform on the other side of a rift. It is possible to scramble down all the way and also to traverse left around the tip into the impressive, overhung bay.

Kanga-Rubh 30m HVS 5a *
R.Anderson, C.Anderson, 2 Jul 2000
From the platform, step down into the rift, bridge across it then climb steeply up the obvious line leading into the right-facing black groove. Follow the groove over a bulge and go up the reddish coloured quartzy groove and crack to belay by a large boulder.

SEILEBHIG (SHEILAVIG)

(NB 005 306) Map p21

This is the prominent small, grassy headland to the south-west of Tràigh Mhangarstaidh. It gives a pleasant short walk and is a superb wave watching spot, especially when there is a big sea running. Two obvious squat, flat topped stacks lie just offshore and contain some walls of perfect pink gneiss, well seen from the road. The southern stack is a deep water soloing venue and is separated from its neighbour by a narrow rift through which the sea surges. There are also two easy climbs in the bay on the south side of the headland.

Approach: Although there is a quicker and more direct route, the best approach is from the small quarry bowl parking place **(NB 0124 3073)** for the beach at Tràigh Mhangarstaidh. Walk down the track towards the beach for 200m, then contour the hillside southwards above the beach, past a ruin; 10min.

Seilebhig Point

(NB 0046 3052) Tidal SE facing

There are two climbs in the bay on the south side of the headland point, on a small wall above the boulder beach.

Long Time Coming S 4a
C.Murray, S.Black, 2002
Go through an overlap left of an arete on the south-west side to gain a large, hanging slab.

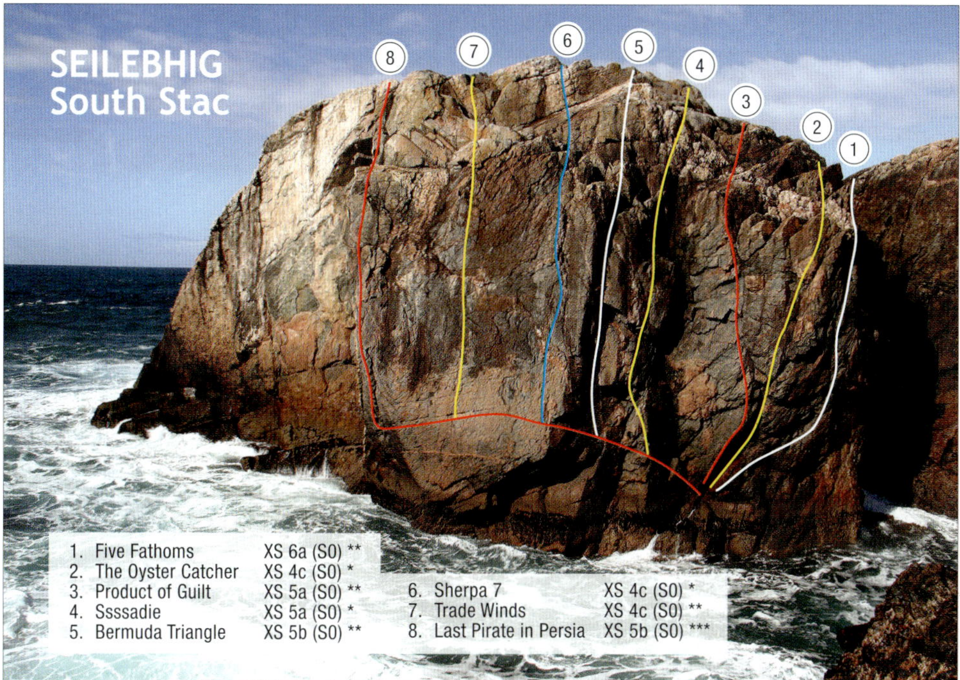

Jubilee Jaunt VD
C.Murray, S.Black, 2002
The corner on the far left of the slab.

Sgeir Seilebhig

The South Stac

(NB 0037 3051) Tidal SE facing

Two well battered stacks lie just offshore. The southernmost of these presents a beautiful south facing shield of perfect clean gneiss opposite the headland tip. To the right of centre is a chimney slot and just to the right is a diagonal crack emerging from a tight niche; 'the changing room'. The sea regularly swamps these stacks. However, on the occasions that it is calm the routes are safe, so don a wetsuit, swim across the 10m channel and have fun!

Routes are described from the changing room niche, right to left.

1 Five Fathoms 10m XS 6a (S0) **
J.Lines (DWS), 16 Jun 2007
Gain a traverse line out right from the niche and follow holds up the hideously leaning prow; short and intense.

2 The Oyster Catcher 10m XS 4c (S0) *
J.Lines (DWS), 16 Jun 2007
The diagonal crack above the niche has good holds and water.

3 Product of Guilt 10m XS 5a (S0) **
J.Lines (DWS), 16 Jun 2007
The crack sprouting directly from the niche is excellent.

4 Ssssadie 14m XS 5a (S0) *
J.Lines (DWS), 16 Jun 2007
Step left round the chimney to climb a short rib to the overlap and make pleasant moves through this.

5 Bermuda Triangle 14m XS 5b (S0) **
J.Lines (DWS), 16 Jun 2007
Traverse left from the chimney and just before reaching the right arete of the shield, forge up superb layback cracks.

6 Sherpa 7 15m XS 4c (S0) *
J.Lines (DWS), 16 Jun 2007
Traverse across and tackle the right arete of the shield on its left side.

7 Trade Winds 16m XS 4c (S0) **
J.Lines (DWS), 16 Jun 2007
The centre of the shield is a great soloing experience. A number of variations exist.

8 Last Pirate in Persia 18m XS 5b (S0) ***
J.Lines (DWS), 16 Jun 2007
Traverse all the way to the left arete and climb it in a superb position on great rock. Probably the best route here; tremendous!

UIG CENTRAL

ÀIRD MHÒR MHANGARSTAIDH

Maps p20 & opposite

West of the beautiful expanse of sand at Tràigh Uige lies the large headland extending northwards from the beach at Tràigh Mhangarstaidh, around to the bay at Camus Uig. Since it contains a number of the area's major geos it is home to the largest concentration of routes on the sea-cliffs.

Directions: Follow the road south past the shop at Timsgarry (Timsgearraidh) and 'Uig sands' to where the road drops down across the river by the Abhainn Dearg Distillery. Continue up the other side past the turning for Carnish and to a road on the right leading to the hamlet of Mangersta (Mangurstadh).

The first climbing areas in this section are perhaps best approached by continuing past this turn off for about 1km to park in the small quarry bowl on the left; this is the parking for the beach at Tràigh Mhangarstaidh.

For the rest of the climbing areas, take the road right, signed to Mangurstadh. The first areas mentioned above can also be approached from here by following the road which loops round left to its end at the houses. For all the other areas, take the road that doubles back uphill to the right from the houses. After passing through a gate at the top of the hill, the road continues past a barn to end at a small shed and the NATS (National Air Traffic Systems) Comms Station building and aerial on the tip of the headland where there is space to park off the road in various places.

At the time of writing Vodafone mobile reception is almost non-existent in this part of the island. However, it is worth knowing that just before the road rounds the bend to descend to the aerial there is a small 'window' where a Vodafone mobile signal can usually be picked from the big mast at Acha Mòr near Stornoway; there is a parking space on the left just before the bend.

ÀIRD MHÒR MHANGARSTAIDH SOUTH

Map opposite

This is the stretch of south-west facing coast extending northwards from the beach at Tràigh Mhangarstaidh to Screaming Geòdha and Lèirigeo. The first areas lie on the north side of the beach at Tràigh Mhangurstadh.

Sròn na Faing

(NB 0075 3095) Non-tidal S facing

On the small headland on the far side of the beach at Tràigh Mhangarstaidh there is an obvious triangular pillar of rock. Care is needed with some loose rock near the top. The belay is on a rope from boulders well back.

Approach: From the small quarry bowl parking place **(NB 0124 3073)** for the beach, walk down the track and cross the sands (10min).

Ocean Drive 18m E1 5b
K.Archer, A.Norton, 28 Jul 1996
Climb a crack-line on the front face of the pillar to a niche then follow a diagonal crack to ledges.

Body Surfin' in a Body Bag 16m VS 4c
K.Archer, A.Norton, 28 Jul 1996
The pillar forms a corner 3m to the right at its junction with the face. Follow the corner passing a bulge at two-thirds height.

Mhangarstaidh bay and headland (photo Rab Anderson)

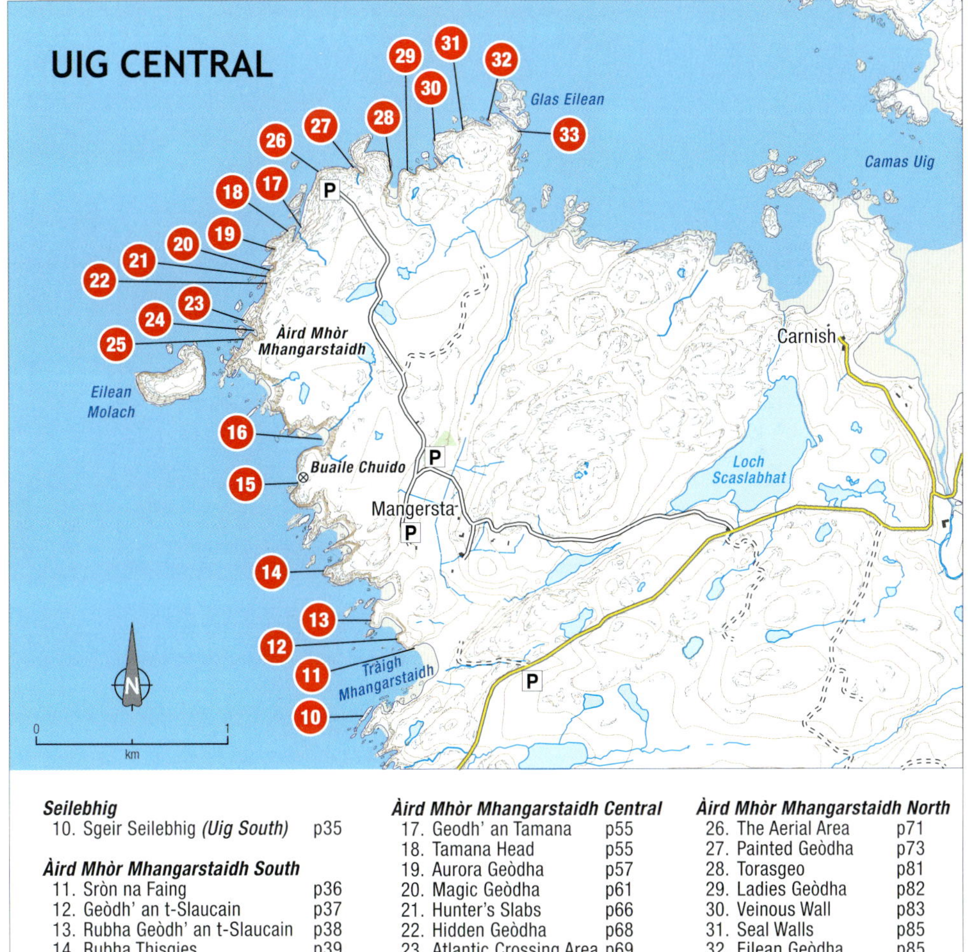

Geodh' an t-Slaucain

(NB 0065 3095) Tidal W facing Map above

North-westwards from the beach at Tràigh Mhangarstaidh, this is the first geo encountered. It is in fact more of a bay and is characterised by a secluded stretch of sand hemmed in between tall cliffs of variable quality. There is one route on an obvious fin of rock at the southern extremity of the bay, which is effectively the headland between the two beaches.

Approach: From the small quarry bowl parking place for Tràigh Mhangarstaidh, walk down the track, cross the sands and go up the slope past the top of Sròn na Faing (13min). It is also easy to reach from the road-end at the hamlet of Mangersta.

Descent: From the north corner of the bay, at low tide and in calm conditions, scramble down steep grass and traverse the secluded beach; see the approach for the Rabbit Walls Area. More likely though, it may be necessary to abseil down the line of the route, which requires back ropes.

Morning Star 25m VS 4b **

K.Archer, A.Norton, 6 Aug 1998

From the undercut base of the fin, pull around the seaward face and climb it just right of the arete. Gain the arete above a niche and follow it to the top.

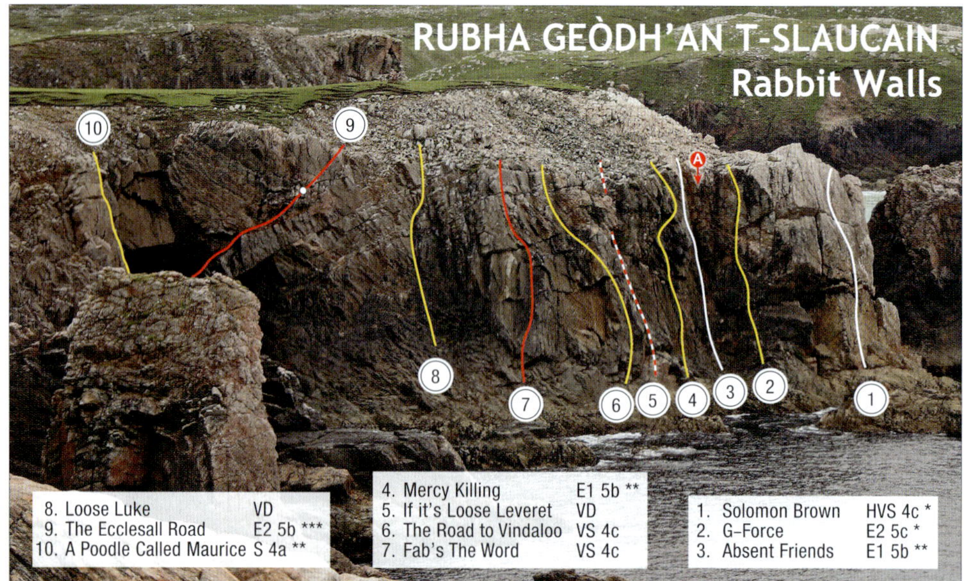

Rubha Geodh' an t-Slaucain

The Rabbit Walls

(NB 0049 3105) Tidal NW facing Map p37

These north-west facing walls lie on the headland forming the northern side of Geodh' an t-Slaucain. A small stack, Stac a' Chais, lies just off the end of the headland.

Approach: From the small quarry bowl parking place for Tràigh Mhangarstaidh, walk down the track, cross the beach and climb the slope at the far side. Follow the edge of the Geodh' an t-Slaucain bay northwards across the top of old lazy beds to locate a narrow grassy neck, which forms a slight crest with two small bumps. Pass between the bumps and drop down to a level grassy ridge that runs out to sea (15min). Part way down it is possible to scramble down steep grass to the secluded beach at Geòdh' an t-Slaucain. An approach can also be made from the road-end at the hamlet of Mangersta, which is slightly closer.

Descent: From the seaward end, abseil down a corner on the north side. Take care of the loose ground on the cliff-top.

Routes are described from right to left, facing in.

1 Solomon Brown 15m HVS 4c *
K.Archer, C.Archer, 29 May 2000
Scramble right from the base of the abseil corner to sea-level ledges at the end of the promontory; the route takes the centre of the prominent slab, right of a wide cleft. Climb the lower slab to the break, follow the corner at the base of the steeper central section, then trend left before moving back right again to the second break. Place the last runners and climb the scoop before trending left to finish.

2 G-Force 15m E2 5c *
M.Garthwaite, R.Anderson, 25 Jul 2005
The bottomless steep crack in the right wall of the abseil corner, gained by moving up and left to it.

3 Absent Friends 18m E1 5b **
K.Archer, C.Archer, 2 Jun 2000
The fine slabby corner. Follow the corner to gain a hanging slab then go up this to an overlap. Move up and follow a second slab to a technical finish up the final steep corner.

4 Mercy Killing 22m E1 5b **
A.Norton, K.Archer, 8 Aug 1998
Just left again, follow a cracked slab to a corner (wet) and climb this to an overhang. Traverse right and pull up into a worrying looking crack to finish.

5 If it's Loose Leveret 20m VD
A.Norton, K.Archer, 7 Aug 1998
The corner of the slab gives a cautious escape route. Follow the corner, then onto a rib and up easy but loose ground.

6 The Road to Vindaloo 15m VS 4c
K.Archer, C.Archer, 31 May 2000
A little way to the left, around a short bad step, is the base of a prominent slabby rib, well seen from the

abseil. From the base of the slabby rib, climb a scoop trending right to gain the arete and follow this, then the final wall to the top.

7 Fab's The Word 20m VS 4c
K.Archer, C.Archer, 12 Aug 1998
Some 10m to the left again is a slabby corner with an overhung cracked rib. Climb up to the rib and turn it on the right. Follow a groove to small ledges and make an awkward pull onto the upper slab which leads to the top.

8 Loose Luke 20m VD
A.Norton, L.Norton, 12 Aug 1998
Some 3m left again, follow a slabby blunt arete then step left to finish up the headwall.

Scramble left again and the next two routes can be seen on a series of overhung slabs that form a small geo.

Descent: Abseil down the arete of the left wall.

9 The Ecclesall Road 50m E2 ***
A.Norton, K.Archer, 4 Aug 1998
A rightwards rising line to the right of the blocky arete of the abseil. Start on a small pedestal 5m up from the base of the arete.
1. 25m 5a Descend a ramp on the left wall towards the left corner. Gain this then follow the back of the second slab to a corner below an overhung groove.
2. 25m 5b Make difficult moves to gain the arete of the right wall and traverse around this into a niche. Traverse rightwards along a break (mediocre protection) to where the break meets easier ground.

10 A Poodle Called Maurice 22m S 4a **
K.Archer, A.Norton, 10 Aug 1998
The line of the abseil, starting 5m down from The Ecclesall Road. Climb the blocky arete on its right side into a corner that leads to a slab. Follow this, then finish up the left wall; belay on the abseil rope.

Rubha Thisgeis

(NB 0030 3125) Non-tidal SW facing Map p37

Lying close to the road end at the hamlet of Mangersta, Rubha Thisgeis is a triple pronged headland. The bay to the north is split in two by a thin ridge with a natural arch through it to give Berie Beag and Berie Mòr, whose north side is formed by the narrow promontory of Stac Dhomhnaill Chaim.

Directions: At the foot of the hill in Mangersta, instead of swinging right up the hill towards the aerial, continue to the road end and park considerately.

Approach: Go through a gate into the fields, then head westwards up the hill, cross the fence and drop down to the headland. The routes are on the central prong with sea cave inlets either side (5min).

Descent: Abseil down the line of a central chimney-groove to good ledges.

The left-hand buttress has two grooves.

Outside Left 15m HVS 5a
R.Anderson, C.Anderson, 22 Jul 2005
The left-hand ramped-groove and crack.

Inside Right 15m HVS 5a
R.Anderson, C.Anderson, 22 Jul 2005
The right-hand groove and ramp going around the roof and back left.

Right of the abseil the right-hand buttress starts as a slab.

Nosed Out 15m HVS 4c
R.Anderson, C.Anderson, 22 Jul 2005
Climb the left-hand crack in the slab, pull over the steepening and go right onto the nose to finish on a platform.

In the Groove 17m E2 5b **
R.Anderson, C.Anderson, 22 Jul 2005
A lovely route up the groove in the edge. Awkwardly gain the groove and climb it around a steepening to the top.

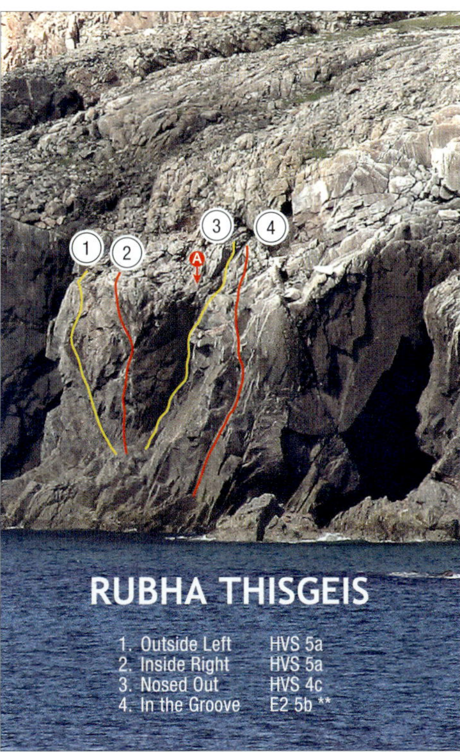

Buaile Chuido (Screaming Geòdha)

(NB 0017 3176) Map p37

This is the highest point on this stretch of coast and therefore the biggest cliff hereabouts. It is an awesome place with climbs ranking amongst the best in the country. There are a number of walls. The Mangersta Slabs enjoy a sunny south-westerly aspect, as do the Upper and Lower Tiers and the main West Face, or Screaming Wall. The North-West Face only catches the sun in the late afternoon and early evening. The geo can be affected by salt spray since it faces full into the westerly seas.

The cliff is arranged in a number of sections. The southern, or right-hand section lies to the right side of a large flat mid-height platform known as the Middle Platform and takes the form of a fine sweep of smooth, granite-like slabs that drops straight into the sea: the Mangersta Slabs. Above the Middle Platform, the Upper Tier West Face runs the length of the platform and turns the edge to form the Upper Tier North-West Face. Beneath these, the Lower Tier West Face extends left from the Mangersta Slabs to turn the edge to the superb and steep Lower Tier North-West Face which is hidden below the north end of Middle Platform. These tiers form a right-angle where they abut the West Face, the stupendous face above and on the far side of a huge arched sea cave. This is the Screaming Wall which is effectively split in two by the huge sea cave, into Screaming Wall Right and Screaming Wall Left. The Far West Face lies just beyond the Screaming Wall, before the edge is turned into Lèirgeo, the deep bay to the north.

A fabulous little bothy has been constructed on the very cliff edge in the angle of the slope just below the highpoint of Buaile Chuido, at the top of the corner between the West Face and the North-West Face. At this point the slabs slope down above the top of the North-West Face towards the Middle Platform. The bothy is not a climbers' doss and is regularly frequented by locals and visitors. Although there should be no problem with staying for the odd night it is not a suitable place for climbers to base themselves for length of time. Anyone wishing to stay here should ask the Norgroves at 3 Mangersta. Please leave the bothy tidy and shut the door (**www.lindanorgrovefoundation.org/site/bothy**).

Directions: Follow the road out to Mangersta and take the right fork which doubles back up the hill away from the houses. Either park off the road just before the gate across the road at the top of the hill **(NB 008 319)**, or at one of the spots beyond the gate, but not at the barn.

Approach: If parking just before the gate, cross the roadside fence via a stile then follow the fence which runs westwards at right-angles from the road and the gate. If parking beyond the gate, head south-west to meet this fence at some point and follow it. The fence runs into a big geo, Lèirigeo, and can be crossed in a couple of places by stiles. Ahead, the long, flat grassy highpoint is the top of Buaile Chuido. Aim for a small boulder on the shoulder just above a grassy depression on the left side of this highpoint then go straight on to gain the sloping rocks around the cliff-top (15min).

Descent: Climbs on the Mangersta Slabs, The Upper Tier West Face, The Lower Tier West Face, The Upper Tier North-West Face, The Lower Tier North-West Face and routes on the Screaming Wall Right, are gained by going southwards back up the rock step from the bothy then heading down the slabs slightly left to locate a shallow depression which slopes towards the sea. Follow this depression down to a notch then make a short scramble down a ramp, or beside it, to gain the south end of the spacious Middle Platform. There are boulders on this platform which provide abseil anchors for access to most of the climbs at sea-level.

The Prozac Link (E4) Dave MacLeod & Natalie Berry (photo Chris Prescott / Hot Aches)

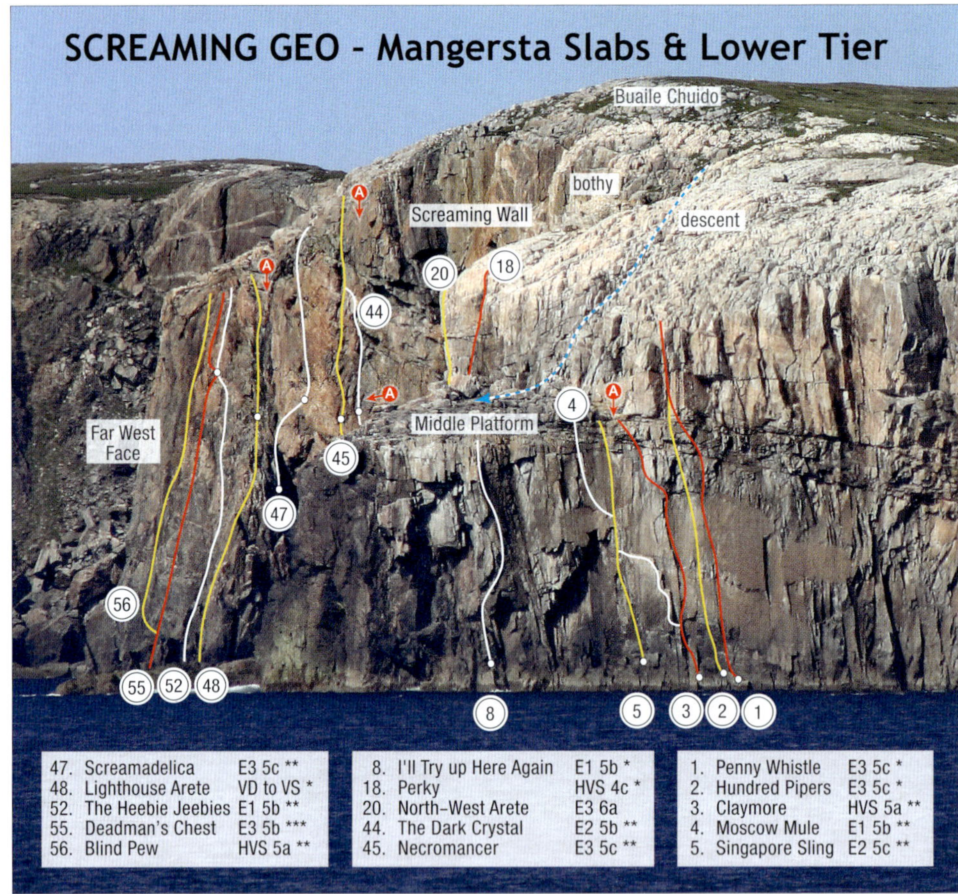

Mangersta Slabs and Lower Tier West Face

(NB 0015 3170) Tidal W facing

At the southern end of the Middle Platform, the sweep of smooth slab can be seen down and to the right (facing in). The adjoining walls of the Lower Tier West Face lie to the left beneath the platform.

Descent: The first four climbs start from a fine sea-level ledge, gained by making a right-slanting diagonal abseil from the corner at the right end of the Middle Platform, pretty much down the line of Claymore. Singapore Sling starts from a ledge to the left which lies directly below the abseil anchors.

Climbs are described from right to left. There is some confusion with regard to a few of the earlier routes here.

1 Penny Whistle 45m E3 5c *

J.Moran, D.Pearce, 5 May 1985

Unfortunately the top third of this climb and Hundred Pipers involve some quite serious climbing on suspect rock. From the right end of the ledge, climb a groove straight up to a broken band then go leftwards to finish up the easier corner.

2 Hundred Pipers 45m E3 5c *

D.Cuthbertson, G.Latter, 6 May 1985

Start directly below a large open corner-groove which is high on the face above the horizontal band. Pull over a bulge and follow thin cracks up the slab on superb rock. Weave through the horizontal band and climb a slim quartzy groove to finish up the easier corner as for Penny Whistle.

3 Claymore 30m HVS 5a **

I.Sykes, I.Sutherland, 1970s

The line of slim corners and cracks above the left end of the ledge. Step left and climb a right-facing corner to a ledge at 6m. Step right into a thin crack (often wet) and climb this through an awkward bulge to a ledge on the left (sometimes full of water). Move back right and go up a shallow groove to a small footledge (old peg). Now traverse left (crux), then move up into a short left-facing corner and climb this before trending left over a bulge to finish on the Middle Platform.

4 Moscow Mule 30m E1 5b **
D.Cuthbertson, L.Clegg, C.Henderson, Jun 1988
Follow Claymore to the ledge at 6m then take the obvious hand-traverse line across to the left edge. Climb a crack for 1m or so, then make a trying move left across an overlap to a jug and finish up the groove above.

The next climb starts from a ledge further left, directly beneath the right end of the Middle Platform.

5 Singapore Sling 30m E2 5c **
D.Cuthbertson, L.Clegg, C.Henderson, Jun 1988
A fine direct through Moscow Mule. From the right end of the ledge, move up then right around the edge and climb a thin crack in the smooth slab with some difficulty to join the crux of Moscow Mule. Climb this and the tricky slabby wall above, going slightly left to finish.

The previous guide describes the following route which is also supposed to start from the Singapore Sling ledge, but it is unsure where it actually lies and how it relates to the other climbs.

6 Let's Go Down to the Water Line E1 5b
M.Tighe and Party, 1980s
Make a rising left traverse to reach a prominent platform ledge. Continue along a flake-crack and the natural line of least resistance. Belay before reaching the Middle Platform to reduce rope drag.

The old guide also mentions two routes at about E1 above the platform ledge mentioned in the previous route; one climbs more or less directly above into a prominent groove, the other works back up and right. Again, it is unsure where these are and how they relate to the other climbs.

The next two routes are further to the left.

7 Groovy Thing 30m E4 5c *
A.Robb, C.Pulley, 14 Jul 2006
This climbs a groove whose base is gained directly by abseil from a large block, about 10m north of the end of the Middle Platform. Climb quite boldly to bear left at the top. It would appear it was initially an attempt to climb the next route.

Singapore Sling (E2) Donie O'Sullivan (photo Crispin Waddy)

8 I'll Try up Here Again 30m E1 5b *
D.Ashworth, C.Lofthouse, May 1993
Reached by abseil down an obvious VS looking corner some 15m left of Claymore, this takes an improbable line up some steep ground. Climb an easy wall to a steep crack, then pull onto a small slab left of an overhang and step down to a crucial foothold at the bottom of a slab on the left of the abseil corner. Climb around the overhang and follow the nose to the top.

Upper Tier West Face

Non-tidal W facing Diagrams p42 & above

A number of climbs lie on the short walls above the Middle Platform. As with the other routes on this cliff, they are described from right to left, as met from where the scramble down gains the platform. This section ends at an arete where the edge is turned to the Upper Tier of the North-West Face.

9 Right Track 10m VD *
The right-hand of a pair of tramline cracks.

10 Left Track 10m VD *
The left-hand tramline crack.

On the left there is a shallow, roofed recess propped up by a 2m high monolith.

11 Katrin's Cream 10m S 4a *
M.Sullivan, J.Garbutt, 22 Jul 1997
Immediately right of the recess, climb a left-slanting crack then a right-facing groove.

12 Screaming Miss Molly 10m VS 4b *
M.Sullivan, J.Garbutt, 22 Jul 1997
Bridge up between the monolith and the right-hand wall of the recess then climb a left-slanting crack.

13 Screaming Sandhoppers 10m S 4a *
M.Sullivan, J.Garbutt, 22 Jul 1997
Start off the monolith and climb a left-slanting crack.

14 Inner Demons 10m HVS 5a *
G.Latter, 14 Jul 2006
Just left of Screaming Sandhoppers is a left-facing groove capped by a block. Climb the crack 2m left of the groove, step up right to pull over the block overhang and finish up the crack above.

15 Rubik 10m E1 5a
A.Moles, A.Yakunin, 10 Aug 2014
The slab and arete immediately left of Inner Demons; dubious gear in the upper half.

16 Ruble 10m E2 5a
A.Moles, A.Yakunin, 10 Aug 2014
The larger right-hand of three left-facing leaning corner-grooves; little protection and some snappy holds.

17 Dubeedoo 10m E1 5a
R.Anderson, C.Anderson, 31 Mar 2008
The central of the three left-facing leaning corner-grooves; dubious rock and protection.

The next routes are 25m further left at the end of the platform.

18 Perky 10m HVS 4c *
C Henderson L.Clegg, 1988
The stepped corner 5m right of the left arete.

19 Pinky 10m E1 5b *
G.Lovick, S.Mayers, Jul 1993
The crack just right of the arete.

20 North-West Arete 15m E3 6a *
S.Crowe, K.Magog, 16 May 1999 (also left finish)
The left-hand arete is climbed mainly on its right side, escaping right near the top. A bold left finish at E5/6 6b requires some cleaning.

Upper Tier North-West Face

Non-tidal NW facing Diagrams below & p50

This is the continuation face around the arete at the end of the Middle Platform. The bothy sits above the corner at the far end.

Descent: From the end of the Middle Platform, go around the edge and along a ledge.

21 It's Raining Rocks! 20m E3 6a *
G.Latter, N.Clement, 29 May 1996
Climb the crack just left of the arete to a horizontal break as for In the Shop on the Hill. Where that routes goes left up a scooped groove continue up the crack above.

22 In the Shop on the Hill 20m E2 5c *
L.Clegg, D.Cuthbertson, C.Henderson, Jun 1988
Climb the crack just left of the arete to a horizontal break, then go left and up with difficulty to the base of a scoop. After a difficult move the scoop eases slightly.

23 Whirlwind 20m E8 6c (F8a) *
D.MacLeod, May 2005
The exposed crack up the centre of the wall where the ledge narrows. The first section of crack to the horizontal is serious with poor gear and snappy holds. Above, the climbing gets steadily harder but is better protected, culminating in a tricky crux right at the top.

Descent: The next routes can be approached directly by abseil from beside the bothy, which avoids a long traverse to reach the belay and the disturbance of any nesting birds. Large cams are useful for the belay. Damn

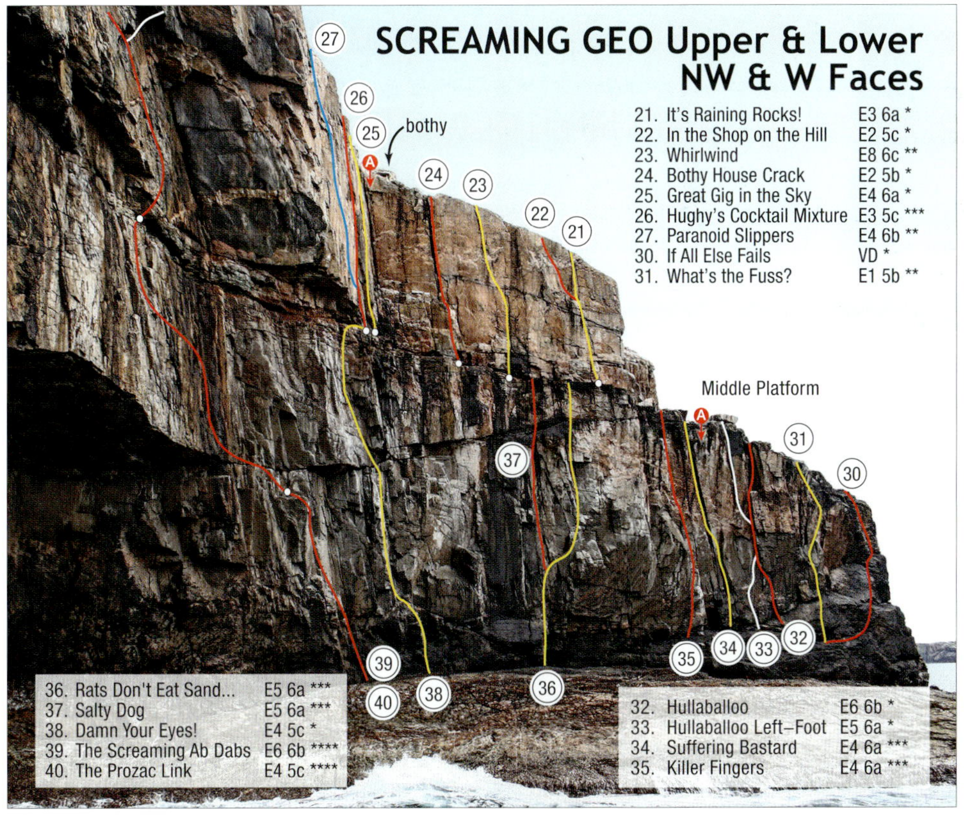

Your Eyes on the Lower Tier can be used as a lower pitch.

24 Bothy House Crack 25m E2 5b *
P.Robins, B.Bransby, 12 Jun 2004
The off-width finishing close to the bothy.

Upper Tier West Face

Non-tidal W Facing Diagram p50

A corner is now formed where the face changes direction and the next five climbs take lines on the upper part of the Screaming Wall Right.

25 Great Gig in the Sky 25m E4 6a *
K.Magog, S.Crowe, 5 Jul 2003
This climbs the wall between the corner and the crack of Hughy's Cocktail Mixture. Climb up the right side of a strip of dark coloured rock and finish up the right-hand crack in the upper wall.

26 Hughy's Cocktail Mixture 25m E3 5c ***
L.Clegg, D.Cuthbertson, C.Henderson, Jun 1988
The splendid crack in the left wall of the corner. Pull round the overhang in a fine position and layback the crack. Sustained but slightly easier climbing follows; pull up right to a ledge and climb the central of three cracks to finish.

Paranoid Slippers (E4) Niall McNair (photo Steve Crowe)

27 Paranoid Slippers 30m E4 6b ***
G.Farquhar, R.Campbell, N.Clement, 29 May 1996
This takes the pink feldspar wall to the left of Hughy's Cocktail Mixture. Pull over the overhang as for that route, traverse left on the lip (crux) then move up and left to better holds. Continue up left to a sentry box and exit this up leftwards, passing a horizontal break to finish left of a wide crack, on the arete overlooking Shadow Dancer.
Variation: **27a Paranoid Alternative Finish**
N.McNair, D.McLeod, 5 Jul 2003
From the top of the sentry box, go up and right to climb the crack just left of the central crack taken by Hughy's Cocktail Mixture.

28 Exit Point 40m E7 6c ***
T.Emmet, D.MacLeod, 1 Jun 2010
Follow Paranoid Slippers to just beyond its crux traverse. Step up then make a rising traverse left at the edge of the vertical wall until it is possible to access an undercut groove in the spectacular hanging arete. This is just above the flake of Shadow Dancer. Follow the groove to a good rest below a roof. Make a long reach through the roof and hard moves above onto the hanging upper arete. After a few moves up the arete the climbing eases off rapidly.

29 Shadow Dancer 40m E7 6b ***
S.Mayers, J.Lovick, Jul 1993
A wild and strenuous route taking a line of sickening exposure up the hanging arete to the right of Screaming Ab Dabs. Follow Paranoid Slippers to the good holds then make another committing move left to the line proper; an overhanging flake-crack. Climb this ever leftwards to eventually reach a brief respite under a roof. Pull directly over this, then trend right past a peg to the base of a corner which leads easily to the top. A double set of cams and some long extension slings are helpful.

Lower Tier North-West Face

Tidal NW facing Diagrams p45 & p54

A deceptively steep wall lies below the north end of the Middle Platform and runs towards the back of the geo. The wall can be greasy and may require the sun to help dry it out. The wave washed platform at the base remains clear of the sea for some time unless the swell is up, at which point it gets swamped.

Descent: Abseil from a choice of good boulders and cracks on the Middle Platform. The boulder closest to the edge out in front of Pinky facilitates an abseil down the hanging, left-facing corner of Hullaballoo towards the right side of the wall.

Climbs are again described from right to left and the first routes lie above the lower part of a raised shelf which slants easily up rightwards.

Killer Fingers (E4) Robert Durran
(photo Rab Anderson)

30 If All Else Fails 25m VD *
D.Cuthbertson, L.Clegg, C.Henderson, Jun 1988
From the right end of the lower raised shelf, climb up to the left end of a slab (good belay). Climb the slab via a short vague crack on its right side then continue rightwards along a series of narrow ledges to finish up a fine little exposed wall.
Variation: **30a Direct Finish E1 ***
About halfway along the traverse of the normal route, climb into a short hanging crack in a groove; short but steep.

31 What's the Fuss? 20m E1 5b **
R.Anderson, N.Morrison, W.Moir, 11 Aug 2006
Start just right of Hullaballoo where the wall forms a blunt edge at the left end of the main slab. Climb to the left end of the slab to gain the steeper rocks at a triangular shaped roofed recess. Step over this then move up and left into a short leaning groove. Pull out right around the blunt edge and climb steeply up left to easier ground leading to the platform.

32 Hullaballoo 20m E6 6b *
S.Mayers, Jul 1993
The left-facing stepped corner towards the right side of the wall. Climb the intermittent cracks just right of the corner for 7m then move awkwardly into the corner to follow it and the wall above more easily to the top.

33 Hullaballoo Left-Foot 20m E5 6a *
B.Bransby, P.Robins, 10 Jun 2004
A pitch based on Hullaballoo. From directly below the main corner, climb up and left (fiddly gear) then back right into the corner. Follow this then step left into a slim hanging ramp-come-groove leading up leftwards to the top.

34 Suffering Bastard 25m E4 6a ***
D.Cuthbertson, L.Clegg, C.Henderson, Jun 1988
The prominent crack system to the left of Hullaballoo gives a brilliant well protected pitch. A big cam is useful for the final groove, but not essential. An undercut start leads to the base of the overhanging cracks. Climb these with an awkward transfer into the left-hand crack. Finish up a superb bomb bay groove.

35 Killer Fingers 30m E4 6a ***
D.Cuthbertson, L.Clegg, C.Henderson, Jun 1988
Immediately right of the central overhanging face is an obvious slab with a layback crack above. An undercut start and a two stepped corner lead to a crack on the right side of the slab. Climb the crack and arrange protection then step down and hand-traverse left. Make a difficult move to reach the layback which leads to the top. The boldness of the climb depends on how far up the crack protection is placed before the traverse left.

36 Rats Don't Eat Sandwiches 30m E5 6a ***
L.Houlding, J.Pickles, 9 Jun 2004
Start as for Salty Dog but traverse right at about 10m to a ledge. Climb the slim groove above to a roof and pull through this to gain a ledge then on to the top.

37 Salty Dog 30m E5 6a ***
D.Cuthbertson, L.Clegg, C.Henderson, Jun 1988
The twin crack system on the left side of the central overhanging face, immediately right of a smooth black slabby rib. Climb the undercut left-hand groove and continue up the crack with some deviation. Reach the final small bottomless groove with some difficulty (small wires); this leads to the top.

38 Damn Your Eyes! 30m E4 5c *
P.Robins, B.Bransby, 9 Jun 2004
Starting 5m right of The Screaming Ab Dabs the following route takes a groove line and provides a good starting pitch for Paranoid Slippers on the tier above. Climb a short corner to a sloping ledge and break. Step left and climb into the main groove, moving left to the vague arete which leads to the main horizontal break. Continue up the slanting groove above, climbing mainly on the left wall; there is no gear above the horizontal break but the climbing is only 5b.

Screaming Wall West Face

Tidal W facing Diagram p50

This impressive wall Extends leftwards from the corner between the faces, running out over the huge sea cave. The wall is in two sections; Screaming Wall Right, accessed from the right side of the cave and Screaming Wall Left, accessed from the left side of the sea cave.

Screaming Wall Right

39 The Screaming Ab Dabs 75m E6 ****
D.Cuthbertson, L.Clegg, C.Henderson, Jun 1988
A magnificent climb which takes a committing and impressive line up the right side of the huge sea cave to attack the upper overhangs. The crux is short but hard and in an intimidating position. The lower part is shared by The Prozac Link. Start at the left end of the Lower Tier, on the left wall of a corner.
1. 20m 5c The Yosemite Crack. Climb an undercut groove, then move left and climb a white crack to a perfect ledge.
2. 25m 5b Traverse of the Gods. Traverse left along the exposed horizontal break then move up to a ledge on the right. Make a rising left traverse across an orangy brown coloured wall to gain a small ledge at the girdling break; large cams are useful for the belay.
3. 30m 6b The Moonlight Cooler Pitch. Move right over a bulge and follow a line of black pockets going left to a large but secure block under the roof; possible belay. Move right and use undercuts to gain an obvious ramp hold above the lip (cam under the roof and a Friend 00 in a small diagonal quartz crack above it). Pull over the roof with difficulty and continue slightly left to better holds beneath the next overhang. Climb this by means of a horizontal crack and finish up the quartzy corner above. Beware of rope drag.

The Prozac Link (E4) Martin Kocsis (photo Mike Hutton)

40 The Prozac Link 95m E4 ****

H.Jones, G.Huxter, 29 May 1996

Rated as one of the best E4's in the country, this is a brilliant hybrid which combines tremendous situations with superb climbing in a committing situation. The line is that of a rising traverse above the huge sea cave and retreat from higher up would be difficult. The lower section is common with The Screaming Ab Dabs. Start at the left end of the Lower Tier, on the left wall of a corner.

1. 20m 5c Climb an undercut groove then move left and climb a white crack to a perfect ledge and belay.
2. 25m 5b Traverse left along the exposed horizontal break then move up to a ledge on the right. Make a rising left traverse across an orangy brown coloured wall to gain a small ledge at the girdling break: large cams useful for the belay.
3. 30m 5c Move right over a bulge and follow a line of black pockets going left to a large but secure block under the roof: The Screaming Ab Dabs goes up through the roofs above here. Move left round the front of the block onto large holds, then continue traversing leftwards to belay beneath a curious downwards-pointing flake.
4. 20m 5c Continue leftwards up and across a white quartzy wall then go round the roof onto a pink pegmatite wall and climb directly to a ramp which leads rightwards to the top.

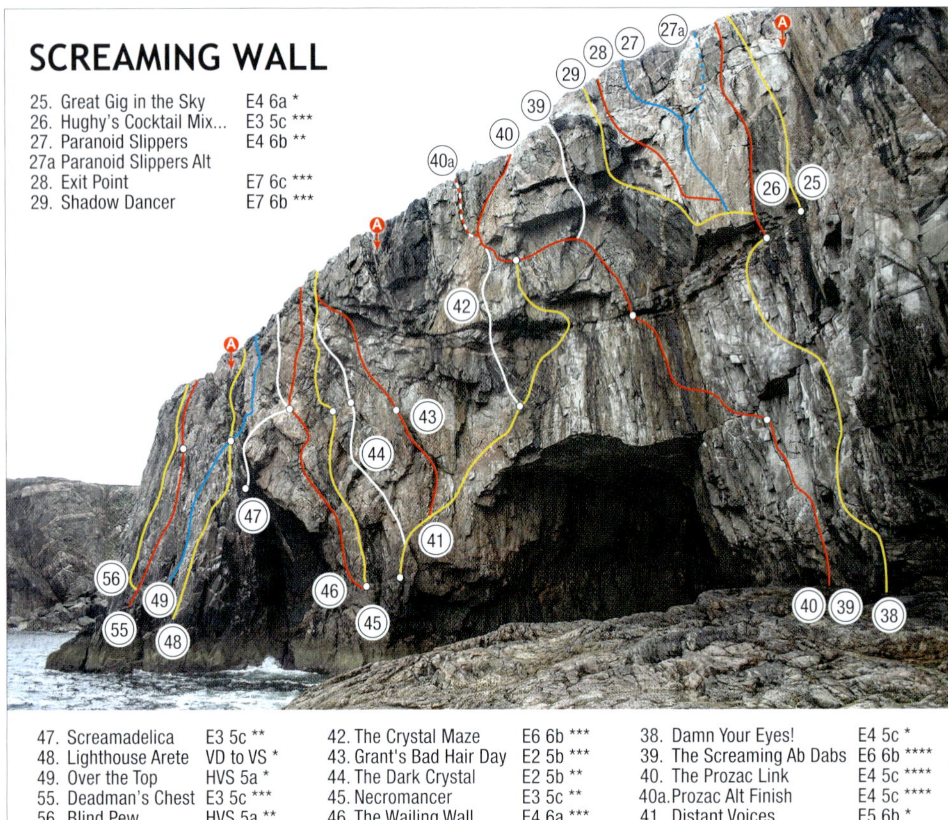

Variation: **40a Prozac Alternative Finish**
P.Robins, B.Bransby and Others, Jun 2004
This maintains the diagonal line with no change in grade, or quality.
4. 25m Climb up and left round the roof to gain the ramp then climb the crack up the headwall on the left.

Screaming Wall Left

The expanse of rock left of the cave; the first four climbs start from the same good ledge, whilst the other two start from a ledge a little lower down to the left.

Descent: From the bothy, head northwards over the top towards the highest point of Buaile Chuido to locate large blocks above the centre of the wall. A 50m abseil gains good ledges for the first four climbs and a 60m abseil down and left gains a ledge below the other two.

41 Distant Voices 60m E5 *
M.Tompkins, S.Mayers, Jun 1993
This climbs up the left side of the sea cave to break through the roofs above.
1. 20m 5c Common with The Crystal Maze; take a line up and right to a stance on a small ledge about 5m above the lip of the cave.
2. 20m 6b Climb easily up right to a break in the roof, then go back across left above the roof to the comfort of some good holds on the rib. The next roof is easier and leads to a good stance at a downward-pointing flake as for The Prozac Link.
3. 20m 5c As for The Prozac Link, up left round the roofs to finish up the ramp.

42 The Crystal Maze 50m E6 ***
S.Mayers, G.Lovick, Jun 1993
1. 20m 5c Common with Distant Voices; climb up and right to a stance on a small ledge about 5m above the lip of the cave.
2. 30m 6b Climb the overhanging black wall above the stance (just right of a slim black corner-groove) to the roof. Cross the roof to the right of the pink feldspar rock, moving slightly right at the horizontal break then climb the wall above to a small overhang. Pass this on its left to a quartzy wall (junction with The Prozac Link and Distant Voices) then climb to an easy right-slanting ramp and the top.

43 Grant's Bad Hair Day 50m E2 ***
H.Jones, G.Huxter, 29 May 1996
1. 20m 5a Traverse right until below a shattered corner then move up this and onto the front face of a precarious block (treat with care). Move up to a ledge and belay.
2. 30m 5b Follow fault-lines easily up and left, aiming for the left-hand end of a big overhang. Move left round the arete beneath the overhang in an exhilarating position and continue easily up and left to finish up a crack-corner, as for The Dark Crystal.

44 The Dark Crystal 50m E2 **
S.Mayers, G.Lovick, Jun 1993
1. 25m 5b Trend up and left from the stance to reach the base of two grooves. The left-hand groove leads to blocky ledges and a belay.
2. 25m 5b Continue up and slightly left to finish up an obvious corner.

The next two climbs start from a non-tidal black ledge 8m diagonally down and left.

45 Necromancer 60m E3 **
K.Pyke, G.Huxter, 10 Jul 1997
This links the prominent black crystalline bands and crack-line on the left side of Screaming Wall; well seen from the bothy.
1. 30m 5c Follow black crystalline rock always trending up and left, steeply at times, on a faint prow. For the final 5m, move right up a corner to gain an airy square-cut perch.
2. 30m 5b Move left to gain the crack system and jam securely until stepping left into an obvious corner-line. Finish directly as for The Dark Crystal.

46 The Wailing Wall 50m E4 ***
M.Garthwaite, R.Anderson, 10 Jul 2010
Start at the same point as Necromancer.
1. 25m 6a Move left to climb a groove and wall, then step left to a small alcove barring access to an overhung left-leaning ramp. Follow this to a good flake above a short jam crack, then step right and climb to a small nose. Improbable moves across the smooth white wall on the left gains good holds visible at its top left edge. Pull up left to a small footledge; junction with Screamadelica.
2. 25m 5b Climb the red wall up and right in an amazing position to a short quartzy groove then a horizontal break. Move up and right to the arete and finish up an inset groove in this.

The next climbs lie just to the left but are accessed from the Far West Face.

Far West Face

Partially Tidal W facing Diagrams p42, p50 & p54

To the left of the Screaming Wall and separated from it by a deep cleft, is the obvious stepped ridge of Lighthouse Arete. To the left of the ridge is a wall of lovely rock which extends north to the edge formed at the entrance of Lèirigeo.

Descent: From the grassy highpoint of Buaile Chuido, drop down north-west to a blockstrewn slope. Head diagonally south across this to beneath a 4m high light coloured wall, with two large blocks (old tat). A 50m abseil from threads beneath the blocks leads over ledges and down grooves to the pedestal base of the ridge of Lighthouse Arete.

The first climb is actually on the far left end of the orange coloured Screaming Wall Left and is gained by abseil past the ledge mid-way up Lighthouse Arete then down the side of the deep cleft. The second pitches of Over the Top and Off the Shelf take lines just to the left. Climbs are described from right to left.

47 Screamadelica 30m E3 5c **
M.Garthwaite, R.Anderson, 10 Jul 2010
A spectacular climb which steps across the top of the cleft separating Lighthouse Arete from the main cliff. Start from a belay on a footledge inside the cleft, some 5m from its top. Climb up and bridge the void onto a foothold below an overlap then climb rightwards into a hanging groove. At the top of the groove step right to small footledges for The Wailing Wall belay. Climb straight up via a downward-pointing tooth and its short right-facing corner then continue directly up the wall to a horizontal break where a step left gains the finishing holds.

48 Lighthouse Arete 45m VD to VS **
M.Tighe, B.Newton and Party, 9 Jun 1987
This is the obvious stepped ridge, or pedestal, on the left side of the geo, to the left of the deep cleft at the end of The Screaming Wall. It provides an atmospheric outing climbed in two pitches. Whilst the climb itself is not outstanding, the approach, the position and the setting are, hence the stars. There are various routes up the initial section which has good rock, the easiest being about VD with the hardest being **The Quiet Man**, VS 4b (G.Latter, J.Rabey, 15 Apr 1999) which takes a line of faint grooves. The fine first pitches of Over the Top and Off the Shelf can also be climbed in conjunction with the route. From a belay on the ledge above the deep cleft, go left up the obvious line then finish up right to reach the abseil blocks.

A splendidly situated non-tidal sloping shelf runs north from the base of Lighthouse Arete, around a step, then below an alcove containing a ledge with a prominent spike, to end at tidal ledges beneath a smooth wall.

49 Over the Top 45m HVS **
R.Anderson, C.Anderson, 10 Jul 2010
Start some 5m to the right of the step on the sloping shelf and just right of a deep groove.
1. 20m 4c Climb a thin crack-line up perfect rock, step left onto a ledge then continue to a belay on the ledge of Lighthouse Arete at the top of the cleft.

Grant's Bad Hair Day (E2) Ian Burton (photo Ferdia Earle)

2. 25m 5a Climb up right to the base of the obvious corner then move up right around the edge onto the left side of the Screaming Wall just left of Screamadelica. Climb a thin crack-line to beneath a roof, then either finish leftwards around the roof to easy ground or go up right which is quite scary.

50 Off the Shelf 45m HVS **
R.Anderson, C.Anderson, 10 Jul 2010
Start on top of the step on the shelf, left of the deep groove.
1. 20m 5a Climb the crack up the right side of the edge to the left of the groove to belay on the ledge of Lighthouse Arete.
2. 25m 5a Climb up right into the base of the obvious corner and follow this to its top on great rock, then continue to the abseil blocks.

51 Port a' Bheul 45m VS *
F.Macleod, F.T.Macleod, 14 May 1999
Start just to the left of Off the Shelf, at the prominent spike in the alcove above the mid-point of the sloping platform.
1. 25m 4b Climb an overhanging, cracked wall between two grooves to a roof. Step left to an arete and go up to a ledge with a block.
2. 20m 4b Traverse left to the exposed arete then go up a wall and either finish left up obvious left-sloping handrails, or up right as for Lighthouse Arete.

52 The Heebie-Jeebies 50m E1 **
G.Latter, J.Rabey, 15 Apr 1999
Start at the prominent spike in the alcove above the mid-point of the sloping platform.
1. 30m 5a Follow a left-slanting pink ramp, continuing up a black ramp across the top edge of a smooth wall and below a pink feldspar wall.
2. 20m 5b Climb a thin crack to a ledge, step left and go up a shallow groove to another ledge. Step right and continue more easily through the recess at the top of the wall to belay further back.

On the left, a wide recessed fault runs up the side of a lovely smooth wall which lies beneath the ramp of Heebie-Jeebies.

53 Pirates 45m E1 **
R.Anderson, T.Prentice, 12 Jul 2007
Start on a small pedestal ledge at the foot of the recessed fault; a fine first pitch.
1. 25m 5b Climb the right side of the recess, then pull onto the ramp of Heebie-Jeebies. Move up and climb a short corner above the ramp to a fine perch on the blocky ledge of Port a' Bheul.
2. 20m 5a Step right and climb above the block to ledges, then go up and right to finish up the top section of Lighthouse Arete.

The following climbs start from the tidal ledge beneath the smooth wall; an entertaining spot!

54 Half 'tache Jack 50m E1 **
T.Prentice, R.Anderson, 11 Jul 2007
1. 30m 5a Climb a crack up the right side of the smooth wall to gain a sloping ledge cutting across the wall. An alternative, less water-troubled start pulls onto this ledge at the same grade by stepping across from the small pedestal ledge in the recess to the right. Climb another short wall, then move up right and climb a shallow corner to gain the ramp of Heebie-Jeebies, which is followed to its belay.
2. 20m 4b Step up right and climb blocky ground to the top.

55 Deadman's Chest 50m E3 ***
R.Anderson, T.Prentice, 11 Jul 2007
Absorbing climbing up the centre of the smooth, slabby wall; small wires.
1. 30m 5b Climb a left-slanting crack to a ledge (possible belay that can be gained from the right via the alternate start to Half'tache Jack), then a right-slanting crack. Dodging around, find a line up the centre of the wall, through a steepening, then up a short corner to step right and belay as for Heebie-Jeebies.
2. 20m 4c Move left and climb the left side of the pink feldspar headwall to a ramp leading up right and a final pull leading into the recess at the top of the wall. A large block on the rubble strewn slope above provides a good thread.

56 Blind Pew 50m HVS 5a **
T.Prentice, R.Anderson, 11 Jul 2007
Climb the initial crack of Deadman's Chest to the ledge, then go left to easier but sparsely protected climbing following a system of stepped grooves and short corners up the left side of the smooth wall.

Lèirigeo

(NB 004 321) Map p37

This deep and broad geo lies immediately to the north of Buaile Chuido.

South Side

(NB 0020 3192) Tidal NW facing Diagram p54

This is the big wall on the south side of Lèirigeo. It lies around the edge from the Far West Face on Screaming Geo, of which it is effectively the continuation. The wall drops straight into the sea and is characterised by a steep lower section and a slabby upper wall. Two dog-leg cracks split the face. Climbs are described right to left.

Descent: Abseil from large blocks above the wall.

57 Conundrum 50m E4 6b
G.Huxter, K.Pyke, 8 Sep 1996
The right-hand dog-leg crack. Start from sea-level ledges 5m right of the crack.
1. 25m 6b Follow an easy blocky right-facing open corner to below a groove. Tricky moves lead up the groove to an overhang at 10m. Move right under the overhang with hard moves up the steep wall continuing

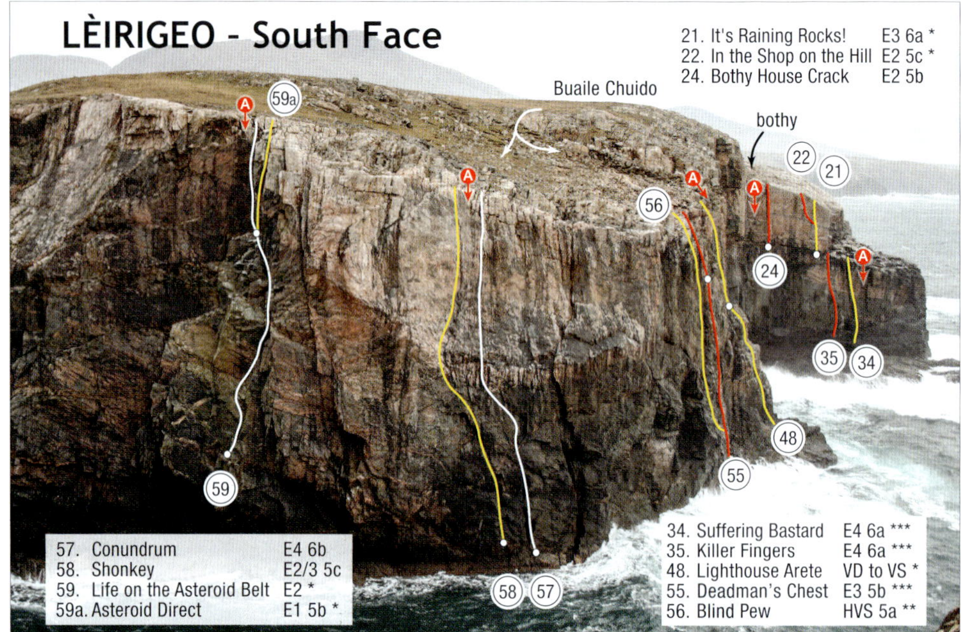

up the overhanging groove. Move right to a small ledge and belay.
2. 25m 5a Move left from the belay and follow a right-trending quartz band towards increasingly easy ground and the top.

58 Shonkey 50m E2/3 5c
T.Fryer, I.Taylor, 6 Jun 2003
The left-hand dog-leg crack is started from a small stance 5m above the high tide mark. Some suspect rock in the upper half. Trend left following the crack to below roofs. Move left 1m to pull through at the point of least resistance and continue more easily on quartzy rock to a slab. Follow discontinuous cracks to the top.

The next two climbs lie further into the geo and finish in the arete of a prominent corner in the top section of the north-west face.

59 Life on the Asteroid Belt 50m E2 *
R.I.Jones, A.Wardle, 8 Sep 2008
Abseil down the corner and right of the large spike under the ledge above the overhung lower wall and left-facing corner-flake system.
1. 35m 5b Climb the steep right-slanting ramp for 4m to a small overhang. Traverse left and up to a ledge (bold). Climb a right-slanting cracked groove to a left-facing overhung corner. Pull through right onto the arete and step back over the corner into another corner. Pull through an overhang and climb easy ground right of a large spike to the bottom of the corner.
2. 15m 4c The fine corner-crack.

59a Asteroid Direct E1 *
R.I.Jones, A.Wardle, 8 Sep 2008
2. 15m 5b 5m right of the corner is a right-facing overhung corner that borders the right side of the wall. Climb this to the top.

North Side

(NB 0015 3206) West facing Map p37
The following two routes are on the fin-shaped headland forming the northern side of the geo, well seen from Screaming Geo. The triangular pink wall has several quartzy lines. The routes are to the right of a prominent corner system which splits the face at its highest point.

Descent: Abseil from a large block to a small ledge just above high tide level.

Rick Campbell's Motorway Adventure 30m HVS 5a
G.Huxter, K.Pyke, 8 Sep 1996
A tricky move leads to a corner. Climb this and the slab above to reach a steep crack. Trend right past a quartzy flake to the top; belay well back.

Crab Sunday 30m E2 5a
K.Pyke, G.Huxter, 8 Sep 1996
From the belay, move up and left for 3m, then go directly up the slab to a large flake corner-crack at half-height. Climb this (crux) until the angle eases; block belay well back.

ÀIRD MHÒR MHANGARSTAIDH CENTRAL

Maps p20 & p37

This is the stretch of coast that runs south-westwards from the NATS (National Air Traffic Systems) Comms Station building and aerial at the road-end. It extends towards the island of Eilean Molach, which lies just off the coast where the Àird Mhòr Mhangarstaidh headland turns to run south-eastwards. Two of the area's major geos, Aurora Geòdha and Magic Geòdha, are located here and lie in a raised rocky headland known as The Flannan Area. The northern end of this headland is formed by the black wall of Tamana Head which is obvious from the road-end. The climbing is described in a north to south direction, as met on the approach from the road-end at the aerial.

Approach: From the parking at the road-end, go slightly uphill from a small shed then contour southwards. Cross a small burn then drop into a shallow bouldery trough in front of the raised rocky headland. Geodh' an Tamana lies down to the right. Ahead, a short scramble up slabs enables one to probably locate the back of Magic Geòdha first, with Aurora Geòdha overlapping it a little further seaward to the north-west (10min).

Geodh' an Tamana

(NB 0025 3300) Partially Tidal SW facing Map p37

This long and narrow inlet runs southwards past the skerry Sgeir Tamana from just west of the aerial. The northern end of the rocky promontory containing Magic and Aurora Geos has a distinct, slabby black tail which descends northwards into the sea and this forms the west side of Geodh' an Tamana. The south-west facing wall of the geo rises above large boulders and is quite sheltered.

Descent: From the shallow bouldery trough at the foot of the rocky promontory containing Magic and Aurora Geos, walk northwards down the gently angled, slabby black tail on the west side of the geo to reach the bottom.

Dry Dock 25m E1 5b *
C.King, R.Kenyon, 6 Jun 1993
An impressive route which takes the crack up the highest point of the steep wall. Start at the two large boulders at the end of the slabby tail. Climb easily up a corner-crack then move up left and go over an overlap. Continue up the crack and finish up a corner.

Birdsong 25m E3 5c **
G. Huxter, K. Pyke, 11 Jul 1997
Start on a large flat-topped boulder beneath a prominent orange corner to the left of Dry Dock. Follow a groove-crack to gain the orange corner and climb this on good holds to a ledge. Step right and go up 5m, then move right onto another sloping ledge to gain the base of an overhanging corner. Move left along the ledge and pull onto an easy ramp to finish. A direct finish up the corner is 6a.

Tamana Head

(NB 0019 3302) Partially tidal NW facing Map p37

Prominently seen from the road, this is the black coloured, north facing wall on the rocky Flannan Area headland. It lies on the other side of the slabby black tail that forms the west side of Geodh' an Tamana.

Approach: Scramble up slabs beyond the top of Aurora Geòdha and head out to the north-western tip of the headland where a short drop gains a platform on the edge. This is at the top of a corner climbed by Fair Play.

Descent: Abseil down the corner to good ledges.

The first three routes are left of the corner.

Left Winger 35m E2 5b *
R.Anderson, C.Anderson, 12 Jul 2004
The leftmost route. Follow Centre Forward to the left of the edge, then just to its left, climb a short right-angled groove capped by a bulge and finish up the slim groove above.

Centre Forward 35m E2 5b *
R.Anderson, C.Anderson, 11 Jul 2004
From the base of the corner-crack, climb easily up left beneath an obvious hanging groove in the edge. Just around the edge from this groove, move up right towards it to enter a short groove to its left and climb this to the top.

Centre Half 30m VS 4c *
R.Anderson, C.Anderson, 12 Jul 2004
A line just left of the corner. Climb easily up left to below the hanging groove in the bulging edge. Pull up into a V-groove beneath the bulge, then go up right to gain the slab left of the corner, then go left and finish up the edge.

Fair Play 30m HS 4b *
R.Anderson, C.Anderson, 11 Jul 2004
The crack in the main corner leads up left past a right-hand finish, which is the upper line of the abseil approach.

Left to Wander 30m E1 5b *
R.Anderson, C.Anderson, 11 Jul 2004
Step across right from the base of the corner-crack to a short groove and awkwardly climb this, then thin cracks up right to a recess which is climbed on its left. Continue in the same line to the top.

Right to Roam 30m E1 5b *
R.Anderson, C.Anderson, 11 Jul 2004
From the base of the groove of Left to Wander, step right to a flake hold then move boldly up to a short groove. A few pulls gain the easier upper groove, which is climbed to its top. Step right and finish up a thin crack.

The next group of climbs lie to the right where a large slab slopes down to the sea. The slab has a prominent black sidewall to its right.

Descent: From the ledge at the top of the previous routes, an abseil can be made down the large slab to gain ledges just above the high water mark.

Tamana Chimney 30m VD **
R.Anderson, C.Anderson, 11 Jul 2004
The chimney formed between the slab and the sidewall.

Sideburn 30m E4 6a **
M.Garthwaite, R.Anderson, 30 Jun 2007
The crack in the black sidewall. Step across the base of Tamana Chimney onto the wall and make difficult moves up the wall to a short leaning groove where further trying moves gain a crack. Climb the crack to the edge, traverse left into the centre of the wall then climb up and left to pull into a groove and finish.

Rubber Ducked 30m HVS 5a **
M.Garthwaite, R.Anderson, 30 Jun 2007
Start at barnacle level at the base of the sidewall. Step up right to climb the wall then slim grooves and cracks up the edge.

Duck Dive 30m E1 5b **
R.Anderson, M.Garthwaite, 30 Jun 2007
The lovely crack to the right of the edge. Either belay as for Rubber Ducked, or move up right onto a small ledge at the base of the crack.

The crack to the right is Bounty Hunters, which is gained along with another three routes from further south where there is a recess at the top of the cliff. This is a short way west from the top of Newton's Law in Aurora Geòdha.

Descent: Abseil into the square-cut recess beside a chimney-crack to gain the foot of a narrow south facing wall with an aesthetic arete up its left side.

Bounty Hunters 25m S 4b **
R.Anderson, C.Anderson, 9 Jul 2006
The fine crack to the right of Duck Dive is gained by a left traverse around the aesthetic arete.

Mutineer's Return 25m VS 4b **
G.Huxter, G.Kirk, 11 Jul 1997
The aesthetic left arete is climbed in an exposed position.

Sidewalk 25m E1 5b *
K.Pyke, G.Huxter, A.Leary, 11 Jul 1997
Climb a crack in the side wall right of the arete to thinner moves leading diagonally right then continue on a rising rightward line following the length of the wall on good holds and ledges.

Ceol na Mara 25m S 4b
F.Macleod, F.T.Macleod, 14 May 1999
The chimney-crack which runs parallel to the side wall.

Sideburn (E4) Mark Garthwaite (photo Rab Anderson)

Aurora Geòdha

(NB 0011 3294) Map p37

This geo lies in the middle of the raised rocky headland known as The Flannan Area. It is located by scrambling up slabs from where one arrives at the shallow trough and walking some 20m across the flat highpoint to where the ground unexpectedly opens up. The geo is deep and quite narrow, and with the sea normally rushing into a cave at its northern end there can be much spray flying around. As well as being atmospheric this does mean that the starts of some routes can be greasy at times. The climbing is described from left to right in a clockwise direction when facing west out to sea, starting with the Seaward Side, or East Face.

Seaward Side - East Face and North Wall

Non-tidal SE & SW facing

On the seaward side of the geo the corner-lines of Newton's Law and Star of the Sea are obvious, running up the angles formed between the East Face and the back, or North Wall to the right, which forms an arch over the sea cave.

Descent: The climbs are all reached directly down the lines, or adjacent ones, to belay on ledges above the sea.

The first three climbs lie on the lower left-hand side, taking obvious crack-lines in the slabby wall right of a chimney fault and are reached by abseiling down the crest then the fault.

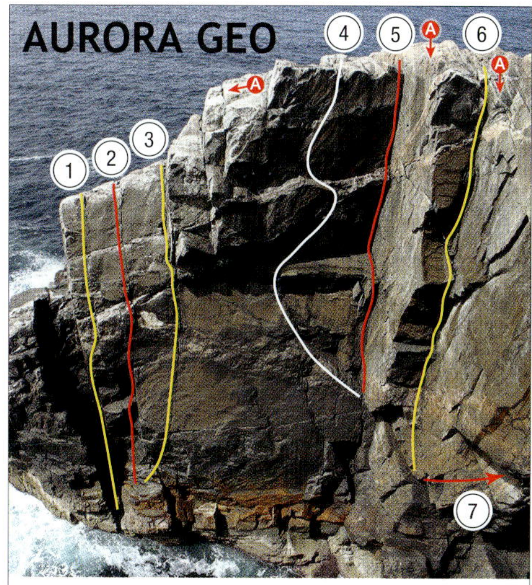

Seaward Side

1. Southern Belle HVS 5b *
2. Grand Central E1 5b **
3. Great Northern E2 5c **
4. Wonder Wall E5 6a **
5. Newton's Law E1 5b **
6. Star of the Sea E1 5b **
7. Romancing the Moose E5 6a ***

1 Southern Belle 30m HVS 5b *

R.Anderson, C.Anderson, 13 Jul 2004

From the base of a rusty coloured recess climb the chimney-fault to ledges, step right and climb a shallow, stepped groove to finish up a thin crack just right of the edge of the slabby wall.

2 Grand Central 30m E1 5b **

R.Anderson, C.Anderson, 13 Jul 2004

Start from a good ledge 5m right of the base of the chimney-fault. Step up left and climb the central, stepped groove to a good ledge, then climb a shallow corner to the slab and climb the crack up its centre.

3 Great Northern 30m E2 5c **

R.Anderson, C.Anderson, 14 Jul 2004

Start from the same ledge as Grand Central. Step up right and climb a shallow groove to the slab then finish up the prominent crack and corner. An alternative finish can be made by moving right to climb a steep little corner.

4 Wonder Wall 30m E5 6a **

D.Etherington, May 1998

Start from the left-hand end of the ledge at the foot of the open corner of Newton's Law. Go directly up to a sloping ledge and move right to the right-hand end of an overhang. Make moves up a thin crack to a small quartzy band, move back left for 3m and make difficult moves up a thin crack trending rightwards. Originally climbed with preplaced gear and graded E4.

5 Newton's Law 30m E1 5b **

B.Newton, M.Tighe (aid), 1974; FFA unknown

The prominent, open two-stepped corner is climbed directly.

6 Star of the Sea 30m E1 5b **

M.Tighe, B.Newton, 1974

Despite being sometimes wet, this is a fine, well protected climb taking the line of the zigzag corner formed in the angle between the faces.

7 Romancing the Moose 30m E5 6a ***

K.Pyke, G.Huxter, 7 Sep 1996

This lies on the North Wall above the sea cave and is a route of contrast in a committing situation. From the foot of Star of the Sea, teeter gingerly along the lip of the hanging slab to a good rest beneath the roof (RP's). Jam wildly rightwards through the roof to gain then climb an awkward crack and at its top move right to gain the headwall. Climb steeply through the quartzy bands to good finishing jugs in the centre.

8 Should Have Gone To Kilnsey 25m E6 6b **
J.Cook, R.Burden, 15 Jun 2013
Good climbing in a great position. Climb the corner in the angle between the North Wall and the East Face (Corner Climb) until feet are level with the first overlap on the Romancing the Moose headwall. After placing gear in the corner, head leftwards to reach a dirty looking crack and a break in the centre of the headwall (gear). Continue straight up, taking a line about 2 to 3m to the right of Romancing the Moose, moving slightly left into a groove at the top.

Landward Side

Non-tidal NW facing

Extending rightwards from the sea cave and the corner formed by the angle between the faces is the West Face. Set back from this is the superb tarblack-coloured Cioch Wall, named after the block at its right end. Due to the fact that the majority of the routes start from ledges well above the sea, this can be a good and atmospheric place to climb when there is a big sea running. It should be noted that the black rock is particularly slippery when wet, so take care on the ledges!

Descent: For most of the Landward Side climbs, abseil down the line of Immaculate Crack from a convenient large spike some 5m back from the edge. This gains the left end of the fine ledge that runs beneath the Cioch Wall. Some of the climbs left of President's Chimney can be gained by continuing the abseil below the ledge beneath Immaculate Crack, whilst the others will require either a tricky left traverse, or a more direct abseil approach to be made. For routes to the right of the Cioch shaped block, abseil directly to their bases.

West Face

Diagram below

This grey coloured section of cliff protrudes from the rest of the landward side and drops straight into the sea. There are two smooth walls on the right side and a number of crack-lines, including two divergent cracks that start in the centre. A sloping ledge runs along the base of the climbs.

9 Corner Climb 25m E3 5c *
G.Huxter, K.Pyke, 7 Sep 1996
This follows the corner in the angle between the faces right of the sea cave. Climb up 5m to a hard move through an overhang. Continue more easily up the corner to the top

7. Romancing the Moose	E5 6a ***	14. A.N.Other	VS 5a **	22. Cioch Crack	VS 4c *
8. Should Have Gone To...	E6 6b **	15. Who Knows?	VS 5a **	23. Poultry in Motion	E2 5b **
9. Corner Climb	E3 5c *	16. The Pie Party	E2 5b **	24. Chicken Run	E1 5c ***
10. Cormorant Corner	E1 5b **	18. Immaculate Crack	VS 4b *	25. Look Back In Anger	E3 6a *
11. Shag Crack	HVS 5a/b *	19. Things Are Looking Up	E3 5c **	26. Don't Look Now	E2 5c **
12. Anonymous	E2 5c **	20. The Roaring Foam	E3 5c ***	27. The Vee	VS 4c **
13. Who Cares!	E1 5b *	21. Ocean View	E3 5c *	28. Black Friday	E2 5b *

10 Cormorant Corner 30m E1 5b **
M.Tighe, I.Sutherland, I.Sykes, 1975
Climb up and left into a hanging ramp below an overhang. Climb the overhang to reach a crack which gets easier towards the top.

11 Shag Crack 30m HVS 5a/b *
M.Tighe, I.Donaldson, 1975
The left-hand of two divergent cracks sports an awkward move over the overhang.

12 Anonymous 30m E2 5c **
M.Tighe & Party 1975; R.Anderson, C.Anderson, 30 Jul 2007
The right-hand of the two divergent cracks. Climb up and left to a ledge on Shag Crack, then step right and climb the crack. Originally graded VS 5a but rock scars indicate that the sea has carried out alterations.

13 Who Cares! 30m E1 5b *
R.Anderson, C.Anderson, 30 Jul 2007
The thin crack and wall just left of and parallel to the crack of A.N.Other.

14 A.N.Other 30m VS 5a **
A.Cunningham, L.Hughes, 10 May 1998
The crack-line running up the left side of the left-hand smooth wall.

15 Who Knows? 30m VS 5a **
R.Anderson, C.Anderson, 29 Jul 2007
The crack-line between the two smooth walls. Start from a ledge at the right edge of the wall and traverse left to the crack. Just below the large ledge move left onto the wall and climb to the top.

16 The Pie Party 30m E2 **
A.Tibbs, H.Tibbs, 27 Jul 2006
The crack-line up the centre of the first smooth wall, which sits in front of President's Chimney. Start on ledges at the right edge of the wall.
1. 13m 5b Climb a crack that starts on the edge and follow this up left onto the fine wall. When it blanks out finish boldly up and right to a platform.
2. 15m The easy arete above.

The Cioch Wall

Diagram opposite

Set back from the West Face and running rightwards from a deep chimney above a fine ledge is the tarblack-coloured Cioch Wall, with its distinctive Cioch shaped block sitting towards the right end. There are further climbs on the right side of the block.

17 President's Chimney 20m VD *
M.Tighe, J.Paterson, 1970s
Climb the deep chimney with some back and foot moves towards the top. An escape route (M) is possible by climbing the chimney until a move left leads onto a large ledge and a finish up the exposed blocky arete.

18 Immaculate Crack 20m VS 4b *
I.Sykes, I.Sutherland, 1970's
The obvious crack above the start of President's Chimney gives a sustained climb.

19 Things are Looking Up 25m E3 5c **
R. Everett, Sep 2001
Previously recorded as an E1 5c named and climbed by G.Latter, R.Campbell in 1993 but they confirm this was not what they climbed! Name kept. Make a few moves up Immaculate Crack, then step right and climb a crack-line leading to a slab. Move left then go up and right through a quartzy section. A fine and intricate climb.

20 The Roaring Foam 25m E3 5c ***
Unknown, 1994
Start some 4m right of the chimney and follow the thin crack which leans rightwards in its upper half; superb, sustained and well protected.

21 Ocean View 28m E3 5c *
W.Moir, N.Morrison, 7 Aug 2006
Climb the thin crack 2m right of The Roaring Foam (small RPs) to reach the top of a pinnacle-flake. Traverse right to gain the wide crack of Cioch Crack and go a short way up this before returning left along a small ramp. Gain a hidden crack and finish up the flakes to its right.

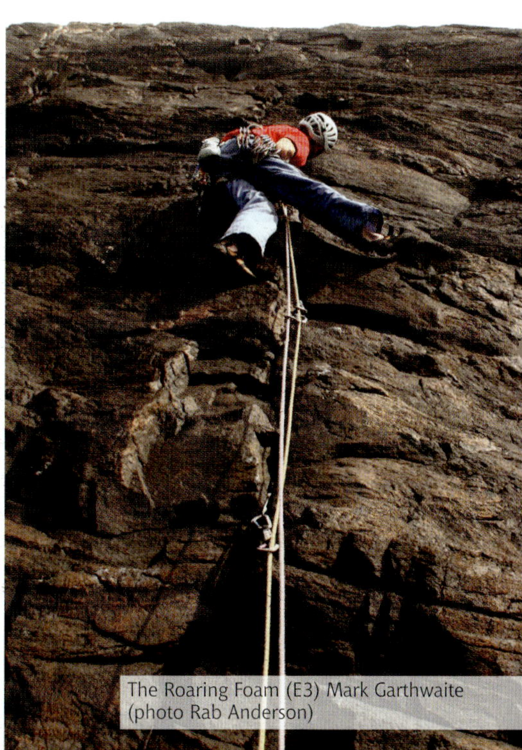

The Roaring Foam (E3) Mark Garthwaite (photo Rab Anderson)

22 Cioch Crack 20m VS 4c *
R.Anderson, C.Anderson, 1 Jul 1997
The wide crack in the centre of the wall can be wet and slimy at times but when dry it provides a pleasant climb.
Variation: **22a Alternate Start - Grease a Break! E2 5b**
R.Anderson, C.Anderson, 1 Jul 1997
The crack immediately to the left runs into the main crack part way up.

23 Poultry in Motion 20m E2 5b **
M.Dale, M.Bock, 30 May 2000
Immediately to the right of Cioch Crack, climb the thin crack and slim ramp then carry on up the thin continuation crack.

24 Chicken Run 20m E1 5c ***
M.Tighe, J.Paterson, 1979
The fine straight crack which starts 2m left of the Cioch.
Variation: **24a Indirect Line 20m HVS 5a ****
M.Tighe, J.Paterson, 1979
The original line is good; start as for the normal route and break out left up the obvious line to join then finish up Poultry in Motion.

25 Look Back in Anger 20m E3 6a *
R.Campbell, G.Latter, Jun 1993
Start from the left edge of the Cioch shaped block and climb the nasty thin crack.

The next climbs are located on the section of wall beyond the Cioch-shaped block and are best approached directly by abseil; there is a convenient fin of rock some 10m back from the edge, in line with the obvious top of The Vee. The climbs can also be reached by traversing around the seaward side of the Cioch.

26 Don't Look Now 20m E2 5c **
G.Latter, R.Campbell, Jun 1993
Good climbing up the intermittent thin crack on the right side of the Cioch. Gain the crack from the platform by a scary move across the abyss. The crack can also be gained from the left side of the Cioch by climbing a short way up Look Back in Anger to a ledge, then stepping right; previously recorded as **Black Affronted** (E2 5c, 1994; no FA details).

27 The Vee 20m VS 4c **
M.Tighe, J.Paterson, 1985
The first prominent V-groove to the right of the Cioch provides a fine climb starting from ledges at its foot.

28 Black Friday 20m E2 5b *
R.Anderson, C Anderson, 13 Apr 2007
The rib to the right of The Vee. Climb easily to a ledge where some awkward moves are followed by easier climbing.

29 Gannet Crack 20m HVS 5b *
M.Tighe, E.Sherstone, 1993
Some 10m to the right of The Vee is another prominent groove, gained by thin cracks above a ledge and climbed awkwardly to reach easier ground.

30 The Zed 20m HS 4b *
M.Tighe, J.Paterson, 1985
A zigzag line to the right of Gannet Crack.

Chicken Run (E1) Mark Jarvie (photo Rab Anderson)

Magic Geòdha

(NB 0015 3290) Map p37

Some 50m south along the rocky crest from the head of Aurora Geòdha the ground opens up to reveal another impressive, deep and even narrower geo with a floor of white boulders. The starts of climbs from the base of the geo can often be worryingly greasy, especially early in the day. However, the sun does reach the depths and any dampness soon disappears.

The landward side is a splendid wall of steep west-facing grey rock, the West Face, with the recessed Black Wall forming its right side which turns into the north-facing South End. The seaward side of the geo takes the form of a tall overhung slab, the East Face, which turns to the southwards facing Red Wall. The climbing is described clockwise around the geo when facing out to sea, starting with the Red Wall at the seaward entrance.

Descent: The best and probably the safest way to access the majority of the climbs here is to walk south beyond the steep West Face on the landward side to a flat platform on the cliff edge. This is directly opposite the Red Wall on the other side of the geo and at the top of the slabby Black Wall. A 30m abseil from here gains large ledges at the foot of the Black Wall which are well above the sea and from where either of two ramps can be easily descended to the boulder filled floor.

Seaward Side

Non-tidal SW & SE facing Diagrams p61 & p62

Red Wall

This is actually the butt end of the promontory which separates Aurora Geo from Magic Geo. Readily seen from the opposite side of the geo, the wall is characterised by three diagonal crack-lines, to the left of which are two chimney-grooves (The Flannan Chimneys). There are times when it may be easier to gain the large ledge at the base of the wall directly by abseil; it should be easy to determine from above when the boulder that enables access from the floor of the geo is clear of the water.

1 Flannan Chimney Left-Hand 25m HS 4b *
M.Tighe, J.Paterson, May 1979
At half-height, the chimney flares and protection is awkward to arrange.

2 Flannan Chimney Right-Hand 25m S 4a *
M.Tighe, J.Paterson, May 1979
This sports a difficult move going right round an overhang at half-height.

3 Flannan Crack 25m VS 4c ***
M.Tighe, J.Paterson, May 1979
The obvious right-slanting crack gives a fine and atmospheric route, especially when the swell is up.

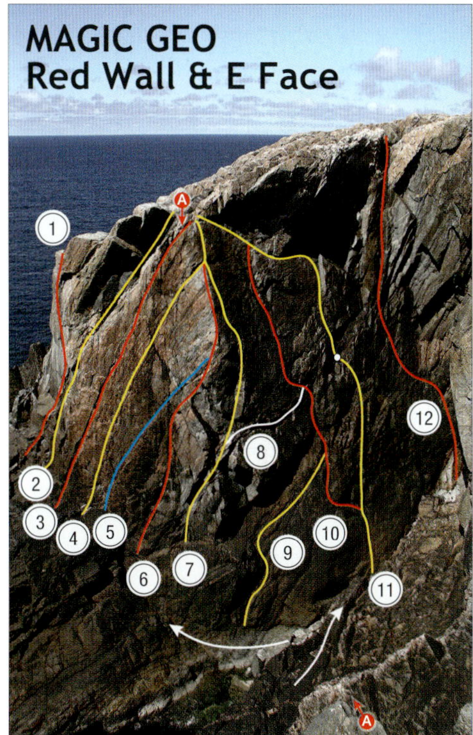

1.	Flannan Chimney Left-hand	HS 4b *
2.	Flannan Chimney Right-hand	S 4a *
3.	Flannan Crack	VS 4c **
4.	Campa Crack	E1 5a **
5.	Gas	E3 5b *
6.	Limka	E2 5b **
7.	Flannan Edge	E3 5c **
8.	Flannan Slab Left-hand	HVS 5a *
9.	Flannan Slab Direct	E1 5b ***
10.	Bubbles	HVS 5a ***
11.	Flannan Slab	VS 5a ***
12.	Kissing the Pink	E2 5b *

4 Campa Crack 30m E1 5a **
D.Cuthbertson, P.Moores, 7 Jun 1985
Climb the next crack to the right; the main difficulties are in the first 5m.

5 Gas 30m E3 5b *
T.Fryer, I.Taylor, 1 Jun 2003
From the base of Campa Crack, follow a right-slanting pink dyke to join Limka after 20m.

6 Limka 35m E2 5b **
P.Moores, D.Cuthbertson, 7 Jun 1985
Start to the right of Gas, then trend up and right following the obvious line. Finish up the arete between the two faces.

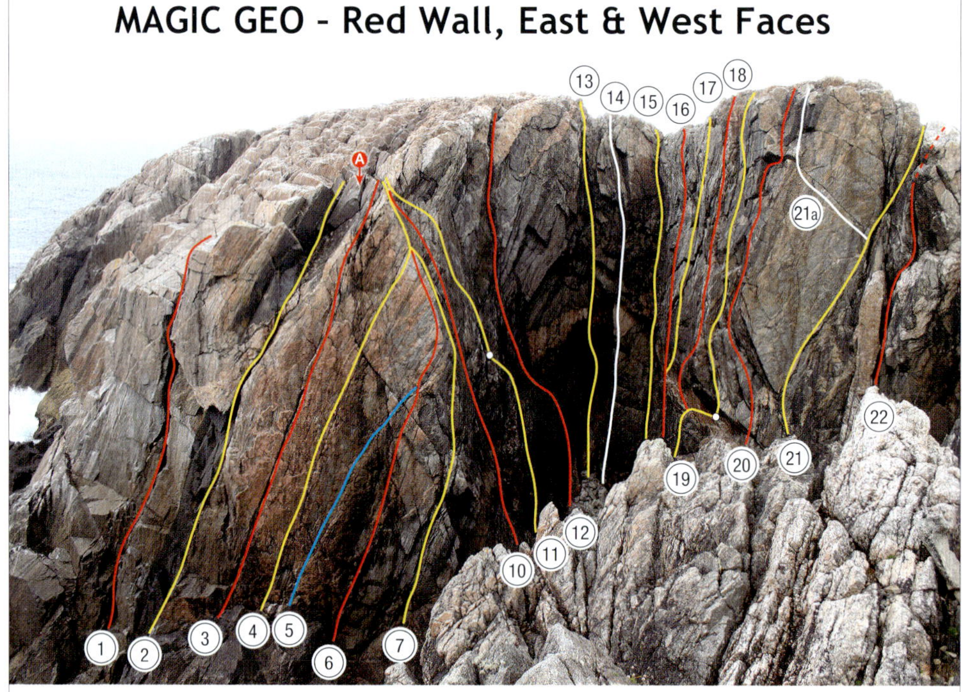

1. Flannan Chimney LH	HS 4b *	10. Bubbles	HVS 5a ***	17. The Sorcerer	E5 6a ***
2. Flannan Chimney RH	S 4a *	11. Flannan Slab	VS 5a ***	18. Gimp Route	E4 5c *
3. Flannan Crack	VS 4c **	12. Kissing the Pink	E2 5b *	19. The Alchemist	E4 6a *
4. Campa Crack	E1 5a **	13. The Crimebusters of The Sea	E5 6a **	20. Am Burrach	E4 6a **
5. Gas	E3 5b *	14. The Eagle Has Landed	E6 6b **	21. Island Life	VS 5a **
6. Limka	E2 5b **	15. Queen's Freebie	E4 6b *	21a. Island Fling	VS 5a **
7. Flannan Edge	E3 5c **	16. The Magician	E5 6a ***	22. Solitary Chimneys	D/VD *

East Face

The overhung slabby wall that runs into the back of the geo above the narrow boulder filled floor. The starts of the climbs can be greasy at times.

7 Flannan Edge 35m E3 5c **

R.Anderson, C.Anderson, 14 Jul 2004

The blunt edge between the Red Wall and the East Face. Start mid-way between the floor of the geo and the ledge at the foot of the Red Wall. The first section is common with Flannan Slab Left-hand. Gain then climb a shallow right-slanting chimney-fault around the edge to a flake-ledge. Climb the quartzy groove on the right side of the edge to a shallow recess below a small roof, move up, then traverse left above the roof onto the edge and climb this to the top.

8 Flannan Slab Left-hand 40m HVS *

M.Tighe, C.Davies, 1978

Originally recorded as Flannan Slab Direct but not really direct and now a variation.

1. 10m 5a Climb the shallow fault common with Flannan Edge to the flake-ledge.
2. 35m 5a Hand-traverse horizontally right for 6m, step up and gain another flake, then follow a line of good holds and left-facing flakes as for Flannan Slab Direct and finish leftwards as for Flannan Slab.

9 Flannan Slab Direct 40m E1 5b ***

M.Tighe, M.O'Brian, 1980s

Start near the left end of the wall, beneath the mid-point of a large slanting overhang 15m up the wall. Climb a shallow groove with difficulty (crux) to better holds in another groove that leads to a large ledge on the left arete below the left-hand end of the large slanting overhang. Step back down and traverse right to easier ground, then climb a series of left-facing flakes and corners to a finish up the slab just right of the final arete.

10 Bubbles 40m HVS 5a ***

C.King, R.Kenyon, 6 Jun 1993

Although climbed after the other Flannan Slab routes and having parts in common, this fine hybrid is probably the best and most direct line on the slab. Climb Flannan Slab to the ledge at 3m then move left into the base of the line of left-facing flakes and corners that the other Flannan Slab routes traverse into. Climb all the way to the top of this line to join Flannan Slab then finish leftwards by either a foot-traverse of the lower break, or a hand-traverse of the upper break.

11 Flannan Slab 45m VS ***
M.Tighe, J.Paterson, May 1978
This splendid route with its two contrasting pitches starts towards the centre of the face, beneath the line of a thin crack leading to a ledge.
1. 25m 5a Climb the thin crack to reach a ledge at 3m; awkward when greasy but reasonable protection. Continue to another ledge, then go up and left on widely spaced holds and protection to another ledge (often partly water filled) and belay; if required there is further gear just over the bulge.
2. 25m 5a Pull over the bulge to gain then climb a prominent short left-facing corner to reach an old peg runner. Traverse left (crux), then go up to good holds and continue the traverse leftwards to finish on the edge; care should be taken to extend runners.

12 Kissing the Pink 40m E2 5b *
S.Maclean, N.Williams, May 1986; Direct finish R.Robins, B.Bransby, Jun 2004
The corner at the right-hand side of the face has a blind crux high on the route. The original start going up and right to climb a short overhanging corner to a ramp appears to have been removed by the sea. Instead, where the geo narrows opposite the corner of Queens Freebie climb a crack to reach the ramp at a large pegmatite band, move left into another groove, then continue to the top. The obvious direct finish (E3) is quite loose.

13 The Crimebusters of the Sea 40m E5 6a **
P.Robins, B.Bransby, 11 Jun 2004
A marvellous outing up the obvious line of weakness in the back of the geo. Starting at the back, climb the left wall to a flake leading into the pink cave. Shuffle and wriggle outwards and upwards to an easier finish in the wider chimney.

14 The Eagle has Landed 40m E6 6b **
P.Robins, B.Bransby, 11 Jun 2004
Another splendid journey up the back of the geo, climbing the obvious lower arete then through the bulge and into the slim finishing groove. The arete is climbed direct and is bold. Going through the bulges is the crux (small cams useful) gaining a block ledge. Step right and go up the pleasant wall and into the finishing groove.

Landward Side

Non-tidal NW & NE facing

West Face

Diagrams opposite & p64

Rising above the narrow boulder filled floor is an impressive steep wall of grey rock containing some long, thin crack-lines.

15 Queen's Freebie 40m E4 6b *
D.Cuthbertson, P.Moores, Jun 1985
The corner at the left-hand end of the wall sports a desperate move over the mid-height bulge.

16 The Magician 40m E5 6a ***
J.Moran, D.Pearce, 5 May 1985
This impressive route, high in its grade, climbs the vague crack to the left of a long thin crack which almost touches the ground, and to the left of a short corner-ramp in the centre of the face. Start about 7m right of Queen's Freebie. Climb boldly up and left to gain a red band and the start of the crack. Climb the sustained and strenuous crack (thankfully well protected) veering right towards the top.

17 The Sorcerer 40m E5 6a ***
J.Moran, D.Pearce, 5 May 1985
Another bold route. Start up The Magician, then climb a ramp on the right and go back left to a flakey corner. Pull over this, then traverse right to finish up the groove above.

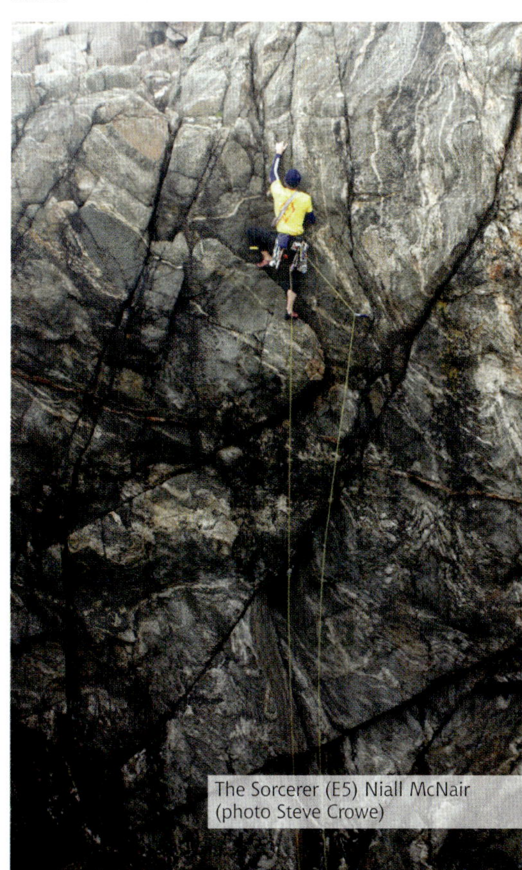

The Sorcerer (E5) Niall McNair (photo Steve Crowe)

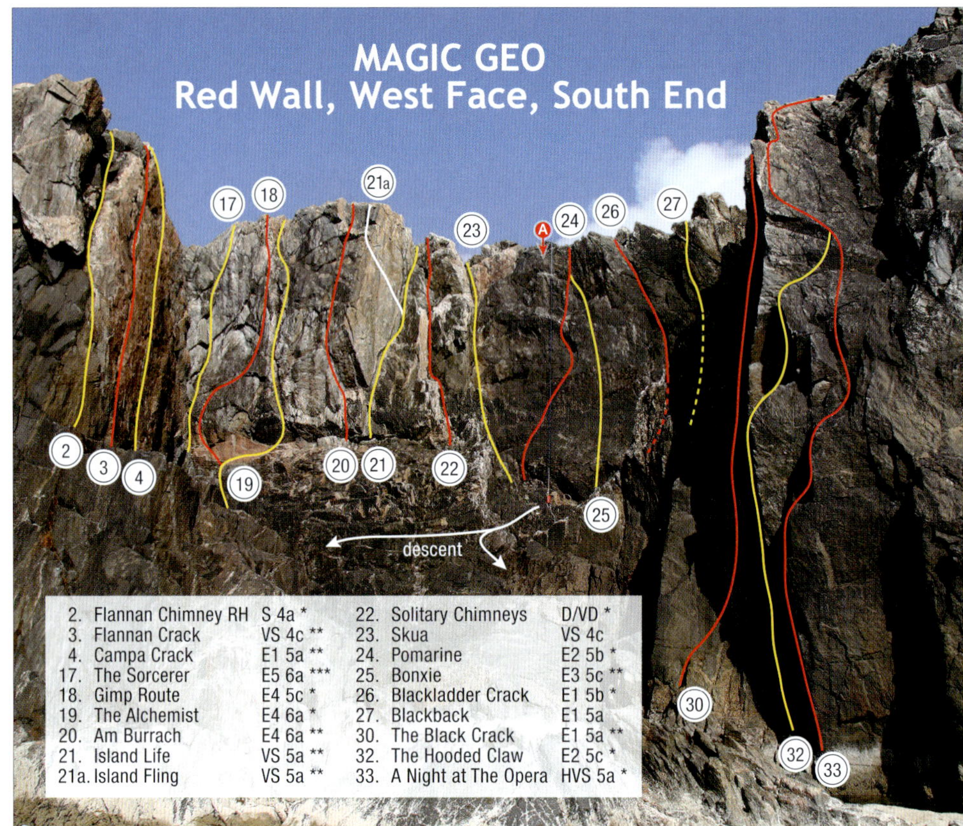

18 Gimp Route 40m E4 5c *
B.Bransby, P.Robins, 11 Jun 2004
Start up The Alchemist and climb this up its initial corner to the ledges, then move left and using a flake pull through the bulge. Traverse right along a thin seam to gain a ramp which soon becomes a crack, just left of The Alchemist. Go direct to the top.

19 The Alchemist 50m E4 *
N.Clement, G.Latter, 25 May 1996
This takes the groove and bottomless chimney towards the right side of the wall.
1. 20m 5c Climb the prominent deep black V-groove which soon eases, then head diagonally right to belay on the large ledge directly beneath the steep leaning groove.
2. 30m 6a Strenuously climb the innocuous looking groove with difficulty to better holds on the left wall at 6m. The chimney-groove above provides a pleasant easier finish.

20 Am Burrach 25m E4 6a **
R.Campbell, G.Latter, Jun 1993
The last line on this part of the wall is a shallow, right-facing groove in the upper wall, to the right of the wide crack of The Alchemist and just left of the arete. Starting from the large mid-way ledge, climb the shallow right-facing groove and pull left to good holds. Climb the thin continuation crack leading into a shallow groove and easier climbing.

21 Island Life 25m VS 5a **
R.Anderson, C.Anderson, 12 Jul 2000
The corner to the right of the overhanging arete which marks the right end of the steep West Face gives a good route. Scramble up leftwards to belay on the shelf beneath the corner. Climb this direct with a steep but well protected start. It is possible to avoid the steep start by climbing up and left into the line from the right to give a S.
Variation: **21a Island Fling VS 5a ****
B.Rose, L.Mackay, 8 May 2002
A spectacular finish to Island Life, taking the obvious incut ledge and slanting crack across the left wall to finish by pulling round the arete in a fine position.

22 Solitary Chimneys 25m D/VD *
Lochaber MC, 1970s
The chimney-cracks formed by a vertical quartzy vein between the two corners.

Black Wall

Diagram opposite

This steep slabby wall forms the recessed right-hand section of the landward side of the geo. The best abseil approach for this geo is down the centre of the wall. There is a good flat area on the cliff-top for gearing-up.

23 Skua 30m VS 4c
R.Anderson, C.Anderson, 11 Jul 2000
The right-facing corner-crack which runs up the left side of the wall.

24 Pomarine 30m E2 5b *
R.Anderson, C.Anderson 10 Jul 2000
Start at the foot of the corner of Skua and move up to gain a break which slants rightwards across the wall. Make a few moves along the break then stand on it to gain holds and pull onto the slabby wall to gain the base of a short groove. Climb the groove and continue to a finish up a slim short corner.

25 Bonxie 30m E3 5c **
R.Anderson, C.Anderson 10 Jul 2000
Start towards the right side of the wall, below a thin crack-line just left of a prominent shattered crack-line at a water trough on the ledge. A steep using undercuts gains the thin crack-line which is followed to a finish up the short corner of Pomarine.

26 Blackladder Crack 30m E1 5b *
R.Anderson, C.Anderson, 11 Jul 2000
The prominent shattered crack-line running up the right side of the main part of the wall has an awkward start.

27 Blackback 25m E1 5a
R.Anderson, M.Atkins, P.Allen, 10 Jun 2006
Start up on the right, in the trough below the right side of the wall. Climb a line of weakness to a recess at the start of the steeper upper section, step left and climb the obvious crack, then pull right out of this to finish.

South End

Diagrams above & opposite

To the right of the Black Wall the cliff turns to face north. There is a broken area of quartzy rock then a steeper, black mitre-shaped wall whose right edge drops into the sea. The mitre-shaped wall has three cracks running up it, the central of which is The Black Crack. The wall is reached by scrambling easily down and across from the foot of the Black Wall then making a short climb to good ledges.

28 Foaming Grooves 30m S 4a
The grooves forming the right side of the recessed slabby bay to the right of the Black Wall. It is not sure exactly where the route goes but there is a fair amount of easy rock between the Black Wall and the steeper mitre-shaped wall.

MAGIC GEO - South End

29.	Last Orders	HVS 5a *
30.	The Black Crack	E1 5a **
31.	Too Wild for Feral Fyffe	E4 6a *
32.	The Hooded Claw	E2 5c *
33.	A Night at The Opera	HVS 5a *

29 Last Orders 40m HVS 5a *
R.Anderson, C.Anderson, 14 Jul 2000
The left-hand of the three cracks on the mitre-shaped wall. Start from ledges at the foot of a corner left of the main corner-groove running up beneath the cracks (a start can also be made up The Black Crack). Climb the corner and move up quartzy rock into the main corner-groove and climb the cracks left of The Black Crack.

30 The Black Crack 40m E1 5a **
Lochaber MC, 1970s
The central crack on the mitre-shaped wall; start from ledges just above the waterline. Climb the wide corner-groove which runs up the left side of the wall to gain the crack then climb this past a small and usually water filled ledge.

31 Too Wild for Feral Fyffe 40m E4 6a *
E.Tresidder, T.Bridgeland, 9 Jun 2003
The prominent blind crack right of The Black Crack gives

good climbing with lots of poor small gear (RPs and aliens), and one crucial Friend 2.5 at half-height. Start as for The Hooded Claw but continue up the crack where that route goes right.

32 The Hooded Claw 40m E2 5c *

R.Anderson, C.Anderson, 11 Jul 2000

From ledges just above the waterline, step up right onto a rib and climb to the base of the prominent but blind right-hand crack. Traverse hard right into the obvious V shaped recess on the arete. Climb the recess, step right to pull up and go back left to climb the arete in a fine position.

33 A Night at the Opera 35m HVS *

D.Cuthbertson and another, Oct 1985

This is the last accessible line on the wall; start slightly further right and lower down, on a small ledge at the foot of a slim corner in the arete.

1. 10m 5a Climb the awkward corner to a ledge.
2. 25m 4c Move up and right, then go left to a quartzy seam at the edge of the slab and finish up this.

Neptune's Staircase (HVS) Chris Anderson (photo Rab Anderson)

Hunter's Slabs

(NB 0010 3285) Tidal & Non-tidal NW facing Map p37 Diagram opposite

The outer wall of Aurora Geo runs into two lovely clean slabs, some 40m high, which sweep down to the sea from beneath a prominent Aiguille-like block on the cliff-top. The slabs are split by a gully-trough and chimney feature beneath the north end of the Aiguille. Some routes have apparently been climbed here in the past but never recorded. Given the grades, the perfect nature of the rock and the outstanding setting, a number of climbs have now been recorded for others to enjoy.

The first climbs lie on the section of wall between the entrance to Magic Geòdha and the slabs themselves. These climbs are gained by abseil and start from small ledges just above the water. A pink quartz-like block on the cliff-top marks the top of the wall. Just to the north of this is the top of the wide groove which The Hooded Claw and A Night at the Opera finish up the left side of.

Descent: The pink block on the cliff-top, or a thread beneath it, provides a convenient anchor. From its north side this allows Drink Awareness and Spirit of the Deep to be gained. From its south side, the white top of Nemo's Corner can be seen and this allows this climb, together with Neptune's Staircase and Davy Jones' Locker, to be accessed.

1 Drink Awareness 40m E3 5b *

R.Anderson, C.Anderson, 7 Jul 2011

Start from a well-positioned small ledge some 5m above the high tide mark on the front of the buttress to the left of Neptune's Staircase, with good wires at the base of the corner at the right end. Move off the left end of the ledge and go up towards the left edge to place a nut in a small left-facing corner. The initial moves are bold and a fall could put you straight into the water, so the correct belay position is vital, as are low tide and a calm sea! Move up right to a break (spike) then continue above to the left end of a handrail (gear) before moving across left into the base of the big groove. Either climb this easily to the top, or climb up and out right onto the front face and finish as for Spirit of the Deep.

2 Spirit of the Deep 40m HVS 4c **

R.Anderson, C.Anderson, 7 Jul 2011

Start from the same ledge as Drink Awareness. Climb the corner above the right end of the ledge to a ledge beneath the roof, traverse right then pull up to reach the edge of the groove of Neptune's Staircase. Step left above the roof and climb the front of the buttress passing the left side of a projection to reach the top.

3 Neptune's Staircase 50m HVS 4c **

R.Anderson, C.Anderson, 7 Jul 2011

This finishes on the north side of the large pink block on the cliff-top but is approached from the other side,

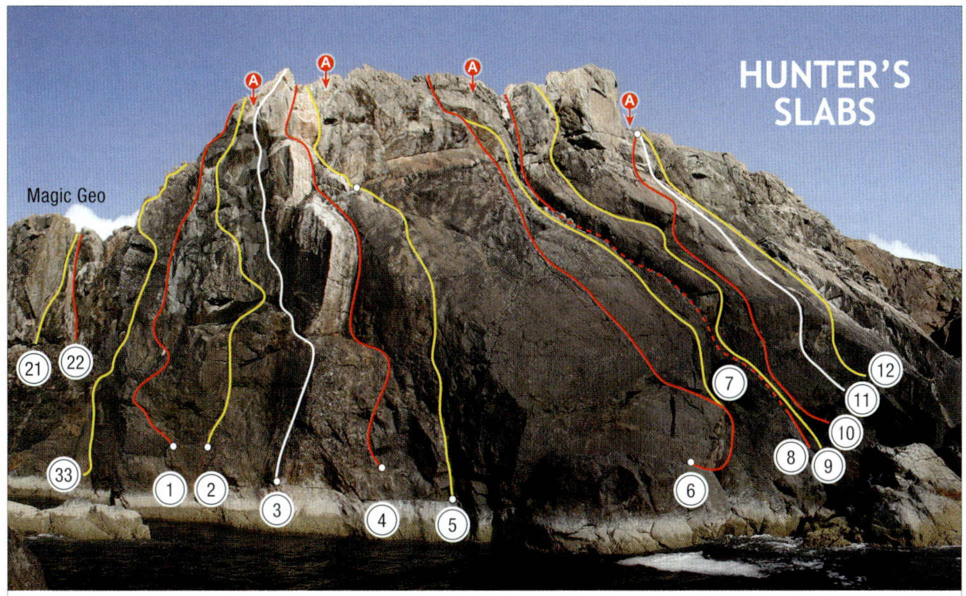

1. Drink Awareness	E3 5b *	6. Hunter's Slab	S 4b **	11. Petit Dru	VD **	
2. Spirit of the Deep	HVS 4c **	7. Hunter's Edge	S 4b **	12. The Walkers Spur	VD **	
3. Neptune's Staircase	HVS 4c **	8. The Trough	S 4a *	21. Island Life	VS 5a **	(Magic Geo)
4. Nemo's Corner	HVS 4c **	9. Du Midi	VS 5a *	22. Solitary Chimneys	D/VD *	(Magic Geo)
5. Davy Jones' Locker	E1 5b *	10. Aiguille Direct	VS 5a **	33. A Night at The Opera	HVS 5a *	(Magic Geo)

down the white corner of Nemo's Corner to reach a small ledge with good gear just above the high water mark. Climb a thin crack and the edge to the right to reach the ledge beneath Nemo's Corner, then traverse left and climb the staircase.

4 Nemo's Corner 40m HVS 4c **

R.Anderson, C.Anderson, 7 Jul 2011

On the left side of the Left-hand Slab there is an obvious right-angled corner which has a white left wall. Abseil down the right wall then slant right from the base of the corner to gain a small black ledge just above the high tide mark (good wires). Climb up and left then traverse left into the corner which is climbed to easier ground leading up the left side of the slab to reach the top.

5 Davy Jones' Locker 45m E1 *

R.Anderson, C.Anderson, 7 Jul 2011

This is gained as for Nemo's Corner but on the abseil slant further right to gain a narrow seaweed covered ledge just down and right from the start of that route (good wires).

1. 25m 5b Climb the crack above the right end of the ledge, then step left and climb up onto the Left-hand Slab. Move up and left along the lip of the slab then move up to a crack and belay on the shelf above
2. 20m 5b Move up the slab then climb leftwards up the stepped corner-line in the headwall.

Left-hand Slab

Descent: From the north side of the Aiguille-like block on the cliff-top, abseil directly down the slab to a splendid ledge.

6 Hunter's Slab 40m S 4b **

R.Anderson, C.Anderson, 15 Jul 2008

The central crack-line up the left-hand sweep of slabs; either start from a small ledge at the foot of the slab, or continue down a short wall (occasionally greasy) to the splendid large ledge beneath the base. Direct access up the short wall is bold and difficult; instead step right off the end of the ledge to climb up and back left to the small ledge at the start of the slab. Climb the crack on perfect rock to below the final steepening then move right and climb to the top.

7 Hunter's Edge 40m S 4b **

R.Anderson, C.Anderson, 16 Jul 2009

Start from the large lower ledge as for Hunter's Slab. Climb to another ledge up on the right; alternative start point. Climb up to the left of a short but steep crack (a 5a variation) then move right into the crack and climb this and the edge of the slab to finish as for Hunter's Slab.

8 The Trough 35m S 4a *
R.Anderson, C.Anderson, 16 Jul 2009
The gully-trough and chimney feature which splits the slabs is climbed mainly on the right wall to a short crux at the top; surprisingly good.

Right-hand Slab

Descent: One option is to abseil down the left side of the slab from the north side of the Aiguille, into the base of the gully-trough; watch the chimney-crack, it eats abseil ropes! The other which is probably better, is to scramble down boulders on the south side of the Aiguille to a ledge and abseil down the centre of the slab to the ledges which girdle the base.

9 Du Midi 40m VS 5a *
R.Anderson, C.Anderson, 13 Jul 2009
Start from the ledge at the base of the trough; obvious spike. Climb the wall which guards the base of the slab up left to a ledge then awkwardly up right onto a ledge then up onto the slab. Follow the line of weakness and the slab left of it, up around the left side of an overlap, then climb a short groove leading up left to the top.

10 Aiguille Direct 40m VS 5a **
R.Anderson, C.Anderson, 13 Jul 2009
Start just right of Du Midi and climb the obvious line steeply onto the slab then follow a line of weakness for a short way before climbing up to the right side of an overlap. Move up right, then back left above the overlap before climbing directly to the ledges below the right side of the Aiguille.

The Walkers Spur (VD) Chris Anderson
(photo Rab Anderson)

11 Petit Dru 40m VD **
R.Anderson, C.Anderson, 13 Jul 2009
Start from the right end of the ledge beneath the slab and climb the left side of a flake like feature to gain a crack-line slanting leftwards up the slab to reach the ledge beneath the right side of the Aiguille.

12 The Walkers Spur 45m VD **
R.Anderson, C.Anderson, 13 Jul 2009
Start at the same point as Petit Dru and climb up right onto the slab then climb the right edge up leftwards to the ledge beneath the right side of the Aiguille. At the start, it is possible to scramble down towards the sea to gain the edge from lower down.

Hidden Geòdha

(NB 0009 3275) Tidal NW facing Map p37

This lies tucked away immediately south of Hunter's Slabs. It is sheltered by the small rock island lying out in front, with the result that it can be possible to escape from the wind and the effects of the sea.

Descent: Immediately behind the Aiguille, a fault drops down behind the slabs. This is actually the line of a narrow, deep cave below, which forms the back of the geo. Instead of dropping down here, traverse over blocks, drop down a small step and go horizontally across the top of some slabs for 40m. At this point the geo is still out of sight. A large pointed flake takes three large linked slings and provides a useful anchor for an abseil down the sloping corner of Hidden Gem to good ledges a short way above the sea. Slippery ledges lead leftwards to the base of Spiny Norman and a ledge a short way up in a niche on the left; it should be possible to abseil directly to here by slanting left on the abseil.

There are three routes described from right to left.

Hidden Gem 35m S 4a **
M.Tighe, J.Paterson and Party, May 1983
The obvious sloping corner-crack is climbed direct.

Spiny Norman 35m HVS 5b **
M.Tighe, J.Paterson and Party, May 1983
Some 12m to the left, climb the obvious, superb, and well protected open corner.

Stormin Normin 35m E1 5b **
R.Anderson, C.Anderson, 11 Jul 2001
Slightly eliminate but very good climbing taking the arete and crack-line just left of the open corner of Spiny Norman. Step onto the left arete then climb this until forced up right into a crack and continue up this until pushed into the corner at the top.

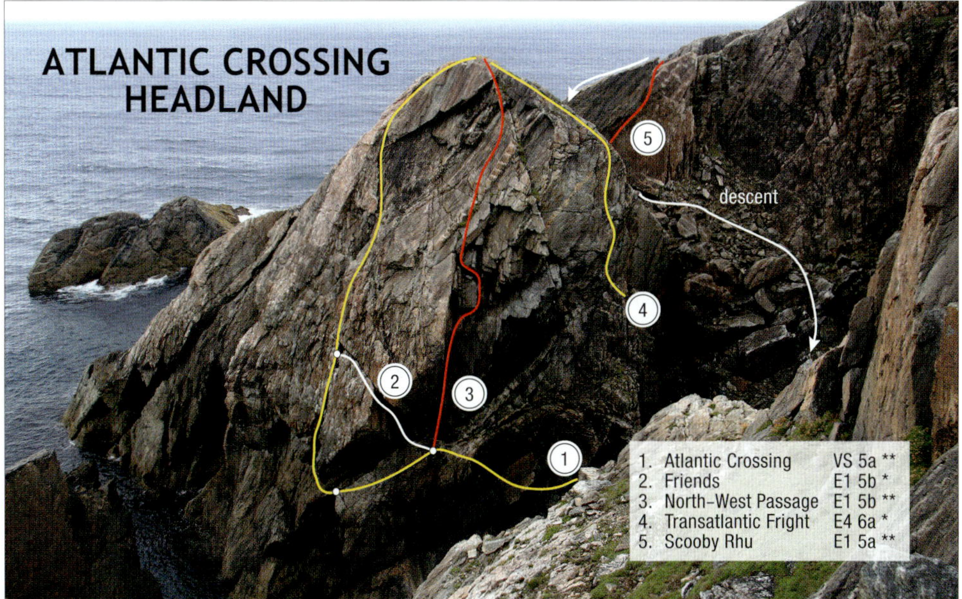

Atlantic Crossing Headland

(NB 9995 3262) Non-tidal W facing Map p37

This distinctive Cioch-like headland block is a few hundred metres further south-west along the coast from the Magic and Aurora Geòdhas area.

Approach: From the parking area at the aerial, contour the hillside well above the coastline, going beyond the rocky promontory of The Flannan Area containing Aurora and Magic Geos to reach a large bay with solitary fence post at its top (15min). The triangular headland block is obvious on the north side.

Descent: Go down the ridge which connects the headland block to the mainland which is slabby on the right and overhung on the left to reach a notch. Descend a ramp on the left then scramble down through the boulder field.

1 Atlantic Crossing 100m VS **

M.Tighe, J.Paterson, May 1979

This is a rising girdle of the headland block. Start where a boulder choke abuts the main face and forms an obvious V-shape.

1. 25m 5a Climb awkwardly down the smooth boulder and step onto the main wall. Either ascend 1m or so to an overhang and traverse left, or go left almost immediately which is steep but on good holds. Bear in mind that the second is potentially in for a big swing here! Continue left across a series of grooves to a prominent spike.

2. 15m 4a Continue left to belay in an exposed position on the buttress edge above a bottomless corner.

2. 15m 5a Make an awkward step round the corner on the left onto a slab; a belly flop works! Climb a bottomless chimney-groove on the left to a small ledge and belay in a sentry box.

3. 45m 4b Climb the cracked wall and slab above, trending left near the top.

2 Friends 15m E1 5b *

M.Tighe, E.Nichols, B.Newton, 1986

A short but sensational variation to Atlantic Crossing. Belay beneath the corner taken by North-West Passage, about two-thirds of the way along the first pitch of Atlantic Crossing. Climb the crack which springs leftwards out of the niche to the left of North-West Passage to join Atlantic Crossing on its third pitch, above the sentry box.

3 North-West Passage 35m E1 5b **

Unknown, 1988

This takes the line of an obvious right-facing hanging corner situated about two-thirds of the way along the first pitch of Atlantic Crossing. Belay beneath the corner. Pull into the corner with difficulty and continue to some block overhangs (suspect). Turn these on the right, then traverse back left to exit onto the slabs at a point where the overlap begins to go back right. Follow the line of least resistance to the top.

4 Transatlantic Fright 25m E4 6a

K.Magog, S.Crowe, 19 Jun 2000

This climbs the crack in the headwall right of North-West Passage. The wall is gained by scrambling up to a pinnacle below the crack (loose rock). Trend up and left from the belay to a small overlap. Pull over this to a rest in a niche. Move left to gain the base of the crack and follow this to the top.

5 Scooby Rhu 15m E1 5a **
M.Tighe, J.Paterson, May 1979
A fine layback starts from the foot of the descent ramp and is short but well protected.

6 Waiting for the Crossing 45m VD/S **
R.Pettner, J.Ison, 2 Jun 2000
The obvious flake-groove on the left-hand side of the wall, about halfway down the scree to Atlantic Crossing on the left as you descend. Follow the groove and arete above, which looks about VS.

Two climbs have been recorded on the easy-angled triangular slab above the descent and lead to the top of the headland block although it is not sure how they relate.

Atlantic Bimbling 30m D *
G.Sewell, E.Mulholland, 24 Jul 2015
Start 1m left of where the down climb meets the boulders at the base of the slab. Climb directly up the slab parallel to the down climb for about 10m to a break then follow a crack trending left.

Mr Pudding 30m D
N.Wood, C.Wakefield, 8 May 2013
Climb the slab above the boulders above the descent on good rock.

Seal Bay

(NB 0002 3253) Non-tidal NW facing Map p37

A number of routes have apparently been climbed on the slabs immediately to the south, opposite the start to Atlantic Crossing. However, only a few climbs have been recorded. The right side of the slabs terminate in a distinctive wide protruding pink feldspar quartz-like vein which forms an arete leading to a large boulder on the cliff-top. A solitary wooden fence post sits just back from the top of the slabs.

Sunset Rib 70m D **
M.Tighe, J.Paterson, May 1978
The pleasant rib up the middle of the slabs. From the top of a quartzy pedestal, step up and go right to a belay on a ledge. Take the easiest line up the slabby rib; an optional belay can be taken before the top with easier climbing to finish.

Descent: The following two routes are gained either directly by a long 70m abseil down the right side of the slabs, or by an abseil from the wooden fence post, down the loose gully on the right side of the slabs. It is also possible to scramble in at low tide beneath Photographer's Corner on Seal Slabs on the south side of the bay.

The Bungling Trundler 70m HVS **
R.Pettner, J.Ison, 2 Jun 2000
This takes the easiest line through the roofs at the back of Seal Bay. Start directly below two notches in the line of roofs halfway up.
1. 45m 5a Step onto a hanging nose and follow walls left of the corners to the two notches in the roof. Balance into the right-hand groove (crux) and onto the slab above to reach a ledge.
2. 35m Go up and right to the obvious flake by black crystals. Follow this and a flake above to the top of Sunset Rib.

The Great Pretender 50m D **
M.Garthwaite, R.Anderson, 10 Jul 2010
The distinctive, wide protruding pink quartz-like feldspar arete which forms the right side of the slabs.

Seal Slabs

(NB 9995 3251) Tidal NW facing Map p37

The following routes are located on the south side of Seal Bay at the left end of an extensive area of easy slabs which terminate in a line of left-facing corners facing the Atlantic Crossing headland block. A cluster of huge boulders sits on the cliff-top above the slabs.

Descent: Either by scrambling down easy slabs further west then making a long sea-level traverse back in, or by an abseil down the slabs from the cluster of cliff-top boulders.

Photographer's Corner 60m VS 4c *
M.Tighe and Party, 16 Sep 1986
The line of slabby left-facing corners which faces Atlantic Crossing; climb direct in two pitches.

Snapper's Rib 60m S *
R.Anderson, C.Anderson, 14 Jul 2010
The slabby rib to the right of Photographer's Corner; this forms the left side of the easy slabs.
1. 30m 4b Easy slabs lead to the mid-way steepening which is taken up the left edge overlooking Photographer's Corner, then around some blocks above to a ledge.
2. 30m 4a Gain the top of the rib via the left edge then move up and traverse right across grass to ledges in the middle of the cliff-top blocks.

Papparazzi Groove 60m D *
R.Anderson, C.Anderson, 14 Jul 2010
On the right of Snapper's Rib easy slabs sweep up left into a deep black groove which is climbed to a finish up the right side of Snapper's Rib.

There is a low-level girdle somewhere hereabouts called **Sholmaru** (D), which starts from the foot of a broad slab-ramp immediately south of Seal Bay and finishes at a feature called the neck. Sholmaru can be linked with **Lonmaru** (VS/HVS) which starts at the neck and takes a natural fault-line 20m above sea-level and goes right to an exposed corner where a tricky descending traverse leads into a rock bay. From here there is a choice of exits. It is unsure where these routes are.

The north-facing cliff to the side of Seal Bay apparently contains a HVS. It is loose and not recommended, but if in doubt with regards to its exact location, the exit from the climb apparently resembles a grass version of the Spider on the North Face of the Eiger!

ÀIRD MHÒR MHANGARSTAIDH NORTH

Maps p20 & p37

Running northwards from the aerial, this section of the headland includes Painted Geòdha, one of the area's major geos. The climbing is described as met in a south to north direction from the road end.

The Aerial Area

(NB 0039 3331) Partially Tidal W to N facing

Comprising The Hooded Slabs, The Hooded Wall and The Channel Walls, and located on the tip of the headland 100m to the north-west of the aerial at the road end, this is one of the quickest cliffs to access.

Approach: From the parking at the road-end, walk north-west past the aerial towards the Flannan Isles in the same line as the road for 100m and descend slabby rock a short way to reach a boulder wedged in a tilted shelf or trough that runs along the top of the cliff (2min). The recessed section of the Hooded Wall lies over the top here.

The Hooded Slabs

These slabs form the outer right (south) side of the recessed section of the Hooded Wall. A protruding slab forms the right edge of the Hooded Wall with a corner to its right then another corner before easier slabs.

Descent: From the wedged boulder on the cliff-top, go south along the trough for about 10m and rig an abseil down the slab; the line of Niche Corner is obvious down to the right. By continuing south down the trough it is possible to scramble in from the southern end. At low tide it is also possible to step across right from beneath the Hooded Wall.

Climbs are described from right to left.

1 Wide Buoy 20m VS 5a *
R.Anderson, C.Anderson, 9 Jul 2006
At the right end, the wide crack in the right-angled corner around the edge to the right of Walking the Plank.

2 Walking the Plank 25m HVS 5a *
R. Anderson, C.Anderson, 9 Jul 2006
From a belay at the foot of Niche Corner, move up right. Bypass a greasy crack in a short steep step by holds on its right, then move up the groove to climb the slender ramp in the black wall. Finish up the bold slabby arete.

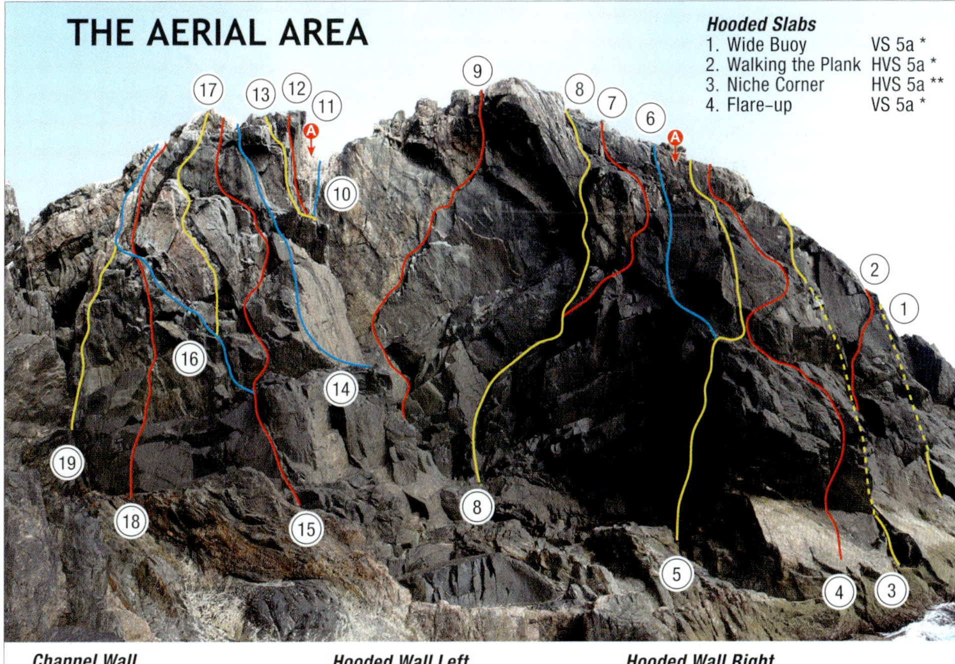

Channel Wall
15. Side Trawler HVS 5b *
16. Cross Channel HVS 4c **
17. Full Fathom Five E3 5c **
18. Blind Alley E3 5c *
19. Taller Better! E3 5b/c *

Hooded Wall Left
10. Bare Black E3 5c **
11. Pitch Black E2 6a
12. Black is Black E1 5b **
13. Paint it Black E2 5b *
14. Black Edged HVS 4c

Hooded Wall Right
5. Buoys From The Black Stuff VS 4c **
6. Buoy On The Brink E2 5c *
7. Buoyancy Aid HVS 4c *
8. Buoys In The Hood E1 5b *
9. Learning To Crawl E4 5c *

3 Niche Corner 25m HVS 5a **
R. Anderson, C.Anderson, 9 Jul 2006
The corner-crack, forming the right side of the protruding slab; an accommodating belay niche sits at its base.

4 Flare-up 30m VS 5a *
R.Anderson, C.Anderson, 4 Jul 2006
The flared slot in the narrow wall and the centre of the protruding slab just around the right edge of the Hooded Wall recess; three of the Hooded Wall routes gain this slab higher up. Climb the slot and continue to a ledge. Step left to make a move up a crack as for Buoys From the Black Stuff, then move up right to climb a shallow groove in the slab and finish up a crack in a short wall.

The Hooded Wall

Diagram p71

This is a recessed section, or bay, between the Hooded Slabs and a jutting prow which forms the left, or north, retaining wall of the recess. A huge fin of rock forms a barrier at the mouth of the bay and between this and the cliff-top there is a deep and narrow channel which runs through to the north side of the headland, both are visible from the Tamana Head and Aurora Geòdha area to the south, as well as the coastline further north. It is a reasonably sheltered bay and waves tend to be broken up by the seaward wall of the fin, although spray does fly about a bit in heavier seas.

Descent: About 10m to the north of and down the slab from the wedged boulder on the cliff-top there is a notch which looks out over the recessed section. An abseil through the notch, overhanging and down the line of Bare Black, deposits one at the foot of the Hooded Wall at the start of the thin crack of Black is Black, which runs up the left retaining wall.

Continuing from right to left, the first three climbs are on the southern side of the bay and finish up the narrow protruding slab of The Hooded Slabs, which forms the right-hand side of this section.

5 Buoys From the Black Stuff 30m VS 4c **
R.Anderson, C.Anderson, 3 Jul 1997
The crack leading out onto the lower right edge of the recessed, or hooded section, to gain the left side of The Hooded Slabs. Climb the crack to the edge, step right and climb a crack which leads to slabby ground then the top.

6 Buoy on the Brink 30m E2 5c *
R.Anderson, C.Anderson, 20 Jul 2017
Climb the initial crack of Buoys From the Black Stuff to the slab. Step left to the edge and wobble up onto a foothold where a small wire protects the placement of a good micro-cam on the left. Teeter up to gain a slot then climb up and right to an easy finish.

7 Buoyancy Aid 30m HVS 4c *
R.Anderson, C.Anderson, 3 Jul 1997
Follow Buoys in the Hood (the two lower shelves are blind and often greasy) to just below its groove and thin crack leading to the edge then traverse right around onto the edge where a crack leads to the top.

8 Buoys in the Hood 30m E1 5b *
R.Anderson, C.Anderson, 28 Jun 1997
Takes a mid-height line up the right side of the hooded section, starting from the centre of the wall. Climb stepped grooves up and then rightwards to the base of a groove with a thin crack in it at the right side of the hooded section. Climb this and continue to the top.

9 Learning to Crawl 35m E4 5c *
M.Garthwaite, R.Anderson, 4 Jun 2017
This climbs the extremely steep finishing groove which forms the hood over this section. Start at the foot of the abseil line (Bare Black) and climb the obvious stepped line rightwards up the back wall to a ledge. Draw breath and boldly climb the groove up right to exit; the wedged boulder lies just above.

The next routes are located on the northern side, or left retaining wall of the recessed section, starting with the line of the abseil.

10 Bare Black 30m E3 5c **
R.Anderson, 4 Jul 2006
The abseil line; the steep groove at the back of the recessed area. Often greasy until later in the day but when dry it gives some interesting climbing and is better than it looks.

11 Pitch Black 30m E2 6a
R.Anderson, C.Anderson, 11 Jul 1998
At the back left corner of the recess behind the abseil line, a flared, left-leaning groove leads awkwardly to Black is Black, finish up this.

12 Black is Black 30m E1 5b **
R.Anderson, C.Anderson, 28 Jun 1997
The thin crack running up the black wall just left of Pitch Black.

13 Paint it Black 30m E2 5b *
R.Anderson, C.Anderson, 3 Jul 1997
The left-facing corner-groove just to the left forces one out right onto a good ledge near its top. Climb the wall above onto the edge and climb up left to the top of the prow.

14 Black Edged 30m HVS 4c
R.Anderson, C.Anderson, 11 Jul 1998
A short crack left of Paint it Black leads onto the arete of the prow, which is followed to a finish up left.

The Channel Walls

These lie either side of the deep and narrow channel which separates the seaward fin of rock from the cliff. An easy scramble around the left retaining wall of the Hooded Wall recess leads to the channel.

West Wall

Diagram p71

The steeper west facing landward side.

15 Side Trawler 25m HVS 5b *
R.Anderson, C.Anderson, 4 Jul 2006
Start in the channel and zigzag up the right side of the wall, just left of the edge, to gain a ledge below the top. A long reach up right is followed by a stiff pull to gain the top.

16 Cross Channel 25m HVS 4c **
R.Anderson, C.Anderson, 20 Jul 2017
A good diagonal line across the steep wall. Follow Side Trawler to the first ledge then go up and left across the wall to join Blind Alley and finish up the pegmatite spike to the left of that climb.

17 Full Fathom Five 25m E3 5c **
R.Anderson, 20 Jul 2017
The pink flake and handrail in the right-hand section of the wall. Climb up and left as for Cross Channel to below the handrail. A poor spike half-protects the move to the rail which is then climbed left. Make a stiff pull using a small flake to gain the ledge above and flop onto this. Step left, wobble up to jugs on the lip and pull over to finish; it would be less tenuous to step right and pull over as for Side Trawler.

18 Blind Alley 25m E3 5c *
R.Anderson, C.Anderson, 28 Jun 1997
From the floor of the channel, climb to a ledge then move awkwardly up a short corner in the centre of the wall. Continue directly above to the base of a pegmatite vein, then go up and around left passing the base of a blind groove to climb a pegmatite flake to the top.

19 Taller Better! 25m E3 5b/c *
R.Anderson, 20 Jul 2017
The left side of the wall. Make easy but balancy moves for 5m up a stepped black groove with no gear to gain a ledge where two small wires can be placed. Make a long stretch up right to a good hold and pull onto the ledge (spike up left) and gear. Step right and continue up to finish via the spike of Cross Channel.

The following routes lie at the northern end of the channel. Climb through the channel, easiest by a higher line on the West Wall, then scramble up to belay on the neck, before the rocks drop down again.

The Great Divide 30m E1 5a *
R.Anderson, C.Anderson, 3 Jul 1999
A short, steep greasy crack proves difficult to protect. Instead climb the fin on the seaward side and step across onto the landward side. Move up to ledges and traverse left into the middle of the wall. Boldly climb a line of weakness up right then continue to the top.
Variation: **The Great Divide Direct 30m E2 5c ****
R.Anderson, C.Anderson, 7 Jul 1999
Where the original route traverses left, climb straight up to a horizontal break, traverse right and make an awkward pull into the crack above. Climb the crack to the top.

East Wall

Four routes are located on the landward facing wall on the southern end of the huge fin which forms the seaward barrier to the Hooded Wall recess. They all finish at the same point so take a sling to leave behind. Again routes are described right to left.

Dorsal Crack 15m S 4b **
R.Anderson, C.Anderson, 4 Jul 2006
The obvious left-slanting crack.

Mickey Fin 15m S 4b *
R.Anderson, C.Anderson, 4 Jul 2006
The crack just around the edge to the left to join Dorsal Crack; pull out right and climb the edge of the slab.

Finlandia 15m VS 5a *
R.Anderson, C.Anderson, 4 Jul 2006
The slab and thin crack in the wall just left of Mickey Fin.

Findaloo 15m HVS 5a *
R.Anderson, C.Anderson, 4 Jul 2006
The slab and short corner to gain the crest.

Painted Geòdha (Sloc an Duilisg)

(NB 0061 3332) Partially Tidal SW & NE facing
Map p37

Properly named Sloc an Duilisg, this picturesque geo offers a large number of quality climbs and has the shortest approach in the area. It is not greatly affected by tides and is fairly sheltered with the main Painted Wall enjoying a sunny south-westerly aspect. The climbers' name for the geo comes from the fact that it was thought to bear some resemblance to the Black Canyon of the Gunnison in the United States. It is an apt name though, because when the sun hits the main Painted Wall later in the day it looks as if it has been created by the bold brush strokes of an artist.

Approach: From the parking area at the shed just before the road end, walk north across flat ground and in a minute the ground suddenly opens up to reveal a deep geo with the main Painted Wall on the far side strikingly obvious. A large tidal pool fills the floor of the geo.

Descent: In the middle of the south side of the geo it is possible to scramble down grass and rock to gain the base, from where most routes can be reached. The

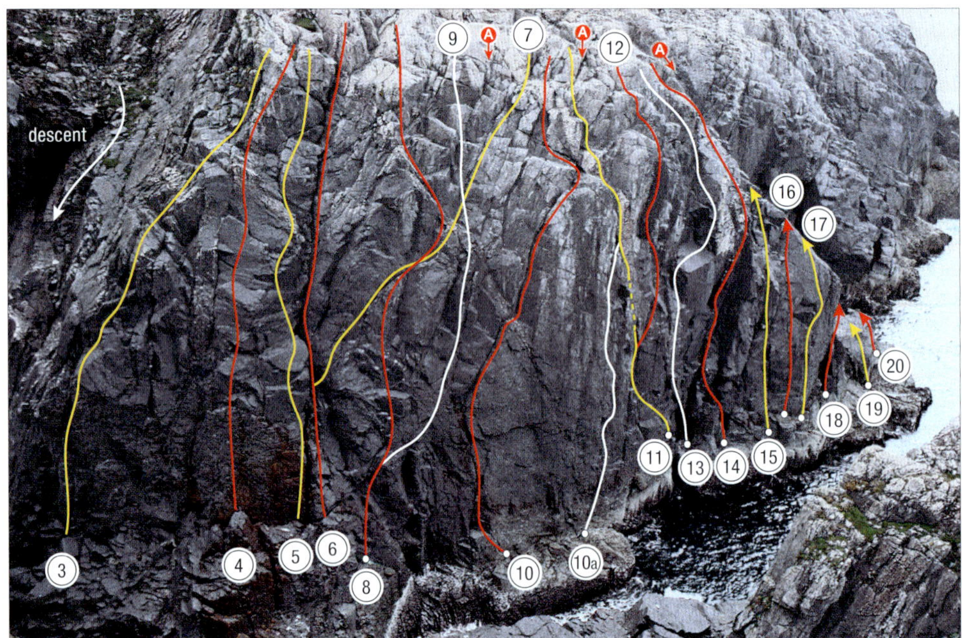

PAINTED GEO - Painted Black Wall

3. Arrival	VS 4c	9. Black Rain	E2 5b **	15. Gear Shifting	E3 5b/c **
4. Rust in Time	HS 4b *	10. Black Foot	E2 5c **	16. Divided Loyalty	E2 5c *
5. Bristles Arete	VD	10a. Black in Time	E5 6a **	17. First Cut	E3 5b **
6. Rub Down	VD	11. Vein Hope	E2 5c **	18. Foaming at The Mouth	E1 5b **
7. Stripper	S 4a *	12. Feint Chance	E2 5b **	19. Edged Out	HVS 4c *
8. Black Rushin'	E1/2 5b *	13. Long Shot	E1 5b **	20. Veinity Fare	VS 4c/5a *
		14. Wide-open	E1 5b *		

depths can take time to dry, so the preferred method is to abseil in directly.

There are three main walls; Lower Painted Wall and the Painted Wall on the north side, then on the south side, the Painted Black Wall. Climbs are described from left to right starting with the South Side then the North Side.

South Side

The roadward side of the geo comprises two sections split by the scramble descent to the base.

Landward End

Non-tidal NE facing

Left of the descent gully, the wall is split into two parts by an area of rockfall higher up, left of which is an obvious flake-line and wide crack.

1 Coal Mining 40m E3 5c/6a

R.Anderson, C.Anderson, 30 Jun 2001

The crack-line up the left side of the left-hand section of the wall. A few good difficult moves up the crack lead to deteriorating rock up which one is forced to climb to reach unpleasant ground then a shelf. The rock on the headwall is poor, so escape rightwards along the shelf.

2 At the Face 30m E1 5a *

R.Anderson, C.Anderson, 30 Jun 2001

The crack and ledges just left of centre on the right-hand section of the wall. Gain a ledge, move up to a spike and continue directly above past ledges and flat holds to reach a slab, finish up this and go rightwards on the shelf.

Painted Black Wall

(NB 0058 3334) Tidal NE facing Diagram above

The tarblack wall that drops into the sea at the mouth of the geo. The wall is split into two sections by a crack-line and chimney. The smaller left-hand section is triangular shaped and lies beneath the descent gully; this is above the tidal narrows where there is a large ledge below the wall. The bigger right-hand section drops directly into the sea and at low tide ledges below the routes are exposed; the line of Black Foot, a crack-line which kinks right is obvious. When dry the rock is excellent and tacky. However, due to the aspect, the routes can become greasy and harder.

The first routes are on the smaller triangular wall beneath and to the right of the descent gully, starting from a spacious ledge.

Descent: Routes on the small triangular wall can be accessed by traversing out towards the sea along the flat ledge from the base of the descent gully, as can the first two routes on the main wall to the right. An abseil down the crack-line and chimney of Rub Down can also gain the base of the wall. Black Foot and the routes to the right are approached directly by abseil to their bases.

3 Arrival 25m VS 4c

R.Anderson, C.Anderson, 1 Jul 2000

Start just right of a rounded boulder in a pool on the ledge. Climb steeply up a shallow groove-flange to flakey holds, then gain a thin crack and climb this and the shallow groove to its right to a wider short crack leading to easy ground.

4 Rust in Time 25m HS 4b *

R.Anderson, C.Anderson, 1 Jul 2000

Just right of Arrival are some shallow grooves, then a rusty coloured wall above the highest part of the ledge formed by a pointed boulder feature. Start on top of this feature, climb to a spike and continue straight up good rock to easier ground leading to the top.

5 Bristles Arete 25m VD *

R.Henderson, E.Pirie, 27 Apr 1995

The arete left of the crack-line and chimney at the right end of the ledge.

6 Rub Down 25m VD *

R.Henderson, E.Pirie, 27 Apr 1995

At the right end of the ledge, climb the crack-line and chimney which runs up the left side of the larger seaward part of the wall.

7 Stripper 25m S 4a *

R.Henderson, E.Pirie, 27 Apr 1995

Climb Rub Down for 5m then follow the obvious right-trending crack-line.

The next climbs start from the right end of the ledge at the foot of the crack-line and chimney and take lines to its right, left of the obvious crack of Black Foot.

8 Black Rushin' 40m E1/2 5b *

R.Anderson, C.Anderson, 3 Jul 2000

From the right end of the ledge, step down and move right to a short flake-crack. Climb this to a nest of holds and a spike runner then gain the ledge above. Climb the clean-cut groove just above and follow the obvious continuation line up right then back left to finish.

9 Black Rain 40m E2 5b **

R.Anderson, C.Anderson, 3 Jul 2000

Start as for Black Rushin' and from the short flake-crack, swing right into a groove and climb this, passing the right end of the ledge in the middle of that route. Continue up the groove to finish up the easier quartzy crack-line.

10 Black Foot 30m E2 5c **

D.Ashworth, C.Lofthouse, May 1993

The obvious crack-line which kinks right; start from a tidal ledge reached directly by abseil. Climb the crack through a bulge trending right and move up to a ledge with difficulty. Follow the obvious line left to the top.

10a Black in Time 30m E5 6a **

M.Garthwaite, R.Anderson, 11 Jun 2018

Climb the thin crack-line right of centre on the fine central wall boldly to a large ledge and finish up Vein Hope; microwires essential.

The next climbs lie on the right side of the wall, right of the crack of Black Foot, and are accessed by abseil directly to ledges at their foot. The first three routes share the same belay ledge below a big left-slanting pink pegmatite streak and wide crack, well seen from the opposite side of the geo and easily found from above when viewed down the groove of Feint Chance.

11 Vein Hope 40m E2 5c **

R.Anderson, C.Anderson, 6 Jul 2000

The wide crack and big left-slanting quartz-like streak which runs into the centre of the wall. Gain a recess then climb the wide crack and continue up the left-slanting line to the top.

12 Feint Chance 40m E2 5b **

R.Anderson, C.Anderson, 6 Jul 2000

Gain the recess beneath the wide crack on Vein Hope, then pull out right and move up to ledges beside Long Shot. Step left and climb the corner-groove to the top (the line of the abseil).

13 Long Shot 40m E1 5b **

R.Anderson, C.Anderson, 3 Jul 2000

Move to the right end of the ledge, then up around the edge to climb the fine wall just right of the quartz-like seam to ledges. Climb a short groove and pull out right onto a shelf, then climb the crack through the wide groove above, moving left onto a shelf and finishing on a higher shelf.

The next climb is gained by abseiling along the top, then down to good ledges in a recess beneath a wide crack below an obvious V-groove in the right side of the wall.

14 Wide-open 40m E1 5b *

R.Anderson, C.Anderson, 6 Jul 2000

Step up left and climb around into the V-groove and

follow this past ledges, up a steeper section and on up to easier ground leading to the top.

The following climbs lie at the far end of the Black Wall just around the edge from the base of the large west facing slab that forms the outer edge of the geo. They can be gained by abseiling down the large west facing slab, then making an easy traverse around the edge on tidal ledges to a good ledge at their base.

15 Gear Shifting 50m E3 5b/c **
R.Anderson, C.Anderson, 16 Jul 2003
The crack-line at the left end of the ledge immediately left of a wider crack. Move up left into the crack-line and climb this to a blocky protrusion, then climb steeply up thin cracks to easier ground leading to the slab. Finish up the slab.

16 Divided Loyalty 50m E2 5c *
R.Anderson, C.Anderson, 16 Jul 2003
The wider crack immediately left of First Cut leads to ledges where moves up right gain a V-groove leading to the slab and an easy finish.

17 First Cut 50m E3 5b **
R.Anderson, C.Anderson, 16 Jul 2003
The thin crack in the blunt edge a short way left of the right edge. Boldly climb the thin crack to a ledge then continue up the edge to the right of a groove.

18 Foaming at the Mouth 50m E1 5b **
R.Anderson, C.Anderson, 16 Jul 2003
Move up right and bridge across a short chimney to gain the right edge of the wall then climb the thinner, right-hand of two cracks to gain the slab via a short V-slot. Finish easily.

The following routes start at the base of a short wall at the foot of the outer slab.

19 Edged Out 50m HVS 4c *
R.Anderson, C.Anderson, 7 Jul 2003
Climb the slabby left arete of the short wall to a junction with Foaming at the Mouth then climb the right side of the arete to finish easily up the slab.

20 Veinity Fare 50m VS 4c/5a *
R.Anderson, C.Anderson, 7 Jul 2003
Climb a wide quartz-like vein in the centre of the short wall and follow the slab easily to the top.

North Side

Starting at the seaward end with the Lower Painted Wall, the routes are described left to right to the main Painted Wall itself and the back of the geo.

Lower Painted Wall - The Friendly Wall

(NB 0060 3334) Partially Tidal SW facing
Diagrams p77 & p78

This lies to the left of the main Painted Wall, at the entrance to the geo, at a lower level; opposite the Painted Black Wall. There is an obvious notched fault towards the centre of the cliff, separating it into two parts: a left-hand seaward wall which is affected by the sea and a more sheltered non-tidal right-hand landward section. There are a number of lines and although they do suffer a little from being close to each other, it is a friendly place with a sunny aspect and the climbing is good with much to go at.

Descent: Walk across the top of the Painted Wall and scramble down to a narrow neck then go up the other side and down slabs to the top of the wall. Gain the base of the wall by abseil down the notched fault in the centre.

The first routes lie on the left-hand section of the wall, where sloping ledges slant down leftwards into the sea. This section is tidal and affected by the swell.

21 Isle be Back 20m E1 5b *
A.Leary, G.Kirk, 9 Jul 1997
Start at the left end of the sloping ledges in the centre of the wall. Climb a short corner for 2m and step left onto a small ledge then go up and leftwards to reach the base of a groove come crack. Pull out leftwards and climb the wall to the top.

22 Becalmed 20m HVS 5a **
R.Anderson, C.Anderson, 6 Jul 2003
Start as for Isle be Back and where that route steps left after the shallow corner, continue straight up a crack-line and finish up a slim quartzy groove

23 Beguiled 20m HVS 4c **
R.Anderson, C.Anderson, 6 Jul 2003
A direct line up the juggy wall and crack 2m right of Becalmed.

24 Bewildered 20m E1/2 5b *
R.Anderson, C.Anderson, 5 Jul 2003
The thin crack between Beguiled and Bewitched.

25 Bewitched 20m E1 5a/b **
R.Anderson, C.Anderson, 5 Jul 2003
The thin crack immediately left of the arete taken by Swell Time. Pull over the initial steepening and climb the crack to the top.

26 Swell Time 20m E1 5b *
G.Kirk. A.Leary, 9 Jul 1997
Start just left of the descent fault under a hanging arete. Pull over the overhang onto the wall above, then move leftwards and follow the left side of the arete to a fine steep finish.

The next routes are on the non-tidal right-hand section of wall, which has good ledges beneath it.

27 Crimp Cocktail 20m E2 5c *
G.Kirk, D.Howard, 10 Jul 1997
Start mid-way between the descent and the next route. Climb a small flake and pull onto a tiny ledge at 6m.

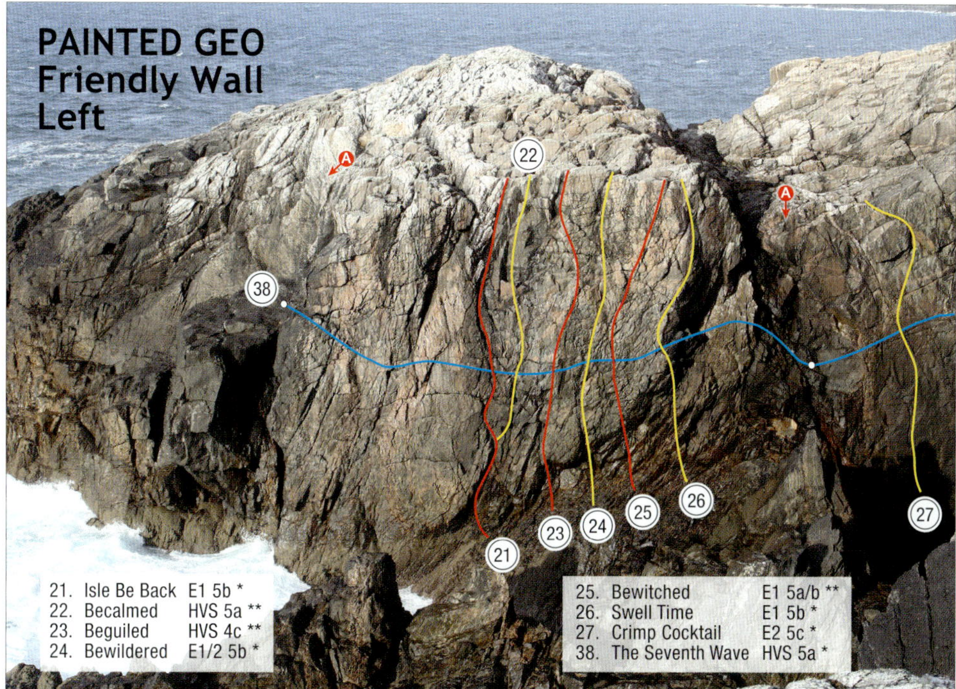

Climb the crack and wall above then move rightwards to beneath an overhang. Follow the crack leftwards through the overhang to the top.

28 Callum's Grasp 20m HVS 5a *
K.Pyke, G.Huxter, 9 Jul 1997
Start at the centre of the crag at a shattered left crack-line. Follow this then go straight up the final flake with great jugs and gear.

29 A Stretch in Time 20m E2 5c *
R.Anderson, C.Anderson, 3 Jul 2000
Start 2m right of Callum's Grasp beneath a small roof. Climb a left slanting crack through the left side of the roof and cross Callum's Grasp to climb the crack to the left of the final flake on that route (probably the finish to Crimp Cocktail).

30 Named by Proxy 20m HVS 5b *
G.Huxter, K.Pyke, 9 Jul 1997
Start directly below a small roof 2m right of Callum's Grasp. Pull through the right side of the roof then continue more easily to the top.

31 Fangs for the Memory 20m VS 4c **
R.Anderson, C.Anderson, 2 Jul 2000
The crack-line which runs up the wall to pass the right side of the small roof, immediately right of Named by Proxy but independent from it in the upper section; just! Climb up onto two upward-pointing fangs of rock at the base of the crack, pull over a minute overlap and continue up the crack to finish directly, just left of a series of shallow left-facing grooves.

32 Legability 20m E1 5a *
D.Ashworth C.Lofthouse, May 1993
This, the original climb on the wall, probably starts from the base of Fangs for the Memory or Torn Away and climbs right onto, or as for Torn Away before moving up then left to Named by Proxy to finish up this or Fangs for the Memory. Start up a right-slanting crack through a bulge. Climb leftwards through a quartzy band to ledges then follow the crack on the left and climb a wall to the top.

33 Torn Away 20m E1 5b *
R.Anderson, C.Anderson, 2 Jul 2000
The obvious left-facing corner and groove line in the centre of the wall; start a short way above where the ramp at the base of the wall rises up rightwards. Climb a crack to the base of the corner, step left, make a stretchy move up and go back right to finish up the corner.

34 High Fidelity 20m E2 5b *
R.Anderson, C.Anderson, 2 Jul 2000
The crack-line immediately right of Torn Away. Move up the ramp to the base of the crack and climb this up a shallow left-facing groove. Step right onto the edge and continue above by a crack, stepping left to go over the capping roof by a thin crack.

The ramp beneath the wall now levels out after the step and there are another three routes off the flat ledge here.

35 Northern Rock 15m E2 5b *

R.Anderson, C.Anderson, 8 Jul 2000

The leftmost line starting from the left end of the ledge lies immediately to the right of High Fidelity. A flat topped hold close to the edge provides a spike runner. Gain the slanting ramp above, then climb the crack and wall just to its right, left of a short corner.

36 Friends Provident 15m E3 5c *

R.Anderson, C.Anderson, 8 Jul 2000

The central line. Climb thin cracks, step up right to the left end of a tiny overlap and gain the sloping ramp. Step up right then climb the wall and cracks just right of a short corner.

37 Standard Life 15m E2 5b *

R.Anderson, C.Anderson, 8 Jul 2000

The rightmost line starts just before the edge where the ledge steps down. A groove leading into a short flared chimney feature bounds the line to the right. Just right of this is the easy-angled right edge of the crag which looks about D/VD. Climb thin cracks up and right towards the edge overlooking the groove, then pull back left and gain the top of the sloping ramp. Finish up slabby rock.

38 The Seventh Wave 80m HVS *

K.Archer, A.Norton, 1 Aug 1996

A girdle traverse of both parts of the Lower Left Painted Wall. Go to the far end of the wall and abseil to a ledge on the left arete.

1. 35m 5a Descend from the ledge to a line of flakes that leads to the break and follow this to cross a section of rounded holds. Regain the break, the becomes less continuous, and follow it to black ledges that lead into the fault between the two sections of the wall. Descend slightly to a stance.

2. 45m 5a Cross the fault, traverse below a block overhang. Continue traversing rightwards to a short corner, passing this to gain a rightwards-rising pink band, which leads to a belay on the arete.

Painted Wall

(NB 0062 3332) Non-tidal SW facing
Diagram opposite

A beautiful wall of banded gneiss. In the shade the wall can look as if it is seeping, however this is normally just the dark streaks of colour. The right-facing corner of Director's Corner is obvious on the left, as is the central crack of Gravity Man with the wide right-slanting pink vein of The Painted Wall just to its right.

Descent: All of the routes except Gloss are reached, either by abseil directly to ledges at their bases (Gravity Man provides a useful line for most routes), or by scram-

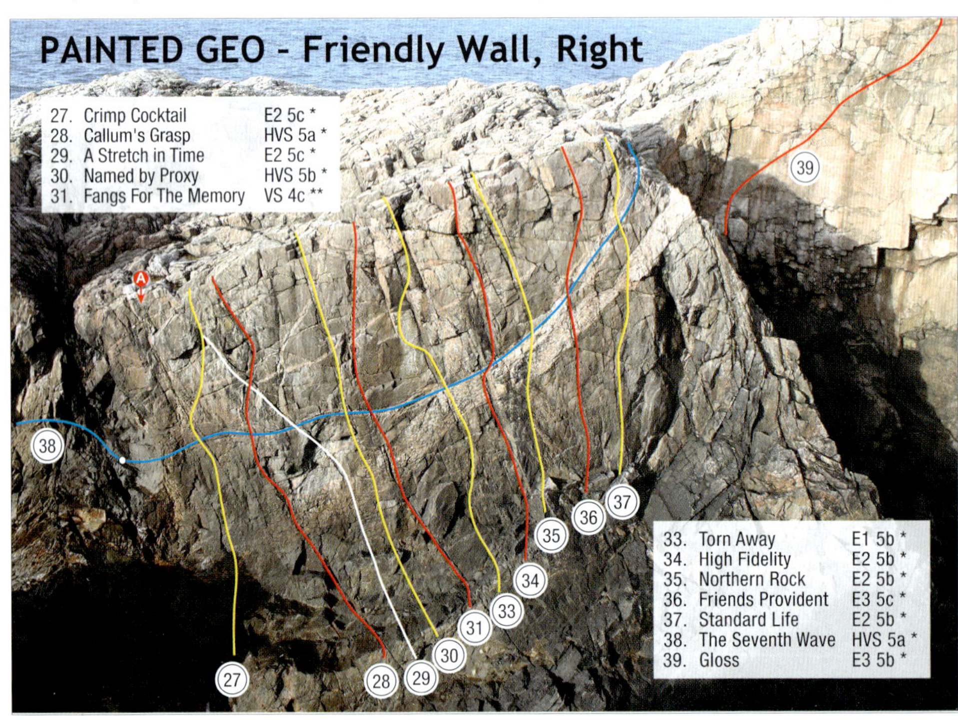

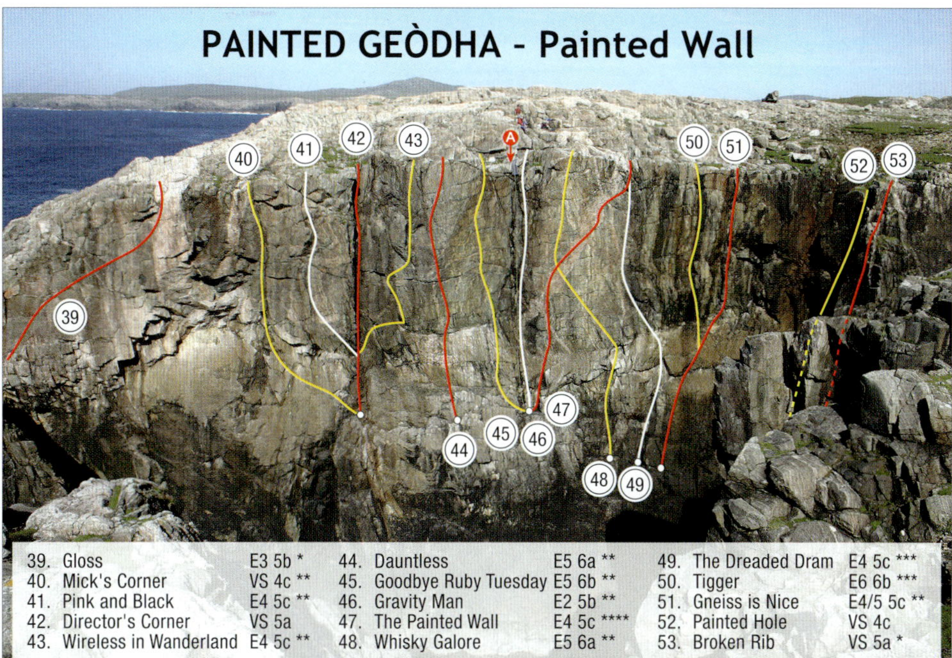

bling down the descent gully on the south side, crossing the geo and climbing to the ledges beneath them.

39 Gloss 20m E3 5b *
N.Dalzell, J.Ashdown, May 1993
Start at the left margin of the wall, from the neck between the Lower Left Painted Wall and the main Painted Wall itself. Traverse awkwardly onto the pink undercut slab then move up to a series of breaks and footholds. Follow these rightwards to beneath an overhang below the top and exit with care up a quartz-like vein that forms a short corner on the right of the overhang.

40 Mick's Corner 25m VS 4c **
M.Tighe, J.Paterson, 1979
The shallow corner at the left side of the wall, reached by trending leftwards on slabby rock from a good ledge beneath the line of Director's Corner.

41 Pink and Black 20m E4 5c **
G.Latter, 7 Jun 1985
An attractive climb up the wall between Mick's Corner and Director's Corner. Start as for Director's Corner and on entering the corner, swing leftwards from the left arete to gain twin diagonal cracks. Continue straight up, following a black seam to gain a good incut ledge. Finish more easily.

42 Director's Corner 20m VS 5a
I.Sykes, I.Sutherland, 1970s
The central corner is worth doing, although it is a bit loose in places.

43 Wireless in Wanderland 20m E4 5c **
I.Taylor, T.Fryer, 16 Jul 2012
From the foot of Director's Corner, traverse hard right to a left-facing corner. Follow the corner to a roof then make bold moves up and right to gain the right side of a pinnacle flake. From the top of the pinnacle, finish steeply just left of the arete above.

44 Dauntless 21m E5 6a **
G.Latter, D.Cuthberson, 7 May 1985
A difficult and sustained but reasonably well protected pitch. Start approximately 6m right of Director's Corner. Climb the quartzy wall to a break, then continue to a second break and go left into a scoop to the right of a pinnacle flake. Now go back right, aiming for twin diagonal breaks near the top and follow these right a short way before finishing strenuously above.

45 Goodbye Ruby Tuesday 20m E5 6b **
G.Huxter, K.Pyke, 9 Sep 1996
A fine, sustained and strenuous eliminate, taking a direct line up the wall; small cams useful. Start in the centre of the wall, 2m left of Gravity Man. Go up the flakey white band to where the wall steepens. A series of powerful moves between breaks leads to good finishing jugs in the centre of the wall.

46 Gravity Man 20m E2 5b **
M.Tighe, W.Newton (aid) 1980s, FFA M.Tighe, the next day
The steep central crack, recorded in the previous guide as Motion Control.

Painted Wall (E4) Rab Anderson (photo Cubby Images)

47 The Painted Wall 20m E4 5c ****

D.Cuthbertson, G.Latter, 5 May 1985

One of the area's classics, this follows the obvious pink band that rises rightwards across the wall. From the ledge at the foot of Gravity Man, go up right to horizontal breaks beneath the band then gain a spike up on its left. Move up the band to breaks before crossing the band and finishing up its right side.

48 Whisky Galore 25m E5 6a **
D.Cuthbertson, G.Latter, 5 May 1985
A bold climb which starts from a ledge about 8m down and right of Gravity Man. Climb a slanting groove to a prominent niche on the right side of an overlap. Pull out of this and go leftwards above the overlap. Cross The Painted Wall and ascend to a good hold and some doubtful protection. Climb strenuously up the bulging wall above to finish via a short crack on the left.

49 The Dreaded Dram 25m E4 5c ***
D.Cuthbertson, G.Latter, 7 May 1985
Good climbing protected by small wires. Start to the right of Whisky Galore, beneath an obvious short black groove. Climb the black groove and the obvious continuation to the steep upper section. A series of vague short cracks leads to the final moves of The Painted Wall.

50 Tigger 25m E6 6b ***
A.Coull, G.Lennox, Jul 2011
Start as for Gneiss is Nice. Climb the short, steep wall onto the slab and move up to the overlap. Pull over this and head directly up to below the bulge. Climb straight up through the steep bulge on positive holds then trend right to the obvious large flake. Launch directly up the striped wall to eventually gain good holds and the top.

51 Gneiss is Nice 25m E4/5 5c **
G.Sutcliffe, D.Cuthbertson, Jun 1994
Start on the highest ledge to the right of the black groove of The Dreaded Dram. Ascend a vague crack in the wall to a horizontal break and protection. Pull onto the slab above and go up to the overlap. Traverse right then move up to the base of a prominent overhanging groove and strenuously climb this.

52 Painted Hole 50m VS
I.Donaldson, I.Sykes, 1980s
The repulsive chimney-line formed in the angle between the Painted Wall and the back wall.
1. 20m 4b Ascend the back of the slimy chimney to a chockstone.
2. 30m 4c Climb out under the overhang by a bomb bay chimney and exit through a hole onto the top.

53 Broken Rib 25m VS 5a *
I.Sutherland, I.Sykes, 1970s
The obvious black prow on the back wall at the far right end of the Painted Wall. Scramble to a large ledge then make a bold start and follow the line of least resistance up the prow.

Torasgeo

(NB 007 332) Map p37

Lying to the north of the road, this is the big geo that is seen ahead on rounding the bend on the final downhill stretch to the aerial.

Approach: Walk south-east on grass from the parking area at the aerial. The wall is best viewed from opposite by contouring around the grassy bowl formed around the back of the geo (10min).

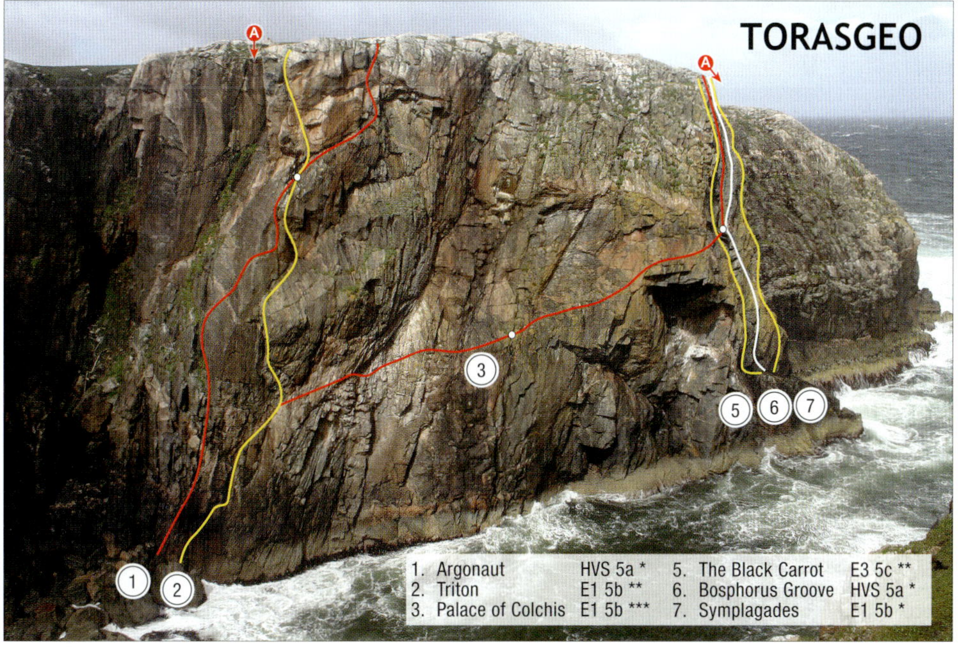

West Wall

(NB 0075 3324) Non-tidal S & E facing Diagram p81

The following climbs lie on the usually sheltered wall on the left side of the geo.

Descent: The first climbs are approached by a 55m abseil from a convenient boulder by going down a vegetated corner to a large boulder cove exposed at all states of the tide; this is some 30m north of an obvious decaying stack, or fin. The climbs further right are also approached by abseil.

1 Argonaut 55m HVS *
P.Donnithorne, E.Alsford, 4 Jun 2006
Start below the slab.
1. 35m 5a Trend up and right across broken grooves, then back up left, up a short groove abutting the main slab. Follow the obvious red seam up right to the right edge of the slab and follow this to a slabby ledge.
2. 20m 5a Follow the tapering ramp up rightwards to its end then steeply up into a groove which leads past a bulge to the top.

2 Triton 55m E1 **
E.Alsford, P.Donnithorne, 7 Jun 2006
Takes the groove line just right of the arete right of the previous route. Start immediately to its right by the largest boulder.
1. 30m 5b Traverse right just above the high water mark for 3m to an obvious shallow, slabby groove. Ascend this until forced right on big holds to beneath a steep corner and go up this past a bulge to a large sloping ledge.
2. 25m 5b The corner above leads to another slabby ledge (the belay of Argonaut). Launch up the orange wall above, slightly leftwards to finish up a short groove in the arete.

3 Palace of Colchis 80m E1 ***
E.Alsford, P.Donnithorne, 10 Jun 2006
A spectacular traverse of the West Wall.
1. 40m 5b Follow Triton for 13m to below the steep corner. Continue by the obvious white juggy line, steeply up rightwards with good positions, until it is possible to step down right onto brown slabs. Keep traversing horizontally right to a small vegetated stance.
2. 30m 5b Continue in the same line across an orange wall, above the large roof, to a spike on the arete. Continue traversing, crossing The Black Carrot, to belay on a ledge in the obvious corner of Bosphorus Groove.
3. 10m 5b Step left and follow the fine thin crack in the streaky wall above. This is between The Black Carrot and Bosphorus Groove.

4 Air Time 55m E2 5c **
J.Barlow, C.Barnes, 29 Aug 2015
Hard to place this route, which was recorded on UKC.
1. 5c From the boulders at the base of Argonaut, traverse rightwards on good holds along a break past the chimney of Triton to a steeply overhanging groove. Climb the groove on good holds to a technical slab above (crux). Belay on the sloping ledge above.
2. 5b Traverse right along the belay ledge and finish directly up; common with Argonaut.
Below the right-hand end of the West Wall there is a commodious non-tidal ledge with a short chimney at its left end. The next two climbs start at the bottom of the chimney.

5 The Black Carrot 45m E3 5c **
P.Donnithorne, E.Alsford, 8 Jun 2006
Move left onto a ledge and pull onto a pink slab. Move left along this, under small roofs and up with difficulty to quartzy footholds on the arete. A small groove leads to big flakes. Trend up and left more easily to reach the black carrot and climb the crack forming its left side to a small ledge. Climb a short groove leftwards to finish over blocks.

6 Bosphorus Groove 45m HVS 5a *
E.Alsford, P.Donnithorne, 8 Jun 2006
From the top of the chimney, move left to climb the obvious left-slanting groove line. Move left under steep ground and pull up into a corner; optional belay here, common to the end of the second pitch on Palace Of Colchis. Continue up the twin cracks in the right wall to an easier angled finish.

7 Symplagades 45m E1 5b *
P.Donnithorne, E.Alsford, 8 Jun 2006
This is based on the right edge of the wall; approach from the commodious ledge by scrambling rightwards along a thin ledge to a slabby corner. Climb the corner for 10m then make a rising rightwards traverse to some gigantic flakes. Step right and climb the arete to the top.

The next areas lie on the section of coast to the north-east of the deep inlet of Torasgeo.

Ladies' Geòdha

(NB 009 333) Tidal N facing Map p37

On the east side of the deep inlet of Torasgeo is a headland promontory called Rubha Gheasbridh. There is a geo to its east which is characterised by an obvious pink feldspar arete, which is the line of Ladies who Lunch.

Approach: Walk downhill around Torasgeo to the headland and the geo (15min).

Descent: Abseil to ledges above the high water mark.

Ladies Who Lunch 35m E5 6a **
G.Huxter, K.Pyke, 6 Sep 1996
Step left and climb through a small overlap then move left again to the arete. Climb this for 5m to a rest. Swing back right and pull through a small overhang to beneath a gently overhanging wall. Place a high RP and make wild moves up the arete. Easier climbing on snappy ground leads to the top and a large block belay.

Out All Night 35m E3 5c
G.Huxter, K.Pyke, 9 Jul 1997
Start as for Ladies Who Lunch and climb for 6m above to gain a right-facing corner system. Follow the corner for 14m until it steepens, then step right into a hanging groove with suspect rock to finish.

Rubha nan Lagan Tiorma

The Veinous Wall

(NB 0100 3341) Partially Tidal SW facing
Map p37 Diagram below

This small headland lies on the far side of the bay beyond Torasgeo, at the entrance to Geòdha nan Sgiod. When looking eastwards across the bay from the top of the Painted Wall, a steep south-west facing wall with a north-west facing slab to its right is obvious. The seaward end of the wall has a distinctive wide diagonal white vein slanting across it, the line of Veinous Trap.

Approach: This and the other sections of cliff here are perhaps better approached by parking on the left just before the bend and the final downhill section of the road. Walk north-eastwards following the high ground, avoiding the drop down and climb back up from Torasgeo. Continue past Ladies' Geòdha, beyond a geo split by a narrow ridge of rock with an arch through it, and walk out to a flat, boulder strewn area where the cliff can be viewed (15min).

Descent: Directly by abseil for the first four climbs and by an easy scramble down the ramp and slab on the landward side of the wall for the other climbs.

1 Veinous Trap 20m HVS 4c/5a **
A.Cunningham, K.Geddes, 27 Apr 1995
At the seaward end, start from the lowest point of the distinctive diagonal white vein and hand-traverse its top.

2 A Step in the Deep Blue 25m HVS 5a **
M.Kocsis, M.Hutton, May 2012
A swinging hand-traverse along the lowest break on the distinctive diagonal white vein; steep, hard moves to start and steeper, juggy ones to finish.

The next two climbs start from a good ledge on the high tide mark in an overhung alcove beneath the white vein. A recessed, narrow pink pegmatite band runs rightwards up the cliff from the alcove. The alcove is gained by abseil but at low tide and in calm seas it can be traversed into by stepping across the tidal trench from the foot of the slab on the right.

3 Intravenous Grip 25m HVS 5b **
R.Anderson, C.Anderson, 17 Jul 2014
The obvious line which cuts through Veinous Trap and A Step in the Deep Blue. Go up and right as for Band on the Run then pull out left to ledges. Move up the crack of A Step in the Deep Blue then pull up left and climb the flake-crack in the white vein of Veinous Trap and continue above to a puzzling exit into the groove above the bulge.

4 Band on the Run 25m E2 5c **
R.Anderson, C.Anderson, 17 Jul 2014
Climb the narrow pink pegmatite band up rightwards to a slim groove just below the top and finish up this.

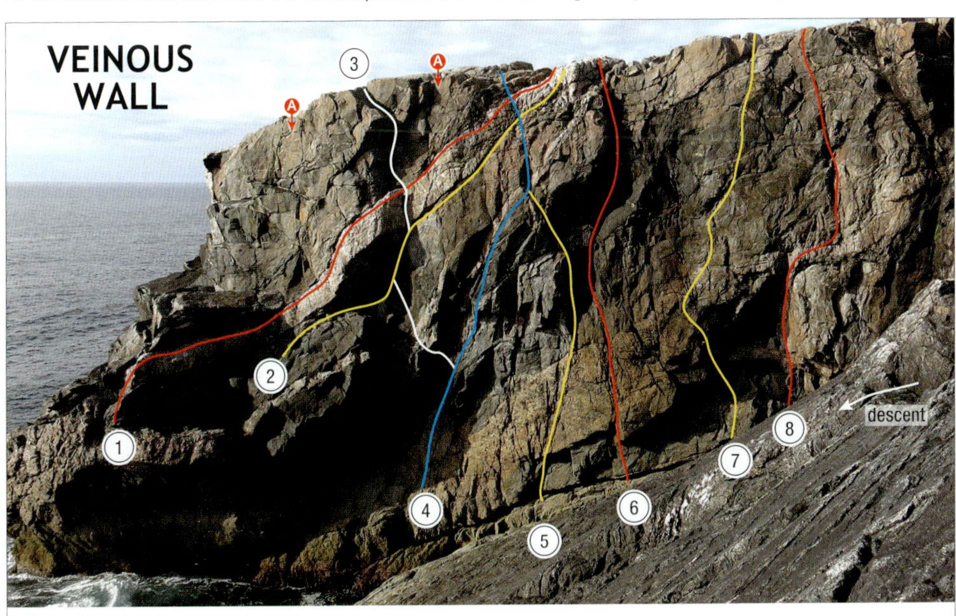

1. Veinous Trap HVS 4c/5a **	4. Band on The Run E2 5c **	6. Sea Shepherd VS 4c **
2. A Step in The Deep Blue HVS 5a **	5. Mysteries of The Deep E1 5b **	7. Fishy Stuff E4 5c **
3. Intravenous HVS 5b **		8. Peeping Reaper E3 6a **

Fishy Stuff (E4) Paul Mitchell (photo Mike Hutton)

The remaining routes are on the side above the landward slab.

5 Mysteries of the Deep 25m E1 5b **
A.Turner, M.Hutton, May 2012
Start at the foot of the descent slab and below the top end of the distinctive diagonal quartzy vein where there is a recess in the wall above. Follow a vague crack up to the left side of the recess then exit out left with a difficult move and climb the wall above.

6 Sea Shepherd 25m VS 4c **
A.Turner, M.Hutton, May 2012
Climb the crack on the right side of the recess and exit this out right by stepping onto the slab to follow a right-facing corner.

7 Fishy Stuff 25m E4 5c **
P.Mitchell, M.Hutton, May 2012
Start 3m to the left of Peeping Reaper. Climb to the overlap and fix some dubious protection (small cam and RP). Crux moves round the overlap lead to better holds and good gear. Follow the wall above on good crimps then veer right towards the top on improving holds. A fine route despite the bold start.

8 Peeping Reaper 25m E3 6a **
A.Turner, M.Hutton, May 2012
Towards the right side of the wall, make awkward moves off the ground into a left-facing corner. Place awkward above head runners on the right wall before launching into a couple of tricky bridging moves leading to a good jug and gear. Step rightwards into an obvious left-facing corner and follow this pleasantly to the top.

The next climbs lie on the non-tidal north-west facing landward slab. Descending, traverse beneath the slab to the foot of Veinous Wall, where it forms a prominent but normally wet and slimy corner.

9 Seething 20m VD *
R.Anderson, C.Anderson, 10 Jul 2000
Some 5m right of the wet and slimy corner at the left end of the slab, climb a shallow corner-groove leading around the right side of a blocky feature then continue direct to the top.

10 Tempest 18m VD/S *
R.Anderson, C.Anderson, 10 Jul 2000
Just right of Seething and slightly higher up the access ramp is an obvious groove. Climb this to the top, passing two horizontal breaks on the final short headwall.

Seal Walls

(NB 0116 3348) Non-tidal NW facing Map p37

Lying on the far side of the Rubha nan Lagan Tiorma headland, this wall runs north-eastwards from a narrow-entranced sea cave beyond the Veinous Wall. The wall is severely undercut on the right where it overlooks a tidal trench entering the sea cave. To the left the wall turns an edge to form a tar-black vertical section before turning into another cave where it decreases in height to slabby rocks running into Eilean Geòdha where the coastline turns into the bay of Camus Uig. The tar-black section contains three routes up obvious cracks.

Descent: Abseil directly to non-tidal ledges just above the sea.

Slippery Customer 30m E2 5b
R.Anderson, C.Anderson, 5 Jul 1997
The crack-line up the left side of the wall contains some suspect rock. Start as for Signed Sealed and Delivered and go left to another crack. On the initial section the climbing is perhaps slightly easier on the left but the gear is better just on the right. Move up left into the easier upper section.

Signed, Sealed and Delivered 30m E2 5c *
R.Anderson, C.Anderson, 4 Jul 1997
The main central crack-line is slightly flawed by some suspect rock near the top.

Flapping About 30m E4 6a *
R.Anderson, C.Anderson, 4 Jul 1997
The crack-line just to the right of the main central crack-line

Eilean Geòdha

(NB 0128 3350) Partially Tidal SW facing Map p37 Diagram p88

A pleasant little geo just beyond the Seal Walls, before the island of Glas Eilean, where the Àird Mhòr Mhangarstaidh cliffs dip into the sea at Camus Uig. It is a long tidal inlet with a south-west facing wall of slabby rock dissected by quartz-like seams, well viewed from the opposite side.

Approach: As for the Veinous Wall then along the coastline past the Seal Walls (20min). A more direct but unsighted line can be taken across grassy ground.

Descent: In lower tide states, perhaps best by abseil down the north-east corner of the geo where the climbs on the slab at the eastern side of the inlet are accessible from the boulders. At other times abseil directly to ledges above the high tide mark. It is also possible to scramble down the slab on the south side at low tide. Climbs further seaward are reached by abseil directly to ledges.

Climbs are described left to right from the seaward tip; the first starts just left of a huge wedge of rock.

1 Roquefort Wedge 20m S 4b
R.Anderson, C.Anderson, 14 Jul 2014
A chimney and wide crack form the left side of the wedge of rock. To the left of this is a wide crack above a good ledge. Climb the crack.

A full height corner lies to the right, and the next three routes start from an accommodating ledge to the left of the corner, down and right from the wedge of rock.

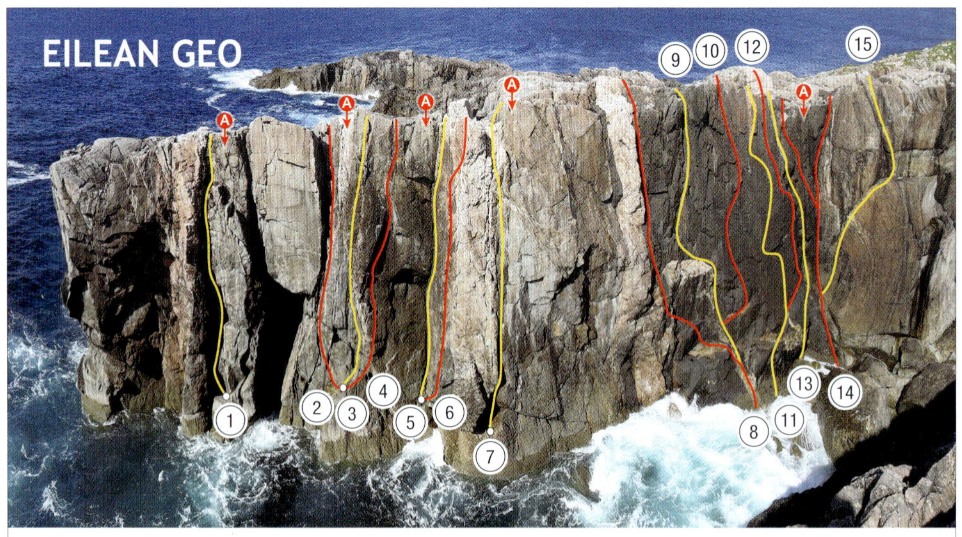

1. Blue Rinse	S 4b	6. Sea Pink	E3 5c ***	11. Eager Weaver	E2 5b *
2. Aqua Marine	VS 4c *	7. Bad Dose of The Grump	S 4b	12. Splendid Sun	HVS 5b *
3. Deep Blue	HVS 4c *	8. Takeaway	VS 4c *	13. Slim Reaper	E1/2 5b *
4. Cyanosis	E2 5b *	9. Breakout	HVS 4c	14. Jack Corner	VS 4c
5. Red Veil	E2 5b *	10. Wish You Were Here	HVS 4c **	15. Flakeout	E1 5b **

2 Aqua Marine 20m VS 4c *
R.Anderson, C.Anderson, 3 Jul 1997
From the left side of the ledge, gain the crack up on the left and follow this up the right side of the wedge of rock.

3 Deep Blue 20m HVS 4c *
R.Anderson, C.Anderson, 3 Jul 1997
The pink pegmatite streak which springs from the right side of the ledge.

4 Cyanosis 20m E2 5b *
R.Anderson, C.Anderson, 14 Jul 2014
Gain the base of a short, right-leaning sharp edged groove and climb this to pull onto a small ledge. Step up right to finish up a thin crack.

The next two climbs are gained by abseiling down the large corner to ledges.

5 Red Veil 20m E2 5b *
R.Anderson, C.Anderson, 8 Jul 2003
Climb the corner.

6 Sea Pink 20m E3 5c ***
R.Anderson, C.Anderson, 3 Jul 1997
An excellent climb up the crack in the smooth pink feldspar wall right of the corner. Near the top the holds force moves out right into a groove on the edge.

7 Bad Dose of the Grump 20m S 4b
I.Taylor, T.Fryer, Apr 2014
The crack up the right side of the white quartz-like band in the centre of the geo.

8 Takeaway 20m VS 4c *
R.Anderson, C.Anderson, 8 Jul 2003
Follows the right side of the large full height vein just left of Breakout, gained by starting as for that route to the accommodating ledge, or directly, tide permitting.

9 Breakout 20m HVS 4c
R.Anderson, C.Anderson, 3 Jul 1997
Some 5m left of the north-east corner, climb a wide quartzy vein up left to an accommodating ledge, from whose right side the vein leads through a notch to a quartzy ledge. Finish up the right side of the groove above.

10 Wish You Were Here 20m HVS 4c **
M.Kocsis, M.Hutton, Jun 2014
Start as for Breakout up the quartzy vein to ledges then traverse up right above a short leaning wall to climb the centre of the slab.

11 Eager Weaver 20m E2 5b *
R.Anderson, C. Anderson, 14 Oct 2014
From the foot of the quartzy vein, climb up and right to a good ledge above the high tide line then climb the slab 2m left of the edge. Initially go up left then move right at a small overlap towards a rock scar; there is a

crucial Rock 1 high on the right. Gain a handrail above then go left and move up to the base of a pink pegmatite streak just below the top (micro-wires). Move up right to good holds then step up right to finish as for Splendid Sun.

12 Splendid Sun 20m HVS 5b *
M.Kocsis, R.Batt Jun 2012
This takes the right side of the black slab at the eastern end of the inlet, gaining the ledge at the start as for Eager Weaver. Protection is tricky to arrange but the difficulties are short lived.

13 Slim Reaper 20m E1/2 5b *
R.Anderson, C.Anderson, 14 Oct 2014
The clean-cut corner-groove up the right side of the slab to the right of Splendid Sun. Gain holds on the left edge (gear) then step awkwardly right into the groove and climb it; the gear improves higher up.

14 Jack Corner 20m VS 4c
R.Anderson, C.Anderson, 14 Oct 2014
The groove and crack-line up the north-east corner of the geo lead to a choice of finishes. The groove on the left has an awkward move or two and is more difficult than the crack on the right.

15 Flakeout 20m E1 5b **
R.Anderson, C.Anderson, 3 Jul 1997
Climb the obvious left to right slanting flake on the back wall of the geo, just right of the north-east corner. From the ledge at two-thirds height, step left and climb to the top.

Glas Eilean

(NB 0142 3348) Tidal SW facing Map p37

Just beyond Eilean Geòdha is the island of Glas Eilean itself, which can be traversed across to at most states of the tide. Towards the south-east corner is a narrow inlet with a sheltered south-west-facing wall where there are some deep water solos.

Descent: A short abseil in to the left gives access to the first climb. The others can be reached by a short abseil down the right side of the cliff. It is also possible to traverse along the bottom to start all the climbs.

Way Out West 15m F6c S1 **
A.Turner (DWS), Jun 2012
Traverse in from the left on easy ground to reach the break at one-third height. Surmount the small roof on incredible jams and large holds. Pull round (crux) onto improving jams and finish more easily up the twin cracks.

Standing on the Edge of Time 15m F6b S0 **
A.Turner (DWS), Jun 2012
Climb the slabby wall and left arete on the right-hand side of the large overhung block. Traverse rightwards onto a grassy ledge to finish.

A Grand Day Out 10m F6b S0 *
A.Turner (DWS), Jun 2012
The easiest way up the wall 2m to the right of a large jutting corner

Crack with a View 10m F6a S0 **
A.Turner, M.Hutton (DWS), Jun 2012
The obvious crack on the far right-hand side of the cliff. Never harder than 5a and the perfect warm up. Delightful

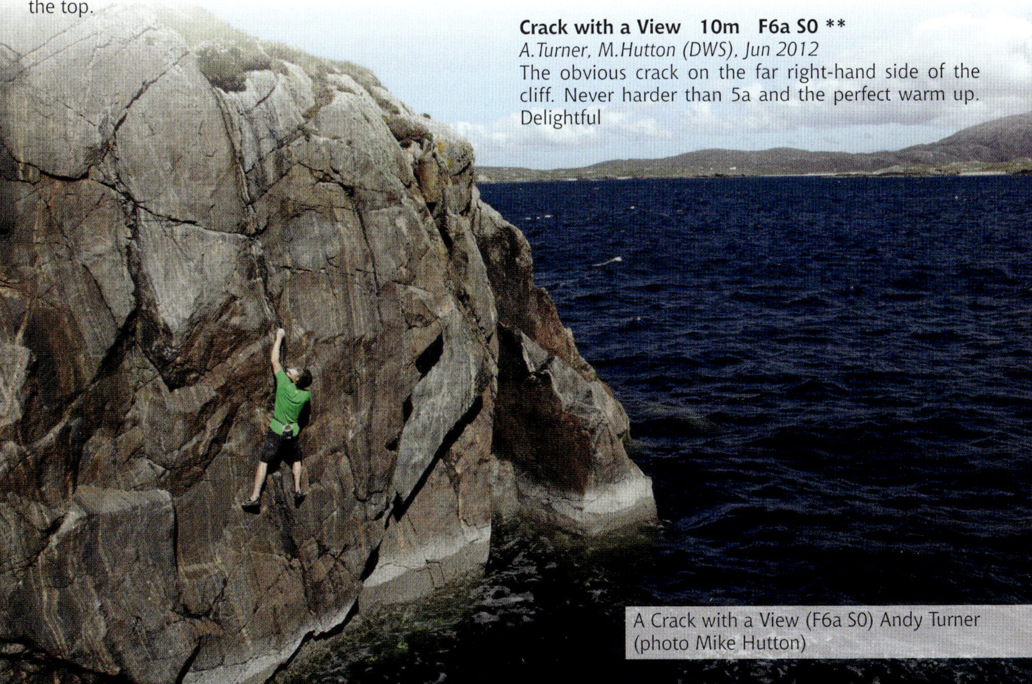

A Crack with a View (F6a S0) Andy Turner (photo Mike Hutton)

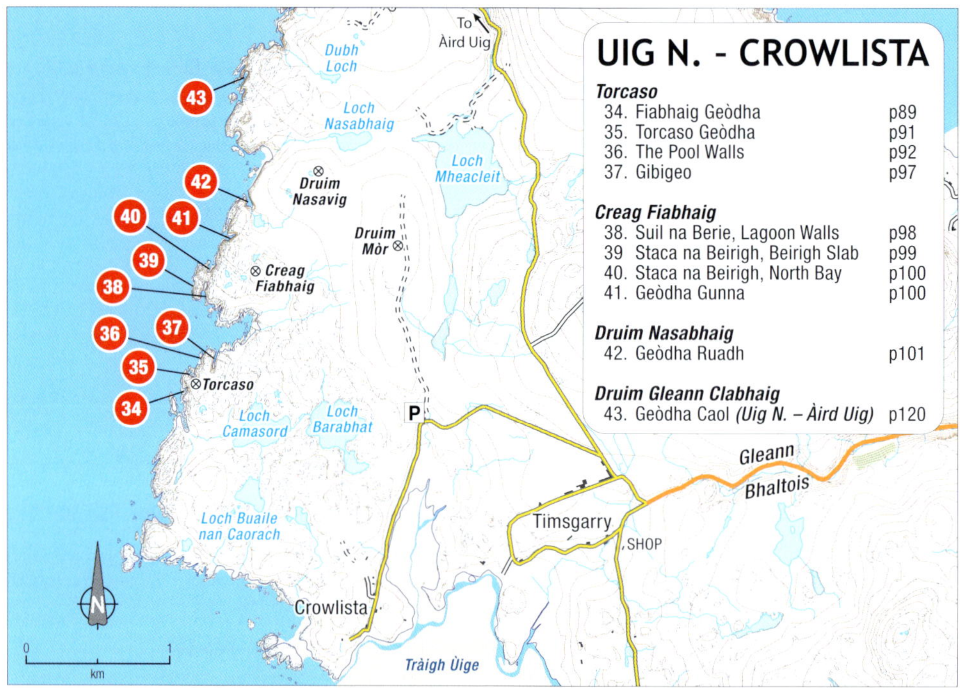

UIG NORTH - CROWLISTA

Maps p20 & above

Crowlista (Cradhlastadh) is the hamlet at the end of the road which loops around the north side of Camas Uig (Uig Bay). The coastline to the west of Crowlista is accessed from the road out to the hamlet and runs northwards for some 3km from Seilebhig Hill over the highpoint of Torcaso to the large bay of Bàgh Fiabhaig, then from the waisted headland of Staca na Berie to the large bay formed by Geòdha Nasabhaig to the south of the Àird Uig coastline.

Directions: Turn north off the B8011 at the top of Gleann Bhaltois meltwater channel, 350m north of the Community Shop at Timsgarry; signed to Àird Uig. Follow the road uphill past the turn off for the Community Centre, then just beyond the houses and the small industrial units, turn left and take the road towards Crowlista; the Torcaso highpoint on the coast is visible ahead. At the bottom of the hill, 1km short of the hamlet, park in a lay-by on a bend in the road **(NB 0452 3492)** where a rough track breaks off right up the hill. All of the climbing areas in this section can be approached from here, either by heading up the hill and across to them, or by walking up the track for 1km, or so and then heading across to the coast.

The climbing is split into two main areas, named after the highpoints on the coast; firstly Torcaso to the south of the large bay of Bàgh Fiabhaig, then Creag Fiabhaig and Druim Nasabhaig to the north of the bay.

TORCASO

Map above

There are four areas of climbing around the highpoint of Torcaso; Fiabhaig Geòdha, Torcaso Geòdha, the Pool Walls and Gibigeo. These are described in that order, in a south to north direction.

Further south, small crags on Seilebhig Hill **(NB 026 343)** apparently provide some climbing on short clean rock, as does the area around Geòdha Ruadh Meall Stèidhnoill **(NB 027 347)**, although no routes have been recorded.

Approach: Walk towards Crowlista for 50m or so, then leave the road to pass through a series of three gates and climb steeply uphill beside a fence, following this to where it turns away north. The cairned highpoint of Torcaso can now be seen ahead and is gained around the north side of Loch Barabhat. Head for a prominent boulder, then either step over the fence just past it, or use the gate further right, and follow the fence a short way round the right side of a knoll. Cut the corner and pass through a gate in another fence to open ground. Go rightwards around a small knoll, Cnoc Mairstean, and pick up a vague sheep track heading off slightly right of the Torcaso highpoint to skirt the right side of a flat boggy area. Follow the line of an old wall a short way toward the bay, then cross the wall and continue uphill towards the summit cairn, passing the head of the south to north running incision of Gibigeo before the final short pull to the top (25 to 30min).

Fiabhaig Geòdha is the narrow south-westward running geo to the south-west of the summit cairn, whilst Torcaso Geòdha is the big westward running geo immediately north-west of the cairn. The Pool Walls lie 100m or so to the north of Torcaso Geòdha, on a small headland formed between it and the deep inlet of Gibigeo which runs northwards into the bay.

Fiabhaig Geòdha

(NB 0290 3525) Map opposite

Lying to the south side of the summit cairn of Torcaso, this fine narrow geo runs at a right angle to Torcaso Geòdha, southwards to the sea and the skerry of Sgeir Fiabhaig Tarras.

Landward Side - Left

Partially Tidal NW facing Diagram p90

At the left side, a groove and triangular roof are obvious then the fault of The Big Easy which runs diagonally up from right to left across the face beneath a steep wall split by a pair of thin tramline cracks. To the right is a corner-groove, the right wall of which is split by a fine, steep crack. Then there is an edge, and around this a right-angled corner before the wall decreases in height and continues rightwards into the sea.

Descent: Abseil down the exit corner of The Big Easy, or the tramline cracks in the centre of the wall. Another option is to abseil down the corner of Gillie Mot.

The climbs all start from a good ledge system that runs beneath the wall.

1 Groove Is In the Heart 40m E3 5c **
M.Garthwaite, R.Anderson, 23 Jul 2002
At the left end of the main wall is a striking groove and corner-line that terminates at a triangular roof. At low tide traverse the tapering ledge just above the sea and gain a belay ledge in the corner. Climb the corner and go out left around the roof then up the headwall.

2 West Side Story 40m E2 5b ***
R.Anderson, C.Anderson, 12 Jul 2016
The slim ramp and groove line running up the wall to the right of Groove Is In the Heart. Start at the lowest ledges then climb up and left to a narrow ledge at the foot of the ramp; a belay can be taken here if the sea is low enough. Climb the ramp (small wires and a cam on the right wall) to a ledge and continue up the groove. Exit steeply on good holds and continue awkwardly above, stepping left then back right to finish more easily.

A huge flake-line used to sit in the middle of the wall and form part of the slanting fault but the winter 2015 storms have removed this and left a series of flat ledges. Kelpie Dancing (E1) used to climb the front of the flake and the routes either side have been altered.

3 Dobhrainn 40m E2 5c **
R.Anderson, C.Anderson, 8 Jul 2001 & 12 Jul 2016
The groove and corner-line running up the wall just left of the main diagonal fault-line. Move up and left into the line and follow this past a difficult section to a ledge. Move up right to gain the edge of the fault then continue up and leftwards to the top.

4 The Big Easy 30m S 4b
R.Anderson, C.Anderson, 8 Jul 2001, 12 Jul 2016
Climb up left on white rock scarred ledges, pull out right to gain then climb the fault-line and finish out rightwards on black rock.

5 A Streetcar Named Desire 25m E5 6b ***
R.Anderson, C.Anderson, 8 Jul 2001
The thin tramline cracks in the centre of the west face. With the removal of the flake this will now be more difficult and serious since the outside edge of the initial part of the flake that stood here was used to gain a point where small wires could be placed to protect the stretchy and blind placement of a Rock 8, or 7 in the base of the right-hand crack. Moves are made right past the wire before stepping up left to the base of the left-hand crack which is climbed to the top.

Groove Is In the Heart (E3) Mark Garthwaite (photo Chris Anderson)

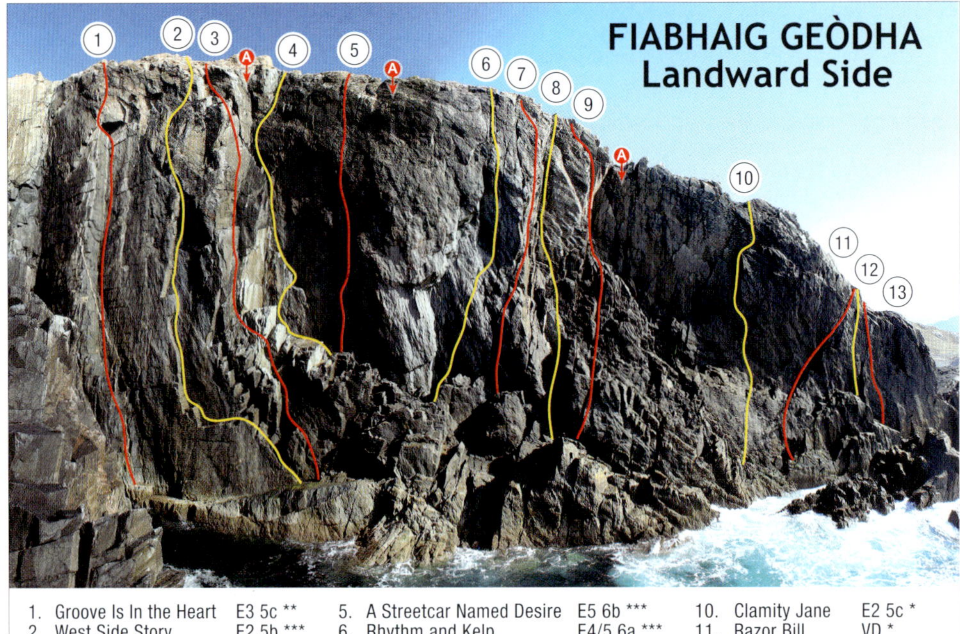

1. Groove Is In the Heart	E3 5c **	5. A Streetcar Named Desire	E5 6b ***	10. Clamity Jane	E2 5c *
2. West Side Story	E2 5b ***	6. Rhythm and Kelp	E4/5 6a ***	11. Razor Bill	VD *
3. Dobhrainn	E2 5c **	7. Kitty Wake	E2 5c *	12. Ian Tern	S 4b
4. The Big Easy	S 4b	8. Gillie Mot	HVS 4c	13. Full Mark	S 4b
		9. Sandy Piper	HVS 4c		

On the right there are two crack-lines between a steep leaning corner-groove and the edge on the right.

6 Rhythm and Kelp 25m E4/5 6a ***
R.Anderson, C.Anderson, 20 Jul 2001
A superb route up the steep left-hand crack-line, between the groove and the edge.

7 Kitty Wake 30m E2 5c *
R.Anderson, C.Anderson, 8 Jul 2001
This takes the right-hand crack-line to go up and around the edge and finish up a widening crack just left of a right-angled corner.

8 Gillie Mot 35m HVS 4c
R.Anderson, C.Anderson, 8 Jul 2001
The right-angled corner, gained from low down. Go up a short crack leading into a V-groove, then easy ground leads to its base.

9 Sandy Piper 35m HVS 4c
R.Anderson, C.Anderson, 8 Jul 2001
Immediately to the right of the start of Gillie Mot, climb a short, steep crack then easier broken ground to finish up parallel jam cracks between the right-angled corner and another corner on the right.

Landward Side - Right

Non-tidal NW facing Diagram above

The wall, less high now, continues rightwards above two ledge systems. The lower of which leads to two large spikes above a tidal channel.

10 Clamity Jane 25m E2 5c *
R.Anderson, C.Anderson, 15 Oct 2015
The obvious short left-facing black corner. Start from the lower ledge about 5m to the left of the two large spikes and climb cracks leading into the corner.

11 Razor Bill 25m VD *
R.Anderson, C.Anderson, 15 Oct 2015
Further right is a right-slanting crack; this can either be gained from the upper ledge or from the two large spikes lower down.

12 Ian Tern 15m S 4b
R.Anderson, C.Anderson, 15 Oct 2015
Start on the upper ledge to the left of a pinnacle feature and climb crack-lines to reach the top of the diagonal crack of Razor Bill.

13 Full Mark 15m S 4b
R.Anderson, C.Anderson, 15 Oct 2015
Start on the upper ledge to the right of the pinnacle feature, layback onto its top and continue up cracks.

Seaward Side

Tidal SE facing

The opposite side of the geo is formed by a slab which is reached by going over the top towards Torcaso Geòdha a way before scrambling down and traversing back left to the top. A crack-line and pink pegmatite vein slant up and across the slab from its bottom left side. The rock is good but needs to dry if spray has been flying about.

Descent: Abseil directly to the base of the climbs.

Northern Slant 35m D **
R.Anderson, C.Anderson, 5 Apr 2016
From good ledges on the left side of the slab, climb the right slanting crack-line and pink vein.

Much Ado about Nowt 25m HVS 4c
R.Anderson, C.Anderson, 5 Apr 2016
Abseil down the centre of the slab into a shallow groove and crack-line just above the high tide mark. Awkward hanging belay (on the rope) on a small foothold below a larger foothold; it might be preferable to place gear in the crack and extend this for the belay. The upper foothold enables the leader to start. Climb the groove and crack and finish more easily up the slab crossing Northern Slant.

Short and Stout 25m E1/2 5b
R.Anderson, C.Anderson, 5 Apr 2016
Belay above the tide mark, down and left on the large flake feature towards the back of the geo. Awkwardly pull over the left side of a small roof into a crack then continue up the slab.

All At Sea 30m HVS 5a **
R.Anderson, C.Anderson, 5 Apr 2016
At low tide and in calm seas it is possible to start off the inner of two pink boulders on the floor at the back of the geo. Climb a crack in a barnacle covered corner to gain the spike on top of the obvious flake feature; well protected and climbable when wet. Step right and climb a smooth groove to the roof and either take this directly or pull out left then step right and climb the crack to the top.

Torcaso Geòdha

(NB 0295 3533) Map p88

The back of this geo lies immediately to the north-west of the cairned highpoint of Torcaso. The first two routes lie on the black rock of south side of the geo.

South Side

Tidal NE facing

Towards the seaward end of the geo, just to the right of a sea cave and a huge rock scar from the 2015 storms, is an area of black rock which protrudes slightly to form a pillar with a pedestal at its base. The first two climbs take crack-lines up the pillar.

Descent: Scramble down towards the top of the pillar, then abseil through a notch to a ledge at the top of the pillar and down between the crack-lines to a small, flat ledge at its base. At low tide and in calm seas it should be possible to scramble down into the geo from the seaward promontory.

No Hiding Place 25m E1 5b **
R.Anderson, C.Anderson, 17 Jul 1998
The left-hand crack-line.

Running Scared 25m E1 5b ***
R.Anderson, C.Anderson, 17 Jul 1998
Step right around the edge into a corner and climb the right-hand crack-line on perfect rock.

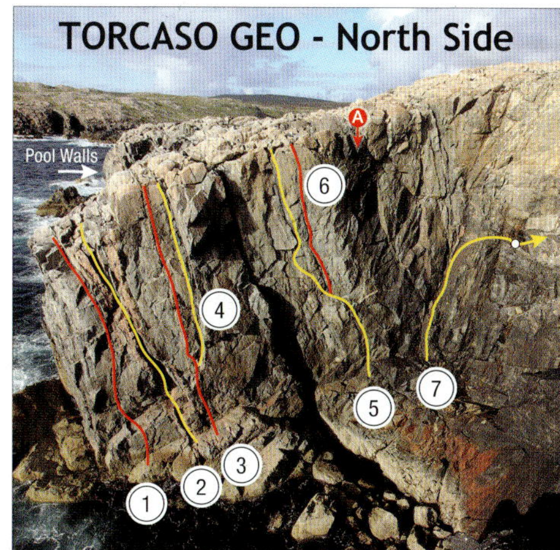

1.	Happy Returns	E2 5c **
2.	Generation Gap	HVS/E1 5b *
3.	Life in the Old Dog Yet	E3 5c **
4.	42nd Street	E2 5c **
5.	Das Boat	E4/5 6a ***
6.	Ein Schiff Voller Narren	E5/6 6b **
7.	Escape From Victory	VS 4b

North Side

Non-tidal SW facing Diagram above

The north side of the geo. Just before the arete forming the extreme seaward end, there is an obvious slanting chimney-crack with a pink pegmatite vein to its right then a long corner.

Descent: Abseil down or just to the side of the long corner of 42nd Street, to ledges just above the sea.

1 Happy Returns 20m E2 5c **
R.Anderson, C.Anderson, 6 Jul 1999
Just left of the chimney, climb the crack in the black wall and then its continuation.

2 Generation Gap 25m HVS/E1 5b *
R.Anderson, C.Anderson, 6 Jul 1999
The slanting chimney-crack.

3 Life in the Old Dog Yet 30m E3 5c **
R.Anderson, C.Anderson, 6 Jul 1999
The pink pegmatite vein just right of the chimney. Either follow the initial crack of 42nd Street, or a line just to its left to join it at the higher ledge. Move up the corner of 42nd Street until it is possible to traverse left into the middle of the wall (jugs) then move up the vein to a roof and ledges just above. The fine crack in the headwall leads to the top.

4 42nd Street 30m E2 5c **
R.Anderson, C.Anderson, 6 Jul 1999
The long corner-line gained by a crack leading from the lower ledge to the higher ledge.

Descent: By abseil; probably best down the corner-line at the right end of the wall. The rock is a bit loose at the top.

5 Das Boat 30m E4/5 6a ***
B.Fyffe, T.Stone, May 2008
This takes the obvious diagonal cracked-groove to the right of the left-leaning chimney-corner towards the centre of the wall. Climb the cracks and block rib to ledges as for Ein Schiff Voller Narren then move up and left around a quartzy shield to a point underneath the right side of a huge downward-pointing flake. Trend back right into the left-facing groove-corner and power up this, then up to the huge flake to finish up the groove and crack above.

6 Ein Schiff Voller Narren 30m E5/6 6b **
P.Thorburn, B.Fyffe, Jun 2005
This takes a crack in the wall to the right of the left-leaning chimney-corner towards the centre of the wall. Climb a left-slanting crack to ledges, then climb a vague block rib and finish up the crack just right of the arete above.

The final route is an escape route starting from ledges at the north-east corner of the geo. Some, if not all of this back wall may have been subsequently altered by the sea.

7 Escape From Victory 50m VS 4b
R Anderson, C.Anderson, 11 Jul 1999
1. 20m 4b Climb the corner on good black rock, then traverse right and step down to a good ledge on the back wall.
2. 30m 4b Traverse ledges across the back wall and finish up a short V-groove in the south-east corner of the geo.

The Pool Walls

(NB 0302 3540) Partially Tidal N, W & NW facing Map p88

About 50m to the north of Torcaso Geòdha, easy slabs lead down to a point overlooking a small bay around a lovely tidal pool. The top of the main wall at the back of the bay is identifiable by its leaning tombstone appearance. The base of the wall above the pool remains clear of the water for quite a number of hours and good ledges below most of the climbs enable the climbs to be accessed for much of the time.

Descent: Abseil down the north side of the bay beyond the highpoint, down the slabs at the top of Deeply Panned, past a platform then a wide, deep corner-crack to the northern edge of the pool. An abseil can also be made from the south side of the highpoint, down Fabulously Fruity on the Back Wall to gain the southern edge of the pool, passing the ledges on the huge boulder feature forming the base of the wall.

Climbs are described left to right, starting with those on the north side of the bay.

North Side

W facing Diagrams p93 & p94

The north side of the bay is defined by a chimney then an obvious arete which leads to a flat topped tower feature forming its edge. Extending leftwards from here is a smooth crack-lined and water-worn outer wall of perfect rock. The first climbs start beneath a groove about 15m along from the edge, above a highly active tidal trench. The wall extends beyond this but drops straight into the tidal trench. A stance beneath the groove is only possible at low tide in calm seas.

1 Tidal Race 25m HVS 5a *
R.Anderson, C.Anderson, 13 Oct 2015
Move up into the foot of the groove 15m along from the edge then pull round the left rib to climb a thin crack. Finish up a big and easy V-groove on the right.

2 Trench Warfare 25m HVS 5a **
R.Anderson, C.Anderson, 13 Oct 2015
Move up into the foot of the groove then step up right and climb twin cracks to a finish up the big V-groove.

The next few climbs can be gained from a non-tidal pedestal ledge which extends leftwards from the foot of the left-hand chimney crack and the arete forming the edge of the bay.

3 Over the Top 25m E2 5c *
R.Anderson, C.Anderson, 13 Oct 2015
Place side runners high in Special Forces then step down left and climb a short, leaning flake feature in a shallow groove. From holds at its top gain better holds on the left then pull onto the wall and continue up a thin crack to finish up a crack in the left edge of the tower.

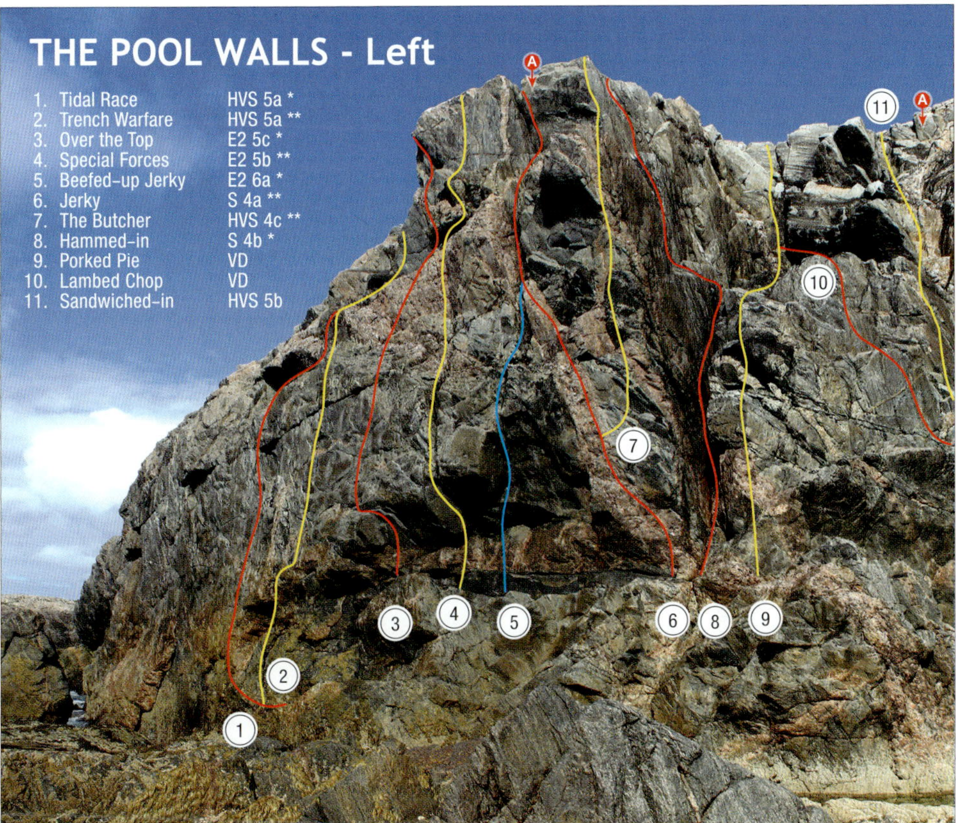

4 Special Forces 25m E2 5b **
R.Anderson, C.Anderson, 13 Oct 2015
The obvious undercut crack, gained by stepping left off the pedestal belay. Continue up a short corner and finish up the centre of the tower.

5 Beefed-up Jerky 25m E2 6a *
R.Anderson, 13 Oct 2015
To the left of the arete is a line giving direct entry into the crack of the original route. Some perplexing moves up a short groove past a small wire (high side runner in pink rock to the right useful) to gain a slot then a thin crack leading to the wide crack.

6 Jerky 25m S 4a **
R.Anderson, C.Anderson, 13 Jul 2001
Start below the chimney and the arete forming the outer edge of the bay. Step left onto the edge then swing left after a few moves on pink feldspar and climb the obvious crack to the top.

7 The Butcher 25m HVS 4c **
R.Anderson, C.Anderson, 9 Jul 2001
The prominent arete above the chimney. Step left onto the edge to climb pink rock then move around onto the right-hand side in the middle. Continue up the arete to a sloping ledge. Move right and climb the right side of the upper arete to the top.

8 Hammed-in 25m S 4b *
R.Anderson, C.Anderson, 15 Jul 2015
Climb the left-hand chimney to gain the large platform between the tops of the two chimney cracks. Finish up a crack in the wall on the left.

9 Porked Pie 25m VD
R.Anderson, C.Anderson, 13 Oct 2015
Climb the edge to the right of the chimney to gain the large platform then finish up the groove at the back.

To the left of the chimney-fault is the wide and deep chimney-crack of the northern abseil line.

10 Lambed Chop 25m VD
R.Anderson, C.Anderson, 13 Oct 2015
Climb the crack-line to the left of the deep right-hand chimney-crack to gain the platform then finish up the groove as for Porked Pie.

8. Hammed-in	S 4b *	14. Northern Exposure	VS 4c *	20. Puddle Duck	E1 5c *
9. Porked Pie	VD	15. Southern Comfort	HVS 4c **	21. Flannantastique	HVS 5a ***
10. Lambed Chop	VD	16. Tomb Raider	E4/5 6b **	22. Fabulously Fruity	E2 5b **
11. Sandwiched-in	HVS 5b	17. Big Fun	VD ***	23. Gloriously Nutty	E3 5c/6a ***
12. Deeply Panned	VS 4c **	18. Pond Life	E2 5c **	24. Amazingly Spicy	E1 5b *
13. Shared-out	VS 4c *	19. Pool Shark	E1 5b **	25. Sideshow	HS 4b *

11 Sandwiched-in 25m HVS 5b

R.Anderson, C.Anderson, 13 Oct 2015

Climb the wall between Lambed Chop and Deeply Panned to gain the platform then step across the gap on the right and climb the washed out quartz-like pink groove.

12 Deeply Panned 25m VS 4c **

R.Anderson, C.Anderson, 24 Jul 2015

Make a few awkward moves up the wall to the left of the deep chimney-crack then move up the crack to just below the platform and climb the groove on the right of the crack past the left side of a grey rock scar. Finish up the crack in the easy slab.

13 Shared-out 25m VS 4c *

R.Anderson, C.Anderson, 22 Jul 2015

Climb Deeply Panned then pull out right and climb the groove line immediately to its right, past the right side of a grey rock scar. Finish up the last few moves of Northern Exposure.

The Back Wall

W facing Diagrams above & p96

The next three climbs start at the left side of the fine back wall and like those on the right side of the wall they are quite close together but offer good climbing.

14 Northern Exposure 25m VS 4c *

R.Anderson, C.Anderson, 13 Jul 2001

Climb a wide crack to a ledge as for Southern Comfort then step left and climb a short crack to a sloping ledge. Continue up a short corner to another sloping ledge and finish up the left-hand parallel groove.

15 Southern Comfort 25m HVS 4c **

R.Anderson, C.Anderson, 9 Jul 2001

This takes the left-hand side of the main, leaning central section. Climb a wide crack to a ledge then take the wide corner-crack to a sloping ledge. Step right across the top of the corner and climb the right-hand groove running up the left side of the headwall.

16 Tomb Raider 25m E4/5 6b **
R.Anderson, C.Anderson, 13 Jul 2001
The steep cracks running up the left side of the central leaning wall. Climb to the ledge just right of the corner of Southern Comfort and climb the thin cracks in the wall to pull onto a shelf; this is an eliminate, avoid stepping out left. Climb tramline cracks up the wall and where these veer off right move up with difficulty and pull directly onto the shelf above. Cracks in the left side of the tombstone headwall lead to the top.

A huge boulder like feature forms the base of the wall to the right. It is easy enough to climb over this to get to the climbs on the other side and vice versa.

17 Big Fun 35m VD ***
R.Anderson, C.Anderson, 22 Jul 2015
A rising traverse across the right side of the wall. Climb to ledges on top of the boulder then follow the traverse line across the wall to a ledge beside the black pillar forming the right side of the wall. Move up and climb a short corner then easier ground to the left of the pillar.

The following four routes can be started by scrambling to a good ledge on top of the boulder feature.

18 Pond Life 25m E2 5c **
R.Anderson, C.Anderson, 29 Jun 1997
From the top of the boulder, step left, climb an awkward leaning section and continue steeply up a thin crack.

19 Pool Shark 25m E1 5b **
R.Anderson, C.Anderson, 29 Jun 1997
A few feet right of the previous route, climb onto the very top of the boulder and follow another crack straight to the top with a steeper middle section.

20 Puddle Duck 25m E1 5c *
R.Anderson, C.Anderson, 29 Jun 1997
Eliminate climbing immediately right of Pool Shark. Step up right into a steep groove and make an awkward move to holds. Continue directly up a groove with an awkward exit onto a small slab and carry on to the top.

21 Flannantastique 25m HVS 5a ***
R.Anderson, C.Anderson, 15 Jul 2015
From a ledge on the right side of the boulder, climb a slab up right to a wide crack in the leaning wall. Gain the shallow groove and crack above, then climb this to a ledge and finish up a crack.

Fabulously Fruity (E2) Paul McCarthy (photo Steve Grey)

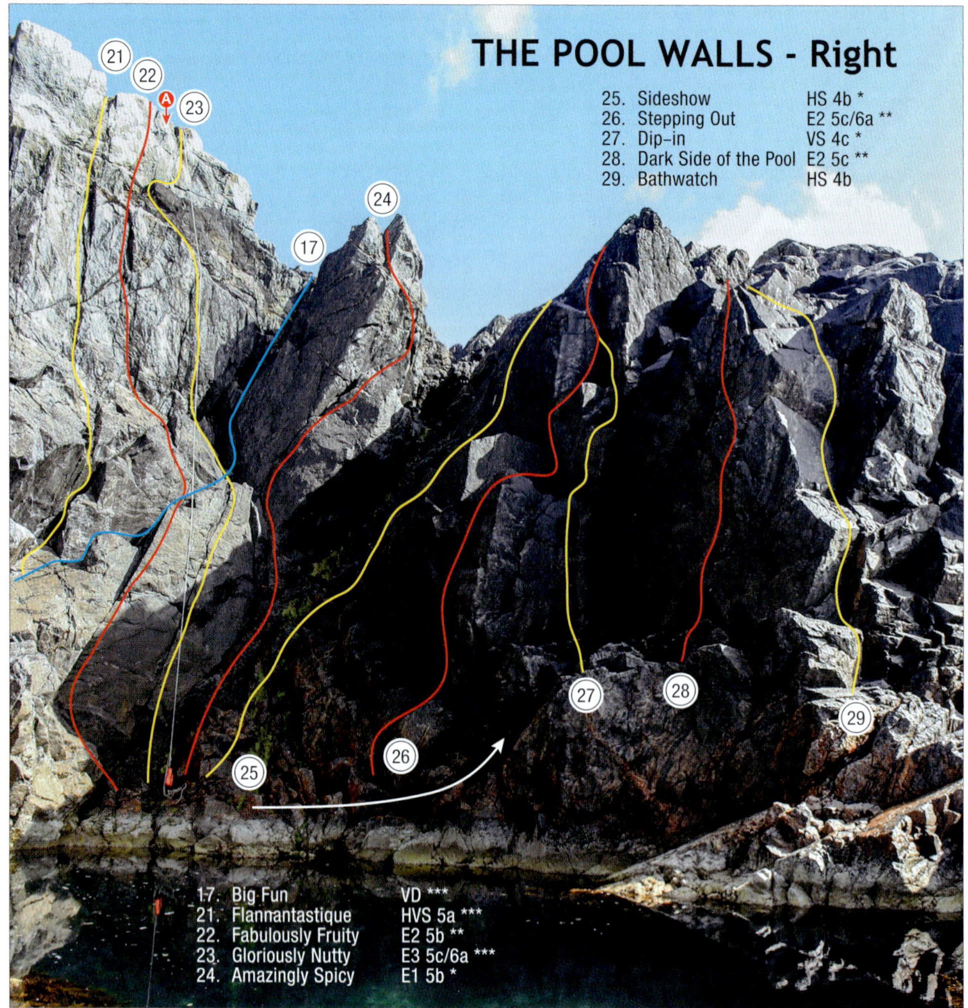

The next four routes start from the edge of the pool beneath a smooth wall at the right side of the boulder feature.

22 Fabulously Fruity 30m E2 5b **

R.Anderson, C.Anderson, 22 Jul 2015

Move up left and climb the slanting crack in the left side of the smooth wall. Cross the traverse line and climb a groove and the continuation crack above, just right of Flannantastique.

23 Gloriously Nutty 30m E3 5c/6a ***

R.Anderson, C.Anderson, 22 Jul 2015

Climb the slanting crack in the right side of the smooth wall to ledges then go up left and climb an awkward short crack to a ledge. Go left around a black intrusion to climb the short final wall.

Variation: **23a Gloriously Fruity 30m E2 5c *****

The lower crack of Gloriously Nutty and the top of Fabulously Fruity.

24 Amazingly Spicy 30m E1 5b *

R.Anderson, C.Anderson, 22 Jul 2015

This gains then climbs the wide diagonal crack in the leaning pillar which forms the upper right side of the wall. Climb slabby rock easily right then step up left into the base of the corner at the right side of the wall, and climb to the ledge at the end of the traverse of Big Fun. Step right and climb a wide crack to its top, then stand up and pull over the bulge to gain the top of the pillar.

South Side

N facing Diagram opposite

The next climbs lie on the black rock on the south side of the pool, to the right of easy slabs. There are two tower like features either side of a central chimney.

25 Sideshow 25m HS 4b *
R.Anderson, C.Anderson, 24 Jul 2015
From the ledge at the side of the pool, climb cracked slabs up the left side of the left-hand tower.

26 Stepping Out 20m E2 5c/6a **
R.Anderson, C.Anderson, 13 Jul 2001
On the tower left of the central chimney, climb a short crack to a series of stepped corners and cracks and follow these to the top.

The next three climbs start from a higher ledge above the pool.

27 Dip-in 20m VS 4c *
R.Anderson, C.Anderson, 24 Jul 2015
Climb up left from the foot of the central chimney to a ledge on the right side of the tower then climb the edge on the right to another ledge and finish up the corner on the left as for Stepping Out.

28 Dark Side of the Pool 15m E2 5c **
R.Anderson, C.Anderson, 24 Jul 2015
Climb the thin crack up the front of the right-hand tower; short but absorbing.

29 Bathwatch 15m HS 4b
R.Anderson, C.Anderson, 24 Jul 2015
The corner in the edge of the right side of the tower.

Gibigeo

(NB 0309 3535) Tidal NW facing Map p88

Originally named Deep Geo, this is the deep and narrow geo that is met on the approach, running north to south off Bàgh Fiabhaig. There are two climbs starting from the base of a hanging corner-crack system on the west facing wall, some 30m from the south end of the geo.

Descent: Abseil down the corner to a hanging stance.

Consequences 30m E4 6a
K.Pyke, G.Huxter, 12 Jul 1997
Make tricky moves up a blank wall and corner (RP's) to a half rest under an overhang. Turn the overhang on its right to gain the arete and step back left to follow the final groove line in an excellent position.

Fright of the Cormorant 25m E1 5b *
G.Kirk, D.Howard, 12 Jul 1997
The crack in the left wall of the corner, starting from sloping ledges. Climb the corner for 4m then follow the crack in its steep left wall to the top.

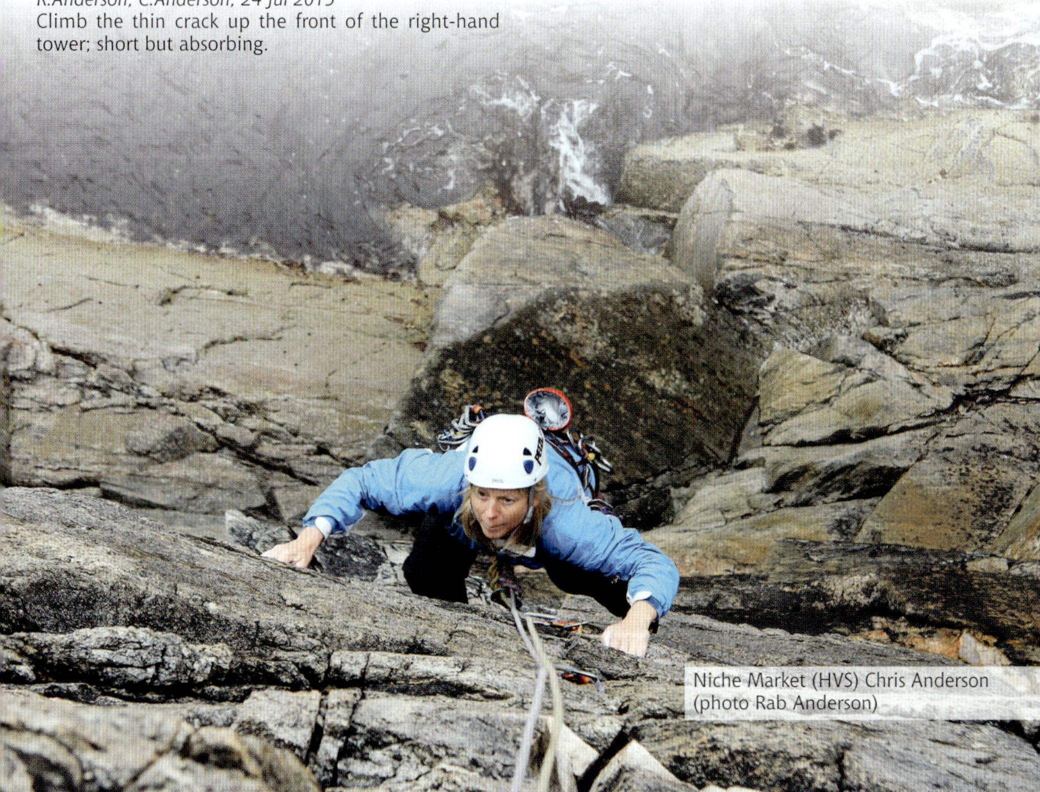

Niche Market (HVS) Chris Anderson (photo Rab Anderson)

CREAG FIABHAIG & DRUIM NASABHAIG

Map p88

These are the highpoints behind the section of coast between the large bays of Bàgh Fiabhaig and Geòdha Nasabhaig.

Approach: From the parking area on the bend at the bottom of the hill, 1km short of the hamlet of Crowlista, walk north (uphill) on the track passing through a gate. Go through another gate and continue to where the track levels out, then 100m past a gate in the fence on the right. Break off left at a corner in the fence and head west to the coast. The cairned highpoint of Creag Fiabhaig can be seen ahead. Staca na Beirigh lies beyond this with Geòdha Gunna then Geòdha Ruadh, and Geòdha Nasabaig running northwards to the right. Initially head downhill, passing to the right of a cairn on the knoll of Cnoc Mòr, then cross a small burn to pass around the head of a shallow valley running into the bay (30min).

Staca na Beirigh and Suil na Beirie

(NB 030 359) Partially Tidal SW & SE facing Map p88

The prominent capped headland on the north side of the large bay of Bàgh Fiabhaig is Staca na Beirigh. It takes the form of a waisted headland, connected to the main landmass by a narrow neck which separates the large inlet of Suil na Beirie to the south from the smaller North Bay inlet to the north. The Suil na Beirie inlet has been referred to as The Lagoon, with the flanking walls called The Lagoon Walls. The area has apparently been explored in the past, although none of these explorations have been recorded. The remote and exposed situation with the outlook across the bay to the Uig Hills is splendid.

The Staca Na Beirigh headland itself has two distinctive highpoints, a northern one and a southern one. The northern highpoint is penetrated by a hole, or gloop, the bottom of which can be reached by a D traverse around to the north at low tide; otherwise you can abseil in. There are apparently three routes back out of the hole from VD to VS, all up obvious fault-lines, but no further details have been forthcoming. Some chimneys on the south-west (seaward) side have also apparently been climbed but not recorded. Beneath the southern highpoint the Beirigh slab is obvious at the entrance to the Suil na Beirigh (The Lagoon) inlet.

Climbs on the landward Lagoon Wall of Suil na Beirigh are described first, then those on the Beirigh Slab opposite and finally those around the North Bay on the north side of Staca na Beirigh.

The Lagoon Wall

(NB 0308 3587) Tidal W facing

This is the landward or eastern side of Suil na Beirie. There have apparently been explorations here in the past, as well as on the opposite side to the right of the Beirigh Slab. Ledges at the base of the wall appear to remain clear of the tide for some time.

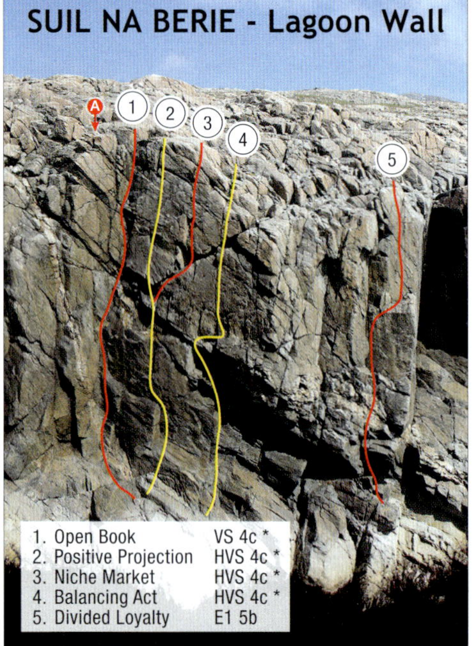

Descent: Abseil down the corner of Open Book towards the north end of the wall, opposite a recessed section of wall right of the Beirigh Slab on the other side of The Lagoon.

1 Open Book 25m VS 4c *
R.Anderson, C.Anderson, 9 Jul 2012
The large, open slabby corner.

2 Positive Projection 25m HVS 4c *
R.Anderson, C.Anderson, 9 Jul 2012
Some 5m to the right of the slabby corner climb a short right-facing corner and continue to the right side of a projecting shelf. Move up onto the shelf then climb a thin crack in the fine rock just right of the slabby corner.

3 Niche Market 25m HVS 4c *
R.Anderson, C.Anderson, 9 Jul 2012
Climb to the projecting shelf on Positive Projection then go up and right to a niche and climb the crack which springs from its top.

4 Balancing Act 25m HVS 4c *
R.Anderson, C.Anderson, 9 Jul 2012
Climb to an alcove beneath the roof then move up left to pull over the left side of the roof. Traverse right on the lip then climb the crack above.

5 Divided Loyalty 25m E1 5b
R.Anderson, C.Anderson, 9 Jul 2012
Around the edge from Balancing Act is a corner and groove line running up a tower feature just left of a deep corner. Pull over the initial bulges and climb the corner-groove to a shelf on the right. Climb the wall right of the final groove to an awkward finish.

The Beirigh Slab

(NB 0305 3585) Tidal SE facing Diagram below

Beneath the southern highpoint of Staca na Beirigh and towards the south-east corner of the headland there is an obvious steep slab. It is well seen across the Suil na Beirie inlet from the top of The Lagoon Wall.

Approach: Head for the northern highpoint on the Staca Na Beirigh headland and go down an obvious slabby depression and groove. At the bottom an easy short scramble gains the boulder field at the neck. On the other side, ascend a slabby shelf up left to white quartz-like rock at a ledge on the edge, then scramble down a slanting ledge system to gain the saddle between the two highpoints. Scramble up onto the southern highpoint and walk out to the top of the slab.

Descent: Abseil down a corner to a good but tidal pedestal at the base of the slab.

1 Crowlista Crawl 25m HVS 5b **
R.Anderson, C.Anderson, 4 Jul 2012
The left-hand of three crack-lines which starts through a scoop is easier after the initial moves. Finish up the corner.

2 Laguna Drive 25m HVS 5a **
R.Anderson, C.Anderson, 4 Jul 2012
Climb up to a ledge, then step left to follow the central crack-line to a shared finish up the corner with Crowlista Crawl.

3 Island Dancer 25m E1 5b *
R.Anderson, C.Anderson, 4 Jul 2012
Climb up to a ledge and follow the right-hand crack-line which slants up right to finish up the centre of the slab.

4 Vegas Shuffle 25m E3 5c *
R.Anderson, C.Anderson, 5 Jul 2012
Good climbing but some friable rock and awkward to place gear makes this a somewhat tenuous outing; micro-wires are useful. Climb up to a ledge, step right then launch up the hairline crack in the centre of the slab.

5 Stornoway Stagger 25m E1 5b *
R.Anderson, C.Anderson, 5 Jul 2012
Dodges the difficult lower half of the previous route then finishes out right. Move up and right to climb a crack-line to the right of Vegas Shuffle. At mid-height the natural line leads left into this route which can either be followed to the top, or broken out of to climb another thin crack on the right.

6 Lewisian Tango 30m E1 5b **
R.Anderson, C.Anderson, 5 Jul 2012
Move up and right then traverse right all the way to a crack on the edge of the slab. Climb the crack to a ledge, step left and climb the right edge of the slab to the top.

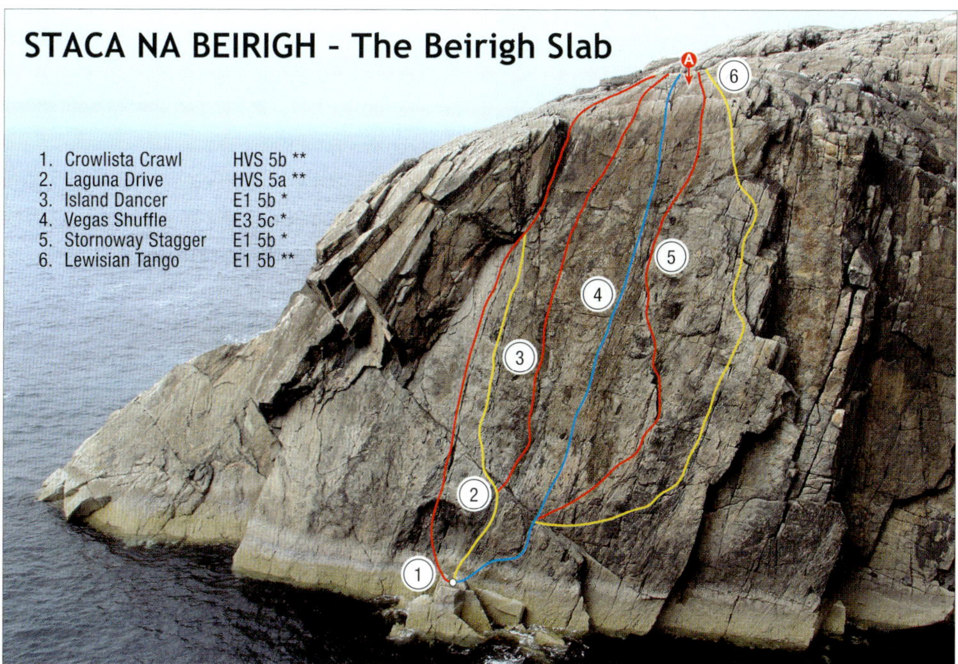

North Bay

(NB 0309 3602) Non-tidal NE facing

Below the northern top of Staca na Beirigh there is a sheltered rocky bay. On the Staca na Beirigh side a slabby rib of blocky corners overlooks a right-angled, quartzy corner, then a series of crack-lines through an upper section of quartzy rock.

Approach: As for the Beirigh Slab to gain the boulder field, then go right.

Cornerstones 30m S 4a
R.Anderson, C.Anderson, 11 Jul 2003
The central corner system in the slabby rib.

Edgeway 30m VD
R.Anderson, C.Anderson, 11 Jul 2003
The slabby right arete just right of Cornerstones.

Whitecap 30m VS 4c *
R.Anderson, C.Anderson, 11 Jul 2003
The thin crack just right of the quartzy right-angled corner.

Red Wall

(NB 0317 3606) Tidal SW facing

Overlooking the bay on the north side of Staca na Beirigh there is a largish broken cliff above a huge rockfall. Just north of this, there is a south facing reddish coloured wall with an obvious hole in it. To access the top of this wall, walk over the top of the crag with the rockfall to locate a wide fault running down its side.

Rabid Wanderings (E3) Glenda Huxter & Kath Pyke (photo Alan Leary)

Descent: An abseil down the red wall gains a spacious ledge below the hole which is a body sized solution pocket. Continue the abseil to ledges just above the sea at the base of a large right to left slanting fault.

The Hole Solution 30m E2 5b *
R.Anderson, C.Anderson, 9 Jul 2003
1. 10m 5b Climb into a V-groove then go right to the arete and climb to the spacious ledge.
2. 20m 5b Move up and left into the hole then climb thin cracks to the top.

Geòdha Gunna

(NB 0332 3624) Tidal SW facing Map p88 Diagram p101

About 300m north of Staca na Beirigh is an impressive large geo. The centre of the north side of the geo has a deep sea cave with an imposing wall to its right. To the left of the cave there is a tall slab slanting up leftwards. Climbs are described from right to left.

Descent: Three climbs lie on the imposing wall right of the sea cave; gained by abseil to sea-level ledges.

1 Rabid Wanderings 45m E3 5c *
G.Huxter, K.Pyke, 14 Jul 1997
Climb the central crack and groove system for 20m before moving out rightwards and taking a diagonal line up to the right end of an overhang. Pull through this (crux) and continue straight to the top.

2 Lucid Visions 45m E4 ***
G.Huxter, K.Pyke, 14 Jul 1997
A brilliant out-there route on a rising and exposed traverse leftwards through hanging grooves to finish up the steep headwall.
1. 25m 5c Climb Rabid Wanderings for 3m before weaving up and leftwards into hanging grooves, to gain a good and exposed stance.
2. 20m 5c Move up and left onto the headwall and follow a thin crack leftwards on steep ground to finish.

3 Captain Oates 45m E4 ****
D.O'Sullivan, C.Waddy (alt), 23 May 2018
Another of the Lewis Sea Cliffs' must-do climbs, this is a stunning route of ever increasing wild exposure; probably E5 if the last two pitches are linked. Start as for the previous two climbs.
1. 20m 5b Where Lucid Visions leaves Rabid Wanderings, follow a roof-capped left-leaning groove system to belay where a rightwards rising pegmatite fault crosses the cliff.
2. 15m 6a Traverse wildly left along the lip of the roof until it is possible to pull up into a rest in a short groove. Leave this leftwards in a magnificent position, then pull up to belay on spikes in another groove.
3. 10m 6b Climb a thin crack to a desperate short corner, from which slapping the top is the crux. An easier alternative (6a) traverses big holds left to the arete, to finish up a short jam crack.

To the left of the cave there is a tall east-facing slab.

Descent: Locate the top of the slab and abseil to ledges.

4 Little Gem 30m VS 4b *
M.Tighe, W.Newton and Party, 1980s
The tall slab which butts against the north wall to form a corner. A small cam in the right crack protects the initial tricky moves up the slab, after which the corner is followed to the top on improving holds and protection.

5 Gun Run 30m HS 4b *
M.Tighe, A.Gillespie, T.McLachlan, 29 May 2000
Start 10m left of Little Gem at a broken black groove. Climb the groove for 8m then make a difficult move right onto the slab, which is followed to the top.

Around the corner from Gun Run is a broken wall with broken ledges just on the high tide line.

6 Pop Gun 20m HVS 4c
M.Tighe, R.McLachlan, T. McLachlan, 29 May 2000
A few metres around the corner from Gun Run, climb a hanging crack and chimney-line and exit onto the slab part way up Gun Run.

7 Gun Crack 30m HVS 5b *
M.Tighe, R.McLachlan, T.McLachlan, 29 May 2000
Left again is a fine crack and open groove; rather gymnastic.

At the north-west corner of the geo, where the south and west-facing walls meet, there is a small recess from which springs a fabulous crack and corner, curving gently rightwards to the top of the cliff.

Descent: Abseil in to the north off big blocks, down a corner (S 4b), and traverse a non-tidal ledge under a wall with five routes (2018, details online).

8 The Legend of Finlay MacIver 25m E1 5b ***
M.Tighe, K.Tighe, 29 May 2008
The crack and corner gives wonderful climbing on perfect rock with excellent protection.

Geòdha Ruadh

(NB 0345 3643) Tidal SW facing Map p88

Some 200m to the north of Geòdha Gunna is a big northwards running geo, which has a beautiful orange slab with a Separate Reality style crack through the headwall on its north-east side.

Brutal Reality 30m E6 6b ***
S.Mayers, G.Lovick, Jul 1993
Reached by abseil, the pleasant slab is followed by the brutally overhanging hand-crack.

There are two HVS 5a routes to the left, one up the pink band, the other just to its right.

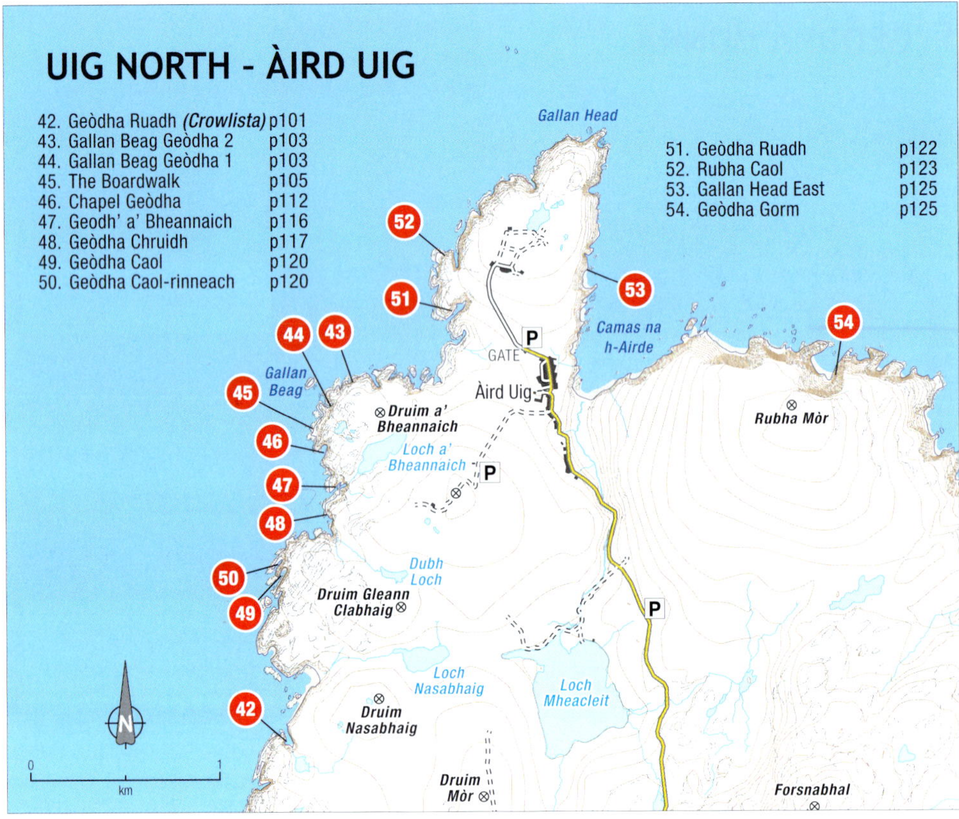

UIG NORTH - ÀIRD UIG

Maps p20 & above

Accessed from the hamlet and former Ministry of Defence base at Àird Uig, this is the stretch of coast running northwards from the large bay formed by Geòdha Nasabhaig at the northern end of the Crowlista section. The coast is broken into three sections by the highpoints between the main bays; Druim Gleann Clabhaig between Geòdha Nasabhaig and Geòdha Chruidh, then Druim a' Bheannaich between Geòdha Chruidh and Camus Geòdachan an Duilisg, and finally the major headland of Gallan Head (An Gallan Uigeach) between Camus Geòdachan an Duilisg and Camus na h-Airde.

The climbing areas are described as met when approached from the parking at Àird Uig; north to south for the initial areas on Druim a' Bheannaich and Druim Gleann Clabhaig, then south to north on Gallan Head.

Directions: Turn north off the B8011 at the top of the Gleann Bhaltois meltwater channel, 350m north of the shop at Timsgarry, and continue past the turn offs to firstly the Community Centre, then Crowlista (Cradhlastadh) to reach the hamlet of Àird Uig.

Go past the houses then the buildings of the former Ministry of Defence base for the surveillance station on the Gallan Head peninsula beyond. The road effectively ends at a decrepit fence across the headland a few hundred metres beyond the last house, which is now a cafe called The Edge. The former MOD surveillance station lies beyond and the ground is littered with abandoned debris and the concrete bases and rings for the aerials that once adorned the site. The area is being cleared of as much debris is as possible.

There is a convenient parking spot on the left about 100m beyond the gate at the last building, The Edge Cafe, a short way before the fence across the headland. All three sections of coast can be approached from here.

For the climbing around Druim a' Bheannaich and Druim Gleann Clabhaig it is possible to drive up a rough peat track that heads westwards between the houses just past the cattle grid in Àird Uig. This track goes uphill to some old MOD buildings on Cnoc na Lìana Mòire and a little closer to some of the cliffs in this section. It is perhaps better to pull off the track and park at the top of the hill, rather than continue as it isn't suitable for vehicles.

DRUIM A' BHEANNAICH

This is the section of coast around the Druim a' Bheannaich highpoint to the north-west of Loch a' Beannaich. This loch lies in a shallow trough between Druim a' Bheannaich and the higher Cnoc na Lìana Mòire highpoint west of Àird Uig, to which the peat track goes to and where there are some old MOD buildings.

The initial stretch of this coast runs west from the large bay of Camus Geòdachan an Duilisg past some big unattractive north facing geos, which can be seen from the road, to the highest point of Druim a' Bheannaich itself. Out in front of this is Geòdha Dubh Faing a' Bheannaich, a deeply incised geo of poor rock, grass and birds. From there the coastline turns south-westwards to run in front of the small wave-battered island of Gallan Beag where the first climbs lie in Gallan Beag Geòdha 2 and Gallan Beag Geòdha 1. Just south from these is the section of cliff known as The Boardwalk, beyond which the coastline changes direction again to run past Chapel Geo then Geodh' a' Bheannaich to the large bay formed by Geòdha Chruidh. On the south side of this bay is the coastline in front of the Druim Gleann Clabhaig highpoint.

Approach: This is described to Loch a' Bheannaich, and from there for each of the geos, or cliffs. From the parking spot just beyond the gate at the north end of Àird Uig, step across the fence then descend to the burn and cross this before rising up the hag-riven slope to gain the north-east end of Loch a' Bheannaich.

Gallan Beag Geòdha 2

(NB 0395 3825) Non-tidal NW facing Map opposite

Immediately to the north of The Boardwalk there are two small geos opposite the small wave-battered island of Gallan Beag. The island can be seen when looking south from the parking spot just outside Àird Uig. The geos are Gallan Beag 1 and Gallan Beag 2 with the latter being the first encountered. The southern end of the geo is formed by a tunnel-like sea cave. The wall to the north of the cave has two obvious ramp-lines running up it before an area of grooves and corners where the edge is turned into another area of rock.

Approach: From Loch a' Bheannaich, go out to the coast just west of the deeply incised Geòdha Dubh Faing a' Bheannaich. Head towards the island of Gallan Beag past some small isolated boulders and drop down boulder-strewn slopes. An obvious large platformed area extends from the top of the tunnel-like sea cave at the southern end of Gallan Beag 2 around Gallan Beag 1 and out to the point overlooking Gallan Beag itself. Instead of heading down to this platformed area, cut back right (facing out) down a boulder-strewn ramp, almost to its end (15min).

Descent: Abseil from a large block at the end of the approach ramp. Down a steep corner to ledges above the high tide mark, which run the length of the wall rightwards to the entrance of the tunnel like sea cave.

The first three climbs start from a pedestal at the left end of the wall where the ledge peters out.

Every Which Way 25m VS 4c
R.Anderson, C.Anderson, 19 Jul 2002
From the pedestal, go left around the edge, follow a groove then step down left to a short, cracked wall. Climb the wall and continue up the left side of the tower to finish.

Little Boomey 25m VS 5a **
R.Anderson, C.Anderson, 15 Jul 2002
From the pedestal, climb black rock just right of the edge to reach an obvious crack. Climb the crack and then grooves leading out onto the left-bounding edge where easy rocks lead to the top.

Rawsons Retreat 25m HVS 4c *
R.Anderson, C.Anderson, 19 Jul 2002
From the pedestal, step up right and climb a thin crack in the initial short, leaning wall, then continue up somewhat eliminately between Little Boomey and the groove of Jacob's Creek to finish up the obvious groove in the final eaves.

Jacob's Creek 25m HVS 5a **
R.Anderson, C.Anderson, 15 Jul 2002
From the base of the abseil groove, climb up and left into cracks leading to a short V-groove. Climb the groove, pull out right, then step back left through the final eaves.

Leftwing 25m HVS 5a **
R.Anderson, C.Anderson, 15 Jul 2002
The edge left of the abseil groove. Climb black rock and shallow grooves left of the groove to beneath the final steepening. Step up right, then pull steeply up left into a crack and finish up this in a fine position.

Rightwing 25m HVS 4c *
R.Anderson, C.Anderson, 15 Jul 2002
The edge right of the abseil groove. From the foot of the groove, climb a V-groove up right, then back left onto the edge. Continue to below the steep upper rocks and make a few bold moves up the edge, then move up and swing left to easier ground leading to the top.

Savage Slant 40m HVS 4c
R.Anderson, C.Anderson, 19 Jul 2002
The obvious right-slanting ramp.

Gallan Beag Geòdha 1

(NB 0385 3822) Non-tidal NW facing Map p102 Diagram p104

The southern of the two small geos opposite the little island of Gallan Beag. The Boardwalk lies just to the south. A narrow inlet cuts into the large platformed area leading out towards the Gallan Beag. The wall overlooking this narrow inlet is composed of excellent water-washed rock with a number of obvious corner-lines. In the centre of the wall the line of Further Adventures in Paradise is obvious as a right-angled corner. Climbs are described starting at the northern seaward end.

Approach: As for Gallen Beag 1 then scramble down to the platformed area and walk rightwards along the top of a narrow geo towards the end of the promontory, above the tunnel-like sea cave at the southern end of Gallan Beag 2.

Descent: Abseil down adjacent lines to ledges.

1 Eightsome Reel 25m VD
R.Anderson, C.Anderson, 13 Jul 2003
The corner and steps at the left end of the wall.

2 S'Mad 25m VS 4c *
M.Tighe, K.Tighe, 24 Jun 2001
The larger corner running up the left side of the main section of wall; either finish up the crack just left of the corner, or the corner itself.

3 Spanish Windlash 25m HVS 5a **
K.Tighe, M.Tighe, 24 Jun 2001
The slim corner running up the middle of the wall; originally given HS, so you might find it easier, or not!

4 Competitive Stress Disorder 25m E3 5c **
R.Anderson, C.Anderson, 13 Jul 2003
Climb thin cracks in the black wall between the slim corner and the arete to an awkward finish just left of the final moves of The Ruby.

5 The Ruby 25m HVS 5a **
M.Tighe, K.Tighe, 24 Jun 2001
The right arete of the black wall. Move out right onto the arete to climb this on the right and then on the left; originally graded MVS.

6 Further Adventures in Paradise 25m E2 5c **
M.Tighe, K.Tighe, 24 Jun 2001
The central right-angled corner. Stiff at the original grade of E1 5b; a number of ascents confirm the current grade.

The arete to the right is broad and has a good ledge on it. Scramble out to this from the base of the corner.

7 Seven 25m E2 5b **
R.Anderson, C.Anderson, 13 Jul 2003
Climb a crack just left of the edge to a steepening, then pull over left onto the wall (small cam useful), then climb to a break, move up right, then pull steeply up left and finish more easily.

8 Grooved Arete 25m VS 4c **
M.Tighe, K.Tighe, 24 Jun 2001
Climb cracks in the front of the broad arete which can be gained from the foot of the central corner.

9 Swirlpool 25m VS 4b *
M.Tighe, K.Tighe, 24 Jun 2001
Just right of grooved arete is an open corner with a black slab to the right. Abseil down to sea-level and tackle a tricky sloping chimney, the broken corner above and the corner slab above that.

The Boardwalk

(NB 037 380) Map p102

South of the small island of Gallan Beag, section of cliff runs to where the coastline turns the edge to then run south-eastwards past Chapel Geòdha. At the foot of the cliff 'The Boardwalk' is a large non-tidal shelf with an elevated section. At its northern end the cliff culminates in an area of messy broken rock, platforms and inlets leading to the platformed area above Gallan Beag Geòdha 1.

The northern end, or left side of this cliff, is formed by a less steep stepped area of black rock left of the prominent corner of Chapel Crack. This is Boardwalk Left. The central area, Boardwalk Central, is much higher, steeper and more imposing and lies above a bay filled with large boulders and non-tidal storm pools. To the right of this the cliff decreases in height to meet a slabby ramp which rises up then around the edge, overlooking Chapel Geòdha. This is Boardwalk Right, and beneath the ramp at its foot is another cliff: Under The Boardwalk.

Approach: From the northern end of Loch a' Bheannaich, go partway along the west side of the loch then head north-west through a grassy depression past the ruin of the small chapel Tigh a' Bheannaich (The Blessing House). Continue past a small pool to reach a small lochan. One option is to head south-west from here to first reach the runoff into the back of Chapel Geo, then on the north side of this locate the south-west corner of the cliff-top where it is possible to scramble down to the shelf under Boardwalk Right. Another option, perhaps better, especially for the first time visitor, is to head down north-west from the far side of the small lochan to a small pool that this runs into, the runoff from which goes down a depression and trickles down easy slabs at the north end of Boardwalk Left. Go through a gap on the left behind the pool and head down to the cliff-top where there is an enormous boulder **(NB 0373 3800)** perched on the edge, at the top of the prominent corner of Chapel Crack (20min).

Descent: From the Chapel Geo side and pretty much overlooking this geo, make a short down-climb, or abseil, to gain a slabby shelf that slants easily down to the south-west end of the Boardwalk.

From the enormous boulder on the cliff-top above Chapel Crack, a smaller boulder on the left (facing out) provides a good thread to facilitate an abseil down the steep grooves of Groove Armada onto the Boardwalk.

Boardwalk Left

Non-tidal NW facing Diagram p106

This is the area of less uniformly steep, stepped black rock extending leftwards above the boardwalk. It runs from the obvious right-angled corner of Chapel Crack to slabbier ground at the left end of the cliff. Water from the small lochans above drains down the easier-angled slabs at the left end of this area. A series of storm pools lie in a trough along the base of the cliff below the Boardwalk. The first climb lies at the far left end of the slabby section where a corner is formed with steeper more broken rocks.

1 Northern Lights 20m VS 4c
G.Pinkerton, C.Acheson, 31 Jul 2005
At the far left end of the cliff there is a left-curving crack rising above a slabby corner at the junction of the slabby black rocks with an area of steeper broken cliff. Climb the crack, with delicate bridging in the lower section.

The next three climbs lie at the left end of the main section of cliff before the angle eases. They start from a ledge in the trough below the cliff, at the left end of a small storm pool with three boulders in it. A short V-shaped recess is prominent above.

2 Lost Waltz 25m HVS 4c/5a *
R.Anderson, C.Anderson, 12 Jul 2015
Go up and left and climb the groove to the left of the prominent short V-shaped recess to gain the large upper ledge. There is a choice of two finishes up short cracks; the left-hand crack being harder.

3 Northern Soul 25m VS 4b **
R.Anderson, C.Anderson, 16 Jul 2002
Gain the prominent short V-shaped recess and climb through it to gain the large upper ledge then finish up the obvious short, right-slanting crack.

4 Hokey Pokey 30m E1 5a
R.Anderson, C.Anderson, 12 Jul 2015
Start as for Northern Soul then move up to a short leaning wall immediately to the right. Place a wire in Northern Soul then stretch for good holds (sideways wire on left) and pull into a groove. Move up left and pull onto the large upper ledge (poor wire on the left). The upper wall is climbed by good holds up the left side of an area of white quartz, with a stretch to good finishing holds.

5 Hebridean Three Step 30m E3/4 **
R.Anderson, C.Anderson, 12 Jul 2015
Belay down and right from Northern Soul, on a small ledge above the storm pool with three boulders in it. A large spike on the wall above can be lassoed for the belay.
1. 20m 5c Climb the vicious short crack on the right then continue easily up and right to a short right-leaning groove. There is no suitable gear above the initial crack, so stretch in an extended wire (rock 5 or 6), or boldly boulder up and place an equivalent sized cam. A few testing moves up the groove gain the large upper ledge.
2. 10m 5c Move up to the base of a thin crack and make a few bouldery moves to finish.

6 Hippy Shake 30m E1 5b *
R.Anderson, C.Anderson, 6 Jul 2008
Start beneath a rock scar between the storm pool with three boulders in it and another one to the right. Climb a groove up the left side of the rock scar then a short steep crack to gain the large upper ledge and finish by a short right-leaning series of holds.

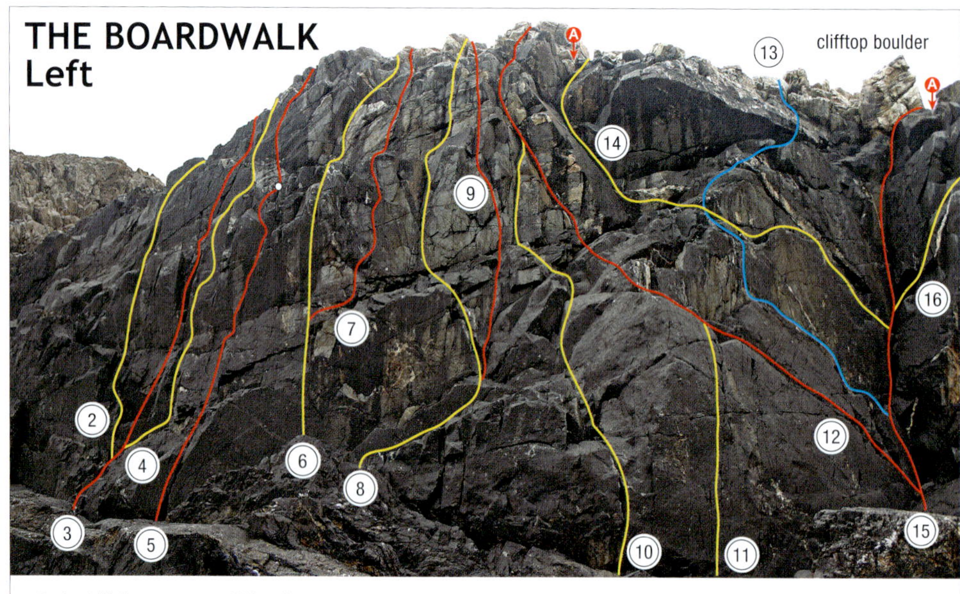

2. Lost Waltz	HVS 4c/5a *	7. Soft Shoe Shuffle	E1 5a *	12. Diving Board	S 4a *
3. Northern Soul	VS 4b **	8. Colonel Huff	HS 4b **	13. Ventura Highway	VS 4c *
4. Hokey Pokey	E1 5a	9. Disco Fever	HS 4b *	14. Around the Bend	S 4a *
5. Hebridean Three Step	E3 5c **	10. Funky Groove	HS 4b *	15. Chapel Crack	VS 4c **
6. Hippy Shake	E1 5b *	11. Storm	XS 6a (S2) **	16. Sallie's Dilemma	VS 4c *

7 Soft Shoe Shuffle 30m E1 5a *
R.Anderson, C.Anderson, 12 Jul 2015
Start as for Hippy Shake then pull out right across the rock scar and climb to a short wall. Step up (gear in small horizontal crack) then move up and right to good holds and gain the upper ledge. Finish up a short crack. Eliminate and a bit sparse on protection but good rock and holds.

8 Colonel Huff 30m HS 4b **
M.Tighe and Party, 16 Sep 1986
Start between the storm pool with three boulders in it and another storm pool to the right. Follow a black shelf up right, then head up left to climb a steeper crack, then the prominent V-shaped groove to gain the large upper ledge. Finish up a short steep wall; the crack on the left is another option.

9 Disco Fever 30m HS 4b *
R.Anderson, C.Anderson, 16 Jul 2002
Go up the black shelf as for Colonel Huff, then climb up to the right of this and pull left into a short groove. Finish up the edge left of the groove of Diving Board.

10 Funky Groove 30m HS 4b *
R.Anderson, C.Anderson, 16 Jul 2002
Immediately to the left of a deep storm pool with a large boulder in it, climb the obvious short crack then go up and left to climb a short groove just right of Disco Fever to finish up the groove of Diving Board.

11 Storm 10m XS 6a (S2) **
C.Waddy (DWS), Jun 2014
The line of thin cracks above the deep storm pool; seriousness is dependent on the depth of the pool.

To the right of the deep storm pool with a large boulder in it is a prominent right-angled corner, which is the line of Chapel Crack. Three traverse lines lead out left above the storm pool from the base of the corner and are gained by scrambling to a ledge at the foot of the corner.

12 Diving Board 30m S 4a *
M.Tighe and Party, 16 Sep 1986
From the bottom of the corner, climb diagonally left and follow the lower traverse line (possible belay at 15m) then climb up 6m and take a narrow, broken slab on the left to the top.

13 Ventura Highway 30m VS 4c *
P.Allen, M.Atkins, 6 Aug 2006
Move up into the corner of Chapel Crack then follow the middle traverse line until moves up a wall lead across the upper gangway of Around the Bend. Continue up and rightwards under the roof then pull around its right side to finish.

14 Around the Bend 30m S 4a *
M.Tighe and Party, 16 Sep 1986
Make a few moves up the corner of Chapel Crack then

go out left and follow the upper traverse line which leads to a finish up the slabby corner on the left.

15 Chapel Crack 20m VS 4c **

M.Tighe and Party, 16 Sep 1986

The crack in the right-angled corner leads directly to the huge boulder on top of the cliff; optional through route to finish. Opinions vary on the grade, so you might find easier, or not!

16 Sallie's Dilemma 25m VS 4c *

M.Tighe and Party, 16 Sep 1986

Break out right halfway up Chapel Crack and follow a short curving groove, with a mantelshelf at the top. A broad ramp leads off to the right. An original direct finish used aid, but this is 5c and now the top of Groove Armada.

Boardwalk Central

Non-tidal NW facing Diagram p108

This extends rightwards from Chapel Crack to an area of storm pools and large boulders where a short descent has to be made off the Boardwalk. The cliff increases in height here and the rock also changes in appearance becoming steeper and brown-coloured, especially at the highest point above the large boulders. The first climb takes the line of the abseil to the right of the corner of Chapel Crack.

17 Groove Armada 15m E4 6a **

R.Anderson, C.Anderson, 26 Jul 2002

The wall and steep V-grooves right of Chapel Crack; short but testing. Scramble up black rock to belay on a shelf below the line.

The following climbs all start from the large bouldered bay with storm pools. The first takes the obvious corner and crack above the leftmost boulder beside a pool. There may have been some wave damage to the first three or four climbs.

18 Bloody Hand 30m E1 5b *

M.Tighe and Party, 1980s

Move up and left to climb a stepped corner into the base of the crack. Climb the crack and its left edge to the top.

19 Magic Dragon 30m E4 6b **

R.Anderson, C.Anderson, 26 Jul 2002

If you listen you might hear it! The crack-line immediately to the right of Bloody Hand, gained by a hand-traverse rightwards from the corner.

20 Divided Fears 30m E3 5c **

R.Anderson, M.Garthwaite, 21 Jul 2002

The obvious crack-line in the left wall of the large corner with a chimney-crack up it. The crack is formed between two distinct types and colours of rock.

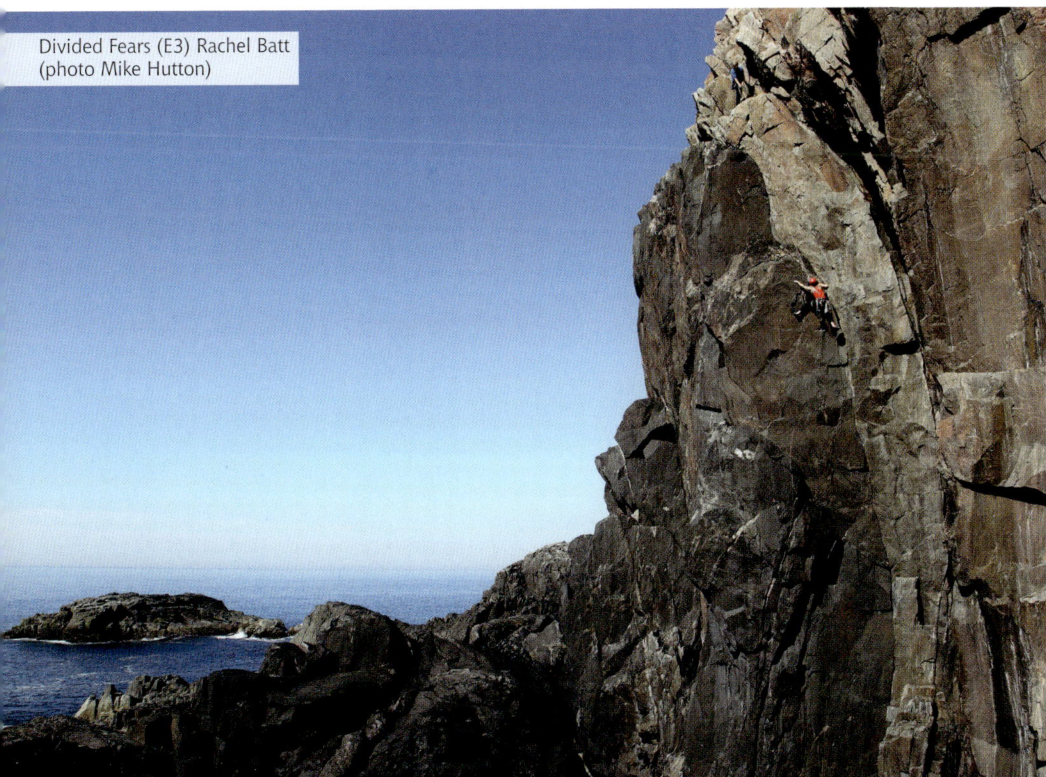

Divided Fears (E3) Rachel Batt (photo Mike Hutton)

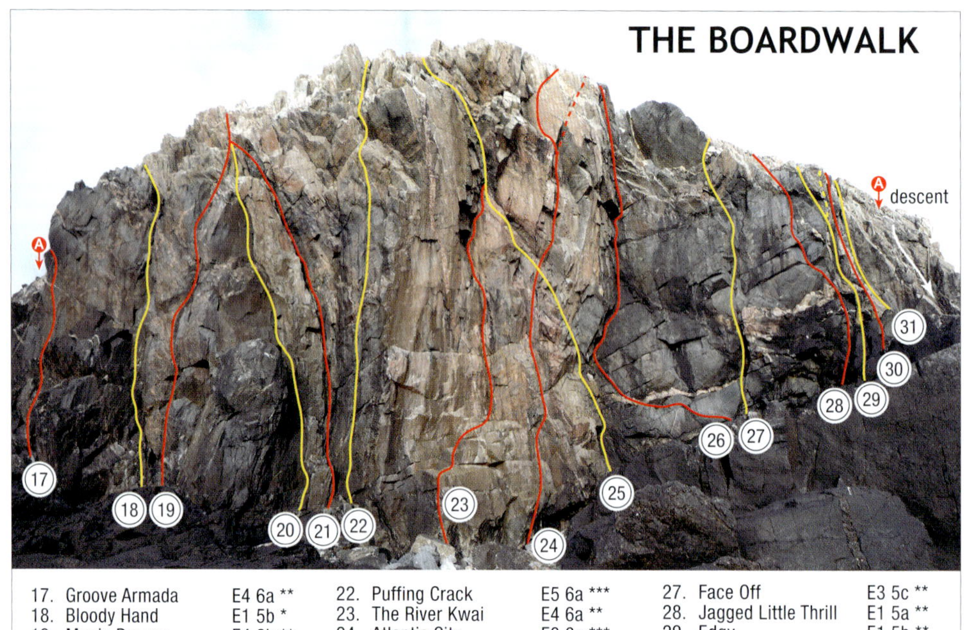

17. Groove Armada	E4 6a **	22. Puffing Crack	E5 6a ***	27. Face Off	E3 5c **
18. Bloody Hand	E1 5b *	23. The River Kwai	E4 6a **	28. Jagged Little Thrill	E1 5a **
19. Magic Dragon	E4 6b **	24. Atlantic City	E3 6a ***	29. Edgy	E1 5b **
20. Divided Fears	E3 5c **	25. A Bridge Too Far	E3 5c/6a **	30. Quartzvein Crack	HVS 4c *
21. Coloured Rain	E2 5b **	26. Shadows in the Sun	E2 5b **	31. Twostep Crack	VS 4c *

21 Coloured Rain 30m E2 5b **
M.Tighe, J.Stevenson, 7 May 1988
The chimney-crack in the large corner.

22 Puffing Crack 30m E5 6a ***
M.Garthwaite, R.Anderson, 21 Jul 2002
The thin cracks running up the impending right wall of the big corner, climbed directly all the way.

Just around an impressive arete is another big corner, partway up which is a square-topped sentry box feature.

23 The River Kwai 35m E4 6a **
M.Garthwaite, R.Anderson, 22 Jul 2002
Start off a boulder to the right of a storm pool and scramble rightwards up the edge to belay at the foot of the corner. Climb the corner through the sentry box to a common finish with A Bridge Too Far.

24 Atlantic City 35m E3 6a ***
R.Anderson, 5 Jul 2006
An obvious line cutting through A Bridge Too Far. Start on a boulder directly below the corner-line of The River Kwai and 5m left of A Bridge Too Far. Move up and right into a corner, then step right around the edge and climb thin cracks to a ledge. Pull up and around right into a groove, then right again onto a slab, at the junction with A Bridge Too Far. Climb the steep groove above with interest and pull out left from the inverted V-shape to finish.

Variation: **24a Alt Finish E5 6a/6b**
S.Williams, 25 Jun 2016
From the exit to the inverted V-shaped, finish spectacularly up the thin crack.

25 A Bridge Too Far 35m E3 5c/6a **
M.Garthwaite, R.Anderson, 22 Jul 2002
Just to the right is an obvious crack-line slanting up left, into the top corner taken by The River Kwai. This line is most obvious when viewed straight on from the slabby shelf to the right. Start from a boulder in the right corner of the boulder bay, beneath an undercut crack. Move off the ground with difficulty. The vertically challenged will have a problem, although there are two ways to get off the ground, or the start of Atlantic City can be used. Follow the crack-line up left in a stupendous position to a steep finish.

26 Shadows in the Sun 35m E2 5b **
M.Tighe, I.Sutherland, B.Newton, 7 May 1988
The big corner to the right with a wide crack. The direct undercut start, taken by A Bridge Too Far, is avoided by a 12m traverse from the right starting on the shelf. Climb the corner and its overhangs direct for a strenuous finish.

Atlantic City (E3) Sam Williams (photo Euan Ryan)

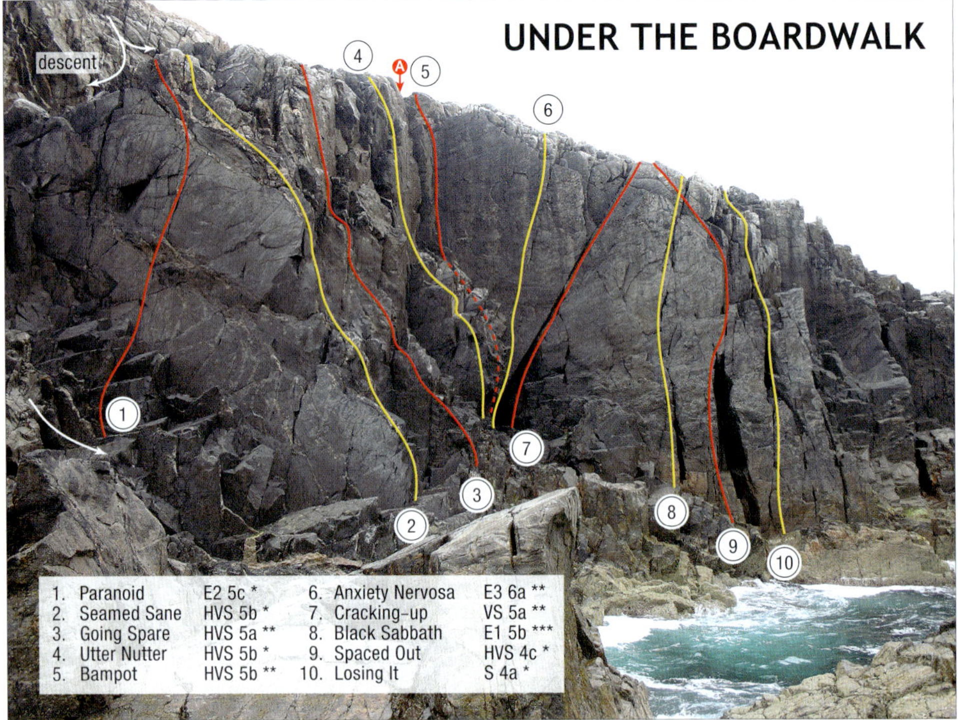

1. Paranoid	E2 5c *		6. Anxiety Nervosa	E3 6a **
2. Seamed Sane	HVS 5b *		7. Cracking-up	VS 5a **
3. Going Spare	HVS 5a **		8. Black Sabbath	E1 5b ***
4. Utter Nutter	HVS 5b *		9. Spaced Out	HVS 4c *
5. Bampot	HVS 5b **		10. Losing It	S 4a *

Boardwalk Right

Non-tidal NW facing Diagram p108

Above and right of the area of boulders and storm pools, a ramp slants up rightwards around the edge beneath walls that diminish in height to end overlooking Chapel Geo. The short wall near the top of the ramp, just before Chapel Geo, is used as a means of descent for this crag and the north-west side of Chapel Geo.

27 Face Off 30m E3 5c **

R.Anderson, C.Anderson, 18 Apr 2003

The obvious groove line just right of Shadows in the Sun. Climb directly into, then up, a left-facing groove line and continue via a right-facing groove line to easier ground leading to the top.

28 Jagged Little Thrill 15m E1 5a **

R.Anderson, C.Anderson, 17 Apr 2003

Climb up to the right-bounding arete and go steeply up its left side via a shallow groove, stepping left at the top to pull over the final jutting shelf.

29 Edgy 15m E1 5b **

R.Anderson, C.Anderson, 17 Apr 2003

Climb a crack in the arete to a finish on its left side. The arete can be finished directly at E2 (M.Atkins, P.Allen, Aug 2006).

30 Quartzvein Crack 15m HVS 4c *

R.Anderson, C.Anderson, 22 Sep 2002

The steep quartzy crack just right of the arete.

31 Twostep Crack 15m VS 4c *

R.Anderson, C.Anderson, 22 Sep 2002

Just to the right, a crack runs up slabby rock, through an obvious diagonal break and on up steeper rock to the top. Climb this crack.

Under The Boardwalk

(NB 0369 3793) Tidal SW & NW facing Diagram above

This small cliff of fine rock is located at sea-level on the headland beneath the ramp that rises up the far right end of the Boardwalk. The North-West Side of Chapel Geo forms the other side of the cliff. There are two walls, a more featured area of south-west facing ribs and deep cracks on the left, separated from a north-west facing wall of smooth, black rock by a right-angled corner.

Descent: From the storm pools and large boulders at the foot of Boardwalk Right, go through a trough then descend stepped rock and traverse across to the cliff. The alternative is to abseil in from the top of the slabby shelf, down the corner between the faces.

1 Paranoid 20m E2 5c *
R.Anderson, C.Anderson, 22 Sep 2002
On the left-hand section of the cliff, just before the right edge is turned, there is a fine wall of steep, slabby, grey rock. Climb a thin crack through a quartzy patch in the centre of this wall.

2 Seamed Sane 25m HVS 5b *
R.Anderson, C.Anderson, 22 Sep 2002
Just right of the edge, a quartzy seam runs the height of the wall. Climb this seam up and around the edge to finish up a short crack.

3 Going Spare 25m HVS 5a **
R.Anderson, C.Anderson, 22 Sep 2002
On the right is a stepped rib of rock, with a corner on its left and a wide crack on its right. Climb the centre of the stepped rib. The groove line on the left of the middle section gives a route of VS 4b **.

4 Utter Nutter 25m HVS 5b *
R.Anderson, C.Anderson, 22 Sep 2002
Just left of the deep chimney-crack next to the right-angled corner, is a protruding rib. Climb the centre of this rib, firstly up steep black rock, then up a thin crack.

5 Bampot 25m HVS 5b **
R.Anderson, C.Anderson, 25 Jul 2002
The corner running up the left side of the black wall, next to the face and immediately right of the deep chimney-crack.

6 Anxiety Nervosa 20m E3 6a **
M.Garthwaite, R.Anderson, 21 Jul 2002
The thin crack running up the wall just left of the central diagonal crack. Aptly named!

7 Cracking-up 20m VS 5a **
R.Anderson, M.Garthwaite, 21 Jul 2002
The central diagonal crack.

8 Black Sabbath 20m E1 5b ***
R.Anderson, C.Anderson, 22 Sep 2002
The right-hand crack.

9 Spaced Out 25m HVS 4c *
R.Anderson, C.Anderson, 19 Jul 2003
Immediately right of Black Sabbath, climb thin cracks just left of a chimney then step across this and gain a ledge. Climb onto a ramp and follow this across the top of the wall.

10 Losing It 25m S 4a *
G.Latter, K.Latter, Apr 2005
The obvious line at the right end of wall, starting few metres right of the chimney. Continue more easily after a short steep start.

Black Sabbath (E1) Shauna Clarke (photo Robert Durran)

Chapel Geòdha

(NB 037 379) Map p102

This large rectangular-shaped geo lies a short distance from the south-west end of Loch a' Bheannaich, at a point just before the coastline turns to run northwards past the Boardwalk. In the past it has also been called May Day Geo.

Approach: From the northern end of Loch a' Bheannaich, go along the west side of the loch to locate the ruin of a small building (the chapel Tigh a' Bheannaich) at the entrance to a grassy depression. Going north-west through the depression accesses the Boardwalk past a small pool then a small lochan. This lochan lies in line with the back of Chapel Geo which sits in a dip.

To access the south side of the geo it is better to go south-west through a shallow grassy depression between two cairned points then drop westwards to the cliff-top. This brings one to a point above the main cliff, at the start of the short Upper Wall and at the top of a diagonal fault running down beneath this into the geo. This is also at the top of Cor Blimey Corner on the Main Wall (20min).

To access the north side of the geo, go north-west through the grassy depression to the small lochan. Locate the back of the geo then find the down-climb leading to the top of the ramp leading to Boardwalk Right, from where the top of the north side can be reached.

South-East Side

The South-East Side consists of a steep, cracked black wall at the seaward end, followed by a series of corners and aretes running into the geo. Above this is the diagonal fault, or shelf, which drops down left towards the back of the geo from a huge block on the edge. A number of shorter routes start from the shelf, all easily gained from the top of the Main Wall.

Upper Wall

Non Tidal SW facing Diagram above

The climbs on the wall above the shelf are described as met descending the shelf, from right to left.

Descent: The first five climbs start above the block and require no descent and those below it are gained by scrambling down and around the block, or by abseil from a thread in the boulder behind it. The territory under the block may be occupied by a fulmar.

1 Shortie 5m D
R.Henderson, 1 May 1995
A broken right-facing corner where the upper wall starts to heighten.

2 Gale Force 8 8m VS 5a *
A.Cunningham, F.Fotheringham, 1 May 1995
A few metres left of Shortie, pull over an undercut nose into thin cracks.

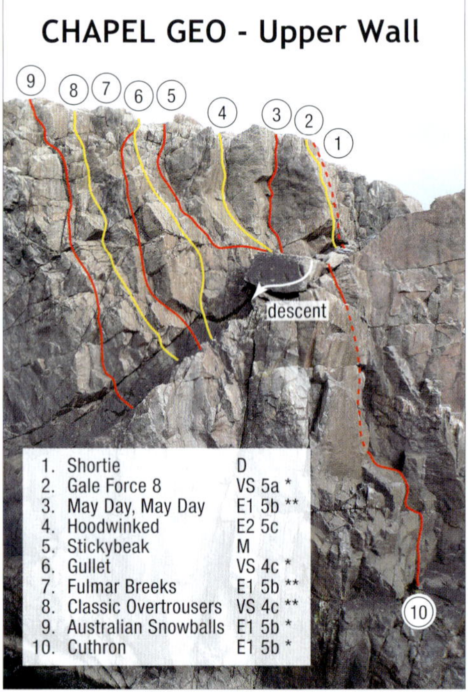

3 May Day, May Day 10m E1 5b **
F.Fotheringham, A.Cunningham, 1 May 1995
Start beside the huge block and climb the overhanging corner-crack.

4 Hoodwinked 10m E2 5c
R.Anderson, 1 Aug 2007
The right-angled corner to the left has a nippy finish.

5 Stickybeak 15m M
R.Henderson, 1 May 1995
From the end of the ledge beside the huge block, step left and climb a slabby left-facing corner.

The next group of climbs lie below the huge block on the sloping lower part of the shelf.

6 Gullet 20m VS 4c *
R.Anderson, C.Anderson, 2 Aug 2007
The cracks left of the corner of Stickybeak. Climb a short corner, step left at the steepening and climb the crack.

7 Fulmar Breeks 20m E1 5b **
R.Anderson, C.Anderson, 2 Aug 2007
Start just around the arete from Gullet, climb to a roof, move left then climb the corner and ensuing layback crack to gain a ledge. Finish right to avoid a block.

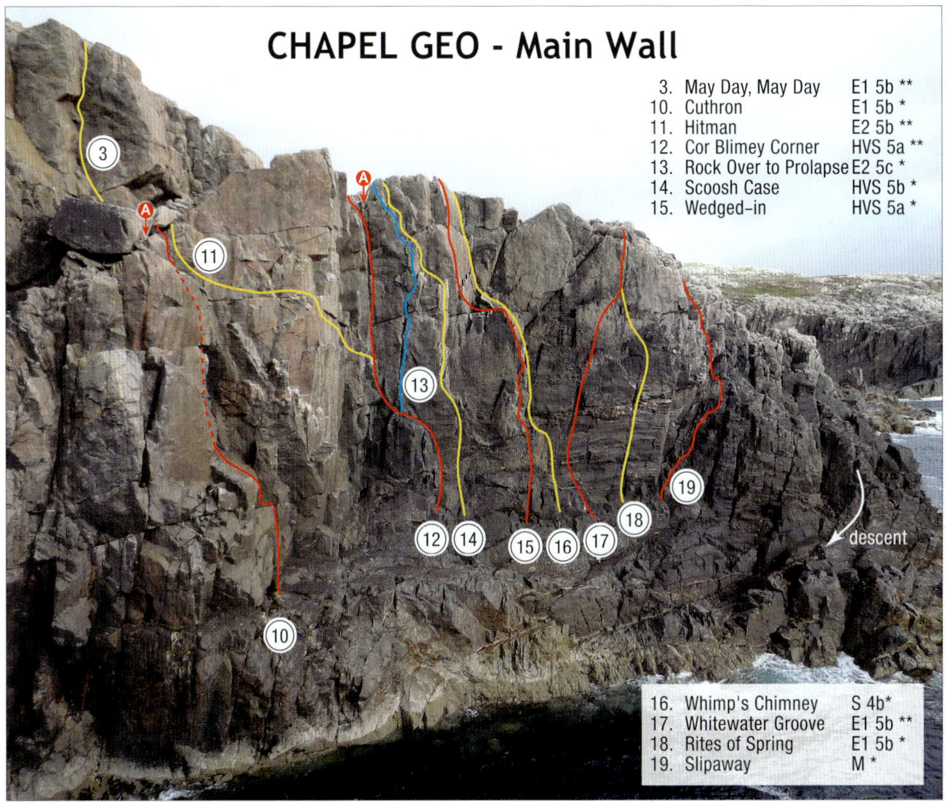

8 Classic Overtrousers 25m VS 4c **
I.Sherrington, R.Henderson, 1 May 1995
The stepped series of ramps and corners immediately left of Fulmar Breeks, trending slightly left.

9 Australian Snowballs 25m E1 5b *
R.Henderson, I.Sherrington, 1 May 1995
Start 3m left again and climb another corner system, with the crux at 5m at a short, overhanging corner.

Main Wall

Non-tidal NW facing Diagram above

The next climbs are located below the shelf, on the larger lower wall, and are described left to right. A good ledge runs beneath the climbs. The most identifiable features are a large flake, which forms a chimney-cleft taken by Whimp's Chimney, and a right-angled corner to the left taken by Cor Blimey Corner.

Descent: Scramble off the end of the promontory to tidal ledges and cut back beneath the climbs. The line of Slipway can be descended when the tide is in. An abseil can also be made down the line of Cor Blimey Corner which tops out at the obvious notch on the cliff-top, or down Cuthron from the thread in the block close to the foot of May Day, May Day.

10 Cuthron 25m E1 5b *
M.Tighe and Party, 16 Sep 1986
Towards the left end of the cliff and just before the ledge narrows, there is a corner containing a prominent, slightly overhanging crack high up. Reach this via a short corner; there is an opportunity to break out left partway up.

Another climb has been recorded here and may be the same as, or similar to, Cuthron; **The End of the World is Knee High** (E1 5b ***; I.Sherrington, T.Walker, 1 May 1995). Traverse left along the platforms to corners before it narrows at a patch of seaweed. Climb a layback crack system until forced to step right then continue up the top system.

11 Hitman 35m E2 5b **
M.Tighe, B.Newton, 8 May 1988
Follow Cor Blimey Corner for about 12m, then move out left and make some trying moves to a ledge. Now continue the left trend and make a sensational pull up around the corner to a very fine and airy left traverse to finish at the top of Cuthron.

12 Cor Blimey Corner 30m HVS 5a **
M.Tighe and party, 16 Sep 1986
The corner in the centre of the wall. Climb the initial corner to a ledge then continue up the main corner in a fine position.

13 Rock Over to Prolapse 30m E2 5c *
M.Garthwaite, R.Anderson 2 Jun 2017
Climb to the ledges partway up Cor Blimey Corner then climb the crack in the right wall until forced out right where the edge leads to the top.

14 Scoosh Case 30m HVS 5a/5b **
J.Stevenson, I.Sutherland, 8 May 1988
From the foot of Cor Blimey Corner, climb the stepped line up the wall of the rib between the corner and Whimp's Chimney; after a hard start trend left.

15 Wedged-in 30m HVS 5a *
R.Anderson, C.Anderson, 14 Jul 2008
The rib immediately left of Whimp's Chimney. Climb to a ledge, go left around the edge and pull onto a pedestal, then pull back round the edge and continue to a large block on a ledge. Above, climb close to the edge to a finish up the edge.

Rock Over to Prolapse (E2) Mark Garthwaite (photo Rab Anderson)

16 Whimp's Chimney 40m S 4b *
M.Tighe and Party, 16 Sep 1986
Climb the prominent chimney-cleft direct, surmounting the chockstone at half-height with difficulty.

17 Whitewater Groove 25m E1 5b **
R.Henderson, I.Sherrington, 1 May 1995
Towards the right end of the cliff, climb the left-hand groove on the steep black wall and curve rightwards to finish via the fine thin crack in the headwall.

18 Rites of Spring 25m E1 5b *
I.Sherrington, R.Henderson, 1 May 1995
The right-hand groove on the steep black wall leads to a finish up the crack of Whitewater Groove.

19 Slipaway 30m M *
R.Anderson, C.Anderson, 13 Jul 2008
The corner-groove at the right end of the main wall; up right, then back left to the top.

The back wall of the geo appears to have been climbed by **Here Today Gone Tomorrow** (E4 6a, S.Mayers, G.Lovick, Jul 1993) which followed a vague crack until it became easier to move right onto the wall at about 25m. At the time of the first ascent the buttress was severely undermined and like the name suggests, the route appears to no longer exist.

North-West Side

Partially Tidal SE facing Diagram opposite

This is on the opposite side of the geo from the Main Wall. From the top of the wall, a ramp leads north-west under a short wall to the Boardwalk, whilst Under the Boardwalk lies just over the top. The wall catches the sun early on and provides a pleasant venue until the opposite side, or The Boardwalk cliffs, come into the sun. The wall is seamed with crack-lines and a large flake is obvious at the entrance to the geo, to the right of which a large pink pegmatite vein runs the full height of the wall.

Descent: Scramble, or abseil, down the short wall close to the edge of the geo onto a ramp as for the southern approach to the Boardwalk. Head south-east over the rise and drop down to an obvious gap on the cliff-top from where an abseil gains good, generally non-tidal ledges at the foot of the wall.

Climbs are described from left to right with the first three routes being on the large flake, which contains a number of crack-lines on perfect rock that can pretty much be climbed anywhere. All three start from a ledge on the right.

20 Mayfair 25m VS 4b *
R.Anderson, C.Anderson, 9 Jul 2008
Step down and traverse left across a ledge system with a step, then climb the crack up the left side of the flake.

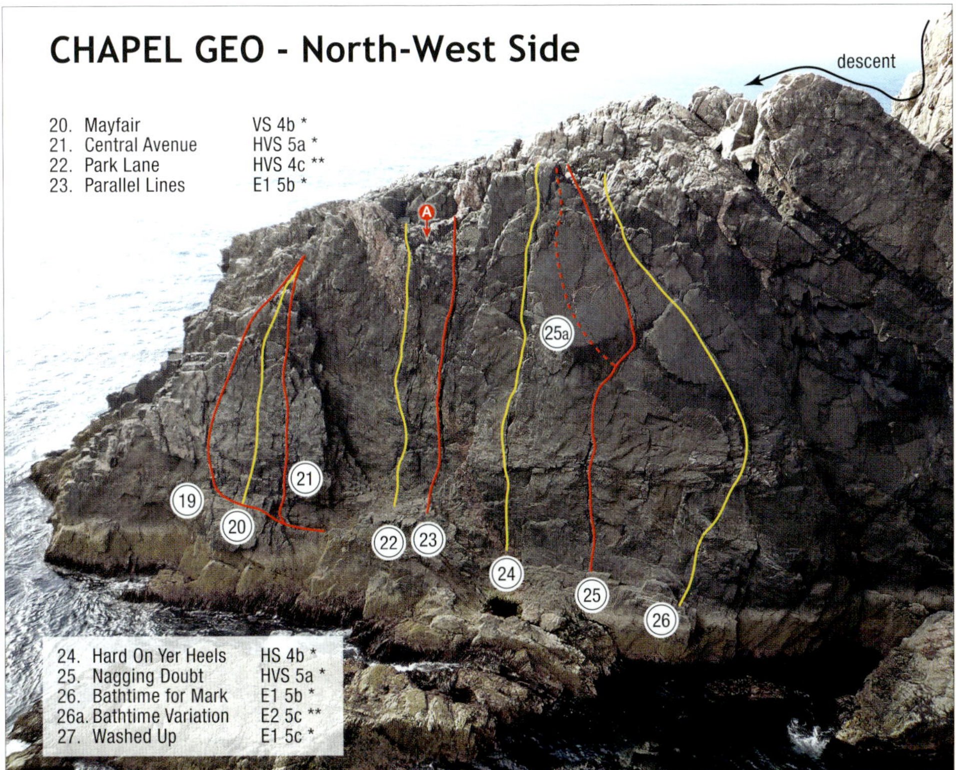

21 Central Avenue 25m HVS 5a *
R.Anderson, C.Anderson, 9 Jul 2008
Step down and traverse across the ledge system with a step then climb the thin crack up the centre of the flake. There is another crack immediately to the left and this looks easier.

22 Park Lane 25m HVS 4c **
R.Anderson, C.Anderson, 9 Jul 2008
Step down and traverse across then climb the thin crack-line just left of the right edge of the flake.

The wall to the right contains an obvious crack-line with a pair of parallel cracks to its left.

23 Parallel Lines 20m E1 5b *
R.Anderson, C.Anderson, 8 Jul 2008
Pretty much climb the left-hand of the parallel cracks in its entirety, although at half-height where it cuts through the pink pegmatite band it is possible to use the right-hand crack to ease matters.

24 Hard On Yer Heels 20m HS 4b *
A.Cunningham, F.Fotheringham, 1 May 1995
The obvious crack which cuts through the pink pegmatite band just above its start.

25 Nagging Doubt 25m HVS 5a *
R.Anderson, C.Anderson, 8 Jul 2008
The fine crack-line which starts at the foot of the pink pegmatite band leads into a black groove which is climbed to the top.

26 Bathtime for Mark 25m E1 5b *
R.Benton, A.Callum, 30 May 2002
The central crack-line starting 3m right of the pegmatite band. Climb the steep crack then follow flakes rightwards to a good ledge. Trend leftwards easily to the top.
Variation: **26a Bathtime Variation E2 5c ****
M.Jarvie, R.Durran, Jul 2011
After climbing the initial crack, go left to finish up the arete overlooking the corner-groove; the crux is thought to be the crack of the original line!

27 Washed Up 25m E1 5c *
R.Anderson, C.Anderson, 9 Jul 2008
The crack-line at the right end of the wall, immediately right of a slim, angular groove. From the end of the ledge, climb the crack to ledges then follow a diagonal crack through black rock and finish directly.

Geodh' a' Bheannaich

(NB 038 377) Tidal SE facing Map p102 Diagram p118

This is the geo into which the Loch a' Bheannaich outflow enters beside an old boundary wall. The north side of the geo is formed by a distinctive slabby fin of reddish coloured rock which contains a cave halfway along it, to the left of which is an obvious wide crack taken by Juggy Crack. On the north side of the fin are the Platform Walls then the Recess Walls, which form part of a shallow platformed bay between the geo itself and Chapel Geòdha.

Approach: Go down either side of Loch a' Bheannaich then follow the outflow and cross the old wall. Keeping to the south side allows the main north side to be viewed from directly opposite (20min).

Descent: Abseil to ledges at the base of the slab.

Routes are described left to right from the end of the fin running towards the cave.

The first routes are on the end of the fin and can be accessed from the Platform Walls on the north side. There is a dark vein on the left, split by a deep fault (also a line of descent) with a pink vein on the right.

1 Rock Goby 15m VD *
K.Geddes, A.Cunningham, 28 Apr 1995
The cracks up the left side of the dark area.

2 Squat Lobster 15m VD *
K.Geddes, A.Cunningham, 28 Apr 1995
Climb cracks up the middle of the dark area.

3 Langustine 15m S 4a *
A.Cunningham, K.Geddes, 28 Apr 1995
Follow a narrow pink pegmatite vein on the right of the dark area.

4 Small Fry 20m HS 4b
T.Walker, I.Sherrington, 28 Apr 1995
Climb by ramps on the right side of the pink vein.

The next routes lie on the main slabby wall of the reddish coloured fin.

5 Feather Star 25m D *
K.Geddes, A.Cunningham, 28 Apr 1995
Start 3m right of the left edge up wide cracks; avoid the bulge on the left to finish via the final moves of Small Fry.

6 Echinoderm 25m VS 4c *
A.Cunningham, K.Geddes, 28 Apr 1995
A few metres left of the wide crack climb into a left-facing hanging corner, moving right round the bulge and finish up the top crack.

7 Juggy Crack 25m S 4a **
The obvious wide crack. Start from a ledge above high water next to a little cave.

8 Nightmare of Prickly Starfish 25m S *
R.Henderson, E.Pirie, 28 Apr 1995
Just to the right of the wide crack, start up twin cracks and finish via the left one.

9 Ride a Wild Starfish 25m D
E.Pirie, R.Henderson, 28 Apr 1995
Climb the arete on the left of the cave.

Platform Walls

(NB 0378 3776) Tidal SW facing

The next routes are on the steep north side of the fin and at the back of a large platformed bay where various dark and light liquorice allsorts veins are obvious.

Descent: In the middle of the steeper north side a scramble leads onto the platformed bay.

At the back of the bay is a white quartz-like cross high up (the saltire), with wide quartz-like veins running up either side.

Saltire Left 25m VD **
T.Walker, I.Sherrington, 28 Apr 1995
Takes the stepped rib through the left side of the quartzy cross.

Saltire Right 25m S 4b **
K.Geddes, A.Cunningham, 28 Apr 1995
Climb by the stepped quartzy rib through the right side of the cross with hard moves over the first step.

Baltic Tellin 25m E1 5b *
A.Cunningham, K.Geddes, 28 Apr 1995
A few metres to the left of the descent is a steep, deep crack. Take to the wall on the right of the crack moving leftwards onto easier ground. Finish by the steep crack through the top bulge.

Recess Walls

(NB 0375 3778) Non-tidal S facing

Some 30m further left of the saltire are a number of corners and grooves in a shallow square-cut recess between Geodh' a' Bheannaich and Chapel Geo. The recess can be located on the cliff-top, as can the big exit corner of Seal Dive.

Descent: Abseil down a deep groove at the back of the recess just right of Seal Dive. Ledges at the bottom appear safe from all but the biggest seas and they can be traversed left to a deep rift where The Abyss starts, or rightwards towards the Platform Walls, which is an alternative approach.

From the slabby shelf at the base of the big groove forming the back of the recess, traverse left to a narrow, deep slot. Routes are described left to right.

The Abyss 35m HVS *
R.Henderson, E.Pirie, 28 Apr 1995
Start at the narrow, deep slot dropping to the sea.

1. 20m 4b Bridge the slot and climb the left-hand corner to a ledge.
2. 15m 5a Continue up the steep fault-line to easier ground.

Pushed Over 30m E2 5b
R.Anderson, C.Anderson, 18 Apr 2003
Just to the right of The Abyss climb a short corner and crack leading to a ledge at the base of a wide crack. Contrive moves up the wall just left of the crack, directly into a shallow groove, and follow this to the top.

Edged Out 30m E3 5b
R.Anderson, C.Anderson, 18 Apr 2003
Climb to the ledge as for the previous route, then continue up the wide crack onto the edge, just left of the upper corner of Seal Dive, then make some bold moves to a large hold and some gear. Finish up the short groove above.

Seal Dive 35m VS *
E.Pirie, R.Henderson, 28 Apr 1995
Takes the big right-facing corner high up with a black ramp below.
1. 20m 4b From sea-facing ledges, climb a clean crack to a ledge below the corner.
2. 15m 4c/5a Climb the corner.

Heatwave 35m D
R.Anderson, C.Anderson, 18 Apr 2003
From the shelf at the base of the left-hand corner forming the square-cut recess, climb up right towards a higher recess then follow corners and ledges back up left to the top of the left-hand corner.

DRUIM GLEANN CLABHAIG

Map p102

Lying out in front of the highpoint of Druim Gleann Clabhaig, this is the southernmost stretch of coast accessed from Àird Uig. It extends southwards from the large bay formed by Geòdha Chruidh, to the large bay of Geòdha Nasabhaig marking the northern end of the Crowlista section.

The north side of Geòdha Chruidh comprises Bassett's Wall, Bassett's Buttress and Allsorts Wall. Beyond this to the south, on the north-west-facing stretch of coast, lie the parallel running geos of Geòdha Caol and Geòdha Caol-rinneach which hold some climbs. Just south again is the large sink-like hole of Seilaro beyond which the coastline turns to face south-west and run into Geòdha Nasabhaig. Geòdha-Seilaro is located here, where there are apparently some unrecorded climbs.

Geòdha Chruidh

(NB 037 374) Map p102

Lying about 100m south of Geodh' a' Bheannaich, this large horseshoe-shaped geo effectively breaks this section of coast into two. The climbing is on the north side, with an impressive, deep and narrow cleft that runs the full height of the cliff. Bassett's Buttress lies immediately north (left) of the cleft and runs into the seaward Bassett's Wall. Allsorts Wall lies to the south (right) of the cleft and is much bigger, much looser and much more of a disappointment than the other two good sections of cliff.

Approach: From the southern end of Loch a' Bheannaich, continue south-westwards opposite the fin of reddish coloured rock in Geodh' a' Bheannaich towards a small headland overlooking the entrance to Geòdha Cruidh. This is defined by a deep and narrow full height cleft, on the north side of which a square-cut projection covered in yellow lichen helps one locate the top of Bassett's Buttress. From there, head down and out to some large boulders above Bassett's Wall (20min).

Bassett's Wall

(NB 0372 3759) Non-tidal SW facing Diagram p118

The seaward section of cliff is a recessed, golden coloured wall.

Descent: Abseil from the large boulders (thread) to good ledges either side of a sea filled rift. The seaward end of the cliff can be gained by an easy scramble down, but the rift prevents a traverse being made across to the other climbs. On the landward side of the rift there are various starting ledges, depending on sea state.

The first three climbs start from the same ledge to the left of the tidal rift.

10 Black Seamed 30m VS 4c **
R.Anderson, C.Anderson, 29 Jul 2005
Climb a black seam at the left end of the wall to join Seamstress at the top of its initial crack. Hand-traverse a slab leftwards then climb stepped corners to the top.

11 Seamstress 30m HVS 5a **
R.Anderson, C.Anderson, 29 Jul 2005
Climb slabby black rock to gain the crack springing from the left side of the rift. Awkwardly enter the crack then take the left branch to a junction with Black Seamed. Step right and climb cracks in the edge to a ledge then follow the obvious line easily up right to finish.

12 Fully Fashioned 30m E1 5b **
R.Anderson, C.Anderson, 29 Jul 2005
Start as for Seamstress and after entering the crack take the right-hand branch to a ledge, then climb the slots in the wall to reach a ledge and finish more easily.

13 Knock Knees 30m E2 5b **
R.Anderson, C.Anderson, 27 Jul 2005
This starts on the right side of the tidal rift, from the lower of two ledges overlooking the rift. Climb the left edge to the next ledge. Make a couple of bold moves up left across the wall to the edge then climb the crack to reach blocky ground and a junction with Footfall. Step left then make a few tricky moves to gain a ledge and finish up the crack above.

Geodh'a' Bheannaich p116
1. Rock Goby VD *
2. Squat Lobster VD *
3. Langustine S 4a *
4. Small Fry HS 4b
7. Juggy Crack S 4a **
Bassett's Buttress p119
18. Jellied Babes S 4b *
19. Bertie's Crack VS 4b *
20. Better Together VS 4c **
21. OK UK VS 4b/c *
descent
Bassett's Wall p117
10. Black Seamed VS 4c **
11. Seamstress HVS 5a **
12. Fully Fashioned E1 5b **
13. Knock Knees E2 5b **
14. Footfall HVS 4c *
15. Toerag E2 5b
16. Fudge Fingers E3 6a ***
17. Crimson Tide HVS 5b **
GEÒDHA CHRUIDH

14 Footfall 30m HVS 4c *
R.Anderson, C.Anderson, 27 Jul 2005
The obvious stepped line up the centre of the wall. Climb up and left into the line and finish up the slab above. Not very well protected.

15 Toerag 30m E2 5b
R.Anderson, C.Anderson, 27 Jul 2005
An unsatisfactory route up the wall right of Footfall. It has gear but the rock keeps forcing moves into Footfall, up which it also finishes.

16 Fudge Fingers 40m E3 6a ***
R.Anderson, C.Anderson, 27 Jul 2005
The tramline cracks in the right side of the wall, started from just above sea-level. Climb past one ledge then gain another; the easy 20m lower section can be missed out. In the central section step right, then back left. Follow the cracks around the left side of the roof and continue to the top.

17 Crimson Tide 50m HVS 5b **
M.Tighe, K.Tighe 19 Sep 2014
A girdle of Bassett's Wall. Follow Fully Fashioned to the ledge at the top of its initial crack then make a long stride right to a ledge on Footfall. Go delicately up and right until below the overhangs and traverse under these into the corner. Descend a little and follow a fault-line out and around onto Bassett's Buttress and finish up Jellied Babes.

At the junction of Bassett's Wall with Bassett's Buttress, there is a deep corner-chimney line which has been top-roped at around E2.

Bassett's Buttress

(NB 0373 3756) Non-tidal SW facing
Diagram opposite

The narrow buttress on the left (north) side of the deep cleft.

Descent: Abseil down a depression in the centre of the buttress to good ledges.

18 Jellied Babes 45m S 4b *
R.Anderson, C.Anderson, 27 Jul 2005
The crack up the left side of the buttress leads to a short steep corner, avoid on the right to then regain the line to finish.

19 Bertie's Crack 45m VS 4b *
R.Anderson, C.Anderson, 27 Jul 2005
Just left of the prominent full-height crack, is a thin crack up the centre of the buttress, following a thin white quartz-like vein. Climb the thin crack to a change of rock type in the recessed section at the top of the cliff and finish easily.

20 Better Together 25m VS 4c **
M.Tighe, 1985; named M.Tighe, K.Tighe, 21 Sep 2014
The prominent wide full height crack-line just right of centre.

21 OK UK 45m VS 4b/c *
M.Tighe, 1985; named M.Tighe, K.Tighe, 21 Sep 2014
This takes the right-hand edge and upper corner of the buttress. Start from sea-level ledges at a 2m flake and continue up a short steep wall on immaculate rock. More good rock leads to the upper corner, which is a little fragile, but well protected.

Allsorts Wall

(NB 0374 3751) Tidal SW & W facing

The large cliff to the south (right) of the cleft contains some impressive looking crack-lines, quartz-like veins and black bands running pretty much vertically through it. Allsorts of rock and allsorts of looseness!

Descent: Directly by abseil.

Loose Liquorice 50m HVS 5a
M.Garthwaite, R.Anderson, 26 Jun 2007
This takes the wide black seam that narrows with height and runs into a corner to the left of a pointed roof on the arete. Climb the seam, the corner, another corner and blocky ground above. On the first ascent a dangerous loose block had to be left looming over the start, a few moves up the initial narrow section of the seam, just left of a corner where a piece of old gear hints at an earlier ascent of something here.

Fudge Fingers (E3) Chris Anderson (photo Rab Anderson)

Geòdha Caol

South-East Wall

(NB 0345 3730) Tidal SE facing Map p102

Located on the minor headland of Rubha Geòdha Chruidh to the south-west of Geòdha Chruidh, this atmospheric geo is one of a pair of parallel geos. It takes the form of a deep and narrow south-westward running inlet. On its north-west side it is separated from the narrow inlet of Geòdha Caol-rinneach by a 10m wide promontory. The climbs are on the slabby wall which runs along the length of the narrow promontory to form the north-west side of the geo.

Approach: From the parking at Àird Uig, gain the south-west end of Loch a' Bheannaich then head south-west past Geodh' a' Bheannaich and the small headland overlooking Geòdha Cruidh. Go around the head of the geo and continuing southwards for another 200m or so on the far side to reach Geòdha Caol (30min). From the parking on the peat track, continue to the end of the track and descend westwards to the head of Geòdha Chruidh; this is 5 to 10min faster.

Descent: By abseil. For the first three climbs this is to a good square-cut tidal ledge at the foot of a prominent corner partway along the cliff.

Spike Fright 40m VS 4c *
D.Cuthbertson, G.Latter, 8 May 1985
Traverse out left from the prominent corner and climb a crack through the overlap. Continue up an enjoyable wall.

Suenos de Piedra y Mar 40m HVS 5a *
S.Wrigley, M.Dale, 3 Jun 2000
Climb the corner to the left of the thin crack of Into the Sea to just below a big roof where a tricky move left can be made to the arete. Continue more easily up the slab and its right arete.

Into the Sea 40m E1 5b **
G.Latter, D.Cuthbertson, 8 May 1985
Climb up right to a thin crack then follow it into the upper part of the slabby corner which leads to the top.

Scoopy Do 40m VS 4b
Some 30m to the right of the above routes, a right-facing corner ends halfway up the cliff where a diagonal crack and fault cuts across it. To the left of this corner, climb a shallow line of weakness running diagonally up and left. Quite bold.

Geòdha Caol-rinneach

(NB 0342 3731) Non-tidal NW facing Map p102 Diagram above

Running parallel to Geòdha Caol, and separated from this by the slender promontory running along its top, is a tall seaward-facing wall overlooking another narrow inlet. On its north side, a ridge drops seawards from the Rubha Geòdha Chruidh headland and it is possible to scramble down this to view the wall from opposite.

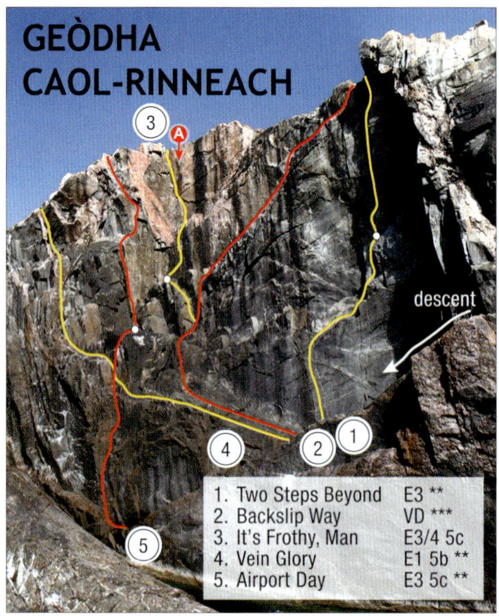

Descent: Either directly by abseil down a recessed section in the wall to the left of a corner (facing out) to a good ledge at the base, or by an easy but thought provoking scramble down a narrow exposed ramp. The ramp starts out along the slender 10m wide promontory, opposite the top of Into the Sea in Geòdha Caol, and slopes down towards the back of the geo to reach the foot of the wall. Although fairly easy it can be greasy in places and there is an undercut drop off into the sea.

1 Two Steps Beyond 45m E3 **
M.Garthwaite, R.Anderson, 26 Jul 2005
1. 25m 5c From the foot of the descent ramp, climb the left-hand cracks in the fine wall and traverse right to below a corner.
2. 20m 5b Climb the corner.

2 Backslip Way 40m VD ***
S.Wrigley, M.Dale, 3 Jun 2000
Including the descent ramp, this is an atmospheric and entertaining outing. From the foot of the ramp, climb stepped corners up leftwards until below the final leaning flake-crack. Follow a black ramp back right to the top, with a tricky section up an overhanging step halfway along.

3 It's Frothy, Man 35m E3/4
M.Garthwaite, R.Anderson, 2 Jun 2017
The central corner; start as for Backslip Way, or abseil to the start.
1. 15m Follow Backslip Way then go up left to ledges below the corner.
2. 20m 5c Place a high wire on the left then move up and right from the base of the corner to holds (gear) then pull up left to gain the ledge at the foot of the upper corner, which is climbed to the top.

4 Vein Glory 30m E1 5b **

R.Anderson, C.Anderson, 20 Apr 2003

At the base of the ramp a 2ft-wide pink vein starts on the floor of the ledge and snakes its way out left and up to the top of the crag. Follow this vein then go up corners and an edge to a small shelf; gear on the right can be arranged and extended. Climb the protruding vein for a steep and spectacular finish.

5 Airport Day 50m E3 **

M.Garthwaite, R.Anderson, 26 Jun 2007

Start at the extreme left end of the ramp where it enters the sea, at the base of a groove.

1. 25m 5a Pull out left onto the edge of the groove, move up then back into the groove, which is climbed until moves out left gain good holds leading back right to the top of the groove and the pink vein on Vein Glory. Follow this for a short way then go up right to below a prominent crack.

2. 25m 5c Climb the crack to its top, then move up and right around the edge to climb a stepped groove up and across the arete to a finish up the left side.

To the south of Geòdha Caol, past an inlet, is the interesting feature and large sink like hole of Seilaro (perhaps created by a collapsed arch) with its sandy flat-floored base. The coastline turns towards Geòdha Nasabhaig here and contains Geòdha-Seilaro. While there is a fair amount of rock much of it appears to be slabby and although there are rumours of some climbs nothing has been recorded.

Airport Day (E3) Mark Garthwaite (photo Rab Anderson)

GALLAN HEAD (AN GALLAN UIGEACH)

Map p102

Lying to the north of Àird Uig, this is the major headland where the coastline turns into Loch Ròg. The bulk of the headland lies beyond a decrepit fence (to be removed) marking the site of a former MOD/RAF Cold War surveillance station. Apart from one stack on the east side of the headland all the climbing to date is on the west facing section of coast just before the fence, a short distance from Àird Uig. Despite the headland beyond the fence containing a fair amount of coastline there is surprisingly little good rock of any real interest to the climber.

Geòdha Ruadh

(NB 044 385) Map p102

This large and deeply incised geo cuts in towards the road about 400m beyond the gate by the last building at Àird Uig, which is a cafe called The Edge. There are two faces, a distinctive slab on the north-west side which is seen from the approach and a more broken face on the south-east side. The main climbing is on the north-west side and is better than it looks, with excellent rock.

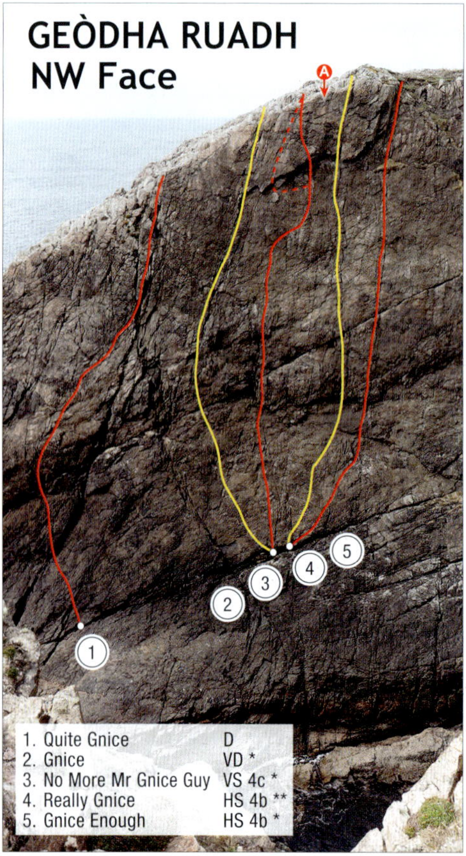

Approach: From the parking spot **(NB 0475 3838)** on the left about 100m beyond the gate at The Edge cafe, walk up the road for 100m and head left (5min).

GEÒDHA RUADH
NW Face

1. Quite Gnice	D
2. Gnice	VD *
3. No More Mr Gnice Guy	VS 4c *
4. Really Gnice	HS 4b **
5. Gnice Enough	HS 4b *

North-West Face

(NB 0445 3855) Non-tidal SE facing
Diagram below

The large slab at the entrance to the geo.

Descent: Either abseil from the cliff-top, or scramble down in a southerly direction and traverse in with one awkward step. For all but the first route it is best to belay in a deep crack which slants across the easy-angled lower section of the slab.

1 Quite Gnice 25m D
A.L.Wielochowski, 7 May 2017
From a flat area at the left end of the easy slab, climb up leftwards at first before slanting rightwards to join an obvious crack system, which is followed to the top.

2 Gnice 30m VD *
A.L.Wielochowski, D.N.Williams, 8 May 2017
Slant leftwards from the bottom crack towards the left-hand end of a thin tapering overhang. Then climb a thin crack system direct to the top.

3 No More Mr Gnice Guy 30m VS 4c *
A.L.Wielochowski, D.N.Williams, 11 May 2017
Go up to a short left-facing corner below the right-hand end of the thin tapering overhang. Climb up directly at first then traverse right on small flakes with difficulty before continuing up to a prominent overhang. Either surmount this direct using excellent flake pockets or step left and cross it without difficulty above a pale flake. Continue easily to the top.

4 Really Gnice 30m HS 4b **
A.L.Wielochowski, D.N.Williams, 8 May 2017
Slant slightly right from the bottom crack to the left-hand side of a small black slab. Then climb a thin crack system direct to the upper overhang. Arrange a belay on the right before finishing direct on amazing holds.

5 Gnice Enough 30m HS 4b *
A.L.Wielochowski, D.N.Williams, 8 May 2017
Slant rightwards from the bottom crack to the right-hand side of a small black slab. Then climb a thin crack system direct to a small grass ledge. Finish more easily just to the right of a right-facing corner.

South-East Face

(NB 0448 3853) Non-tidal NW facing

At the seaward end of this side of the geo, right of the grassier rocks, is an area of more continuous rock. There is one route which follows an obvious left to right rising pegmatite intrusion across the top of the rock.

Descent: Abseil down a grassy gully direct to ledges above the high water mark at the start of the route.

You're So Vein 55m S *
A.L.Wielochowski, D.N.Williams, 11 May 2017
A fun excursion up the left to right-rising pegmatite intrusion. The climbing is mostly easy on good rock and in a fine position.
1. 40m 4a Follow the pegmatite band rightwards via a steep step which requires care with protection for both the leader and the second. Good belay on a comfortable horizontal ledge.
2. 15m Continue traversing over a few easy steps to the top.

Rubha Caol

(NB 044 387) Map p102

This is the minor bird- or anvil-shaped headland to the north of Geòdha Ruadh, between it and the deeply incised and narrow northwards running Geòdha an Truillich to which the fence enclosing the former MOD site runs. The climbing is described from the arrival point at Geòdha an Truillich in an anti-clockwise direction southwards.

Approach: From the parking spot **(NB 0475 3838)** on the left about 100m beyond the gate at the cafe, walk up the road a little and cross behind Geòdha Ruadh. Continue to where the fence across Gallan Head meets the back of Geòdha an Truillich then follow the top of the west side of this geo out to the northern tip of the headland (10min).

The Trullich Headland

North Tip

(NB 0445 3885) Non-tidal N, NW & W facing

This is the area around the northern part or wing of the bird-shaped Rubha Caol headland. The first group of climbs lie out on the tip, on the west side of Geòdha an Trullich where there is a slabby black corner, to the left of which the slabby arete of True Grit is obvious and can be seen from the top.

Descent: A short way down from the highpoint, a good block on a small platform enables an abseil to be made down the slabby, black corner. Most of the routes can be accessed from here, including those around on the West Face. The sea-level tip of this headland is formed by jagged black ledges, which appear to be clear from all but the roughest seas.

Climbs are described from north to south, left to right.

Tacky When Dry 30m E1 5b *
R.Anderson, C.Anderson, 21 Sep 2002
Climb the groove and crack to the left of the arete of True Grit then cross a small hanging slab and move up towards the big groove at the back. Now go out right across the wall to climb a crack onto the edge to reach easier ground leading to the top.

Over the Edge 30m HVS 5a **
R.Anderson, C.Anderson, 20 Sep 2002
The crack immediately to the left of the arete, climbed direct. Either finish up the top section of True Grit, or easily up the fault.

True Grit 30m HVS 5a **
R.Anderson, C.Anderson, M.Garthwaite, 20 Jul 2002
The crack running up the right side of the fine, slabby arete to the left of the abseil corner. Gain the crack directly, then climb it and the arete, stepping right to finish up a short final arete.

Homerun 30m VS 4c **
R.Anderson, C.Anderson, 20 Sep 2002
The crack which slants diagonally up left across the slab into the final moves of True Grit.

Dumb and Dumber 25m HVS 5a *
R.Anderson, C.Anderson, 20 Sep 2002
Left of the abseil corner and just right of Homerun, climb the slabby groove running up the right side of the slab, move up right along a break, then make a few steep moves up a crack and move up right to finish.

The next climbs are to the right of the abseil corner.

Easy Out 25m VD
M.Garthwaite, R.Anderson, 20 Jul 2002
A line up the slabby black wall of the abseil; left into the corner, then out and up right to finish.

Minor Forty Niner 25m HVS 5a *
R.Anderson, C.Anderson, 7 Jul 2006
The right side of the abseil corner's slabby wall. Climb blocky flake-lines just left of the right arete then follow a thin ramp up right to finish up the edge.

The following climbs lie just around the edge on the true frontal buttress which forms the tip of this headland before it turns the edge to the West Face proper. Around the edge from the abseil corner is an open corner with easy ledges and shelves leading up into it.

Blubber 25m E4 6a *
R.Anderson, 7 Jul 2006
Start at the top of the shelf, below the open corner and beneath a hanging groove. Move up the corner, then bridge up and left (poor RPs). Move past these with difficulty and climb the groove on good gear (Friend 4 useful). Great moves but marred a little by the difficulty in arranging protection at the crux.

Shelved 40m HVS 4c
R.Anderson, C.Anderson, 20 Sep 2002
Start down to the right and on the black rock to the left of the narrow frontal buttress. Gain a short groove, either directly or rightwards up a slabby shelf then climb this. Instead of continuing up into the open corner, pull onto a narrow shelf on the right and follow this around onto the edge of the narrow frontal buttress. Climb the edge and continue on pleasant rock.

Moby Dick 40m E2 5c **
R.Anderson, C.Anderson, 17 Jul 2002
Start beneath twin cracks cutting through the lower, black wall of the narrow, frontal buttress. Climb the cracks, continue through an obvious break in the steep grey wall, then step left and finish up slabby grooves.

Minky 40m HVS 5a **
R.Anderson, C.Anderson, 17 Jul 2002
Just around the edge to the right of Moby Dick, climb a short, wide crack through the lower band of black rock, then its short continuation through the next band. Continue over a reddish slab and climb the centre of the narrow buttress to the top.

West Face

(NB 0442 3878) Non-tidal W facing

The frontal face.

Descent: If the sea does not permit access from the North Tip, abseil directly down the right side (facing in) of the face from a depression on the cliff-top, close to a deep corner groove, to a tilted slab and pedestal. Three climbs start from the pedestal and two from lower down, beneath the imposing main face.

Bonaventure 40m E2 5c ***
M.Garthwaite, R.Anderson, 20 Jul 2002
An impressive route up the centre of the imposing West Face. Start in the centre of the face beneath the only obvious break in the lower black wall. Climb this, then move up and left to an obvious undercut flange in the overlap. Pull up right into a groove and from the top of this step left to gain a line leading directly into the upper groove, which is climbed to the top.

Swell 40m E2 5c **
M.Garthwaite, R.Anderson, 20 Jul 2002
A parallel line just right of Bonaventure. Break through the lower band, as for Bonaventure, then move up and right, before climbing back up left to a thin crack-line leading over small overlaps to a steepening beneath an obvious short, leaning wall with a break in it. Step up left and move right into the break, then pull boldly through the break to gain a blocky feature and finish more easily.

The next routes start from the pedestal on the right side of the face.

Static Fear 30m E1 5a
R.Anderson, M.Diggins, 20 Jun 2002
Climb the obvious crack-line over a steepening to where it peters out beneath the final eaves, then lurch steeply up right on slightly dubious rock into a shallow groove leading to the top.

Charged 30m E2 5b *
M.Diggins, R.Anderson, 20 Jun 2002
Climb thin cracks directly to the base of the obvious smooth groove. Climb the groove to its top then continue a short way before moving up right to finish more easily.

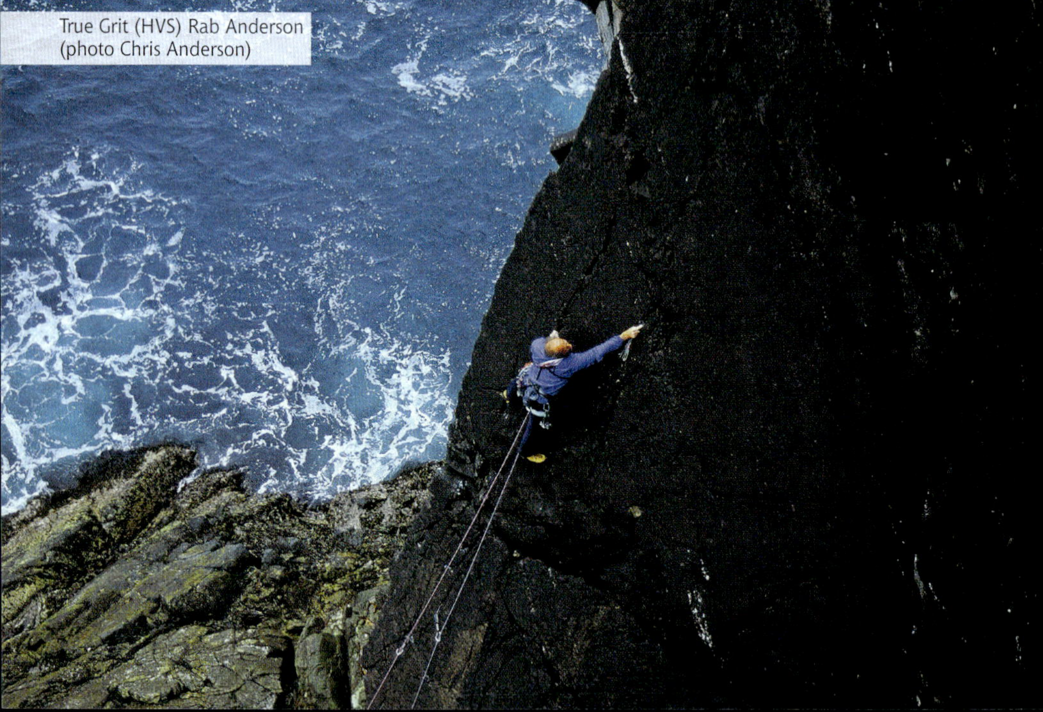
True Grit (HVS) Rab Anderson (photo Chris Anderson)

Cool Running 30m VS 4c **
R.Anderson, M.Diggins, 20 Jun 2002
Step up right and climb thin cracks just right of Charged, which soon widen and lead to a V-shaped groove. Climb the groove, then easier ground to the top.

West Face Continuation

(NB 0440 3875) Tidal W facing

The next climbs lie just to the south. Two of these start from a similar pedestal block belay as that on the right side of The West Face. This is just around the obvious arete with projecting eaves, which forms the right side of the West Face.

Descent: It is possible to traverse across from the right side of the West Face. The alternative is to abseil directly to the southern pedestal, down a slabby crack-seamed wall.

Washing of the Spears 30m E2 5c **
R.Anderson, C.Anderson, 17 Jul 2002
A fine line up the edge forming the left side of the slabby wall. Step up left from the pedestal and climb cracks just right of the edge, staying on the front face to below the final steepening. Climb a left-slanting, thin crack to the top. A groove just to the right should provide an alternative finish at an overall grade of about HVS.

Gallan Cracks 30m VD to S **
R.Anderson, C.Anderson, 17 Jul 2002
The area of slabby rocks above the pedestal can be climbed anywhere on fine rock. A central line between the deeper cracks is probably slightly harder than the cracks themselves.

A short way down and right from the pedestal, almost on the last ledge, is a wide, deep crack.

Thinner Better 35m VS 4c **
R.Anderson, C.Anderson, 21 Sep 2002
Just right of the wide, deep crack, climb a thin crack and continue on fine rock, always just right of the bigger crack and its continuation.

Knight's Move 40m HS 4a **
S.Lenartowicz, C.Humphry, 11 Jun 2013
Start down and right of Thinner Better. Ascend a scoop rightwards to a traverse line which is followed rightwards to a prominent groove. Climb this to the top.

Gallan Head East

Map p102

There have been rumours of some climbing on the main headland beyond the fence but more recent exploration has yielded remarkably little that appears worth developing here. One route has been recorded and this is on a fin-shaped sea stack **(NB 052 387)** in the bay of Camus na h-Airde on the east side, some 400m north of Àird Uig. The stack is accessible at mid to low tide by a 70m abseil descent down a steep grassy slope.

Depth Charge 25m HVS 4b
R.I.Jones, J.Sanders, 15 Jun 2004
Climb a left-facing corner on the south fin, pulling right 2m before the top of the corner to avoid a loose exit. Continue with care to the top. Descend by abseil.

RUBHA MÒR

Map p102

To the east of Àird Uig, this is the 160m highpoint above the bay of Camus na h-Airde. Whilst the map hints at some promising cliff the coastline is generally broken, vegetated and loose.

Geòdha Gorm

(NB 0646 3808) Non-tidal W facing Map p102

This fairly large bay lies 1.5km east of Àird Uig, just north of the highest point of Rubha Mòr. There is one route on the eastern side, on the highest section of cliff where there is a conspicuous intrusion of slabby pink rock some 80m high. The only route so far is not a great climb, although it is certainly an adventurous outing.

Approach: Park beside an old building **(NB 0532 3700)** on the east side of the road about 1km south of Àird Uig. Head north-east across rough moorland for some 1.3km and ascend to the summit of Rubha Mòr. It is probably worth descending the cliff-top on the western side of the bay first to get a good view of the face (25min).

Descent: Go down the cliff-top on the eastern side of the bay to a slight flattening with two in-situ iron stakes. A 75m abseil leads directly to a grassy bay a little above the base of the slab, at the bottom right of the face looking up, and well above the sea. Either belay on the abseil rope, or on blocks set in the grassy terrain further right.

Sunset Boulevard 90m E1 4c
A.L.Wielochowski, D.N.Williams, 9 May 2017
The route gains and follows the left-hand arete; the rock is a bit scary and belays are not plentiful.
1. 30m 4c Make a rising leftwards traverse on suspect rock heading for the left-hand arete. Some 5m before the arete, place a tape over a small stumpy spike. Move left again then step back right to stand on the spike. Step up and make a delicate move to gain a line of weakness leading left to the arete. Excellent belay on a large block-come-flake.
2. 30m 4a Climb a prominent groove and step out right near the top on good holds. Continue more easily up the arete. Eventually traverse left on grassy ground to reach a wide crack for a chockstone and large hex belay.
3. 30m 4b Step back right onto the face and climb slightly rightwards on good holds then traverse left to a ledge where the character of the rock changes. Climb blocky holds with care (no protection) and finish up a short corner.

UIG NORTH-EAST - VALTOS

Maps p20 & right

This section covers the climbing on the Tobha Mòr and Tobha Beag headlands to the north of Valtos (Bhaltos), together with the small crags on the hillside of Beinn na Bheirigh which lie beyond the campsite at the eastern end of the Tràigh na Beirigh sands. Also included are the small offshore islands of Pabaigh Mòr and Pabaigh Beag.

Approach: Turn off the B8011 at the east end of the Gleann Bhaltois meltwater channel and go past the church at the head of the Miavaig (Miabhaig) harbour inlet. At the junction by the Fire Station, the right branch of a loop road leads to Reef (Riof), then the campsite and beach at Tràigh na Bheirigh, then to the hamlets of Kneep (Cnip) and Valtos (Bhaltos). The left branch of the loop road leads past Loch Sgailleir to Cliff (Cliobh) and the beach in the bay at Tràigh na Clibhe, then goes over the hill where it splits, with either branch leading to Valtos, then the campsite.

TOBHA MÒR AND TOBHA BEAG

Lying to the north of Valtos, between the beaches at Tràigh na Clibhe and Tràigh na Beirigh, this two-pronged headland juts into the sea between the bay of Camus na Clibhe and the island of Pabaigh Mòr.

Geòdha Maladail

(NB 0890 3775) Tidal W facing Diagram opposite

This is the big, open geo that splits the headland into two. The west facing side of the geo forms a big and long cliff which gradually diminishes in height northwards as it passes a sea cave, to end near a natural arch on the point. The climbing areas are described as met on the approach, with the geo first then the headland point.

Directions: Park on the grass to the side of the left-hand road that goes from Cliff to Valtos. This is towards the top of the hill just after the road forks, in the vicinity of the cemetery and the water treatment works, overlooking the sands of Tràigh na Clibhe.

Approach: Contour the hillside of Seuchaval and go through the col between this and Tobha Mòr, then drop down to cross the burn which drains into the back of the geo. Follow a sheep track up the hillside over the high-point then down to an old wall which cuts across the headland and runs towards the cliff edge. This is almost at the end of the main west facing wall where it runs into a sea cave before the cliff becomes more broken. There is a grassy hollow on the cliff edge where the old wall takes a bend just before the cliff edge (20min).

Descent: By abseil. Where the path goes through the old wall, a large embedded boulder in the wall can be threaded to provide a convenient abseil point, with a back up in the rocks just in front. Slightly off to the right facing out, the ropes can be run over some rocks and then down the small exit groove of the first route.

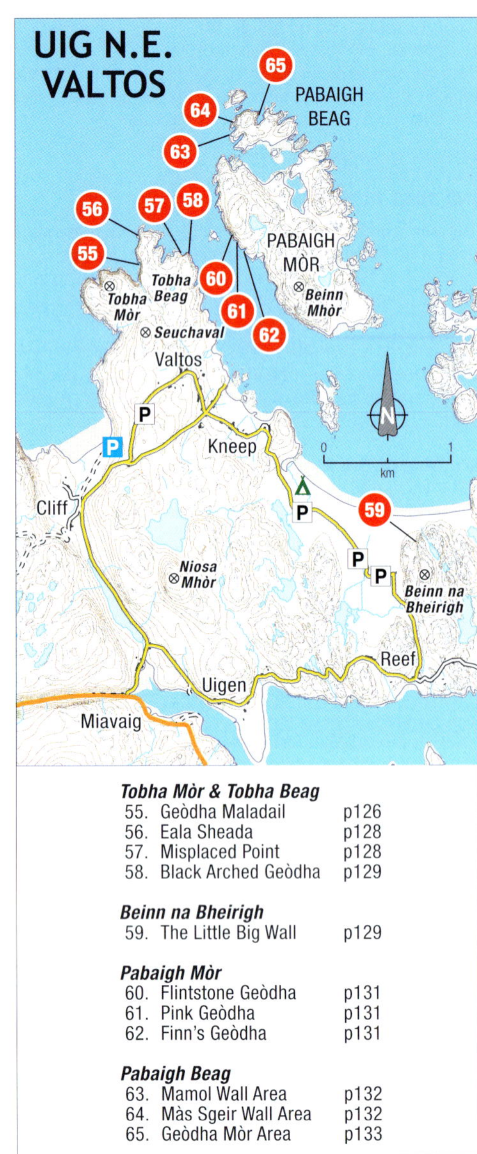

Another abseil point is from a prominent large block about a third of the way south along the cliff from its northern end.

A large tidal shelf runs beneath the cliff and the abseil from the wall gains this close to where it terminates at the sea cave. When the tide is out the shelf can be easily traversed southwards for 100m or so. At the left end of the cliff there are very few breaks in the steep lower band of black rock.

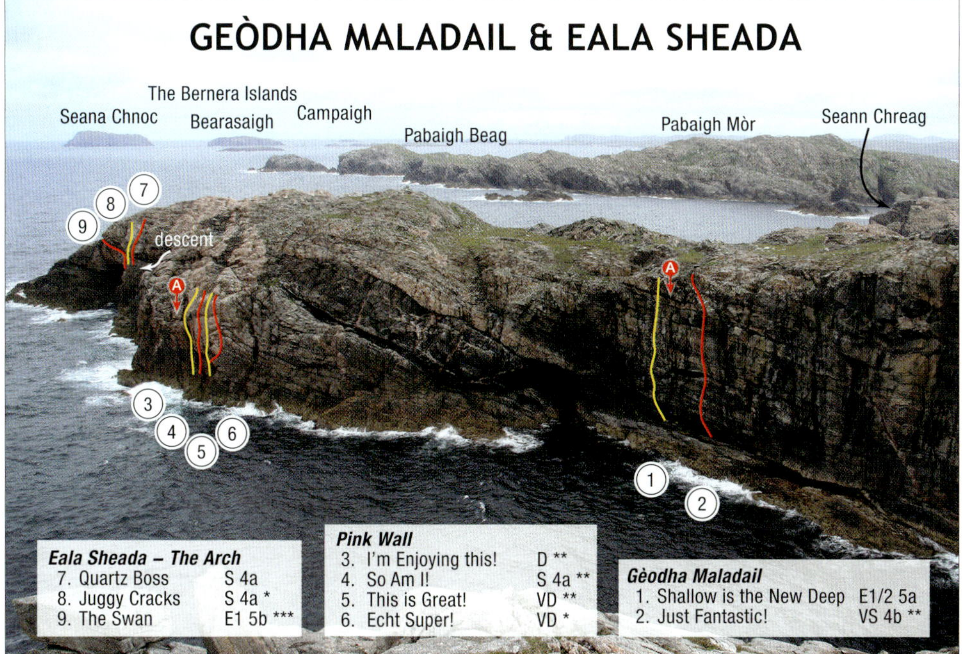

1 Shallow is the New Deep 40m E1/2 5a
R.Anderson, C.Anderson, 19 Apr 2003
This takes the wide, shallow groove that runs the height of the cliff above the initial band of black rock, towards the left end of the shelf. Start just to the right of the groove where there is an obvious break in the steep lower wall. Climb steeply to the break and then move up left and across into the base of the groove. Climb the groove to the top; the gear and the rock are not as one might like at the top.

Some 20m or so further along the shelf to the south, an obvious square-cut tower feature can be identified at the top of the cliff. The next route climbs a crack leading into the blocky corner forming the left side of this tower.

2 Just Fantastic! 35m VS 4b **
G.Latter L.Mackay, 10 May 2002
Start at the left end of a long, narrow tidal pool, at the right end of a long overhang at the base of the cliff. Traverse up left past a groove and climb the slabby wall to the base of an obvious crack. Follow the crack to a recess at the base of the blocky corner running up the left side of the tower and climb this, gingerly in places, to the top.

Pink Wall

(NB 089 379) Tidal W Facing

The next climbs are located on a fine wall of pink pegmatite 200m further north. This is on the other side of the sea cave and below the top of the slight rise beyond the old boundary wall.

Descent: A 25m abseil from a large block gains tidal ledges at the base.

3 I'm Enjoying this! 25m D **
L.Mackay, B.Rose, 10 May 2002
Climb the fine left-slanting fault at the left end and step right to finish up cracks in the beautiful pink slab.

4 So Am I! 22m S 4a **
L.Mackay, B.Rose, 10 May 2002
Climb easy juggy rock, passing to the left of a projecting square block to finish up the short steep crack in the headwall.

5 This is Great! 22m VD **
B.Rose, L.Mackay, 10 May 2002
A direct line up the wall, passing right of the square block, to finish up a crack in the right edge of the steeper headwall.

6 Echt Super! 22m VD *
J.Smith, K.Speidel, 15 Jul 2015
Start up This is Great!, then go up and right onto a large block and ledge. Continue above to another ledge then go left across a slabby ledge to finish up a corner-crack.

Eala Sheada

The Arch

(NB 089 381) Non-tidal W facing Map p126 Diagram p127

The northernmost point of the Tobha Beag headland is formed by the small promontory of Eala Sheada, just north of the Pink Wall. Reach it by continuing north beyond a slight dip on the other side of the rise, past the old wall above Geòdha Maladail.

Descent: Although it is possible to abseil to the start of the routes there are roofs, and locating the correct line is a little difficult. Another option is to scramble down, possibly with the security of a rope. To do so, on the cliff edge about 10m or so beyond the slight dip between the highpoints, look for an easy line leading a short distance down a shallow corner to some ledges. Descend to the ledges then work along and down before traversing the ledge system to beneath the roofs. On the way two easy climbs are passed.

7 Bossanova 20m S 4a
R.Anderson, G.Nicol, 6 Jul 2012
Immediately to the right of the roofs which overhang the ledge system, climb up right to a large blocky feature then squeeze up right to attain a standing position on this. Step left then climb over the obvious quartzy boss and continue to the top.

The Swan (E1) Martin Kocsis (photo Mike Hutton)

8 Juggy Cracks 20m S 4a *
Start at the same point as the previous route and climb a steep but juggy line of cracks.

9 The Swan 30m E1 5b ***
M.Tighe, K.Tighe, J.McClenaghan, 7 May 1999
A spectacular left-rising traverse which climbs above the arch. Start from the left end of the ledge system, beneath the roofs which overhang the start. Follow an obvious horizontal break out left above the initial roofs, then move up to good incuts in the next break. Follow this left and move up to a ledge just below a guano ledge (possible belay). Pull up left to follow the easier wide break to the left beneath the capping roofs, moving left and up past a large flake to the final break. Well protected; take plenty cams.

Seann Chreag (Misplaced Point)

(NB 092 379) Tidal W facing Map p126

To the east of the northernmost point of the Toa Beag headland, a little but perfect off vertical wall drops straight into the sea at the small point of Seann Chreag. In its centre the wall is capped by a short, overhanging headwall. There are some deep water solos.

Descent: The base can be gained at about S by descending easy ground on the north side and traversing in just above sea-level. Alternatively a diagonal fault leads down rightwards, then back left to gain the right end of the cliff at about VS.

Sweet Arete 15m HS 4a (MXS 4a) (S2) *
J.Lines (DWS), 13 Jun 2007
The shapely arete at the left end of the wall.

Wander at Will 15m VS 4b (XS 4b) (S2) **
G.Latter (DWS), 10 May 2002
The arete delineating the right side of the open groove to the right of Sweet Arete.

Diretissima 15m VS 4c (XS 4c) (S2) **
G.Latter (DWS), 10 May 2002
The central line to finish by a shallow V-slot.

It's Ravaging 15m E1 5b (XS 5b) (S2) *
J.Lines (DWS), 13 Jun 2007
The line through the headwall between Diretissima and Stravaiging.

Stravaiging 15m HVS 5a (XS 5a) (S2) ***
G.Latter (DWS), 10 May 2002
The furthest right line, finishing spectacularly on good holds through the overhanging headwall.

The obvious left-slanting diagonal fault in the bigger cliff just to the right has been climbed at D, though it is a bit broken at the top.

Black Arched Geòdha

(NB 093 378) Tidal N facing Map p126

About 100m south from Seann Chreag, this sheltered and cosy eastwards running geo has a number of relatively safe and easy deep water solos.

Descent: Go down an easy black slab on the eastern side, but when halfway down cut in and climb down (4b) onto a strategically positioned ledge. A harder option is to descend the slab to sea-level and traverse in to the ledge just above the water (5b). All the routes start from the ledge.

O.V.D 10m XS 4c (S0) *
J.Lines (DWS), 13 Jun 2007
From the right end of the ledge climb the diagonal crack line.

The Flying Sheep 10m XS 4c (S0) *
J.Lines (DWS), 13 Jun 2007
Traverse further right to gain the right-hand diagonal crack-line.

Day Without End 12m XS 5a (S0) *
J.Lines (DWS), 13 Jun 2007
Traverse further along the lip of the arch and climb the wall just left of a faint groove.

On the Hoof 15m XS 5c (S1) *
J.Lines (DWS), 13 Jun 2007
Continue past Day Without End until you reach some thin cracks in a slab. Climb these on small finger holds.

Black Rum 20m XS 5c (S1) **
J.Lines (DWS), 13 Jun 2007
The whole traverse of the curving archway gives a fun and safe outing.

BEINN NA BHEIRIGH

The Little Big Wall

(NB 1095 3660) Non-tidal Alt 20m W facing Map p126 Diagram below

The hillside at the eastern end of the magnificent Tràigh na Beirigh sands is dotted with small crags and minor bits of rock. One of these is a small, insignificant looking wall not far above the machair. On closer acquaintance the wall is found to be composed of smooth, near perfect gneiss and provides a number of fine climbs, which although short, pack a fair punch and give some excellent moves. The crag is unaffected by the sea so it is a useful little venue. There is also some good bouldering and the Reef campsite is at the other end of the beach. The crag does get used at times for abseiling and there is

a stake on the balcony ledge at the top of the main wall which is unnecessary given that the wall just behind this has some good large wire placements.

Approach: Although there are vehicular tracks leading across the machair towards the crag, one should help protect this rare environment and abide by the signs dissuading one from driving over it. There are various places to park, from where it is a short walk across the machair to a gate down and left of the crag; (5min).

Descent: Scramble down a ramp rightwards from the balcony.

The left end of the wall has a fine staggered crack-line running up it with a pocketed wall to its right, then towards the right side of the smooth central section are some thin crack-lines rising above embedded blocks.

1 Traighding Places 20m HVS 5a *
R.Anderson, C.Anderson, 14 Jul 1998
The corner at the left end of the wall has an awkward exit.

2 Tunes of Glory 20m E5 6b ***
R.Anderson, 9 Jul 1999
A superb route up the staggered crack-line in the left side of the wall. Climb the first crack then move right and climb the upper crack.

3 Rouge Traighder 15m E5 6b **
D.Macleod, 12 Jun 2001
Start below some curving overlaps between Tunes of Glory and Barrier Reef. Climb direct through the bulges and boldly move up the pocketed wall above to reach the good protection crack of Barrier Reef. Continue up with a hard move to gain a thin horizontal then move up and left to join Tunes of Glory for its last few moves.

4 Barrier Reef 20m E5 6a ***
R.Anderson, 16 Jul 1999
Brilliant climbing up the pocketed central wall. Gain the first pocket, then the large pocket and move up left to another large pocket, then go up right to a thin crack and continue to the break then the top. Some large cams are useful for the pockets and micro-wires for the thin cracks.

5 Cnippy Sweetie 15m E7 6b ***
D.Macleod, S.Richardson, 12 Jun 2001
Excellent technical but sparsely protected climbing up the smooth wall between Barrier Reef and Cnip Fit. Climb Barrier Reef to its first pocket then dyno to another pocket a long way up and right, and continue rightwards to a horizontal break (small cams). Climb up and left with difficulty using flanges and a pocket to reach another break (small wire). Finish directly.

Barrier Reef (E5) Iain Small (photo Tony Stone)

The next climbs start from some embedded blocks to the right.

6 Cnip-Fit 15m E5 6a **
R.Anderson, C.Anderson, 14 Jul 1998
Start on the blocks and from a letterbox, swing left into a thin crack then move up this to its top where it is possible to stretch a Rock 6 up and right into a V-slot. Gain the break on the right and follow its diagonal continuation left to pull onto the ledge and finish more easily.

7 Berie-Berie 15m E4 6a **
R.Anderson, C.Anderson, 15 Jul 1998
Start on the blocks and move up past a horizontal break to a flange (small wires). Gain the horizontal break above, (a small horizontal slot just up and right provides additional protection). Climb to another horizontal break then gain the ledge and finish up right as for Milk-Traigh.

8 Milk-Traigh 15m E3 6a *
R.Anderson, C.Anderson, Jul 1997
Just right of the blocks, climb the obvious crack to its end then pull up left to a ledge and finish up right.

9 Rainy Days and Golden Evenings 40m E2 5b *
K.Magog, S.Crowe, 7 Jul 2003
A high level girdle. Start on the right and traverse the break below the top to finish on the left.

PABAIGH MÒR

(NB 096 384) Map p126

This rocky island is one of a small group of islands lying in a sheltered position in Loch Ròg, between Uig and Great Bernera, about 1km north-east of Valtos. The climbing so far, deep water soloing, is found in a number of geos on its west coast, facing the Toa Mòr and Toa Beag headlands.

Flintstone Geòdha

(NB 0963 3809) Map p126

The most northerly geo that holds climbs is directly opposite a rock in the sea and pretty much opposite Eala Sheadha on the mainland shore opposite. It's a fairly shallow geo with a wide crack splitting the back of it. Access the geo from the seaward end on the south side.

Wilma 10m MXS 4a (S1) *
J.Lines (DWS), 13 Jun 2007
Traversing in, gain a big jutting jug in the slab and continue past a slight overlap.

Barney 15m XS 5c (S0) *
J.Lines (DWS), 13 Jun 2007
Gain the obvious sentry box and climb the left edge to below an overlap, traverse left under this and gain the wall above. Traverse back right and reach a ramp, wander off this leftwards.

Bam Bam 15m XS 5b/c (S0) *
J.Lines (DWS), 13 Jun 2007
Traverse leftwards to the right of the central chimney-crack, climb the edge and pull through the roof.

Pebbles 15m XS 5b (S0) **
J.Lines (DWS), 13 Jun 2007
Traverse in to gain and climb the central chimney-crack. At the roof step left and up.

Pink Geòdha

(NB 0969 3800) Map p126

About 50m south of Flintstone Geòdha is a deep cut geo with no climbs as yet; another 50m to the south of this is Pink Geòdha, an orange-pink coloured arch. The routes can be soloed at any state of the tide and are superb.

Perception 10m XS 6a (S0) **
J.Lines (DWS), 13 Jun 2007
From the south side of the geo, traverse in to gain a steep black hanging groove by brilliant move, and continue directly.

Beautiful People 13m XS 6a (S0) **
J.Lines (DWS), 13 Jun 2007
As for Perception until the lip of the arch then make a thin left traverse immediately above the lip to gain better holds and finish direct. Lovely climbing.

Finn's Geòdha

(NB 0976 3794) Map p126

About 100m to the south of Pink Geòdha is a deeper cut geo, which has a smooth black, south facing wall. It would appear this is Geodha' an t-Sneachd, as named on the OS map.

Spongebob 15m XS 5b (S2) *
J.Lines (DWS), 13 Jun 2007
From the seaward end on the north wall, traverse to the centre of the wall and climb it via a yellow lichen strip near the top.

PABAIGH BEAG

(NB 099 389) Map p126

The island of Pabaigh Beag lies to the north of the bigger island of Pabaigh Mòr. Access is by boat and enquiries should be made at Valtos or Miavaig, or at Circebost pier on Bernera. There are several sheltered camping spots on the island but there is no naturally occurring water. Disturbance of the many nesting birds should be kept to the absolute minimum. There is no evidence of land based animals. A visit is worthwhile for those with a sense of adventure and lines remain to be discovered. The climbing areas are described, working clockwise from the west side where Geòdha Dubh is the southernmost and biggest of two geos. Climbs are generally described from right to left.

Mamol Wall Area

(NB 097 388) Non-tidal Map p126

A small buttress just north of Geòdha Dubh.

Struay Lass 16m S 4a
P.Headland, K.Archer, 11 Jun 2013
Climb the wall on the right-hand side of the buttress.

Way To Blue 15m HVS 5b
K.Archer, P.Headland, 11 Jun 2013
Start 5m left of the previous route and climb a short wall to a ledge, then pull onto the upper wall (crux) and follow the pink band of rock to the top.

Màs Sgeir Wall Area

(NB 097 389) Non-tidal Map p126

This extends, on more than one level in several sectors, from the north-west corner of the island. Contour above Geòdha Dubh, the southern of the two geos on the west side of the island, to locate a notch in the skyline on the north-north-west of the island across a broken boulder field. Access to a non-tidal platform is made by scrambling down a gully, the turn left and scramble across the tidal outflow of a short through-cave to arrive at the Scottish Block.

Scottish Block

So called because its western profile looks like a map of Scotland. Routes are described left to right. An abseil descent can also be made down the slabby face if sea conditions prevent access from the descent gully. The first route starts from the ridge on the right-hand side.

Aberdeen 12m E1 5b
K.Archer, P.Headland, 14 Jun 2013
Start on the right arete of the west face. Climb the arete to a niche then make awkward moves to exit on its right to reach the base of a corner system. Climb this until a move left gains the top wall.

Alba 16m VS 4c
K.Archer, P.Headland, 9 Jun 2013
Start at the left-hand corner of the buttress, climb direct to good cam placements then move across to the 'west coast' and follow it without deviation.

The Last Four Things 17m VS 4b
P.Headland, K.Archer, 9 Jun 2013
On the slabby northern face of the Scottish Block, start at the crack on the right-hand corner, move up to the slabby upper section and trend left across the slab to exit on the upper wall at the left-hand side.

4th Birthday Route 14m VS 4c
P.Headland, K.Archer, 15 Jun 2013
In the centre of the slabby northern face climb through a short series of overlaps, once established trend leftwards to exit on the left-hand arete.

The Reivers 16m HVS 5b *
K.Archer, P.Headland, 9 Jun 2013
This follows the deep black blocky V-groove between the Scottish Block and the outflow from the through cave; finish through an overhanging slot.

Dubh Cracks

The black slabs and cracks immediately left of the descent gully.

Distant and Found 16m VS 5a *
P.Headland, K.Archer, 9 Jun 2013
Gain then follow the elegant corner formed by the black slab and wall on the right.

Flame Resistant Rainwear 15m HS 4a
P.Headland, K.Archer, 14 Jun 2013
Climb direct up the stepped arete of the slab which forms the corner of the previous route.

The Bradbeer Legacy 14m HS 4b
K.Archer, P.Headland, 9 Jun 2013
Start 1m left of the previous route and climb the blocky corner to the thin crack.

The Famous Five 15m S 4a
P.Headland, K.Archer, 9 Jun 2013
From 1m left of the previous route, climb the steep wall on large ledges to a platform; continue up the grey wall above.

Dubh Slabs

The black slabs immediately right of the main descent gully.

The Romp 15m S 4a
K.Archer, P.Headland, 14 Jun 2013
From the platform on the right at the base of the descent gully, climb a square-cut niche and from a higher platform climb the buttress on the right.

Màs Sgeir Side Wall

The large grey wall bordering Dubh Slabs is reached by traversing the base of Dubh Slabs, if sea conditions allow, or from the main gully 20m further north by descending slabby ground.

Black House Blues 12m VS 4c
K.Archer, P.Headland, 14 Jun 2013
Start near the left-hand arete of the wall. Climb a crack

then the right-hand corner system to reach and climb the upper wall.

Màs Sgeir Wall

The largest wall on the island is tidal and is accessed by a low-level traverse from either the main descent gully or the Dubh Slabs.

Wild Atlantic Son 22m HVS 5a **
K.Archer, P.Headland, 10 Jun 2013
At the right-hand end of the main wall a wide crack high up can be seen; start below and right of this at a platform. Climb up trending left until an exposed pedestal is reached beneath the final exposed wall, climb this with elation!

Master Chef 24m E1 5b **
P.Headland, K.Archer, 14 Jun 2013
Further left is a blocky wall. Climb past several small ledges to a large platform at the base of a left-trending narrow slab. Place good runners in the back of the crack and climb onto the arete of the slab, then onwards up the slab and short wall above.

Raven 24m HVS 5a
K.Archer, P.Headland, 14 Jun 2013
Start 5m left of the previous route at a large platform, below a slab and overhang. Climb the initial blocky wall then gain the slab via an overlap, climb following the right side-come-corner until the overhang, traverse left under the overhang and continue the line to the top.

To reach the next climb traverse the base of the wall and cross to the small islet, traverse its ridge and drop down to a large barnacle-covered jammed block.

Beesley Street 25m VS 4b *
P.Headland, K.Archer, 10 Jun 2013
From the jammed block follow the arete of the large black slab then move onto the slab to finish.

Geòdha Mòr Area

(NB 099 388) Non-tidal Map p126

The large geo on the east side of the island. There are several sectors nearly all of which are non-tidal although they can be affected by heavy swell. The first area described is the east-facing wall at the end of geo's northern edge.

Promontory Buttress

This can be reached by a short abseil down the centre of the wall to a non-tidal ledge just above the sea.

Gwilym's the Daddy Now? 16m VS 4b
P.Headland, K.Archer, 10 Jun 2013
From the ledge, climb rightwards up the stepped ramp to the centre of the face then continue direct.

Marc O'Polo 15m VS 4b
K.Archer, P.Headland, 10 Jun 2013
From the platform, climb the left side of the wall direct and exit through a corner niche.

Geòdha Mòr Slabs

The large sweep of slabs on the northern side of the geo; descent is by abseil down the right-hand side of the slabs. The rock is loose in places.

Climb If You Will 22m VS 3b
P.Headland, K.Archer, 9 Jun 2013
From the ledge two-thirds down the slab, 3m from the adjoining wall, climb cracks through the short wall then the loose slab above.

Geòdha Mòr South Wall

This is the area of overlapping ledges at the entrance to the geo on its south side. Access is by a short abseil down the wall, two-thirds of the way from the left-hand end to a prominent black ledge above the sea.

Feeding the Rat 12m S 4a
P.Headland, K.Archer, 13 Jun 2013
Traverse 2m right from the belay ledge and climb to the first notch on the left-hand end of the skyline.

Spanking the Moles 15m S 4a
K.Archer, P.Headland, 13 Jun 2013
Traverse 5m right from the belay ledge and climb to the second notch on the skyline.

Only 24hrs from Lincoln 20m S 4a
P.Headland, K.Archer, 13 Jun 2013
A rightwards-rising traverse of the cliff; exit up the third and final corner with a short wall above.

Oystercatcher in flight (photo Rab Anderson)

Great Bernera (Beàrnaraigh)

Maps p19, below & p137

The island of Great Bernera juts into Loch Ròg on the west coast of Lewis, between Uig to the south-west and Carloway (Càrlabhagh) to the north-east. A short stretch of water separates it from the mainland and this is crossed by a bridge.

The climbing is out on the north-west tip of the island, on the west-facing coastline between the two road-ends at Tobson and Bostadh. The principal area is Geòdha Mòr Shlèibhte which lies at the southern end of the Rubha Cuinish headland which forms the north-western tip of Great Bernera. Three of the small islands off the northern tip of Bernera have also been climbed on.

The outlook across Loch Ròg, over a sprinkling of small islands to the sands at Tràigh na Beirigh with the mountains of Uig and Harris beyond, is superb.

The climbing areas are described south to north starting with three small crags on the mainland side of the bridge over to Bernera, on Beinn Sgarastaigh and at Crùlabhig, then onto Bernera itself with Geòdha Mòr, followed by the Geòdha Mòr Shlèibhte area and Creag Rebridh. The three small islands, on which there is climbing, are Bearasaigh, Campaigh and Seana Chnoc; the guide for these islands is online.

Directions: Turn off the main A858 from Stornoway or Carloway at Garynahine (Gearraidh na h-Aibhne), onto the B8011 to Uig. Some 5km along this road, take the single track road northwards. Coming from Uig it is the first left after the turn off to Scaliscro Lodge, after rounding the end of Loch Ròg. Pass the crags at Beinn Sgarastaigh and Crùlabhig, cross the bridge onto the island and go through Breaclete where there is a small shop, petrol and a community cafe. Just beyond Breaclete a road goes off left to Tobson for Geòdha Mòr, whilst continuing straight on leads to the road end at Bostadh and the approach for Geòdha Mòr Shlèibhte and Creag Rebridh.

BEINN SGARASTAIGH

Creag Sgarastaigh

(NB 1918 3213) Alt 20m W facing

This small inland crag is located on Beinn Sgarastaigh (98m) and is visible from the road just before the cattle grid south of Lundal on the road to Bernera. The crag is composed of three rounded buttresses separated by wide cracks.

Approach: Park on a section of old road just before the cattle grid at Lundal. Cross the flats and the Lundal River (a small burn) to gain the raised ground of Druim a' Chruidh, then follow this to the sea and cut across to the crag (10min).

1 Thunderbolt 15m E2 5c *
R.Anderson, C.Anderson, 6 Jul 2010
The crack-line up the left side of the left-hand buttress.

2 Scaramouche 15m E1 5b *
R.Anderson, C.Anderson, 4 Apr 2008
Lovely climbing up the crack-line in the centre of the left-hand buttress.

3 Fandango 15m E2 5c *
R.Anderson, 11 Jul 2008
The splendid crack-line up the central buttress is started by a few moves up the big crack on the right. A direct start up the wide crack is 6a.

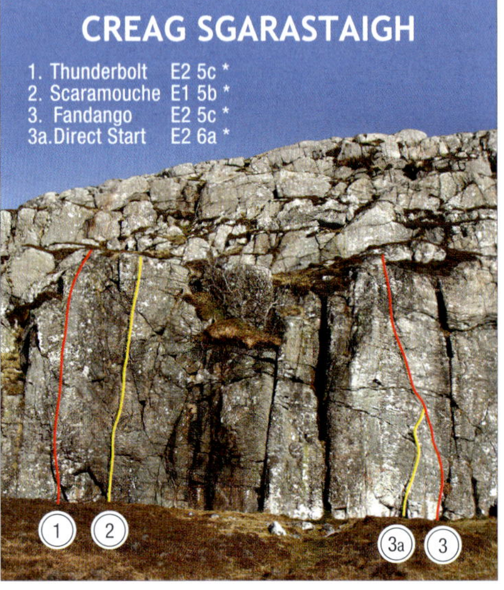

Sgarastaigh Craglets

(NB 1924 3184) Alt 60m SW facing Map opposite

Visible from the road, and rising up the hillside to the right of Creag Sgarastaigh, are some minor crags; useful in combination with that crag and Crùlabhig as quick drying inland venues.

Mini-scule 8m VS 5c *
R.Anderson, 10 Jul 2009
Boulder up a hairline crack right of the edge, step left and climb the crack.

Tiny-tot 8m VS 4c *
R.Anderson, 10 Jul 2009
The wall just right of the hairline crack, then the right-hand crack.

Short-lived 8m VS 5a *
R.Anderson, 10 Jul 2009
Climb to a rock scar and finish up the crack above.

Micro-domo 10m HVS 5b **
R.Anderson, 10 Jul 2009
The thin crack up the middle of the domed right-hand portion of the craglet; great rock and good moves but over far too soon.

DRUIM MÒR

Crùlabhig

(NB 1705 3348) Alt 20m W facing Map opposite Diagram p136

This superb little inland crag is located at the northern end of the ridge of Druim Mor, a mere 100m to the south of the road about 1km before the bridge over to Bernera. It is possible to just squeeze a car off the road without blocking the gate into the field in front of the crag. There is also some pleasant bouldering with a flat grass landing. Due to the sheltered location and the steepness of the crag it is often possible to climb here in adverse sea and weather conditions, making it a most useful venue.

Descent: By a short corner and grassy ramp on the left.

1 Lard of the Pies 15m HVS 5a **
P.Woodhouse and party, 4 Jun 2002
The clean groove and overhang at the left end of the crag. Trend left up the steep lower wall and climb the groove direct to pass the top overhang using a 'bucket' on the left. Good sustained climbing, slightly marred by the exit through thick reed grass, although a sling and crab on the tree facilitates a lower-off.

2 All Hail King Silly 20m E6 6c ***
M.Garthwaite, R.Anderson, 1 Jun 2017
Start as for Lard of the Pies then go up and right to black rock then up left and continue above, to a finish up Mixed Blessing.

3 Chasing Tails 20m E4 6a/b **
R.Anderson, 14 Jul 2006
Start at a short handrail below the steepest bit of the crag. Gain a break then another break and move up to a crack. Traverse right and climb the corner to surmount the roof, the right-hand of two possibilities perhaps being best. Finish up the flange in the headwall.

4 Mixed Blessing 25m E2 5b **
R.Anderson, N.Morrison, W.Moir, M.Atkins, P.Allen, 9 Aug 2006
A good hybrid taking the lower section of The Cruel Crack then the central corner of Chasing Tails before traversing left beneath the roof to cross its left end.

5 The Cruel Crack 20m E2 5c ***
R.Anderson, C.Anderson, 13 Jul 2006
The striking central crack is gained by the corner; cruel by name, cruel by nature!

6 Double or Quits 20m E3 6a **
R.Anderson, M.Garthwaite, 27 Jun 2007
Climb the crack to the right of The Cruel Crack then tackle the bulge and short, roofed corner to exit out left and finish up the wall above.

7 Crimpology 20m E5 6b **
M.Garthwaite, R.Anderson, 27 Jun 2007
Ascend the wall right of Double or Quits, then go left to place gear in that route before moving right to an undercut and making some trying moves to reach holds. A finger traverse leads right to where the bulge can be overcome to reach the short upper wall.

Cruel Crack (E2) Neil Morrison (photo Rab Anderson)

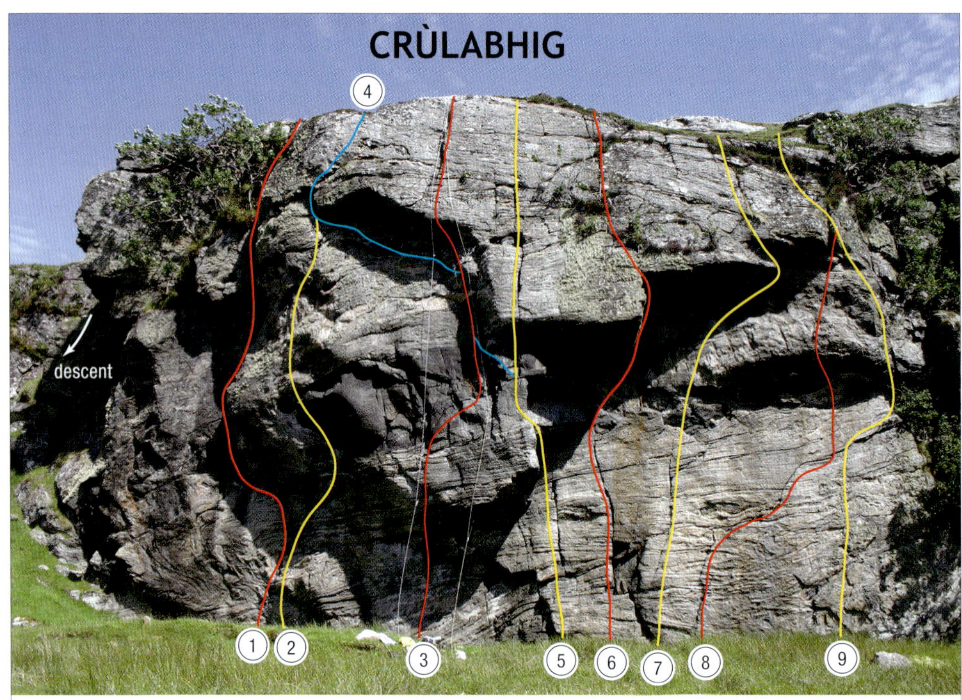

1. Lard of the Pies	HVS 5a **	4. Mixed Blessing	E2 5b **	7. Crimpology	E5 6b **
2. All Hail King Silly	E6 6c ***	5. The Cruel Crack	E2 5c ***	8. Gneiss to See You...	E6 6b ***
3. Chasing Tails	E4 6a/b **	6. Double or Quits	E3 6a **	9. Southern Breeze	E1 5c *

8 Gneiss To See You, To See You Gneiss 20m E6 6b ****

M.Garthwaite, R.Anderson, 3 Jun 2017

Climb a crack up and right, stand in the break and power through the bulge to finish up the groove of Southern Breeze.

9 Southern Breeze 20m E1 5c *

R.Anderson, C.Anderson, 4 Aug 2007

At the right end of the wall, climb past a plaque to a horizontal break then move along this to the right edge of the wall. Climb the crack then move left to finish up a short groove and wall.

The next three climbs are about 100m further right; the first two start just left of a grassy chimney-gully.

Descent: By a rightwards traverse down grassy ledges.

10 The Major's Reserve 20m E1 5b *

R.Anderson, M.Garthwaite, 3 Jun 2017

Start as for Wild Orchid and continue straight up by ledges to a higher ramp. Move up and right then swing out right and cross the headwall to finish up Wild Orchid.

11 Wild Orchid 20m E1 5b **

R.Anderson, M.Garthwaite, 1 Jun 2017

Just left of the grassy chimney-gully gain a short ramp and climb this. Awkwardly move up to the roof (micro cams) and climb the fine crack in the headwall to finish up a recess.

12 Letterbox Wall 10m HVS 5b *

C.Barnes, 29 Aug 2015

Just around the edge to the right of the chimney-gully, climb a short wall with two obvious letterbox-like breaks at one-third and two-thirds height.

TOBSON

Geòdha Mòr

(NB 1329 3856) Non-tidal W facing
Map opposite Diagram p138

This small and accessible geo lies towards the southern end of the north-west tip of Great Bernera. On the north side of the geo there is a good and finely situated wall. Although an approach can be made from Bostadh to the north, the road end at Tobson is much closer.

Directions: Just beyond Breacleite, turn off left and follow the road to its end at Tobson by a small beach. Park off the road and take care not to block the turning area, which is used by vehicles including the local bus.

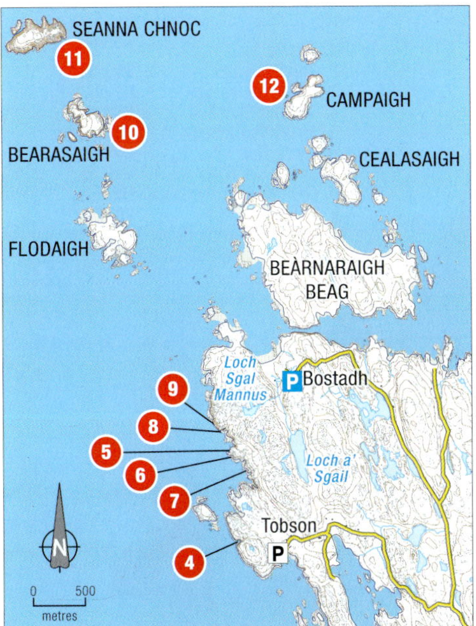

GREAT BERNERA

BERNERA ISLANDS

* www.smc.org.uk/publications/climbing/OuterHebrides

Approach: Follow the stone wall south around the last house, crossing a wooden fence and going through a gate in another fence behind the house. Climb north-west around the highpoint to reach the geo (10min).

Descent: The first two routes are in the geo itself, which can be gained by an easy gully to reach a ledge above sea-level.

Fear of Rejection 15m VS 4c
P.Woodhouse, K.Archer, 28 May 2001
Climb the left-facing corner just right of the overhangs and finish up the face; well protected.

Fresh Westerly 15m VS 5a
P.Woodhouse, K.Archer, 31 May 2001
The crack and arete on the face just right of the previous route.

The next climbs lie to the north of the geo, on the splendid seaward face, where the rock is solid and well cracked.

Descent: About 100m to the north of the geo locate the head of a gully then drop down to the start of the wall. The wall can be viewed from a promontory in front of its north end. A ramp descends southwards beneath the wall to a cave almost at sea-level. A few routes climb easy ground below the top of the ramp.

1 Eeezie 10m D
R.Anderson, C.Anderson, 2 Apr 2008
Short crack and steps left of The Struggler.

2 The Struggler 18m HVS 5a *
P.Woodhouse, K.Archer, 28 May 2001
Start below the ramp and climb easy rock to it, then step up left to the base of a shallow corner. The corner leads to a block overlap where good protection can be arranged before awkward moves gain the top of the block and the short finishing crack.

3 Bernera Five-Oh 15m E1 5b *
R.Anderson, C.Anderson, 2 Apr 2008
An eliminate starting off the ramp in the centre of the wall right of The Struggler. Climb up and left to an awkward finish up thin cracks in the left edge; moving right below these allows an easier finish to be made adjacent to the next climb.

4 Will the Real Eric Jones Please Stand Up 18m HVS 5a **
K.Archer, P.Woodhouse, 28 May 2001
The overlap and left-trending groove opposite the end of the viewing promontory and above the large fallen blocks. Start beneath the ramp, climb to it, then pull over the overlap to gain the groove and follow this before moving slightly left onto the face to make a precarious mantel to finish. A gritstone classic!

5 Tobson's Choice 18m HVS 5a *
K.Archer, P.Woodhouse, 28 May 2001
Climbs around the obvious big roof. Climb easy ground to the ramp then take the steep wall to the right of Eric Jones to reach the roof. Pass this on the left and go up to the bottom of a steep corner which is followed to the top.

6 Prime Cut 15m HVS 5a **
R.Anderson, C.Anderson, 17 Jul 2008
Start beneath the big roof then climb up and around its right side. Either finish directly, or traverse left to finish up a groove.

7 Below the Salt 18m HVS 5a *
K.Archer, A.Norton, 26 Jul 2001
Start from the right edge of a small cave near the foot of the descent ramp. Gain the wall above the cave, traverse left into a shallow corner, then go around this and up to the obvious flake-line which is followed to the top.

8 Geo-graphically Gifted 15m HVS 5b **
K.Archer, A.Norton, 26 Jul 2001
Go up to the base of a niche then climb this and a groove to beneath the overhang. Pull directly over this on surprising holds to a ledge then to the top.

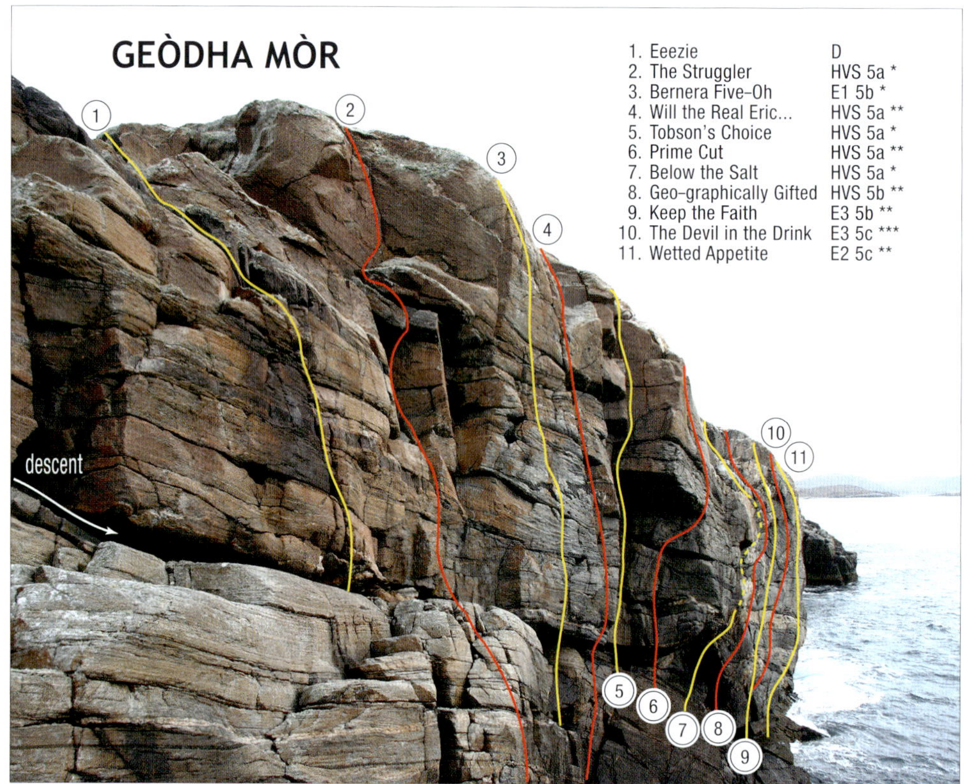

9 Keep the Faith 15m E3 5b **
R.Anderson, C.Anderson, 17 Jul 2008
The left edge of the fine wall. Pull over the roof some 2m right of Geo-graphically Gifted and climb the quartzy wall to steeper moves over a small roof where the temptation to step left should be avoided, for an awkward rounded finish.

10 The Devil in the Drink 15m E3 5c ***
R.Anderson, C.Anderson, 8 Jul 2009
The centre of the wall. Pull over the roof as for Keep the Faith then move up and right to a ledge before climbing the steep upper section directly above a flake feature and past two horizontal breaks.

11 Wetted Appetite 15m E2 5c **
R.Anderson, C.Anderson, 8 Jul 2009
The right edge of the wall. Start beneath the arete then pull onto a shelf beneath an overhang and move awkwardly left into a groove. Climb this to a break then gain the break above and finish directly.

The next two climbs lie to the south towards the seaward end of the geo, in a slabby bay around the edge from the main wall. The rock is a little friable. At low tide and calm seas it is possible to traverse in under the main wall, otherwise access is by abseil to ledges above the sea.

Living in Colour Laughing out Loud 15m HVS 5a
K.Archer, P.Woodhouse, 31 May 2001
Traverse left to the arete, then climb a thin crack and the slab above.

Dogs Dinner 15m VS 4b
K.Archer, P.Woodhouse, 31 May 2001
Climb straight up from the ledges, initially following a crack, then from break to break.

The next route is on the second small slab to the south, reached by abseil down a corner to ledges.

A Fiver in the Fickle Hand of Fate 18m VS 4b
K.Archer, S.Armstrong, 3 Jun 2002
The right-hand crack-line. Step left to the crack and follow it to the top.

The final climb lies just around and into the geo where there is a pedestal.

Say Aye tae a Pie 8m VS 5a
K.Archer, A.Norton, 26 Jul 2001
From the pedestal, climb the slab on the right before moving back left to pull onto the upper face by an interesting move.

RUBHA CUINISH

This is the headland which forms the north-west tip of Great Bernera. The climbing lies on the southern side of the highpoint (c50m) and is approached from the road end overlooking the beautifully situated sands of Tràigh Bostadh.

Directions: Just beyond Breaclete, pass the turnoff to Tobson and continue straight on then curve round to the car park at the road-end above the beach at Bostadh. There are public toilets here, a cemetery and an Iron Age village where one of the dwellings has been reconstructed.

Geòdha Mòr Shlèibhte (Creag Liam)

(NB 1328 3942) Partially Tidal NW facing
Map p137 Diagram p140

Towards the north-west tip of Bernera, this superb little headland juts out into Loch Ròg, a short walk from the road-end at Bostadh. The name is a bit of a mouthful and it has also been called Creag Liam. There are a number of outstanding climbs and deep water solos here in a tremendous setting.

Approach: Contour south-west across the hillside above the reconstructed dwelling, cross the burn and head uphill beside a small side burn to reach Loch Sgal Mannus. Follow the south side and a short distance beyond the loch, drop down south-west towards the obvious headland. Most of the climbs are out on the far tip where there is a yellow coloured lichenous promontory between two corners (1km, 20min).

Descent: Climbs towards the landward side are reached directly by abseil to the lowest convenient ledge. For climbs towards the seaward end, at lower states of the tide, it is possible to scramble to the base of the cliff from the seaward tip and traverse back along. The alternative is to abseil in, down one or other of the corners taken by Na Fir Clis and Body and Soul, which lie either side of the promontory.

Climbs are described from the land out to the seaward tip. The fabulous arete of Mega Tsunami is obvious and delineates the two main areas of the cliff. To the left of this arete the cliff is darker and is comprised of a series of grooves and aretes dropping into the sea. Shags nest on the inland part of the cliff and in the cave at the back of the geo.

1 Minor ripples 20m XS 5b (S3) *
D.Laing (DWS), 18 Jun 2007
Towards the left end of the cliff is an obvious hanging slab with a crack splitting its centre. Gain the slab via a slight arete and overlap then climb the slab to finally finish via a wacky overlap.

To the right is a buttress with an A-shaped roofed niche at its top, taken by the next two climbs.

2 Focus 20m XS 5b (F6a) (S3) **
J.Lines (DWS), 18 Jun 2007
Take the left-hand crack-line into the left edge of the A shaped niche, step up and left onto a ledge, then either finish direct via one hard move or dangerously traverse left to gain the top (XXS 5b; S3+).
Variation: **2a Right-hand Finish XS 5c (S1/2) ****
J.Lines (DWS), 14 Jun 2007
A good and safer deep water solo finish. Below the A-shaped niche, take the obvious hand-traverse right to finish as for Shockwaves Right-hand.

3 Shockwaves 20m XS 5c (S2/3) ***
J.Lines (DWS), 14 Jun 2007
From the right edge of the buttress, climb the crimpy arete (crux) to gain a small ledge, continue to the base of the A-shaped niche. Tackle the right edge of this to gain some flat jugs on the right wall and swing round the ludicrous arete in a mind boggling position to finish.
Variation: **3a Right-hand Finish XS 5c (S1/2) ****
J.Lines (DWS), 14 Jun 2007
A safer deep water solo. Traverse right at the base of the A-shaped niche to gain ledges.

4 Tremors 25m F6c (S2) *
J.Lines (DWS), 20 Jun 2012
The buttress between Shockwaves and Mini Tsunami. Climb a vertical wall, moving left at the top to beneath a slight tapering ramp which is climbed to a ledge. Using sidepulls, move out left over the void and use the hanging prow to gain the ledge above. Scramble out easily on the left.

5 Pillar Groove 25m VS 4c
A.Cunningham, F.Macleod, 18 May 1999
The third open groove to the left of the Mega Tsunami arete has a huge, tapered block set into its left side. Start directly below the block, from a small black ledge above the undercut base. Climb around the right side of the block then chimney into the crack on the right to finish.

6 Mini Tsunami 25m XS 4a (S2) **
J.Lines (DWS), 18 Jun 2007
The curving stepped arete just left of the groove of High Pressure is a delight; finish slightly right up a groove and slot.

7 High Pressure 25m VS 4b
A.Cunningham, F.Macleod, 18 May 1999
A line up the left side of the first groove left of the arete of Mega Tsunami. From a small grey ramp stance, climb a line of flake-cracks and ledges.

8 Aftershock 25m F7a+ (S2) **
J.Lines (DWS), 20 Jun 2012
The left wall of the Mega Tsunami arete. Climb the wall just left of the arete to a notch at the overlap. Layback the crack-line to a vague quartz-like seam then find a hidden finger slot on the right and cross through for a good flat hold. Slap up the hanging rib to gain a pink boss hold and continue up the line, on hidden slots, which bends slightly into a blocky finishing groove.

The arete taken by Mega Tsunami is obvious. Westwards towards the tip from here, the next section of cliff is a recessed bay formed between two right-angled corners, then the yellow-coloured lichenous promontory on the cliff-top beyond which are two further corners.

9 Mega Tsunami 30m E6 6a (S2) ***

D.Cuthbertson, J.George, 16 Jun 2001; J. Lines (DWS), Jun 2007

The ships prow of an arete gives a superb climb and an amazing deep water solo. Fails a four star rating as a rest is possible by going out right (and then returning) before the steep final prow is climbed. From the foot of Roag Rage, traverse left along the lower of two breaks to reach a groove beneath an overhang in the arete. Climb up to and over the overhang to the base of a short, steep, smooth open groove. Climb this to a large hold out on the right, step back left and ascend a groove in the arete to an undercut flake. The next section kicks out to provide a strenuous finale up the thin discontinuous crack just right of the prow.

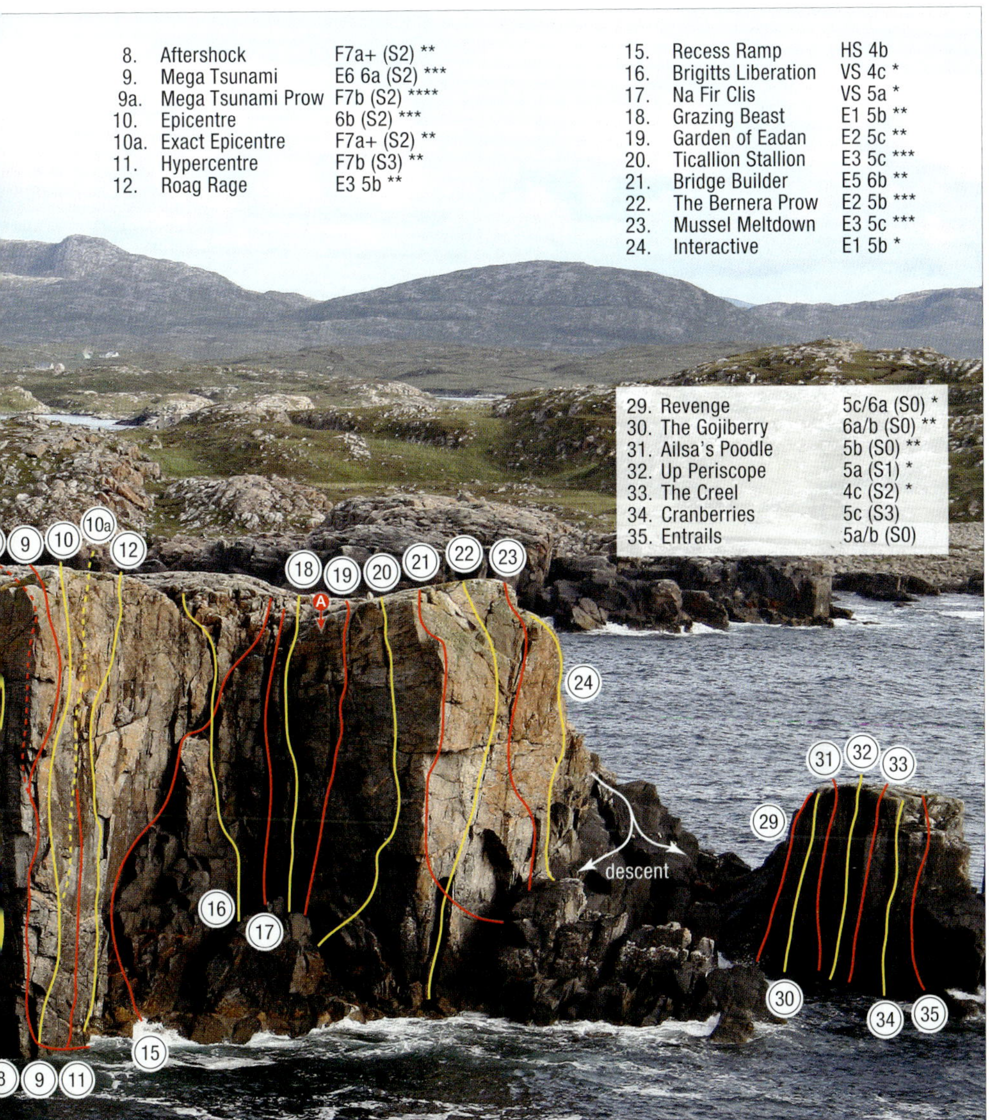

Variation: **9a Mega Tsunami Prow Finish 30m F7b (S2) ******
J.Lines (DWS), 20 Jun 2012
A brilliant world class DWS. Climb Mega Tsunami to the jug come sidepull where that route goes up the pocketed crack on the right. Reach left around the prow and climb the underside of this via a series of compression moves to the break. Move onto the right side and then back to finish on the very prow.

10 Epicentre 25m XS 6b (S2) ***
J.Lines (DWS), 18 Jun 2007
This superb route threads its way up the wall to the right of the arete. Traverse leftwards to the seat rest at the base of Mega Tsunami. Climb up and rightwards to an impasse, crimp up and snatch leftwards to gain a small ledge (crux S0/1). Make a tricky mantel onto it, then thin moves up the wall to gain better holds leading up right. Take the obvious handrail leftwards and follow the slight groove just right of the arete to the top.

Mega Tsunami (E6) Ferdia Earle
(photo Malcolm Scott)

Variation: **10a Exact Epicentre 25m F7a+ (S2) ****
J.Lines (DWS), 20 Jun 2012
A direct on Epicentre. Where that route goes left at the impasse, go up and undercut the overlap making hard moves to gain a flat hold in the blank wall. Make a further hard move using a slot on the right to gain a flake hold above. Follow flakes more easily up and right to a ledge and an easy groove to the top.

11 Hypercentre 25m F7b (S3) **
J.Lines (DWS), 20 Jun 2012
The wall right of Epicentre. Traverse in from the right to gain the centre of the wall. Climb easily to a big pink pocket where a thin seam leads to an overlap where it turns into a tiny corner. Climb just left of the seam to layback off the corner to reach small holds on the wall above. Flake holds soon appear and are followed to the final easy groove as for Exact Epicentre.

12 Roag Rage 25m E3 5b **
R.Anderson, C.Anderson, 4 Jul 2000
The crack up the right side of the smooth wall right of Mega Tsunami. Start at the base of the crack at low tide. Climb the crack to its top, stand up and stretch leftwards for holds and continue to ledges. The thin continuation crack immediately left of the edge provides a fine finish.

13 The Bostadh Strangler 25m E2 5c ***
R.Anderson, C.Anderson, 4 Jul 2000
The overhung stepped corner and wide crack left of the main corner.

14 Great Northern 20m HVS 5a **
A.Cunningham, F.Macleod, 7 Apr 1998
The right-angled corner-crack in the landward side of the recessed bay.

15 Recess Ramp 20m HS 4b
A.Cunningham, F.Macleod, 18 May 1999
Start right of the corner and climb a stepped diagonal line rightwards to finish at the top of the right-hand corner.

16 Brigitts Liberation 20m VS 4c *
B.Hogge, J.Cunningham, A.Cunningham, 15 Sep 1996
Start just left of the right-hand corner and climb a left-trending stepped black dyke to finish through an awkward slot in the same line.

17 Na Fir Clis 15m VS 5a *
F.Macleod, A.Cunningham, 7 Apr 1998
The right-angled corner at the seaward side of the recessed bay.

18 Grazing Beast 20m E1 5b **
A.Cunningham, F.Macleod, 7 Apr 1998
To the right of the corner, climb a steep black crack then an awkward curving jam crack to finish.

19 Garden of Eadan 20m E2 5c **
A.Cunningham, L.Hughes, 18 May 1998
The fine, steep crack up the middle of the wall.

20 Ticallion Stallion 20m E3 5c ***
L.Hughes, A.Cunningham, 11 May 1998
The superb crack-line, just before the right edge. Climb up to the left of the undercut crack and move rightwards to gain it at a small roof.

21 Bridge Builder 20m E5 6b **
D.MacLeod, T.Emmett, 2 Jun 1010
The arete left of The Bernera Prow is gained by a logical approach from the right (especially in high seas). Start right of the crack of The Bernera Prow. Move leftwards across the wall on big holds and go up to a bulge on the arete. Climb over this, just right of the arete (crux) to better holds above.

22 The Bernera Prow 20m E2 5b ***
A.Cunningham, L.Hughes, 11 May 1998
The overhanging crack in the front of the promontory, started from the left corner of the prow. Climb the groove to the roof, swing right into the crack and jam wildly up this to the top.

23 Mussel Meltdown 20m E3 5c ***
R.Anderson, M.Garthwaite, 29 Jun 2007
The wall and thin crack right of The Bernera Prow. Start at the high point of the ridge, at the foot of the arete of Interactive. Make difficult moves up, then left above the roof to gain the crack and climb this to the top.

24 Interactive 15m E1 5b *
A.Cunningham, L.Hughes, 11 May 1998
Awkward cracks and shallow corners in the left arete of the obvious corner. Start at the top of the ridge below the arete and swing right into the first crack.

25 Deepest Blue 15m E2 5c *
S.Muir, D.MacLeod, Jun 2005
A line up the right side of the arete.

26 Body and Soul 20m VS 4c **
A.Cunningham, B.Hogge, J.Cunningham, 15 Sep 1996
The right-facing corner-crack.

27 Barnacle Butter 20m E4 5c ***
M.Garthwaite, R.Anderson, 29 Jun 2007
The steep wall between the two corners. Climb up and left to holds, then up right into a scooped area before moving up left. Continue above across breaks to finish centrally.

28 Conception Corner 20m VS 4c **
A.Cunningham, B.Hogge, J.Cunningham, 15 Sep 1996
The corner-crack at the seaward end.

Leumadair Mòr

The Submarine

Tidal NE facing Diagram p141

The headland tip of Geòdha Mòr Shlèibhte features a short, east-facing vertical wall which drops into a trench, pretty much opposite Conception Corner. This hosts a number of short but good and usually safe, deep water solos. Aptly, a leumadair is a dolphin.

Descent: At the southern, or left end, is a kind of white flake which is the start of the traverse (5b *), used to access the routes. The traverse towards the north end can be climbed at either high or low water; the right-hand routes can also be accessed from the north.

29 Revenge 8m XS 5c/6a (S0) *
J.Lines (DWS), 14 Jun 2007
The leftmost non-line on the face relents to a few lovely tenuous moves.

30 The Gojiberry 10m XS 6a/b (S0) **
J.Lines (DWS), 14 Jun 2007
The thin crack gives brilliant but surprisingly difficult moves.

31 Ailsa's Poodle 10m XS 5b (S0) **
J.Lines (DWS), 14 Jun 2007
The central crack-line is a superb DWS experience.

32 Up Periscope 10m XS 5a (S1) *
J.Lines (DWS), 14 Jun 2007
The ragged cracks to the right give another enjoyable climb; finish slightly left.

33 The Creel 10m XS 4c (S2) *
J.Lines (DWS), 14 Jun 2007
The central groove, but be careful with the reef at the bottom.

34 Cranberries 10m XS 5c (S3)
J.Lines (DWS), 14 Jun 2007
The blunt arete to the right, climbed on its left side is slightly eliminate and not one to fall off. You have been warned!

35 Entrails 10m XS 5a/b (S0)
J.Lines (DWS), 14 Jun 2007
A thin crack low down is climbed by one good move to a ledge, before taking the short wall above just left of the arete. Can be gained easily from the right; low to mid tide is a necessity.

Slanting Geòdha

(NB 1331 3935) Tidal S & W facing Map p137

This is the small geo some 60m to the south of Geòdha Mòr Shlèibhte, behind its seaward tip, confusingly named Geòdh' Shlèibhte on maps. There is a south facing wall and a west-facing wall with a corner formed in the angle between the two.

Descent: The south facing wall can be easily accessed by descending a ramp down the left side and the west facing wall can be accessed by scrambling down and traversing in from the seaward tip on the right. Routes are described left to right, with the first two starting from the south-facing, or left-hand wall.

Wee Gem 15m VD *
R.Anderson, C.Anderson, 13 Jul 2000
At the base of the corner between the two walls is a deep recess with a wide crack coming out its left side to run up the slabby left wall. Climb the slabby left wall of the corner via the deep recess and the wide crack.

Right On 15m E1 5b **
R.Anderson, C.Anderson, 13 Jul 2000
The right side of the corner via the steep crack and blocky holds, then step left to climb the short headwall.

The west-facing wall has a mini Cioch-shaped block at its base with at least four diagonal lines slanting right to left up the wall from the block.

A Different Slant 20m E1 5b **
R.Anderson, C.Anderson, 13 Jul 2000
Moving left from the block, this is the second of the four diagonal lines. From the base of the Cioch-shaped block step down left past two flat topped spikes to a third pointed spike and climb the diagonal crack running leftwards up the wall.

Tir nan Og 20m E1 5b *
A.Cunningham, F.Macleod, 24 Apr 1998
Hand-traverse the obvious diagonal break that starts from the top of the Cioch-shaped block.

S.A.M.S Slab

(NB 1341 3922) Tidal SW facing Map p137

Some 300m south of Geòdha Mòr Shlèibhte there is a slab with an obvious crack up it; this can be descended to its right.

The Iranian Problem 10m VS 4c *
D.Laing, 19 Jun 2007
The left-hand side of the slab via a crack-line.

S.A.M.S 10m VD
D.Laing, 19 Jun 2007
The crack up the centre of the slab.
There are another two climbs a short distance to the right (south), left of a wall with two prominent crack-lines, either on the ridge of rock which faces S.A.M.S Slab or in the geo formed on the other side.

Shrimp Arete 10m VS 4b **
D.Laing, 19 Jun 2007
Climb the left-hand arete of the wall on its right-hand side.

Talking to Shrimps 10m VS 4c
D.Laing, 19 Jun 2007
Climb the obvious corner on the right-hand side of the wall.

Creag Rebridh and Geòdha nam Bàn

(NB 1318 3961) Tidal W facing Map p137

To the north of Geòdha Mòr Shlèibhte there is a domed promontory a few hundred metres to the south-west of the cairned highpoint (c50m) of the Rubha Cuinish headland. On the Geòdha Mòr Shlèibhte side, a long and narrow, square-cut geo lies hard in against the base of the slope at the southern end of this domed area; from here the cliffs run northwards.

Approach: As for Geòdha Mòr Shlèibhte to Loch Sgall Mannus, then head west to a cairn on top of the domed area (15min).

The climbing is described right to left and the first routes are on the south-facing wall at the entrance to Geòdha nam Bàn, a narrow square-cut geo, pretty much running east to west to form the southern extremity of Creag Rebridh. The wall is well seen from the top of Geòdha Mòr Shlèibhte and in certain light, the golden brown coloured face that forms the seaward end resembles a lion's face.

Descent: By abseil from the seaward end; a semiburied block in a hollow of grass at the top of the easy-angled slabs can be used as an anchor. Abseiling into the entrance of the geo gains a narrow tapering ledge, rising from left to right, below the first three climbs. Slanting down a crack and groove gains the other two climbs.

Out of the Box 20m E1 5c *
K.Archer, A.Norton, 30 May 2005
Start at the right end of the narrow tapering ledge. Climb a short overhanging wall via a hard mantelshelf, continue up before moving right to finish up a short corner.

Simba 12m XS 5c (S2) **
J.Lines (DWS), 17 Jun 2007
Start part way along the ledge, just to the right of a thin seam. Launch up and left on finger jugs (don't fall here), until a move back right gains a deep pocket. Climb up past an overlap and flake, veering slightly leftwards. Safer the higher one goes because of the ledge.

Banana Crack 12m XS 5b (S1) **
D.Laing (DWS), 19 Jun 2007
Step left off the left end of the ledge and pull into a pod groove then climb it and continue up the diagonal crack in the upper wall.

The next two climbs are located to the left of the entrance to the geo, on the change of aspect where the cliff runs northwards and there is an obvious large open groove.

To the Max 20m HVS 5b *
A.Cunningham, S.Howie, 19 May 1999
On the abseil, go down the right side of the groove (facing in) to gain a ledge above barnacle level. Climb stepped grooves heading for a seemingly wide crack through the top bulge. Reach over the bulge to discover there is no crack, so pull through the bulge leftwards onto the easy slab to finish.

Bostadh Groove 20m VS 4c **
A.Cunningham, S.Howie, 19 May 1999
Abseil through a slot in the edge and down the line of the route to barnacled rock at low tide, or a ledge on the right if the sea threatens. Follow the groove direct.

The next routes are some 25m to the north and climb the full height of the cliff.

Descent: Go down a vague gully or depression on the south side of the cairned highpoint. This leads to a slab which is traversed leftwards (facing in) to a short corner. Reverse the corner to the top of a ramp. There are two grooves here, to the right of a black arete.

Return of the Absent Friend 40m HVS *
A.Norton, K.Archer (alt), 24 Jul 2001
The prominent left-hand chimney-groove.
1. 20m 5a Climb the groove to a ledge at its top. Take the left-hand layback crack to a large ledge.
2. 20m 4c The slab is ascended using a huge undercut flake to a corner. Climb this and a short layback to finish.

The Moral Low Ground 40m HVS 5a
N.McAllister, P.Woodhouse, 3 Jun 2002
The right-hand groove. From a notch above the platform, follow the groove through an overlap to a ledge. Climb the obvious groove and another overlap (hard but safe), then the wall above trending right.

Part Time Potato Peeler 40m HVS 5a
K.Archer, S.Armstrong, 3 Jun 2002
Climb the steep wall immediately right of The Moral Low Ground to a fierce looking horizontal jamming crack. Follow this to the right arete and pull around this to share a stance with The Moral Low Ground. Take the slab and blocky arete above.

Banking On It 18m VS 4c *
F.Fotheringham, S.Howie, Jul 1997
This climbs the upper tier, gained from the grassy depression and slabby ground to the right. One of the above routes may well use it as a second pitch. Climb an open twisting groove and crack-line bounding the right of the steep prow. Finish via an awkward crack in the steepening before the final easy slabs.

The next climbs are further left, to the north.

Bosta'in 40m VS *
K.Archer, A.Norton, 27 Jul 2001
From the start of Return of the Absent Friend, descend another short corner to gain sea-level ledges. Walk left and the climb starts in the centre of the wall, just right of a rock pool.
1. 25m 4c Step onto the wall and gain a left-rising ramp. Follow this then go up a corner to a ledge beneath an overhang.
2. 15m 4b Climb the chimney and corner at the back of the stance.

Absence Makes the Heart... 40m HVS
K.Archer, A.Norton, 30 May 2005
1. 25m 5a From the overhung slabs left of Bosta'in, traverse into the corner where it abuts the main face and climb this until it is possible to hand-traverse a small ledge, then continue up a corner to reach the stance of Bosta'in
2. 15m 4b Pitch 2 of Bosta'in.

The next route is on the north side of the highpoint. Descend stepped ground and a slabby ramp leftwards until able to cut back right under a short crag above high tide level.

Short Changed 10m HVS 5a *
F.Fotheringham, S.Howie, Jul 1997
Climb a steep right-angled corner-crack.

Garenin (Na Gearrannan)

Maps p19 & right

This section covers the coastline to the south-west then to north of the hamlet of Garenin **(NB 194 442)** near Carloway. There is an isolated climb on a small inland cliff at Tolsta Chaolais some 3 miles (5km) to the south of Carloway, which is described at the end of this section.

Directions: Coming from Uig and the south, follow the A858 past Callanish (Calanais) and the turn-offs to Tolastadh a' Chaolais to reach Carloway (Càrlabhagh) then turn left to Garenin (Na Gearrannan).

Coming from Stornoway, take the A857 north to Barvas (Barabhas) on the west coast, then the A858 southwards, passing through Bragar and Shawbost (Siabost). Pass the turn-offs to Dalbeg and Dalmore to reach Carloway then turn right to Garenin.

Continue past the Blue Pig Studio (gallery cafe with home baking) to the road end where there is a car park at a restored Blackhouse Village with a hostel, cafe and public toilets.

GARENIN SOUTH-WEST

There are two climbing areas on the headlands of Rubha Eacleit and Rubha Talanish. Beyond this, Àird Laimisiadair with its lighthouse marks the entrance to Loch Ròg, opposite the Bernera Islands.

RUBHA EACLEIT

(NB 1859 4396) Non-tidal & Tidal NW & SW facing Map above

This small headland is the second encountered to the south-west of Na Gearrannan.

Approach: Go through a gate, walk downhill through the Blackhouse Village then exit by another gate and cross the boulder beach in the bay overlooking Loch Garenin. On the other side, go through a gate then head uphill south-westwards and cut across the neck behind the bigger headland of Rubha nan Gearranan. Now drop down past the head of Geòdha a' Mhaide to cross a fence by a stile then go up the short rise to the headland of Rubha Eacleit (20min).

On the narrow north-west face, gained by a traverse in from the north, a HS at the north-west end and a good E3 5c crack up the front face have apparently been climbed. From here, at low tide in calm seas, it is possible to view the steep south-west facing continuation of this cliff, which lies around the edge to the right, overlooking Druidigeo. A barnacle-covered flat ledge runs along the base of the cliff at the left end but is unfortunately interrupted by a short leaning wall which prevents it from being traversed. The first climb takes a crack in the left side of the wall above the short leaning wall at sea-level, whilst the second takes the obvious left-facing roofed corner.

Viva Las Vaguely Arsed 25m E2 5c **
M.Garthwaite, R.Anderson, 12 July 2009
Either climb a groove up the left side of the short leaning wall from the left end of the barnacle ledge at the base of the cliff, to a slab then step right to a foothold on the lip of the leaning wall, or abseil in from up on the left to a hanging belay on the foothold. Once established, move up and right to climb the crack and corner above.

Lillylicious 25m E3 5c ***
M.Garthwaite, R.Anderson, 11 Jul 2009
At low tide and with slack water, abseil directly to the barnacle ledge at the foot of the left-facing roofed corner. A swing in is required to gain the ledge and there is gear at the foot of the corner. Climb the corner with interest over two steepenings.

RUBHA TALANISH

(NB 1796 4364) Non-tidal NE facing Map above Diagram opposite

This headland lies on the west side of the bay opposite Rubha Eacleit. The climbing is on the north-east tip just beyond a small geo. A protruding roofed buttress and the right-hand skyline arete are both prominent on the approach. A black slab lies between the two and there are some large boulders along the base of the cliff.

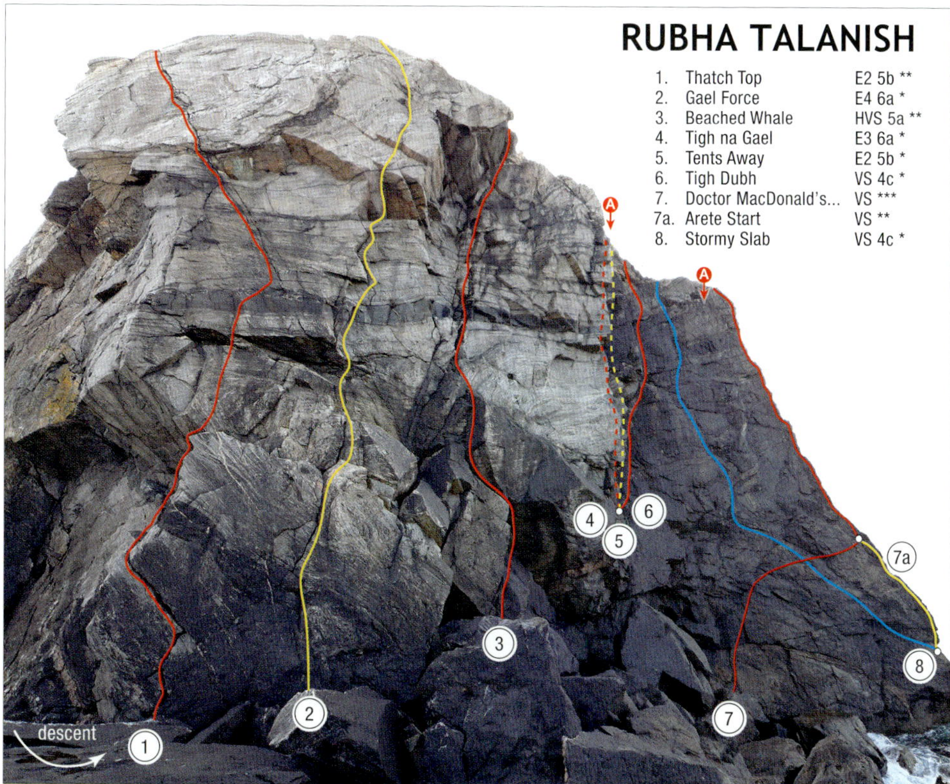

Approach: Continue around the bay from Rubha Eacleit past the end of Loch Dubh na Glaic towards the buttress on the far side of the bay. Just beyond some sheep pens, head uphill to Rubha Talanish where there is a cairn (40min). A shorter approach can be made from the road end at Borrowston (Borghastan), **(NB 189 424)**, but it is less attractive and the ground underfoot is more tedious (20min).

Descent: By abseil; either directly to the routes or into the small bay on the landward side off a boulder to go down a rubble slope followed by scrambling over boulders.

1 Thatch Top 30m E2 5b **
I.Small, A.Hume, 18 Aug 2001
The landward end of the cliff forms a buttress with a double overlap. Climb a thin crack on the front of a large flake at the base of the buttress. Cross the overlap and gain a thin diagonal crack (small wire), then follow this through a second overlap to finish up the fine headwall.

2 Gael Force 30m E4 6a *
I.Small, S.Jensen, 20 May 2007
The right edge of the buttress. Start just left of Beached Whale from the large boulders. Delicately gain a diagonal crack left of an overhung recess, then follow it to a flake crevasse and ledges. Tackle the wall above from a recess below an overlap, making bold moves out right to gain a crack leading to a sloping ledge on the arete. Surmount the overhang above on the right and follow the pocketed wall.

3 Beached Whale 30m HVS 5a **
I.Small, A.Hume, 18 Aug 2001
The large corner-line to the right; climb a steep corner and awkward diagonal crack leading left to the main corner then ascend this directly.

The next three climbs start from a ledge at the base of the corner to the right gained by abseil.

4 Tigh na Gael 25m E3 6a *
I.Small, S.Jensen, 20 May 2007
This climbs the left wall of the corner. Climb an awkward crack to gain the hanging corner left of Tents Away. Follow this then take the fine crack in the left wall, passing a bulge to finish up the widening crack.

5 Tents Away 25m E2 5b *
I.Small, A.Hume, 18 Aug 2001
Climb a steep corner and transfer left to gain the main corner-line. At the headwall, finish strenuously rightwards via a flake.

6 Tigh Dubh 25m VS 4c *
I.Small, A.Hume, 18 Aug 2001
The corner-line at the left end of the slab; there is a ledge at the base of the corner.

7 Doctor MacDonald's Farewell to Lewis 60m VS ***
M.Tighe, K.Tighe, H.Clark, 21 Jul 2000
This climbs across the black slab onto the right-bounding arete. Start from the jumble of huge boulders at the bottom of the slab, just above the high tide mark.
1. 30m Make a tricky move up the little apron slab to gain a diagonal fault-line which heads up right to join the arete, delineating the north-east and north-west faces. Belay on a small ledge in a fine position.
2. 30m Follow the arete via cracks and small corners to the top.
Variation: **7a Arete Start 35m VS ****
I.Small, A.Hume, 18 Aug 2001
Gained by abseil, the arete can be climbed in its entirety starting from a sloping ledge above the high tide mark.

8 Stormy Slab 35m VS 4c *
I.Small, A.Hume, 18 Aug 2001
Start from the sloping ledge at the base of the arete, as for the Arete Start to Doctor MacDonalds Farewell. Climb the slab to the left of the arete via grooves and a final overlap.

GARENIN NORTH
ÀIRD MHÒR

Map p146

This is the big headland and 87m highpoint to the north of Garenin. There are three climbing areas: Creag Ruadh, A' Bheirigh and Tiumpan Head

Creag Ruadh

(NB 189 447) Tidal SW facing Map p146

This is an esoteric little crag on the south-west side of the headland overlooking the bay formed by Loch Garenin. The cliff is difficult to view, even from the opposite side of the bay. Just north of a small geo (Geòdha Ruadh), three small 8 to 10m stacks lie close in by the shore, overlooked by bigger 20 to 30m cliffs. The stacks are a swimming rather than a climbing challenge, though the central one is joined to the mainland by a precarious bridge.

Lillylicious (E3, p146) Mark Garthwaite
(photo Rab Anderson)

Approach: From the Blackhouse Village, head northwards on the waymarked coastal trail towards the highpoint of Àird Mhor and after about 500m break off left and go around the head of Geòdha Ruadh to the cliffs, which are hard to see from above. Once located, the three little stacks provide a reference point.

Gneiss Little Wall 20m HVS 5b **
M.Tighe, J.Armour, Jul 1999
About 50m south of the southern stack is a fine wall reached by abseil into a little rocky alcove. It is also possible to traverse into here from Geòdha Ruadh. Go out left under a grey rock platform and pull onto the wall, which has good protection once found.

Red Slab 20m VD *
M.Tighe, A.Gillespie, Jul 1999
The fine little diagonal slab overlooked by Gneiss Little Wall and just south of South Stack.

Marine Exposure 30m VS 4c
M.Tighe, K.Tighe, 28 Aug 2000
A diagonal abseil past an overhang leads to an alcove immediately opposite the most northerly rocks of North Stack. Climb diagonally up left to the left-hand edge of an overhang. Pull through this and climb the steep wall and slab above. Good protection where it is needed on the overhang.

A' Bheirigh

(NB 187 450) Map p146

To the west of the highest point of Àird Mhòr, a prominent 64m high headland juts out into the sea. There is a fine little cliff here and it is a great place to explore.

Approach: From the Blackhouse Village, head northwards on the waymarked coastal trail. Pass Geòdha Ruadh and climb uphill almost to the Àird Mhòr highpoint before going down left to locate a line of 8m high bluffs. These have to be negotiated in descent to reach slopes leading to the neck between two impressive geos: Geòdh' an t-Seabhaig on the left and Geòdha nan Sgalag on the right. Cross the neck and climb onto A' Bheirigh (25min). This is a worthwhile walk in its own right.

On the return, or in continuing out to Tiumpan Head, a splendidly exposed sheep track cuts beneath the bluffs and above Geòdha nan Sgalag on the north side; keep an eye out for the point where this cuts back right to breach the bluffs.

The first route is a traverse line out onto the furthest north-western promontory, Gob a' Chuthail. To find the start, scramble down on the north side until the line can be seen 8 to 10m above the sea. The start is characterised by a bottomless chimney dropping into the sea.

The Gunnel 50m VD **
M.Tighe, K.Tighe, 30 Aug 2000
Follow the traverse line going gently downhill in a fine, exposed position above the sea to arrive at the neck of a little promontory jutting out to sea; the North Landing. On a calm, dry day at low tide it is possible to continue the traverse right around the headland by going down into a boulder choke and up right over a greasy keystone onto a diagonal ramp-line. Failing this, the only option for the VD climber is to reverse the traverse.

A fine crag overlooks the North Landing with two excellent routes.

Red Velvet 30m E1 5b **
M.Tighe, K.Tighe, 30 Aug 2000
The central crack and corner-line can be started via Ard Cuan, or by a short little wall immediately below the line.

Ard Cuan 50m VS 4c **
M.Tighe, K.Tighe, J.Winter, N.McCougan, 8 Jun 2004
The diagonal crack-line that goes out left from the North Landing, crossing Red Velvet low down; exciting and well protected. It might be useful to belay partway along to avoid rope drag.

On the south-west side of the headland, the cliffs are more broken with a myriad of little walls, chimneys and corners all the way down to the sea. Going down, west, from the highpoint over yellow lichenous rock, there are two diagonal ramp-lines running towards the North Landing, the upper one of which is a continuation of The Gunnel. Both ramps can be scrambled down at grades M to D. Towards the bottom of the lower ramp there is a tunnel under a boulder; the next route starts here.

The Loom 40m VD **
K.Tighe, M.Tighe, 20 Aug 2000
Go out on an exposed ledge on the wall above the tunnel and climb up to the second ramp-line where a little corner chimney-line leads to the top.

The Weaver 35m VD *
K.Tighe, M.Tighe, 30 Aug 2000
About 10m back up the ramp from the previous route, zigzag up the wall and head for a chimney in the upper part of the crag.

Tiumpan Head

(NB 1915 4535) Tidal NW facing Map p146

The headland to the north of the Àird Mhòr high point holds an excellent cliff characterised by striking pink and black banding in the near perfect gneiss. There is an unusual variety of quality climbs.

Approach: From the Blackhouse Village, follow the waymarked coastal trail to the highpoint of Àird Mhòr. Leave the trail here and descend gradually northwards for a further 300m to arrive at the headland (25min).

To help with identification there is a tiny rock islet Sgeir na h-Oishir (the Oyster Skerry) a few metres offshore. A little grassy hollow, a few metres back from the sloping, boulder strewn cliff-top provides a good base.

Routes are difficult to identify from above. The main feature to look for when peering over the edge is the big right-angled corner of Clais Mòr, which is opposite the northern end of the Oyster Skerry and has a big, smooth, black boilerplate slab on its south side. There is only one route north of Clais Mòr and climbs are described southwards from here, left to right as if facing the cliff.

Descent: By abseil. It is possible to descend black slabs to the north, if dry.

Sinuous Chimney 30m E1 5b *
M.Tighe, K.Tighe, 27 Aug 2002
The deep and elongated S-shaped chimney-cleft a few metres left of Clais Mòr. Make some steep, difficult moves up a rib on the right and layback around onto the face. This leads to somewhat easier climbing and better protection in the chimney proper.

Clais Mòr 40m E3 5c ***
M.Tighe, K.Tighe, 26 Jun 2006
The big corner-chimney gives an excellent tussle with wide, wide bridging and excellent protection.

Olive Oil 45m HVS 5b **
M.Tighe, K.Tighe, 27 Aug 2002
Start a couple of metres up Clais Mòr where a ramp goes out right across the black wall. Follow the ramp and make an airy move around the corner, difficult to protect for the second; 15m. Go up and left into a leaning recess and climb delicately up the slab to a steep exit on the left.

On the right, the next feature of the cliff is another corner, though not quite of the same proportions as the one taken by Clais Mòr. The next climb starts from a fine ledge at the bottom of this corner, just above the high tide mark.

Popeye 30m HVS 5a *
M.Tighe, I.Lee, 24 May 2001
Start from the ledge at the bottom of the corner. Step left around the corner and climb a rib for 15m before going delicately left over an overlap to reach the corner slab of Olive Oil, which is followed to the top.

English Spinach 30m E1 5b ***
M.Tighe, K.Tighe, 28 Aug 2000
The fabulous corner is climbed on near perfect rock with perfect protection.

There is an unclimbed slabby corner to the right before the crag becomes more broken and the routes a bit shorter. A number of climbs start from a big, broken ledge system 8 to 10m above the sea and they are characterised by some striking white, orange and black vertical banding.

Orange & Black 20m HVS 5a *
M.Tighe, I.Lee, G.Anderson, 24 May 2001
Between the two different colours of rock at the left side of the wall, a fine jam crack leads to a mid-way platform. The continuation of the fault-line has a crux at the top.

The Bay 20m VS 4c
M.Tighe, I.Lee, G.Anderson, 24 May 2001
Climb a shallow bay in the middle of the wall, then a tricky little black wall and short diagonal fault with a brown-white quartzy vein on the left, followed by easier ground to the top.

The Vein 20m HVS 5a
M.Tighe, K.Tighe, J.Cargill, 21 Jun 2001
The eroded out, white quartzy vein in the upper part of the cliff, just right of centre.

Black Honey 20m S 4a **
M.Tighe, K.Tighe, 30 Aug 2000
A few metres right of The Vein, climb a fault-line containing unusual rough, black, honeycombed rock.

The cliff now falls back into a big geo with a very pronounced pink and black banded cliff at the back: the Liquorice Quarry. The cliff is severely undercut at the bottom.

BEANNAN MÒR

Carragh Liath

(NB 1978 3811) Alt 25m NW facing

South of Carloway, the village of Tolsta Chaolais sits beside Loch a' Bhaile on a minor loop road and is overlooked by a broken crag on the west side of Beannan Mòr (77m), a small knoll on the west side of the A858. Approached in 10min, it provides a single sheltered line on its north end that remains relatively dry when everywhere else is wet.

Beannan Crack 10m E1 5b **
R.Jones, C.Jones, 18 Apr 2012
Climb the hanging crack, pulling out left through the roof.

Dalbeg (Dail Beag)

Maps p19 & below

This section covers the stretch of coast around Dalbeg **(NB 228 458)**, a hamlet located behind a fine beach in a bay, Bàgh Dail Beag, just off the A858 on the west coast between Carloway (Càrlabhagh) and Shawbost (Siabost).

The coastline here has been split into three: Dalbeg South, covering the cliffs between the beaches at Dalbeg and Dalmore to the south; Dalbeg and Àird Dalbeg itself (the main area overlooking the bay); and Dalbeg North, the coastline running northwards towards Rubha na Beirghe which is covered under the Shawbost section.

Directions: Coming from the south and the Uig area, follow the A858 past Callanish (Calanais) and Carloway (Càrlabhagh), pass the Dalmore turn off and turn left downhill to Dalbeg. Continue to the parking area at the road end beside the lovely lily covered Loch Dhailbeag and the fine beach in the bay, Bàgh Dhail Beag. This is about 1hr from the Uig sea-cliffs area.

Coming from Stornoway, take the A857 north to Barabhas (Barvas) on the west coast the head south on the A858 passing through Bragar and Shawbost (Siabost). Just after Loch Raoinebhat take the minor road on the right. This is some 30min from Stornoway.

Going in either direction from Dalbeg there is a waymarked coastal trail.

Dalbeg South

1.	Geòdha na Mua	p152
2.	Storm Geòdha	p152

Dalbeg

3.	Dalbeg Buttress	p152
4.	Cave Slab	p156
5.	Black Geòdha	p156
6.	Small West Wall	p158
7.	Mid West Wall & Big West Wall	p159
8.	Unnamed Geòdha	p161
9.	Preacher Geòdha	p162

Dalbeg North

10.	Solus Wall	p163
11.	Creagan Ben Guidamol	p163

Rubha Bratag

12.	Geòdha Bratag	p164

Rubha Na Beirighe

13.	Murray's Rib	p165
14.	North Side	p166
15.	North West Tip	p167

DALBEG SOUTH

Mid-way between the beaches at Dalbeg and Dalmore there is a headland with a few routes at Geòdha na Mua and Storm Geòdha.

Geòdha na Mua

(NB 2195 4585) Non-tidal E facing Map p151

A northwards running geo on the headland between Dalbeg and Dalmore.

Approach: Walk westwards from the Dalbeg parking area, cutting across the Rubha Beag headland to a bay with a boulder beach. Ascend the rise beyond to reach a wide valley with a burn and follow this down to the head of a geo with a large spire in its centre. Scramble easily down the back of the geo (15min). A northwards approach of about the same time and distance can also be made from the Dalmore car park, briefly following the coastal trail.

Prawn in the USA 40m E2 5a/b
H.Jones, G.Huxter, 24 May 1996
On the left-hand side of the geo (facing out), a large block rests against the wall. Just beyond this is a cave with a chimney rising out of its left-hand side. Start just left of the cave. Move up until it is possible to step right onto the slab above the cave. Climb up right into a corner and ascend this for 4m before moving right at a striated area onto a bulging buttress of light grey rock. Follow good holds up right to protection under a bulge. Climb directly through the bulge and go up a left-trending crack to where it becomes horizontal. Move straight up past horizontal breaks to the right edge of the pinnacle by a pink intrusion, then trend left to the top.

Storm Geòdha

(NB 2180 4590) W facing Map p151

A big cliff between the westwards projecting promontory of Rubha na h'Airde and the main headland tip to the north-east.

Approach: Head westwards from Dalbeg as for Geòdha na Mua, passing the head of that geo and Geòdh' a Gharaidh to gain the Rubha na h'Airde promontory (20min). It is about the same time and distance from Dalmore.

Descent: Abseil down easy-angled ground at Rubha na h'Airde and traverse left (north) into the bay. At the left-hand end of the bay there is a wave cut platform below the most compact area of cliff.

The Storm 50m E5 6a ***
G.Huxter, 27 May 1996
This brilliant route starts at the far end of the wave cut platform where an overhang ends in the left-hand of two cracks. Climb the crack for 15m to a ledge. Climb straight up for 3m before moving left to climb a vague flake. Move back right and go up to the notch in the overhang. Exit rightwards over this into a slabby groove and follow this to broken ground and a ledge on the right. There is an inadequate belay at the end of a 50m rope. On the first ascent a rope was left some 25m down the cliff and was used to abseil off. However, an easy traverse right of some 6m leads to the finishing traverse of the next route.

It's HVS Glen but not as we know it 50m E4 5c **
H.Jones, G.Huxter, 24 May 1996
Start from the top of a raised blocky area at the right-hand end of the platform. From the centre of this, go slightly left up a corner-groove to a good ledge beneath a down-pointing spike at 12m. The spike becomes a right-facing hanging corner. Make a few moves up a ramp on the right, then step left into the corner and layback up to a ledge. With hands on the ledge step left to the foot of a crack, then follow the crack with difficulty to a capping block. Chimney up the left-hand side, then continue more easily to a belay at horizontal cracks just below the top as the rope runs out.

DALBEG

ÀIRD DALBEG

The main climbing areas here are on the headland around the highpoint on the north side of the bay.

The first climb is actually in the bay where there are four 10-15m high sea stacks, one to the north and three to the south, which are easily accessible an hour either side of low tide. The southern stack is an easy climb up the landward face. The west and east stack are joined at the high tide mark and the western stack can be climbed by an easy wall (M) from where the stacks join. The outing can be extended to take in the western pinnacle with a downclimb (D) from the top of the stack.

The eastern stack has a cairn on its top and can be accessed by a scramble up the east side (assumed to be the line of first ascent – difficulty not known but probably no more than M/D). The western wall makes for an enjoyable outing and contains one climb.

The Day the Whale Danced 20m VS 4b
R.I.Jones, J.Sanders, 14 Jun 2004
1. Climb the wall to a large perched block, pull around this to its left and belay.
2. An easy scramble gains the top and summit cairn. Descent is by abseil from the belay at the top of the first pitch.

Dalbeg Buttress

(NB 2248 4630) Non-tidal W facing Map p151 Diagram p155

The headland on the north side of the bay is split by an obvious deep slot, which can be seen from the road. A large boulder sits prominently at the top of this. The seaward side of the slot forms a narrow buttress with

Limpet Crack (E3) Andy Turner (photo Mike Hutton)

an arch through it at the bottom. The west facing wall of this buttress overlooks a large wave cut platform and holds some fine routes on good rock.

Approach: Follow the waymarked coastal trail northwards to the top of the headland and break off left (10min).

Descent: From the slope on the seaward side, where the buttress can be seen, it is possible to scramble down a gully towards the sea before traversing right (facing in) onto easy-angled slabs; somewhat loose, exposed and scary! It is perhaps best to abseil in down the slabby corner just back from this where the left side of the cliff meets the slabs; there is a boulder just back from the edge which provides a convenient anchor.

West Wall

On the main wall, two slanting crack-lines are prominent on the left, whilst in the centre, starting at half-height, a groove runs up leftwards. An arch at the right end of the wall has two prominent right-leaning groove lines to its left.

1 Left Edge 35m VS 4c
A ramp forms a corner at the left end of the wall; climb the left edge of the ramp and finish up a short crack.

Limpet Olympics (E5) Neil McNair (photo Steve Crowe)

2 Rampling 35m VD
B.Davison, May 1989
Climb the ramp-line and stepped corner at the left end of the wall; finish carefully.

3 Damp Down 35m E3 6a
B.Davison, A.Cunningham, 24 May 1989
The lower and left-hand of the two slanting crack-lines is a bit artificial as it is possible to step down onto the ramp in a few places. Start up Rampling until it is possible to pull onto the wall using a flake. Make hard moves left along the crack under a small roof to a foothold then go up the left-hand of two cracks to a flat handhold. From this, reach right into the right-hand crack and follow this to the top.

4 Limpet Olympics 40m E5 6a **
N.McNair, K.Magog, S.Crowe, 8 Jul 2003
Starting left of Limpet Crack as for Damp Down, go up and traverse an undercut flake right to Limpet Crack. Break out right to a good jug and gear placement then climb the centre of the headwall direct.

5 Limpet Crack 40m E3 5c ****
A.Cunningham, B.Davison, 17 May 1989
An excellent climb following the compelling right-hand quartzy crack-line which runs up leftwards from the middle of the wall.

6 Flock Talk 40m E8 6c (F8a) **
D.MacLeod, Jun 2005
A hard and serious eliminate taking a fairly central line up the lovely wall of smooth rippled gneiss between Limpet Crack and Tweetie Pie Slalom. The crux is at 15m, a long way above gear and a sprinting belayer might prevent contact with the platform! Climb the first couple of moves of Limpet Crack then break out right across the wall to the large diagonal flake on Tweetie Pie Slalom; good gear, the last for a long way. Step left and climb to a rattly undercut; cams in this do not hold body weight. Step up and climb leftwards across the wall to a desperate long rockover to reach an overhead undercut. Continue left and then up to gain the good jug and gear placement on Limpet Olympics just right of Limpet Crack then climb the easier wall above as for Limpet Olympics.

7 Tweetie Pie Slalom 40m E5 6a ***
D.MacLeod, N.McNair, S.Richardson, 13 Jun 2001
This superb route starts as for Neptune a Calling to then take the logical finish and produce one of the best climbs on the wall. Follow Neptune a Calling to the large flake. Step left and climb direct just left of a shallow corner-groove to a roof. Move left under the roof into a soaring diagonal crack and follow this to the top with sustained interest and good protection.

8 Neptune a Calling 40m E5 6a *
B.Davison, A.Cunningham, 24 May 1989
Climb the blunt rib immediately to the left of Neptune to reach a small roof after 7m. Make difficult moves left

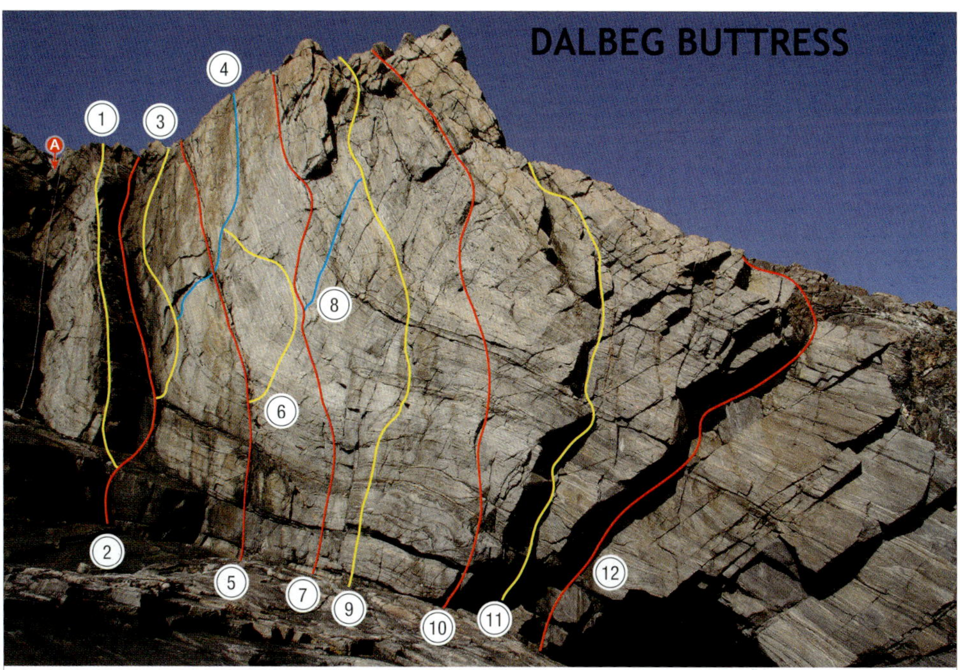

1. Left Edge	VS 4c	5. Limpet Crack	E3 5c ****	9. Neptune	E3 5c ***
2. Rampling	VD	6. Flock Talk	E8 6c **	10. Mercury and Solace	E5 6a **
3. Damp Down	E3 6a	7. Tweetie Pie Slalom	E5 6a ***	11. Wave Watcher	E4 6a *
4. Limpet Olympics	E5 6a **	8. Neptune a Calling	E5 6a *	12. Underneath The Arches	E4 6a *

to a small horizontal slot, then go left again to a vertical crack before moving up to a large flake. Now climb right into a shallow corner-groove then go up into the groove of Neptune and finish as for this.

9 Neptune 40m E3 5c ***

B.Davison, A.Cunningham, 17 May 1989

Start just right of where the wall steps out some 5m right of Limpet Crack. Climb up and step right into a left-facing flange line then follow this to gain the left-slanting groove line which starts at mid-height in the centre of the wall. Follow the grooves up leftwards to the top. A lovely sustained climb.

10 Mercury and Solace 40m E5 6a **

N.McNair, S.Richardson, D.MacLeod, 14 Jun 2001

Excellent but slightly escapable climbing up the wall between Neptune and Wave Watcher. Start on the arete left of Wave Watcher. Climb to a ledge, step up into a groove and move left to a large pocket. Climb directly above this into another groove and move left to gain a crack-line. Climb this (technical) to good holds below the start of a ramp then follow the ragged diagonal crack on the left to gain a ramp and finish directly up the cracked wall.

11 Wave Watcher 45m E4 *

B.Davison, A.Cunningham, 18 May 1989

1. 25m 6a To the left of the arch, a strenuous start enables the left-hand of the two leaning grooves to be climbed.
2. 20m 4c Finish up the left arete of the buttress.

12 Underneath The Arches 45m E4 *

A.Cunningham, B.Davison, 19 May 1989

1. 20m 6a Climb the right-hand leaning groove under the roof to a slab.
2. 25m 4c Finish up the left arete of the buttress.

13 Dalbeg Buttress 60m HVS

B.Davison, A.Cunningham, 17 May 1989

1. 15m 5b From just above the sea, lean across the gap to the right side of the arch. Using an RP1 as a hand-hold, step across the gap and heel hook to get onto a ledge; this can be very slimy and may have to be timed to miss the waves! Once on the ledge, climb up a few metres and belay below an overlap.
2. 20m 5a Go onto the front of the buttress and climb up, weaving through three overlaps, taking the top one by its left arete.
3. 25m 4a Climb the slab above, then the corner in the middle of the slab.

East Wall

On the east, or landward side of the black slot, there is an easy-angled slab with a wall facing to sea, with two corners. There are three routes on this wall.

Celtic Ray 20m VS 4b
P.Mallon, C.McCartney, 1990
The first corner.

Don't Break My Raybans 20m HVS 5a
C.McCartney, P.Mallon, 1990
The wall between the two corners, trending right to the arete to finish.

Born to Fly 20m HVS 5a
C.McCartney, P.Mallon, 1990
The second corner.

Cave Slab

Map p151

This lies just north of Dalbeg Buttress. The left end of the slab is undercut by a large cave, whereas the right side runs to a series of steep grooves below an orange coloured slab with a crack-line running up its centre.

Right Side

Descent: From the scramble descent to Dalbeg Buttress, turn right (facing out) at the top of the descent slab.

The Black Hole 45m E4 6b
B.Davison, A.Cunningham, 20 May 1989
This takes the crack in the overlap at the far left-hand end, starting by moving into a wide undercut niche. Hard moves over the next overlap lead into a short steep corner. Swing right and follow the crack in the slab left of the overhang to finish up a short corner.

Simple Jim 35m E3 6a
A.Cunningham, B.Davison, 19 May 1989
Start by hard moves up the crack 3m right of the last route. Follow the red slab up to a roof then traverse left and pull over the overlap at a quartzy vein. Move up and traverse right to the base of a steep corner and climb this past a huge block to finish leftwards.

Beam Me Up Scotty 30m E1 5b
B.Davison, A.Cunningham, 19 May 1989
Follow a left-trending black ramp-line to pull into a niche at the base of the final crack (crux) then climb the wide crack in the easy red finishing slab.

Bones 30m S 4a
B.Davison, Apr 1989
Start just right of the previous route and climb up to gain the thinner right-hand crack in the red finishing slab.

Kling on Corner 25m E1 5a
B.Davison, A.Cunningham, 19 May 1989
The smooth groove at the right side of the red slab is a bit loose in places.

Left Side

The next climbs lie above the sea at the far left end of the slab. An overlap at the right side, left of which are two grooves, gives access to the extreme left end of Cave Slab.

Descent: Walk round the headland of Cave Slab and abseil down a short seaward facing wall to a sloping platform. At low tide it is possible to reach this around the corner from the seaward end of Black Geòdha and scramble up to the foot of Warp Drive.

Warp Drive 15m HVS 5a **
B.Davison, 25 May 1989
The line of the abseil at the left end; a pocketed wall with a crack and a shallow groove running up it.

Dilithium Crystals 20m HVS 5a **
A.Cunningham, B.Davison, 21 May 1989
Climb a groove 3m to the right on good cracks and pockets.

It's No Good Captain, She's Breaking Up 20m VS 4c *
B.Davison, 25 May 1989
Start up a ramp, harder than it looks, then move into the groove left of the overlap.

Captain's Log 30m HVS 5a *
A.Cunningham, B.Davison, 21 May 1989
Cross the overlap at its lowest point, move over two small overlaps onto the top slab then head towards a groove capped by an overhang. Climb the crack on the left of this to the top.

Black Geòdha

(NB 2246 4635) Non-tidal N & W facing
Map p151 Diagram opposite

The geo north of Dalbeg Buttress is marked by two large cairns on its top. On its northern side a large easy-angled slab runs down to the sea, above which rises a steep back wall left of a sea cave. The geo is well seen from the top of this slab and routes are described from left to right starting with two climbs on the Back Wall.

Back Wall

The first climb takes a direct line up the back wall left of the cave. Its base is reached by scrambling down the easy-angled slab.

1 Parting Shot 45m E4 **
G.Huxter, K.Pyke, 13 Sep 1996
1. 20m 6a Start at the right-hand of two grooves and climb this awkwardly up and right into a hanging groove. Move up then right around an overhang and climb a groove to a fine cave belay. A fine pitch with lovely technical climbing.
2. 25m 5c Move up and left for 3m, then go straight up via a down-pointing fang into the final groove; take care with the rock.

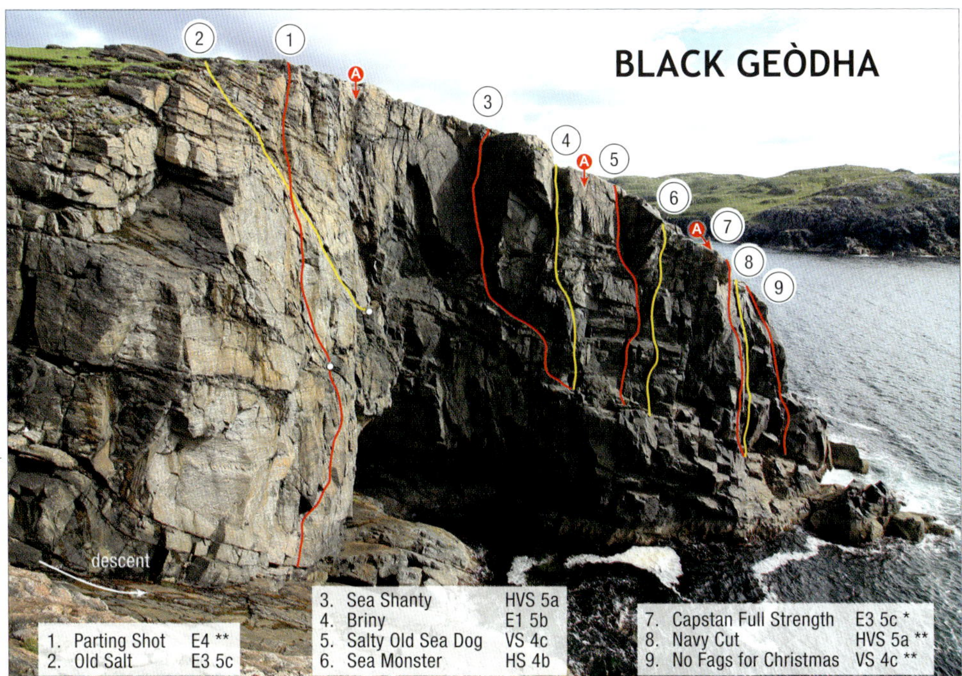

The back wall of the geo has a quartz-like crack running up it starting from a ledge halfway up it above the sea cave. Gain the ledge by a full rope length abseil with the anchor well back.

2 Old Salt 40m E3 5c
B.Davison, A.Cunningham, 22 May 1989
From the left end of the ledge, follow the quartz-like crack diagonally left for about 30m to a ledge. It would be possible to finish up a groove above here. However, the crack continues at ledge level, so step down and follow it left to its end.

South Wall

The black coloured wall on the south side of the geo. A ledge slants up leftwards beneath it from the sea and this ends in the centre by some large flakes.

Descent: Abseil down the wall right of centre and move along the slanting ledge. Climbs at the seaward end can be gained by scrambling down the ledge. An alternative is to go down the grassy slope from the top as far as possible to where a flat topped block on the left (facing out) can be threaded. This facilitates an abseil down slabby rock a short way then over the edge to the right end of the cliff at the start of the slanting ledge. This point can also be reached at low tide by climbing down from the bottom of Warp Drive on Cave Slab.

3 Sea Shanty 40m HVS 5a
A.Cunningham, B.Davison, 21 May 1989
The left-hand and largest of three prominent corners in the upper wall. From the left end of the ledge, move up and left to light-coloured rock and a ledge system trending left. From the bottom of the corner, move up and exit right at its top.

4 Briny 35m E1 5b
B.Davison, A.Cunningham, 22 May 1989
The shorter central corner. From the left end of the ledge, move up a faint blunt rib, directly below the V of the corner above, to some overhanging unstable looking blocks. Weave left through these to the start of a good crack then move into the top corner and climb it.

5 Salty Old Sea Dog 30m VS 4c
B.Davison, A.Cunningham, 22 May 1989
The left-facing right-hand corner. Start 5m right of the previous route and climb a short corner to a ledge. Go up a crack until it is possible to move left into the bottom of the corner and climb this to the top.

6 Sea Monster 30m HS 4b
A.Cunningham, B.Davison, 21 May 1989
Immediately right of the last route is a corner facing the sea. A steep start leads to a ledge at half-height, from where a crack on the left leads to a steep finish.

The next climbs lie at the far right end where the slanting ledge starts.

7 Capstan Full Strength 30m E3 5c *

R.Anderson, C.Anderson, 15 Jul 2009

The groove and slabby wall immediately left of the stepped corner of Navy Cut. Climb the groove (good but awkward to place Rock 4 high on the left in the lip of the bulge) and gain a small ledge (crux). Climb the thin crack above then move up and step left to a hairline crack. Move up again and left to another hairline crack on the edge. Now move up and right to finish up a crack. Lots of small wires and some small cams useful. A more amenable route at about E2 5b would be to climb the lower corner-crack of Navy Cut then step left onto the small ledge.

8 Navy Cut 30m E1 5b **

A.Macfarlane, D.McGimpsey, B.Marshall, 23 Jul 1989

Climb a left-facing corner-crack to a large sloping ledge then go up the corner and left around a Damoclean flake. Continue awkwardly up the groove. An alternative start gains the large sloping ledge from the right by climbing the right side of the arete right of a groove.

9 No Fags for Christmas 30m VS 4c **

B.Marshall, D.McGimpsey, A.Macfarlane, 23 Jul 1989

The groove at the seaward end about 7m right of Navy Cut. Go up the groove for 3m, step left to a ledge, then chimney and layback the flake in the groove above.

On the north side of Black Geòdha, beyond the descent slab to Parting Shot and before the depression leading to the Small West Wall, the headland contains a sea cave split by a striking vertical groove and crack system. Access the base of the line by abseiling down a slab on its north side.

Wads up there? 40m E5 6a **

D.O.Sullivan, C.Waddy, Jun 2014

Gain the line by a short bouldery traverse from the left. Climb to the roof and move left to gain a juggy flake then go strenuously back right above the roof; finish direct. Steep and strenuous and best left until the afternoon to dry out.

Small West Wall

(NB 2243 4640) Non-tidal NW facing

Map p151 Diagram below

This lies out towards the point at the northern end of the headland between Black Geòdha and a deep northwards running geo to its right.

Descent: Walk left down a boulder filled depression then climb down a slabby corner to gain a black rock

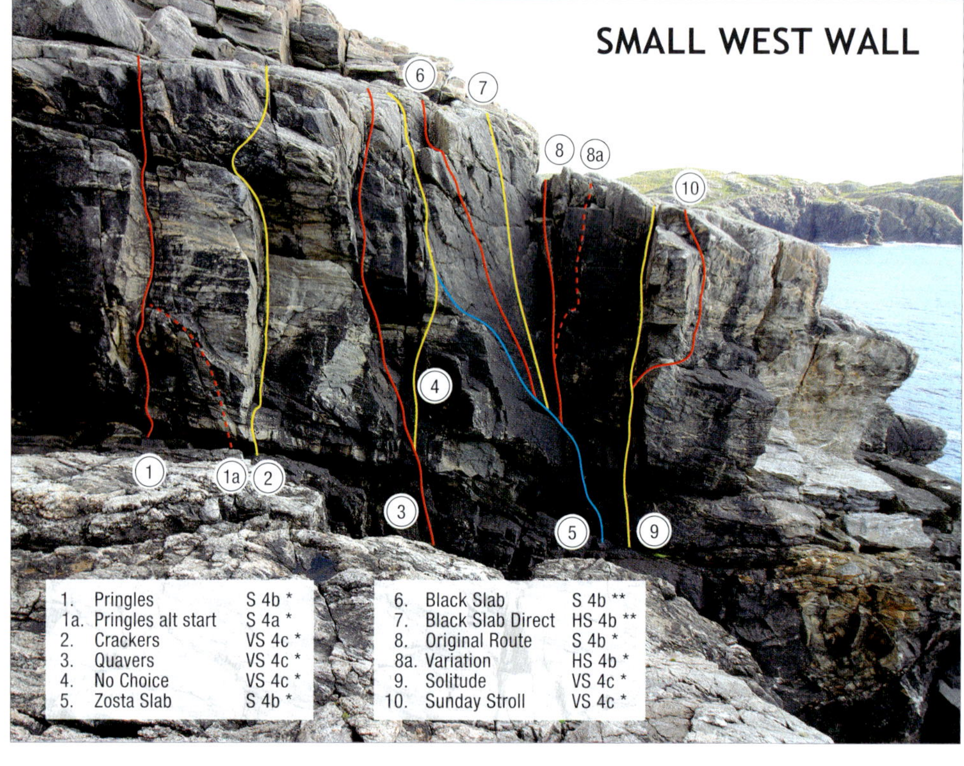

1.	Pringles	S 4b *
1a.	Pringles alt start	S 4a *
2.	Crackers	VS 4c *
3.	Quavers	VS 4c *
4.	No Choice	VS 4c *
5.	Zosta Slab	S 4b *
6.	Black Slab	S 4b **
7.	Black Slab Direct	HS 4b **
8.	Original Route	S 4b *
8a.	Variation	HS 4b *
9.	Solitude	VS 4c *
10.	Sunday Stroll	VS 4c *

platform containing a brackish pool about 20m above the sea. The top of the cliff above Pringles is a useful gearing-up spot, and an alternative is to set up an abseil down that climb from a large boulder.

The left end of the cliff is formed by a series of corners with the first two climbs up the corners being gained from an upper platform. The other climbs lie below this platform above the brackish pool where there is an undercut slab.

1 Pringles 10m S 4b *
K.Geddes, A.Cunningham, 26 Apr 1995
The corner at the extreme left end is often wet. This climb takes the corner to its right. An easier but unprotected start can be made just to the right.

2 Crackers 10m VS 4c *
R.Anderson, C.Anderson, 21 Jul 2017
Climb the corner right of Pringles to the bulge. Bridge up, wire in horizontal break, then swing left and continue to the top.

3 Quavers 12m VS 4c *
R.Anderson, C.Anderson, 21 Jul 2017
The corner immediately left of the slab. Climb steeply up left into the corner as for No Choice and continue to the bulge (large cam or hex useful) then bridge up the groove to a ledge (micro cam and wire) then gain the top.

4 No Choice 12m VS 4c *
A.Cunningham, K.Geddes, 26 Apr 1995
The corner-crack left of the slab. Pull through the initial bulge and turn the next on the right to finish as for Zosta Slab.

5 Zosta Slab 20m S 4b *
I.Sherrington, T.Walker, 26 Apr 1995
Pull through the bulge at the base of the corner of Original Route to gain the right side of the undercut slab then traverse left along the base of the slab and go up cracks in the left edge. There is some similarity between this and the next route.

6 Black Slab 15m S 4b **
Start as for Zosta Slab then climb cracks slanting left.

7 Black Slab Direct 15m HS 4b **
Start as for Zosta Slab then climb directly up the slab just right of centre, past two shallow pockets.

8 Original Route 15m S 4b *
B.Davison, Apr 1989
The corner up the right side of the slab; a variation moves out onto the right wall partway up (HS 4b *).

9 Solitude 15m VS 4c *
B.Davison, May 1989
To the right is another corner with an awkward start.

10 Sunday Stroll 10m VS 4c *
B.Davison, 13 May 1990
Start as for Solitude, then swing right onto the nose of the arete and go round to a ledge. Finish up the wall at the back.

The cliff to the right used to hold three climbs (Hang It, Mongrel and Good Crack) but the sea claimed these during the winter of 2016/17, leaving a large rock scar.

11 Just for the Crack 10m VS 4c *
E.Pirie, R.Henderson, 26 Apr 1995
This climb may still exist. At the right end of the rock scar pull over the nose to climb a right-trending crack.

Mid West Wall and Big West Wall

(NB 2244 4646) Non-tidal NW facing
Map p151 Diagram p160

Forming the headland point out in front of and below the Small West Wall is a wall which increases in height as it runs leftwards to where the cliff turns the edge to run east; here it continues to the entrance of the big, north-running geo which defines the right side of the headland tip. In the centre of the right-hand section, a groove capped by an overhang with a hanging plaque of rock to its left is obvious. Ledges run leftwards beneath the wall to the left-hand section: the Big West Wall.

Descent: Either abseil down the central corner from a thread beneath a block, or scramble down from the platform below the Small West Wall.

Routes are described from right to left. The first three routes are squeezed onto a small wall of good rock at the extreme right end.

12 Rightline 15m E2 5b
R.Anderson, 22 Jul 2016
An eliminate up the right extremity of the wall. Move up and right to the ledge beneath the middle of the wall then go up and right to pockets and continue just left of the edge.

13 Midline 15m E1 5b **
R.Anderson, C. Anderson, 22 Jul 2016
Move up and right to the ledge beneath the middle of the wall. Gain the slanting crack on the right and climb the wall.

14 Leftline 15m E2 5b *
R.Anderson, 22 Jul 2016
Move up and right to a thin crack above the ledge in the middle of the wall. Pull onto the wall using a knobble then pull left to pockets (cam) and from a hold on the left move up and right to finish on better holds.

15 Tea For Two 15m VS 4c *
D.McGimpsey, A.Newey, Jul 1989
The shallow left-facing corner-groove right of the overhang, starting up a crack. A variation start up the slab to the left is possible at 5b.

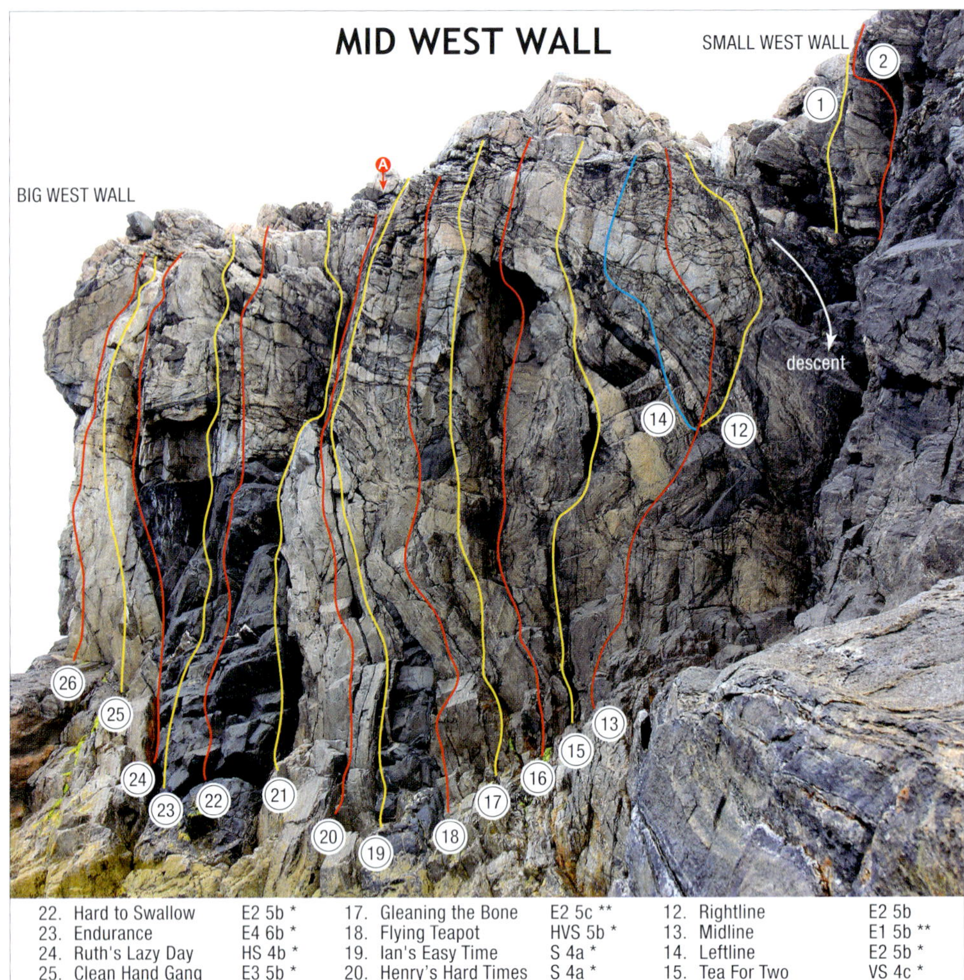

22.	Hard to Swallow	E2 5b *	17.	Gleaning the Bone	E2 5c **	12.	Rightline	E2 5b
23.	Endurance	E4 6b *	18.	Flying Teapot	HVS 5b *	13.	Midline	E1 5b **
24.	Ruth's Lazy Day	HS 4b *	19.	Ian's Easy Time	S 4a *	14.	Leftline	E2 5b *
25.	Clean Hand Gang	E3 5b *	20.	Henry's Hard Times	S 4a *	15.	Tea For Two	VS 4c *
26.	Jessie James	E2 5b *	21.	Mid West Corner	VD *	16.	Down Under	E2 6a *

16 Down Under 15m E2 6a *
B.Davison, A.Macfarlane, 13 May 1990
Climb the groove to the left to the overhang then move over this on good finger jams.

17 Gleaning the Bone 15m E2 5c **
A.Macfarlane, D.Stelfox, 24 Aug 1989
The narrow pillar with the hanging plaque of rock, to the left of the groove.

18 Flying Teapot 15m HVS 5b *
A.Macfarlane, D.McGimpsey, B.Marshall, Jul 1989
The groove left of the narrow pillar.

19 Ian's Easy Time 15m S 4a *
I.Sherrington, T.Walker, 26 Apr 1995
The right edge of the slabby wall.

20 Henry's Hard Times 15m S 4a *
The slabby wall.

21 Mid West Corner 15m VD *
The large central corner.

22 Hard to Swallow 15m E2 5b *
A.Cunningham, K.Geddes, 26 Apr 1995
The crack-line left of the corner; steep and strenuous.

23 Endurance 15m E4 6b *
B.Davison, A.Macfarlane, 21 May 1990
This takes the corner and crack through the right side of the overhang. Climb the corner and make awkward moves up the groove to the overhang. A foothold on the right helps progress through the overhang to the head-wall and a sloping finish.

24 Ruth's Lazy Day 20m HS 4b *
D.McGimpsey, C.Allen, May 1989
Climb the groove left of the overhang.

25 Clean Hand Gang 20m E3 5b *
B.Davison, 24 May 1990
Takes the wall to the left as directly as possible. Start at the right side of the wall, then make moves up and left to a good hold. A long reach to a flat incut leads to good holds trending right to a ledge. Climb the edge of the groove to the top.

26 Jessie James 20m E2 5b *
B.Davison, 24 May 1990
Climb the right side of the arete forming the left end of the wall to a good hold. Move left to good but spaced holds on the arete to a ledge. Finish by moving up and left into Outlaw.

Just around the edge are three grooves. There is some rock scarring here so the routes may be slightly different to when first climbed.

Outlaw 20m E1 5b *
D.McGimpsey, B.Marshall, 23 Jul 1989
Climb the groove immediately left of the arete and exit up the corner.

Robbery Under Arms 20m E1 5b *
A.Macfarlane, D.McGimpsey, Aug 1989
The middle of the three grooves, starting up the left-hand series of cracks and small ledges. Continue up to the hanging nose then step right to finish.

Thuggery 20m HVS 5b *
A.Macfarlane, D.McGimpsey, B.Marshall, 18 Jun 1989
Climb the left-hand groove, starting up a corner past a flake to continue through the roof.

To the left, the wall gains height and becomes the Big West Wall, which curves round towards the entrance to the deep geo to the east. The initial section is capped by an overhang with a corner running through it at either end. The final section contains a recess with two corner climbs up either side. Again routes are described right to left.

Descent: It is possible to traverse across from the Mid West Wall, however the sea does crash in here and the rock can be greasy, so it might be better to abseil down one of the corners.

New World 25m E1 5b *
B.Davison, 17 May 1990
Just right of the overhang that runs along the bottom of the wall is a steep groove. Climb the groove and at its top move right to a ledge, then climb the wall to the prominent corner at the right end of the top roof.

Island of No Return 35m HVS 5a *
B.Davison, 17 May 1990
About 7m left of where the overhang running along the bottom of the wall ends there is a square-cut groove capped by a small roof. Move up to the top of the groove then hand-traverse 4m right to a foothold and ascend cracks to a basalt intrusion. Move to a ledge on the right then go up to another ledge. Traverse left into the bottom of the corner at the left end of the top overhang.

The next four climbs start at a recess about 6m left of Island of No Return.

Chew the Route 30m E4 6a **
K.Pyke, G.Huxter, 11 Sep 1996
This takes the hanging arete leading rightwards from New Addition. Start up the recess as for that route and climb its flake chimney to the ledge. Move right onto the arete to reach a big undercling, gain the crack (crux) then make sustained moves using the arete to a fine belay ledge.

New Addition 40m HVS 5a *
B.Davison, 17 May 1990
Climb the right-hand corner of the recess then take a flake chimney leading to a ledge; continue up the corner to the top.

First Born 40m VS 4c *
B.Davison, 17 May 1990
Climb the left-hand corner of the recess to a ledge then go up a wall before stepping left into a shallow chimney and corner leading to the top.

Crow Road 35m E2 5c *
K.Pyke, G.Huxter, 10 Sep 1996
Start 3m left of First Born at the base of a right-trending groove. Follow the groove right onto the arete and move steeply through a small roof split by a thin crack (crux) to gain a groove leading to the top.

Unnamed Geòdha

(NB 2263 4645) Tidal N facing Map p151

The big northwards running geo between the Big West Wall and Preacher Geòdha appears to have no name. The headland on the east side of this, opposite the Big West Wall, contains one route. Unfortunately, the rock above two-thirds height was found to be very loose.

Descent: Abseil from blocks at the western end of the headland overlooking the end of the Big West Wall. Anchors are set back a few metres west of the abseil line with additional anchors just above the lip.

Lewis Bites Back 35m HS 4a
P.Drew, P.Johnson, 12 Jun 2017
From the foot of the abseil, climb an easy groove for 10m to good ledges. Go directly up the steep wall on big jugs to a ledge below the overhanging headwall then step left to climb a crack and loose ground. The finish is worrying and there are no anchors directly above the route; diagonal belay from the abseil blocks.

Blessed are the Weak (E5) Hertha Taverner-Wood (photo Ferdia Earle)

PREACHER GEÒDHA

1. Blessed are the Weak E5 6a ***
2. Red Hand Gang E2 5b
3. Mr Big Comes Clean E3 5c *
4. A Prophet's Doom E3 6a *

Preacher Geòdha

(NB 2257 4648) Non-tidal NW facing
Map p151 Diagram above

This lies to the east of the headland with the Small West, Mid West and Big West Walls, on the other side of an intervening deep geo and not far from the back of Black Geòdha. Easily viewed from directly opposite, it takes the form of an obvious tall wall, the centre of which is split by a prominent crack emanating from a circular black intrusion. A huge block leans against the base of the left side of the wall and at the top a decrepit fence line runs down to the side of the wall.

Descent: Carefully abseil from a fence post, down the gully to the right.

1 Blessed are the Weak 45m E5 6a ***

G.Huxter, 23 May 1996

Despite an unpleasant start this is a brilliant route which takes a direct line up the left side of the wall. Climb Red Hand Gang for 6m and make a long step left then climb up and leftwards aiming for the centre of a horizontal overlap. Cross this and go directly up to a good ledge. Climb the hanging flake above then go up slightly rightwards on pocketed rock to a crack and finish at the highest point of the cliff; boulder belay.

2 Red Hand Gang 35m E2 5b
D.Stelfox, A.Macfarlane, 28 Aug 1989
The prominent crack emanating from the circular black intrusion; loose.

3 Mr Big Comes Clean 30m E3 5c *
A.Macfarlane, D.McGimpsey, B.Marshall, 30 Jul 1989
Climb the rightmost of three corners right of Red Hand Gang.

4 A Prophet's Doom 20m E3 6a *
A.Macfarlane, D.McGimpsey, 16 Jul 1989
The sustained crack-line 3m right of Mr Big Comes Clean.

DALBEG NORTH

The coastline running north-eastwards towards Shawbost from Àird Dalbeg, past a large bay with stacs and arches.

Solus Wall

(NB 2310 4663) N facing Map p151

A mitre-shaped wall on the north side of the large bay beyond the Àird Bianish promontory and arch.

Approach: From the Àird Dalbeg highpoint, walk downhill to the east for a few hundred metres and cross a drystane dyke at the head of a pebble bay containing an arched split sea stack. On the way down the hill the mitre-shaped wall can be seen on the far side of the bay. Around its corner facing seawards into Geòdha Tolaig Mòr is a stepped wall, a roofed recess, projecting prow and blocks. The wall is protected on the right (west) by a square-cut, bookend buttress with windows, the other side of which is the mitre shaped wall viewed on the approach. Climbs are described from right to left.

Descent: Abseil to good ledges.

Solus 20m HVS 4c
F.Macleod, C.Humphries, 9 Nov 2002
Climb the wall trending right into the bottomless right corner of the roofed recess.

Dealanach 20m VS 4c
F.Macleod, C.Humphries, 26 Oct 2002
The short right-facing corner and crack direct to the left corner of the recess.

An Grian 20m HVS 5a
F.Macleod, C.Humphries, 26 Oct 2002
Climb direct to the left side of the blocks, surmount them and finish up the right corner of the prow.

Rionnag na Maidne 22m E1 5b
F.Macleod, A.Sutton, 30 Dec 2002
The sustained direct off-width V-crack before the central arete.

Tigh Solus 22m S
A.Sutton, F.Macleod, 30 Dec 2002
Start left of the central arete on a low ledge below a left-facing short corner. Climb a fault-line through an overhang to finish across a cracked slab.

Soisgeul 18m S
A.Sutton, F.Macleod, 21 Dec 2002
Climb a series of right-facing corners direct to the overhang. Step left, climb a short wall to a horizontal break and cross an overlap.

CREAGAN BEN GUIDAMOL

(NB 234 456) Alt 60m NW Facing Map p151

A broken and unappealing looking crag on the corner of the road just north of Dalbeg. Previously climbed on in the late 1980s but nothing recorded as others had apparently climbed there before.

On the right-hand side of the crag, directly above a fence line, is a short cliff bisected by a number of crack-lines. Other shorter routes were also climbed around the edge of the buttress at around S. Descents are by easy scrambles.

Shower Dodging 15m HVS 5a *
G.Lynn, M.McMillan, 4 Aug 2010
The series of thinner cracks up the left-hand side of the buttress.

Milestone Route 15m VS 4c
G.Lynn, M.McMillan, 4 Aug 2010
The central crack-line.

Titch's Adventure 15m HS 4b
M.McMillan, G.Lynn, 4 Aug 2010
The right-hand set of cracks leads to a small niche near the top.

Directly above and to the right is another small buttress.

The Chessmen 10m VS 4c
M.McMillan, G.Lynn, 4 Aug 2010
The central flake system.

On the far left section of cliff, slightly recessed in a small grassy bay, are a number of slanting crack-lines.

Smelly Hitchhiker 10m HS 4b
G.Lynn, 5 Aug 2010
The left-hand arete.

Runaway Dog 10m S
G.Lynn, 5 Aug 2010
The left-hand crack which opens into a chimney-slot.

Waiting for a Lift 10m S
G.Lynn, 5 Aug 2010
The next crack to the right.

Shawbost (Siabost)

Maps p19 & p151

North-east from Dalbeg (Dail Beag), the coastline runs past the settlements of South Shawbost (Siabost bho Dheas) and North Shawbost (Siabost bho Thuath). The climbing lies to the west of the road-end at South Shawbost, on the headlands of Rubha Bratag and Rubha na Beirigh.

Directions: Heading north-east on the A858 from Dalbeg, take the first road left, signposted Shawbost bho Dheas. Follow the road to a minor crossroads where the road to the right is signed to the shore. Turn left and after 100m or so park on the right opposite a shed, at the entrance to a rough track, taking care not to obstruct access.

RUBHA BRATAG

This small headland is close to the road-end at South Shawbost.

Geòdha Bratag

The Orpheus Wall

(NB 2397 4737) Partially Tidal W facing
Map p151 Diagram opposite

The west side of the headland is formed by a fine little wall which overlooks the sheltered bay created by the geo. The wall sits above some large boulders and is only affected by the highest tides and rarely affected by the swell.

Approach: Walk south up the road past the house and take the first track off to the right. Pass through a gate and follow the track a short way before heading across the field to cross a fence by a step over stile beside a gate; the waymarked coastal trail crosses here. Cross some lazy beds to reach the top of the small headland of Rubha Bratag, which has a few boulders sitting on it (10min). The prominent cairned headland on the opposite side of the bay is Rubha na Beirighe.

Descent: Drop down to the north of the highpoint and follow a slabby shelf easily down.

The first routes start off the slabby shelf where there is a large left-facing corner.

1 Blowin' A Gale 10m HVS 5a
R.I.Jones, J.Sanders, 13 Jun 2004
Climb the left-facing corner for 4m. Step left to a niche then right to a platform. Pull up into a hanging niche on the left and continue to the top.

2 What Planet Do You Live On? 10m VD
J.Sanders, R.I.Jones, 13 Jun 2004
The large broken crack-line right of the corner.

3 Stolen Moments 10m HS 4b *
J.Sanders, R.I.Jones, 13 Jun 2004
Climb the arete right of What Planet to a hanging slab and finish up a crack.

4 Sirens of the Sea 12m HVS 4c **
R.I.Jones, J.Sanders, 13 Jun 2004
Start 4m right of Stolen Moments and climb to a niche below a leaning wall, then step right to climb the arete and corner above.

5 Toerag 15m VS 4c **
R.Anderson, C.Anderson, 16 Jul 2004
The short corner where the wall turns the edge and properly starts. Climb up right into the corner and follow this to finish as for the previous route.

6 Little Cus 15m E2 5b *
R.Anderson, C.Anderson, 16 Jul 2004
The slim corner just above where the shelf meets the boulders. Climb up and right above a recess to the foot of the corner, then awkwardly climb this, step right and pull over onto a ledge to finish as for Toerag and Sirens of the Sea.

The remaining routes take lines on the fine wall above the boulders. A huge flake-like feature is obvious in the centre at the base of the wall. To the left of this is a recessed roofed section and to the right two thin crack-lines run up the wall before a corner.

7 The Underworld 20m E3 5c *
R.Anderson, C.Anderson, 20 Jul 2004
From the left end of the boulders, climb to a ledge then go up a slim groove to a small triangular roof. Steeply gain the groove above on some creaky holds and continue to a ledge then finish up the short corner of Orpheus.

8 Niflheim 20m E3 5b **
R.Anderson, C.Anderson, 16 Jul 2004
Start beneath the widest part of the roof. Steeply climb a groove to the roof, pull through this and go up a thin crack. Move up and step left to a horizontal break then go leftwards under a small roof to finish up the short corner of Orpheus.

9 Vanaheim 20m E3 5b **
R.Anderson, C.Anderson, 16 Jul 2004
Just left of the huge central flake, climb a shallow line of weakness steeply up the right side of the recessed section and pull onto the wall. Move up left, then follow Niflheim up thin cracks and step left to the horizontal break. Now move right to finish steeply up quartzy orange coloured rock, seamed with thin cracks.

10 Valhalla 20m E2 5b ***
R.Anderson, C.Anderson, 16 Jul 2004
The thin central crack-line, gained up the left side of the flake.

GEÒDHA BRATAG - The Orpheus Wall

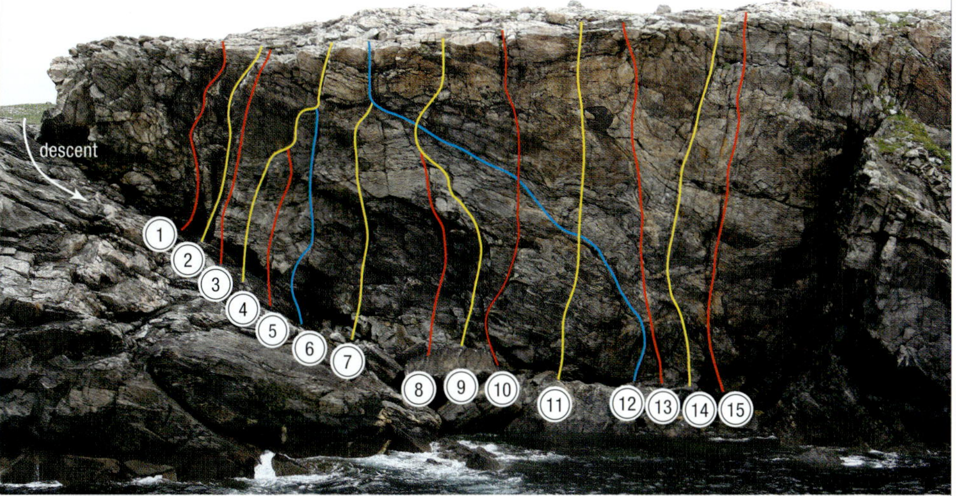

1. Blowin' A Gale	HVS 5a
2. What Planet.......	VD
3. Stolen Moments	HS 4b *
4. Sirens of the Sea	HVS 4c **
5. Toerag	VS 4c **
6. Little Cus	E2 5b *
7. The Underworld	E3 5c *
8. Niflheim	E3 5b **
9. Vanaheim	E3 5b **
10. Valhalla	E2 5b ***
11. Thor Tips	E3 5c **
12. Orpheus	E2 5c **
13. Styx and Stones	E2 5c ***
14. Odin Keep Quiet	E2 5b **
15. Rude Boys	E1 5b **

11 Thor Tips 20m E3 5c **
M.Garthwaite, R.Anderson, 17 Jul 2004
Climb the centre of the flake to pull out right into a slim groove then continue to the top of the flake. Climb directly to the top of the wall passing to the left of a prominent patch of black rock.

12 Orpheus 30m E2 5c **
R.I.Jones, 14 Jun 2004
The original route is a right to left rising traverse. Climb the ramp up the right side of the flake to its top then climb the wall for 2m before traversing up leftwards. A step down and a pull across are made before going up leftwards under a small overhang to finish up a short corner.

13 Styx and Stones 20m E2 5c ***
M.Garthwaite, R.Anderson, 17 Jul 2004
Climb the ramp up the right side of the flake for a short way then climb wavy rock passing the right side of the patch of black rock to finish up a short corner.

14 Odin Keep Quiet 20m E2 5b **
M.Garthwaite, R.Anderson, 17 Jul 2004
Gain a ledge then climb the left-hand of two thin cracks.

15 Rude Boys 20m E1 5b **
R.Anderson, M.Garthwaite, 17 Jul 2004
Gain a ledge then climb the right-hand of two thin cracks

RUBHA NA BEIRGHE

(NB 2355 4745) Tidal N to W facing Map p151

The prominent headland with a cairn, which can be seen when looking west from the road at South Shawbost.

Approach: As for Rubha Bratag by walking south up the road past the house to take the first track off right. Pass through a gate then follow the track a short way before heading across the field to the waymarked coastal trail and cross a fence by a step over stile beside a gate. Continue along the coastal trail a short way, past the head of Geòdha Bratag, then make for the headland. Cross a narrow neck of land and the remains of a wall which form part of an ancient fort. Continue towards a prominent fin of rock jutting out to the north. An arch and sea cave cut all the way through the headland at this point (15min).

Murray's Rib

(NB 2365 4743) Map p151

The prominent fin of rock has a few climbs on the south facing slab, at the entrance to the arch and sea cave.

Approach: Scramble out along the rib above the slab and make a tricky descent to a small platform at the north end then traverse back along the bottom of the slab.

Duck Egg D **
T.McLachlan, K.Tighe, 29 May 2001
The central crack-line.

Stowaway D **
Y.Colwell, M.Morris, 29 May 2001
The little corner.

The slab between and to the right of these routes can be climbed just about anywhere at VD to S.

North Side - The Poacher Area

(NB 2361 4745) Map p151 Diagram right

The next climbs are located on the north side of the headland, on the opposite side of the prominent fin where it forms a shallow sea cave. The rock is distinctly black in colour here.

Descent: A short way along the top, going westwards from the prominent fin, is a small ledge running along the cliff edge just below its top. From here, it is possible to locate the top of a pillar with a corner running down either side. To the left of this pillar is the shallow sea cave into which the north-facing wall of the prominent fin runs. Some way back from the top of the cliff is a large embedded tombstone of a boulder, which can provide an abseil anchor.

The first two climbs start from small ledges just above the high water mark, at the foot of the corner running up the left side of the pillar.

1 It's a Knockout 20m E2 5c **
R.Anderson, M.Garthwaite, 18 Jul 2004
Climb a crack which slants out left above a cave then goes up to an off-width, which provides an entertaining finish; Friend 4 useful.

2 Fistfighter 20m E1 5b **
R.Anderson, M.Garthwaite, 18 Jul 2004
The crack running up the corner.

The next climbs start at the foot of the corner running up the right side of the pillar.

3 The Poacher 25m E1 5b ***
M.Tighe, H.Robertson, K.Colwell, K.Tighe, 29 May 2001
The crack in the corner past an overhang; splendid.

4 Pregnant Pause 30m E3 5c **
M.Garthwaite, R.Anderson, 18 Jul 2004
Move up and right to gain then climb the thin cracks running up the right wall of the corner and follow the obvious line which curves right to gain the arete, which is followed to the top.

The next climb lies just around the right arete, reached by a short traverse along narrow tidal ledges.

5 Internal Exam Crack 20m E1 5b ***
M.Garthwaite, R.Anderson, 18 Jul 2004
Climb the prominent corner-crack to a roof, move right beneath this and finish up the edge.

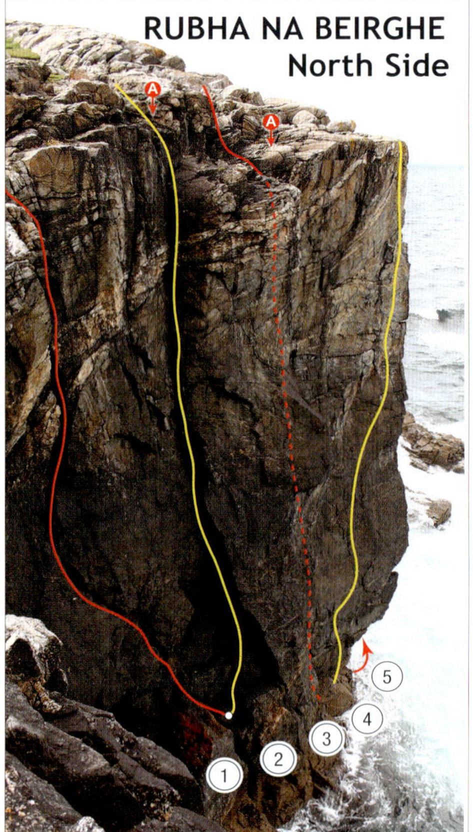

1. It's a Knockout E2 5c **
2. Fistfighter E1 5b **
3. The Poacher E1 5b ***
4. Pregnant Pause E3 5c **
5. Internal Exam Crack E1 5b ***

About 20m right (west) of Internal Exam Crack there are some large boulders on the cliff-top. An abseil from the most north-easterly boulders, through a V-groove just right (looking out to sea) of the edge of the overhanging cliff-top, gives access to the following climb.

6 Soaked By A Wave 25m VS 4c *
R.I.Jones, A.Wardle, 9 Sep 2008
Belay on a small ledge left of overhangs and 8m above the sea. Climb the steep crack-line up the wall to a ledge system beneath the overhanging cliff-top. Climb the wall and V-groove on the left to finish.

For the next climb follow a fault-line from the most north-westerly cairn to the edge of the cliff, then abseil to a hanging belay on a very small stance above an overhang.

7 Above The Swell 20m S 4a *
A.Wardle, R.I.Jones, 9 Sep 2008
Climb cracks up the steep wall to the top.

North West Tip

(NB 2350 4746) Map p151 Diagram p168

The next climbs are located beyond the highest point on the north-west tip of the headland. With the base being tidal and affected by waves, the cliff can only really be accessed at low to mid tide in calmer seas. It can also take the sun to dry the cliff out once the tide has left the base. If caught at the right time it is an excellent cliff.

Descent: On the north side of the tip, on the edge of the cliff a split boulder provides a convenient anchor for an abseil down a slabby black corner.

8 The Surging Sea 25m E1 5b *
R.I.Jones, A.Wardle, 7 Sep 2008
Start 5m left of the corner. Climb the stepped arete, first into a niche, then up the right arete to a sloping ledge. Traverse up left to climb the cornered arete to finish.

9 One Step Beyond 25m HVS 5a **
R.Anderson, M.Garthwaite, 19 Jul 2004
The line of the abseil; the fine slabby black corner.
Variation: **9a Beyond Direct 25m E1 5b ****
R.I.Jones, A.Wardle, 7 Sep 2008
Climb One Step Beyond to the halfway ledge, step right and climb cracks directly up the wall to the top. Moving right around the edge, go down a short step onto a barnacled promontory and ledge running beneath the front face of the headland.

10 Shawbost Pillar 25m E1 5b ***
R.Anderson, M.Garthwaite, 19 Jul 2004
The slim pillar just around the edge is climbed over a steepening to finish up the left edge.

11 North West Passage 25m HVS 5a **
R.Anderson, C.Anderson, 20 Jul 2004
Climb the chimney running up the right side of the pillar to gain the top of a fine sloping quartzy ledge then follow the cracks above.

A short way to the right, above where the shelf narrows, is an obvious corner flanked on either side by slim corner-grooves. These provide the lower sections of the next four climbs and lead to good ledges on which a belay can be taken.

12 Slimline 25m HVS 5b **
R.Anderson, M.Garthwaite, 19 Jul 2004
Climb the left-hand slim corner-groove to gain the base of a sloping quartzy ledge, then finish up the thin crack left of the main corner.

13 Dheas Corner 25m E1 5b **
R.Anderson, C.Anderson, 20 Jul 2004
The central corner; there is a good ledge in the middle.

The Poacher (E1) Shauna Clarke (photo Robert Durran)

14 The Lewisian 25m E3 5c ***
R.Anderson, C.Anderson, 20 Jul 2004
The obvious crack in the upper wall, just right of the corner. Climb the right-hand slim corner-groove to the mid-way ledges then step right and climb a short wall to the base of the crack. Climb this to gain the wide crack which leads to the top.

15 Episiotomy 30m E3 5c ***
M.Garthwaite, R.Anderson, 19 Jul 2004
The prominent right-hand crack in the upper right wall of the corner. Climb either of the previous routes to the mid-way ledges. Step right and climb the short wall in common with The Lewisian, then go right and steeply climb the crack to the top.

The next two climbs are located on the steep undercut frontal section of the headland, a short way right of the previous climbs. They share a common start up a shallow groove, which splits into two distinct grooves a short way up. The start lies just left of a deep tidal pool where a cleft is formed between the main wall and a pinnacle to its right.

16 Knocked Up 30m E5 6a **
M.Garthwaite, R.Anderson, 19 Jul 2004
This climbs the steepest part of the frontal section of the headland. Pull up a shallow groove, step right and move up to a ledge beneath a bulge. Move up left to a corner-groove and climb this until it is possible to pull out right onto the edge. Move up and right steeply, then make some wild moves across left to gain holds and a tenuous finish above.

17 Oh No the Heads Too Big 30m E2 5c **
M.Garthwaite, R.Anderson, 19 Jul 2004
Start as for the previous climb and follow this to the bulge before stepping right to climb the groove. Continue by the obvious line up left to finish.

Behind the pinnacle to the right is an overhung left-facing corner.

Another Doomsday Scenario? 15m E1 5b *
R.I.Jones, A.Wardle, 9 Sep 2008
From a large jammed boulder, climb the corner and make a fine pull through the overhang at the top.

Large Hadron Collider 10m VS 4c
A.Wardle, R.I.Jones, 9 Sep 2008
To the right of the previous climb descend a ramp for 10m then traverse a sloping ledge to a large left-facing corner and climbs this.

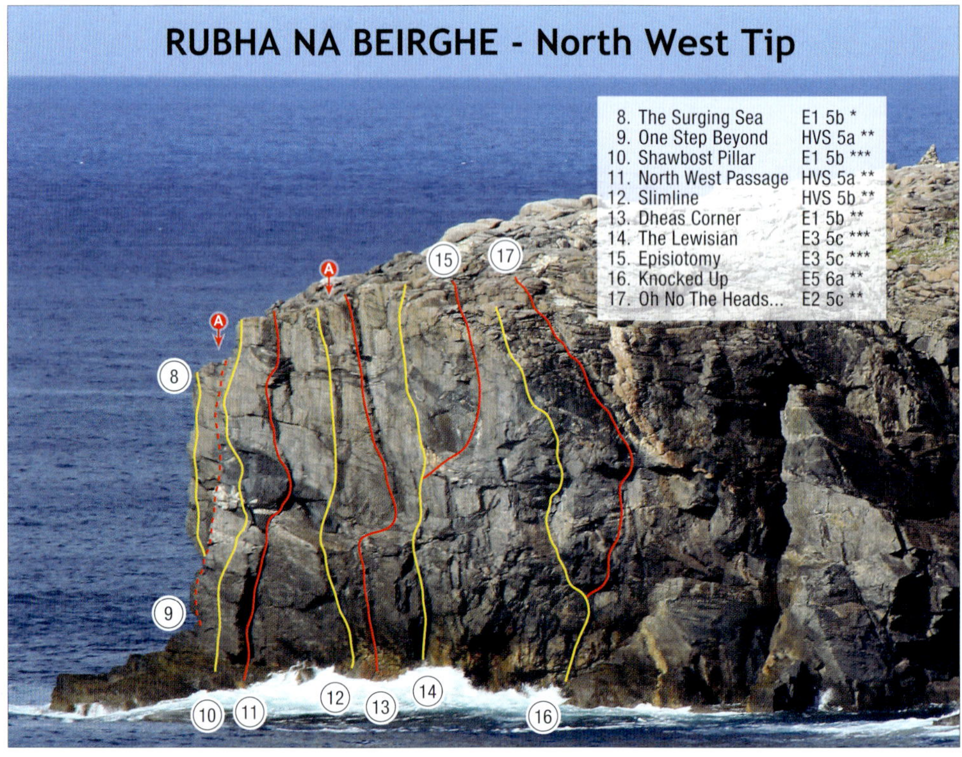

The Lewisian (E3) Robert Durran
(photo Lucy Spark)

Bragar

Maps p19 & right

Two principal headlands are located on the stretch of coast near Bragar to the east of Shawbost. These are Àird Mhòr Bhràgair and Àird Bheag Bhràgair, with most of the climbing being on the former.

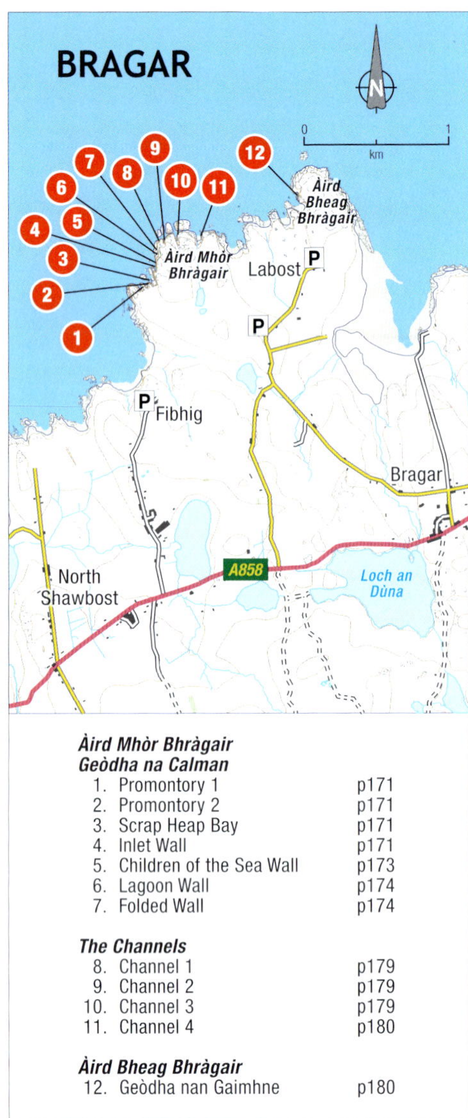

ÀIRD MHÒR BHRÀGAIR

(NB 269 495)

An excellent and fairly complex headland, notable for the popular Folded Wall area where there is a good spread of lower and mid-grade routes. Most of the climbs lie on the west facing side of the headland on a series of northward running walls. Some of the climbs can suffer from greasiness but this often dries later in the day when the sun comes round.

There are two possible approaches to Àird Mhòr Bhràgair.

Directions 1: Turn off the A858 at Siabost bho Thuath at a sign for An Carnan and Fibhig and park on the left at **(NB 268 485)**, just before the two houses at the end of the road.

Approach 1: Walk to the end of the road and go left through a gate in front of the most northerly croft. Go through another gate beside a ruin and descend a grassy slope, crossing a fence to gain the boulder beach. Cross this then head across the field to between the two high-points ahead and cross the fence to reach Scrap Heap Bay (15min). The barbed wire fence running up the slope has to be stepped over or crossed by a rickety step over stile on the coastal trail to the right to gain the Inlet Wall and the Folded Wall.

Directions 2: Another approach can be made by a track which starts at **(NB 277 489)** at Labost on the next road off the A858 to the east. The track is gained by following this road to its junction with the road from Bragar and turning left. The track starts at the top of the hill just beyond a house on the left; there is room for one or two cars to be squeezed off the road on the left, just beyond the start of the track.

Approach 2: Go through a gate and follow the track, going through another gate to where the track ends at a third gate. Cross the fields past Lochan Dubh heading for a prominent boulder on the skyline. Cross the barbed wire fence by a rickety step over a stile just behind this; there is a gate to the right which is the better option until the stile is fixed. The top of the cliff is reached in the vicinity of the Inlet Wall (15min). Following the fence left leads to Scrap Heap Bay.

Scrap Heap Bay is the first landmark at the southern end of the series of west facing walls. A load of scrap and rubbish has been tipped into this bay and although there are no routes in the bay itself, it provides a useful though unattractive landmark. The wall on the east side of this bay runs northwards past the end of a fence to form Stac nan Eun (Stack of the Birds), which is a narrow ridge running out to sea, comprised of a series of three pinnacles.

Opposite Stac nan Eun to the east, on the other side of a deep and narrow inlet, is the Inlet Wall, the biggest wall hereabouts. The northern end of the Inlet Wall has been called the Children of the Sea Wall, beyond which the cliff steps back to form a recessed section, the Lagoon Wall. Just to the north of this recessed section is the fine Folded Wall, which contains a number of excellent routes on perfect rock. Beyond this and running eastwards opposite some offshore skerries is a series of smaller geos and promontories.

Geòdha na Calman

This lies to the west of Scrap Heap Bay, between the Àird Mhòr Bhràgair headland and the smaller headland of Luchair. Two small promontories jut northwards into the sea here, to the west of Scrap Heap Bay.

Promontory 1

(NB 2687 4934) Tidal Map opposite

Some 50m to the west of Scrap Heap Bay is a promontory with a small island and a little triangular witch's hat stack lying to its north. At the north-eastern end of the promontory overlooking the entrance to Scrap Heap Bay and well viewed from opposite is an enormous pillar, some 30m high, which has been cleaved from the cliff face during the January 2015 storms.

The west side of the promontory is formed by a wall that drops into the sea, which can be viewed from the top of Promontory 2, opposite. There are three climbs which are described from right to left.

Descent: Abseil down the right side of the wall to a good ledge at the foot of a steep corner-crack.

Tides Out 30m E2 5c *
M.Garthwaite, R.Anderson, 19 Jul 2014
Climb the corner-crack to ledges then continue up the crack above to a steep finish.

Don't Tie Me Up 30m E3 5c **
M.Garthwaite, R.Anderson, 19 Jul 2014
The central line up the west facing wall. Step across left into a groove and climb this for a few moves before pulling out right to go up and around a projection onto a ledge on its top. Step left and climb the wall.

Tie Me Down 35m E2 5b
M.Garthwaite, R.Anderson, 19 Jul 2014
Step across left into a groove and climb this to ledges then go left and climb blocky ground to a steep finish out left.

There are three climbs on the north-west tip of the promontory.

Descent: Abseil from a little grassy bay on the tip.

September Rain 30m HVS 5a **
M.Tighe, K.Tighe, H.Clarke, C.Clarke, 1 Sep 2002
The left side of the wall is defined by a fine corner-crack. A tricky start leads to a mid-way ledge and interesting crack above; fragile at the top.

Rock Island Line 30m E1 5b *
M.Tighe, K.Tighe, 25 Jun 2003
A few metres to the left is another fine corner-line, which runs the full height of the cliff. This is climbed with jamming, an arm bar and good protection.

Scrap Heap Challenge 30m E1 5b *
M.Tighe, K.Tighe, 25 Jun 2003
A diagonal fault-line starts from the extreme north-west corner of the promontory, first as a groove for a few metres to a big ledge, then as a steep crack-line up the wall to the left of Rock Island Line. The holds tend to be a bit flaky but the climbing is good and well protected.

Promontory 2

(NB 2683 4934) Non-tidal Map p170

To the west of Promontory 1 is a smaller promontory, the foot of which is reached by scrambling down an easy gully on its west side.

Western Rib 20m E2 5b/c
M.Tighe, K.Tighe, 25 Jun 2003
This climbs the nose of the promontory; a gentle little slab leads to a fierce little quartzy wall then some big steps out right to finish.

Tour de Chance 15m E2 5c **
M.Garthwaite, R.Anderson, 14 Jul 2013
The crack-line up the side wall to the right of the nose provides a surprisingly good and technical climb.

Scrap Heap Bay

(NB 2691 4934) Map opposite

There are no climbs in the bay itself and although there is a cave which runs through to the inlet at the south side of the Inlet Wall, this is non-navigable.

Stac Nan Eun (Stack of the Birds) 300m VS *
M.Tighe, K.Tighe, Jul 2000
Though not strictly stacks, these three pinnacles form a narrow ridge running north to south, joined to the mainland, but with sea either side. An old green, mildewed rope was found in 2000, perhaps indicating an earlier ascent. Abseil from a fence post or scramble into Scrap Heap Bay and traverse some 150m to below the lowest point on the ridge, between the northerly, flat topped pinnacle and the middle one (only possible at mid to low tide). Climb up into the small col and bag the big flat-topped northern pinnacle. Return to the col and head south over the next two pinnacles. From the central pinnacle, abseil down the west side to ledges from where a gully and groove line can be ascended back to the cliff-top at about VD. The pinnacles can be climbed from the landward end, but it is a loose, scary affair and misses out lots of fun climbing.

Inlet Wall

(NB 2693 4946) Partially Tidal W facing Map opposite

Heading north, the next climbs are on the Inlet Wall, which sits across the intervening deep and narrow inlet from the Stac Nan Eun ridge. Crossing the barbed wire fence by either stepping over it or using the rickety stile a little further up the slope gains the top of the wall. Although it can't be seen from above, there is a non-navigable through route from Scrap Heap Bay. The wall can be viewed from the top of the cliff at the end of the Stac nan Eun ridge.

Opposite the U-shaped feature on the Stac nan Eun ridge, a cliff-top depression on the cliff-top sits above the main central section of the wall; a useful gearing-up spot.

Climbs are described from the south, right to left (facing in), starting with the Inlet Wall proper, then running northwards to the Children of the Sea Wall.

Descent: The first five climbs lie on the right side of the wall towards the back of the inlet. They are gained by abseil to non-tidal ledges from a block and wires in the south side of the cliff-top depression. This passes a block which marks the exit from Magnificent Seven. A thread under a boulder on the north side of the depression also provides a possible anchor point.

Back in Black 30m E4 5c *

M.Garthwaite, R.Anderson, 21 Jul 2014

The rightmost line on the wall is an obvious layback flake feature up the lower black rock. Gain this and climb it. A step left gains the rest on Blacked Out. Swing back right and traverse into the overhung groove, climb this with difficulty to an easing. Move up and right then continue above to finish by an obvious crack.

Blacked Out 30m E3 5c **

M.Garthwaite, R.Anderson, 20 Jul 2014

Start just left of Back in Black on the upper ledges. Climb up and right via a flared groove (spike) then traverse right and pull up into a rest place beneath a steep shield of rock. Steep and intimidating moves up left lead to moves right and a step into the groove of Back in Black. Climb up and left to finish directly above.

Magnificent Seven 30m E3 5c **

M.Garthwaite, R.Anderson, 19 Jul 2015

Start as for Blacked Out, climbing the flared groove past the spike to the start of the traverse, then pull onto the wall above (small wire) and climb into the base of the big groove. Move up this, then out onto its right rib. Step across the top of the groove and climb directly above to exit by the small block on the cliff-top.

Technical Ecstasy 30m E5 6b ***

M.Garthwaite, R.Anderson, 10 Jun 2018

Belay as for the previous two climbs. Go up left across the seepage line to a flake-crack. Climb onto its top, then go right and undercut a small roof to exit up right before traversing back left to pull up to a ledge. Climb the white streak and crack through the roof to earn a well positioned finish up the headwall.

The Late Show 45m E1 5b ***

M.Garthwaite, R.Anderson, 7 June 2018

Climb to the flake on Technical Ecstasy then step down and traverse a ledge left to climb a groove to gear. Traverse left to Play for Today and follow this to a small alcove then exit left to finish up a short corner.

Sea Dog (E2) Mark Garthwaite (photo Rab Anderson)

The next climb starts from a narrow tidal ledge which runs beneath the wall.

Play for Today 35m E4 6a ***
M.Garthwaite, R.Anderson, 19 Jul 2015
A superb route up the centre of the wall. Start below a left-facing groove and corner. Pull into the groove and climb it up and right, then traverse up left into another groove and climb this to the headwall which is climbed by a thin crack.

At the left end of the main section of the Inlet Wall, the rock steps back to form a full height corner-groove: the line of Sea Dog. This sits opposite the end of the ridge of Stac nan Eun and can be identified from above where a boulder sits on a ledge just beneath the cliff-top, pretty much above the corner.

Descent: On the cliff-top immediately north of the corner-groove a crack and a stubby flake provide good anchors for an abseil down the left wall of the corner to tidal ledges. Slanting down left at the top enables a higher ledge at the foot of the chimney recess of Pot Belly to be gained.

Sea Dog 30m E2 5b ***
M.Tighe, K.Tighe, 15 Jul 2000
The full height corner-groove. Direct entry via the recess at the foot of the line is often greasy but should go when dry. The first ascent traversed in across the wall from the foot of Pot Belly to the left where there is a slightly higher ledge around the edge. A better start can be made from the tidal ledge to the left of the corner by stepping off a pedestal and climbing up and right into it.

Foirfeachd 30m E3 5c ***
M.Garthwaite, R.Anderson, 20 Jul 2014
This climbs the centre of the fine wall left of Sea Dog. From the tidal ledge at the foot of Sea Dog, step off the pedestal onto the wall and climb the centre until moves up left lead to easier ground. Finish up the wall just left of the groove at the top.

Salted Nuts 30m E3 5c **
M.Garthwaite, R.Anderson, 21 Jul 2014
Pull onto the wall as for Sea Dog and Foirfeachd then climb the left edge of the wall to make steep moves into a slim groove which leads to easier ground. Finish up the left wall.

The following three climbs start from a large, slightly higher non-tidal ledge at the foot of the deep and wide chimney recess to the left.

Pigs on the Wing 30m E1 5b **
R.Anderson, C.Anderson, 25 Jul 2014
A climb with much interest, taking the right-slanting groove line from the foot of Pot Belly. Finish up left of blocks via a jug (good wire) in the middle of the wall.

Pot Belly 25m E2 5b **
M.Tighe, I.Lee, G.Anderson, 23 May 2001
The fine, deep and wide peapod-shaped chimney recess. Squirm up the pod with some difficulty and squirm out of it with even more!

Gut Reaction 25m E2 5c ***
R.Anderson, C.Anderson, 25 Jul 2014
The wall and groove left of Pot Belly. Climb up left to a slanting overlap then go up right, to the edge overlooking Pot Belly. Step left across the top of the overlap and climb the groove above to easier ground and the top.

Grey Rib 25m S 4a
K.Tighe, M.Tighe, 15 Jul 2000
Just beyond the top of Pot Belly there is a chasm with an arched overhang at the back of it. This climb takes the rib on the seaward side of the southern end and is a little delicate at times. Abseil directly to its foot or traverse in from Pot Belly.

Children of the Sea Wall

(NB 2693 4951) Tidal W facing Map p170

Formerly known as the Arch Wall, this is the northwards continuation of the Inlet Wall. An arch sat at its northern end but the sea removed this in 2016, creating a big left-facing corner with a pink right wall. The climbs Arch Wall (VS) and High Teas (VS) no longer exist.

Descent: At the northern end of the Inlet Wall a ramp with boulders drops north from the cliff-top towards the Folded Wall. This passes above a wall of fine rock. Boulders on the ramp provide anchors for an abseil down the wall. Ledges at the foot of the wall remain clear of the sea for some time but are affected by the waves, which can be big.

Sea Enema 20m E2 5c **
G.Latter, K.Latter, 10 Aug 2005
The destruction of the arch has removed the lower part of this climb leaving the upper right-slanting crack. It is not known if this can now be climbed.

Children of the Sea 30m E3 5c ***
M.Tighe, K.Tighe, 25 Aug 2004; A.Ellwood, D.Parton, 12 May 2016
The destruction of the arch has removed the lower part of this climb; originally a left to right rising traverse. The wall has been climbed as a straight up route from a tidal pedestal and small cleft at its base. A thin crack leads to a choice; leftwards by the continuation crack or right to ledges below a roof (from where the wall has also been climbed). Take the leftwards continuation then climb up and right to the left side of the obvious guano-stained ledge and finish up the impending headwall on jugs and immaculate rock.

Lagoon Wall

(NB 2695 4954) Non-tidal W facing Map p170

Moving northwards is a fairly large tidal pond, the Lagoon. There is a good ledge at the bottom of the wall, immediately opposite the outflow of the tidal pond. Seepage affects the wall but it does dry later in the day.

Descent: Either by abseil to the ledge, or scramble down the trench at the foot of the Folded Wall and traverse across to it at low tide.

White Magic 20m VS 4c **
M.Tighe, K.Tighe, J.Winter, 15 Jun 2004
From the left side of the ledge, a broad, diagonal quartz-like vein slopes left up the wall. Follow this and the little wall to the top on improving holds.

Sleight of Hand 20m E1 5b **
G.Latter, K.Latter, 10 Aug 2005
The shallow, hanging groove in the centre of the wall to the right of White Magic. Start up a short left-slanting crack, then the groove, finishing up an easy short crack above the ledge at the top.

Sleeping Dogs (VS) Cynthia Crindlay (photo Colin Moody)

Folded Wall

(NB 2695 4956) Non-tidal W facing Map p170 Diagrams opposite & p177

North from the Lagoon is the Folded Wall, a fabulous sweep of perfect gneiss which juts out from the cliff-top. There is a good gearing-up spot in a grassy depression on its top. Platform ledges run beneath the wall, which at the southern end are separated from the wall by a deep trench. The rock dries quickly but the platform ledges can be slippery and there are dropoffs, so take care.

Descent: Abseil directly to the ledges, perhaps best between the corner of Kenny's Cavity and Edge of Distinction, which are identifiable from above; there is a large block on the north side of the gearing-up spot which can be used and on the lower ledge beneath this there is a good crack. It is possible to scramble in by going northwards down a promontory by a series of ramps then making a short down climb into a small bay; looks a bit intimidating from above. There has been some wave damage in this bay and whilst the descent can still be made it might be slightly harder than the original grade of D.

Climbs are described from right to left when looking in from the platforms.

1 First Fold 30m S 4b **
R.Anderson, C.Anderson, 15 Oct 2014
The arete forming the right side of the wall. Scramble down the trench and start near its foot. Climb up right to the obvious fault then go up left and climb the right side of the arete, stepping left then back right to pass the roof on the edge.

The next five climbs start from the platform ledge and involve crossing the trench at the base of the wall. They can also be started directly from the base of the trench by scrambling down into it from the left side and making a few bouldery moves up the lower wall.

2 Two By Three 25m S 4a **
Start as for Number 3 and climb the wall and crack-line 1m or so to the right.

3 Number 3 25m S 4a ***
M.Tighe, K.Tighe, H.Clarke, 20 Jul 2000
Near the right side of the wall, at about one-third height, the rock has been folded into a perfect number 3 shape. Fall across the trench (crux!) then climb the wall directly through the 3 and continue up the crack-line.

4 Three Plus 25m S 4a **
An eliminate up the crack-line through the small roofs between Number 3 and Goodbye Donella.

5 Goodbye Donella 25m HS 4b *
M.Tighe, K.Tighe, H.Clarke, 20 Jul 2000
To the left of Number 3 is a triangular, calcified alcove. A curving fault-line runs through this and goes the full

10.	The Scoop	E1 5b **	5. Goodbye Donella	HS 4b *	1.	First Fold	S 4b **
11.	Left Edge	E1 5b ***	6. Black Recess	VS 4b *	2.	Two By Three	S 4a **
12.	Closer to the Edge	E1 5b ***	7. Sleeping Dogs	VS 4b ***	3.	Number 3	S 4a ***
19.	Snake Dyke	E2 5c ***	8. Fifty Fifty	E1 5b **	4.	Three Plus	S 4a **
			9. Le Slot	E1 5b **			

height of the cliff. Cross the trench and follow the fault all the way with the exit from the alcove being the crux.

6 Black Recess 25m HS 4b **
M.Tighe, K.Tighe, H.Clarke, 20 Jul 2000
A few metres left of and slightly higher than the calcified alcove of Goodbye Donella is a black recess with quartzy veins in the black rock. Cross the trench and head straight up through the recess to the top.

7 Sleeping Dogs 25m VS 4b ***
K.Tighe, M.Tighe, H.Clark, 20 Jul 2000
Start in the middle of the wall 5m left of Black Recess and 5m right of Le Slot, below a small triangular alcove and overhang at one-third height. Climb into the alcove and pull over the small overhang onto the steep wall above on immaculate holds. Continue to the top trending slightly left, or right which is a bit harder but better.

8 Fifty Fifty 25m E1 5b **
R.Anderson, T.Prentice, 6 Jul 2007
An eliminate up the thin crack between Sleeping Dogs and Le Slot, continuing directly to the top in the same way.

9 Le Slot 25m 25m E1 5b **
M.Tighe, K.Tighe, H.Clarke, 20 Jul 2000
At the left end of the trench, low down on the wall, is a narrow 3 to 4m long diagonal slot at the foot of a right-leaning groove. Climb the awkward slot then the groove and the immaculate wall above, directly to the top. An alternative start traverses some 4m into the slot from the right, easier at VS 4c.

The lower section of wall to the left contains three sets of hairline cracks which are taken by the following three routes. The difficulty of these is perhaps more in arranging the initial protection than the actual climbing.

10 The Scoop 25m E1 5b **
M.Tighe, K.Tighe, 10 Jun 2004
Start 2m left of Le Slot below a concave depression just left of centre in the upper part of the wall. Bold moves lead up the lower wall to a tiny triangular niche at the top of the hairline crack from where the halfway ledge can be gained. Easier climbing leads up the scoop.

Number 3 (S) Grahame Nicoll
(photo Laura Nicoll)

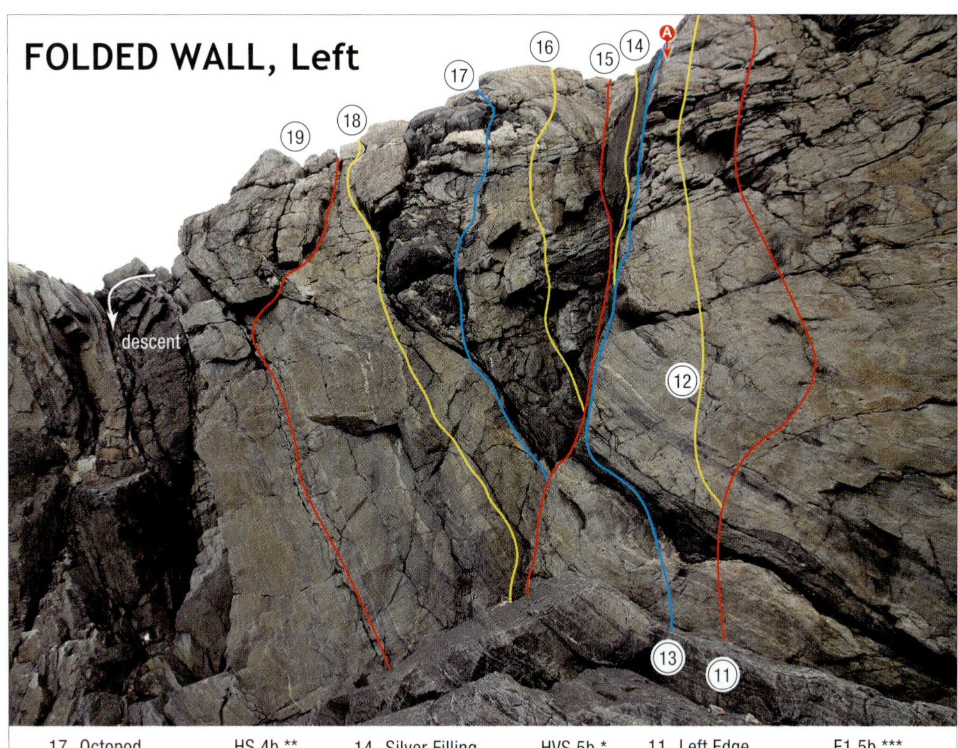

17. Octopod	HS 4b **	14. Silver Filling	HVS 5b *	11. Left Edge	E1 5b ***
18. Squid	E1/2 5b *	15. Kenny's Cavity	VS 4b **	12. Closer to the Edge	E1 5b ***
19. Snake Dyke	E2 5c ***	16. Extraction	E3 5c **	13. Edge of Distinction	HVS 4c **

11 Left Edge 25m E1 5b ***
M.Tighe, K.Tighe, 15 Jul 2000
Start in the centre of the wall, a few metres left from The Scoop and a similar distance in from the left edge. Intricate moves lead up right by a hairline crack to a depression from where the halfway ledge is gained. The steep but juggy upper wall is climbed through a short, roofed corner.

12 Closer to the Edge 25m E1 5b ***
R.Anderson, T.Prentice, 6 Jul 2007
Start as for Left Edge but climb straight up the hairline crack to the right of the edge and continue to the top.

13 Edge of Distinction 25m HVS 4c **
M.Tighe, K.Tighe, J.Winter, 10 Jun 2004
This takes the left edge of the main wall before it turns back into Kenny's Cavity. Climb up and around onto the left side of the edge, awkward to arrange protection, then boldly move back up right onto the edge and finish airily up this.

14 Silver Filling 25m HVS 5b *
R.Anderson, C.Anderson, 15 Oct 2014
An eliminate up the slab between Edge of Distinction and Kenny's Cavity, starting as for the former. Higher up, place good wires in Edge of Distinction then step back left and make some stretchy moves to finish.

15 Kenny's Cavity 25m VS 4b **
M.Tighe, K.Tighe, 11 Jul 2000
The corner-groove around the corner from the main wall gives good climbing.

16 Extraction 25m E3 5c **
R.Anderson, C.Anderson, 15 Oct 2014
Make a few moves up Kenny's Cavity then step onto the left wall and climb a shallow left-facing groove to a small roof, which is surmounted at its widest point. Continue to a finish up the juggy headwall.

17 Octopod 25m HS 4b **
M.Tighe, K.Tighe, 11 Jul 2000
Start at the base of Kenny's Cavity and follow a curving crack-line out left for a few metres before heading straight up the gently bulging wall on excellent jugs. A possible exit right at two-thirds height is better avoided by taking the lovely quartzy wall directly above.

Snake Dyke (E2) Andy Turner
(photo Mike Hutton)

18 Squid 25m E1/2 5b *
M.Tighe, K.Tighe, H.Clark, 20 Jul 2000
Start at the same place as Octopod but climb the much thinner curving crack below the main one, to a ledge at half-height. Now go up the wall into a shallow chimney and finish by a 3m flake-crack.

19 Snake Dyke 25m E2 5c ***
M.Tighe, K.Tighe, 11 Jul 2000
The superb diagonal fault leads to a ledge at half-height and is well protected by small to medium friends. Easier climbing up the brown groove leads to the top.

The wall now falls back into a small bay with the scrambling approach route in the back: **The Exit** (D/VD). Squirm climbed a corner here then went right to Snake Dyke but most of this appears to have been removed by the sea in 2014/15. Beyond this is a short smooth wall, after which the cliff peters out into the sea. Channel 1 lies on the other side of this smooth wall.

The Channels

To the east of, and just behind the Folded Wall, on the north side of Àird Mhòr Bhràgair, there is a series of sea inlets and promontories. These are guarded by a similar series of low-lying islands, or skerries, in the sea to the north, which almost mirror their landward neighbours. The channels have been numbered 1 to 4, as have the skerries.

Channel 1

(NB 2696 4961) Map p170

Lying some 25m to the north of the top of the Folded Wall, this narrow channel can be viewed from the ramp leading down northwards from the top of Octopod and Snake Dyke. The first climb is on the north-east tip of this channel and the next two are around the corner to the west, on the north wall opposite Skerry 1.

Sgarbh Beag 25m S 4a
M.Tighe, K.Tighe, J.Winter, N.McGoughan, 7 Jun 2004
Abseil to a good ledge at the north-east corner of Channel 1. Follow big flakes up and slightly left to a big ramp near the top, then finish up a groove in the wall.

Crack and Slab 25m VS 4b
M.Tighe, K.Tighe, 7 Jun 2004
The most westerly line on the wall. Climb a short groove and crack above the belay ledge to a ramp-ledge at mid-height. A delicate, poorly protected slab leads to the top.

D Day 25m HVS 5a/b ***
M.Tighe, K.Tighe, 7 Jun 2004
Almost in the middle of the wall an unclimbed crack runs up into a groove guarded by a short overhanging section. Follow this crack for a few metres and go left into a corner. Pull out and left under an overhang to a little pedestal below the final thought-provoking wall. Sustained and well protected but a touch fragile.

Channel 2

(NB 2700 4962) p170

The small Skerry 2 lies off the entrance. On the west side of the channel there is a big, unclimbed, sloping black slab at the mouth. On the east side a diagonal fault-line, steep at the bottom, starts at the seaward end and slopes up from left to right to give the next climb.

Frigate 25m E1 5b **
M.Tighe, K.Tighe, Y.Colwell, 29 May 2001
Either abseil to the foot, or approach down a series of ledges around the edge on the north side of the promontory. The corner is tricky low down but eases a bit after halfway.

On the north wall of the promontory, there is a fine broken corner-line about a third of the way along.

Ken's Route 25m VS 4c
K.Colwell, R.McLachlan, 29 May 2001
Belay on the apron slab at the bottom and climb the broken corner; trickier than it looks although the protection is good.

Chanel 25m HS 4b
M.Tighe, T.McLachlan, 29 May 2001
Moving east the crag starts to overhang. This route climbs up under the initial overhang before traversing out right to avoid it, and so to the top.

Roberton's Jam 25m E1 5b
H.Roberton, M.Tighe, 29 May 2001
Follow the initial part of Chanel then continue up the crack that cuts through the overhang.

There are fierce overhangs at the eastern end of this promontory opposite Skerry 3.

Channel 3 - Geòdha Braighe

(NB 2708 4964) Map p170

This is a long and narrow inlet with two climbs starting on the west wall around the edge from Roberton's Jam, well viewed from the opposite (eastern side) of the channel. About 10m in from the seaward end of the wall there is a vertical fault-line running the full height of the cliff. The first climb starts at the bottom of the fault-line.

Black Sabbath 45m E2 5b
M.Tighe, H.Clark, 1 Sep 2002
Go out diagonally right across the wall fairly low down to a little platform on the corner. Go around the corner and follow a diagonal, gently overhanging crack-line to the top.

Plumb Line 30m E1 5a/b
M.Tighe, K.Tighe, 16 Jun 2003
This takes the fairly prominent line up the east facing west wall of Channel 3. Belay in a notch some 10m in from the seaward corner, below the fault and just above the high tide mark. Go up and left a few metres to a prominent left-sloping ramp, then go straight up the groove above and exit left on slightly friable rock at 5a, or right up the steeper headwall on better rock at 5b.

Channel 4 - Geòdh' an t-Sruthain

(NB 2726 4965) Map p170

The cliffs now decrease in size. The fence which runs due north from Lochan Dubh ends at the head of this channel near the remains of a rusted-out van lie. The east side of this channel is formed by a low line of cliffs, and three climbs start from the extreme north-west corner of the promontory on this side, below an arete, on a small ledge just below the high tide line; calm sea required.

Seal Play 20m HVS 5a
M.Tighe, J.Cargill, 23 Jun 2001
From the small ledge below the arete go up 1m or so, then right into the bottom of a recess, or bay. Climb the wall and the small diagonal groove on the right.

The Arete 20m HVS 5a *
This climb has not been led. Protection is limited, making it a bold lead or a possible deep-water solo if the tide's in.

The Sting 20m HVS 5a ***
M.Tighe, J.Cargill, 23 Jun 2001
The excellent little crack just left of the arete has great protection and a tricky finish. Sometimes damp at the bottom.

There is another small cliff around 100m east again with an interesting looking traverse line near the top; unfortunately the rock is rather suspect. East again is the rocky bay of Dùnan Croir.

ÀIRD BHEAG BHRÀGAIR

(NB 280 498) Map p170

This small headland lies to the east of Àird Mhòr Bhràgair and the bay of Dùnan Croir and forms the most northerly point of this section of coast.

Geòdha nan Gaimhne

(NB 2794 4986) Partially Tidal W & N facing Map p170

This geo forms the west side of Àird Bheag Bhràgair and contains a small cliff that can be seen from Àird Mhòr Bhràgair. This comprises a low, smooth west-facing wall which sits in a small inlet, and a bigger north-west-facing roofed wall overlooking a bay with easy-angled slabs on its north side. The small west-facing wall can be viewed from opposite. A good non-tidal ledge runs beneath this wall to where it ends at an arete, where the rocks turn to form the bigger north-west facing wall (tidal).

Directions: Take any of the roads leaving the A858 to the east of Siabost bho Thuath and follow the road to its end at Labost. There is room to park on the right at **(NB 280 294)**, just before the last houses.

Approach: Walk to the turning circle at the road-end, step over the fence and walk out to the headland (10min).

Descent: Abseil down the middle of the wall to the ledge which runs beneath it.

Climbs are described from right to left.

One for the Road 12m HS 4b
R.Anderson, M.Garthwaite, 19 Jul 2015
The obvious crack in the right side of the smooth central section of the wall.

Two for the Money 12m E2 5c **
M.Garthwaite, R.Anderson, 19 Jul 2015
The right-hand of a pair of thin tramline cracks in the smooth central wall.

Three of a Kind 12m E3 5c *
M.Garthwaite, R.Anderson, 19 Jul 2015
The left-hand of the tramline cracks.

Four Play 12m HVS 5a *
R.Anderson, M.Garthwaite, 19 Jul 2015
The crack up the left side of the smooth central section; gained by stepping across a gap in the ledge.

High Five 20m E3 5c *
M.Garthwaite, R.Anderson, 19 Jul 2015
Start from the far left end of the ledge system beneath the wall. Climb up and left onto the edge, then go up to the roof. Traverse beneath it to a break then pull through to finish.

The cliff now turns the corner into a small tidal bay with easy slabs running down its north side, which can be descended to gain the next route.

Tower of Babel 20m HVS 5a
M.Garthwaite, R.Anderson, 17 Jul 2016
The pillar at the left end of the wall, gained by walking down the slabs. Probably not to remain in place for too long!

Ness (Nis)

Maps p19 & right

This, the northernmost part of the Isle of Lewis, was originally settled by the Norse and is fairly well populated in various ribbon settlements off the main A857. Unsurprisingly, there is a seafaring tradition here and each year a pilgrimage is maintained to Sula Sgeir, a small lump of rock in the sea 40 miles (64km) to the north, to collect young gannets (gugga). Port Ness has a little harbour and a beach which is overlooked by Cafe Sonas, whilst nearby the Cross Keys Inn also provides hospitality. The flatness of the landscape can give Ness a bleak and inhospitable look but this is offset by the big skies, the restless sea and the coastal scenery. It is a wild and spectacular bit of coast to walk. Many climbers visit when the weather is poor elsewhere to watch the waves battering in at the Butt. There is some climbing and bouldering and perhaps more to be found.

THE BUTT OF LEWIS

Lying level with and due west from Sandwood Bay near Cape Wrath on the mainland, this is the most northerly point on Lewis. A lighthouse sits on the tip and can be seen from some distance away on the approach.

Directions: Take the A857 to Ness, then either the B8013 or the B8014 to Eoropie (Eòropaidh) where the road is signposted out to the Butt of Lewis. On the final section of the road out to the lighthouse is a lovely, small east-facing bay is passed called Port Stoth and there are three easy climbs here. Park at the lighthouse. It is 55 miles (88km) from the Uig area and takes about 1hr 30min.

Port Stoth

(NB 5236 6597) Non-tidal S facing Map above

The small east facing sandy bay 600m to the south-east of the lighthouse. There is a small cliff on the north side, at the back of the bay.

Picnic Bay Arete 10m S
G.Lynn, 5 Aug 2010
The bounding left-hand arete, visible from the approach.

Sandy Sandwiches 10m S
G.Lynn, 5 Aug 2010
The crack to the left of the right-hand arete to join the arete near the top; some loose rock.

Bouldering Mat Umbrella 10m VS 4c
G.Lynn, 5 Aug 2010
The right-hand arete; awkward moves low down lead to a loose finish.

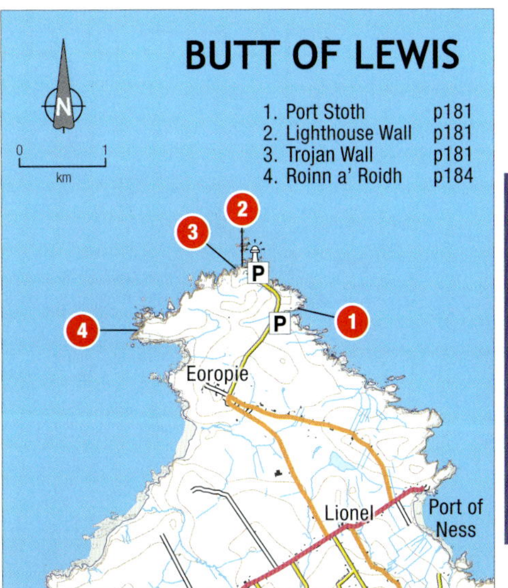

Lighthouse Area

Lighthouse Wall

(NB 519 665) Tidal N facing Map above

Immediately behind the lighthouse is a west facing pillar, gained by abseiling to a narrow ledge from a carefully parked car on the cliff edge; check the handbrake!

Mondeo Man 20m HVS 5a
C.Henderson, R.Durran, 9 Jul 2008
Climb a short, steep crack above the left side of the ledge and finish more easily rightwards.

About 100m to the west of the lighthouse there is a 20m high stack: the Conspiracy Stack. Descent is by abseil from rocks, or stakes (not in-situ, bring your own) to a narrow channel that separates the stack from the mainland. After a large step across, difficult moves are made to a platform and belay.

Northern Conspiracy 20m HS 4b *
R.I.Jones, J.Sanders, 12 Jun 2004
Climb the landward (south) face by a left-slanting groove-ramp with an awkward step left at mid-height to easier ground. Good climbing on good rock.

Trojan Wall

(NB 5184 6650) Tidal W facing Map above Diagram p182

This buttress of rock is often pictured in tourist brochures and postcards of the lighthouse. About 150m to the west of the lighthouse is a sizeable geo which has a large landslip in its south end. Trojan Wall lies on the

1.	Journey Over the Sea	E1 5a/b **
2.	Gneiss Achillies...	HS 4a
3.	Apple of Discord	VS 4c
4.	Agamemnon	HVS 5a ***
5.	Menelaus	HVS 5a **
6.	Helen's Chimney	HS 4b *
7.	Hector	HVS 5a **
8.	Odysseus	VS 4c ***
9.	Aphrodite's Promise	E2 5b ***
10.	How Many Husbands...	HS 4a
11.	Trojan Horse	S 4a *
12.	Messing with the Acheans	HVS 5a ***
13.	Don't Look a Gift Horse...	E1 5b ***
14.	Something About the Iliad	HVS 5a **
15.	Patroclus	E1 5b **
16.	Who's Homer?	VS 4c
17.	Trojan Work Ethic	E4 6a **
18.	Hermione's Exit	VS 4c
19.	Hidden Agenda	S
20.	Sinon	HVS 5a

lighthouse side of the geo and is split into two tiers by a large ledge that becomes a sloping ramp to the north-east. The Lower Tier provides some excellent climbs on fine rock with good protection. It is accessible between mid to low tide. Routes on the Upper Tier are more limited and the rock is loose beyond the area where routes are recorded.

Descent: Abseil down the line of Trojan Horse from stakes (not in-situ) 20m back. An abseil is possible from rocks but not advised as these are poor.

Lower Tier

The wall can be easily viewed from the cliff-top on the west side of the geo. It is split into four distinct sections from left to right; Seaward Buttress, Three Corner Buttress, The Wall and Right End Wall. Right of this the rock is loose and broken. Climbs are described from left to right starting at the large chimney in the corner that separates Seaward Buttress from Three Corner Buttress.

Seaward Buttress

The Buttress at the left end of the wall.

1 Journey Over the Sea 25m E1 5a/b **

R.I.Jones, J.Sanders, 17 Jun 2004

An awesome route taking a line out of the chimney in the corner and crossing the overhanging wall on a rising traverse. From a belay at the base of the chimney, climb up 3m then traverse leftwards on a hanging slab to an exposed position above the sea. Pull strenuously up and left onto the face and continue up a left-slanting crack-line on easier ground.

2 Gneiss Achillies But Not As We Know It! 13m HS 4a
J.Sanders, R.I.Jones, 17 Jun 2004
Climbs the left-hand corner of the chimney on adequate holds; poor protection.

Three Corner Buttress

The buttress to the right of the corner and chimney.

3 Apple of Discord 13m VS 4c
R.I.Jones, A.Wardle, 6 Sep 2008
Climb the right-hand corner of the chimney.

Just to the right is a 5m-wide wall, undercut on its left-hand side.

4 Agamemnon 15m HVS 5a ***
R.I.Jones, J.Sanders, 17 Jun 2004
Start 2m from the left of the 5m wall, climb directly up on good holds and steep ground.

5 Menelaus 15m HVS 5a **
R.I.Jones, J.Sanders, 17 Jun 2004
Pull onto the 5m wall from the right side, trend slightly left and then straight up on good holds.

6 Helen's Chimney 15m HS 4b *
J.Sanders, R.I.Jones, 18 Jun 2004
The crack-corner and chimney on the right.

7 Hector 15m HVS 5a **
A.Wardle, R.I.Jones, 6 Sep 2008
The arete right of Helen's Chimney.

8 Odysseus 15m VS 4c ***
R.I.Jones, J.Sanders, 12 Jun 2004
The central of the three corners gives excellent climbing with the crux saved for the last few moves.

9 Aphrodite's Promise 15m E2 5b ***
R.I.Jones, A.Wardle, 6 Sep 2008
The excellent overhanging arete right of Odysseus. Pull out right through the overhang and then left onto the wall right of Odysseus to finish.

The Wall

The following climbs take the wall to the right of the third corner, forming the right side of Three Corner Buttress.

10 How Many Husbands Does A Beautiful Girl Get? 15m HS 4a
A.Wardle, R.I.Jones, 10 Sep 2008
Climb the corner, stepping right at the overhang to finish as for Trojan Horse.

11 Trojan Horse 27m S *
J.Sanders, R.I.Jones, 12 Jun 2004
This climbs both tiers, taking a line just right of the corner.
1. 3c 15m Climb a left-slanting crack 2m right of the corner.
2. 4a 12m Climb the middle of the upper wall directly through the bulge.

12 Messing with the Achaeans 15m HVS 5a ***
R.I.Jones, J.Sanders, 17 Jun 2004
Start 2m right of Trojan Horse and climb the centre of the wall direct through steep ground to a hanging niche. Pull through this on the left and continue to the top.

13 Don't Look a Gift Horse in the Mouth 15m E1 5b ***
R.I.Jones, J.Sanders, 17 Jun 2004
A metre to the right, climb up and rightwards above a right-facing overhanging corner. Pull up and rightwards through steep ground and climb the wall direct, trending right of the orange wall to reach the top.

14 Something About the Iliad 15m HVS 5a **
R.I.Jones, J.Sanders, 12 Jun 2004
Climb the wall 4m to the right to an overhang at 5m. Take this on the right and move up to a right-facing hanging-corner. Climb the corner and pull out left onto the wall above and then continue to the top.

Right End Wall

15 Patroclus 15m E1 5b **
A.Wardle, R.I.Jones, 6 Sep 2008
Start by a niche and left of a short pillar. Climb the wall and step left at the overhang then climb the chimney to an airy finish.

16 Who's Homer? 15m VS 4c
R.I.Jones, J.Sanders, 17 Jun 2004
Climb a short pillar in the centre of the wall and step right onto a hanging slab. Follow good holds in a rising traverse. Pull up and right into a niche and climb to the top with care.

Upper Tier

About 5m to the left of the second pitch of Trojan Horse, the wall turns the edge and beyond the left arete is a north-facing wall above a sloping non-tidal shelf. Near the arete is a crack leading into a shallow groove. This is reached by abseil from a poor spike near the edge, backed up by an old metal spike well back along the top of the Upper Tier.

17 Trojan Work Ethic 25m E4 6a **
R.Durran, C.Henderson, 9 Jul 2008
Climb the crack and get into the shallow groove, all hard work, then continue steadily to the top.

The next climbs are around the edge to the right, to the left of the top pitch of Trojan Horse, and are gained by the normal abseil down that line.

18 Hermione's Exit 18m VS 4c
A.Wardle, R.I.Jones, 6 Sep 2008
Climb the left-facing corner-groove on the left side of the wall. Step left and go up the next short corner then traverse right under the hanging niche on the final headwall to finish. Finishing up the niche is 5b but the protection and rock are poor.

The middle of the main wall is taken by the second pitch of Trojan Horse and the next is to its right.

19 Hidden Agenda 15m S
J.Sanders, R.I.Jones, 12 Jun 2004
Climb the wall 2m right of Trojan Horse to a small overhang at mid-height. Pull out rightwards into a right-facing corner and climb to the top.

20 Sinon 12m HVS 5a
R.I.Jones, A.Wardle, 10 Sep 2008
Pull up the right arete, onto the wall left of the arete, and climb to an overhang; junction with Hidden Agenda. Pull onto the pillar above from the right and climb this in a fine position.

Far Right Buttress

The cliff immediately right of Trojan Wall is loose and unstable; 30m south of this wall is another buttress with two prominent right-facing corners in the lower section. The shallow left-hand corner angles up leftwards; the right-hand corner is vertical to a shallow roof and is bounded by a rib on the left. The two climbs provide good climbing but also some loose rock.

Descent: Abseil from old in-situ stakes.

Wit Amidst Folly 35m HVS 5a
R.Jones, C.Jones, 16 Apr 2012
Start below and just right of the left-hand corner. Climb the wall right of the corner, trending slightly rightwards to pull out onto a halfway ledge just left of a broken hanging rib. Step left and directly up with care to finish right of a detached corner-crack.

Another Case for Dr Lightfoot 35m E1 5a
R.Jones, C.Jones, 16 Apr 2012
Start below the right-hand corner. Climb the corner and then the right side of the rib to the halfway ledge. Climb a shallow chimney and pull out left onto a shallow roof. Climb up for 3m then traverse rightwards to finish up a right-facing corner.

Roinn a' Roidh

(NB 507 658) Non-tidal W facing Map p181 Diagram above

This is the most westerly point of the Butt of Lewis headland. Just north of a cairn with a stone serpent at its base is a geo which contains an obvious wall, well seen from the south side. This is just north of the western tip, the Toll a' Roidh, which has an arch through it known as the Eye of the Butt of Lewis.

Approach: Walk along the top of the cliffs from the lighthouse car park, following the waymarked coastal trail (20min).

Descent: Although the base of the climbs can be gained by a traverse of the opposite wall of the geo and stepping over a gap onto the wall, stakes (not in-situ) are required for the belay on top and can therefore be used for abseil access.

1 Knucker 25m E1 5b
A.Wardle, R.I.Jones, 6 Sep 2008
Climb the slanting crack-line on the left of the wall and right of the niche to the overhang. Traverse left around the overhang and pull right onto the wall above to finish.

2 Nagini 25m E2 5b ***
R.I.Jones, A.Wardle, 6 Sep 2008
Start from a ledge under the overhang on the right side of the wall; climb up leftwards to the wall just left of a right-facing hanging corner. Climb the wall and shallow, capped groove-crack above to pull out left, then go rightwards to a ledge and niche above to finish.

Some climbing and bouldering has been claimed on other sections of the coast hereabouts, some of it unappealing. This is at places named The Boneyard Crag, Ramrageo and Creag Dubh out towards Skigersta but a visit by the author and others has revealed little to substantiate wild claims! No doubt further investigation will reveal climbing but unfortunately for the meantime the information is discounted. There is good bouldering to be had and definitely more to be properly and truthfully documented.

THE EAST COAST

Map p19

Three small areas on the east side of Lewis are covered in this section: Tolsta to the north of Stornoway, the Eye Peninsula to the east and Caitiosbhal to the south.

TOLSTA (TOLASTADH)

The settlements of New Tolsta and North Tolsta lie on north-east coast to the north of Stornoway. Beyond the sands of Tràigh Mhòr and Tràigh Ghearadha there is an isolated cliff at Dùn Othail. The beach at Tràigh Ghearadha has some small tidal sea stacks and there is apparently some bouldering here.

Dùn Othail

(NB 542 515) N, E & S facing Map p19

This tower lies on a small headland beyond the road end at Tolsta.

Directions: Take the A857 north out of Stornoway and at Newmarket on the edge of town, turn right and follow the B895 up the east coast through Tunga, Coll and Back to the parking area at the road end beyond Tolsta. This is at the northern end of the lovely 2.5km long stretch of sand that is Tràigh Mhòr, and above the smaller beach of Tràigh Ghearadha with its sea stacks. The car park at the northern end of Tràigh Mhòr has toilets.

Approach: Walk north up the peat track, crossing the Bridge to Nowhere which was part of Lord Leverhulme's plan to build a road up the coast to Ness. This is now a waymarked Heritage Trail. Follow the track, from which the castle-like crag becomes visible, and when it ends continue on the route ahead which swings back towards the 89m highpoint on the coast to the side of Dùn Othail (3km; 45min).

North Wall

Although the bay just north of the tower offers a few possible routes, the first climbs are some 400m north of the tower, on a wall with four large boulders at the bottom.

Descent: Abseil down the wall.

Haar 15m S
A.Macfarlane, D.McGimpsey, 5 Jul 1989
Climb the slabby wall immediately above the four large boulders.

The Milky Bar Kid 20m VS
A.Macfarlane, D.McGimpsey, 15 Jul 1989
North of the four boulders is a large, arched roof, then a south facing corner. Start up a ramp on the right of the corner, then move into the main corner-chimney.
Variation: **Direct Start E1 5c**
Start up the steep jamming crack that forms the bottom of the chimney.

The Grey Tower

From the previous routes, and the coast just to the north of the dun, it is possible to look back and see two obvious corner-lines on the grey tower on the dun itself.

Descent: Abseil from the neck of land joining the tower to the mainland. It also appears possible to scramble delicately down on the north side.

Celtic Swing 65m E1 *
A.Macfarlane, D.McGimpsey, 5 Jul 1989
This follows the right-hand corner.
1. 4a Climb the wall and corner to belay on a ledge with some loose rock.
2. 5b/c Step up from the belay, then traverse left to a short corner and go up right to a large ledge. Alternatively, climb straight up a crack from the belay then go left to the large ledge. From the ledge, take the left-hand crack to a belay.
3. 4c Follow the corner to below a large pillar and traverse left to exit.

Druid 65m E2 ***
A.Macfarlane, D.McGimpsey, 20 Jun 1989
A companion route which following the left-hand corner.
1. 10m 5a Climb the wall to the right of the corner to belay on the ledge.
2. 35m 5b Step around the corner and climb it to an obvious large ledge and belay.
3. 20m 5a Continue up the corner to finish.

The next climbs lie on the south side of the tower.

Looksee Crack 50m VS
J.R.Mackenzie, A.McDonald, 14 Aug 1971
Start by a big detached flake. Climb behind this to a recess and overhang. Further laybacks to a heather ledge, a wall to the right, a broad terrace and a choice of corners lead to the summit.

Below the grass on the south side of the tower are three obvious open corners at sea-level: the Open Books.

State of Mind 20m E1 5a
A.Macfarlane, D.McGimpsey, 13 Aug 1989
The right-hand corner.

Cloud Burst 20m E2 5b
B.Davison, A.Nisbet, 13 Aug 1989
The left-hand corner.

THE EYE PENINSULA (AN RUBHA)

Map p19

Separated from Stornoway by a narrow isthmus, this peninsula extends eastward into the sea. There are sea-cliffs of a variable nature near the village of Upper Bayble (Pabail Uarach).

Directions: Take the A866 east past the airport onto the Eye Peninsula then turn off right, either before or after Garrabost, and follow the road to where it ends beyond

Upper Bayble. Vehicles can be taken as far as the aircraft beacon **(NB 544 319)**.

Descent: Walk left and contour the cliff edge to follow a path down a grassy gully. At sea-level, cross blocks and the route starts by a slab. This is due east from the beacon.

Jacob's Ladder 80m S
A.McDonald, A.McDonald, 29 Aug 1971
1. 15m Climb the slab and corner to grass and belay below a crack.
2. 40m Go up the crack, step left to an overhang and go over this, then traverse right to a groove. Climb a slab to a shallow chimney which is taken to a grassy recess.
3. 25m Gain a corner and climb this.
Variation: **Alternative Finish 25m VS**
J.R.Mackenzie, A.McDonald, 12 Dec 1972
3a Traverse right over grass and then slabs, then hand-traverse across the steep face on good holds before swinging over a bulge to a small ledge. Traverse right to a corner, climb this, then go up the slab for a short distance before hand-traversing left to a sloping shelf. Finish by surmounting the arete and an easy slab.

SOUTH LOCHS

This area of Lewis lies to the south of Stornoway and south of Loch Eireasort, the sea loch that bites deep into the island.

Caitiosbhal

(NB 406 171) Alt 50m S facing Map p19

These roadside crags lie on the hillside of Caitiosbhal in the South Lochs area of Pairc, about 1km to the west of Calbost. They are of good quality gneiss and although they are not very steep they are pleasantly situated overlooking Loch Mirceabhat.

Directions: Turn south off the main A859 Stornoway to Tarbert road at the west end of Ballalan (Baille Ailein), at the end of Loch Eireasort, and follow the B8060 through Cearsiader and Gearraidh Bhaird. The crags can be reached on a loop road, either through Taobh a' Ghlinne, or Marbhig. Park at the top of the hill before the road descends to Calbost; there is space off the road by the bridge over the outflow from Loch Beag Caitiosbhal.

Approach: Walk down the road and go uphill to the slabs (2min).

Left-hand Slab

1 Far Left 28m M *
C.Grindley, C.Moody, 12 May 2008
The left-hand of two lines on the slab.

2 Yellow Patches 28m M *
C.Moody, C.Grindley, 12 May 2008
The right-hand line on the slab.

3 Upper Cracks 18m VD *
C.Moody, 12 May 2008
Up and right of the slab is a crack in a short wall, climb this to a grassy ledge then move left and climb another crack.

Right-hand Slab

4 One 20m M
C.Moody, 12 May 2008
The far left-hand route.

5 Two 22m M **
C.Moody, C.Grindley, 12 May 2008
The fine left-hand, easy-angled crack.

6 Three 24m M **
C.Grindley, C.Moody, 12 May 2008
Walk up the right-hand crack.

Juniper Buttress

This lies right of the slabs and is slightly steeper; descend off right.

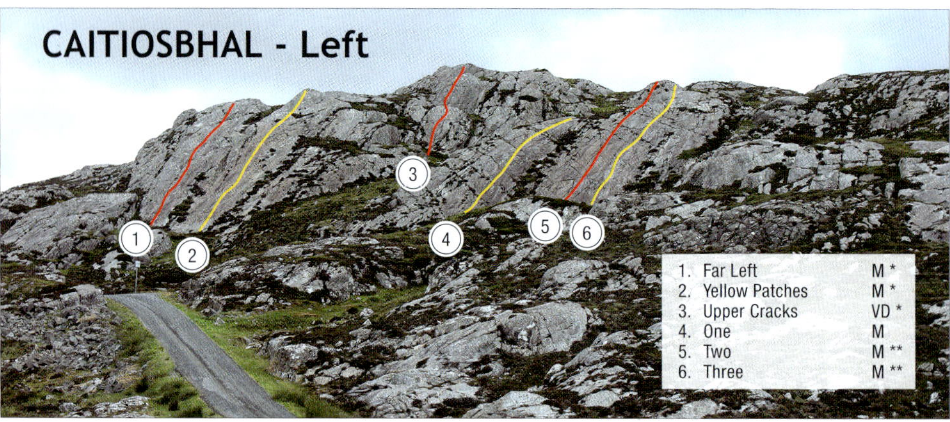

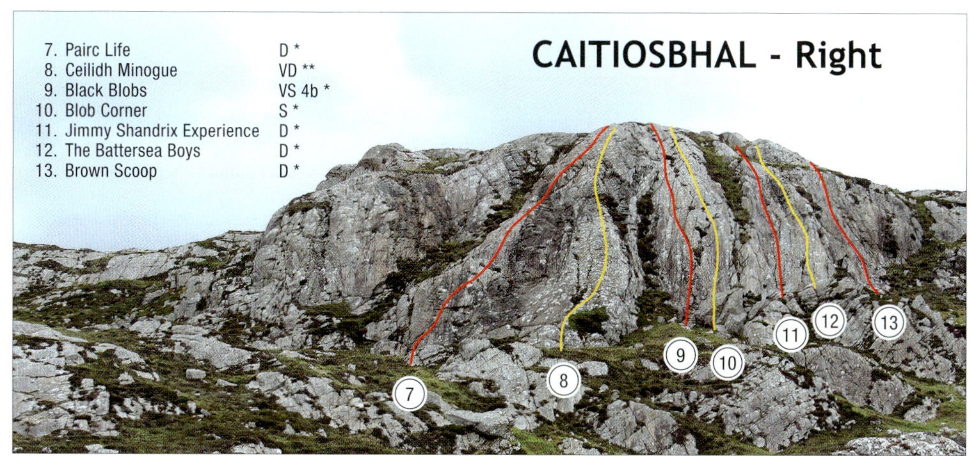

7 Pairc Life 45m D *
R.Anderson, C.Anderson, 10 Jul 2012
Start at the lowest rocks left of Ceilidh Minogue and climb the slabby rib, then slant up right to finish just left of that route.

8 Ceilidh Minogue 40m VD **
C.Moody, C.Grindley, 12 May 2008
Fine climbing up the longest bit of rock. Start at the toe of the buttress left of an embedded spike. Climb up then move right above a large juniper bush and climb the rib.

9 Black Blobs 25m VS 4b *
C.Grindley, C.Moody, 12 May 2008
Start at a grassy corner and rib .Climb up on black blobs then continue up the rounded rib above.

10 Blob Corner 25m S *
C.Grindley, C.Moody, 12 May 2008
Climb just right of a slanting corner with heather patches.

11 The Jimmy Shandrix Experience 15m D *
C.Moody, C.Grindley, 12 May 2008
The fine scoop to the right of a vegetated corner.

12 The Battersea Boys 15m D *
C.Moody, 12 May 2008
Start 2m right of The Jimmy Shandrix Experience and climb another scoop past a clump of heather at 4m.

13 Brown Scoop 15m D *
C.Moody, 12 May 2008
Start 5m right at quartz crystals and climb pleasantly up.

Ceilidh Minogue (VD) Rab Anderson (photo Chris Anderson)

The Uig Hills

Maps p19 & opposite

Although the main focus of attention for climbers' visiting the Uig area is undoubtedly the climbing on the sea-cliffs, one cannot fail to be impressed by the splendid coastal backdrop formed by the Uig Hills. These wild and remarkably rugged hills form two principal chains running in a south-north direction towards the sands at Uig Bay (Camus Uig). These chains are split by the beautifully sculpted Glen Raonasgail, whose classic U-shaped sides and bealach are prominent when viewed from the north. The highest hill in Lewis, the conical shaped Mealaisbhal, sits at the northern end of the westerly chain of hills and contains a large north face of broken rock, which is where some of the early routes on Lewis were pioneered.

There is a large amount of rock in the hills, although much of it is too broken, too slabby or too small to be of great interest. Of particular note however is the very fine and conspicuous sweep of slabs forming the north face of Griomabhal at the southern end of the westerly chain; the Tealasdail, or Griomabhal Slabs. These offer some lovely routes at a reasonable grade in a tremendous setting. At the southern end of the eastern chain of hills is the incongruous rounded lump of Tamanasbhal which hides a magnificent cliff tucked away on its east face: Creag Dhubh Dhìobadail, one of the country's finest, biggest and least frequented mountain crags. Sgorran Dubh Teinneasabhal lies on the next hill north and contains some of the early mountaineering style routes climbed in the hills. At the northern end of this chain the rocky Beannan a' Dheas holds some shorter climbs, as does Sneihabhal together with its rocky nose Sròn ri Gaoth, the outlying hill to the south of Suaineabhal on the other side of the loch of the same name.

Despite their rather modest altitude these rugged mountains have much character and are of interest to both the climber and the walker. Although small in comparison to the hills of the mainland it is worth ascending any of these hills for the tremendous panorama that extends on one side across the wave-torn Atlantic coastline out to The Flannnan Isles and St Kilda and on the other across the Minch to the mainland. No visit to the area is complete without a walk to the summit of one of the hills and even better to one of the fine inland crags where there is good adventurous climbing to be had in splendid surroundings.

There are six main climbing areas: the Glen Tealasdail or Griomabhal Slabs; Creagan Tealasdale; Creag Dhubh Dhìobadail; Sgorran Dubh Teinneasabhal; Beannan a' Dheas and finally the crags on the east side of Loch Suaineabhal on Suaineabhal and Sneibhal.

GRIOMABHAL

Tealasdail Slabs

(NB 012 220) Alt 250m N facing
Map opposite Diagram p190

Visible from much of the Uig coastline, these prominent slabs lie on Griomabhal (497m), the southernmost of the western chain of hills, and are set in a splendid position overlooking the dark waters of the Dubh Loch at the head of Gleann Tealasdail. The rock is a mix of gneiss and quartz-like pegmatite giving excellent slab climbing on clean sound rock which leads to an abrupt top-out on the summit of Griomabhal.

The nature of the rock means that it is possible to climb almost anywhere. The cliff is slow to dry after the winter but thereafter it dries fairly quickly after rain and although there are weeps it is usually possible to dodge them, connecting the available dry rock. The steeply inclined grassy terrace of Golden Gully separates the Main Slab from the shorter left-hand East Buttress. On the steeper lower half of the Main Slab the lines are more independent and above this the rock type changes to produce a tapering sweep of unbroken quartz-like pegmatite where the slab narrows and the routes are forced together. Protection and belays can be a bit scarce at times. An early guidebook described the slabs as 'hopeless and manifestly unclimbable'.

Some of the earlier routes have seen few ascents and as well as descriptions being awkward to figure out, the lines prove difficult to precisely place on the diagram, so this should only be used as a rough indicator.

Directions: Follow the B8011 past the turn off signed to Mangurstadh and go through Islivig then Breanish to reach the end of the road at a slipway in the bay at Camas Mol Linnis **(NB 9935 2343)**. There are various places to park around the bay and at the road-end; please leave the turning space at the end clear.

Approach: Head south to a boulder beach then go uphill and cross a fence beside a burn. Climb uphill and go rightwards through a gap between cairned knolls, then continue rising across a second burn. A third burn is reached in the upper reaches of Gleann Tealasdail and followed to the Dubh Loch (2.5km, 1hr). Steep grass leads to the foot of the climbs which are described from right to left.

Descent: Both the east and west shoulders of Griomabhal can be descended, although the left-hand east flank is more convenient, especially if rucksacks have been left below. This is achieved by heading east down the shoulder for 400m to the north end of a tiny lochan, then dropping steeply down a shallow gully-fault, on its left side, to gain the west end of Loch Bràighe Griomabhal before heading west through the gap. It is worthwhile having the second carry a sac with lightweight boots, or trainers.

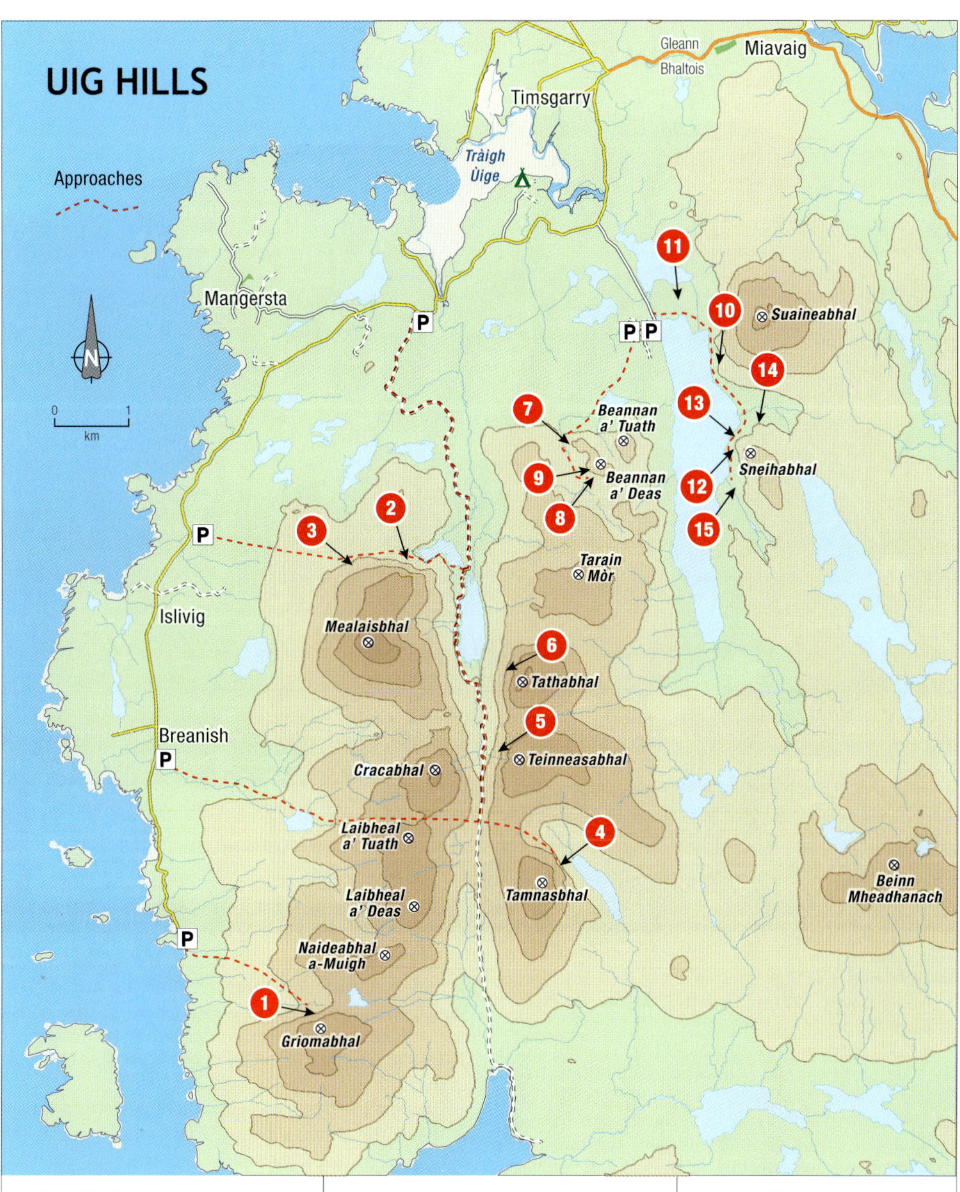
UIG HILLS
Approaches
0 1
km
Gleann Bhaltois
Miavaig
Timsgarry
Tràigh Ùige
Mangersta
Islivig
Breanish
Suaineabhal
Beannan a' Tuath
Beannan a' Deas
Sneihabhal
Tarain Mòr
Mealaisbhal
Tathabhal
Teinneasabhal
Cracabhal
Laibheal a' Tuath
Laibheal a' Deas
Tamnasbhal
Naideabhal a-Muigh
Griomabhal
Beinn Mheadhanach

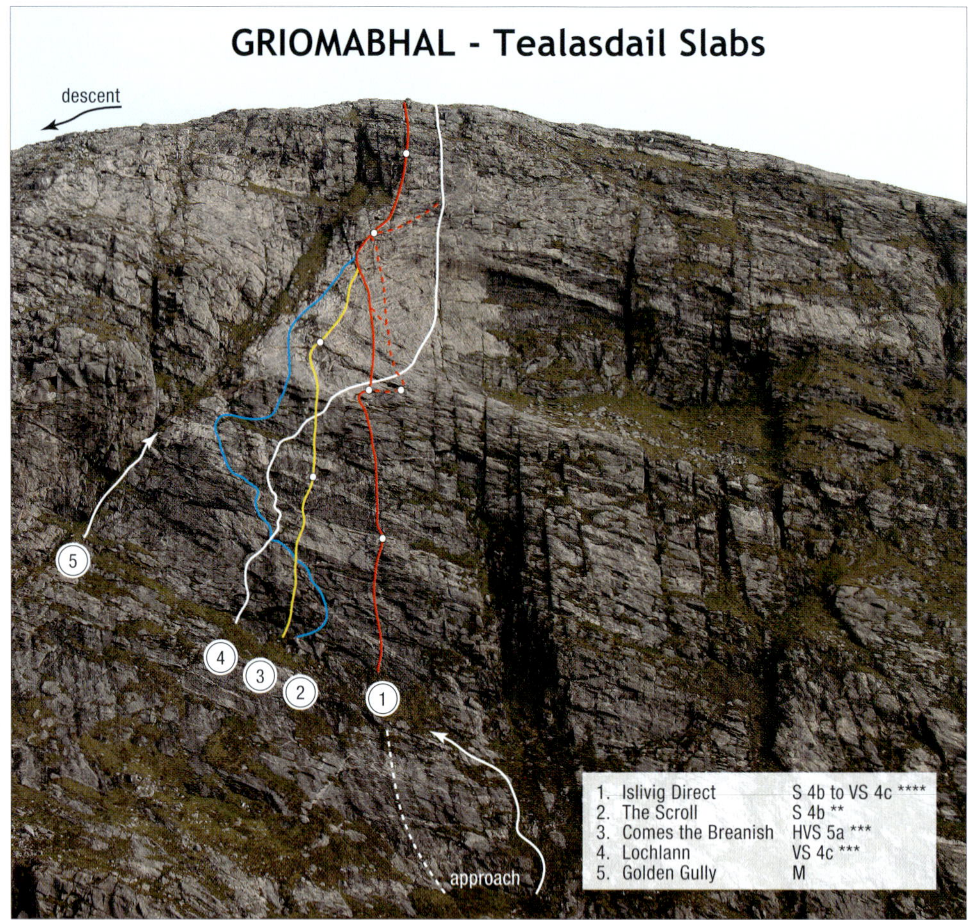

Main Slab

1 Islivig Direct 270m HS 4b to VS 4c ****

R.Sharp, W.Sproul, 8 Jun 1969

A magnificent outing taking a direct line from the foot of the slabs to the summit. A lower band of easy slabs can be climbed in one long pitch to a sitting belay (no gear) on the grass terrace beneath the main slabs, thereby avoiding the grassy slope to the right. The start of the route proper is towards the right side of the slab and about 50m to the left of the grassy gully bordering the right side of the slabs.

1. 60m 4b A long first pitch up grooves, cracks, walls and corners leads to a good belay at the left end of a grass ledge.

2. 60m 4b Continuing in a similar fashion, another long pitch with possible intermediate belays leads to the left end of a terrace below the upper slabs. The terrace runs beneath an overlap which slants up from right to left and there is now a choice.

3a. 60m 4b From the left end of the terrace, follow a thin crack-line up and over the two principal overlaps. Continue up a more defined crack (possible belay) which leads towards Golden Gully. Just below a grass ledge climb up to the upper cracks and belay below or above a small overlap.

3b. 60m 4b/4c From the right end of the terrace, where it meets the overlap, follow a thin crack through the next overlap with reasonable protection to where it fades, then move into the crack on the left to continue as for 3a. Instead of moving left, it is better but harder to continue straight up the slab over two minor overlaps and up the right side of a dark streak with the odd bit of protection, to reach a belay at the small overlap beneath the upper cracks after 60m.

4, 5. 90m 4b, 4a A choice of lines up various cracks lead to an abrupt finish at the summit. It is also possible to slant up right to join the upper crack-line of Lochlann.

2 The Scroll 300m S **
J.Ball, M.Reeves, 13 Aug 1970
Start beneath the right side of the central overlaps on the main slab, below and left of a line of weakness which slants up left. The top section is likely to be similar to or the same as Islivig Direct and Comes the Breanish. Pegs used for belays on the original ascent.
1. 35m Go right for about 10m, then follow a weakness trending left above the start to a small grass ledge.
2. 35m Continue trending left to a good rock ledge.
3. 25m Go straight up to the end of a long grass ledge just right of Golden Gully.
4. 40m Move 10m right and down the grass to a small groove. Ascend the slab directly until the angle eases. Continue by trending right to a small ledge.
5. 40m Go diagonally right to a grassy ledge.
6. 45m Climb straight up to a rock ledge.
7. 40m Climb diagonally right to a crack-line which leads to a small ledge.
8. 40m Climb a crack then more broken slabs.

3 Comes the Breanish 275m HVS ***
R.Anderson, C.Anderson, 16 Jul 1998
Start beneath the right side of the central overlaps, at the same point as The Scroll and right of Lochlann. A fine direct making the best use of the rope.
1. 55m 4c Step right and climb straight up to the left-trending weakness of The Scroll, then continue straight up onto a quartzy protuberance. Climb a thin crack past a small, narrow, wedged block to reach a white slab (Lochlann and The Scroll belay over to the left). Continue straight up passing a block on its right side to belay higher up beneath an overlap at the top of a short, right-facing corner; wires in a horizontal in the overlap. A superb and generally well protected pitch on perfect rock.
2. 55m 5a This takes the middle of the main seepage area and although it can be climbed fairly direct when wet, it will be better if dry. Step left and pull onto the white quartz-like slab above the overlap, then climb straight to the left end of an overlap with a pointed bit in its middle. Climb the bulge on the left, just left of a thin crack (possibly easier further right if dry) and continue to a short, overlapped corner. Climb this, or if wet step right and move over a small overlap, onto a smooth white slab and make a few thin moves to gain a small quartzy overlap (gear) then step left back into the top of the corner. Above the corner, follow slabs, holds and quartzy seams to a small grass ledge then gain a grassy horizontal break and move right to a short, left-facing corner.

Islivig Direct (HS) Eric Parker, Maurice Birkill & Sarah Birkill (photo Ron Kenyon)

3. 55m 4b Step up right, then go up and follow thin cracks in a quartzy line trending up right. Cross a crack-line (junction with Islivig Direct pitch 3a) and continue as for this to a more obvious crack-line which is climbed for a short way to a small ledge just short of the grassy rake of Golden Gully.
4. 55m 4b Move right along the ledge a little to gain then climb twin cracks and continue to reach a ledge occupied by some blocks.
5. 55m 4a Move right and climb easily to a wide crack then on up to the summit.

4 Lochlann 270m VS ***
D.C.Forrest, J.McEwan, 4 Jun 1970
To the left of Islivig Direct and The Scroll, the slabs begin with a series of black overlaps, directly below a slab corner starting 10m up.
1. 30m Climb through the overlaps to gain the corner and follow this to the slabs above. Traverse right to a smooth white slab and climb this to a small ledge left of a larger grass ledge; peg belay originally used.
2. 40m Climb the groove behind the ledge and move right to the end of a ramp running left (assumed to be taken by The Scroll). Follow this then climb a white scoop. Go left to a crack and climb this through several overlaps to a large grass ledge; belay just to the right.
3. 30m Climb the slabs and corners above, going right to take a belay (peg originally used) in a sweep of white water-worn slabs.
4, 5, 6. 170m Go right up slabs, crossing Islivig Direct, and finish up a crack through walls and slabs well to the right.

East Buttress

Golden Gully D
R.Sharp, W.Sproul, May 1968
The steeply inclined grassy terrace separating the main area from that further left.

Joint 120m VS
B.Clarke, K.Tremain, 3 Jun 1972
This takes a line up the wall left of Golden Gully. Scramble 10m up the gully and start from a ledge at the foot of the slabs. On the first pitch pass a flake on its right. On the second, climb a corner-groove at the left end of the overhangs and gain a recess with huge blocks. There is a chimney above, then easier slabs lead to the top.

Reefer 125m S
T.Fletcher, I.Sommerville, 3 Jun 1972
Start at the lowest point of the slabs left of Golden Gully, directly below a prominent square-cut chimney. Follow a crack system for 65m and finish by the chimney and slabs of Joint.

20 Minute Buttress 60m VD
T.Fletcher, I.Sommerville, 3 Jun 1972
The furthest left buttress on the crag. Start at the lowest point and climb straight up using the left-hand V-groove. Finish by easier slabs.

Looking across towards Mealasta from the main slabs, a distinctive south facing outcrop can be seen, which from some angles appears to have a pinnacle. This contains two pleasant one pitch routes. One follows a crack system at VD and the other climbs more directly to the upper crack at VS. An area of west facing slab above Loch Bràighe Griomabhal has also been climbed on. One climb gives 90m of climbing at around D with a short crack in an overlap near the top at D/VD. These are known to be dry when the slabs on Griomabhal are wet.

MEALAISBHAL

At 574m this is the highest hill in Lewis and the most prominent of the Uig Hills, providing a splendid back-drop to the climbing on the Uig sea-cliffs. It sits at the north end of the western chain of hills at the entrance to Gleann Raonasgail.

Creagan Tealasdale

Main Crag

(NB 027 280) Alt 140m N facing Map p189

A large north-facing area of cliff almost 300m high overlooks Loch Mòr na Clibhe on Mula Mac Sgiathain, the termination of the north-east shoulder of Mealais-bhal. Unfortunately much of the rock is too broken and vegetated to afford any continuous climbing. The main cliff is of some historical value but it could perhaps do with a modern look-over and may yield further climbs, although these are perhaps likely to be more mountain-eering in nature. Some recent climbs have been done on Far West Buttress, the small compact crag at the west end.

Approach: Via the bikeable estate track up Gleann Raonasgail as for Creag Dhubh Dhìobidail and Sgorran Dubh Teinneasabhal to reach Loch Mòr na Clibhe then break off right (4.5km, 1hr 15min on foot). Another approach can be made from just north of Islivig, by approaching as for the Far West Buttress (3km, 1hr).

The eastern section above Loch Mòr na Clibhe forms a narrow corrie where the face is cleft from almost the corrie floor to the top by a large fissure called the Polla Glas. On closer inspection this comprises a main gully and to its left a discontinuous lesser gully which starts about one-third of the way up the main gully. The North Rib of the Polla Glas was climbed by W.Ewing and G.R.Symmers in Aug 1933 but few details are available. The eastern side of the corrie gives cleaner rock and the buttress on this side, East Buttress, close to the gully, gives a Grade 2/3 scrambling route with an optional pitch of D; see Highland Scrambles North. To the right of the ridge, adjacent to the Polla Glas, a grass terrace slopes up to the right. Below the terrace three shallow gullies divide the rock into three buttresses and another insignificant buttress at the left end. Above the grass terrace the crags are rather broken, but they are more continuous above the right-hand buttress where the grass terrace virtually terminates.

Descent: Down to the track via the grassy depression above Loch Raonasgail. An alternative is the slope to the north-west then skirting back under the Far West Buttress to follow the glen east to Loch Mòr na Clibhe.

Central Buttress 210m D
R.G.Folkard, M.deV.Wills, Miss J.Fox, 5 Aug 1948
Start in the centre of the buttress to the left of a black section of rock; cairn. Climb to a stance and belay below a small overhang (30m). Continue up the slab on the left to easier ground then traverse right to a stance behind a block. Continue to traverse right and climb a slab next to a long greasy crack to a stance and belay (30m). Scramble to the terrace (45m). Walk right along the terrace to a small rock pinnacle just beyond a large area of overhanging black rock; cairn. Climb the pinnacle and traverse the ridge on the other side to a heather ledge at the foot of a vertical wall. Climb the wall on the right and continue directly by 90m of varied climbing ending in a grassy rake. Follow the rake to the left for a few metres to climb a 15m chimney and finish by an interesting exit over a large chockstone at the top. A 5m slab leads to easy ground.

The Porker 85m S
M.H.Moar, G.Lawson, 15 Sep 1970
This lies on the same buttress as Central Buttress. Near the middle of the buttress is a recess bounded on the right by overlapping slabs. Still further right is a just distinguishable waterslide. The climb follows the overlapping slabs. Start at an obvious ramp leading up right to the slabs proper; cairn.
1. 20m Move up the ramp, then go straight up the ensuing grooves.
2. 20m Continue up cracks and slabs to a flake and a belay above.
3. 45m Climb the vertical crack behind the stance, and from the top of the crack step left onto a large slab. Traverse left and up across slabs above a recess to join slabs which initially bound the left-hand side of the recess, then climb directly over easy rock to the terrace.

Far West Buttress

(NB 0215 2815) Alt 220m N facing Map p189 Diagram above

Readily seen from the road, this is the small compact buttress at the far west end of the Main Crag. It overlooks a splendid boulder field; the Carnaichean Tealasdale.

Approach: This can be by the bikeable track up Gleann Raonasgail then by walking under the Main Crag; see above. However, it is more quickly reached by parking either side of the culvert **(NB 9990 2867)** which takes the burn under the road near Islivig where there is a bend at the low point just south of the parking for Àird Feinis. From there, follow the north side of the shallow streamway eastwards toward the crag, which can be seen (2.3km, 45min).

Descent: down the gully west of the crag.

CREAGAN TEALASDALE
Far West Buttress

1. Fray Bentos E1 *
2. Ergot Kernel E4 ***
3. Caledonian McBrain... E1 ***
4. Grime of the Century E5 6b ***

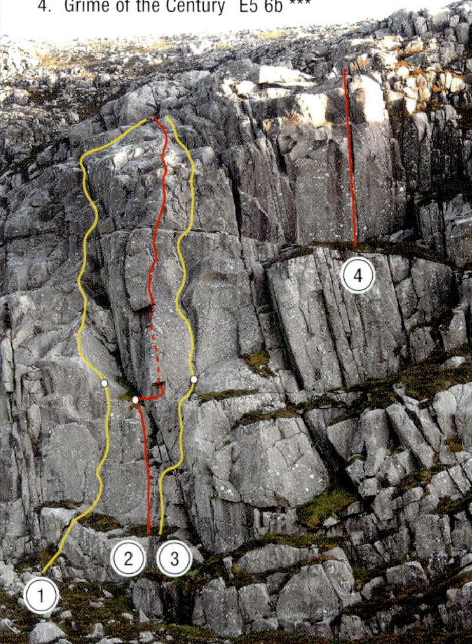

The first climb lies up the left side of the grassy groove which runs up the left side of the central roofed pillar.

1 Fray Bentos 50m E1 *
P.Graham, M.Scott, 3 Oct 2016
A slightly wandering line but with some good moves and rock.
1. 5b 20m Climb a big right-facing flake to a ledge. Move right for 2m and climb the flake and crack system to a large ledge.
2. 5b 30m Follow the vague rib-line to the left of the big vegetated corner, until it merges with the corner after about 20m. Continue up the corner to the top

The next two climbs are on the central roofed pillar.

2 Ergot Kernel 50m E4 ***
M.Scott, P.Graham, 4 Oct 2016
A superb route up the groove and crack in the pillar; the second pitch offers brilliant jamming and bridging up a peapod groove.
1. 20m 4b Follow the easiest line, leading from the right, to a large ledge below and slightly left of the groove.

2. 30m 6a Climb the groove with interest to a good rest below the roof. Pull round the roof and jam wildly up the continuation crack to reach easier ground which leads to the top.

3 Caledonian McBrain Justice E1 ***
P.Graham, M.Scott, 3 Oct 2016
The chimney and attractive groove up the right side of the roofed pillar.
1. 20m 5b The gaping chimney; approached from the left, it is friendlier than it appears. Belay below the attractive groove.
2. 30m 5b The lovely groove and continuation cracks above.

The final climb lies on the wall above the upper grass ledge to the right of the central pillar.

4 Grime of the Century 25m E5 6b ***
M.Scott, P.Graham, 3 Oct 2016
A superb finger-crack splits the pristine wall; very sustained and technical for the first 12m but easier above. Slightly awkward to get to but well worth the effort; either scramble up the gully to the right and abseil in, or climb the previous route.

Grime of the Century (E5) Ferdia Earle (photo Malcolm Scott)

TAMANASBHAL

Creag Dhubh Dhìobadail

(NB 046 239) Alt 180m NE facing Map p189 Diagram opposite

Apart from Sròn Uladail in Harris, Creag Dhubh Dhìobadail is the most important mountain cliff on the island. It is not as overhanging as Sròn Uladail is, but for quality it is unsurpassed and arguably one of the finest mountain crags in Scotland. The cliff lies hidden away on the side of Tamanasbhal (467m), a great rounded lump of a hill that displays no sign of what lies lurking along its eastern flanks. Almost a kilometre in length, the central wall drops in one dramatic sweep to the corrie floor some 200m below. The cliff is superbly set in a fine corrie overlooking Loch Dhìobadail. Although extensive, there are few lines of weakness breaking the cliff's defences and as a result there are not many climbs. The nature of the climbing is sustained and requires a bold approach, particularly as protection is not always plentiful due to the compact nature of the rock. The cliff faces north-east, catching the sun in the morning, so an early start is worth the effort. After prolonged periods of rain the cliff takes at least three or four days of good weather to come into condition. Once dry, however, it doesn't appear to be greatly affected by shorter spells of bad weather, although there are some persistent seepage lines. A word of warning: beware the dreaded midge and in summer pick a day when there is a breeze blowing. When the sun leaves the crag, and it does so quite early, all hell can break loose! There is good camping beside the loch below the cliff.

Since the cliff lies on the far side of the hill from the prominent bealach between the two chains of hills it is only reached after some effort. There are two ways to approach the cliff.

Directions: Follow the B8011 as for the directions to the Uig Sea Cliffs on p20. Cross the river which flows into the southern end of Uig sands, turn left past the Abhainn Dearg distillery and park near the top of the hill where a track heads south, just beyond the entrance to a disused gravel pit, towards the shaped valley between the hills **(NB 0315 3135)**. There are a number of places to park without blocking access, or passing places.

Approach 1: On foot or mountain bike, by following the estate track which goes all the way up Gleann Raonasgail to cross the prominent Bealach Raonasgail before descending to the shores of Loch Tamnabhaigh in the south. The track passes Creagan Tealsdale, which lies to the right, then runs beneath Sgorran Dubh Teinnasval on the left side of the glen. There is a locked gate about 1km along the track. From the Bealach Raonasgail (7.8km, 2hr on foot), ascend the short slope on the left, almost due east, to the grassy Braigh Bhuidhe bealach (c350m) between Teinneasabhal and Tamanasbhal to gain the head of the large Coire Dhìobadail. Drop down then make a long slanting descent south-eastwards into

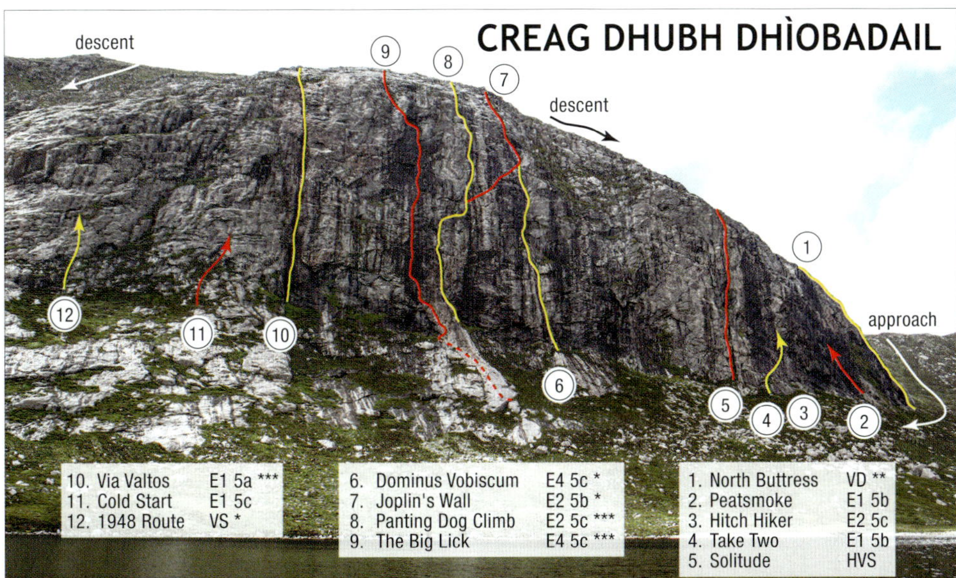

the corrie and contour the hillside, whereupon the crag looms impressively into sight, majestically overlooking the end of Loch Dhìobadail (9km, 2hr 30min on foot).

Approach 2: On foot, this is shorter and quicker, although the terrain is rougher with a bit more ascent and descent. Start from Breanish, near the end of the B8011; park at the road bridge **(NB 9922 2568)** over the burn. Follow the track up the north bank of the burn then cross over before the boggy flats and head uphill into the corrie containing Loch na Clibhe. Traverse the north shore, then ascend the north side of the burn closest to Laibheal a' Tuath, up an obvious ramp which can be seen from the road, to reach the col between Cracabhal and Laibheal a' Tuath. Descend to the Bealach Raonasgail (4.8km, 1hr 30min). Ascend the other side to the bealach and drop into Coire Dhìobadail to gain the cliff (total 6km, 2hr).

Descent: Down either end of the cliff; slippy and toe crushing. It is worthwhile considering having the second carry a sac with boots or trainers.

In the centre of the highest part of the cliff, above an obvious tongue of red slabs, the wall is marked by black streaks and features a large flying-saucer shaped depression in the middle of the face. No substances required to make this out, although some may have to visualise harder than others! This wall is bounded on the left by the prominent crack-line of Via Valtos, left of which are two slanting rakes, and on the right by the less well defined crack-line of Solitude. Due to the compact nature of the rock some of the lines are difficult to figure out from the ground. Climbs are described from right to left, as met on the approach.

1 North Buttress 120m VD **

J.Ball, H.Ball, 1968

This is on the slabby right side of the cliff; the first section rounded on the descent. The climb avoids any difficulty, but takes a more or less central line up the buttress. Runners and belays are relatively scarce. Start on the left edge of the buttress, below a rib, about 3m up from the lowest point.

1. 35m Climb the rib, first on its side, then on the front and again on the side where the angle is easier. Continue right along a rake to a belay.

2. 35m Move slightly left and climb the slab above, steeply at first, then continue on a direct line to a grass ledge. Go left to another broad ledge and belay.

3. 35m Move right up the rake and continue up a right-trending crack-line which continues to a belay on the right.

4. 15m Move left and climb directly up the wall.

The next climb is some 50m to the left, just beyond an area of extremely steep grass.

2 Peatsmoke 115m E1

J.L.Bermudez, J.Walker, N.Wilson, 13 May 1996

At the right end of the main face, a rib of rock extrudes below the line of the base of the crag. There is a left-facing corner on this rib. Scramble up the rib to the left of the corner to where it steepens.

1. 25m 4b Climb steep slabs to the left of the left-facing corner to an overlap. Climb over this at its left end, move right to easier climbing then move left to a narrow boulder -trewn ledge.

2. 25m 5b Step back right and climb grooves to a sloping ledge. Climb the obvious overhanging corner

above, exiting right at the top, then step back left to an excellent ledge; a strenuous pitch.
3. 40m 4c Climb the obvious left-slanting ramp above and continue in the same line eventually to traverse slightly left to a wet groove.
4. 25m 4b Traverse about 5m right and climb a left-slanting ramp, then step right at its top and finish up slabs.

Some 80m to the left, the crack-line of Solitude is obvious, breaching the cliff's defences to the left of some roofs.

3 Hitch Hiker 160m E2
A.Macfarlane, B.Davison, Apr 1990
Start up slabs below and left of an obvious roof, at the foot of a right-slanting ramp about 10m right of the crack-line of Solitude.
1. 40m 5b Start up the slabby ramp-line as for Take Two, trending right to belay on a small ledge after passing a quartzy band using 3 points of aid; wet.
2. 40m 5c Move up a steep groove to a sloping ledge below the right-hand end of a large roof, then traverse left to a ledge at the other end of the roof.
3. 40m 4c Hand-traverse right to the arete then climb a ramp-line trending left.
4. 40m 4c Move left to finish up a corner and a left-trending groove.

4 Take Two 120m E1
C.Watts, S.Vietoris, 1 Jun 1981
Start as for Hitch Hiker.
1. 20m 4c Ascend the right-slanting ramp until an awkward move leads left to a ledge. Climb a corner, move right round a bulge and go up to a narrow ledge.
2. 25m 5b Climb up and right to a black niche. Move round right, then go left and climb a steep quartzy rib to a large sloping ledge. Climb a thin groove then move left to a cramped niche.
3. 40m 5b Move left onto a pedestal, then make a strenuous move up to the top of a slanting crack-line. Trend right over blocks and flakes to belay at the right end of a left-slanting ramp-line.
4. 35m 4c Move up the ramp and surmount an overhang. Continue to the foot of an obvious square-cut chimney-corner and climb this to the top.

5 Solitude 170m HVS
J.Ball, M.Reeves, 1970
The cliff's main right-hand crack is indefinite in its middle section. Scramble to the foot of the crack.
1. 35m Climb the crack using holds on the left at the steep section. Eventually climb the wall on the left and move up to the foot of a large recess.
2. 30m Climb the right edge of the recess then follow indefinite rocks and some grass to a vegetated ledge.
3. 20m Continue in the same line to a niche at the foot of the upper section of the crack; poor stance and belay.
4. 15m Climb twin flakes just left of the crack. Step right and go up a steep crack-line (sling for aid on FA) to a poor stance in a slabby niche.
5. 15m The crack now divides. Take the vertical left-hand weakness to a ledge then move left and climb a short groove to the foot of a prominent chimney.
6. 50m Climb the steep chimney then the gully to easier rocks.

6 Dominus Vobiscum 125m E4 *
C.Waddy, A.Wainwright, 4 Jun 1995
Start at the obvious curving corner-groove low down on the wall, some 80m left of Solitude and 30m right of the obvious tongue of slab extending below the cliff.
1. 45m 5b Climb the obvious curving corner into a short chimney and belay on ledges; spikes.
2. 50m 5c Climb a short corner, then go left and back right, heading for an obvious right-facing flake in a shallow groove; the right-hand of two flakes. Climb this to ledges then move boldly up and right on slopers to a ledge. Continue up to belay in a niche.
3. 30m 5b Step right, then climb easy slabs to a belay. Scramble off.

The impressive central section of the cliff is flanked by the curving corner-groove of Dominus Vobiscum on the right and the crack-line of Via Valtos on the left. A lovely tongue of pinkish-coloured slab extrudes from the base of the cliff here. Running down to the ground just left of the slab tongue is a full height black weep which passes through the right side of the flying-saucer shaped depression in the centre of the cliff.

7 Joplin's Wall 205m E2 *
G.Cohen, R.Archibold, 3 Jun 1974
The original climb up this section of cliff and the first to breach the impressive central defences. It would appear that Panting Dog Climb pretty much follows the first three pitches of this climb before continuing straight up whilst this climb finishes out right up a prominent right-slanting ramp. Start at the top right of the tongue of slabs on the highest grass ledge.
1. 35m 5b Step left onto the tongue, climb to a short black groove, exit left and zigzag up the slabby wall above to a short groove. Climb this and step right from its top to an excellent niche.
2. 35m 5b Climb the black corner above and continue fairly easily to a short right-facing groove beneath a smooth band. Traverse the wall to the right of the groove for 3m or so, until beneath the middle of an overhang. Step up to the overhang and traverse left on underclings to a small perched block, above which a short wall leads to easier climbing into a prominent depression. Continue diagonally right to belay in a chimney-crack system at a point level with a horizontal fault on the right.
3. 25m 5a Make an exposed traverse right along the horizontal fault, with bulging rock above, for about 8m, then climb steeply to gain easier ground
4, 5, 6. 110m 4c Climb up and right to gain then follow the big ramp which runs diagonally right towards the top.

8 Panting Dog Climb 180m E2 ***
M.Fowler, A.Strapcans, 20 Jul 1980
An excellent climb which takes a direct line above the tongue of slabs. The first pitch is common with Joplin's Wall and it then takes a similar but more direct line for the next two pitches before continuing straight up a series of prominent corners where Joplin's Wall goes right. Start on the highest grass ledge to the right of the tongue.
1. 35m 5b Step onto the tongue, climb to a short black groove, exit left and zigzag up the slabby wall above to a short groove. Climb this and step right from its top to an excellent rock niche.
2. 30m 5b Climb the black corner above and continue up an easy crack. Move right and climb up and under the slanting overhang until it is possible to traverse right to a prominent grass ledge.
3. 30m 5b Traverse horizontally right to a line of weakness in the wall above. Climb this to overhangs, move left onto a slab and pull through the bulges to a good stance at the foot of the obvious corner system.
4. 25m 5a Climb the corners to belay beneath a right-slanting corner with an overhanging left wall.
5. 30m 5c Ascend the corner, avoiding the large rocking block on its right (crux), to reach good ledges on the left. Step right then undercut and layback an easy-angled slab to belay on the next ledge.
6. 30m 4c Easier climbing leads to the top.

9 The Big Lick 175m E4 ***
M.Fowler, A.Meyers, 1 Jul 1981
This impressive, bold and sustained climb takes a line from the left side of the tongue of slabs to reach the right side of the large flying saucer shaped depression in the centre of the cliff. Start at the upper left-hand side of the tongue of slabs; the slabs can be climbed as a gentle warm up.
1. 25m 5c Step right onto the front of the tongue and climb past the overlap. Trend left across groove lines to reach a good jug beneath a black bulge at the top of the most prominent groove. Make hard moves up left then go up to a thin flake which leads to a ledge.
2. 20m 5c Climb the left-hand groove above the left end of the ledge to its capping overhang. Move round the right-hand side of this to a ledge then move up to belay on the next one.
3. 45m 5b/c Surmount the overhang directly above the stance to gain the area of slabby rock. Climb this directly to a stance at the upper right-hand extremity of the black flying saucer shaped depression.
4. 20m 5b/c Gain a pinnacle flake on the right and step left from its top to climb boldly up the wall of quartz rock. Continue more or less straight up to a good ledge about 10m below overhangs.
5. 25m 5b Step down left from the stance and traverse horizontally left on an exposed sloping ledge. Climb a corner for 5m, then move left again to belay on a ledge beneath a light coloured area of rock.
6. 40m 5c Above are three groove lines. Gain a sloping ledge in the middle groove by an awkward move from the right-hand groove. Continue with difficulty until it is possible to move into the left-hand groove which gives easier climbing to the top. It is also possible to climb the left-hand line which is cleaner and in a superb position.

10 Via Valtos 150m E1 ***
A.W.Ewing, W.Sproul (4 pegs), Spring 1970; FFA R.Archbold, G.Cohen, Jul 1974
The prominent crack-line running up the left side of the central wall. Unfortunately it is often wet but when dry it gives a fine climb.
1. 40m 5a Climb straight up the crack to a grass patch.
2. 35m 5b Move out onto the left wall, then go up to an overhung corner with a sloping slab above.
3. 30m 5a Step up and right, then go left into the crack and climb straight up to a ledge.
4. 45m 5a Go right then left to gain and climb an overhung corner, then move left into the crack. Continue by a chimney and finish more easily.

The Big Lick, P5 (E4) Blair Fyffe (photo Tony Stone)

11 Cold Start 180m E1
A.Macfarlane, J.Norgrove, 28 Apr 1991
Start some 20m left of Via Valtos.
1. 5a Climb up and slightly right to a faint crack-groove. Ascend this to a stance below a smallish roof.
2. 5c Step right into a corner and go up to the right-hand side of a large sloping shelf.
3. 4c Move across to re-belay at the left side of the shelf before traversing 5m left to climb slabby rock to belay left of a long roof.
4. 5b Move up and left to an obvious corner-crack system and climb this.
5, 6. 4a, 4b Trend right and up to the top.

12 1948 Route 180m VS *
W.Sproul, R.Sharp, 1969
This takes a crack system rising diagonally right on the left-hand section of the cliff, best seen from halfway down the side of the loch. It is the line attempted by Folkard in 1948. Start beneath the two slanting rakes left of Via Valtos and climb over slabs and grass to the overhung base with a grass filled crack leading up right.
1. 40m Climb up and right; peg belay.
2. 40m A continuation crack leads to twin cracks.
3. 25m Take the right-hand crack (2 peg runners on FA) with a steep finish to another crack.
4. 35m Go left into a crack and climb up right to a slab; peg belay.
5. 40m Continue directly up broken rocks to finish.

13 South Buttress 155m VS *
J.Grieve, M.Reeves, 1968
With the exception of pitch 3, the standard is generally VD to S. On the left side of the cliff, left of Via Valtos, are two obvious slanting rakes. Left again, this takes a less obvious slanting line, starting up slabs.
1. 35m Climb slabs trending right to a ledge; flake belay above.
2. 30m Continue slanting right up slabs to a thread belay under a bulging wall.
3. 25m Move up left of a prominent little overhang, step back right and climb the bulging wall, moving right at its top to a stance; thread belay above.
4. 30m Move up to a corner, slanting right. Climb this and exit left at the top onto a heather ledge.
5. 35m Continue directly up a steep wall to easier ground.

TEINNEASABHAL

Sgorran Dubh Teinneasabhal

(NB 038 253) Alt 260m W facing Map p189 Diagram opposite

This face is located on the west flank of Teinneasbhal (497m) near the head of Glen Raonasgail, above the track through the glen between the two chains of hills. It is passed beneath on the northern approach along the track to Creag Dhubh Dhìobadail. Although distant, it can be seen from the road. Little is known about the cliff and there appears to be some confusion over the naming of the features and therefore where the lines actually go, particularly the early climbs.

A stone shoot, Great Gully, forks halfway up the face and splits it roughly into three parts: North Buttress to the left, Central Buttress between the forks, and South Buttress to the right of the right-hand fork. Right again are three parallel gullies (numbered 3 to 1) with No.1 being the right-hand and nearest to the next buttress, Far South Buttress. North Buttress is broken and gives little more than a scramble. Central Buttress has a steep lower part, avoided via the stone shoot. The upper part also offers scrambling with harder variations, all leading to the summit. South Buttress offers the better climbing.

Approach: Along the bikeable estate track up Gleann Raonasgail as for Creag Dhubh Dhìobadail to just short of the Bealach Raonasgail (7km, 1hr 45min on foot).

Descent: By the south-west shoulder to the Bealach Raonasgail.

1 North Buttress 120m M
G.S.Johnstone, S.Johnstone, Autumn 1952
The sprawling buttress on the left. Follow the edge above the northern trifurcation of Great Gully. There are some good but easy slabs near the top. There is a Grade 3 scramble in this vicinity starting up the lower slabs; see Highland Scrambles North.

2 South Buttress 145m S
R.G.Folkard, M.deV.Wills, 4 Aug 1948
Start at the lowest part of the main buttress overlooking Great Gully.
1. 15m Climb a steep rib to a grass platform then traverse left onto a triangular rock projecting over the gully and climb a slab to a small stance; thread belay.
2. 25m Climb mainly on slabs to a platform.
3. 15m Either climb the crack above or the slab on the right, then continue to the foot of a grassy rake sloping up to the left.
4. 20m At the far end of the rake, climb another slab to a roomy niche.
5. 20m Go straight up to a heather and moss slope, then climb to a good stance and belay behind a pile of blocks. The slabs leading upwards from here are at a fairly high angle and a huge overlapping slab blocks the way except to the right. Still higher there is a considerable overhang guarding the final exit.
6. 25m Traverse right and up until level with the base of an overlapping slab, then continue straight up, keeping a metre or so away from its right edge. Halfway up it, traverse left and surmount the overlap by a delicate move and continue to a fine stance in a sheltered nook behind a pile of rocks.
7. 25m Climb out on the right and traverse left immediately below the final overhang to a small ledge. Surmount the overhang on good holds then climb easier rocks until it is possible to scramble onto the roof of the overhang. Scrambling leads to the top.

3 Nosferatu 180m VS
B.Clarke, K.Tremain, 4 Jun 1972
Start by scrambling about 5m up to the right from the start of South Buttress; peg belay below a slab.

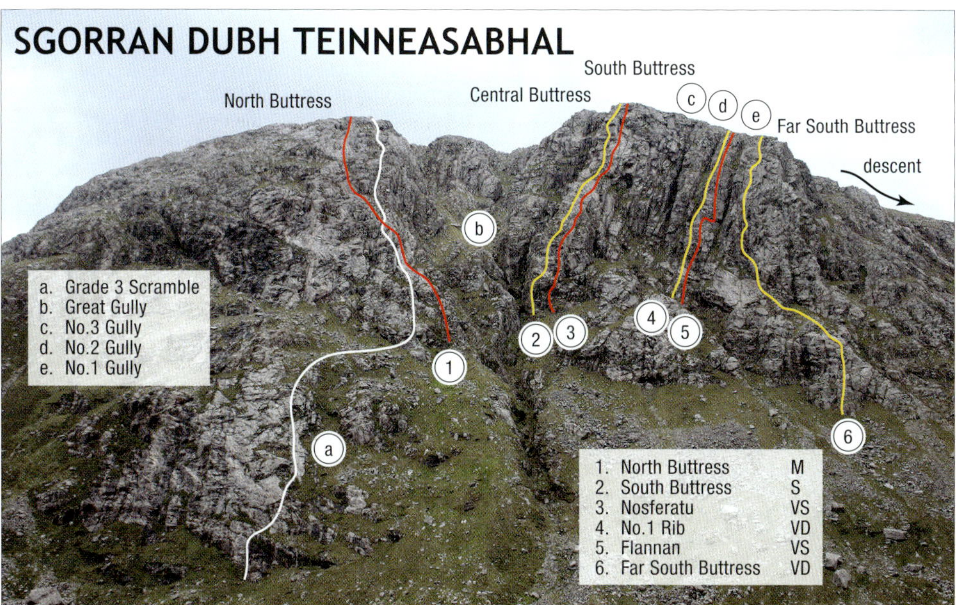

1. 15m Climb the slab to belay below a corner.
2. 40m Traverse right, climb a wall then go up a slab and groove to a niche on the arete. Climb the arete to a stance.
3. 40m Continue up the arete to a ledge.
4. 20m Climb a short corner to the terrace and cross this to the right; peg belay.
5. 30m Climb a groove just left of the arete, then take a short slab into a corner. Traverse right under an overhang and go up to a ledge. Move right and climb a slab on the arete to a grassy recess; peg belay.
6. 35m Step left and climb the slab above (peg runner) to a grassy niche. Traverse the slab on the left, move up a corner then climb an overlap on the right to reach the top.

The three gullies, numbered 1 to 3 starting from that nearest Far South Buttress, are well defined for most of their height. No.2 is hardly a gully at all when seen close up.

4 No.1 Rib 140m VD

R.G.Folkard, M.deV.Wills, Miss J.Fox, 4 Aug 1948

The loose rib between No.1 and No.2 Gully. Start at a tongue of rock coming down from the rib into No.2 Gully.

1. 30m Scramble up an easy slab to a stance, then climb the rib above to a small stance beside the gully.
2. 15m Climb a wall to a fine stance among a pile of immense, apparently firm, blocks.
3. 15m Continue up the wall above, passing some large insecure looking blocks, to a poor stance and belay just above a sloping platform.
4. 20m First climb a small rib, then ascend either a delicate slab on the right or a strenuous crack on the left and finish up the wall on the right to a small stance and poor belay.
5. 10m Near the top of the nose above, the holds virtually disappear but the angle soon eases; stance and small belay. Traditionalists should note that on the first ascent the leader wore socks here, commenting that it would be at least S in boots!
6. 25m A small wall leads directly up a rib to a grassy stance.
7. 25m The rib is now easy and rather broken.

5 Flannan 120m VS

T.Fletcher, J.Macdougall, 4 Jun 1972

This takes a line up No.1 Rib, as the first ascentionists couldn't make the buttress fit the description of No1 Rib given above. Start at an earth ledge below the rib and at the side of No.2 gully. Climb a right-slanting groove onto the crest of the rib and climb this to a peg belay below an obvious corner (35m). Make a descending traverse to the right for 6m then go straight up the overlapping wall overlooking No.1 Gully to a peg belay on a large grassy ledge below a steep slab with a prominent chimney above. Climb the slab and the chimney, then move left onto the crest of the rib and follow it to the top.

6 Far South Buttress 100m VD

R.G.Folkard, Miss J.Fox, 3 Aug 1948

The buttress was climbed by W.Ewing and G.R.Symmers in Aug 1933; other than being forced rightwards off the central line there are no further details. The 1948 climb takes a more direct line, pretty much overlooking the parallel gullies on the left. Start on a grassy shelf, just left of and a little above the lowest point of the lower section of the buttress.

Moderate climbing for 25m gains a grassy shelf which is followed by 25m or so of scrambling to reach the foot of a large slab, lowest at its right end. This lower portion can be avoided by walking up the grassy shelf to the right.

1. 10m Climb the large slab to a grass slope, then climb the overhanging chimney in the wall on the right on good holds to a stance.
2. 20m Traverse left along sloping ledges to below a black groove, then climb the groove on awkward holds until an escape can be made onto the rock platform on the left.
3. 25m Climb the corner above the belay for about 6m, then traverse left to a line of weakness going up to a grass slope and good stance.
4. 30m Continue up, trending slightly right and passing an overhanging rectangular block on the right, to a stance and belay just left of a small overhang.
5. 15m Step into and climb a small crack on the right, then continue up the slab to a grass platform. Easy climbing leads to a broad ledge.

TATHABHAL

West Face

Map p189

This is the slightly higher hill (515m) just to the north of Teinneasabhal. There is one described route on the west side of the south-west ridge, overlooking Gleann Raonasgail. There are two Moderate scrambles, one up the south-west shoulder and the other up the north-west rib, with some climbing up to VD; see Highland Scrambles North.

All About Lewis 90m S

C.Rumsey, 1990

1. 45m Climb the slab just right of the prominent corner on the lower right side of the face.
2. 45m Trend leftwards and climb short walls to the summit.

BEANNAN A' DEAS

There are three crags on this conspicuous small hill (252m) which, along with its partner Beannan a' Tuath, lies between the entrance to Glen Raonasgail and Loch Suaineabhal. The hill contains a fair amount of rock. An area of slabs on the north-west side is prominent and can be seen from the road along the coast. There is also a small buttress beneath the west top and a good crag tucked away around the back a short distance away. There are also numerous small walls and buttresses that will provide short routes. The prominent sweep of slabs should produce some longer but quite easy fun routes at about M to VD on good clean rock.

Directions: Turn south off the B8011 just over the bridge across the river 1.8km past the shop at Timsgarry. Follow the road to Loch Suaineabhal and then go up the hill to park beside the Uig water treatment plant at Loch a' Lighe Beag.

Approach: Walk up the track on the east side a short way then break off right down to the loch to gain the next lochan, Loch Deireadh Langa, on a vague ATV track following a line of intermittent posts and manholes marking the line of a buried pipeline. This continues past the west side of Loch a' Bheannan to follow its burn west for 400m and then south into the narrow glen between Beannan a' Deas and Flodrasgairbhe Mòr. The north-west Face lies above the burn at the entrance to this glen (2km, 40min). South Crag is reached by continuing to Loch Bealach Euna Clibh, then going along its east shore to the end and around the back to climb the hillside above two old sheilings, possibly beehive dwellings, to reach the crag (3km, 1hr). Summit Buttress is some 5-10 min away.

North-West Face

(NB 051 295) Alt 150m NW facing Map p189

This lies on the prominent and extensive sweep of slabs on the north-west side of the hill, visible from the road. Much of the slabs are set at a fairly easy angle but there is an obvious steeper triangular shaped slab which defines the lower left side of the main mass of slab. The right side of this appears to be taken by a line climbed by W.Ewing and G.R.Symmers in Aug 1933 whilst to the left is a steep crack. The crag is easily combined with South Crag and Summit Buttress to give a pleasant day out in the hills.

Descent: Perhaps best rightwards (south) to gain easy ground descending from the summit of the hill.

The Geal Crack 90m VS **

A.MacDonald, J.R.Mackenzie, 18 Aug 1971

Just left of centre on the triangular area of steeper rock is a fine curving quartzy crack.

1. 30m 4c Gain the crack and climb it to a ledge then gain a bigger ledge just above.
2. 60m 4a Easy slabs; more difficult ground can be found on the right.

South Crag

(NB 055 290) Alt 200m S facing Map p189
Diagram opposite

This is located not far below the summit of Beannan a' Deas, overlooking the pasture of Àirigh a Beannain. The rock is good, the setting pleasant and being tucked away round the back of the hill there is a feeling of isolation; a useful retreat from the coast when it is being battered by the sea. From just above the left side of the crag, a grassy ledge system leads up and across to Summit Buttress, with which it can be combined.

Descent: Probably easiest down the left-hand side.

1 Roll On 30m S 4a *

R.Anderson, C.Anderson, 12 July 2017

At the base of the left side of the crag is a large flake feature. Climb the left side of this and cross the left-

1. Roll On	S 4b *	4. Wind and Withering	E2 5b **	8. Commitment	E2 5c **
2. Stroll On	HS 4b **	5. Crunch	E2 5b *	9. What a Day	E2 5b **
3. Wandering Zig Zag	E1 5a *	6. Blown Away	E2 5b *	10. The Neb	VS 5a *
		7. Diagonal	HVS 5b ***		

slanting fault to gain the upper crack which slants right across the cracked slab above. Move up and climb the slab to gain the top of the left-trending diagonal crack up the left side of the central section, then go right up a short step by a crack and finish easily on the top.

2 Stroll On 30m HS 4b **

R.Anderson, C.Anderson, 12 July 2017

Climb the centre of the flake and cross the fault to gain a right-slanting crack. Step up and go up right across the middle of the slab to the left-trending diagonal crack up the left side of the central section. Swing out right on a handrail then move up and climb a crack to the top.

3 Wandering Zig Zag 30m E1 5a *

K.Neal, A.Van Lopik, 8 Jun 2006

At the left end of the central section, climb the obvious left-trending diagonal crack for 4m, step right onto the slab and follow a right-trending crack up and right to a rounded blunt nose. Place some gear and hand-traverse left to the top; quite bold.

4 Wind and Withering 30m E2 5b **

R.Anderson, C.Anderson, 11 Jul 2006

From the blocks just right of Wandering Zig Zag, pull over onto the start of a narrow shelf in the middle of the lower bulge, then pull round onto the slab and continue to horizontal breaks. Climb past a short, thin crack to gain the crack of Wandering Zig Zag then go up and right before stepping back left to climb the blunt nose direct to finish.

5 Crunch 30m E2 5b *

K.Neal, A.Van Lopik, 8 Jun 2006

A direct line up the centre of the crag with some suspect rock and fairly poor protection until half-height. Start beneath the niche and pull onto a flake-crack then make a couple of moves rightwards before pulling through onto a narrow shelf in the middle of the bulge. Head slightly leftwards via a thin crack to gain the left side of the triangular niche then follow shallow parallel cracks and go right to the top.

6 Blown Away 30m E2 5b *

R.Anderson, C.Anderson, 11 Jul 2006

Follow Crunch to the narrow shelf in the bulge, reach up right to a good crack then go up right and across Diagonal to climb the right side of the niche.

7 Diagonal 30m HVS 5b ***

K.Neal, A.Van Lopik, 8 Jun 2006

The obvious right to left line through the triangular niche. Go up a short crack in the slab then make a stiff pull over the bulge and continue into the niche. Climb the crack up the back of the niche and continue to the top.

8 Commitment 30m E2 5c **

K.Neal, A.Van Lopik, 10 Jun 2006

A fine route through the roof at the right end of the lower bulge. Climb a thin crack to gain the right end of the roof, traverse left then steeply climb the crack to gain the ramp on the right and finish up easier ground.

Diagonal (HVS) Rab Anderson
(photo Chris Anderson)

9 What a Day 30m E2 5b **
K.Neal, A.Van Lopik, 10 Jun 2006
Start up the same crack as Commitment then traverse right to finish up a lovely crack; small gear.

10 The Neb 30m VS 5a *
K.Neal, A.Van Lopik, 10 Jun 2006
Climb to the prominent flake at the right-hand side and gain a standing position on it by a tricky move then continue to the top via cracks.

Summit Buttress

(NB 054 292) Alt 220m W facing Map p189 Diagram below

This small buttress sits beneath the west top of Beannan a' Deas, a short distance uphill from South Crag and is easily combined with that; a grassy ledge system runs down from the right side of Summit Buttress to South Crag. The outlook is particularly fine. It is possibly the buttress on which some climbs were made in 1933 by W.Ewing and G.R.Symmers. There is a broken north- facing wall and a cleaner looking west-facing wall. Unfortunately, despite initially looking good the west-facing wall only runs to any decent height towards its right side, which is where the rock is of good quality; the left side appears to have some suspect rock.

Descent: Down the right side by going south a short way towards a tiny lochan to cut down across slabs.

1 Off the Rails 25m S 4a *
R.Anderson, C.Anderson, 12 July 2017
Start just left of Left on the Line then climb up and left to take a direct line up good rock.

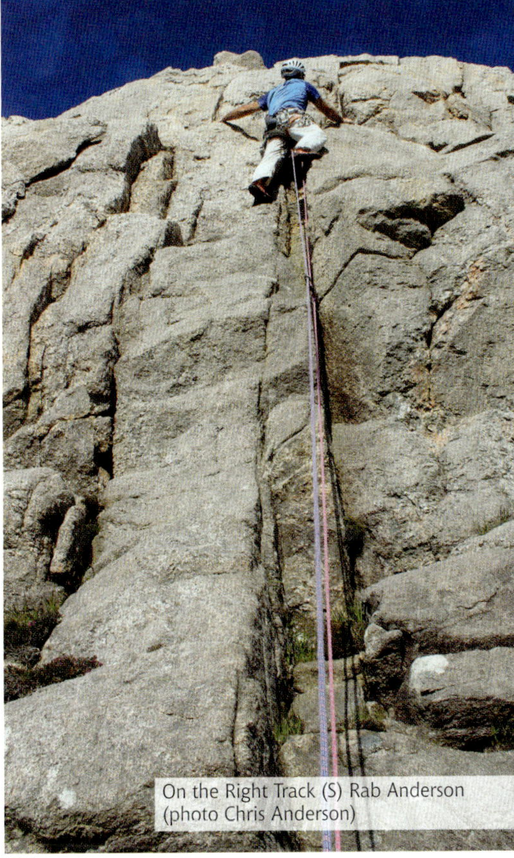
On the Right Track (S) Rab Anderson (photo Chris Anderson)

2 Left on the Line 25m S 4b **
R.Anderson, C.Anderson, 8 Jul 2013
The left-hand of a pair of parallel crack-lines.

3 On the Right Track 25m S 4a **
R.Anderson, C.Anderson, 12 July 2017
The right-hand crack.

4 In the Lane 25m VS 4c *
R.Anderson, C.Anderson, 8 Jul 2013
Just left of the edge, climb a short crack and continue up a crack-line.

5 Outside Edge 25m VS 5b *
R.Anderson, C.Anderson, 8 Jul 2013
Make an awkward start up a crack in the edge and continue up the edge.

There is rumoured to be some climbing on the neighbouring Beannan a' Tuath to the east and although there is much exposed rock here and on the neighbouring Tarain; nothing has come to light.

SUAINEABHAL

West Face

(NB 071 306) Alt 30m W facing Map p189

The large, domed shape of Suaineabhal (429m) is a distinctive landform and the length of its west side overlooking the head of Loch Suaineabhal is composed of much rock, most of it fairly broken and vegetated. Towards its right side, right of the rocks known as Creagan Gorma, a broad rocky spur descends towards the loch. There is one climb on the principal area of rock on the left side of the spur, which is well left of the West Slabs Grade 3 scramble up the right side of the spur; see Highland Scrambles North. Although from a distance the cliff looks retiring, on closer inspection it forms a fine concave sweep of slabs leading to walls and a nose.

Approach: Turn off the B8011 just over the bridge 1.8km past the shop at Timsgarry and take the road to Loch Suaineabhal to park opposite the weir. Cross the weir and follow the side of the loch to the south of the Euscleit Mòr knoll to gain the upper of two paths that run beneath the cliff to reach a small and narrow stony gully leading to the base of the slabs (1km, 20min).

Descent: The second narrow gully nearest to Suaineabhal, close to Creagan Gorma to the north, can be descended although there is a scrambling section. The first narrow gully requires an abseil off a block on the left. Alternatively, continue right to join the West Slabs scramble leading to the top of the hill.

Arcadia 106m HVS 5a **

J.Mackenzie, E.Mackenzie, 26 Jun 2013

An enjoyable and well protected route once above the slabs. The prominent but shallow right-facing corner and wall that form the third pitch, together with the deep groove right of a prow that forms the fourth pitch, are clearly visible from below, both just left of the final nose. Move right from the little gully beneath the undercut start and begin just left of a pair of parallel dark water streak marks.

1. 27m 4a or 4c Either take the crack on the right at 4c, or the much easier the shallow break just left to move up slabs to a short wall. Climb this to reach a grey slab and up this to a stance.
2. 20m 4b Move up and slightly left over blocks left of a honeysuckle bush to move left onto a ledge below the steep wall and shallow right-facing corner.
3. 20m 5a Climb the crack right of the corner to move left into it on top of a huge hollow flake and continue up to a curved overhang. Move right then up and right to a hidden airy stance below a deep but hidden groove; a fine pitch.
4. 12m Climb the deep blocky groove to an overhanging crack and move left below this to another hidden eyrie stance.
5. 12m 4c Above the stance is a wall split by a right-trending flake-crack. Climb this to a ledge.
6. 15m Easily up the nice rib to a large grass patch.

The climb continues for a further 50m or so by Grade 2 scrambling via a steepening rib and easy-angled slab to the shoulder where the descent gully lies on the left.

Euscleit Mòr

(NB 066 312) Alt 40m W facing Map p189

This is the small knoll that lies at the foot of Suaineabhal at the north end of Loch Suaineabhal, Point 85m on the OS 1:50k map. It contains a line of crags which face the road and although fairly broken, the rock is of good quality gneiss with areas of coarsely crystalline red pegmatite. A grassy central gully splits the crag.

Approach: Park opposite the weir at the north end of the loch and approach as for Suaineabhal, crossing the weir to reach the crags (5min).

Descent: By the grassy central gully, or at either end.

Black Pudding 20m VD *

G.Nicoll, A.Nicoll, L.Nicoll, M.Nicoll, C.Pasteur, 13 Jul 2015

Start 20m left of the grassy central gully at the right end of a quartzy overhang. Surmount the overhang and climb leftwards up a fine slab. Finish up a crack and niche.

Practice Rib 20m D

E.Mackenzie, J.Mackenzie, 21 Jun 2013

Immediately right of the grassy central gully is a rib and slab. Climb the juggy overhang then go up slabs to a ledge. Continue up the slabby arete to the top, initially delicate.

Solstice Pillar 20m HS 4b **

J.Mackenzie, E.Mackenzie, 21 Jun 2013

Well right of Practice Rib, the striking red pillar is the most obvious line on the crag. It is much easier than it looks and climbs the pegmatite wall on generous holds to a scoop before continuing up the wall via a crack to a ledge at 15m. Continue up the easy rib to the top.

SNEIHABHAL

This small 253m hill lies to the south of Suaineabhal overlooking Loch Suaineabhal. The OS place the name Sròn ri Gaoith beside the summit, but in reality this probably refers to the prominent rocky nose which drops north-west from the summit and the nearby name of Sneihabhal should apply to the whole hill. Hidden Buttress lies out of sight to the south of the rocky nose, facing south-west, on the other side of a gully which slants up the side of the nose. Gil Mileabhat Crag lies some 500m further south from Hidden Buttress facing south-west on the hillside above the loch. Ardroil Buttress is thought to lie on the frontal part of the nose itself with whilst Flannan Buttress is thought to lie on a knoll some 400m to the north-east.

Sròn ri Gaoith

Hidden Buttress

(NB 073 292) Alt 20m SW facing Map p189 Diagram below

Hidden Buttress lies to the side of the frontal nose of Sròn ri Gaoith and cannot be seen from the approach to the north, hence the name. However, from the parking at the northern end of Loch Suaineabhal it is possible to see the suggested line of the top of the cliff where it slants down the hillside straight into the loch.

Directions: As for Beannan a' Dheas and Suaineabhal to park by the weir at the north end of Loch Suaineabhal.

Approach: Cross the gap in the weir and follow the east shore beneath the large and rambling west face of Suaineabhal. A vague path rises around the shoulder of the hill to avoid steep broken rocks which drop into the loch, before descending to the shore again. The nose of Sròn ri Gaoith lies ahead and a broken cliff facing north-west is obvious, perhaps Ardroil Buttress. Hidden Buttress runs straight into the loch and it is not possible to traverse the lochside to reach it. Instead climb the hillside to pass beneath what is thought to be Ardroil Buttress and follow a gully-ramp up and over the top of the crag. Care should be taken in the gully for there is a nasty step in the middle and there is some unstable rock; a return has to be made this way but it should be possible to rope the awkward bit if required. At the top, traverse along a shelf, then drop down heathery slopes and approach from the south side (3km, 1hr 30min).

Descent: Rightwards and back down via the approach.

The cliff rises straight out of the water at its left-hand end and forms a right-rising band of rock, about 30m high, extending for over 150m up the hillside. Spike Fright traverses across the lowest part of the crag just above the water; in 2001 this was equipped with in-situ runners and a tyrolean to short-cut the walk back and avoid the gully. The left-hand section of the crag is steep, but appears rather broken and of doubtful solidity. The cliff slants up rightwards from the water for some 50m to a large, vegetated and overhung corner system, bordered on its lower right half by a band of big black overhangs. These form the left-hand limit of the best section of crag; a sea of slabs and left-slanting overlaps, up and right of which the crag degenerates into shorter vegetated walls.

Climbs are described from right to left as met on the approach.

1 Where Eagles Nest 35m HVS 4c ***

R.D.Everett, D.Gaffney, Sep 2001

This superb climb starts 10m up and right of the ramp-line of Election Special, below the right end of a line of overhangs that slant up and left to the top of the crag. Traverse directly beneath the roofs, with a tricky step up a short overhanging corner to a higher level after 10m. Continue directly under the roofs in a splendid position with exemplary protection. At about 20m make an exposed step across an open corner to very exposed ledge, junction with Con John, and continue in the same line as for that route to the top.

2 Con John 35m HVS 4c *
J.Stevenson, A.Birrel, 1 Sep 1987
Climb the left-slanting ramp-line of Election Special for 10m, then go up right and move hard left into an obvious groove below the overhangs. Pull out left onto the exposed ledge on the previous route and continue up this to the top.

3 Election Special 35m HS 4b *
B.Newton, M.Tighe, 1974
Cutting through the centre of the main slabs is a left-slanting, slabby ramp-line that starts to the right of large blocks. Follow the line leftwards to a fine stance at 20m then continue in the same line under overhangs to where they fade; finish up a short steep wall with care.

4 Hidden Treasure 35m E2 5b **
R.D.Everett, D.Gaffney, Sep 2001
Below the line of Election Special is an impressive wall with an obvious narrow ledge at half-height, from which rises an easy looking corner on its left. Below the ledge is a large plinth embedded in the ground. Start at a large spike 5m right of the plinth.

1. 20m 5b Climb a thin crack to an undercut block at 5m (runners), then step down left and follow edges and footledges quite boldly horizontally left for 5m to a short corner (RP2). Swing left onto the ledge in the middle of the wall, then climb the thin steep crack directly above to join Election Special and belay on its fine stance. A direct start would be possible at a similar technical grade, but there would be no gear and the landing is awful. Even as it is there is ground fall potential from the traverse.

2. 15m 5a Directly above is a small overhung square-cut sentry box. Climb the gently impending wall above, first leftwards then swinging rightwards past the sentry box to join the finish of Where Eagles Nest.

5 The Eyrie 50m E1 5b **
M.Tighe, B.Newton, J.Pollard, 1974
Some 50m left of Election Special, in the centre of the crag, is a prominent fault-line with small overhangs. Start by climbing left under double overhangs then follow the fault directly to the top in two pitches.

6 Ventus 40m HS 4b *
M.Tighe, A.Scoular, 1 Sep 1987
About 40m left of Eyrie is another fault. Climb the line of least resistance to the left of the fault.

7 Spike Fright 12m VS 4c
I.Sykes, I.Sutherland, 1987
Climb a left-rising line just before the crag peters out on the left. This is the only low-level way off and is a serious little route due to a rather large flake which sits just beneath the surface of the water!

Once Bitten (HVS) Rab Anderson (photo Chris Anderson)

Ardroil Buttress

This was described as a prominent crag overlooking Loch Suaineabhal. It is possibly the obvious buttress rising above the gully-ramp on the approach to Hidden Buttress.

Direct Route 90m VD
G.M.Wallace, J.Crombie, 24 Oct 1971
Start at a wide corner and go left beneath an overhang to follow the true crest.

Flannan Buttress

This was described as an outlying crag some 400m, or so to the north of Ardroil Buttress. It could be the cliff on the north-east side of the nose, on the knoll known as Cleite an Eoin.

Original Route 120m VD
G.M.Wallace, J.Crombie, 3 Oct 1971
Start at the lowest rocks, climb to an overhang and pass it by a groove on the left. Take the rib on the left and move back right until above an overhang. Follow the crest to the summit.

Gil Mileabhat Crag

(NB 073 287) Alt 60m SW facing Map p189 Diagram right

This sits on the hillside above Loch Suaineabhal, some 500m further south from Hidden Buttress, overlooking Gil Mileabhat, the gorge and burn that drains from the small Loch na Gile. The cliff presents itself as a sweep of steep clean slab some 60m high. A terrace cuts across the middle of the crag.

Approach: The cliff can be approach from the northern end of Loch Suaineabhal passing over Hidden Buttress, from which it is some 15min from. This involves an ascent and descent of the unpleasant Sròn ri Gaoth gully (3.5km, 1hr 45min). An alternative approach, which takes the same time, can be made by parking at the start of the track at **(NB 115 292)** above the south end of Loch Croistean and heading west across rough ground up the Abhainn Todail to the knoll of Oirchleit. Here the traditional cairned route crossing the narrow neck between the lochans to the north-east is joined (another alternative). Follow this around the head of Loch Gruineabhat, then along the eastern flanks of Sneihabhal to go around the end of the hill until above the Gearraidh Mileabhat beehive bothans **(NB 078 281)**. Instead of descending to the bothans, stay high and traverse around the north side of a knoll then drop down to the crag (5.5km, 1hr 45min). There is much rock on the hillside and although there is nothing big, some of it is perhaps worth exploring. The walk through the wilderness is as much part of the day as the climbing.

Descent: Traverse right and descend heathery slopes.

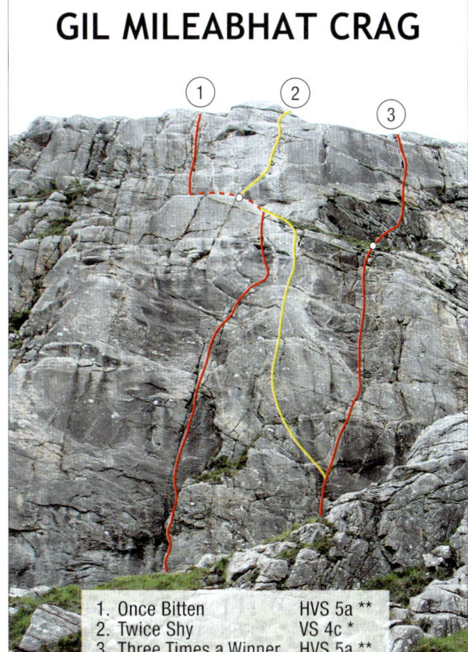

1 Once Bitten 55m HVS **
R.Anderson, C.Anderson, 11 Jul 2012
The obvious central crack-line which starts at a large flake.
1. 30m 5a Climb the flake, step left into the crack and climb to where it fades at a ledge. Move right then thinly up left to easier ground and a short crack leading to the terrace.
2. 25m 4c Climb cracks up on the left to gain another terrace and finish up cracks in a short wall.

2 Twice Shy 55m VS *
R.Anderson, C.Anderson, 11 Jul 2012
Start towards the right side of the crag beneath a finger forming a crack and flake-line.
1. 30m 4c Make a few moves up the finger as for Three Times a Winner then step left and take a central line between it and the previous route to reach the terrace.
2. 25m 4b Move up and right to climb a fine pegmatite vein to the next terrace where there is a choice of finishes.

3 Three Times a Winner 55m HVS **
R.Anderson, C.Anderson, 11 Jul 2012
Start at the same point as Twice Shy.
1. 30m 4b Climb the finger and continue up the crack-line and scoop to the terrace.
2. 25m 5a Move up right and climb a thin crack via some lovely moves to reach the next terrace and finish easily up a short wall.

HARRIS (Na Hearadh)

www.visitouterhebrides.co.uk
www.explore-harris.com
www.isle-of-lewis.com

Notable for the fabulous beaches on its west coast and for a fine range of hills in the north, the Isle of Harris is a beautiful place. Contrary to the name it is not actually an island on its own and it shares its island domain with the larger Isle of Lewis. The boundary between the two 'isles' occurs just north of Scaladale where they are joined by a 10km neck of land between two sea lochs: Loch Rèasort on the west and Loch Seaforth on the east. There is only one road through this neck of land, the A859, and this provides the only link for climbers travelling between Lewis and Harris.

The North Harris and South Harris divide is more evident and takes the form of a much narrower neck of land some 600m wide between east and west

Loch Tarbert at the principal town and ferry port of Tarbert (An Tairbeart).

Maps: Lewis and Harris are covered by OS 1:25000 Explorer Series Sheets 455, 456, 457, 458, 459 & 460 and OS 1:50000 Landranger Series Sheets 8, 13, 14 & 18.

Ferries: Lewis & Harris can be reached by Caledonian Macbrayne vehicle and passenger ferry service <**www.calmac.co.uk**> (**0800 0665000**). Ullapool to Stornoway (Lewis), Uig (Skye) to Tarbert (Harris) and Berneray (North Uist) to Leverburgh (South Harris).
City Link buses connect with the ferries at Ullapool and Uig (Skye).

Flights: Loganair (Scotland's Airline) fly to Stornoway on Lewis and Benbecula in the Uists (as well as Barra) <**www.loganair.co.uk**>. Flybe through their partnership with Eastern Airways fly to Stornoway <**www.flybe.com**> and <**www.easternairways.com**>.

On-island Transport: There are good bus services and a number of car hire companies. Comhairle nan Eilean Siar (Western Isles Council) <**www.cne-siar.gov.uk**> has bus timetables and travel information as does Visit Outer Hebrides <**www.visitouterhebrides.co.uk**>.

Drive times: Between the island ferry ports of Stornoway and Tarbert it is 36 miles (57km) or about a 50min drive. Between Leverburgh and Tarbert it is 20 miles (32km, 30min drive). Between Tarbert and Timsgarry in the Uig Sea-Cliffs area it is 55 miles (88km, 1hr 15min drive). It takes about 1hr 30min to drive from Timsgarry to the start of the walk for Sròn Uladail, or vice versa.

Amenities: For anyone arriving via Stornoway it is possible to shop here since this is the only place with a major supermarket, in the form of a Co-op and a Tesco. On Harris, Tarbert and Leverburgh have small general stores with most provisions and both have petrol stations. On the mainland, Ullapool has a Tesco and on Skye, Portree has a large Co-op on the road out to the ferry at Uig.

Accommodation: Climbers visiting Harris usually camp in the vicinity of their chosen crag, or at one of the nearby fabulous beaches. There is a good site in a lovely location by the dunes and the beach at Horgobost **(NB 049 968)**. The ferry port of Tarbert offers all the usual amenities as well as a small number of B&Bs, guesthouses and hotels. Check <**www.visitouterhebrides.co.uk**> or at the Tourist Information office in Tarbert.

Mobile Phones: See the Lewis introduction on page 9 for information on mobile phone antennae on Lewis and Harris.

Harris Hills and Outcrops

North Harris (Ceann a' Tuath na Hearadh)

A splendid range of rugged hills is located in North Harris, the highest being An Cliseam, or Clisham (799m), which is a Corbett and also the highest hill in the Outer Hebrides. The majority of the climbing is on two main cliffs. The first is Sròn Uladail, or the anglicised Strone Ulladale as some will know it, in Gleann Uladail, and Creag Mò in Gleann Sgaladail. Despite their fine situations the other crags are seldom visited, although further investigation may well reward those with a sense of adventure.

ULABHAL

Sròn Uladail (Strone Ulladale)

(NB 080 133) Alt 160m W to NE facing
Map opposite Diagrams p212 & p225

Mighty Sròn Uladail (442m) sits sphinx-like at the head of Gleann Uladail. It forms the end of the long northern ridge of Ulabhal, a northern top of Oireabhal, which terminates abruptly in an imposing great prow of overhanging rock that towers 270m above Loch Uladail. The Sròn is without doubt one of the most impressive pieces of rock architecture in the British Isles and the walk through the hills to view it is a popular excursion.

The approach to the cliff is via Gleann Chliostair which runs northwards from the B887 Huisinis road at Amhuinnsuidhe on the coast, on the south side of the North Harris Hills. Creating a through route between the principal hills of Tiorga Mòr to the west and Oireabhal and Ulabhal to the east, this glen links with Gleann Uladail to reach the sea at the head of the fiord-like inlet of Loch Rèasort.

Directions: Some 4km north of Tarbert, turn west off the main A859 to Stornoway at the Ceann an Ora Bridge and take the B887 towards Hushinish (Huisinis). Follow this to just before the gates to Amhuinnsuidhe (Abhainn Suidhe), where a tarmac road on the right **(NB 0530 0780)** is signposted to Chliostair Power Station and Marine Harvest's Amhuinnsuidhe Hatchery. Parking is awkward. Do not park in the entrance since large vehicles require this for turning. There is limited space beside the gates to Amhuinnsuidhe and some 50m up the track where the riverside verge is just wide enough to accommodate a number of vehicles opposite a passing place. There is also limited parking at the locked gate 400m further up the tarmac road where the track forks right to the fish farm.

Approach: Walk or cycle along the track past the power station to a dam at the southern end of Loch Chliostair (3.2km, 45min). Continue along an excellent path, first on the east side of the loch and then by the west bank of Loch Aiseabhat before dropping down to the Sròn (4.3km, 1hr 15min; total distance 8km, 2hr).

Descent: Grassy slopes with intermittent deer tracks lead right (south) beyond South Buttress where a grassy gully gains the far end of the crag, below which the approach path can be joined after its descent from Loch Aiseabhat.

There is good camping by the river and numerous boulders under which it would be possible to bivouac. Either way, be prepared to do battle with the fearsome Harris midge!

The rock is a form of Lewisian Gneiss, mostly excellent but quite varied and sometimes a bit slate-like in texture. Bands of mica schist and areas of quartzy rock add further variety to the climbing which is most definitely for those with a sense of adventure and a strong head (as well as arms). The rock dries quickly after rain, particularly on the North-West Face, which appears to be virtually unaffected by even the most adverse conditions. When it rains the sheep scuttle off up the hillside to shelter beneath the overhangs and happily munch away in the dry some distance out from the base of the cliff! The North-East and West Faces require several dry days to come into condition, especially the obvious weep lines between the giant inverted staircase and South Buttress at the end. For the harder routes, microcams can be very helpful!

Routes are described from left to right starting with those on the seldom visited, more broken and buttressed North-East Face, around the edge from the main rock bastion, followed by the North-West Face and then the West Face.

North-East Face

This lies out of sight around the edge from the principal rock bastion, to the left of the actual nose, or prow, of the Sròn itself. This side of the Sròn is split by two huge gullies; on the left, Great Gully runs full height and on the right a vague gully runs up from the foot of the face to the equally imposing Great Recess, or Amphitheatre, which starts halfway up and runs to the top.

Great Gully Buttress

This is the largest and most continuous mass of rock on this side of the Sròn. Steep slopes of heather and grass guard its foot. Higher up to the left of Great Gully, and level with the Amphitheatre, there are three buttresses on which the exploratory climbers first climbed. One of these buttresses is climbed by Irens' Route, which was also used to gain the others.

Iron Butterfly 270m HVS/A2

P.Macdonald, I.G.Rowe, May 1969

The main difficulties are concentrated in the first 120m. The steep lower section is breached by an overhung left-slanting fault leading to easier rocks above, which give excellent climbing. Climb steep and dangerous grass to reach the rock at 60m.

1. 30m Climb to a tree on a ledge, then move left and climb a short strenuous crack system to an eyrie below the overhung fault.
2. 35m Move down and right into the fault and climb it leftwards to a large ledge (8 pegs and nuts for aid).
3. 35m Move left to surmount the bulge (peg for aid) onto a slab, then go right into a corner, which leads to a belay. Easier rocks lead to the summit.

Tyke 190m S

R.B.Evans, L.A.Hawarth, Mrs. A.Evans, May 1961

This lies immediately left of Great Gully. The rock is very good after a vegetated start. Scramble up 45m of steep heather to a small rowan. Gain the second rowan to the right, then climb slabs moving right and go up over a bulge to a small stance and peg belay below an overhang. Traverse right below the bulge, then follow easier rock overlooking the gully to a good platform below a steep groove. From a gangway on the left, enter the steep groove and climb it to a terrace where the angle eases. Pleasant slabs lead to the top.

Great Gully 300m VS

R.B.Evans, L.A.Hawarth, Mrs. A.Evans, May 1961

A poor climb with more vegetation than rock. Evil looking cave pitches are avoided on the left but a square amphitheatre at one-third height (the crux) is unavoidable and is climbed in two pitches. The first goes up a left-slanting groove (10m); the second traverses right and up a groove through an overhang (25m).

No.1 Buttress 75m D

R.G.Folkard, M.deV.Wills, Miss J.Fox, 30 Jul 1948

The right-hand buttress, between Great Gully and the top left fork. From the base of Amphitheatre Buttress, climb a steep grass rake leading to Great Gully. Start in the gully fork to the left of the buttress, a few metres or so above its base. The gully above has two parallel overhanging chimneys; make a short traverse into a groove on the left and climb to a grass slope above the overhang (20m). Now traverse right onto the buttress to some large blocks and climb this to the top, keeping as much to the right as possible; 50m of climbing then scrambling.

No.2 Buttress is to the left of the fork and is described under Irens' Route.

No.3 Buttress 80m D

R.G.Folkard, M.deV.Wills, Miss J.Fox, 29 Jul 1948

The left-hand buttress is separated from No.2 Buttress by yet another branch which stems from Great Gully. Gain it from the lower grass slopes of the Amphitheatre by an airy walk along a ledge to enter Great Gully. The departure on the other side is more awkward and involves two pitches of about D. Now follow a grassy rake past the base of No.2 Buttress. The buttress proper begins from the grass on the left (cairn) and gives a somewhat artificial route with 45m of climbing then 35m of scrambling.

Lower Crag and Upper Crag

The mass of rock and vegetation to the right of Great Gully has a mid-height grassy terrace which cuts across below the Amphitheatre, or Great Recess, gained from beneath the nose by a ramp of grass and rock followed by Irens' Route. Where this ramp crosses the line of the nose itself there is a grassy alp known as Rush Platform. The terrace effectively forms a sort of lower and upper tier, which the pioneers called Lower Crag and Upper Crag. Above the terrace, the tapering buttress between the two gullies is Amphitheatre Buttress. Various lines were apparently climbed on the lower tier to the right of Great Gully but most are too broken and vegetated to be worthwhile.

Direct Route 355m HS
G.J.Fraser, Miss E.M.Baldwin, Apr 1958
This direct line on Amphitheatre Buttress starts at the base of the cliff to the right of Great Gully. It crosses the 1948 Route at about its 10th pitch but thereafter apparently takes a line somewhat to the right. It is said to be a fine climb and although vegetated in the middle, the final section gives beautiful clean climbing. With modern day ropes and protection it will be possible to string pitches together. In a grassy bay below the steepening of Great Gully, the buttress base forms a steep wall. Start at the middle of this wall beneath a corner-crack.
1. 10m Climb the wall bearing left, then go back to a niche below the corner.
2. 25m Leave the niche on the right, then go straight up vegetation and a rock wall to a good ledge and belay.
3. 20m Follow a grassy rake to the right, then climb a steep clean wall until it is possible to move right to a ledge.
4. 10m Leave the right end of the ledge and climb a crack with a small tree alongside.
5. 20m Climb a crack and a broken groove leading right to a large platform.
6. 10m Ascend a small overhang direct, on the left.
7. 40m Easy grass leads to a short wall.
8. 20m Climb the wall around a large block and continue over slabs.
9. 20m Easy climbing leads to a belay in a gully 6m above the foot and to the right of the next wall.
10. 20m Move onto the wall above the belay, then climb straight up to beneath a V-chimney.
11. 15m Climb the chimney, pulling out awkwardly at the top onto a good ledge.
12. 20m Go up the slab above on small holds.
13. 20m Traverse up right towards an exposed stance at the tapering foot of the final tower.
14. 20m Climb just to the left of the rib on steep good holds; chockstone belay beside a protruding flake.
15. 15m Avoid the easy looking groove, and move onto the face of the buttress. Climb close to its edge then move right onto a sloping ledge.
16. 30m Continue straight up grooves from the right-hand edge of the ledge. At 15m, move right around a rib. Climb a quartzy block into a crack and go up this to a platform under an overhang.
17. 40m Take the overhang at its right then go straight up the narrow crest of the buttress; finish up a wide chimney.

Amphitheatre Approach 95m D
R.G.Folkard, M.deV.Wills, Miss J.Fox, 30 Jul 1948
Start below and right of the Amphitheatre and scramble to the foot of the rock and heather buttress immediately left of a wet black wall (cairn). After the first pitch the climbing is on clean rock.
1. 35m Steep climbing, occasionally on rock, leads to a grass slope; block belay.
2. 20m Starting at the back of a large grass recess, right of a gully, climb a steep slab until it is possible to step into the gully above a small cave, then go up the gully to a rock platform and belay on the left.
3. 25m Climb up left, then go straight up to a thread belay.
4. 15m Continue to a block belay on grass slopes leading to the Amphitheatre.

Irens' Route 195m VD
H.J.Irens, F.Solari, A.Kinnear, 2 Jul 1938
The route climbs the full extent of the face, starting beneath the overhanging nose of the main rock bastion itself. It then takes a long leftward trend, crossing Great Gully to finish up No.2 Buttress. Details of this and other early routes have been recorded in the Rucksack Club Journal and perhaps the Yorkshire Ramblers Club Journal. Described by Irens as a good mountaineering route, the exact line taken in relation to Slab Route on the Lower Crag, as climbed by Folkard's party in 1948, is uncertain with the 1938 description simply stating "Easy slabs to amphitheatre at foot of the great recess." The 1948 Slab Route description has been used here. At the time of the1938 ascent a local shepherd mentioned that prior to 1914 a German party had apparently made an un-roped ascent by nearly the same route.

Start from a grass platform on a small rock buttress slightly right of the nose. A long tongue of slabby rock stretches down to the platform and gives a pitch of 30m. About 60m of easier climbing follows, trending left. Climb the steeper rocks directly to Rush Platform (35m). A short descending left traverse leads to the grass slopes of the Amphitheatre. From the left-hand base of Amphitheatre Buttress, ascend a grassy rake to enter Great Gully. Cross the gully leftwards by steep grass to a buttress divided by two chimneys. Climb the right-hand chimney until a difficult traverse leads across the left-hand chimney to another rib. The buttress above provides exposed but not difficult climbing on sound clean rock.

Amphitheatre Buttress 165m S
R.G.Folkard, M.deV.Wills, 28 Jul 1948
This is the tapering buttress between the Amphitheatre and Great Gully. Start at the foot of the buttress; originally reached by what was known as the Slab Start, probably common with Irens' Route.
1. 30m Climb a grassy rake to establish a position on the buttress, make an ascending traverse to a small cave; poor stance and belay.
2. 45m Traverse right until the wall can be climbed to a grass ledge. The slab above leads to a heather ledge. Climb a 12m wall, first left then right, where heather

3
8
5
10a
10b
10
13
14
15
11
16
17
4
6
7
16
14
1
2
3
12
8
10
11
SRÒN ULADAIL

1. Inversion HVS 5a *
2. Mosskill Grooves E6 6b ***
3. The Scoop E7 6b ****
4. The Scoop (Aid) A3 ***
5. Knuckle Sandwich E7 6c ***
6. Knucklehead A4
7. The Nose A5
8. The Usual Suspects E8/9 7a ***
10. The Chisel E7 6b ****
10a. Gloaming Finish 6b ***
10b. Roaming Finish 6a ***
11. Stone E5 6a ****
12. The Occasional Table E6 6b
13. Kismet E5 6a/b ****
14. White Dwarf E5 6b ***
15. Premonition E6 6b ***
16. The Orphan E5 6a *
17. The Second Coming E5 6b **
18. Beyond the Ranges E4 5c **
19. Cuinas E4 6a *
20. Flakeway to the Stairs E2 5c *
21. Palace of Swords Reversed E5 6b ***
22. The Missing Link E5 6a **
23. Big Luigi E4 6a ***
24. Wee Eck E5 6b *
25. The Beautiful South E7 6b **
26. Crackhead E4 6a *
27. Solar Wind E3 5c *
31. The Serpents Head E2 5c **
33. Prelude S 4a *
34. Midgard VD *

leads to a small stance. It is possible to split this pitch.
3. 30m Climb the wall above to the left to below an overhang, then bypass this to the right. Regain the rock above the overhang as soon as possible then continue to a good stance overlooking Great Gully.
4. 20m Climb the rib above to a commodious platform, which has a huge boulder at its back and overlooks Great Gully.
5. 25m The Crux. Climb the wall on the right by combined tactics, then follow a short slab and the small holdless rib above until scrambling leads to a good stance; cairn. The leader climbed this pitch with one boot removed!
6. 15m Scrambling leads to the top.

North-West and West Faces

Diagrams p212 & p225

The massively overhanging North-West Face is the recessed area to the right of the nose. It contains a central, deep-set line of roofed corners and grooves which are followed by the celebrated climb The Scoop. The next principal feature to the right is one of the most identifiable features on the cliff, the large mid-height corner-groove taken by The Chisel. Right again, above the toe of the cliff, the West Face is at its highest and contains an area of equally impressive yet less steep corners and groove lines; in its upper third the long corner-crack of Stone is obvious. This massive wall extends rightwards for almost 1km, passing a giant inverted staircase then an area of black stained, slabby grooves to terminate at the slabby South Buttress.

Climbs are described beginning with one around the edge of the nose, on the North-East Face, then those on the compelling and massively overhanging face of the nose itself. There is a degree of uncertainty in the relationship of a number of the climbs here, particularly in their upper sections.

1 Inversion 170m HVS *

M.A.Reeves, J.Ball, 15 Aug 1965

An intricate route of great character which weaves its way up a steep bit of cliff; exposed with amazing positions throughout but quite dirty. Start from Rush Platform, gained by climbing up the ramp beneath the main face as for Irens' Route (125m). The climbing begins at a cairn in the centre of a steep clean face.
1. 25m 5a Go up steep rocks then climb a shallow groove until it is possible to go right beneath a large overhang to a vertical black groove. Climb this, then follow a short rib on the right to a good ledge beneath the first great overhanging barrier (chockstone belay).
2. 10m 4c Traverse right beneath the roof to a cracked overhanging weakness on the edge. Climb this on surprising holds then continue to a small stance with fine belays.
3. 20m 5a The second barrier of overhangs is now above. Traverse left round a corner to a cracked overhanging groove. Climb this (difficult) to a roof, step down left then reach over the roof to a hidden edge. Mantelshelf up in a remarkable position to a slanting niche then go awkwardly out right to an easier wall above. Climb the wall to a stance level with an obvious right-traversing line.
4. 25m 4c Traverse down right then move up to an edge at about 12m. Climb the bulge above to the left of a cracked chimney (loose blocks), then trend left awkwardly to a small ledge on the nose. Go straight up a slab for 4m then climb diagonally right to a large triangular grassy stance.
5. 35m 4b Climb straight up the broad edge above, going slightly right on delicate slabby rock to a shallow black groove. Go up left, then move back right up a short grassy rake to a belay beneath very steep rock.
6. 25m 4c Go left onto a large block then climb a steep nose to easier ground.
7. 30m Easy rocks lead to the top.

Variation: **Inversion Direct E1 5b**

S.Gillies, G.Gavell, May 1997

3a. 30m This avoids the traverses of pitches 3 and 4 by climbing an obvious crack above the belay to emerge on the "edge at about 12m" of pitch 4. Finish as for the rest of that pitch.

2 Mosskill Grooves 100m E6 ***

B.Moon, J.Dawes, P.Pritchard, 1989

This climbs the prominent ramp-groove to the left of The Scoop, starting up and left of that route.
1. 40m 6b Pull over a bulge into a capped right-facing corner. Traverse right to a poor peg and move up into the huge right-facing corner. Climb this to nut belays at the top.
2. 30m 6a Climb the overhanging crack and chimney-line directly above the belay to a sloping ledge and small nut belay.
3. 30m 5c Go right across slabs to join The Scoop and belay as for this at the end of pitch 6. On the first ascent the line was climbed to a junction with The Scoop then abseiled back down. Otherwise finish as for The Scoop pitches 7 and 8.

3 The Scoop 205m E7 ****

J.Dawes, P.Pritchard, 6-12 Aug 1987

One of the most prestigious lines on British rock; it is an amazing climb which gives a serious and committing undertaking of awe-inspiring steepness. It is possible to abseil off after pitch 3 but thereafter it would be problematic. Start up the slope below the huge scooped corner-line which runs up towards the highest point of the prow. Scramble up some delicate slabs to an in-situ peg belay.
1. 20m 6b A rude awakening! Draw breath, step down and move up to an overhang. Climb this and a short wall (passing an old bolt) with a delicate pinch move onto a sloping ramp. Ascend the awkward overhanging wall above then move right to a hanging belay.
2. 25m 6b Move right and climb a short steep crack in the back of the groove to a ledge with numerous pegs; possible belay. Step right and go up a cracked rib to enter the fine open corner above then climb this to a comfortable ledge on the left.

The Scoop, P5 (E7) Tony Stone
(photo Iain Small)

3. 25m 6a Continue up the corner-groove to a roof then make thin moves left and continue up to a hanging belay below the main corner.
4. 25m 6b The aid version climbs straight up here. Instead, climb the exposed 'flying groove' out left by a series of wild layback and undercut moves. The groove above leads to an overhang which is turned on the left by an extremely exposed barn door move around the arete. Continue strenuously up a thin crack and a huge flake to the sanctuary of a lie-down sofa ledge.
5. 15m 5c Step down onto the huge flake and traverse left in a sensational position. Continue the traverse line with increasing difficulty to a corner below the left end of the roof (hanging belay). The blade pegs are in poor condition and there is little else, so it may be better to continue!
6. 25m 6a An awkward move gains the groove above. Take the left arete to a slab then follow a slim undercut groove right to a good ledge under the imposing capping roof.
7. 20m 6a A serious pitch. Move right and up to peg runners then climb back down and traverse right to a bulge. Make a series of committing moves through the bulge to a line of welcome jugs leading to a belay on the lip of the overhang, using nuts, cams and a peg.
8. 50m 5a Traverse left under a block overhang and go up to a ledge, turning any difficulties on the left. Now climb rightwards to the edge, which leads to top.

4 The Scoop (Original Aid Version) 170m A3 ***
D.Scott, G.Lee, J.Upton, M.Terry, Jun 1969
Although superseded by the free version, this gets climbed because of its inclusion in the book Hard Rock (to make ticking it more difficult!). At the time it was a tremendous achievement with 30hrs of very hard aid climbing spread over several days. Despite modern equipment it is still a difficult and demanding undertaking. Those attempting the aid version should make use of as many alternatives to pegs as possible.
1, 2 and 3. 70m A3, A2 and A2/3. As for the free version.
4. 25m A3 Where the 'flying groove' of the free version goes out left, climb a corner of red quartzy rock to a big block overhang. Go out left and continue to the next roof, then make a spectacular pendulum out left to the sofa ledge shared with the free version.
5. 30m A3 Tension back to the corner and return to the roof. Turn a block on the left (handle with care), then continue up a smaller block overhang. Reach round horizontally right 2m and go up until the narrow crack peters out. Using the bolt, place a high peg on the right. Follow this line until it is possible to look up the final pitch, now vertical. Belay on the sloping slab on the right.
6. 45m HVS/A1 Climb up and right and follow a thin crack up a brown wet streak on the wall with a mixture of aid and free moves. Continue more easily over sloping blocks to the end of the climb, then scramble to the top.

5 Knuckle Sandwich E7 ***
J.Dawes, P.Pritchard, 1987
Starting up The Scoop, this then essentially climbs the middle section of Knucklehead to finish by the upper section of The Nose.
1. 6b Climb the first pitch of The Scoop to a perched block belay.
2. 5b Traverse easily up right to a white ledge and poor bolt belay.
3. 6c Climb the overhanging thin crack directly above the belay to a tiny ledge. Climb up and right on big loose flakes to old bolts beneath an overhang. Pull desperately round this and go up to a hanging belay below the band of roofs.
4. 5a Traverse right to below the first big corner.
5. 6b Climb the corner to a difficult traverse right on overhanging quartz. Continue with difficulty to a small ledge.
6. 6a Climb perfect rock straight to the top.

6 Knucklehead 165m A4
P.Lloyd, T.King, 1977
Another impressive aid route, which is now partly followed by Knuckle Sandwich. The original top section continues straight up to join The Scoop above the final overhangs.

7 The Nose 150m A5
D.Scott, G.Lee, D.Hennick, 1972
This famous aid climb takes the demarcation line between the North-West and West Faces, between The Scoop and Sidewinder. The line was partially freed at E7 6b by J.Dawes and N.Craine in 1994. The top section is climbed by Knuckle Sandwich.

8 The Usual Suspects 130m E8/9 7a ***
D.MacLeod, T.Emmett, 28 Aug 2010
A spectacular voyage up the steepest part of the cliff, climbing terrain normally associated with hard sport routes. It is generally well-protected and the rock is excellent apart from a couple of metres on pitch 2. Televised by the BBC, the first ascent was made in heavy rain after a long wet spell. Start with a short scramble up to a large sloping ledge beneath the largest overhangs of the lower part of the cliff and underneath a ludicrously steep left-facing groove. This is just left of The Chisel and well down and right from the start of The Scoop.
1. 40m 6b From a large block, traverse right a couple of metres to a large flake and move up to a niche with a big loose boulder. Pull over the bulge and climb leftwards up the wall on improving holds to a big square jug (good gear). Hard moves though the bulging crack above gain a sloping shelf at the base of the left-facing groove. Climb the groove on good holds for some distance to a good bridging rest beneath an overhang. With excellent protection, make a desperate move to gain a standing position above the overhang but beneath the next bigger overhang. Traverse left to a stopping place and continue with hard moves getting established on a big undercut flake. Follow this left then up to its termination and take a hanging belay. A big pitch!

2. 25m 7a Straight off the belay desperate crux moves on tiny holds lead rightwards without respite or protection to a superbly positioned flake-line on the lip and good cams. Turn the lip using the flake then pull left to gain another flake-crack. Follow this with thuggy climbing to a block below a perched ledge above and to the right. Arrange good cams, the last gear on the pitch. Pull right onto the ledge. Move up on big suspect holds then climb diagonally leftwards (6a) to gain the most welcome belay ledges of Knuckle Sandwich (old bolt and small cams).
3. 35m 6b Start up the thin crack of Knuckle Sandwich for 4m (small wires) to a sloping shelf leading right to gain a huge detached flake. Layback up this and make difficult moves on slopers and edges over the bulge to a smooth rounded slab. Step right onto a spike for a no hands rest and good cams. Return and climb the big flakes with difficulty at first to a junction with Knuckle Sandwich below a bulge. Arrange crucial gear then make a long fingery traverse rightwards across the wall in a fantastic position. Mantel onto a big flat hold and move up to a belay directly above.
4. 15m 6b This pitch climbs the roof and thin cracks just left of the arete looming overhead. Arrange crucial small cams in the roof then use crimps on the small sidewall to pull round into the roof and out on improving holds to a huge jug on the lip. Climb the wall cracks above with some technical moves but good protection to a ledge.
5. 45m 6b/c From the left edge of the ledge, clip a poor knifeblade and make a very tenuous move laybacking the small arete to gain better holds. More tricky moves on small edges lead leftwards to gain an obvious line of spiky jugs leading diagonally into a big open groove. Climb this past a couple of bulges to a right-trending line of jugs below bulges. Step up then left and go straight up the final 15m headwall; 5b when dry but serious when wet.

9 Sidewinder 165m A5/HVS
D.Scott, G.Lee, 1971
This takes a line in the vicinity of the wide corner in the middle of the face taken by The Chisel (possibly immediately to its left) to finish up the large corner above.

10 The Chisel 150m E7 ****
C.Waddy, B.Drury, J.Biddle, 1989, 1 rest point; FFA G.Smith, C.Waddy, 1994
Another truly outstanding climb, this is rated as perhaps the best climb on the cliff. It takes a line through the prominent wide chiselled-out corner in the middle of the face with an undercut flake on its left wall.
1. 20m 5b Start below and left of orange walls about 15m down and right of the start of The Nose. Move up and right through overlaps until a wide break leads down and right onto an obvious hanging wall. Continue right to belay in a central crack.
2. 35m 6a Climb the crack until it becomes a groove. Follow this as it curves right. At its top, traverse right to an arete and boldly climb this to ledges. A better protected variation (6a/b) is possible by taking a shallow groove to the ledge, starting about 3m before the arete.
3. 10m 5c Layback flakes on the left then traverse right to a large ledge.
4. 10m 6a Climb up right to the large horizontal break under the roof that is the most obvious horizontal line on the cliff. Step left and pull steeply into the main groove to gain a hanging belay.
5. 20m 6b Now climb the main groove with difficulty and continue up left along the obvious undercut flake until it finally eases near the arete. Pull over the roof to gain a footledge; very strenuous and exposed but well protected.
6. 20m 6a Climb a short groove to a lichenous bulge then move right and go up through this until a very exposed step right leads to a short, open groove. Climb this then a crack to pull out left onto a perfect square ledge.
7. 15m 6a Climb the corner above until it gets hard then step right into a quartzy groove leading to the top.
Variation: **10a The Gloaming Finish *****
C.Waddy, G.Smith, 1994
This left-hand finish is noted as being slow to dry and on the two known ascents a rest was used on the final pitch due to wet rock, although it was felt this wouldn't be too hard when dry.

The Usual Suspects, P2 (E9) Dave MacLeod (photo Brian Hall)

Stone, P5 (E5) Ramon Marin
(photo Crispin Waddy)

6. 20m 6a Climb a short groove, then traverse left along a break until it eases.
7. 20m 6a Step left and climb a roof into an obvious corner then follow this until a short traverse across a hanging wall leads to a ledge; grade allows for a wet section.
8. 15m 6b Mantel onto the slab above and step right to a crack-groove. Climb this steeply into double narrow grooves and go up these until a gritstone-like sloping rail leads to the top.
Variation: **10b The Roaming Finish** ***
T.Stone and I.Small, 14 Jun 2011
Another fine finish which although a little bold, provides excellent climbing on good clean rock.
6. 40m 6a Climb the groove above the belay to the lichenous bulge then traverse right for about 5m to pull round onto a sloping ledge at the bottom of a vague groove. Move up the groove then trend right again to step airily into the base of another groove. Climb this groove and then the rib on its right to reach the base of a quartzy wall with a sloping gneiss footrail rising leftward below it. Climb up and follow the footrail left across to the quartzy wall to move around the blunt arete and up onto a ledge. Move up the slim groove immediately above to a good ledge with a giant cracked flake.
7. 20m 5b Climb up to the obvious overhanging quartz crack above the belay and follow this to a dirty off-width at the back of a huge corner. Avoid the off-width and instead traverse across to cracks in the left wall of the corner; follow these pleasantly to the top.

11 Stone 200m E5 ****
K.Spence, J.Porteous, 22-23 May 1969; FFA: M.Fowler, A.Meyers, 1981
This sensational climb was the first to breach the Sròn's central defences at Scottish VS and A2; now free and rated as soft for the grade. A golden eagle is known to nest on Stone and it is up to those wishing to attempt the route to check beforehand whether the eagle has chosen this as a nest site that year. It is an offence to willfully disturb the nest site of such a bird. There is information on birds on the Mountaineering Scotland website. The climb starts at the lowest rocks beneath an obvious open corner.
1. 25m 5a Climb the corner to a large flake on the right wall.
2. 35m 4b Descend a little, traverse right on the slab beneath the overlap, then go up an obvious break to a slab under another roof.
3. 25m 5c Traverse left on a slab under the roof to a ledge. Go left again to climb an overhanging quartzy groove and exit left below its top to a ledge. A variation on this pitch from a 1968 attempt (M.Reeves, J.Grieve) climbs two short walls then a cracked wall into a cave before traversing left to the quartzy ramp.
4. 25m 4a An easy quartzy ramp leads to a ledge beneath a big corner with twin cracks.
5. 45m 6a Climb the corner-crack then transfer into the right-hand crack and climb it; strenuous and sustained but very well protected. The move right can either be made low down, or higher up when the corner-crack becomes off-width at the bulge. Belay on the upper of two grass ledges below a corner.
6. 45m 5b Climb the corner until a small ledge on the right arete can be reached then traverse right into easier grooves leading to the top.

12 The Occasional Table E6 6b *
J.Dawes, N.Craine, 1994
This relatively short though serious route climbs directly out of the first pitch of Stone. It can be used as an alternative start to a number of the other routes on this bit of wall. From the belay at the top of pitch 1 on Stone, continue steeply straight up to a sloping ledge; the Occasional Table. Make hard moves up and left to a dirty sloping ledge, continue up to a larger sloping ledge then move right to belay at a vertical crack.

The next four climbs all start with basically the same pitch, which leads to a stance either partway up, or at the top of pitch 4 on Stone at the foot of the corner.

13 Kismet 140m E5 ****
C.Waddy, R.Rogers, 1989; alt top pitch M.Gardiner, C.Waddy, D.O'Sullivan, 4 Jun 2016
Another amazing climb which, after crossing Stone, gets into the first corner-groove to the right of the big corner on The Chisel. Start some 60m above and right of Stone, above the lower slabs, and as far left as is possible to easily go from the giant inverted staircase.
1. 40m 6a Traverse left along an obvious break then go steeply up a diagonal crack to a high niche. Alternatively, climb immediately up a short wall past inverted flakes (5c) then continue easily left to the high niche. Step under the bottom right corner of the orange quartzy wall that forms the underside of the ramp on pitch 4 of Stone and continue until a thin crack leads up to the ramp. Belay level with a razor-thin flake which leads horizontally left. Alternatively, climb the first three pitches of Stone.
2. 15m 6a Follow the flake left until it fades, then climb a shallow groove to a ledge under a large roof formed by the main horizontal break.
3. 10m 6a Climb flakes across the roof and belay immediately in a large groove right of the main groove of The Chisel. This can easily be linked with the previous pitch.
4. 25m 6a Step right and climb a crack in the arete between the two main corners until it joins the right-hand corner (White Dwarf). Follow this to its belay then traverse right to a ledge.
5. 20m 6a Climb a shallow groove until it blanks out at 12m then hand-traverse round a blank pillar and pull up to a superbly appointed belay seat like a pew (with a view!).
6. 15m 6a Step up and traverse left into an open groove which leads to cracks (junction with The Chisel) and pull out left onto the perfect square ledge.
7. 15m 6a If dry it is logical to finish as for The Chisel, up the corner above until it gets hard then step right into a quartzy groove which leads to the top. The alternative is to climb the open corner-groove on the

right then traverse right to the arete and finish up the groove of White Dwarf. An earlier variation finish (1994, A.Donson) traverses right for 6m past the corner-groove to follow good holds up the arete of the groove to finish as for White Dwarf; graded 5b, this was attempted on the 2016 ascent and found to be hard!

13a Kismet Original Finish
Climbed as an exploratory traverse across the top of the cliff.
7. 25m 6b Step down left onto a hanging slab and cross this to easier climbing leading to the large top corner-groove of Sidewinder. The Roaming Finish to The Chisel belays here then climbs cracks in the left wall of the corner (5b). The original finish to Kismet continues left towards The Gloaming Finish to The Chisel before gaining the top.

14 White Dwarf 140m E5 ***
C.Waddy, A.Ford, 1989
Starting as for Kismet, this takes the next groove to the right, cutting through that route twice to head direct for the top. It is very Comici-esqué after the first pitch.
1. 45m 6a As for Kismet, but continue up the ramp to belay at the top of pitch 4 on Stone.
2. 15m 5c Gain the large break which leads awkwardly left into the bottom of a large corner, the second corner right of The Chisel.
3. 20m 6a Strenuously climb the corner to belay at its top.
4. 20m 6b Climb up and left, then go up a little overhanging groove through a bulge. A steep crack leads to Kismet's pew stance.
5. 15m 6b Climb straight up (initially footless) then go boldly into an acute-angled corner which leads to a ledge.
6. 25m 5c Continue directly until a wet mantel gains the top.

15 Premonition 115m E6 ***
C.Waddy, G.Smith, 1994; FFA A.Coull, G.Lennox, Jul 2011
Another excellent climb, which starts as for Kismet and White Dwarf then takes a line immediately left of the corner-crack of Stone.
1. 45m 6a Follow Kismet and White Dwarf to the top of pitch 4 on Stone.
2. 20m 6b Climb the cracks in the left retaining wall of the corner of Stone until a traverse left leads to a rest in a hanging groove. Climb out the top of this to a thin ledge then go up to a larger ledge.
3. 25m 6b Climb the left-leaning corner-groove above and pull over a roof in an amazing position to gain a short crack (the first ascent gained this point by pulling out of the corner-groove into a groove on the right to climb this past a peg then step left at its top with 2 rest points). Climb the crack then hand-traverse wildly right to a belay.
4. 25 6a A short crack-groove on the left leads to a ledge. Continue up cracks and grooves directly, and more easily, to the top.

16 The Orphan 115m E5 *
C.Waddy, A.Donson, 1992
This follows grooves to the right of Stone. Most of the climb was ascended in adverse weather, so the grade and description may not be entirely correct!
1. 45m 6a Climb as for the previous three routes to below the corner-crack on Stone.
2. 10m 5c/6a Traverse right along the lip of the roof below the right wall of Stone's corner.
3. 25m 5c Climb various grooves until forced horizontally right to reach the third pitch of The Second Coming at an open groove. Move up and left and belay under a roof.
4. 20m 5c Continue up a groove to belay below a tower.
5. 15m 6a Climb steeply into a groove on the left side of the tower to finish.

17 The Second Coming 75m E5 **
C.Waddy, R.Rogers, 1992
Start to the right of the previous routes but to the left of Beyond the Ranges, below an obvious black, cracked arete. The description was written up at a later date and may be inaccurate! Certainly, the pitch lengths don't tally to the length of the neighbouring routes.
1. 25m 5b Climb to the arete and go up it on quartzy cracks.
2. 10m 6a Traverse right along the lip of the roof, then go up and back left until above the previous belay.
3. 20m 5c Climb grooves and ledges to a tower of rock.
4. 20m 6b Climb a crack-groove on the right until it leans back and eases, then continue to the top.

18 Beyond the Ranges 110m E4 **
D.Cuthbertson, P.Moores, May 1985
This lies to the left of the giant inverted staircase, on a slightly projecting buttress between Stone and Flakeway to the Stairs, but closer to the latter. It takes a line of right-facing corners and flakes just right of a pink pegmatite intrusion. Start near the left end of a terrace, gained after 60m of scrambling.
1. 45m 5c Climb the corner rightwards, then go back left under an overhang. Move up then back right to a ledge, climb through a break, then move left and make an awkward move left again to a large flake. Pull into a quartzy crack above with a loose flake hold. Traverse right to a footledge, move up then traverse back left across suspect but probably well keyed blocks. Now climb a quartzy groove, pull out left in a superb position and continue to a fine ledge and belay.
2. 35m 5b Climb the corner-groove above with a tricky move onto a ledge. Climb a short brown groove then go right to belay at the foot of an obvious layback corner.
3. 30m 5a Climb the corner to a ledge with a block then traverse left to another ledge with a block. Go back right and up to the top.

19 Cuinas 90m E4 *
C.Waddy, R.Rogers, 1989
It is not quite sure where this goes and how it relates to the routes either side of it. Start at a short corner in black

Kismet, P6 (E5) Mike Gardiner
(photo Crispin Waddy)

rock about 30m left of the giant inverted staircase, and below an obvious small right-trending corner-overlap at 30m.
1. 40m 6a Climb up to the corner-overlap via cracks and flakes, then continue up it and belay on ledges beyond.
2. 25m 5c Climb an open groove to ledges and belay.
3. 25m 5b Continue up an open groove to the top.

20 Flakeway to the Stairs 135m E2 *
C.Watts, S.Vietoris, 1 Jun 1981; FFA: A.MacFarlane, B.Davison, Jul 1990
This climbs a line of flakes to the left of the giant inverted staircase.
1. 35m 5a Climb diagonally left along a fragile ramp to overhanging and detached block flakes. Climb these strenuously to a small ledge beneath a roof.
2. 25m 5b Traverse right beneath the roof. Climb a crack on the right of the flake until it fades. Move left to a second flake, then climb a wide crack.
3. 20m 5c Descend left and around a corner then move left and go up the wall to a ledge.
4. 55m 5a Climb the ramp and surmount the overhang. Continue to the foot of an obvious square-cut chimney-corner and climb this to the top. A more direct finish goes up a corner left of the stance (probably Cuinas).

The huge inverted staircase has been climbed to about two-thirds height (three of the five steps), but was found to be loose and nasty. About 15m right of the inverted staircase is a large corner; the next four climbs begin here with a common start.

21 Palace of Swords Reversed 90m E5 ***
C.Waddy, R.Rogers, 1989
1. 25m 5c Climb the large corner then step left and climb a slim flake-crack which leads back into the corner above. Continue up the corner to a ledge on the right.
2. 20m 6b Climb the wall round an overhang above and left of the belay, then continue to a ledge (possible belay). Now climb the left-hand groove above (steeper than the right-hand one, but it has holds) past a peg runner to a ledge.
3. 20m 6a/b Step left off the ledge and go boldly up the wall round a roof into a groove that leads to a belay below a large roof.
4. 25m 6a Traverse horizontally right along a slab, then go up left above a roof and continue round an overhanging arete where easy ground leads to the top.

22 The Missing Link 80m E5 **
C.Waddy, A.Donson, 1992
1. 25m 5c Palace of Swords Reversed, pitch 1.
2. 20m 6a Step off the right side of the ledge onto an awkward ramp. This leads to a wide layback crack. Avoid this by an arete which leads boldly to a belay below a groove.
3. 20m 5c Climb the groove to belay at the right end of the traverse of Palace of Swords Reversed, pitch 4.
4. 15m 6a Finish as for Palace of Swords Reversed.

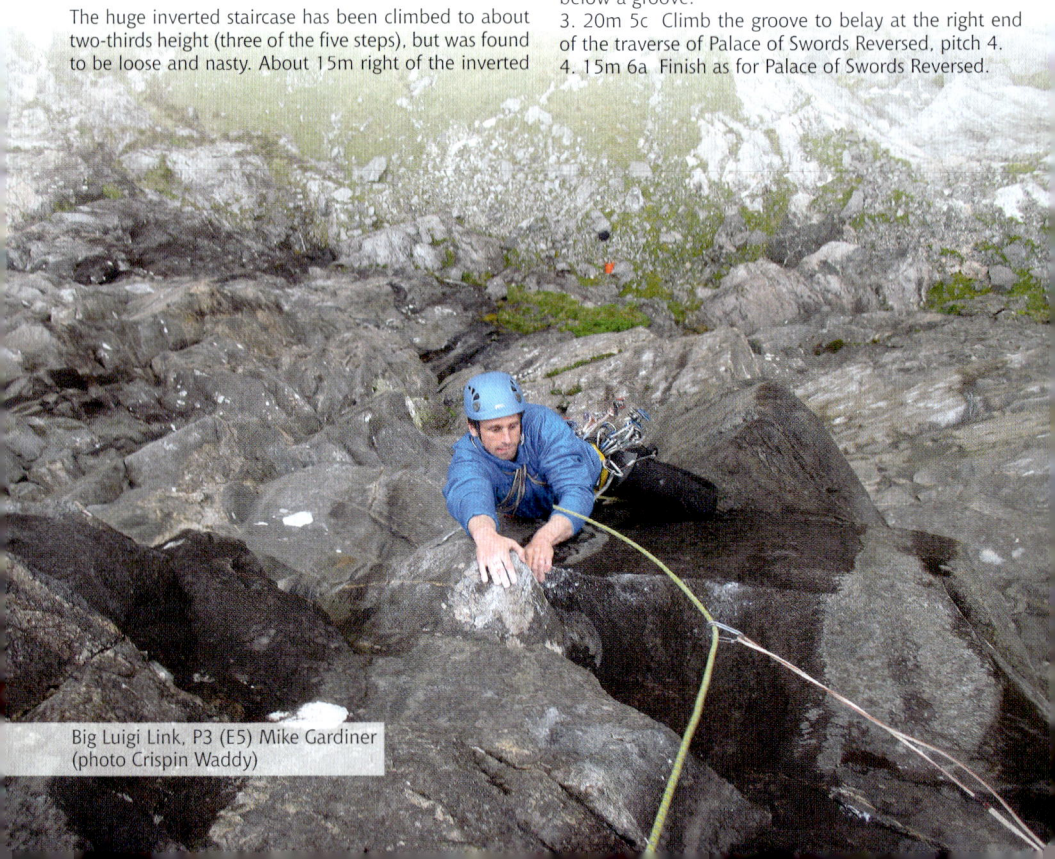

Big Luigi Link, P3 (E5) Mike Gardiner (photo Crispin Waddy)

23 Big Luigi 75m E4/5 ***
C.Waddy, J.Biddle, 1989
1. 25m 5c Palace of Swords Reversed, pitch 1.
2. 25m 6a Follow the second pitch of The Missing Link onto the ramp, then continue right along quartzy rock into a groove. Climb this to cracks in a black wall which lead via a short horizontal traverse to a belay.
3. 25m 5c Climb more or less directly in a straight line via grooves and cracks to the top.

23a The Big Luigi Link 80m E4/5 ***
M.Gardiner, D.O'Sullivan, C.Waddy, 3 Jun 2016
There is some confusion on the precise line of Big Luigi. This climb, and in particular the top pitch, is said to be superb.
1. 25m 5c Palace of Swords Reversed, pitch 1.
2. 25m 6a Step awkwardly off the right end of the ledge and move down 1m to an obvious quartzy jug. Now climb steeply up and slightly right into a slim groove left of the arete, which is followed more easily to a belay straight above the previous one.
3. 30m 5c Follow the groove above, curving left until an intimidating but remarkably easy traverse leads left to finally gain an undercut nose in a fantastic position. From this the finish eases above.

24 Wee Eck 95m E5 *
I.Small, P.Nolan, Jun 2009
1. 25m 5c As for the previous three routes.
2. 25m 6b Follow Big Luigi into the quartzy groove then swing out onto the right arete to gain a good footledge. Hard moves right lead to a corner which is followed to a good square-cut ledge.
3. 25m 6a Step right off the ledge, climb a white groove to an overlap, then follow the break out right around the arete to a footledge. Take the bulges above on the right to a long thin ledge.
4. 20m Take an easy corner on the right to easier ground.

25 The Beautiful South 75m E7 **
D.Turnbull, J.Arran, 22 May 1998
The hanging corners between Palace of Swords Reversed and Crackhead.
1. 25m 5b Climb into a left-trending open groove and continue to a good stance in an alcove below a narrow roof beneath blank rock.
2. 20m 6b Move up right to a flake and hidden peg runner (very poor). Make bold moves up to the bulge (peg runner), then move immediately left to a 120° overhanging wall. Climb this with difficulty to easier ground leading to corners above.
3. 30m 5c Move up and rightwards up blank corners, then back left to join the easy exit ramp.

26 Crackhead 65m E4 *
C.Waddy, A.Donson, 1992
This starts some 45m right of Palace of Swords Reversed, directly below an obvious straight crack in the right side of a wall guarded by roofs. 2018 Note: C.Waddy thinks there may have been rockfall at the roofs on pitch 1.
1. 25m 5c Climb up to a break in the roof which leads to a narrow slab. This leads right to a belay in the base of the crack.
2. 20m 6a Climb the crack until near its top, where it becomes necessary to step left into a niche. Pull out of this to slabs.
3. 20m 4c Climb slabs to join and finish up Midgard.

Four climbs were added at the right end in 2018 on rock that is described as being generally exceptionally fine. These climbs and those also added on South Buttress at the same time are said to be good and would be given more stars elsewhere were it not for their length compared to the existing climbs here. However, due to their size and location, it is possible to rig an abseil to allow a number to climbed.

27 Solar Wind 40m E3 5c *
C.Waddy, D.O'Sullivan 28 May 2018
Parts of this climb may coincide with Borealis and some, if not all, may coincide with the earlier Aurora which it now supersedes since aid was used on that route. The climb takes the groove system about 15m left of the obvious crack taken by The Serpents Head. Climb into the groove from the left and follow it with an awkward move left and up small stepped ledges to the 'ultimate nut slot'. Step right and continue until a step left gains good quartzy holds, from where difficult climbing leads rightwards past an ancient peg to a ledge. Move left to a steeper crack under an overhang and left of the main groove line, then follow this past a niche to a belay on Midgard.

28 Aurora 200m HVS & Aid
J.Grieve, M.A.Reeves, E.Jones, 31 May 1967
Precisely locating this line has proved difficult. However, it has effectively been superseded by Solar Wind, although the description has been retained for historical interest. Start at a vague weakness of grooves 40m left of Prelude
1. 35m Climb easily at first towards a small triangular overhang; a peg was used on the FA to reach good holds over bulge. Move right then go straight up a groove to a sloping rock stance on the right (peg belay).
2. 10m Step back left across the groove to a steep wall. Climb this and exit left to an excellent rock stance; 2 pegs & 2 slings used for aid.
3. 10m Use a shoulder to reach a ledge up and right. Move right under a bulge then go up and back left above it. Continue up a groove to a good rock ledge on the left (peg belay).
4. 45m Move a metre or so right to a corner-crack and climb this to a long narrow grassy rake. Cross this and climb steep slabs trending left towards an overhang-capped bay. On reaching bulges, pull up (peg runner) and traverse right to a small stance below large perched blocks.
5. 10m Traverse right to an overhanging corner-crack and climb this (2 slings for aid), pulling out right beneath the roof to a good ledge.
6 & 7. 90m Follow slabs and grass to easy ground.

29 Borealis 80m E2 **
A.Macfarlane, D.McGimpsey, 14 Jul 1989
Start as for Aurora.
1. 20m 5a Climb the groove to a sizeable ledge directly below a triangular roof.
2. 30m 5b Traverse right to a right-facing corner. Climb this to a sloping ledge. Move left to another right-facing corner and climb this to a belay ledge, as for Midgard.
3. 30m 4c Climb a slab to a left-facing corner-chimney.

30 One Flew Over 35m E5 6b ***
D.O'Sullivan, C.Waddy, C.Plant, 28 May 2018
Brilliant climbing on perfect rock; small wires and cams useful. Start 8m left of The Serpents Head, directly below a thin crack with a peg at half height. Follow a short thin crack for a few metres and traverse up right to breach the large overlap at its right side. Continue up until it is possible to traverse back left to the base of the thin crack. Crux moves past the peg gain an undercut under the overlap on the right. Undercut right 2m then go straight up on good edges. Continue more easily to a left-facing groove then trend right to finish.

31 The Serpents Head 95m E2 *
C.Waddy, C.Plant, 27 May 2018
The obvious straight crack.
1. 35m 5c Climb up to the crack and follow it with a short diversion right on hollow flakes (junction with So, That is Running Out of Gas) to a long ledge. Climb part way up the diagonal overlap then rock-over using good flakes above it. Continue to belay on Midgard next to a petrified snake's head.
2. 60m 4c Continue over the roof above and on up a slabby tongue of rock, some, or much of which may coincide with Prelude.

32 So, That is Running Out of Gas 85m E3 *
C.Plant ,D.O'Sullivan, C.Waddy May 2018
Start below and right of The Serpent's Head; easier for the tall.
1. 35m 6a Climb a flake to a short left-facing corner (junction with The Serpents Head) taking care with some less sound rock just before it. Break out right at the top of the corner then go up the wall to an overlap and at a point where a lump of rock comes down, make hard moves over onto a ledge. Awkwardly leave the ledge to gain easier ground and make a leftward traverse to belay as for The Serpents Head.
2. 50m 4c Finish as for The Serpents Head, or more easily up Midgard.

33 Prelude 170m S 4a *
M.A.Reeves, J.Grieve, 28 May 1967
This starts in the same general weakness as Midgard, crossing this and taking a direct route up the wall; originally climbed in error for Midgard. Start just left of a light-coloured tongue of rock about 30m left of The Gangway.
1. 35m Climb an obvious cracked groove left of a pillar then go up rightwards to ledges.
2. 35m Go up right for a metre or so then back left up a sort of gangway to a weakness in bulges above. Step up and traverse 10m horizontally right by a smooth sloping ledge to an easy groove. Climb this and bear left on slabs.
3, 4 & 5. 100m Continue straight up with increasing interest, keeping in the centre of a clean ribbon of slabs; belay as required.

34 Midgard 180m VD *
R.B.Evans, L.A.Hawarth, Mrs. A.Evans, May 1961
A fine route with exposed situations, taking the easiest line up this section of wall. Start about 25m left of The Gangway at the lowest point of a tongue of rock.
1. 20m Go up slabby rock on the left to a band of yellow rock. Move right along a ledge to a belay.
2. 20m Move up right for 6m, then step left and traverse right again to belay below an overhang at the obvious traverse line.
3. 30m 3. 30m Follow the traverse left into a corner then go up slabs and a grass patch to a small flake belay.
4, 5 & 6. 110m Continue the traverse to the base of a second grass patch. Move down a little and go across to an easy gangway which leads to the top.

South Buttress

The buttress at the extreme right end of the west wall is split into two tiers by The Gangway.

35 The Gangway D
R.B.Evans, L.A.Hawarth, Mrs. A.Evans, May 1961
The left to right rising gangway which splits South Buttress. Start via a steep corner and a short traverse left, then 60m of pleasant slabs lead to scrambling; belay as required.

36 Not Found 50m E1 *
C.Plant, P.Reeve, May 2018
Start 15m up and left from Eureka, at a slight groove beneath an overlap.
1. 30m 5b Climb the left-facing groove and short right-facing fault to the centre of the overhang where a long reach left is made to sloping ledge. Gain the slab above by moving right over the steepening and go up the slab to white rock which is followed to an exit right to ledges; belay beneath a left-facing corner.
2. 20m 5b Climb the left-facing sickle groove exiting onto the arete and so up to the gangway. Finish as for Eureka; there are opportunities to do independent finishing pitches from the gangway.

37 Eureka 135m HVS ***
J.Grieve, E.Jones, 1 Jun 1967
A direct line up the front of South Buttress following a line of grooves on the lower tier then the bulging nose above The Gangway. Start beneath this nose at a line of thinly defined cracks just right of a brown bulge at the left end of the lower tier.
1. 20m 4b Go straight up grooves until a 3m traverse leads to an overhung slabby ledge on the left.
2. 25m 4c Move right and climb a short wall to a small ledge beneath a steep brown groove. Climb the groove to the heather gangway.

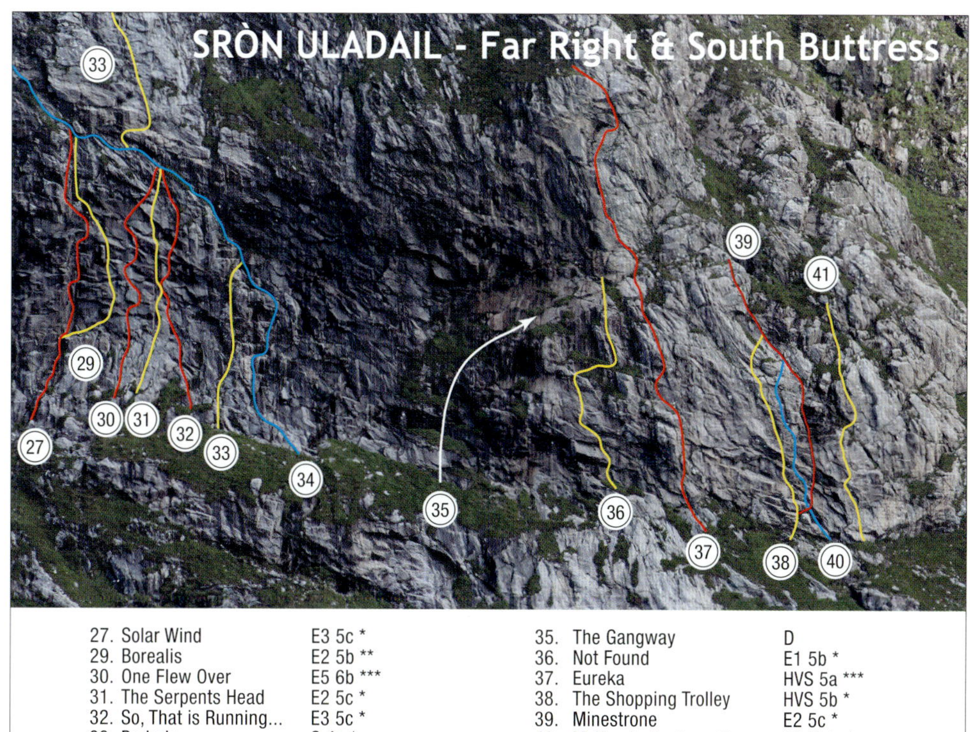

27. Solar Wind	E3 5c *	35. The Gangway	D
29. Borealis	E2 5b **	36. Not Found	E1 5b *
30. One Flew Over	E5 6b ***	37. Eureka	HVS 5a ***
31. The Serpents Head	E2 5c *	38. The Shopping Trolley	HVS 5b *
32. So, That is Running...	E3 5c *	39. Minestrone	E2 5c *
33. Prelude	S 4a *	40. Mother is the Invention...	E3 5b/c *
34. Midgard	VD *	41. Minuet	E1 5b *

3. 45m 5a Climb directly up the steep nose above and move left to pull over the bulge to gain a recessed slab. Climb this to its top right corner.
4. 15m 5a Climb an alarmingly overhanging crack on magnificent holds.
5. 30m Finish up easy walls and ledges.

38 The Shopping Trolley 30m HVS 5b *
C.Plant, C.Waddy, May 2018
Start 15m right of Eureka, from an obvious perched boulder sat on a head height ledge. Step off the boulder and head leftward up the fault-line over two steepenings to an easing finish.

39 Minestrone 30m E2 5c *
C.Waddy, C.Plant, 26 May 2018
From the perched boulder, climb up and right into a crack that leads to a belay on the slabs.

40 Mother is the Invention of Necessity 30m E3 5b/c *
C.Plant, C.Waddy, May 2018
Start just right of The Shopping Trolley. Climb the area of slabby rock directly beneath the overhang wending right and left finding reasonable but often spaced gear, to a tricky move onto a ledge on the left of the overhang. A corner is climbed for a few moves before heading right at a break to finish.

41 Minuet 30m E1 5b *
C.Waddy, C.Plant, 26 May 2018
Start on the right side of a brown streak which is the last part of the slab to dry. Climb easily up rightwards to gain a series of left-facing short corners which then lead to the right side of a large ledge near the top. Step right onto an obvious tower then follow the crack and arete to the top.

42 South Buttress 110m S 4a
R.B.Evans, L.A.Hawarth, Mrs. A.Evans, May 1961
Start halfway along the steep lower wall and climb 4m to a large obvious block belay. Move up onto the slab on the left, then make a long traverse right under overhangs until a smooth wall leads to a ledge and belay below overhangs. A broken gangway leads through the overhangs and scrambling follows to The Gangway. Climb the upper wall to a belay below a prominent overhang, and turn this by a groove on the right.

Other routes were apparently climbed on South Buttress by Grieve, Jones & Reeves in 1967 but considered too discontinuous to be worth recording.

TIORGA BEAG

Creagan Leathan

(NB 050 135)   Alt 200m   E facing   Map p208

This crag lies on the hillside opposite Sròn Uladail.

Approach: As for Sròn Uladail, then cross the burn and climb the hillside (8km, 2hr).

Descent: Down either end of the crag.

Little Red Rooster   65m   HVS *

M.Fowler, A.Meyers, 2 Jul 1981

This takes the obvious red streak of rock on the left side of the steepest buttress. Start from a grass ledge where the crag steepens, about 5m right of some piled blocks.

1. 35m 4b Climb the wall more or less directly until, at about 15m, it is possible to move right into an obvious wide crack. Follow this for 6m, then trend left to a rock stance below an easy left-slanting ramp.
2. 15m 5a Climb the ramp until it ends, then ascend wet, broken-looking rock on the right to belay just left of a very wet corner.
3. 15m 4b Trend left and finish up a pink right-slanting groove.

Grey Rib   75m   HVS **

M.Fowler, A.Meyers, 2 Jul 1981

The obvious grey rib right of Little Red Rooster gives better climbing than that route. Start directly below the rib on a grass ledge.

1. 35m 5a Climb the rib to a stance.
2. 40m 5b Move back onto the front of the rib and, keeping to the crest, follow this to the top. A good pitch.

Windwhistle   90m   VD

R.B.Evans, L.A.Hawarth, Mrs. A.Evans, May 1961

This goes up the most attractive continuous rock in the centre of the crag, finishing up an exposed wall.

TARAN MÒR

(NB 034 155)   Alt   200m   N facing   Map p208

This small 303m hill lies at the north-west end of the North Harris Hills above the sea at Loch Rèasort. On the northern side of the hill overlooking the loch the buttresses are broken with ledges and grass rakes and feature slabs at a relatively easy angle. However, a deep, almost hidden, gully splits the mountain and its walls give a few pitches of steeper climbing. The approach is made from the road end at Huisinis **(NA 992 121)** and on the way in Huiseabhal Mòr is passed and this contains some scrambles including a Grade 3, gained from the cottage at Loch na Cleabhaig; see Highland Scrambles North.

Sundowner   135m   S

R.Sharp, W.Sproul, 11 Jun 1969

Start at the foot of the buttress forming the left gully wall at a large boulder. Climb a corner to a ledge with jumbled blocks. Climb up left into a chimney system. Some way above, climb a crack in a wall and finish up slabs.

UISGNEABHAL MÒR

Sròn Scourst

Map p208

Gleann Mhiabhaig is the next major south to north running glen to the east of Gleann Uladail, which it joins at the eastern end of Loch Reàsort. Towards the northern head of the glen, the long ridge running off Teileasbhal terminates in the rocky prow of Sròn Àrd on which there is no known climbing. Further south, about a third of the way along the glen, on the east side of Loch Scourst, there is a conspicuous promontory which forms the termination of the north-west ridge of Uisgneabhal Mòr.

This is Sròn Scourst and although similar to Sròn Uladail in some ways, closer inspection reveals a buttress that does not live up to the expectations it hints at from afar. Unfortunately it is nowhere near as steep, continuous or impressive as its neighbour and little has been recorded on the buttress.

Some unsatisfactory routes have apparently been climbed on the north-west face. **Sron Scourst Gully** (D), the big gully running up the north side of the nose, is solid but wet with luxuriant vegetation and impressive rock scenery (E.C.W.Rudge, D.R.Henderson, 7 Sep 1947). There is a scramble somewhere on the north-west flank, descended by a gully to the north (H.J. Irens, F.Solari, A.Kinnear, Jun 1938). There is a more recent good Grade 3 scramble which takes an exposed and improbable but unobvious line starting at **(NB 105 099)** about 300m beyond Loch Scourst; see SMC Journal 2010. One climb is described.

Directions: Turn west off the main A859 to Stornoway at the Ceann an Ora Bridge and take the B887 towards Hushinish (Huisinis) to the head of the deep sea loch inlet of Loch Mhiabhaig There is parking either side of the bridge over the river flowing into the loch.

Approach: A good track runs along the floor of the glen to Sròn Scourst (4km, 50min) and on to Sròn Àrd.

Direct Route   90m   S

C.J.M.Slesser, D.J.Bennet, 5 Aug 1967

A direct line up the west end of the promontory. Under the steepest part of the cliff there are the remains of a fence at a smooth vertical wall; start a few metres north of this. Climb broken rocks with a right traverse to a vertical chimney. Go up this for 5m then traverse right to an exposed ledge. Climb more or less directly up steep rocks to a broad ledge 45m above the start. Continue slightly rightwards to a short awkward groove, above which the climb deteriorates.

CLISHAM (AN CLISEAM)

At 799m, this is the highest peak in the Outer Hebrides, and a Corbett. On the south-west side of the peak are the Coire Dubh Slabs which are some 250m high and on the north side is Aonaig Mhòr where there are a few winter climbs recorded.

Coire Dubh Slabs

(NB 1472 0728) Alt 430m SW facing Map p208

The Coire Dubh Slabs are composed of the finest quality clean grey gneiss and give friction climbing. There are numerous possibilities of easier but grassy lines which are often wet. The slabs are bounded on the left by a narrow gully and on the right by a straight grassy gully. The quickest drying lines are the balder slabs. The slabs are sub-divided into three by two left-slanting rakes, the first above the lowest spur of slabs and the second, starting from the gully, separating the main slabs from the upper slabs. The main slabs are characterised by a clean line of slabs well left of the gully and the upper slabs by a square-cut recess and three curving overlapped corners to its left.

Approach: One option is to turn off the A859 just north of Tarbert and go 1km along the B887 to Bunavoneader (Bun Abhainn Eadarra) and from there follow the path a short way to then break off and follow the burn into the coire. Quicker though, is from higher up at the west end of Loch na Ciste where there is a slip road lay-by off the A859 at **(NB 159 051)**. Slopes by the burn lead to a bealach where the southern spur of An Cliseam can be contoured before descending to a bright green grass patch within Coire Dubh; a short ascent then leads to the lowest point of the slabs (1hr 15min). The main walkers' approach to An Cliseam begins from a small car park some 2km further north-east along the road.

Coire Dubh Rib 250m D
G.S.Johnstone, S.Johnstone, Autumn 1952
This appears to take the defined rib that borders the straight grassy gully. It avoids the upper slabs then re-enters higher to finish up broken ground. Start at the bottom right-hand corner formed by the rake and the straight grassy gully. Stay 15 to 30m from the grassy gully for 150m then break out into the gully. Traverse left to finish on slabs at a gentler angle. A better and harder route would bear left after 120m to avoid the gully.

The Harris Jig 250m HVS 5a **
J.Mackenzie, E.Austin, 10 Jul 2009
A very pleasant outing taking the most continuous rock, often straightforward, left of the straight grassy gully; pitches two and four are particularly good. Start 12m left of the base of the rocks at a left-facing corner.
1. 50m 4a Go easily up the corner to overlaps which are taken centrally to easier ground and a belay on the rake directly below a small pointed block that is left of a much bigger one.
2. 50m 5a Climb the smoother slabs below the smaller pointed block, past a short corner beneath a bigger balder slab which is bounded by a wet and grassy corner on the right. The slab has a partially cleaned thin crack for quite good gear nearer the corner. Climb the slab left of the cleaned crack direct to an overlap, all on lovely friction. Move right and break leftwards through the overlap to belay at the smaller pointed block.
3. 50m Move left and up coarsely crystalline rock to the second rake at a black wet patch of slab, taking an overlap above this to arrive below the square-cut recess in the upper slabs.
4. 35m 5a The recess encloses a smooth friction slab, entirely without cracks. To its left the recess has a wet corner leading to a double overlap that runs across the top of the slab. Wet streaks often run beneath this overlap. Climb up the slab moving into the corner at about halfway up, depending on confidence. The alcove at the top of the corner beneath the overlaps is well protected but can be wet. Move right to a dry flange and mantel onto the slab between the overlaps then traverse back left to the alcove and up this to belays in a recess on the left.
5. 40m Step left and up a red feldspar slab easily followed by scrambling to belays beneath a nice slab on the right.
6. 25m Climb the pleasant slab.
Scrambling remains to the top.

The rib left of the slabs gives a Grade 2 scramble with variations possible; the half-height overhangs are avoided by pink steps on the left. The slabs are also climbed by a Grade 3 scramble (see Highland Scrambles North), starting at a broken rib below the right-hand edge. It is unsure how the scrambles relate to the two climbs.

Aonaig Mhòr

(NB 155 079) Alt 450m N facing Map p208

This lies on the north side of the mountain where there are numerous possibilities for winter climbs of grade II/III of 60m to 110m.

Approach: Either from the north-east up Gleann Sgaladail past Sgùrr Sgaladail, or from the south-east from the car park at **(NB 174 058)** used for the standard ascent of An Cliseam and going through the col between An Cliseam and Tomnabhal.

Pairc 90m III
A.Macfarlane, Dec 1989
The obvious icefall on the right-hand side of the cliff.

Leodhas 110m III
A.Macfarlane, P.Macfarlane, 13 Mar 1992
The right-hand buttress, immediately right of Pairc.

Incarnation 100m III, 4
A.Latham, A.Latham, 22 Dec 2010
There is an obvious frozen waterfall at **(NB 154 079)** and the climb takes the left side of this; it is unsure how it relates to Pairc. Scramble for 10m up a left-trending ramp to the first stance. Climb interesting ground for 10m, followed by an easy snowslope to a belay below the corner on the left (40m). Move left to a blocky

corner. Climb the corner and then up mixed rock and ice up the obvious weakness (40m). Move up and left to a roof and from a large flake, step out right round the arete. Finish up the pleasant icefall, trending left at the top.

Cnoc a' Chaisteal **(NB 143 101)** is the crag at the north end of a spur which descends from Mullach an Langa at the end of the ridge which extends from Mulla bho Dheas over Mulla bho Thuath. This has been climbed at its western end up a rib of square-cut blocks which leads to a sloping platform and a loose, notched block at the top. To the left the face is steeper and less broken.

MÒ BHÌOGADAIL

Creag Mò

(NB 172 097) Alt 150m SE facing Map p208 Diagram opposite

Mò Bhìogadail is a minor northern outlier of Clisham and sits at the entrance to Gleann Sgaladail to the side of fiord-like Loch Seaforth. The hill's eastern slopes terminate in Creag Mò, a large cliff which dominates the surroundings. The cliff can be clearly seen from the A859 nearby. Although the cliff is a bit loose and vegetated in parts, many of the climbs are a lot better than their appearance would suggest.

Directions: Heading north from Tarbert, the A859 to Stornoway drops steeply down the hill towards sea-level again after swinging round the flanks of Clisham. Creag Mò can be seen straight ahead here. At the foot of the hill, where the road swings round over a bridge across the Abhainn Sgaladail, there is off-road parking at **(NB 183 099)** on the west side of the road, on the north side of the bridge. This is just south-west of the Scaladale Outdoor Centre.

Approach: Follow a stalkers' path on the north side of the river for 1km before heading directly up the hillside to the crag (40min).

Descent: Down either side of the crag.

The most obvious feature of the cliff is an impressive central amphitheatre in the middle of which lies the prominent line of Central Grooves. A short grassy terrace runs right from here and splits the left side of the right wing into two tiers. Where the overhangs of the amphitheatre peter out on the left, a crack springs up towards the overhangs; this is the line of King Lear. Some 40m left again and low down is a long roof, crossed by Little Bo Peep, which guards an area of slabby grooves above. The crag now tapers down to the left, becoming more broken and vegetated. Climbs are described from left to right.

The first climb would appear to lie on an area of rock at the far left end, 150m or so to the left of the main crag.

1 The Corner 50m VS 4c

The obvious brown corner at the left-hand end of the crag. Start 3m right of the corner. Climb slabby rock trending left then go up the corner to a ledge. Climb a series of short steep corners to a large ledge. Climb an overhanging rock band into a corner and continue to a grass ledge. Another short pitch can be made by ascending the steep wall above, or walk off left.

About 40m to the left of the central amphitheatre there is a long wide overhang just above the base of the crag; three climbs start here.

2 Little Bo Peep 75m E1

M.Fowler, A.Strapcans, 8 Jul 1980

This takes a crack through the overhang and the slabby rocks above. Scramble to an old peg below the overhang.

1. 35m 5b Move left and climb the crack through the overhang, climb up right more easily and surmount an awkward bulge to reach ledges.
2. 40m 5b Trend diagonally right for 5m, then follow a discontinuous crack up the centre of the buttress until it is possible to climb up left to belay on grass ledges.

Grassy scrambling to finish.

3 King Billy 50m HVS

A.Macfarlane, D.Stelfox, 26 Aug 1989

1. 4c Start up the wall immediately right of the overhang of Little Bo Peep and climb to a grass ledge.
2. 5a Climb the wall trending right into a corner. Follow this, then exit left through a roof.

Grassy scrambling to finish.

4 Herbivore 110m HVS *

P.T.Newell, C.G.Winfield, 6 Aug 1969

A good route despite its name. Start right of King Billy at a short slab.

1. 30m 4a Climb the right edge of the slab to a grassy niche below a small overhang. Step left and take this at an obvious weakness. Continue rightwards up grass and rock to belay at the base of a corner.
2. 20m 5a Move up the corner and go round a bulge to a ledge on the right. Carry on up the corner, using a thin flake, to reach a small ledge on the left wall. Continue up and left again to a larger ledge below a corner.
3. 15m Climb the corner for about 4m, traverse right to a shallow depression, step down and traverse a small grass platform and jammed flake to belay at the base of a corner.
4. 10m 5a Climb the leaning corner and exit right over heather.
5. 35m Swing up left onto a slab, cross this to a corner and ascend an obvious scoop on the left wall to a ledge. Go left again and climb a short corner to finish up steep vegetation.

Variation: **4a Direct Variation E3 6a ***

B.Davison, A.Macfarlane, 19 May 1990

Follow Herbivore until it traverses right mid-way up the obvious corner. Continue up the corner with difficulty to a sloping finish.

CREAG MÒ

2. Little Bo Peep	E1 5b	8. Central Grooves	E6 6b *	14. Miny	S
3. King Billy	HVS 5a	9. The Mighty Chondrion	E7 6c **	15. Footpad	VS 4c
4. Herbivore	HVS 5a *	10. The Realm	E8 6c ***	16. MacBeth	VS 5a
4a. Herbivore Direct	E3 6a *	11. Drive Station	E5 6a **	16a. MacBeth Var.	HVS 5a
5. Wee Gommie	HVS 5a *	12. Stellar Crack	E3 5c **	17. Impact	HVS 4c
6. King Lear	E2 5b **	13. Antipodean Exile	E2 5b **	18. Smeagol	HS
7. Last Resort	E5 6a **			19. Gollum	S

5 Wee Gommie 100m HVS *

S.Vietoris, C.Watts, 1980

Despite vegetation this is quite a good route; start about 10m left of King Lear. Climb a shallow pink groove, then trend left into deeper grooves and finish up a short slanting chimney. Climbed in four pitches (5a, 5a, 5a, -); the last two are the same as Herbivore pitches 4 and 5.

6 King Lear 95m E2 **

M.Fowler, A.Strapcans, 8 Jul 1980

The obvious crack-line and the steep wall above. A spectacular outing with intimidating positions, excellent in its middle section. Start about 5m left of the overhangs of the amphitheatre at a short groove with a mossy tree on its left wall.

1. 10m 4c Climb the groove and move right to belay beneath a corner.

2. 15m 5b Move diagonally right up the wall to gain the crack, then follow this until it is possible to move right to an excellent exposed stance above the overhangs.

3. 25m 5b Climb the wall above, trending right, to a ledge round the corner on the right. Pull through the overhang above the left end of the ledge and climb up left to a prominent short crack which often oozes. Climb this vile crack to a good stance.

4. 45m 4c The grassy ramp on the right leads to a short wall and the top.

7 Last Resort 90m E5 **

C.Muskett, D.MacLeod, Apr 2014

An excellent route taking the big brown slab on the left side of the amphitheatre.

1. 45m 5c Start below a grossly overhanging flake system in the left wall of the amphitheatre. Pull up on steep jugs and swing immediately left and up to gain a system of exciting steep flakes. Follow these to a good belay ledge at the top of the flake.

2. 45m 6a Climb the 40m brown slab above, following left-trending lines of weakness with spaced protection to eventually pull over onto an easy finishing slab at the top. An intricate pitch on great rock.

8 Central Grooves 75m E6 *

S.Meyers, G.Lovick, 1993

A difficult and serious climb which takes the obvious central grooves of the amphitheatre.

1. 20m 5c Start up a loose black wall below a break in the roof and an obvious groove. Climb this to a poor peg (the high point of an earlier attempt), then move left over loose ledges to a worrying hanging stance on cams.

2. 45m 6b Climb up right to make some difficult and

committing moves past a peg into the base of the next groove. Follow this, moving slightly left at a sloping ledge, then finish direct.
3. 10m A short scramble gains the top.

9 The Mighty Chondrion 60m E7 6c **
D.MacLeod, M.Sakano, 6 Apr 2017
The central fault at the back of the main amphitheatre gives two contrasting pitches, with strenuous but well protected horizontal roof climbing on the first.
1. 20m 6c Climb a flake-crack to the border with the roof. Pass a couple of dubious holds in the soft rock patch here to gain the roof crack. Arrange gear with difficulty and make hard moves to a resting position with a knee-bar in the wide crack (Camalot 3.5). Hard moves lead to improving holds rounding the lip to gain a short chimney and a small ledge over the lip.
2. 40m 5c A very traditional pitch up the wide fault, often climbing on the right wall or arete of the fault, or not if this is affected by drips from an overhead seep. Continue to the large grassy terrace and belay. Either escape right along this, or climb another short easy pitch to the top.

10 The Realm 80m E8 ***
T.Emmet, D.MacLeod, 31 May 2010
Start below the curving flake feature in the huge horizontal roof.
1. 30m 6c Move easily up to the roof and carefully arrange various cams in the roof, taking care with soft flaky rock. The rock improves immediately you begin the flake. Launch out across this on big holds until they run out at halfway. A sustained bouldery sequence leads out to and around the lip to gain a standing position on a good foothold above the roof. Step right and belay.
2. 50m 6b Move up the wall a couple of metres and make a delicate traverse left on poor sloping edges to gain a very welcome runner in a thin crack. Make a hard move to get established in the crack. Continue up this with excellent climbing, moving left below the stepped overlaps to successive wall cracks leading to the top.

11 Drive Station 40m E5 6a **
C.Muskett, D.MacLeod, Apr 2014
An exciting and exposed line which gains a crack in the left side of an impressive 40m blank wall towards the right-hand side of the main wall. Start right of the roof system below the crack-line in the wall above. Move left into a small curving groove and climb this until it is possible to move rightwards with difficulty to the thin crack. Follow this to easier ground just below the top.

12 Stellar Crack 40m E3 5c **
D.MacLeod, C.Muskett, Apr 2014
An excellent climb up the crack system at the right-hand end of the main wall, just right of the impressive blank wall. Good protection and strenuous climbing with a worrying loose block near the top that can be delicately avoided, or perhaps trundled by the second?

13 Antipodean Exile 40m E2 5b **
A.Macfarlane, D.McGimpsey, 8 Jul 1989
On the right side of the central overhanging amphitheatre, a grass ledge and terrace lead rightwards to a blunt arete on the right side of a smooth clean wall. Start just left of the arete. Climb up to the incipient crack. It is possible to step left into the main crack and follow this, but if it is wet, traverse right and go up the arete. Climb the double cracks and a shallow chimney to the top.

The following climbs lie on the right wing and may be quite hard to place.

14 Miny 105m S
R.B.Evans, L.A.Hawarth, Mrs A.Evans, May 1961
This, the first climb on the crag, starts below the easily accessible grass terrace at the left side of the lower wall. Footpad may follow the lower section. Go up slabs past a small sapling to the grass terrace. From the right end of the terrace, a steep groove leads to the top.

15 Footpad 105m VS
B.Clarke, J.Macdougall, 1 Jun 1972
Below and right of the amphitheatre is a white slabby arete; scramble up steep grass and belay under a small overhang. The first pitch may be the same as, or similar to, Miny.
1. 40m Step left and climb the grooved arete, then climb a wall to the grassy terrace beneath the smooth wall at the right side of the amphitheatre.
2. 20m Descend slabby grooves and grass diagonally right until it is possible to step into a groove. Climb the groove to a grass pedestal on the right.
3. 20m From the right end of the pedestal, climb a steep crack and a chimney to a small stance.
4. 25m Continue up the groove above, stepping out right at the top.

16 MacBeth 85m VS
M.Fowler, A.Strapcans, Jul 1980
Scramble up to belay beneath the grey flecked buttress forming the most continuous and steepest piece of rock right of Miny and Footpad.
1. 30m 4c Climb up to a shallow groove which leads to an overhang. Pass this on the right and move back left above it. A short wall of better rock leads to a grass ledge on the right.
2. 20m 5a Step left from the end of the ledge and climb a wall and a crack until it is possible to move left to another grass ledge, which is probably the Footpad pedestal.
3. 35m 4c The crack above the right end of the ledge leads to easier climbing and the top; possibly the same as Footpad.

16a MacBeth Variation 85m HVS
A.Macfarlane, D.McGimpsey, 8 Jul 1989
Start a little down and left of Macbeth below a corner-groove.
1. 35m 5a Climb the groove past loose blocks and a short overhanging wall then continue until level with the first belay of MacBeth. Traverse briefly left then go up a

The Mighty Chondrion (E7) Dave MacLeod
(photo Chris Prescott / Hot Aches)

rounded edge to belay below some roofs.
2. 15m 4c Climb a chimney to the grass ledge below the third pitch of MacBeth.
3. 35m 4c Finish up MacBeth and Footpad.

17 Impact 85m HVS
K.Woods, D.Macmorris, 26 Jul 2014
Start down to the right of the previous climbs at the lowest rocks, at the left-hand of two continuous areas of rock, just right of some stepped overhangs.
1. 25m 4c Climb the grey wall direct up cracks and blocks to a grassy ledge. Quite loose.
2. 20m 4a Move up and right through the line of least resistance to traverse a terrace right almost to its end. Block belay.
3. 25m 4b Continue to the end of traverse (escapable here) then climb straight up through a broad groove and pull over to grass ledge.
4. 15m Traverse right along the grass ledge then go up an easy vegetated groove.
Scramble left then up right to the top.

18 Smeagol 100m HS
M.A.Reeves, J.Ball, 26 Aug 1965
A direct line on good rock which leads to the prominent cracked-corner of Gollum. Start at the clean right edge of a vegetated recess a few metres left of the start of Gollum.
1. 25m Go up, trending left to a small ledge on an edge. Move right across a steep wall to a short groove which is climbed to a poor ledge.
2. 20m Step left to a good rock ledge then climb the interesting rock above directly, past loose blocks, to the left end of a large ledge.
3. 20m Move awkwardly left to a shallow bay, climb a groove on the left to a slab which leads to easy ground. Continue easily to below the corner of Gollum.
4. 35m Climb the corner to the top.

19 Gollum 100m S
M.A.Reeves, B.Reeves, 23 Aug 1965
Start towards the right side of the lower wall at an obvious easy-angled slabby rib (cairn).
1. 30m Go up the rib to a steep groove and climb this to a ledge on the left. Go up a slab to an overlap and move over this then trend right to a steep little wall. Ascend this and move a metre or so left to a stance on large detached blocks.
2. 35m Climb a slab on small holds, then go up a short groove splitting the steep wall above. Walk up a grassy rake to some large blocks and get onto the wall above at an obvious left traverse. At the end of this, go up right to a large grassy bay, then walk 10m left to a prominent cracked-corner.
3. 35m Climb the corner to the top.

The final two climbs are on a smaller crag over to the right.

20 Lost Gandulf 20m VS
S.Stupart, M.Moss, 27 Jul 1997
Two obvious diagonal cracks run rightwards for the full height of the crag from a terrace. Climb the crack, with two deviations out right onto a slab.

21 Shelob 15m S
M.Allan, S.Marvell, 27 Jul 1997
The right-trending crack 15m to the right of Lost Gandulf. Most interesting at the top.

TOMNABHAL

Sgùrr Sgaladail

(NB 163 085) Alt 180m NE facing Map p208 Diagram opposite

Visible from the road, Sgùrr Sgaladail can be clearly seen looking up Gleann Sgaladail past Creag Mò. It is a big dark foreboding cliff nearly 1km long and over 200m high which dominates the head of the glen. Unfortunately, although there is a fair amount of unclimbed rock, there is much vegetation and the cliff is wet, dank and dingy. It requires a prolonged spell of good weather for the cliff to come into condition and even then it is doubtful whether the seepage ever dries completely.

Approach: Park as for Creag Mò and follow the rough path up Gleann Sgaladail. Continue to the bend in the river before heading up to the foot of the cliff (2.5km, 1hr).

Descent: Down the north-west shoulder towards Loch Mhisteam then either cut back right to descend the grassy rake beneath the crag, or continue downhill to the burn issuing from the loch.

The main face rises above a grassy rake and is bounded by East Gully on the left and West Gully on the right. To the right of West Gully the cliff is more broken and vegetated. The steepest section of cliff is formed by a black wall, defined on the left by the gully-groove of Miolnir and on the right by a vegetated depression and a line of shallow grooves running full height. West Buttress lies to the left of West Gully. Apart from at the left end, the more continuous areas of rock are guarded by turf ledges and slabs. There has been some confusion on the locations of Central Gully and West Gully, together with the adjacent routes; see 1998 and 2002 SMC Journals. However, given the vile nature of this cliff, this is unlikely to be fully resolved unless by someone with a particular bent for this sort of thing.

1 Sideshow 105m HVS
A.Macfarlane, D.McGimpsey, Jul 1990
Start below a roof just right of East Gully.
1. 40m 5a Break through the small roof and continue to a stance.
2. 25m 4c Climb up to a quartzy vein and move right.
3. 40m 4c Move right to follow a continuous rib of rock to the top.

2 Miolnir 140m VS *
R.B.Evans, L.A.Hawarth, A.Evans (1pa), May 1961; FFA A.Macfarlane, B.Davison, 1990
The obvious feature left of centre on the main face is the prominent gully cleft which develops into an overhung

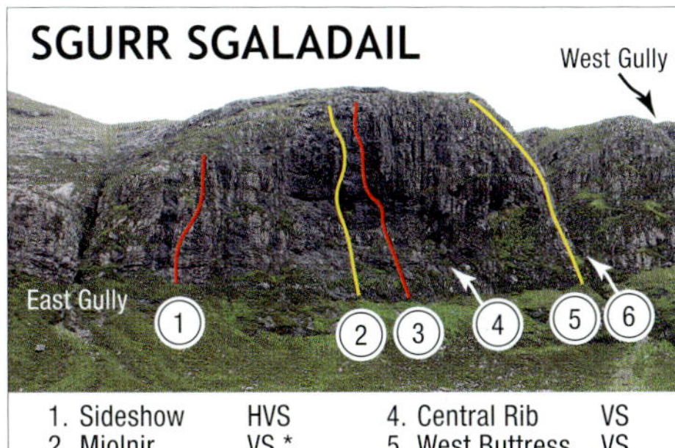

groove. This climb takes the lower part of the cleft then breaks out left to ascend a deep V-groove. A fine steep route

Gain the gully after 30m of slabs on the left. Follow the steepening gully for 25m. Go up a groove on the right, then move back into a chimney to reach a boulder-strewn platform; belay on a smaller ledge 4m to the left. Climb a steep wall above to below an overhang. Move right and climb the deep groove to a ledge on the left. Pull over the overhang (crux, 4c), then go left to a stance and belay. Finish up the steep corner above.

3 Panorama 175m E2

M.Fowler, A.Meyers, 30 Jun 1981

On the steepest section of cliff to the right of Miolnir is a black wall with a prominent line of overhangs slanting diagonally up from right to left. The climb goes directly up the wall to the start of the diagonal overhangs. Start by scrambling up rock and grass for 75m to the highest ledge to the right of a wet groove-gully bounding the steep area on the right.

1. 25m Move down left and cross the wet groove-gully to gain an ascending line of steps on the far side. Trend left to belay next to a large loose block.
2. 30m 5b Move left above the overhangs and trend up left to the obvious depression in the face about 30m below the start of the diagonal line of overhangs. Cross the depression leftwards on sloping holds and pass the overhang above on the left. Move delicately right above to a stance and dubious thread belay.
3. 25m 5b Climb steeply just right of the stance and surmount an overhang to gain the foot of a deep groove. Follow this until it is possible to move left on very wet rock to a wet stance and poor belays below dripping overhangs.
4. 25m 5c Move back right and ascend an exposed right-slanting ramp. From its end move up left to a sloping ledge with difficulty. Traverse delicately right for 3m to belay on nuts.
5. 35m 5b Move back left and surmount the overhang to gain a ledge beneath a deep long groove. Climb this and a short continuation groove to a ledge.
6. 35m 5a Ascend the grooves directly above and continue up short awkward walls to the top.

4 Central Rib VS

N.S.Tennant, M.K.Tennant, 1954

Takes the area of rock between Central Gully and West Buttress; no further details are available. Given the previous confusion on Central and West Gullies it is unsure where this route is, although the name and grade suggest that it could well be the same as, or in the vicinity of West Buttress.

5 West Buttress 225m VS

A.Powling, D.Yates, 8 Jul 1969

A direct line up the buttress right of the main crag; start at the lowest rocks just left of a gully. Given the grade and the more continuous nature of the climbing it is likely that this route is actually on the obvious buttress to the left of the main Central Gully (see next climb), in which case it is not actually West Buttress!

1. 35m Follow grass up left, then go back right to a stance at a pinnacle.
2. 35m Go straight up over rock and grass to a stance below a small overhang.
3. 20m Break out right, then go up to a small stance beneath a long crack.
4. 30m Climb the crack for 12m, then trend right to a thin crack very near the right edge of the buttress. Climb this, step left then climb the face to a grass stance.
5. 15m Move up to a greasy crack which leads (crux) to another grass stance. About 90m of scrambling remains.

6 Central Gully 230m

M.Botterill, A.H, 11 May 1930

There has been confusion as to where this, the first recorded route here, goes and therefore where the neighbouring climbs lie. It is likely that over the years Central and West Gullies have been confused. From the original description (1932 YRC Journal) which notes three gullies, it seems clear that Central Gully is just that, the obvious central gully, not the shallow depression up the face right of Panorama. The gully above the initial grass terrace was originally described as having scree and jammed boulders. At the penultimate pitch a traverse was made out onto the western buttress where a chimney provided the onward link.

MULLA

Loch Beag Crag

(NB 220 028) Alt 170m SW facing Map p208

There is a small roadside crag on the minor road to Reinigeadal which leaves the A859 on the high section to the east of Clisham. The crag is on the knoll of Mulla above Loch Beag, just south of Loch Mòr. These lochs lie opposite and beneath Tòdun, the shapely hill seen from the high section of the A859 between Tarbert and Stornoway. The Scaladale Outdoor Centre use the crag.

Lower Tier

This contains five climbs. **Route 1** and **Route 2** follow vague cracks and grooves at VD and S; **Route 3** goes straight up the right side of the capping boulder at S; **Route 4** is a diagonal line to the top bulge at HS 4b and **Route 5** is a direct to the top of the diagonal at VS 4c/5a.

Upper Tier

Though short the climbs are on perfect gritstone-like gneiss. From the Lower Tier an 'Easter Island statue' is obvious up and right. This contains three routes.

The Maoi 8m E2 5c **
J.Mackenzie, A.James, 21 Apr 2016
The block-topped slab is climbed directly up the middle to the top block. Step right to finish. Immaculate.

Maoi Grooves 8m VS 5a *
A.James, J.Mackenzie, 21 Apr 2016
Just right of the slab are curving grooves. A tricky start below the left one is followed by easier climbing.

Maoi Cracks 8m S 4a
A.James, J.Mackenzie, 21 Apr 2016
The wall just to the right via twin cracks with a clump of heather. Pleasant if undistinguished.

Well to the left of The Maoi is a much taller thinner buttress with a groove on the left.

Avoiding the Issue 16m VS 4c
J.Mackenzie, A.James, 21 Apr 2016
An open chimney lies left of a rather dirty lower groove. Climb this and step back right then climb up to horizontal cracks. Traverse left delicately below a smooth block to arrive at a heathery bay and finish up this.

SGAOTH ÀIRD

(NB 162 045) Alt 450m N Facing Map p208

Lying to the south of and opposite Clisham, this hill forms part of a small but rugged group of attractive hills located at the south-eastern end of the North Harris Hills range. They lie on the east side of the A859 between Tarbert and Stornoway where they form a west-facing horseshoe around Glen Skeaudale above the Ceann an Ora Bridge at West Loch Tarbert, at the point where the B887 to Huisinis leaves the A859.

With its summit located at **(NB 166 040)**, Sgaoth Àird (559m) and its western neighbour Sgaoth Iosal form the north side of the horseshoe. However, the climbing on Sgaoth Àird lies on the opposite side of the hill overlooking the A859 to the north where there are 150m crags. These are broken into numerous buttresses, of which only the three at the west end have climbs. From right to left, the first is Slab Wall which climbs a belt of steep 75m slabs left of the parallel cracks that split this face. A narrow cleft separates Slab Wall from No.1 Buttress, which has an obvious steep nose, visible from the road and with a semidetached block forming the east wall of the gully. Left of No.1 Buttress is a gully with a scree cone. Next is No.2 Buttress which is divided by a left-slanting gully shelf.

Directions: At the highest point of the A859, after the initial climb up from West Loch Tarbert, is the small Loch na Ciste which sits beneath the spur that falls north from the shoulder of the hill. There are two loops of old road either side of the loch for parking.

Approach: By the north spur (30min).

Haudes 40m VS
H.Small, J.W.Graham, Jul 1966
A bold route which climbs the obvious nose of No.1 Buttress. Start in a narrow gully right of the nose and below a steep groove in the left wall.
1. 20m 4c Climb a steep groove (peg runner) to belay on top of a pinnacle.
2. 20m Climb the steep wall above to a block belay. Finish by a scramble up right via a small pinnacle overhanging the gully.
Variation: **Alternative Finish S**
P.Macdonald, I.G.Rowe, May 1969
From the top of the pinnacle, traverse 5m right and climb the edge of the buttress.

No.2 Buttress 150m VD
G.S.Johnstone, S.Johnstone, Autumn 1952
Scramble up the edge of the eastern section of the buttress overlooking the gully shelf. After 75m the rock becomes continuous and steep. Climb the last short slab direct.

SGAOTH IOSAL

(NB 155 045) Alt 450m N Facing Map p208

Sgaoth Iosal (531m) is the next hill west from Sgaoth Àird and is the final hill in the circuit of Glen Skeaudale. The northern slopes hold four buttresses numbered 1 to 4, west to east, then almost under the summit itself, Pinnacle Buttress. These buttresses overlook the A859 and are easily accessible from there. There are some easy climbs and scrambles.

No.1 Buttress D
G.S.Johnstone, S.Johnstone, Autumn 1952
A three pitch climb described as being good and on wonderful rock.

Pinnacle Buttress M
G.S.Johnstone, S.Johnstone, Autumn 1952
This is climbed on its southern edge by a fantastic profusion of jugs.

Sròn a' Sgaoth

(NB 1461 0396) Alt 304m SW facing Map p208 Diagram opposite

This is the western termination of the summit shoulder of Sgaoth Iosal. There are some crags on the west and south-west prow of the hill overlooking the A859 on the initial climb north of Tarbert. The rock is good quality gneiss, mostly very clean but blocky higher up. Steep slabs with a prominent brown water worn streak lie on the right, facing south-west, whilst a steeper nose lies above and left, facing west. The old guide refers to steep slabs here offering climbing but gives no descriptions.

Directions: Towards the top of the initial climb up from the Ceann an Ora Bridge at West Loch Tarbert, park just off the road at the entrance to the wind turbine site.

Approach: Cross the road and ascend the steep hillside. It is possibly easiest to keep right of the lower continuation of a scree-filled gully to the left of the crag and weave up grassy areas. A short, broken rock step is taken by a left-trending line to reach a grass terrace beneath the crags (30min).

Descent: Down a gully bounding the nose on the left (north-west) of the routes. The terrace at the base of the crag is gained by taking the second grass niche leftwards from the scree filled gully.

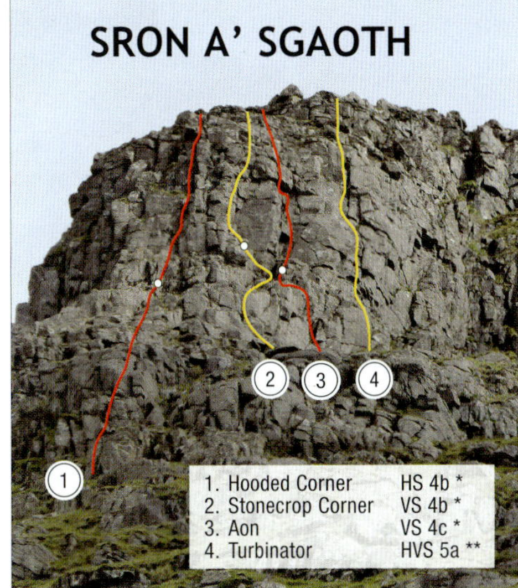

1 Hooded Corner 65m HS 4b *

J.Mackenzie, A.James, 19 Apr 2016

Start at the nose on the left of the crag overlooking the shallow gully, a bit mossy but an obvious line. A prominent jutting block has a straight corner to its left which provides the route.

1. 35m. From the toe of the buttress, climb straight up to a steeper exit (some loose rock) then cross a grassy terrace and belay below a clean slab.
2. 30m 4b Climb the slab to the base of the corner and go up the corner steeply on flat holds. Continue in a good position to exit by the jutting block.

The crag is now split by two corners with a tier of rock below.

2 Stonecrop Corner 40m VS 4b *

J.Mackenzie, A.James, 20 Jun 2017

This climbs the less obvious left-hand corner, starting from the lower tier at a big flake. A pleasant climb, easier than it looks.

1. 20m From the flake, climb twin cracks up a short steep step to the shelf above. Move right to the bollard on Aon then back up left to an exposed stance.
2. 20m Climb the left wall of the corner to the capping bulge, step right then go over it and continue to a good thread belay above.

3 Aon 32m VS 4b/c *

J.Mackenzie, E.Austin, 5 Jul 2009

The right-hand corner with an overhang at the top; a nice well-protected climb on excellent holds.

1. 15m Climb the lowest rocks above blocks and move up right to a bollard below the right-hand corner.
2. 17m Climb the corner, stepping left under the overhang to pull over this to gain the top and a thread belay a little higher.

4 Turbinator 35m HVS 5a **

J.Mackenzie, A.James, 20 Jun 2017

To the right of the two corners the crag swings right and steepens. This climb takes the prominent crack-line left of a right-trending line of overhangs. A short step leads to the undercut crack, up which some good moves lead to a wide crack (Friend 4). Continue up the crack past stable blocks.

The slabs to the right of the nose are the lowest situated crags on the face. There is a steep lower wall on the left with a grass shelf above the brown water streak to the right, and less continuous slabs right again. Though the lines are aesthetically contrived, they give the best climbing.

Da 60m VS 4c *

J.Mackenzie, E.Austin, 5 Jul 2009

1. 25m 4c The lower wall has a little curving crack leading to a wall and bulge at the top. Climb the crack and wall to near the bulge, move left to twin thin cracks at a rust coloured section (much easier if the route is started to the left but not so good) then up a short wall moving right (avoiding the grass shelf) to belays in a little corner above a ledge.
2. 35m 4b Step right and climb just right of a bulge (Friend 4 hole) then climb to a little ledge and corner on the right. Climb the corner then short walls to belay at a thin sling spike.
3. 40m Scrambling leads to the top.

Tri 60m VS 4b *

J.Mackenzie, E.Austin, 5 Jul 2009

This climbs the brown water-worn streak 6m to the right of Da. Start at a gravel patch.

1. 30m 4b Climb letterbox holds up and right over shelves, including a mantelshelf, then straight up to belay by the corner of Da.
2. 30m 4a Move left and climb the diagonal shelf left of

Stonecrop Corner (VS) Andrew James (photo John Mackenzie)

the overhang to enter an arched niche and wide crack to the left of grass. Climb the wide crack to belay as for Da.
3. 40m Scrambling to finish.

To the left of the grassy gully, which is left of the nose of the hill, are three buttresses. The smaller one adjacent to the gully provides the next climb.

Mistaken Identity 40m VD
A.James, J.Mackenzie, 20 Jun 2017
On the left-hand side of this crag, overlooking the gully that separates it from the next one on the left, there is a fine lower slab of perfect rock.
1. 15m Climb the perfect slab.
2. 25m Unfortunately, the promise is not maintained and the route becomes a blocky scramble taken on the left.

GIOLABHAL GLAS

(NB 141 029) Alt 300m N Facing Map p208

Giolabhal Glas (475m) is the highpoint on the south side of the corrie. At the end of its north-west ridge is Giolabhal Dubh whose north face, the Geòdhan Dubh, holds a line of six buttresses; from left to right A, B, C, D and E. Buttresses A, C and D give good scrambles up to Grade 3 on superb rock. Buttresses E and F are short and easy although F has a Grade 3 start. Buttress B has steep greasy walls with insecure greasy ground. See Highland Scrambles North. The old guide notes some climbing here, which is likely to be the same as the scrambles.

Black Face Gully 200m I
A.Macfarlane, 1991
The middle of the five gullies between the buttresses.

Lochan Crag

(NB 1536 0267) Alt 350m N facing Map p208 Diagram opposite

East of the summit of Giolabhal Glas itself, below two small lochans on its north-east shoulder, is Lochan Crag. Despite an arduous approach a visit is worthwhile. There is apparently another shorter but steeper crag a few hundred metres to the north-east, not described here.

The crag is composed of the best quality grey gneiss, often compact lower down but with better cracks and protection higher up where it steepens. Being at fairly high altitude, the outlook is fine and the rock dries quickly, apart from the slabby left side which appears to have a semi-permanent weep. The rock is a pleasure to climb on and sports some great bollards for slings. On the right of the crag is a shelf that is near the level with the top of the initial pitches.

Directions: Before the A859 climbs the hill north of Tarbert, turn off the A859 at the Ceann an Ora bridge onto the B887 where there is a car park by the new houses.

Approach: Cross the A859 and the bridge then go up the right-hand (south) bank of the Skeaudale River. Rough moraine-hummocked ground leads up Glen Skeaudale for about 1.5km below steep slopes to where a left-slanting heather rake just west of a small ravine is followed up steep ground close to small outcrops, until a line of crags runs west across the hillside. These crags form a broken lower tier to the hidden Lochan

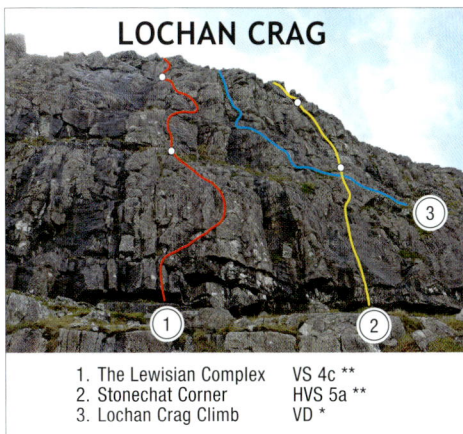

1. The Lewisian Complex VS 4c **
2. Stonechat Corner HVS 5a **
3. Lochan Crag Climb VD *

Crag whose far left boundary is marked by a prominent pinnacle on the skyline. Contour under these lower crags to where they end then scramble up leftwards to the broad terrace below Lochan Crag (1hr 30min).

Descent: To the west, left looking out, down a stony rake that curves back right to the shelf and then across some scree to the foot of the crag.

1 The Lewisian Complex 75m VS 4c **

J.Mackenzie, E.Mackenzie, 24 Jun 2013

A good varied climb, low in the grade, taking the rib to the right of the slab. Start right of the usually wet slab by a black undercut wall.

1. 20m 4b/c Starting from a low shelf, surmount the overhang via great jugs (sling) to gain a right-trending ramp. Follow this to a shallow corner and climb it and easier rocks above to a grass stance.
2. 20m 4c Move left onto a rib then up this to a grass patch just right of the wet slab. Traverse right (hidden hold) into a stone niche then move up left delicately to reach and climb a steep groove to a stance. A good varied pitch.
3. 20m 4a Move up the slab edge on the left then step right above some grass to climb shelves and corners to a commodious stance on the left.
4. 15m Climb into and up a short corner and scramble above to a thread belay.

To the right of the rib there is an open corner high up with a wet continuation below. Just right again is a fine hanging slab with a shallow groove on its left and a deep left-facing corner higher up that marks the right-hand end of the crag.

2 Stonechat Corner 80m HVS 5a **

J.Mackenzie, E.Mackenzie, 24 Jun 2013

This has very good contrasting pitches on perfect rock, the climb taking the hanging slab and deep corner above. Protection improves with height.

1. 25m 4c Gain the slab from the left via the shallow groove and continue up and slightly right up a rib to a small stance just above a lone spike. A good but quite bold pitch.
2. 20m 5a Climb up to the double corner then go up this with joy (well protected) and step left to its continuation to a good alcove stance.
3. 15m 4a Move up left to a short broken corner of blocks and climb this to a stance.
4. 20m Scramble to the top.

3 Lochan Crag Climb 60m VD *

G.S.Johnstone, Mrs.S.Johnstone, Autumn 1952

From the grass shelf on the right, this traverses slabs leftwards to reach the upper part of the central groove on the face. Start on a ledge about 15m from the west edge of the buttress. Zigzag up to a rock recess surmounted by a prominent V-chimney, which slightly overhangs the recess. The traverse into the recess provides an interesting excursion on steep slabs.

Beinn na Teanga lies to the east of Giolabhal Glas and this has a Grade 1 scramble up slabs on its south side; see Highland Scrambles North.

BEINN A' CHAOLAIS

Sgalpaigh View Crag

(NG 2092 9884) Alt 114m SW facing Map p208

A minor, quick drying crag on the flanks of Beinn a' Chaolais overlooking Gleann a' Chaolais above the road to Scalpay. It takes the form of perfect wall of orange coloured gneiss split by three cracks with a short lower tier.

Directions: Follow the road east from Tarbert and park in the vicinity of Steinis about 1km from the bridge to Scalpay.

Approach: Walk west along the road then cross to the crag (15min).

A bheil e doirbh? 10m VS 5a

J.Mackenzie, E.Mackenzie, 10 Sep 2012

Well, sort of! Approach from the left end of the lower tier and climb the left-slanting crack.

'S e, 's e doirbh a th'ann 10m HVS 5a *

J.Mackenzie, E.Mackenzie, 10 Sep 2012

Quite so, especially at the top. The middle crack has a delicate finish.

Bidh seo nas fhasa 10m VS 4c

J.Mackenzie, E.Mackenzie, 10 Sep 2012

The straight crack on the right; as the name says, apart from the first move!

Caolas Crag

This lies to the east of Tarbert, about about 2km west of the bridge over to Scalpaigh (Scalpay). It is another crag used by the Scaladale Outdoor Centre and there are apparently six climbs.

South Harris (Ceann a' Deas na Hearadh)

Despite a huge amount of exposed rock here, there is surprisingly little climbing in the way of either sea-cliffs, or outcrops, since it appears most of the low rocks have been buffed flat by glaciation. There is however a little climbing and more may yet materialise.

CEANN REAMHAR

Uamascleit

(NB 1300 0000) Alt 100m NE facing Map p208

Uamscleit (281m) sits to the north-east of Ceann Reamhar, Ben Losgaintir's east top, and has a rocky northern face overlooking West Loch Tarbert, well seen from the road just west of Tarbert. The best approach is probably from behind the school and the sports centre at Tarbert. The face is broken by terraces, but at the right of the face the lowest tier forms a fine little buttress. There is a Grade 3 scramble on the left; see Highland Scrambles North.

Cleitior S
K.Crocket, K.Simpson, 29 Jun 1972
A pleasant route taking a rising traverse with fine slab climbing reminiscent of the Etive Slabs; harder more direct lines are possible.

Original Route 60m D
R.W.MacLennan, J.Russell, 27 Jul 1953
Start 15m to the left of shallow grass on the right of the main buttress. Climb a 20m rib then traverse right along the base of a broken slab and across a grass gully. Climb a corner and follow a groove up to the right, then climb a series of short walls and easy slabs to finish.

UABHAL BEAG

Stalwarts Bluff

(NG 1334 9479) Alt 160m SW facing Map p208

This small quick-drying crag lies above the road south of Tarbert, at the southern end of the long hill which rises north-westwards over a number of tops to Beinn Dubh. It takes the form of a steep left-facing sidewall just visible from the road.

Directions: Just over 500m west of the highest point of the A859 south of Tarbert, park at the sheep fanks immediately west of the Roghadal, Geocrab, Manais turn off.

Approach: Cross the road and climb the hillside past the west end of the small Loch an Fheadain (10min).

Bluffer 12m VS 4b *
A.James, J.Mackenzie, 22 Jun 2017
Climb the ramp bounding the sidewall to its top, move up to a girdling crack and step right onto the face to finish.

Puffer 12m VS 4b
A.James, J.Mackenzie, 22 Jun 2017
Climb a slanting crack-line up the sidewall and pull onto the front face to finish up the easier rib on the left.

Suffer 10m VD
A.James, J.Mackenzie, 22 Jun 2017
Climb the slabby front face centrally to finish up a narrow crack.

UABHAL MÒR

Creag na Tri Piosin

(NB 122 958) Alt 80m S facing Map p208 Diagram opposite

Known by the local outdoor centre as Rowan Tree Crag, this small vertical wall of excellent rock lies on Uabhal Mòr on the north side of the glen above the main A859 south from Tarbert. The crag is best seen in profile when heading up the hill from the west towards Tarbert from Seilebost, and the turn off to Luskentyre (Losgaintir).

The base of the crag is pleasantly flat and grassy and the outlook encompassing both east and west coasts is lovely. Some of the grades may be a bit stiff but the climbs are short and generally well protected. The top of the crag has several stakes hammered into cracks, for belays.

Directions: West of the highest point of the A859 south from Tarbert, the intermittent single track road descends towards Luskentyre and becomes double carriageway running alongside a series of lochans. Between the last two lochans, and just before the road narrows to single carriageway, there is a car park on the south side of the road **(NG 119 956)**.

Approach: Cross the road and climb the hillside (10min).

1 Climb C 9m VS 4c
This lies around the corner at the left end of the crag, with a low crux and easier finish.

2 First of Eight 9m VS 4c
B.Davison, 23 May 2014
The crack at the left side of the crag left of a shield of rock halfway up the face; a steep start.

3 Second of Eight 11m E1 5b
B.Davison, 23 May 2014
The next crack 3m right starts at half-height at the left of the overhangs has some hollow sounding blocks.

4 Two Power Three 11m E1 5c **
R.D.Everett, D.Gaffney, Sep 2001
Climb a flake-crack leading to the middle of the band of overhangs left of the central corner-line. Layback over and continue with interest to the top.

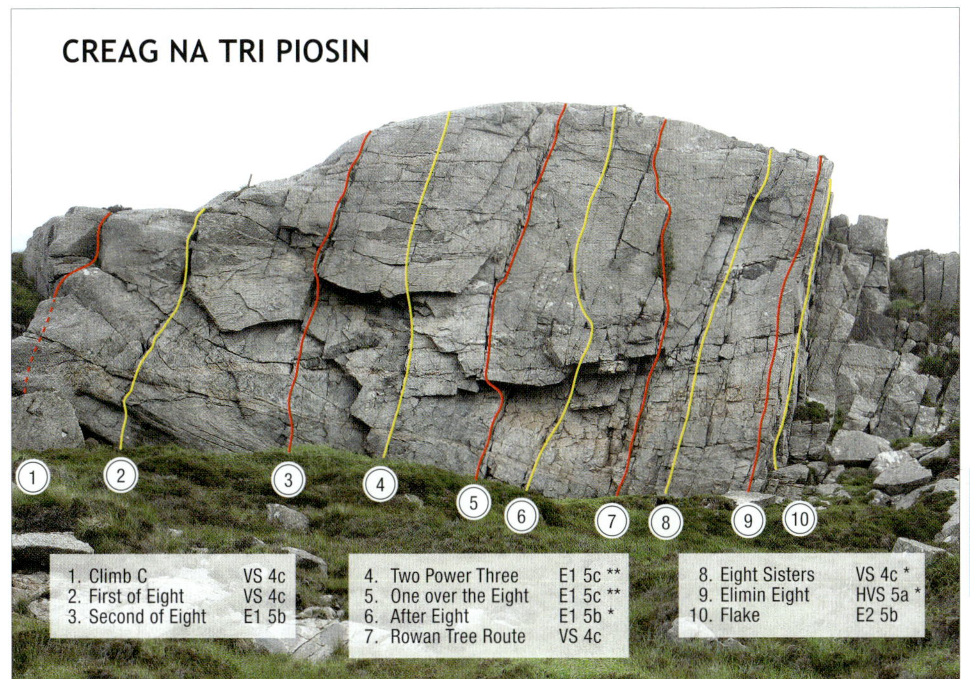

5 One over the Eight 11m E1 5c **
R.D.Everett, D.Gaffney, Sep 2001
The central corner gives a fine sustained climb. Start up a steep crack near the left end of the low band of roofs.

6 After Eight 11m E1 5b *
R.D.Everett, D.Gaffney, Sep 2001
Start below the widest point of the low band of roofs. Climb straight through the roof via a small square-cut recess then climb the wall and finishing crack between the central corner and the crack system to its right.

7 Rowan Tree Route 11m VS 4c
The next crack system right contains the rowan tree. Climb the right side of the overlap to the rowan and finish up the flake-crack.

8 Eight Sisters 11m VS 4c *
D.Gaffney, R.D.Everett, Sep 2001
Start just right of the low band of roofs and climb cracks to finish steeply up the slim right-facing corner.

9 Elimin Eight 11m HVS 5a *
R.D.Everett, D.Gaffney, Sep 2001
The right arete. It is more interesting, but rather artificial, to keep ones right hand on the arete all the way; runners can be placed in the previous climb.

10 Flake 9m E2 5b
B.Davison, 23 May 2014
Around the arete, climb flakes up the overhung wall.

MAOLADH MHICEARRAIG

Creag An-Eoin

(NG 098 948) Alt 100m NE facing Map p208 Diagram p238

This lies on the north-east side of Maoladh Mhicearraig (340m) overlooking the Bealach Eòrabhat, in the glen which provides a through route from one side of the island to the other. The glen runs south of and parallel to the main A859 from where the cliff can be seen in the vicinity of the Luskentre turn off before the road starts to climb towards Tarbert. The route through the glen is known as the Coffin Road since it was used by people taking their dead from the sandy west side of the island to bury them on the peaty east coast. The climbs described are on the main face which has a prominent ledge at three-quarters height.

Directions: On the west side of the causeway at the head of Luskentyre sands, and at the road sign for Seilebost, turn off the A859 onto a loop of old road. It is possible to drive along this to park next to Loch Carran at **(NG 087 961)** but the road is not in the best

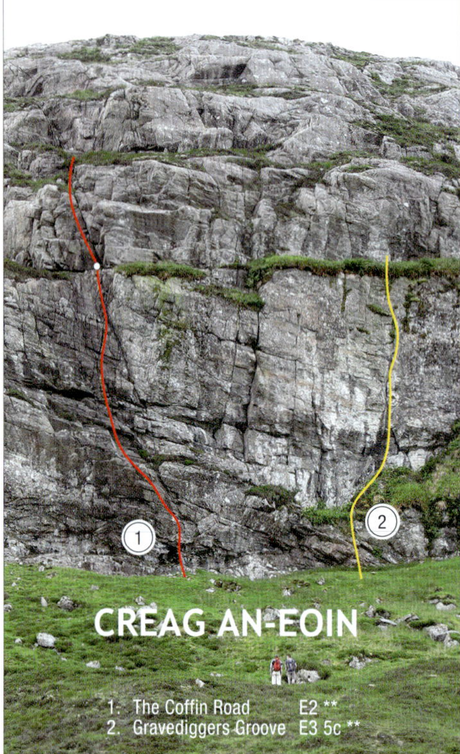

condition and some might prefer to park after a few hundred metres along it.

Approach: Follow a track up the east side of Loch Carran then Loch a' Bhealaich to the Bealach Eòrabhat (20min). A slightly longer approach can be made from the south-east at Àird Mhìghe.

1 The Coffin Road 35m E2 **

G.Nicoll, I.Blackwood, C.Pasteur, 6 Jul 2009

The left-trending line at the left end of the main face.

1. 25m 5c Climb the ramp-groove line through the lower barrier wall then the right edge of the black (mossy) wall above.
2. 10m 4c A short corner leads to scrambling.

2 Gravediggers Groove 25m E3 5c **

G.Nicoll, C.Pasteur, I.Humberstone, 11 Jul 2009

Good sustained climbing up the groove and crack-line at the right end of the main wall. Climb to a ledge and easily up right to the base of a black groove. Climb straight up the groove and crack above to the three-quarters height ledge. Escape off right.

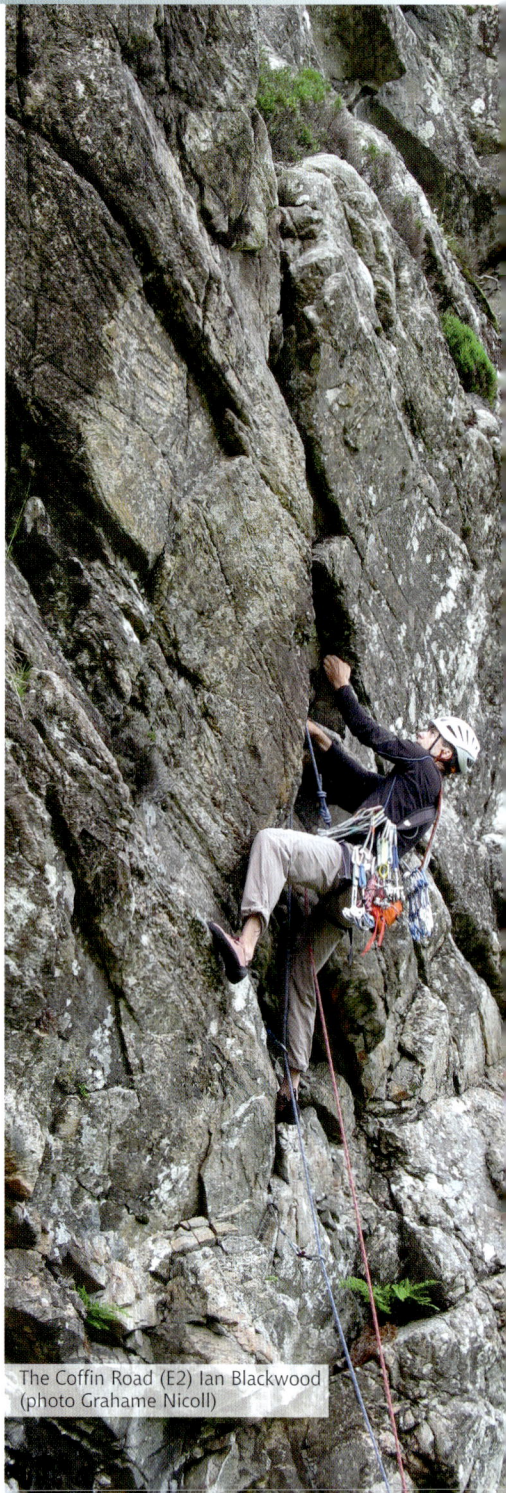

The Coffin Road (E2) Ian Blackwood (photo Grahame Nicoll)

CNOC NAN ADAG

Creag Aisnig

(NG 1627 9346) Alt 30m SW facing Map p208

A little gem of a crag which lies on a small knoll, south of the Cnoc nan Adag (61m) high point, just off The Golden Road, overlooking Loch Harmasaig, between Grosebay (Greosabhagh) and Scadabay (Scadabhagh). A lovely wall of compact pink rock is the main feature.

Directions: Some 6km south of Tarbert on the A859, take the second turning off the A859 and follow this south to Grosebay, then follow the Golden Road east towards Scadabay. After 1km, the crag will be seen on the east side of the loch. Park around the bend just beyond the crag where there is a large space alongside the road.

Approach: Walk 100m back along the road then head across to the crag (2min).

1 The Shining Path 15m E4 5c **
R.Anderson, C.Anderson, 17 Jul 2003
The left side of the central quartzy wall. Start off a boulder at the left side of the wall as for The Golden Road and climb straight up to a small spike. Move up and left around the edge into the main groove, then stretch up the arete to a small hold before pulling back around the edge onto the face to reach a crack-line leading to a narrow shelf. Move right and finish directly.

2 The Golden Road 15m E4 6a ***
R.Anderson, C.Anderson, 14 Jul 2003
Superb climbing up the middle of the wall. Start off the boulder at the left side of the wall as for The Shining Path. Pull up to the first horizontal break then step right into the centre of the wall and climb this to the top.

3 The Ivory Highway 15m E3/4 6a ***
R.Anderson, C.Anderson, 17 Jul 2003
The right edge of the wall. Climb a thin line of weakness to a short V-groove, then pull steeply over onto the quartzy wall and climb to the top break where a step up left gains a short, thin crack leading to the top.

ROINEABHAL

Coire Roineabhal Slabs

(NG 049 862) Alt 200m NW facing Map p208

Roineabhal (460m) is a fine little mountain in the southern tip of Harris, fortunately spared from being turned into a super-quarry for its anorthosite. The area around the summit is notable for the lenses of red garnet imbedded in the gneiss. On its north side there is a well formed corrie which sports long easy-angled slabs on the east side and more broken ones further round to the west and on the back wall. Much of the eastern slabs will be Grade 2 to 3 scrambles at most but one easy climb has been recorded.

Approach: The slabs are best reached by parking by a small track at **(NG 061 852)** and following it and the Abhainn Collam over the shoulder of Tora-cleit to traverse onto the eastern slabs (45min to 1hr).

Descent: Down either side of the corrie or one of the scree filled gullies.

An Aite Boidheach 150m Grade 2 to D **
J.Mackenze, E.Mackenzie, 1 Jul 2013
This follows the steepest and most overlapped section of the eastern slabs, starting at overlapped slabs just left of a white slab, reached by a descending traverse from Tora-cleit. Climb the most continuous line up and slightly left, taking in all the avoidable difficulties en route on superb rough and compact rock. Only a few moves of D at most but easier if the overlaps or smoother slabs are avoided.

The Ivory Highway (E3/4) Rab Anderson
(photo Chris Anderson)

Harris Sea Cliffs

Unlike Lewis, Harris provides very little in the way of sea-cliffs. Other than those on the island of Scarp off the west coast and two climbs on Toe Head in the south-west corner, nothing else has come to light.

SOUTH HARRIS

GOB AN TOBHA (TOE HEAD)

(NF 957 942) Tidal S facing Map p208

Ceapabhal (365m), the prominent isolated hill overlooking the Sound of Taransay, has this rocky headland at its northernmost tip. A large black slab is a prominent feature and the slim buttress to its left (west) offers two climbs, reached by down climbing or abseiling.

Directions: About 4km north of Leverburgh, turn off the A859 for Northton and park at the road end.

Approach: Either go over Ceapabhal and its northern top, or around the west side of the hill which will involve gaining height toward the end to avoid grassy sea-cliffs. As one drops down from the northern summit, the cliffs can be seen in a small bay to the south-west of the headland and are sheltered from the worst of any swell (4km, 1hr 30min).

Toe Arete 15m VD
B.Davison, 22 May 2014
The right arete of the buttress offers a pleasant climb though lacks protection.

Toe Buttress 15m D
B.Davison, 22 May 2014
The centre of the slim buttress offers easy climbing and a crack in its upper half.

SCARP

Map p208

Scarp is an extensive island which lies just offshore to the north of Huisinis. The highest point of the island is Sròn Romul (308m). The central, northern and western areas provide rough walking with much heather and bog. The climbing so far is on the sea-cliffs and the best access to these is to stay close to the coast or to contour around the many bluffs above the lower ground. On the original visit a landing was made opposite the small island of Cearstaigh on the north coast, on the beach at **(NA 964 167)**. Although this is a good landing and camping spot, it is far removed from some of the best climbing areas. There is naturally occurring water on the island.

The rock is mostly Lewisian Gneiss, with many quartz-like pegmatite intrusions. Along the western and south-western coast there are several promising looking geos, some with impending walls. The most extensive area with potential is from Tarta Geòdha (unexplored at the time of writing) through to the flat headland of Mànais.

The most convenient landing and camping place would be on the Mànais headland which would give easier and relatively quick access to the main areas.

Scarp was abandoned in 1971 (though some of the old houses in the village have been restored) and there is much evidence, in many surprising areas, of previous occupation and of the hard and uncompromising life of the inhabitants.

MÀNAIS WALL AREA

Map p208

This extends across three distinct areas, North, Main and South. The Main Wall area is the most extensive. The climbing is described from left to right.

Mànais Wall North

(NA 958 140) Tidal

Descent: Scramble down to the northern end of a tidal platform.

Keys to the World 22m HVS 5b **
P.Headland, K.Archer, 13 Jul 2012
Start from the platform at the far left-hand end of the crag where the two small slabs meet. Climb the left-hand slab to the overhanging corner on the left, surmount this to the second overhang and on to the top.

No Consolation 22m HVS 5a *
K.Archer, P.Headland, 13 Jul 2012
From the same start as the previous route, climb the right-hand slab to the black overhang on the right-hand side and make unusual moves through to the upper cracks. Finish on the left headwall. Constrictive!

Weymouth 22m VS 4c
K.Archer, P.Headland, 13 Jul 2012
Starts where a step-up has to be made on the approach traverse. Go up over easy ground to the base of a slabby corner and climb the short headwall above.

Mànais Wall Main

(NA 958 140) Non-tidal

The first climb starts at the left end of the crag, right of the brown wall.

A Girl Called Cecil 17m VS 4c *
P.Headland, K.Archer, 11Jul 2012
Climb the right-facing corner at the left-hand edge of the large, scooped white triangular wall.

Tide Turner 18m HVS 5a
P.Headland, K.Archer, 9 Jul 2012
The scooped, white triangular wall is followed in its centre until a move right to a short niche; the overhanging crack above is climbed on layaways.

Cabbage, Sweat and Micturation 18m S 4b
K.Archer, P.Headland, 10 Jul 2012
Climb the flake-line which borders the right-hand side of the large, scooped white triangular wall.

Hard Work Kills Horses 18m HVS 5b
P.Headland, K.Archer, 10 Jul 2012
The double open-book corners. Start on the left and climb to a large ledge at the base of the first open book, climb this to a second ledge and on to the top.

Land of Milk and Honey 20m HVS 5b **
K.Archer, P.Headland, 11 Jul 2012
The central right-facing corner of the imposing main wall.

Solarized 24m E2 5b **
P.Headland, K.Archer, 13 Jul 2012
Follow the broken fault-line slightly right of centre in the large imposing wall to an obvious small ledge below the headwall. Arrange small nuts here before traversing right under the headwall to the cracked depression leading to the top. Sustained!

Six Pence in the Pie 14m HVS 5a
K.Archer, P.Headland, 9 Jul 2012
Climb through the X-shaped cracks direct.

Chapter 109 13m HVS 5a
K.Archer, P.Headland, 9 Jul 2012
Start on the left-hand corner of the light brown slab, move to the centre and climb to the notch in the skyline.

Calendar Girl 13m VS 5a *
P.Headland, K.Archer, 9 Jul 2012
The bow-shaped corner bordering the narrow slab of Rocket Ma-a-an; climb the corner to the top.

Rocket Ma-a-an 12m VD
K.Archer, P.Headland, 9 Jul 2012
Follows the laid back narrow slab on the left-hand side of the first bay reached from the descent.

Wicket Chronicles 12m VS 4b
P.Headland, K.Archer, 9 Jul 2012
On the right-hand side of the first bay from the descent is an incut crack. Climb up ledges to the narrow crack and climb this on big holds to the top.

Mànais Wall South

(NA 960 139) Non-tidal

The first climb starts in the black geo to the left of the main wall.

Descent: By abseil.

Donald John MacLennan 21m HVS 4c
P.Headland, K.Archer, 11Jul 2012
This lies on the left-hand wall in the black geo. Climb the slabby wall following the line of 'cemented-in-place' blocks; good gear at half-height.

The next climbs are the wall to the right of the black geo.

Philosophy of Risk 12m HS 4c
P.Headland, K.Archer, 10 Jul 2012
The second crack along from the left-hand arete; climbed on ledges and finger jams.

Whiff Away 12m S 4a
K.Archer, P.Headland, 10 Jul 2012
The third crack along from the left-hand arete of the wall.

Canal Dreams 12m S 4b
K.Archer, P.Headland, 11 Jul 2012
The fourth crack along from the left-hand arete of the wall.

CAOLAS CEARSTAIGH AREA

Map p208

This lies directly opposite the small island of Cearstaigh, adjacent to the beach and is accessed by walking down from either side. Climbs are described left to right.

Caolas Cearstaigh Crag East

(NA 962 168) Non-tidal

Descent: Scramble down to the eastern end of a non-tidal platform.

Don't Fake Life 9m E1 5b *
P.Headland, K.Archer, 12 Jul 2012
The narrow incut recess at the left-hand end of the cliff, on superb light grey rock. Bridge and back-and-foot up the recess.

Number 7 the Beeches 12m E2 5c **
P.Headland, K.Archer, 12 Jul 2012
Climbs the series of short slabs and overhangs in the narrow niche, above a shallow pool. Start on the undercut right side of the pool with a powerful move to start, then traverse the quartz-like band to the niche (Friend 3). Climb the niche direct.

Ticks R Us 17m S 4b
K.Archer, P.Headland, 12 Jul 2012
The short laid-back area immediately left of the central overhang. Start from the toe of the buttress, trend left towards a short headwall and follow this to the top.

Caolas Cearstaigh Crag West

(NA 962 168) Non-tidal

Descent: Scramble down to the western end of the platform.

Jacaranda 24m E2 5b ***
K.Archer, P.Headland, 12 Jul 2012
Start at the weakness at the right end of the ledge that runs from the central corner. Pull through this then traverse easily to the base of an overhanging corner, move up to beneath the overhang, then move out left (small cams). Powerful layback moves on good holds lead to the final corner.

Bouldering on Lewis & Harris

This is not a guide to the bouldering on Lewis & Harris, simply a mention of some venues to explore with more, no doubt, to be found.

Beinn na Bheirigh (NB 109 356)

Small walls and boulders on and around the crags on the hillside to the east of the campsite at the Tràigh na Beirigh sands. Some problems done by R.Anderson but not recorded, these and others subsequently recorded by D.Macleod, N.McNair & J.Sutton.

Aird Feinis (NA 992 294)

Large boulder on a rocky headland in a lovely setting. Some problems done but not recorded by R.Anderson, these and others subsequently recorded by D.Macleod.

Carnaichean Tealasdale (NB 021 283)

Superb boulder field below the Far West Buttress of Creagan Tealasdale on the north flank of Mealaisbhal, 2km from the road. Numerous unrecorded problems left for others to find and enjoy.

Miavaig Boulders (NB 080 346)

Two roadside boulders by the burn running through Glen Valtos. A few problems recorded by J.Sutton.

Crulabhig (NB 171 335)

Traverses and short problems along the base of the cliff.

Tolstadh and Back (NB 536 497)

Bouldering on and around the stacs at the road end on the Tràigh Ghearadha beach and at Back on the east coast north of Stornoway. Sketchy details recorded by S.O'Conor.

Port Nis (NB 539 634)

Tidal bouldering off the beach to the south of the harbour at Nis, close to the northern tip of Lewis. Problems recorded by S.O'Conor, J.Sutton and D.Macleod

Sgiogarstaigh and Creag Dubh (NB 553 620 and NB 557 615)

Apparent bouldering on the coast south of Port Nis. Sketchy details from S.O'Conor.

The Boneyard

Apparent bouldering in caves and coves to the north of and around Eòrpaidh. Sketchy details from S.O'Conor.

South Dell, Nis

Tidal caves and boulders off the beach near South Dell. Sketchy details by S.O'Conor. Probably at Sròn Pheicir **(NB 487 624)** on the west side of Tràigh Dhail.

Scaladail Boulders (NB 190 097)

Large boulder field with only a few big boulders on the north side of the A859 Stornoway to Tarbert road where it climbs the hill above Scaladail. Some problems on two boulders recorded by S.O'Conor and D.Macleod.

Sròn a' Sgaoth (NB 143 041)

Viciously steep wall above a nasty landing, prominently seen above the east side of the road just south of the quarry on the road north of Tarbert. Central crack recorded by S.O'Conor!

Sròn Uladail boulders (NB 076 136)

Numerous large boulders and loads of potential, but perhaps a bit too far to carry a mat.

Tarbert (NG 159 999)

Two boulders on the hillside overlooking the Church of Scotland in Tarbert. Accessed in front of Macleod's Bar up the side of the car park and the wall by the church. Problems recorded by S.O'Conor.

Tarbert, the Lingeadail Boulder (NB 165 005)

Fairly large boulder overlooking Lingeadail some 10min up the hillside above the gritter depot on the Scalpay road outside Tarbert. Problems done by R.Anderson but not recorded.

Aird Mhighe Crag (NF 123 928)

Good little quick drying bouldering crag with some 35 problems although the base can be boggy. Descriptions on the UKC website and the old Scottish Climbs wiki.

The Aird Feinis boulder (photo Chris Anderson)

BARRA (BARRAIGH)

The main interest is the extensive line of sea-cliffs in the south-west.

Access: From Oban by Caledonian MacBrayne ferries; **Tel: 0800 0665000** or **www.calmac.co.uk**. An alternative is from South Uist via Eriskay also by Calmac. There are flights to Barra Airport (at the north-east of the island) from Glasgow; **Tel: 01871 890212** or **www.isleofbarra.com**.

Maps: Ordnance Survey 1:50000 Landranger 31 and 1:25000 Explorer 452

Accommodation: For information about hotels and B&B the local web site is very good, **www.isleofbarra.com**. The Dunard Hostel in Castlebay is to the west of the Calmac pier; **Tel: 01871 810443** or **www.dunardhostel.co.uk**. There are several camp sites, ask at the tourist information office in Castlebay or see **www.isleofbarra.com**.

Amenities: There are cafes, pubs, restaurants and shops. Public transport by minibus is very good except on Sundays, alternatively take a bike.

ÀIRD GHRÈIN

Two gneiss cliffs have been climbed on at the north-west point of Barra, there is potential for more routes here.

Approach: Start from the golf course **(NF 662 042)**. Walk up the track that leads to the comms mast then continue out past the house to Aird Ghrein, 20 to 30min from the golf course.

Creag Eilean nan Eun Mora

(NF 647 049) Partially Tidal SW facing

The small rocky island of Eilean nan Eun is to the north of Àird Ghrèin, the surrounding land is ringed by cliffs. The route below is to the north-west where the cliff north of the island is shorter.

Descent: Walk round north of the island then scramble round below the crag from the west.

North Chimney 20m VD
C.Moody, C.Grindley, 20 Apr 2009
Climb the shallow chimney-line.

Creag Eilean Eun Beaga

(NF 646 048) Non-tidal SSW facing

This clean wall faces the island. The rock is slightly friable in places. The routes finish on a flake ledge; from this ledge scramble up 20m or traverse off and up.

Descent: Abseil in or scramble down either side.

Linking Corners 20m S 4a
C.Moody, C.Grindley, 19 Apr 2009
Climb a shallow right-facing corner at the left side of the crag, step left and climb another corner.

Gaining the Corner 20m VS 4b *
C.Moody, C.Grindley, 20 Apr 2009
Climb the nice wall just left of Right-hand Corner to gain and climb a right-facing corner, step left and continue to the top.

Right-hand Corner 20m S 4a
C.Moody, C.Grindley, 19 Apr 2009
At the right side of the crag is an open chimney feature. Climb the crack left of the chimney then climb the right-facing corner, step left and continue to the top.

BORVE SCHOOL

(NF 656 020) Alt 20m S facing Map left

There is a handy pair of slabs at the school that can be useful for a poor day, the routes were climbed in drizzle.

Approach: Travelling north up the west coast road after the Isle of Barra Hotel is the township of Borve; the school is the last building. From the road cross the fence and walk to the slab in a minute, the right-hand slab in another minute's walk to the east. The first three routes climb the left-hand slab and are not well protected, the last three climb the right-hand slab.

Reading 14m VD *
C.Grindley, C.Moody, 5 May 2010
Follow the crack on the left-hand side with steeper rock high up.

Riting 16m VD *
C.Moody, C.Grindley, 5 May 2010
Climb scoops right of Reading.

Rithmetic 16m VD *
C.Grindley, C.Moody, 5 May 2010
Climb the right-hand crack to the flake then move up left to avoid a grass patch.

Danger of Death 12m D *
C.Moody, C.Grindley, 5 May 2010
Start at the left side of the right-hand slab. Gain and climb the thin crack then continue up and left.

Three Live Wires 12m D *
C.Grindley, C.Moody, 5 May 2010
Start 3m right, climb up left to a thin crack, follow this crack to the top.

Keep Off 12m D *
C.Moody, C.Grindley, 5 May 2010
Start 1m right at the deep crack. Climb the deep crack towards a grass topped bulge, avoid the bulge by a right step then climb to the top.

There are easier looking lines just right.

South-West Barra

Map p248

To the west of Castlebay lies the huge rounded bulk of Beinn Tangabhal, with a long line of sea-cliffs to its west stretching for about 2km. Routes are described from north to south. By public transport (or walking) it is best to approach from the north, as this is nearer Castlebay than the south approach.

Approach: From just south of Isle of Barra Hotel **(NF 649 002)**. Follow the marked path towards Dun Ban for 10 to 15min. Cross the fence where it starts to dip down towards the sea then continue gaining some height. A boulder will be seen on the skyline, aim just above it to round the impressive chasm Lunar Geo. Beyond is the Rock Island Area. Go down the peninsula north of the rocky island to the top of the routes for Hot Wall and Ice Cream Wall. Walk south from the top of the Rock Island Area past a couple of overhanging beaks in the cliff below (seen in silhouette from Hot Wall) to an easier angled wall above a rocky peninsula; Temperance Wall.

LUNAR GEO

(NF 627 001) Non-tidal SW facing Map p248

This is the long impressive chasm attaining some 90m in height, which is passed on the coastal approach to the Rock Island Area.

The Light Side

The following four climbs lie on an excellent 70m wall at the seaward end of the south-west face of the chasm. The most recognisable features are the left-facing corner of Harvest Moon and a wall to its left containing prominent twin cracks.

Descent: By a 60m abseil down the line of the corner of Harvest Moon to a small belay ledge, 7m below and left of the base of the corner and some 10m above the sea. The first three routes start from this ledge, an impressive place! Routes are described from right to left.

Harvest Moon 60m VS **
P.Whillance, C.Grindley, 17 Aug 2009
1. 45m 4c Move up right and climb a rib to gain the base of the corner. Follow the corner throughout and exit onto good ledges on the right.
2. 15m 4b Step left and continue in the same line to the top. Belay well back.

Shine On 50m HVS 5a ***
P.Whillance, C.Grindley, 17 Aug 2009
Climb the centre of the slab, trending slightly left to avoid bulges, then go back right to below a hanging left-facing corner-crack (7m left of Harvest Moon). Climb the crack steeply through the bulges then follow the obvious twin cracks in the upper slab to reach big ledges on the left just below the top.

Lunar Eclipse 50m E2 **
P.Whillance, C.Grindley, 17 Aug 2009
1. 35m 5a Climb the centre of the slab more or less direct to below a right-facing hanging ramp (5m left of Shine On). Follow this steeply leftwards through the bulges and continue up to a good ledge below the smooth headwall.
2. 15m 5b Climb the centre of the clean slab (3m left of the twin cracks of Shine On) with a balancy move to reach a good break. Move right and up a slanting crack to finish at the top of Shine On.

Lunatic Fringe 60m VS ***
P.Whillance, C.Grindley, 18 Aug 2009
Approach via the 60m abseil (as for the previous routes) down the corner of Harvest Moon, but belay 8m further left on good ledges near to the left edge of the slab. A very good route with incredible situations for the grade.
1. 45m 4a Climb the left edge of the slab on good holds until above a line of overhangs to the right. Traverse right on ledges for 4m then up trending rightwards heading for a steep prow. Belay on ledges to the right below a clean headwall (as for Lunar Eclipse).
2. 15m 4b Move back left and climb the wall just right of the prow to a ledge below a short steep groove. Up this to the top.

ROCK ISLAND AREA

Map p248 Diagram p249

This area is around the rocky island at **(NL 624 999)**. Hot Wall overlooks the island from the north, Dubh Slab overlooks the island from the east, Ice Cream Wall is

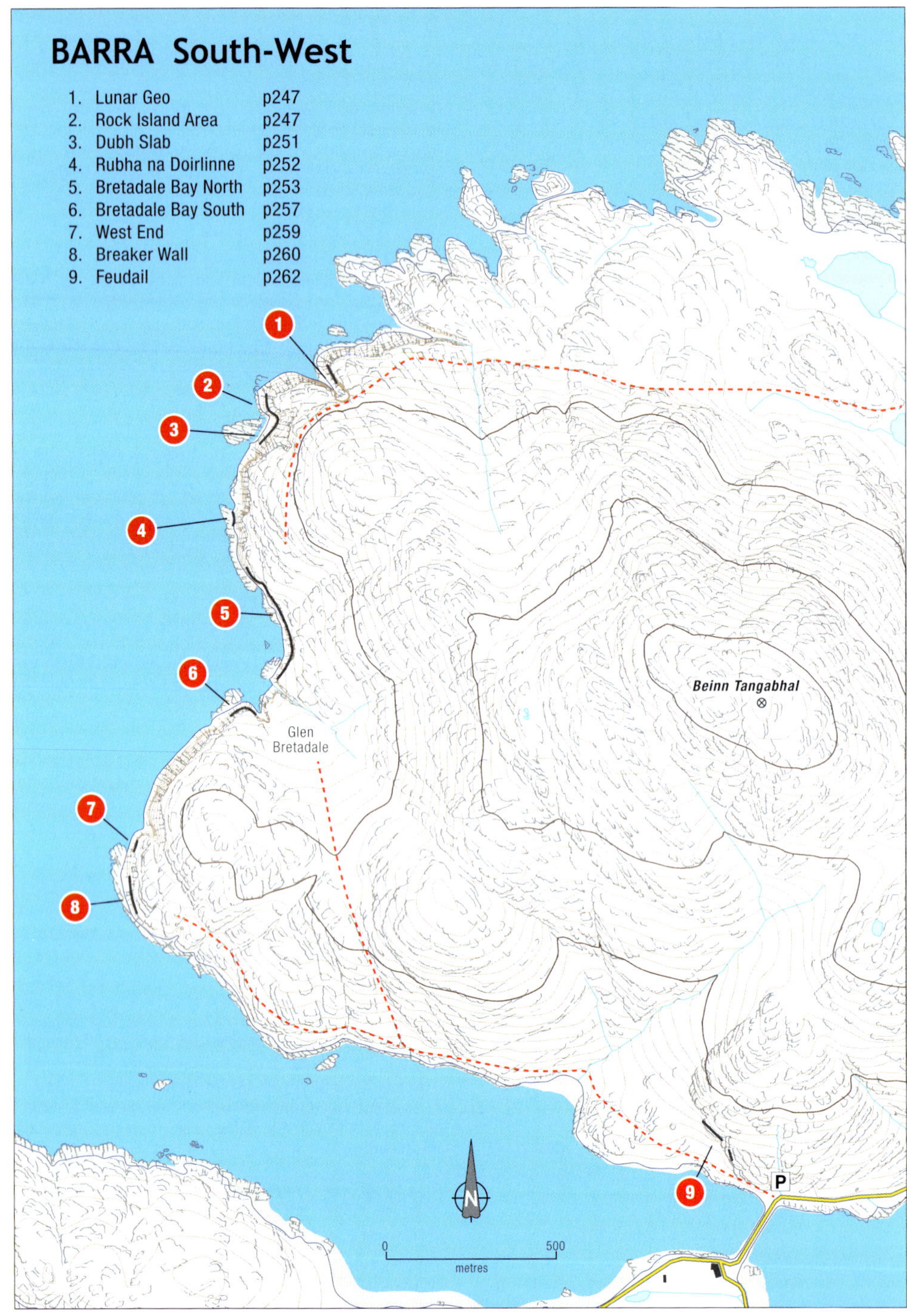
BARRA South-West
1. Lunar Geo p247
2. Rock Island Area p247
3. Dubh Slab p251
4. Rubha na Doirlinne p252
5. Bretadale Bay North p253
6. Bretadale Bay South p257
7. West End p259
8. Breaker Wall p260
9. Feudail p262
Glen Bretadale
Beinn Tangabhal
P
N
0
500
metres

between the two. There may be gulls nesting well above the routes so approach quickly to keep disturbance to a minimum. 50min from the road.

Hot Wall Continuation

(NF 625 000) Alt 20m W facing

This is the continuation of Hot Wall just left (north) of it.

Descent: Abseil in.

Sunset 25m VS 4c **
C.Moody, C.Grindley, 18 Apr 2009
Just left of Sunburst. Climb up the crack-line then continue trending left of the overhanging area.

Sunburst 25m E2 5b **
C.Grindley, C.Moody, 18 Apr 2009
Start just left of Catch the Sun. Climb up the left side of the rib then climb up to an area of grey rock. Step left and climb straight up the overhanging nose to the top. Perhaps over graded.

Catch the Sun 22m VS 5a ***
C.Grindley, C.Moody, 18 Apr 2009
Start 12m left of Thermal at a short right-facing corner. Climb this awkwardly (crux), continue up then move right and finish up the obvious fault.

Hot Wall

Alt 20m SW facing

This short immaculate wall is just north of the rock island on the north side of the rib and can be a sun trap.

Descent: Abseil in.

Edge of the Sun 18m VS 4c **
D.Robinson, K.Williams, 5 Apr 2012
Climb the stepped arete left of Thermal.

Thermal 18m HS 4b **
C.Moody, C.Grindley, 17 Apr 2009
At the left side of the wall is a prominent corner-chimney, climb this using a crack on the left.

Sunspot 18m VS 4b **
C.Grindley, C.Moody, 17 Apr 2009
Start 2m right of Thermal. Move up for 6m step right to gain the vertical crack then continue up slightly left-wards.

Sundae 18m VS 4c **
C.Grindley, C.Moody, 17 Apr 2009
Start up Barrahamas then climb up left to finish at a slot in the skyline.

Barrahamas 18m VS 4c **
C.Moody, C.Grindley, 17 Apr 2009
Start 5m left of the right-hand corner. Climb up and step right to gain and climb crack-line to a horizontal crack. Step right and continue to the top.

Molten 18m S 4a **
C.Moody, C.Grindley, 17 Apr 2009
Climb the left-facing corner at the right side of the wall on amazing holds, to the big ledge (possible escape). Step right and climb up a crack to the horizontal crack, move left to the ramp then up to top.

Under Hot Wall

Non-tidal

Descent: Abseil.

Warm Up 15m S 4a *
C.Moody, C.Grindley, 10 Jun 2009
Pleasant climbing up the slab left of Cool Down.

Cool Down 15m S 4a *
C.Grindley, C.Moody, 10 Jun 2009
Climb the corner-crack below the right end of Hot Wall, pull left to gain the platform below Hot Wall.

Catch the Sun (VS) Cynthia Grindlay (photo Colin Moody)

Ice Cream Gully Wall

Non-tidal S facing

The right side of the Hot Wall area has a number of fine routes. The first route is just left of a black dyke, the other three routes are right of the black dyke.

Descent: Abseil.

Penny Lick 40m D *
C.Moody, C.Grindley, 18 Apr 2009
Right of Hot Wall is a rib with a broad face, this route climbs to the right of the broad face. Abseil down the rib right of Hot Wall to a small ledge above sea-level. Climb up through the open chimney slot, continue up the rib to a ledge below a steep wall. Move right and climb cracks and easier ground.

The next three routes lie on the steep buttress to the right of the black dyke. Abseil approach from a wide platform above and right of the dyke to a good ledge system some 10m above sea-level.

Mr Softee 40m E1 5b **
P.Whillance, C.Grindley, 16 Aug 2009
Takes the left edge of the buttress. From the upper left end of the ledges, climb steeply up the edge overlooking the black chimney for 8m then trend rightwards to reach the big ledge crossing the buttress at 25m. Climb steep cracks on the left side of the buttress to below a prow. Move left and finish up corner-cracks.

Mr Whippy 40m E3 6a ***
P.Whillance, C.Grindley, 16 Aug 2009
The obvious crack-line in the centre of the buttress. Another ascent thought E2 5c; probably dependent on reach.
1. 25m 6a Start from the right side of the ledges and climb a leftwards slanting ramp to below a thin crack in the leaning wall. Difficult moves lead quickly to better holds. Continue up the crack to the big ledge system.
2. 15m 4b Up a right-trending ramp, then go steeply back left to gain the final rightwards leaning crack. This pitch shares a lot of the ground with the second pitch of Hot Fudge Sundae.
Variation: **Alt Finish 5b**
Climb from the left of the belay to a prow. This can be breached on its right side then direct to the top.

Hot Fudge Sundae 40m VS 4b **
C.Grindley, C.Moody, 8 Jun 2009
This route climbs the right side of the buttress to the right, abseil to the ledge system above sea-level.
1. 25m 4a Climb the straight-forward corners just right of the frontal face to an easy fault.
2. 15m 4b Move left to the rib, pull over the bulge and zigzag to the top.

Ice Cream Gully Upper Wall

Alt 50m S facing

There are some fine crack-lines above a grassy base.

Descent: Scramble down to the base by the right side of the wall, or the gully just to the right again, or abseil, or walk in from the south (above Dubh Slab).

Luca 20m S 4a *
C.Moody, C.Grindley, 10 Jun 2009
Start at the left side of the ledge at the base of the upper wall where a ramp comes up from the wall below. Climb a series of cracks to the top, pleasant but escapable.

Nardini 22m VS 4c **
C.Grindley, C.Moody, 10 Jun 2009
Start around the middle of the ledge (right of the previous route). Climb up through an overhang at 6m. Finish steeply up the left-facing flake-corner.

Chocolate Mint Chip 22m VS 4c **
C.Grindley, C.Moody, 9 Jun 2009
Climb the wall just right of the ledge at the base. Climb up slightly left to gain and climb the prominent crack.

Banana Split 18m VS 4b **
C.Grindley, C.Moody, 8 Jun 2009
Start at a slight niche. Climb the crack up and slightly right.

Giannetti 18m VS 4c *
C.Moody, C.Grindley, 9 Jun 2009
Climb the wall to the right finishing up the same route.

Just One Cornetto 16m S 4a
C.Grindley, C.Moody, 8 Jun 2009
Climb past some quartz towards a right-facing corner-crack, finish up this.

Long Slab

Alt 60m NW facing

This is the short slab facing the Ice Cream Gully Upper Wall, above the left side of Dubh Slab.

Descent: Scramble down the gully between the two, or walk in from the slopes just south.

The Finger Crack 8m HVS 5a *
C.Moody, C.Grindley, 9 Jun 2009
This is a short but appealing crack at the left side of the slab.

Piping Slab 15m S 4a *
C.Moody, C.Grindley, 9 Jun 2009
Start towards the right side of the slab. Climb up to and over an easy overlap, then follow the crack up and left.

Hanging Corner 15m VD *
Start just right of Piping Slab. Climb up to bulges, gain and climb the hanging corner.

DUBH SLAB

(NL 625 999) Partially Tidal NW facing
Map p248 Diagrams above & p249

This is the prominent dark sweep of slabs opposite Ice Cream Gully Wall.

Dubh Slab

1. Little Black Sambo VS 4c **
2. Black Gold HVS 5a ***
3. Black Light VS 4c ***
4. Black Velvet VS 5a **
5. Bible Black VS 4c **

Descent: Abseil in or scramble down to the west.

1 Black Magic 35m VS 4c **
C.Grindley, C.Moody, 9 Jun 2009
Abseil down the left side of the slab to a semi-hanging belay below two overlaps. Make awkward moves then climb the easy-angled crack up slightly left up the slab. Good climbing but a little unbalanced.

2 Black Gold 50m HVS 5a ***
P.Whillance, J.Lagoe, C.Grindley, A.Hyslop, C.Moody, 8 Jun 2009
This is the fine obvious central line up thin left-slanting cracks. Abseil to the sloping rock shelf at the base of the right side of the slab. Perhaps one move of 5b.
1. 22m 5a Follow the left-slanting corner containing a thin crack then make awkward moves to gain and climb the continuation crack, belay at the wide right-slanting crack.
2. 28m 5a Traverse left to gain the continuation crack, follow the crack with interest to the top.

3 Black Light 26m VS 4c ***
C.Moody, C.Grindley, 13 Jun 2009
An excellent line. Start a few metres up and right from Black Gold. Climb the undercut flake-line up left to gain a corner-crack, climb the corner-crack with interest to the top.

4 Black Velvet 26m VS 5a **
C.Grindley, C.Moody, 13 Jun 2009
Climb the initial corner of Bible Black for 4m then move leftwards up flakes towards a chimney. Climb the fine thin crack left of the chimney.

5 Bible Black 22m VS 4c **
C.Moody, C.Grindley, 9 Jun 2009
The crack at the right side of the slab, start below flakes in a corner. Climb the corner, step right at the top and finish up the fine steep slab.

There is a pleasant short Severe above these three routes or an easier scramble to the right.

RUBHA NA DOIRLINNE

Temperance Wall

(NL 624 997) Partially Tidal W facing Map p248

There are a number of nice climbs on this wall, which is above a tidal rocky peninsula.

Descent: Abseil.

Coffee Palace 50m VS 4c **
C.Grindley, C.Moody, 7 Jun 2009
Climbs the yellow right-facing corner at the left side of the crag. Start to the right of the corner at the left side of the blunt rib. Climb the stepped shallow corner leftwards then steeply (crux) to easier ground. Move up then left into the corner. Continue up the corner avoiding the roof by going left. Belay on easy rock above.

Band of Hope 50m VS 4b **
C.Grindley, C.Moody, 7 Jun 2009
Start next to the previous route and climb the weakness above. Climb up to the corner and follow it up right of the roof to belay. Go up to the horizontal rail, pull over the bulge at the left side of the rail then continue up more easily.

The Drunkard's Children 60m S 4a **
C.Moody, C.Grindley, 7 Jun 2009
To the right is a 6m high black block. Climb the corner on the right side of the block then continue to easier ground below a steepening, belay. Climb into an awkward recess then move right onto the steep shelf and climb up to the top.

The Bottler 60m S 4a **
C.Moody, C.Grindley, 7 Jun 2009
Climb an easy right-facing corner and continue up and right to belay before the corner becomes vegetated. Hand-traverse left then climb a short corner, exit this on the left, climb to the top past two easy corners.

Teetotal 70m S 4a *
C.Moody, C.Grindley, 8 Jun 2009
Climb the rib just right of the previous route and continue steeply to gain a right-slanting corner-ramp. Finish easily up the ramp, the narrow corner was avoided.

Undercut Rib

Partially Tidal W facing

South of Hot Wall is a barnacle covered rib extending into the sea at Temperance Wall. South of this is another similar rib with an overhanging base.

Descent: Abseil to the platform at the base.

Cake Stand 50m S 4a **
C.Moody, C.Grindley, 18 May 2009
The start is guarded by an overhang. Climb the easiest line which is a short left-facing corner-crack then step right to easier ground. Move up then traverse left to a crack, this is followed to an easier angled area, finish up the corner on the left side of the rib.

More Cake 50m VS 4b *
C.Moody, C.Grindley, 18 May 2009
Start as for Cake Stand then instead of moving left climb the wide crack past the left side of the roof. Follow the continuation crack-line to the top.

Black Stained Top

Alt 25m W facing

To the south is a prominent short black-stained slab at the top of the cliff.

Access: Walk south again along the cliff-top.

Descent: Abseil down Smelly Corner.

A Piece of Coffee Cake 24m VD *
C.Moody, C.Grindley, 18 May 2009
Abseil down Smelly Corner to the third ledge. Climb flake-cracks to the left of that route.

Smelly Corner 24m HS 4b *
C.Moody, C.Grindley, 18 May 2009
Just south of the black slab is the top of a corner, abseil down it past two ledges to a third ledge. Climb back up.

Easy Ground

Partially Tidal W facing

To the south again is an impressive steep wall, and south of this wall are a series of easy ribs and corner-gullies.

Descent: Scramble down one of the corners or abseil in.

Broad Rib 50m M *
C.Moody, C.Grindley, 18 May 2009
Climb the broadest rib (left of centre).

BRETADALE BAY, NORTH

Map p248 Diagram above

This is the north side of the bay containing two stacks.

Approach: Start at the causeway and walk along the vague track towards Breaker Wall. Go past an overhanging crag (Junction Walls) at **(NL 628 982)**, then follow a grassy rake up and left (north-north-west) to the col then drop down into Glen Bretadale; about 1hr from the causeway. Another approach is to walk to Rock Island Area from near the Isle of Barra Hotel and continue along the cliff-tops to reach the bay. Allow 1hr from the hotel.

Barra Wall

(NL 624 997) Partially Tidal SW facing

These excellent routes are on a steep slabby immaculate wall on the north-west point of Bretadale Bay. A raised platform sits at the base of part of the wall separated from the crag by a ravine containing a rock pool. The raised platform connects to the main crag and leads right towards the vertical sea cave.

Descent: Abseil to ledges from a huge block.

Escape Route 40m M
Traverse left from Barra Wall under another wall to reach a dyke, climb this.

The first routes start from the seaweed covered ledges round to the left of the main slab. There is a short steep wall leading to a terrace.

Sushi 35m VS 5a ***
S.Muir, K.Howett, 2005
Climbs the open corner bounding the left side of the smooth central slab. From the lowest of raised ledges, climb off the left side into a shallow corner in the broad rib. This leads into the corner itself. Up this to the capping roof. Traverse right under it until its possible to step back left above it and finish on big holds.

Asahi 35m E3 5c *
S.Muir, K.Howett, 2005
Climbs just right of the open central corner of the slab via the line of a brown streak. From the lowest of raised ledges, take easy rock to the base of the streak (gear in the shallow groove on the left). Go up the wall with difficulty, through a quartz area direct and on up the brown streak to the right end of the capping roof. Exit right up the steeper headwall.

Haute Coiture 45m E2 5b ***
S.Muir, K.Howett, 2005
Tackles the line of a very shallow groove in the centre of the wall. Start on the sea-washed ledges at the left end of a tidal pool.
1. 10m 5b Climb the overhanging wall via a thin flake, then head diagonally right to enter a recess leading left to the ledges.
2. 35m 5b Head up and right over ledges to gain the base of the shallow groove. This leads to a flake-line up to a ledge. From the left end of the ledge climb the slab direct until better holds lead right to an exit.
Variation: **Bad Hair Day 35m E3 5c ****
P.Whillance, C.Grindley, 19 Aug 2009
A variation finish to Haute Coiture. Climb Haute Coiture to the ledge above the flake-line. From the top right end of the ledges climb the slab direct (bold) moving left to exit.

Hot Catwalk Strutt 45m E2 5c ***
K.Howett, S.Muir, 2005
Takes a line just right of Haute Coiture. Start at the left end of a raised ledge below the main crag in the ravine. From the extreme left end of the ledge climb the steep wall to a small stepped roof. Go through these on the right and then up the wall heading left to the arete and gain ledges above (possible belay). Move up to the bigger ledge. Climb the centre of the steep wall via obvious big flakes, then direct to the right side of a higher smaller ledge. Climb directly up the red-brown slab boldly to a small flake to finish.

Cobra 45m E2 5c ***
S.Muir, K.Howett, 2005
Climbs a line right of Hot Catwalk Strutt through the left side of the steeper wall and the fine shallow groove in the upper slab. Start on the small ledge beside Hot Cat. Climb up into a slim ramp immediately right of Hot Cat. This leads to the steep wall which is climbed on huge black flakes and jugs leading to a quartz roof. Step left below the roof and up to better holds leading into the shallow right-facing groove. This leads more easily to the top. A fine pitch, high in the grade.

Snake Charmer 35m E4 5c ***
T.Fryer, I.Taylor, 11 Jun 2011
A fine sustained pitch that slithers up the wall right of Cobra. Start on a ledge up and right from Cobra. Go up a shallow left-slanting groove to a flake, then move up and right to a good ledge. Break through the roof above on monster undercuts and jugs to gain a very shallow groove. Follow this until it peters out and an awkward move leads to better holds. Trend left to finish.

Sunray Canker 45m E1 5a
K.Howett, S.Muir, 2005
This serious route climbs the line of the conspicuous stepped grooves in the centre of the wall, overlooking the vertical sea cave. Marred by some unstable blocks in the top section. Start from the right end of the raised platform. Climb up a slabby corner to a roof. Traverse hard right and up into the line of the grooves which lead in steps with ledges back leftwards into a left-facing corner. Climb this to its top and an impasse. Climb the steep wall via fragile flakes into a chimney. The left wall of this is formed by horribly hollow sounding blocks, so climb with care up the right arete to the top.

Black Gold (HVS, p251) Jonathan Lagoe (photo Colin Moody)

Dancing Walls

Non-tidal W facing

These walls lie immediately right (east) of Barra Wall and extend from the sea cave south to just past the low point in the cliff where a burn runs down over slabs. Routes are described right to left.

Descent: Abseil.

Right (south) of the sea cave is a series of fine grooves, right again is a red banded buttress. The first two routes are on the red banded buttress.

Lilly the Pink 22m VS 4c
T.Carruthers, T.Stephenson, Jun 2004
Climb the obvious flake-crack on the right side of the buttress to the overhang. Step left and up into the steep corner which soon eases, continue to the top. The corner gully just right gives a poor Moderate.

Anniversary Waltz 25m VS 4c **
P.Whillance, A.Hyslop, 29 Sep 2009
This route is on the left side of the buttress, 5m left of the previous route. Climb the right-slanting hand crack then the red left-facing corner-crack.

On the left side of the red banded buttress is a gully of rotten red rock. The next obvious feature is a crack-line about 7m left. Between these features is a brown slab seamed with thin cracks.

Highland Fling 30m E2 5c **
P.Whillance, C.Grindley, 1 Oct 2009
Climb the thin crack in the centre of the brown slab to below a rib. Go up the crack in the left side of the rib to start, then move onto the right side and up to a large ledge below an overhang. Traverse left into the corner and climb the hanging corner to the top.

Buggerama 30m E2/3 5c
R.Strube, T.Carruthers 15 Jun 2004
Climb Highland Fling to a ledge below the big double roofs. Climb through the roofs at the obvious point directly above.

Time Travel 30m E2 5c
R.Strube, S.Tyson, J.Beveridge, 15 Jun 2004
Climbs the crack line 7m left of the rotten gully. Climb the obvious flake crack and short off width to reach the

corner in a black band under a roof. Climb the corner and pass the roof into a hanging curved corner. Exit onto the left arete at the top of Red Groove.

Rock Shoe Shuffle 40m E1 5b **
P.Whillance, C.Grindley, 1 Oct 2009
Start 2m left of the crack of Time Travel. Use a thin crack to gain a leftwards rising foot ledge that leads across the wall to gain the base of a corner. Climb the corner, then follow a series of grooves and ramps trending rightwards and up to the top.

Twinkle Toes 40m E4 5c/6a **
P.Whillance, A.Hyslop, 23 May 2010
Mid-way between the starts of Rock Shoe Shuffle and Strictly Come Climbing is an open shallow groove with a thin flake-crack (the natural starting point for Rock Shoe Shuffle avoided by that route).
1. 12m 5c/6a Climb the shallow groove with increasing difficulty and sparse protection, moving right at the top to belay on good ledges.
2. 28m 5b Climb up rightwards to a steep slim left-facing corner. Up this to its top and pull out left onto a slab (junction with Soft Shoe Shuffle). Continue up slabby ramp rightwards to the top (as for Soft Shoe Shuffle).

Red Groove 40m E4 5c
T.Stephenson, J.Beveridge 15 Jun 2004
Climb the shallow groove of Twinkle Toes until it eases at a sloping ledge marked by quartz. Climb up and right into a stepped corner (Rock Shoe Shuffle) which leads to the top.

Strictly Come Climbing 45m HVS 5a ***
P.Whillance, C.Grindley, 1 Oct 2009
Start at the left-hand end of the non-tidal platform and move up to a large belay ledge below a striking rightwards slanting crack-line. Follow the obvious diagonal line on good holds.

Trip The Light Fantastic 55m E1 5b **
P.Whillance, C.Grindley, A.Hyslop, 22 May 2010
Start as for Strictly Come Climbing at the left-hand end of the non-tidal platform and move up to the large belay ledge.
1. 30m 5b Move up the obvious diagonal, as for Strictly Come Climbing for 5m, then step left and climb a steep slim groove in the wall, pull out left onto a slab. Go up left to a short right-facing corner-crack, this leads to a large belay ledge in the middle of the wall.
2. 25m 4c Climb the slabby corner trending leftwards to reach a short chimney-crack and so to the top.

Carvery Buttress

Non-tidal W facing

South of Dancing Walls is a huge sea cave. Carvery Buttress is just south of the cave. An obvious rounded block belay can be found 15m back from the cliff-top. This is about 150m south of Dancing Walls and about 100m south of the burn. South of Carvery Buttress the cliff grows in height and has a loose finish.

Descent: Abseil from the rounded block to the huge non-tidal block.

Scimitar 35m E3 6a **
P.Whillance, C.Grindley, 26 May 2010
From the huge non-tidal block go down left (north) on the ledge. Climb a short groove to gain a ledge on the left. Follow the stepped arete to the base of a hanging V-groove. Climb the groove and jamming crack through two small roofs to a ledge. Go up rightwards via a short corner to the top.

Sickle Groove 35m E1 5b **
P.Whillance, C.Grindley, C.Moody, A.Hyslop, 25 May 2010
From the block step across onto the cliff. Move left a metre or so then climb the crack-line to big ledge and traverse left into the ramp. Climb up the slabby ramp rightwards then climb the overhanging corner.

Kukri 40m HVS 5a **
P.Whillance, C.Grindley, C.Moody, 25 May 2010
Start as for Sickle Groove, step across onto the main cliff, move left a metre or so then climb the crack-line to ledges on the right. Traverse right to the groove and follow this, then move left and continue up to finish.

The Devil's Horns Area

(NL 625 993)

South from Dancing Walls and Carvery Buttress the cliff-top reaches a high point; south of this is a grey pillar facing the stacks; Baldies Pillar. This is separated from a huge unclimbed black north-west facing wall (called Black Boiler Wall) by a deep geo. Right of Black Boiler Wall are two geos separated by a pillar, right again is the black slab of Comedy Slab facing the two stacks; The Devil's Horns.

Baldies Pillar

Non-tidal SW facing

This is an obvious tall slender slabby pillar. Sloping ledges lie at its foot and a good belay is below a faint shallow groove line.

Descent: Abseil.

Sensible Feet 45m E3/4 6a *
K.Howett, S.Muir, 2005
Go up and left to a small roof above a short rock scarred groove. Pull over and head left to near the arete. Climb up crozzley rock to a steepening. Gain a thin diagonal crack in the smooth slab above and follow this to gain good holds below the final shallow groove. Go up to the groove and traverse the lip of the roof forming its base (leftwards) then continue left (crux) to gain better holds leading towards the left arete. Gain the diagonal crack in the centre of the slab above to finish.

Comedy Slab

Non-tidal W facing

The black slab bounded on the right by a corner that separates it from the slab of Route One. This is directly opposite the stacks. Start from small ledges in the base of this corner.

Descent: Abseil.

Sea Cliff Climbing for Beginners 30m VS 4c **
T.Carruthers, K.Howett, 2003
Traverse left to start. Climb the shattered crack on immaculate rock up the centre of the slab, exit out a steep corner.

Comedy Duck 30m E1 5b *
K.Howett, T.Carruthers, 2003
Climbs directly up the centre of right side of the slab, just left of the corner. Traverse left off the ledge and boldly climb the centre of the slab to a second horizontal crack. Gain the two cracks which split the centre of the slab above, to under the capping wall. Steeply up a slight corner through this to top out.

The Bretadale burn forms a slight canyon (Death Rattle Gulch) just before dropping into the sea and the north side forms the start of the walls leading round towards a sea stack. This gulch can be crossed southwards from the ledges below this wall to reach a large expanse of non-tidal ledges below a steep west facing wall.

Death Rattle Gulch Area

(NL 624 992)

The routes are on walls either side of the gulch. The south facing wall starts deep within the gulch, where its base is cut off by pools fed by the Glen Bretadale burn (and the sea at exceptional tides and storms). Here it forms a smooth slab capped by a huge roof. Further left the wall continues above a raised platform where the burn joins the sea and more permanent pools.

North Gulch Wall

Non-tidal W & S facing

There are some sheltered, short steep routes. The platform continues as the wall turns a corner and disappears where a black slab drops directly into the sea opposite the sea stacks and this marks the end of the north side of the Gulch Area. Routes are described right to left.

Descent: Abseil.

The Mike McCan't Start 18m HVS 5a
J.Beveridge, T.Carruthers, A.Wilde, 2003
Start above the pool. Climb directly up the front of the buttress to the top corner of Norah Batty.

Norah Batty 18m VS 4b
A.McSherry, M.Howard, 2003
Climb the obvious disjointed corner-line up and slightly right. A steady lead!

Un-named 18m E2 5c
A.Wilde, J.Beveridge, T.Carruthers, 2003
Climbs the thin crack in the centre of the wall left of Norah Batty. Start up the wall just right of the lower crack to the roof. Pull through using holds on the right and follow it with a hard move in the upper wall.

Fat Ankles 18m E2 5b
A.McSherry, M.Howard, A.Wilde, 2003
The wall and overlap left of the thin crack.

Route Two 18m VS 4c *
M.Howard, A.McSherry, 2003
The corner to the left in the angle of the crag as it turns to face west, go through a shallow chimney high up

Orangeman Marty McCann 25m E1 5b
A.McSherry, M.Howard, 2003
A rising right to left line left of Route Two.

Route One 30m E1 5b
M.Howard, A.McSherry, 2003
A rising traverse left of Orangeman Marty McCann. Take a diagonal leftwards line across the top of the slab (under the steeper upper wall) to gain a guano covered ledge in the left arete. Finish in a hanging groove right of the corner bounding Comedy Duck.

Pool Hall Crag

Non-tidal W facing

The walls on the south side of the gulch face west out to sea, lying above large tide free ledges. The main section of interest is a very steep west facing wall.

Descent: As for North Gulch Wall.

Hoodie Rib 20m D
C.Moody, C.Grindley, 15 May 2009
This route unfortunately climbs a mixture of gneiss and basalt and it is poorly protected. At the left side of the wall a toe of rock sticks out. Start up this and climb to a platform (an escape should be possible up the glen from here). Continue up to the left of the arete.

Pot Black 10m E3 6a **
J.Beveridge, T.Stephenson, 2004
The steep groove in the steep wall before the rock turns black and less steep.

On The Black 12m VS
T.Carruthers, S.Tyson, 2004
Start up the slick, black groove to the right of the steep wall, move right onto the alarmingly detached rib and climb carefully.

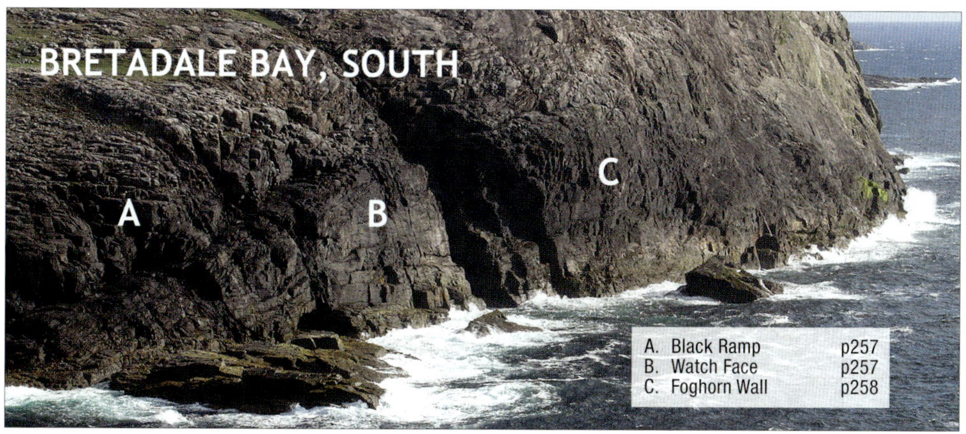

BRETADALE BAY, SOUTH

Map p248

These are the crags on the south side of the bay. The crags and routes are described left to right (east to west).

Black Ramp

Alt 20m N facing Diagram above

South of the stacks is a black ramp which slopes down to the left (east). The base of the routes is higher than most of the crags so they might avoid the sea spray in rough weather.

Descent: Walk down the ramp for about 60m to reach the first sizeable buttress.

Black Eye Corner 14m HVS 5a *
A.Hyslop, C.Moody, 1 Oct 2009
Climb the steep corner on the right-hand side of the buttress to gain ledges. Continue up awkward cracks in the slight corner.

Bleezin Wall 14m E2 5c *
A.Hyslop, C.Moody, 1 Oct 2009
Left of the Black Eye Corner is an overhang at head height, climb the corner left of it then step left and continue to the overhang. Climb the hanging flake above the overhang in the north wall.

An easy line to the left has been climbed by starting up jutting shelves.

Malky the Alky 14m D
C.Moody, 26 May 2010
Right of the overhang of Gubbed is another overhang, between the overhangs is an arete. Climb the right side of the arete then the shallow corner-crack up right.

Gubbed 14m E1 5a *
A.Hyslop, C.Moody, 1 Oct 2009
Down the ramp 20m left of Bleezin Wall is a deep cave like slot. Climb up the back of the slot then continue up cracks in the arete to the left.

Fleein Cracks 14m E2 5c **
A.Hyslop, C.Moody, 1 Oct 2009
Start round left of the deep slot. Climb the short steep crack with a long reach to a horizontal break. Climb the steep parallel cracks above.

Oot Ma Heid 14m D
A.Hyslop, C.Moody, 1 Oct 2009
Start left of the last route. Move up left and step across the chimney. Climb up to cracks in the left wall of the chimney and finish up these.

Watch Face

Tidal NW facing Diagram above

This is the wall below the top of the black ramp.

Descent: At the top of the black ramp is a pile of boulders, about 4m down (east) of the ramp from the last of the pile are twin boulders lying close in to the wall. Abseil from here to a tidal platform; the platform is higher at the left (east) end. To reach the last two routes abseil to a non-tidal ledge from the westmost boulders of the pile.

Time for One More 22m VD *
C.Moody, C.Grindley, 8 May 2010
Start at the left (east) end of the platform. Climb the obvious line up to the left.

Hourglass Crack 30m VS 4b *
C.Moody, C.Grindley, 8 May 2010
Start at the low point of the ledge. Climb the fault above then a finger crack then easier ground.

Lost in Time 24m VS 4b **
C.Moody, C.Grindley, 8 May 2010
Abseil from the pile of boulders to the start of the route. Climb twin cracks then a fine finger-crack.

Who Knows Where the Time Goes? 22m VS 4b **
C.Moody, C.Grindley, 25 May 2010
Start at the right arete of the wall. A bold start gains a horizontal crack, move up and right then climb the crack-line to the ledge.

Foghorn Wall

Alt 15m NW facing Diagram p257

Right (west) of Watch Face is a basalt dyke. Foghorn Wall is west of this and east of the large green slabs. There is a block in the sea which is a useful locator. The first two routes are just east of the block, the other routes are opposite the block.

Approach: From the top of the cliff scramble down from the left or right to avoid a short steep wall at the top, then abseil in. For the first two routes abseil to a ledge from a large, 3m wide, flake leaning against the wall. For the other routes find an anchor point across from the block in the sea and abseil to the ledge. The starting ledges slope down to the right (west).

King Shilling 30m HVS 5a **
P.Whillance, A.Hyslop, C.Grindley, C.Moody, 23 May 2010
Start at the left end of the short ledge. Climb the overhanging crack to a ledge then continue up the corner above.

Penny Black 30m VS 4b **
P.Whillance, A.Hyslop, C.Grindley, C.Moody, 23 May 2010
Start at the right-hand end of the ledge, climb the steep crack-line.

Decimalisation 30m VS 4b **
C.Moody, C.Grindley, 24 May 2010
At the left end of the main ledge is a narrowing. Climb the cracked fault left of this up and slightly right go over a bulge then up.

Crown Corner 30m S 4a *
C.Moody, C.Grindley, 24 May 2010
Start just left of the narrowing in the ledge and climb a left-facing corner-crack then past a bulge with easier climbing above.

Tanners 30m S 4a **
C.Moody, C.Grindley, 23 May 2010
Start at the left end of the ledge, just right of where it narrows. Climb twin cracks.

Florin Flake 30m S 4a **
C.Moody, C.Grindley, 24 May 2010
Climb the line of the flakes then climb up slightly left, step left to avoid the bulge and continue up.

Classic Corner (E3, p262) Pete Whillance (photo Colin Moody)

Half Crown Corner 30m S 4a
C.Moody, C.Grindley, 23 May 2010
About 10m down and right from the twin cracks is a left-facing corner system, climb this. The bulge at the top was avoided by a step right.

Five Bob 30m S 4a **
C.Moody, C.Grindley, 23 May 2010
There are twin cracks 4m right. Climb directly to the shelf then climb the twin cracks.

Gold Guinea 30m S 4a **
C.Moody, C.Grindley, 23 May 2010
Start to the right and climb the left-facing corner-crack.

Penny Tray 50m D *
C.Moody, C.Grindley, 23 May 2010
Start at the right end of the ledge. Follow the shelf rising up right, climb a steep crack then scramble back up left.

WEST END

Map p248

These are the crags at the south-west tip of Barra. They consist of three closely grouped cliffs: Black and Tans Wall, Boulder Walls and Breaker Wall.

Black and Tans Wall

(NL 620 988) Tidal SW facing

North of Boulder Walls a gully cuts through the cliff. This fine wall overlooks the gully to the north of it with a number of ramps on the wall.

Approach: Continue past Breaker Wall to the north.

Descent: Abseil in.

The Darkness Beckons 80m E4 6a ***
P.Whillance, J.Lagoe, 12 Jun 2009
A fine line low in the grade with reasonable but spaced protection. Abseil down from the north end of Boulder Walls at low tide.
1. 30m 6a Climbs the most obvious bottomless crack in the middle of the face. Start right of the crack below the groove in orange rock. Bridge across the gully to gain the wall. Follow the orange groove then climb to the diagonal fault and move up right to place protection. Step down and traverse horizontally left to gain the groove. Follow a crack to ledges on left.
2. 50m 4b Climb up through a band of black rock, then slightly rightwards to the top.

A Second Pitch 45m S 4a *
C.Moody, C.Grindley, 3 May 2010
At the top of the wall are two right-slanting ramps. Abseil to broken ledges at the base of the left-hand ramp. Romp up the ramp to a large flake, escape possible. Climb up a corner on right of the flake then step left and follow a weakness to the overlap, from the right side of the overlap pull up left and continue to the top.

Easy Slab

Alt 50m SW facing

This is the slab on the upper right side of Black and Tans Wall, just above Boulder Walls. The slab is climbable anywhere but the rock is perfect.

Approach: Walk in from the right (east) or uphill from Boulder Walls.

Descent: Walk off to the right (east).

Crevasse Route 16m VD *
C.Moody, C.Grindley, 3 May 2010
Start 10m left of Crescent Climb. Step over the crevasse and climb the slab crossing the slight overlap near the right-hand end.

Pocks 16m HVS 4c *
C.Moody, C.Grindley, 3 May 2010
Start 5m left of Crescent Climb. Climb the slab to the left end of the pock-marked flake then climb the bold slab above.

Crescent Climb 18m VD *
C.Grindley, C.Moody, 3 May 2010
There is a pale block sitting on the slab just above the base; start here. Climb up right to the left-facing corner, carry on up via the left-facing crescent shaped corner-overlap.

Left Block 18m VD *
C.Moody, C.Grindley, 7 May 2010
At the right side of the slab is a long pale block about 1m up. Climb up over the block near the left end then climb a pale streak past another long block below the final bulge. Climb the bulge to easy ground.

Right Block 18m VD *
C.Grindley, C.Moody, 7 May 2010
Climb past the right-hand side of the long block. Finish up the bulge near the right end.

Boulder Walls

Tidal NW facing

Between Black and Tans Wall and Breaker Wall is a length of cliff with huge tidal boulders below.

Descent: Abseil in for most routes.

Diamond Life 35m S 4a *
C.Moody, C.Grindley, 12 Jun 2009
Roughly in the centre of the wall is a large right angled corner with a huge diamond shaped block in the sea below. Abseil into a ledge at the base of the chimney (unclimbed corner-crack below). Climb the chimney to ledges then climb the wide crack in the corner.

Left Corner 20m S 4a
C.Grindley, C.Moody, 12 Jun 2009
This and the next two routes start on big ledges halfway up Diamond Life on the south side of that route; abseil to the ledge. Start up the corner just left of Angry Skies (the first obvious line right of the upper half of Diamond Life) then follow Angry Skies for a couple of moves and move left to a large platform. Climb the corner-crack on the left.

Angry Skies 20m S 4a *
C.Moody, C.Grindley, 12 Jun 2009
Left of Carat are easy corners. Climb the right-hand corners.

Carat 16m VS 4b **
C.Grindley, C.Moody, 12 Jun 2009
Climb the corner-ramp in the middle of the wall up left to a ledge then climb the bulging crack above.

Escape 40m M *
C.Grindley, 12 Jun 2009
Walk left of Breaker Wall at low tide to the second boulder along. Climb pleasantly up a choice of routes.

The Bouldering Cave

Alt 25m W facing

This is a short cliff of overhanging rock above the right end of The Boulder Walls.

Descent: The choices are: Traverse left (west) from the top of the left-hand routes on Breaker Wall; Scramble down and left (west) from above the left end of Breaker Wall; or abseil in.

Stalactite 14m E2 5c **
C.Grindley, C.Moody, 7 May 2010
Start 2m right of the big boulder at the left side of the cliff. Climb up then move awkwardly right onto a protruding ledge. Climb the steep wall above.

Snottite 10m HVS 4b *
C.Moody, C.Grindley, 7 May 2010
A difficult route to grade, climbing on big holds but overhanging with awkward protection so potentially serious. Start 3m left of the long block at the right-hand side of the cliff. Climb overhanging flakes to the left-facing flake-crack. Pull over this then continue easily.

Thag 10m VS 5a
C.Moody, C.Grindley, 2 May 2010
Stand on the long block. Pull onto the undercut wall then continue up.

Gog 10m VS 5a
C.Moody, C.Grindley, 7 May 2010
Start 1m right of the long block. Pull up then climb the short corner and continue up to the left.

BREAKER WALL

(NL 620 987) Partially Tidal SW facing
Map p248 Diagrams below & opposite

This fine wall is the most westerly on Barra. There are reefs out to sea so breakers form in some sea states. The base is a large platform. The north end has some huge barnacle covered boulders (the start of Boulder Walls) and the south end is tidal. Many routes finish at a ledge after 20m, a 20m scramble then leads to the top.

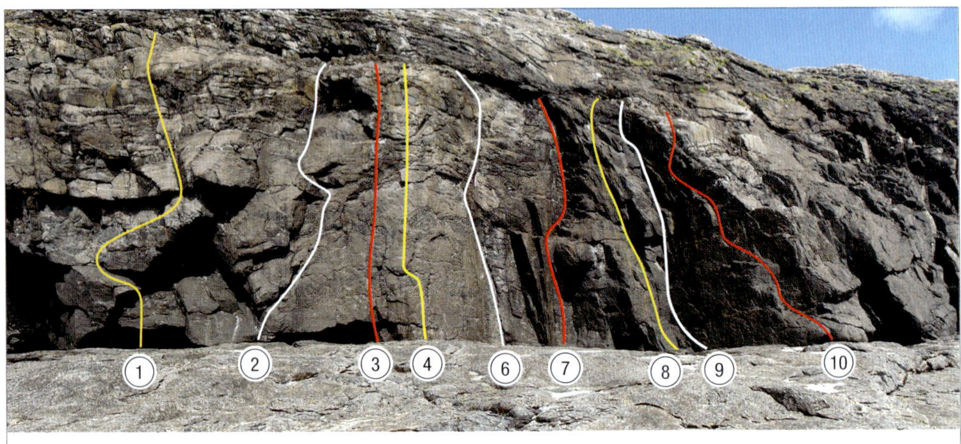

Breaker Wall Left

1. Potted Haugh	HVS 5a **	4. Rib Eye	E1 5a **	8. Frigger's Climb	E1 5a *
2. Sirloin	HVS 5a **	6. Druth's Groove	E2 5b ***	9. Pool Corner	HS 4b **
3. Rump	E1 5a **	7. In Black	HVS 5a **	10. Pool Ramps	VS 4b *

Approach: From the causeway, cross a fence and walk along faint tracks on the north side of the coast (Loch Caolas Bhatarsaigh). Where the coast starts to get craggy gain some height then drop down to the top of the cliff, 40min from the causeway.

Descent: Abseil in, from any of several places to make anchors in the rocks.

The first four routes climb the pillar at the left side.

1 Potted Haugh 20m HVS 5a **
C.Moody, C.Grindley, 2 May 2010
Nice exposed climbing after a brutal start. Left of Sirloin is an undercut slab, left again is a very undercut triangular slab. Gain the triangular slab with difficulty then climb up slightly left to an overhang. Traverse right below the overhang till below a corner-crack on the edge, climb the corner-crack then up to the ledge.

2 Sirloin 20m HVS 5a **
C.Moody, C.Grindley, 17 May 2009
A fine varied climb, starting at a recess in the centre of the pillar at the north end of the wall. Climb up to a triangular block then step left, continue up the corner slightly right to finish over a bulge to the ledge.

3 Rump 20m E1 5a **
C.Grindley, C.Moody, 11 Jun 2009
Steeply climb the crack just left of the arete to an easing of the angle, climb bulges then up to the ledge.

4 Rib Eye 20m E1 5a **
C.Moody, C.Grindley, 17 May 2009
This climbs the left arete of the pillar. Start just right of the arete at a crack. Climb up the crack for a couple of moves then step left and climb steeply to the ledge.

5 Drop In 20m E3 6a **
S.Crowe, K.Magog, 14 Jun 2009
Sustained crimping up the wall left of the leaning corner. Turn the roof at 12m on the left or finish direct.

6 Druth's Groove 20m E2 5b ***
A.Hyslop, J.Lagoe, C.Grindley, C.Moody, 11 Jun 2009
This is low in the grade and gives fine sustained climbing. Climb the steep left-leaning corner, then continue up and slightly right to a step left below the roof to gain the ledge.

7 In Black 25m HVS 5a **
A.Hyslop, J.Lagoe, 11 Jun 2009
Climb up to then through the open chimney, go up the open groove above then pull out right over the bulge.

8 Frigger's Climb 25m E1 5a *
C.Moody, C.Grindley, 11 Jun 2009
Step left above the pool (as for the next route) head up left to climb the brown-stained rib. There is an awkward move at the top and some of the runner placements are not obvious.

9 Pool Corner 20m HS 4b **
C.Moody, C.Grindley, 16 May 2009
To the right of the pillar is a bay, this route climbs the obvious corner at the right side of the bay. Step left above a pool to gain the corner.

10 Pool Ramps 20m VS 4b *
C.Grindley, C.Moody, 1 Sep 2017
Pull onto the shelf left of The Green Boulderer then move left along it. Climb steep corners and ramps to finish just right of Pool Corner.

11 The Green Boulderer 20m VS 4b *
C.Moody, C.Grindley, 16 May 2009
Climb the rib through two bulges to easier ground.

12 Rain Stops Play 20m S 4a *
C.Moody, C.Grindley, 15 May 2009
Climb the recessed corner then easier ground.

13 Escape Direct 20m S 4a *
C.Moody, C.Grindley, 16 May 2009
The rib right of Rain Stops Play.

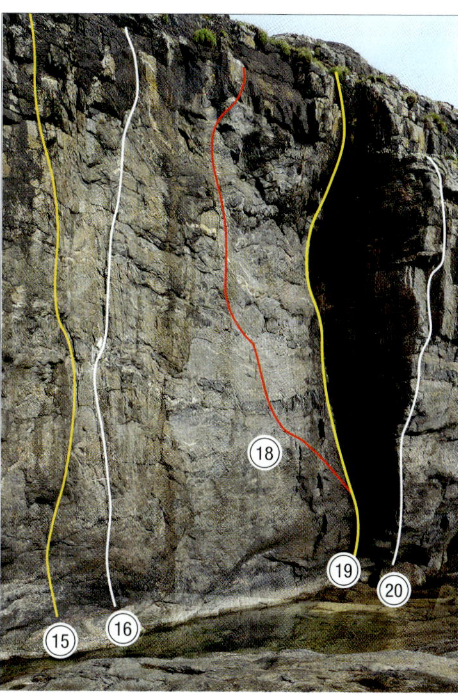

Breaker Wall Right

15.	Party Wave	E4 6a **
16.	Rock Dance	E3 6a **
18.	Missing Musketeers	E3 6a **
19.	Classic Corner	E3 5c ***
20.	Impact Zone	E6 6b ***

14 Escape Route 20m D *
Start at the left side of the rib as for the previous route then climb out right. Follow the crack-line up.

The last routes have tidal starts.

15 Party Wave 35m E4 6a **
S.Crowe, K.Magog, 14 Jun 2009
Start 3m left of Rock Dance. Difficult moves lead up to a small roof. Trend up and right to a shallow groove and a junction with Rock Dance. Follow the groove for a few metres then pull out left to a steep finish.

16 Rock Dance 35m E3 6a **
K.Magog, S.Crowe, 14 Jun 2009
Pull over the initial steep black bulge then make some crimpy moves to a shallow groove and a junction with Party Wave. Continue to a good ledge. Trend up and rightwards to a tricky finish.

17 Old Codger 35m E3 5c *
J.Walker, G.Tyldesley, 9 Jun 2011
Climb the layback flake right of Rock Dance, starting from a tidal island in the middle of a rock pool. From the top of the flake move up and left to finish up Rock Dance or move further left and finish up Party Wave (E2 5b).

18 Missing Musketeers 35m E3 6a **
I.Taylor, T.Fryer, 9 Jun 2011
Go up Classic Corner for 5m, traverse left and go up a thin flake in the middle of the wall to good holds. Go up, then left and pull rightwards through the capping bulge.

19 Classic Corner 35m E3 5c ***
P.Whillance, A.Hyslop, C.Grindley, J.Lagoe, 11 Jun 2009
The stunning left-facing corner-crack at the right side of the wall, low in the grade. The finish is overhanging.

20 Impact Zone 35m E6 6b ***
S.Crowe, K.Magog, 16 Jun 2009
The impressive right arete. A powerful start soon merges into a sustained and technical sequence of moves switching up either side of the arete. This eventually leads to a bold finish on the right.

FEUDAIL

(NL 636 979) Alt 50m SE & SW facing Map p248 Diagram opposite

This is the obvious cliff west of the causeway, it is clearly seen from Vatersay and might offer climbing when many of the sea-cliffs are exposed to the elements.

Approach: Walk west from the causeway to reach the crag, 5min.

1 Flower Power 12m VD
P.Wood, B.Davison, 6 Jun 2015
Walk left from Wild Iris Wall to reach two crack-lines. Climb the left-hand crack.

2 Powerful Poppy 12m VD *
C.Moody, C.Grindley, 3 May 2010
Climb the more prominent right-hand crack.

Wild Iris Wall

This is the main south-east facing wall.

3 Venus Midge Trap 20m VD
C.Moody, 3 May 2010
Climb short steep cracks in the arete at the left end of the wall (where the crag changes direction) and continue up the slabs.

4 Violet Crack 20m VS 4c *
A.Hyslop, P.Whillance, C.Grindley, C.Moody, 25 May 2010
At the left end of the wall are twin cracks. Climb the crack left of the twin cracks (right of red seams) then continue up the slab.

5 Heather Cracks 20m HVS 5a **
A.Hyslop, P.Whillance, C.Grindley, C.Moody, 25 May 2010
Climb the twin cracks at the left side of the wall.

6 When The Boat Comes In 20m E1 5a
P.Tanton, T.Doldone, 6 Jun 2015
Start 5m right of Heather Crack and climb the wall and the two faint cracks in the upper half of the wall.

7 Arny Flapcans 20m E1 5b
M.Payne, P.Fleuriot, 6 Jun 2015
This climbs the slim bottomless slot between When The Boat Comes In and Crazy Daisy. Awkward gear placements in the lower half lead past a slot to a horizontal break near the top.

8 Crazy Daisy 20m HVS 5a *
P.Whillance, A.Hyslop, C.Grindley, C.Moody, 26 May 2010
In the centre of the wall is a grass patch above head height. Start left of the grass patch. Move up right past the left end of the grass then climb the corner past a small overhang. Good varied climbing.

9 Rambling Rose 20m E1 5b *
P.Whillance, A.Hyslop, C.Grindley, C.Moody, 26 May 2010
Start as for the last route then traverse right on the grass patch. Climb up the recess to a small overhang then traverse right on a footledge, with poor holds, to reach a flake. Climb up and exit left.
Variation: **Direct Rambling 20m VS 4c**
P.Wood, B.Davison, 6 Jun 2015
Start 4m right of Rambling Rose and climb the wall just right of a shallow left-facing corner to a grass ledge. Step left to a flake and finish direct as for Rambling Rose.

Upper Tier

SW facing

10 Ivy Groove 12m S 4a
B.Davison, 6 Jun 2015
Climb the shallow open groove up the wall 2m left of Interflora.

11 Interflora 12m S 4a
C.Moody, C.Grindley, 3 May 2010
Start at the right side of the upper tier (above and right

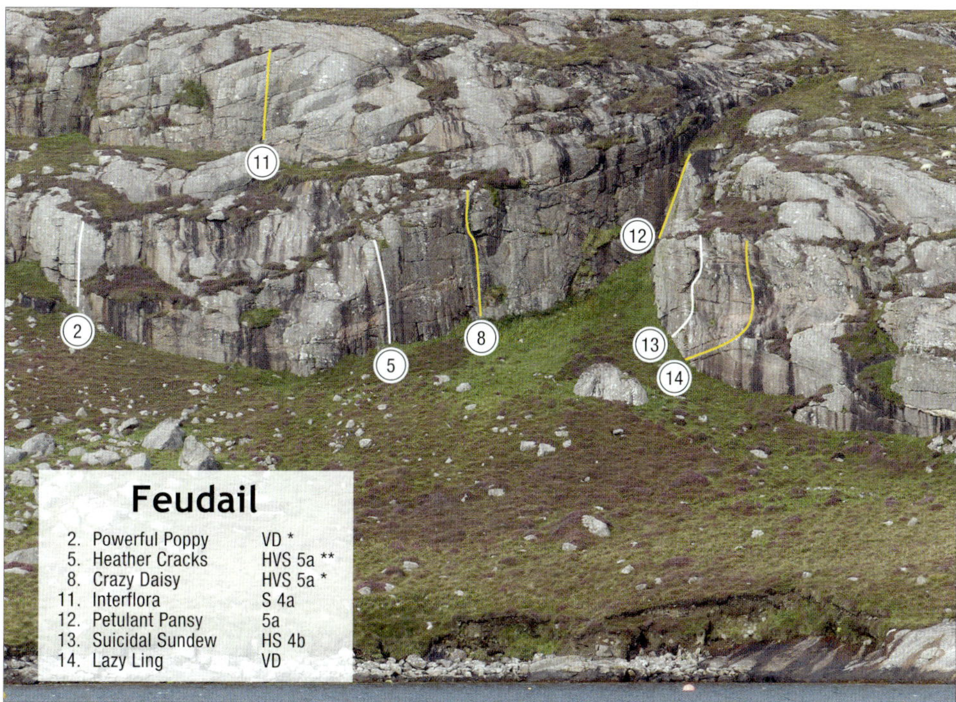

of Powerful Poppy). Climb the corner-crack to a good ledge on the right, continue in the same line to the top.

Right-Hand Crag

The broken slabby wall right of Wild Iris Wall.

12 Petulant Pansy 10m 5a
P.Whillance, 25 May 2010
At the top right end of Wild Iris Wall is a deep crack. Climb the middle of the short slab just right.

13 Suicidal Sundew 20m HS 4b
C.Moody, C.Grindley, P.Whillance, 26 May 2010
Start up left from Lazy Ling. Follow a ledge right then move up slightly right on ledges. Climb the steep wall past slanting crack (this is right of a steep flake-crack) to a ledge, then finish up the bulge above.

14 Lazy Ling 20m VD
P.Whillance, A.Hyslop, 26 May 2010
Traverse right at an obvious horizontal crack then climb the slab. A direct start was climbed up a black streak at 5b.

15 Gracias 20m VD
C.Moody, C.Grindley, 26 May 2010
Start at a grass ramp to the right. Move right above a short steep wall then follow the slab leftwards then up. The direct finish is hard and was avoided (by the leader) by an escape up right.

VATERSAY

Vatersay is the island just to the south of Barra, joined to it by a causeway.

BLACK WATER GULCH

(NL 614 968) Tidal

Black Water Gulch is a narrow geo with steep black walls on either side.

Approach: From Caolas at the north end of the island follow the road west till it ends at a gate at **(NL 623 973)**. Walk across the next field, around the beach at Tràigh Bhàirlais, then follow a vague coastal path westwards to reach a prominent north facing sea inlet. A pleasant 15min walk.

East Face

An impressive wall of steep crack-lines and one very obvious corner.

Graphite Corner 25m E2 5c **
P.Whillance, C.Grindley, 13 May 2011
Takes the obvious right-facing corner on the left side of the wall. Abseil down the line to a small ledge about 12m above sea-level (semi-hanging belay). Follow the corner throughout, steep and sustained.

Coalite Crack 25m E1 5b *
P.Whillance, C.Grindley, 13 May 2011
Access and belay as for Graphite Corner. Climb the corner for 5m then follow the slanting crack diagonally rightwards across the wall. Pull over a small overlap to reach a large flake then go direct up the final wall with a long reach for the top.

Copper-Bottomed Chimney 20m VS 4c *
P.Whillance, C.Grindley, 10 May 2011
Take the right-facing corner and chimney-line towards the right side (seaward end) of the wall. Abseil down the line to a big, rust coloured, non-tidal ledge at the base of the square chimney. Climb the chimney and continue up wide twin cracks to reach the right-hand end of a long ledge. Go up the short crack on the right to the top.

SWALLOW COVE

(NL 613 967) Partially Tidal NW facing Map p246

The Cove consists of a wide amphitheatre of rock and can be viewed as a number of separate crags of different character, at different levels above the sea. For convenience they are described here as Lower Wall, Right Side; Lower Wall, Central; Lower Wall, Left Side; Upper Wall, Rusty Slab; and Upper Wall, The Buttress. Only the Lower Wall, Left Side is affected by tide.

Approach: From Black Water Gulch continue along the rising coastal track for another 5min to reach the big north-west facing inlet of Swallow Cove. Access to the Upper Wall is by descending the boulder strewn slope (care with loose stones) in the middle of the Cove. The Lower Wall can be reached by steep scrambling descents but is perhaps best gained by abseil.

Lower Wall, Right Side

This consists of a black wall with several prominent crack and corner-lines. The base is non-tidal and covered with large boulders. It extends from a deep gully-dyke line at the right-hand end to an easy chimney-ramp descent on the left (directly below the Upper Wall descent slope). Routes are described from right to left.

Sounds of Vatersay 25m HVS 5a **
P.Whillance, C.Grindley, 9 May 2011
Start a few metres left of the deep gully-dyke line, below a blunt arete. Step across from a boulder and climb steeply up ledges on the right edge of the overhanging wall until it is possible to traverse left across a slab to reach the base of a prominent corner. Climb this to the top, a good, improbable looking route.

Annie Jane 25m E2 5c **
P.Whillance, C.Grindley, 9 May 2011
Start as for Sounds of Vatersay. Step across and up steeply for a few metres, then go up left to an overhung ledge below a thin hanging crack. Pull steeply over the bulge (crux) and up the slab leftwards to the base of a V-groove. Climb this to the top, another good route.

The prominent deep chimney of The Causeway is 15m left, providing the starts for the next three routes.

Shipwrecked 20m VS 4c
P.Whillance, C.Grindley, 9 May 2011
Climb the deep chimney on its left side for 5m until it is possible to bridge across and gain a big ledge out to the right. Move right along the ledge a few metres to a corner and follow this to the top.

On the Beach 20m VS 5a
P.Whillance, C.Grindley, 9 May 2011
Start as for Shipwrecked to gain the big ledge on the right of the chimney. Follow twin cracks on the left side of the wall to gain a ledge overlooking the chimney. Move up right and finish around the right side of a hanging prow.

The Causeway 20m VS 4b
P.Whillance, C.Grindley, 9 May 2011
Follows the prominent deep chimney-line throughout.

Just left of The Causeway is an easy chimney-ramp descent that separates the Central and Right Side of the Lower Wall.

Lower Wall, Left Side

The Lower Wall, Left Side is tidal and forms an impressive clean sheet of rock with a line of overhangs near the top. On its left is a short, easy-angled pink corner above largely non-tidal ledges. This corner and the chimney to its right are Difficult in standard and can be used as a means of descent or abseil approach for accessing the next route.

Ocean Drive 25m E2 5c **
P.Whillance, C.Grindley, 13 May 2011
Takes an open groove leading to a hanging flake groove in its upper section, just right of the ledges at the foot of the easy chimney. Step right onto the wall and go up to a good ledge, then move rightwards across the wall to another ledge. Move up over an overlap to gain a flake-crack and ledge. Make a long stride back left to gain the hanging flake groove line. Climb this steeply to ledges and easy ground.

Upper Wall, Rusty Slab

SW facing

A short, brown-coloured fin-slab of rock situated in the middle of the amphitheatre and easily accessed down the central boulder-strewn slope. The rock is superb though the protection is somewhat sparse.

Hirondelle 12m VS 4c
P.Whillance, C.Grindley, 11 May 2011
Takes the obvious line up the left-hand side of the slab.

Start easily up ledges and finish with an awkward move to reach a good ledge on the rib on the left. Scramble off up rightwards.

Out of Africa 12m VS 4c *
P.Whillance, C.Grindley, 13 May 2011
Climbs the thin, rightwards-slanting crack in the middle of the slab. Excellent climbing, with the crux at the top. The lower part can be avoided by starting from a crack up to the right, but why would you want to do that?

Upper Wall, The Buttress

The Buttress is the large area of rock immediately above and to the left of Rusty Slab.

Migration 30m VS 4c
P.Whillance, C.Grindley, 11 May 2011
Takes a rightward-trending line of cracks and corners. Start at a large ledge a few metres left of Hirondelle. Step up right, then move left onto a steep wall and up to gain a large ledge at the foot of the first corner. Climb the corner then traverse right on ledges for 7m to below a curving crack. Up this and a steep corner above to emerge on easy slabs at the top.

GOLDEN WALL

(NL 615 964) Alt 20m SW facing

This fine little wall of golden rock is useful as it is not subjected to the same amount of sea spray as the lower crags.

Approach: Start from the same parking as Black Water Gulch **(NL 623 973)**. Walk south-west then walk over the hill then back left (east) for a short time to reach the crags. Walk down either side.

Copper 12m D
C.Moody, 29 Sep 2009
Start at the left side of the wall. Climb the left-trending crack. There is an easier route to the left.

Kori 12m VS 4c *
C.Grindley, C.Moody, 29 Sep 2009
Climb the fine crack to the right.

Golden Retriever 12m S 4a
P.Whillance, A.Hyslop, 27 May 2010
Climb the obvious groove up the right-hand side of the wall.

ORIGINAL WALL

(NL 621 943) Partially Tidal S facing Map p246

A handful of routes have been climbed here, there is a cairn on the hillside above. The routes were recorded in 2009 but had probably been climbed before.

Approach: Start at the north end of Vatersay village. Walk west along the marked footpath, rise up to the south-west then drop down to the top of the cliffs. These routes are on the least broken cliff, north-west of the big sea-cliff on Beinn Ruilibreac.

Descent: Abseil

Cairn Wall 20m VS 4b *
C.Grindley, C.Moody, 16 Apr 2009
Climb the wall on the left-hand side following a vague corner-line.

Cairn Right 20m S 4a **
C.Grindley, C.Moody, 16 Apr 2009
Climb the wall to the right.

Left Cairn Corner 20m VD *
C.Grindley, C.Moody, 16 Apr 2009
At the right side of the wall are two corners. Climb left of the left-hand corner then up cracks.

Right Cairn Corner 20m S 4a
C.Grindley, C.Moody, 16 Apr 2009
The right-hand corner-crack.

DYKE AREA

(NL 621 940) Non-tidal W facing

South of the above routes is a high area of cliff, and south of this is a 2m wide black dyke that runs south forming a dip, rising up then down again.

Sunny Rib 20m S 4a *
C.Grindley, C.Moody, 16 Apr 2009
Start at the dip in the dyke below two easy left-slanting crack-lines. Climb the rib between the two cracks, pleasant but escapable.

Rising Dyke 20m VD *
C.Grindley, C.Moody, 16 Apr 2009
Start in the same dip as the previous route. Follow the right side of the black dyke as it rises to the south. The fault continues to the south forming vertical walls rising from the sea, with ledges that birds nest on.

BOULDERING

AIRFIELD (NF 699 048)

Problems have been climbed on a boulder near the airfield. The boulder is fairly prominent and can be seen from various locations to the south. Park at **(NF 698 052)** off the road and walk south-east up the hillside for 500m.

JUNCTION WALLS (NL 628 982) Alt 20m SW facing

At the junction of the routes to Breaker Wall and Bretadale Bay. These leaning walls have been played on a little.

CLACH NA CREEL (NL 637 977) Alt 20m

There are some green boulders just west of the causeway, less than 5min walk.

THE BISHOP'S ISLES

These are the Islands of Sandray (Sanndraigh), Lingay (Lingeigh), Pabbay (Pabaigh), Mingulay (Miùghlaigh) and Berneray (Bearnaraigh).

Maps: Ordnance Survey Maps 1:50,000: Landranger 31; 1:25,000: Explorer 452

Lying towards the southern end of the Outer Hebrides island chain, this collection of beautiful and remote islands is also known as The Barra Isles.

Barra is connected to its close southern neighbour Vatersay by a causeway, and these two southernmost inhabited islands have a population of over 1,000. To the south lie a series of uninhabited islands, the first of which is Sandray. There follows a longer stretch of sea leading to Pabbay (the Priest Island), then the notorious Sound of Mingulay followed by the island of Mingulay. South of Mingulay lies the most southern island in the Outer Hebridean chain, Berneray, which is locally known as Barra Head, there being several other islands called Berneray in the Hebrides. All these islands offer excellent sea-cliffs of immaculate, weathered Lewisian Gneiss. All are described in this book except Lingeigh, which is found online; see cover for details.

Natural History: Mingulay and Pabbay were designated Sites of Special Scientific Interest (SSSI) in 1983 and further designated under the EU Habitats Directive as a Special Protection Area in 1994, mainly due to the presence of large numbers of breeding sea birds. If you are interested in birds, you will be pleased to hear that Pabbay, Mingulay and Berneray all support large colonies of puffin, razorbill, fulmar, kittiwake, shag, guillemot (including black guillemot), storm petrel, shearwater, four species of gull and many others. Climbers should take care not to disturb these colonies, although the climbing is likely to be particularly guano-covered and so not attractive. Breeding commences in March for some species, but the majority start nesting in May, and are usually present until mid-July.

Twitchers will also be interested in the fact that Pabbay and Mingulay also have large populations of ground nesting birds. There are great skuas (bonxies) nesting on the summit grass of the hills, and the rare corncrake in the reeds of lazy beds. Numerous snipe, rock pipit, skylark, starling and wren can be found nestingg in the ruins of the cottages, and eider duck often nest inland on the promontories. Buzzard and eagle (including sea eagle) can also be seen hunting on most of the islands.

The islands are also home to large numbers of common seal, which should not be disturbed. Seal pups will be found apparently abandoned; they are not abandoned and must be left alone.

The Bishop's Isles (photo Mike Webster)

The birds are incredibly tolerant of humans compared with those on the mainland. Even so, the majority of routes have been climbed on those crags which are free of nesting birds or on areas of cliff where the routes do not directly disturb any nesting sites.

The larger colonies of gull, Fulmar and Kittiwake are usually shared by Razorbill and Guillemot. These colonies are obvious by their acres of guano and are best avoided (they are in any case highly unpleasant places to climb, even after the nesting period!).

Puffin, razorbill and guillemot sometimes nest as individual pairs, scattered over the more broken areas of cliff which offer little interest for climbing, but they also nest in small groups on horizontal ledges on steep and otherwise impressive climbing venues. Here again they are obvious, and climbing directly through a nesting ledge should be avoided during the nesting period, although climbing to the side seems to cause no disturbance. In fact the birds will be very inquisitive and will rarely fly off as long as you remain relatively quiet and don't surprise them.

In some areas a single pair of guillemot or razorbill will nest on a small ledge. These birds lay eggs directly onto bare ledges, incubating them by placing the eggs on top of their feet. When startled by an approaching climber the eggs can be dislodged and lost forever in the sea. It is best to make an effort to search for these birds on the line of your chosen route whilst abseiling in, and to not continue if they are found. If, after doing everything possible, you do encounter them en-route, do your best to limit disturbance in these situations. Sections of the Giant's Pipes cliff on Berneray are a good example of where care should be taken.

Corncrake is probably the rarest species encountered and it is best to avoid the taller foliage of lazy beds as much as possible to reduce any disturbance. You will know if they are in residence, as their distinctive croak will keep you awake all night and camping well away from these areas also ensures you get undisturbed sleep! The sound of snipe 'drumming' cannot be avoided and will keep light sleepers awake no matter where you camp.

Many archaeological artefacts litter these islands. On Pabbay, neolithic chambered tombs have been identified, and a 6th-century Pictish symbol stone; a similar stone has been found on Berneray. Iron Age evidence has been excavated from a midden beside the village on Mingulay along with coins and bronze pins, from the Early Christian or Pictish period. The islands were stocked with sheep in 1911 and the following summer the last inhabitants departed. The Barra Isles Sheepstock Company owned the island and sheep remained until 1999. In April 2000 Mingulay, Pabbay, and Berneray were sold to the National Trust for Scotland who removed all but a handful of the, now feral, sheep.

The abandoned cottages that make up the village in Mingulay, like the other island village areas, are Scheduled Monuments. While they have become filled with sand in relatively recent times, it is important not to disturb any ruins, and not to use them as shelters or latrines as they are important to the local people of Barra as a memorial to those who lived on the island many years ago. The islands and buildings are still visited regularly by descendants to remember their forbears, so please don't disturb them in any way, and treat all these ancient sites with respect;. Apart from visits for day trips, climbers have become the 'inhabitants', albeit transitory, of these island.

Camping and Health Issues: The National Trust for Scotland (NTS) now own and manage the islands of Pabbay, Mingulay and Berneray. The following advice is issued as a guide from the NTS and the Mountaineering Scotland.

Ensure your visit has as little impact on the islands as possible. Follow advice about wild camping and sanitation in the outdoors so as not to pollute the available water supplies. Take ALL your rubbish back off the island with you; don't be tempted to burn it.

Camping: On Mingulay the preferred climbers' campsite is on the flat ground beside the old school house (the small habitable cottage to the south of the bay) and not near the remains of the old village. On Pabbay the preferred area is to the south of the stream in the village bay. Open fires should ONLY be lit on the beach.

Obviously there are no toilets on the islands. If you are a small group, then using common sense and advice given by Mountaineering Scotland and Scottish Natural Heritage will suffice. Large groups of eight or more need to think seriously about digging latrines. The main issue

here is where to place them and how best to operate them. Good advice on this is contained in 'The Expedition Handbook' by the Expedition Advisory Service, and NTS suggest the best area to bury human waste is in the inter-tidal zone on the beach.

Fresh water burns exist on Sandray, Pabbay and Mingulay and can usually be relied upon throughout the summer, except during droughts. They have proven to be drinkable without chemical treatment (but after boiling) so far and every effort should be made to keep them clean. There are two old wells on Berneray, neither of which are clean and they can dry to stagnant pools in summer. Take enough water to last your trip. There is little or no running water on Lingeigh, unless it has been very wet.

The island of Pabbay used to be infested with various species of tick. In places, particularly around the flat grassy area near the beach, they were a real nuisance, but this seems to have abated in recent years. Although there is no evidence that the island's ticks carry Lyme disease, care should be taken between May and September.

All the islands suffer to some extent with midges, although Berneray seems the worst; hope for a slight breeze.

The islands are prone to fairly constant winds and this, in sunny weather with reflection off the sea, can quickly lead to sunburn, not something normally associated with Scotland. If you are fair skinned, take precautions.

Emergencies: Because of the remoteness relative to rescue, come prepared with an expedition-scale first aid kit in case the worst should happen, as mobile phone reception is poor to non-existent. There is an Orange mast in the north-west of Barra and this can sometimes allow reception from Mingulay and Pabbay, although freak O2 reception has been found on occasion from Sandray. The remote situation should not be underestimated, and climbers could consider some other means of communication such as marine band VHF or satellite phone. As a minimum it is worth taking some flares for serious situations (there is a lifeboat based in Castlebay).

Despite all of the above possible options for getting help, none can be completely relied upon. The weather can be extreme and groups have been known to be stranded with little food, so come prepared and be self-sufficient.

Climbing Ethics: From its earliest development in 1993 most ascents have been on-sight, an approach adhered to by most activists. While a few pegs have been placed, in-situ gear is uncommon, probably a wise policy given the hostile and corrosive nature of the environment. There is generally ample natural protection on most routes and if a line is too unprotected for you, then it is best left for bolder future climbers to on-sight.

Access to the climbs: Descent to most of the cliff bases has involved abseiling, as they are inaccessible without calm seas and a boat. A 150m static rope is long enough for most of the larger cliffs on Mingulay, but descent to Creag na Beastie on Berneray requires a rope of over 250m. Rope protectors are essential as the rock is incredibly rough. Stakes are generally unnecessary as there are usually ample natural belays. Where descent is possible by foot (or scrambling, sea-level traversing) then this is the described method.

Access: Barra is served by a regular ferry service from Oban, and by flights. To get to the islands south of Barra requires either a private yacht or a boat charter from Barra (although a few hardy folk have paddled out and climbed). The best months for access to these islands are likely to be May to September. Outside this period the seas are generally too rough to make the necessary landings. In 2017 the main charter boat available was the Boy James, skippered by Francis Gillies. Francis transports groups of tourists, twitchers and climbers out to the islands during the summer months, from April until he finishes for the season at the end of September. The boat is capable of carrying 12 people plus gear, and runs out of Castlebay. Contact Francis directly (tel: 01871 810679 (W) or 07970 554147 (M) or email: **mingulayboattrips@outlook.com**).

Camping on Mingulay (photo Rob Greenwood)

Razorbill & Puffin
(photo Cynthia Grindley)

The Priest (E1) The Great Arch, Pabbay
Mike Hammell & Martin Kocsis (photo George Gilmore)

SANDRAY (SANNDRAIGH)

This small, uninhabited island lies some 8km to the south of Barra. There are several beautiful beaches on the island. The biggest beaches lie on the east side, one to the north and one to the south connected by extensive sand dunes. The islands are still owned by the Barra Islands Sheepstock Company, and sheep are grazed here through the year.

There are no huge crags on this island but it does offer particularly immaculate rock. The climbs are concentrated on the west coast towards the south-west tip with a few smaller ones on the south coast. The cliffs are described starting in the north and running in order down the west coast and then along the south coast.

Camping: The best campsite for visiting climbers lies in the bay in the north-west corner, beside the remains of the old village of Sheader, with a large area of flat machair and reliable fresh water in a small stream on the hillside to the east. However, there is also a good water supply from the beautiful Lochan nan Cuilce beside The Galleries and better fresh running water can be had on the south coast from the small stream of Gleann Mòr beside the deep water solo crag.

RUBHA SHEADAIR

The headland to the west of Sheader shelters the campsite from any westerly winds, and forms the extreme north-west tip of the island. On the west side of its highest point are a series of easily accessible walls.

The Rune Stones Cliff

(NL 629 921) Partially Tidal SW facing
Diagrams p272, p273, p274 & p275

This is a series of three distinct walls separated by steeper right-angled walls between them, forming corners and aretes. Huge rounded boulders litter the base of the cliff below the main central area, inspiring the name. A rock ramp lies below the most northerly section, named Lifeline Wall, whilst the middle wall has been named Stone Wall. The southern wall, Shark Skin Wall, is wave-washed at all tides.

Descent: Gain Lifeline Wall and Stone Wall from the north, down a ramp with a boulder at its base. Climbs above the ramp are accessible at all tides. Beyond this access is possible from mid-tide by boulder hopping across to Stone Wall. Shark Skin Wall is gained from the south down a deep gully.

Lifeline Wall

Lifeline Wall is undercut by a roof along its entire length above the ramp. The wall increases in height and turns a slight angle where the ramp steepens to drop into a permanent rock pool at the base, surrounded by boulders.

The first substantial piece of rock is an orange-coloured wall, just right of this boulder. To its right is a bulging buttress. Right again it is undercut by a roof, which increases in size, a horizontal flake-crack being very prominent. Right of this is a big but broken right to left fault, followed by two further smaller faults. The wall then turns a slight angle and the ramp drops into

View of Skye from Sandray (photo Ron Kenyon)

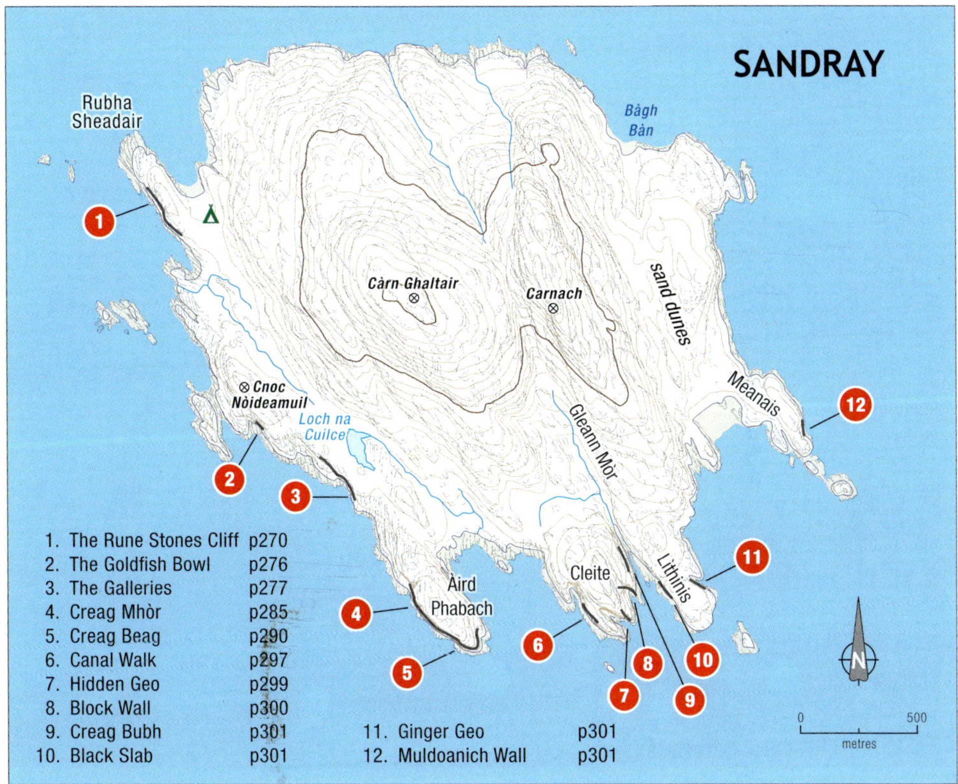

the rock pool. The most prominent feature on the wall above the pool is a stepped fault cutting left to right. Below this, just above the pool, is a sentry box recess capped by a roof. The routes are described left to right as approached down the ramp.

1 First Born First 10m S 4a
R.K.Howett, 3 Jun 2007
Right of the boulder, the orange wall is bounded on its left by a vertical corner-fault, leading onto the descent ramp. Climb the wall on jugs leading right into the corner.

2 Eden Valley Sub Aqua Club 15m VS 4c
T.Carruthers, S.Tyson, 26 May 2002
The crispy, orange-coloured wall starting up a tiny left diagonal crack is finished direct.

3 Agent Orange 15m VS 4c **
T.Carruthers, M.Howard, 13 Sep 2001
The obvious crack through the orange wall.

4 Super Soaker 15m VS 5a *
R.K.Howett, K.Howett, 31 May 2015
Start up Birth Stone to the ledge. Follow the diagonal line leftwards into the top of Agent Orange.

5 Birth Stone 15m E1 5a **
K.Howett, T.Rankin, 17 May 2000
Climbs direct up the steep bulging buttress right of the orange wall. Strenuous.

6 Horizontal Pleasures 15m VS 5a *
T.Carruthers, M.Howard, 13 Sep 2001
A corner and bulge above. A hard start through the roof.

7 The Complete Angler 15m VS 5a
T.Carruthers, S.Tyson, 26 May 2002
The right arete of Horizontal Pleasures, starting up that route.
Variation: **Direct Start E3 6a/b**
K.Howett 27 May 2002
Climb direct through the roof and a slot to gain the arete. A high boulder problem, serious without a mat.

8 Horizontal Horizons 15m E2 5c **
T.Rankin, K.Howett, 17 May 2000
Climb the obvious horizontal flake rightwards under the roof onto a ledge in the lip. Pull steeply into a standing position and jugs then head up the steep wall above. Strenuous.

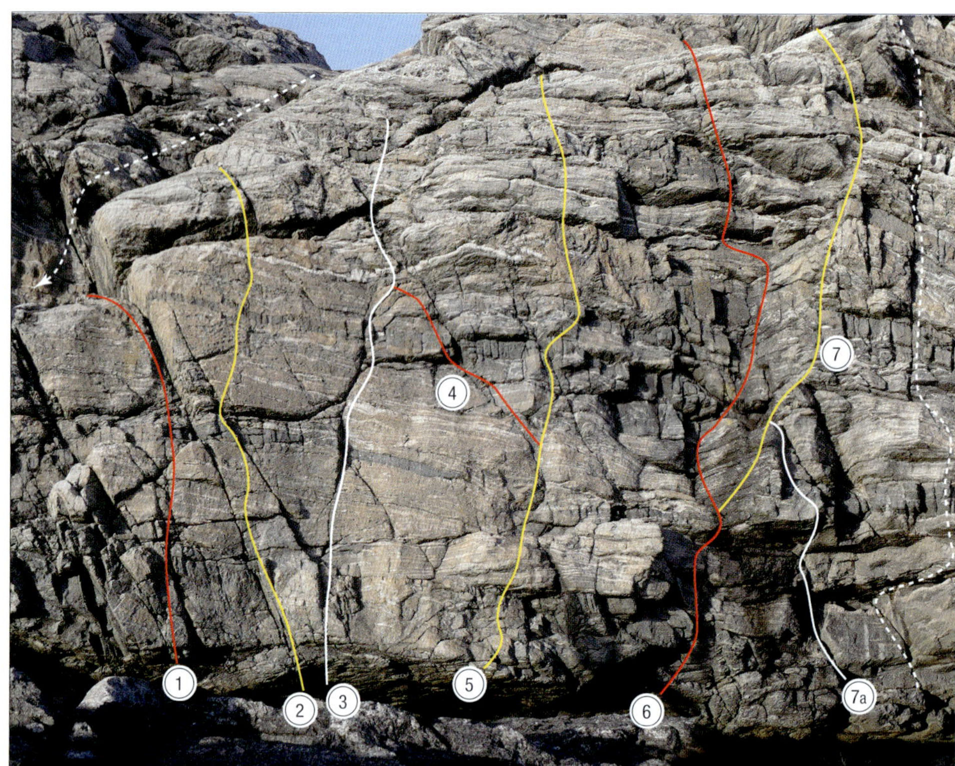

RUBHA SHEADAIR - Lifeline Wall, Left-hand, left

1. First Born First	S 4a	4. Super Soaker	VS 5a *	7. The Complete Angler	VS 5a
2. Sub Aqua Club	HVS 5a *	5. Birth Stone	E1 5a **	7a. Direct	E3 6a/b
3. Agent Orange	VS 4c **	6. Horizontal Pleasures	VS 5a *		

9 Forging the Future 15m HVS 5b *
T.Rankin, 17 May 2000
Start 2m right of Horizontal Horizons, make hard moves through the roof to the ledge and gain an obvious spike jug. Climb direct to join the end of the big fault of Border Reiver and finish up this.

10 Mystic Smeg 15m HVS 5a *
T.Stevenson, J.Beveridge, 26 May 2002
Start between Forging the Future and the base of the big diagonal fault at an obvious break in the roof. Go through the roof on jugs and the easy wall to gain the fault at mid-height. Pull out steeply right to an obvious big flake and go up the wall to the top.

11 Border Reiver 20m VD
T.Carruthers, M.Howard, 2001
The big right to left diagonal fault is easy after a steep start.

12 Crystal Balls 15m VS 4b
K.Howett, 18 May 2000
Climb the smaller diagonal fault to the right, starting through the roof where the bigger fault of Border Reiver starts.

13 Van Gogh's Lug 15m E1 5b *
T.Stevenson, J.Beveridge, 26 May 2002
Climbs the slight rib defining the lower half of the big fault. Climb Crystal Balls to gain the rib on the right, go up this to where it blanks out. Make harder moves up the wall above, leftwards, to better holds.

14 Short Palm Line 15m HS 4b **
K.Howett, 18 May 2000
Climb the next diagonal fault to the right. Pull through the lower roof into a short leftwards-slanting corner. Pull out right into the fault and follow it left to easy ground.

RUBHA SHEADAIR - Lifeline Wall, Left-hand, right

8.	Horizontal Horizons	E2 5c **	11.	Border Reiver	VD	14.	Short Palm Life	HS 4b **
9.	Forging the Future	HVS 5b *	12.	Crystal Balls	VS 4b	15.	Wankle	E1 5b
10.	Mystic Smeg	HVS 5a *	13.	Van Gogh's Lug	E1 5b *	16.	Big Apple Crumble	HVS 5b *

15 Wankle 15m E1 5b
K.Howett, S.Paterson 23 Apr 2017
Squeezed in up the blank looking wall just before Big Apple Crumble. Start below an obvious juggy flake at 5m. Gain the jugs. Pull onto the blank wall above and reach over the bulge to gain a black diorite band. Go up a thin crack in the orange wall above to easy ledges.

16 Big Apple Crumble 15m HVS 5b *
T.Carruthers, M.Howard, 13 Sep 2001
Start where a jammed block lies deep in the back under the roof. Go through the roof via obvious holds in a hanging V-groove to gain a shallow left-facing groove. Go up this to the base of a left-diagonal brown groove and step right to a ledge. Follow the leftmost cracks in the headwall right of the brown groove (A Pulse is Good).

The main section of the wall now starts as the ramp descends into the rock pool and the lower roof is at its lowest point. A stepped series of ledges and left-facing shallow corners cuts across the face from above here, left to right, finishing above the centre of the cliff (Lifeline).

17 A Pulse is Good 20m VS 4c **
K.Howett, 27 May 2002
Just right of Big Apple Crumble, as the ledges dip, the undercut wall sticks out in a slight prow with obvious holds. Pull through the roof via these holds to gain the left end of a little black overlap. Go up into a shallow broken groove to gain the left-diagonal brown groove. Follow this more easily to the top.

18 Playing the Cards 20m VS 4c **
T.Rankin, 18 May 2000
Start at the lowest point of the roof. Pull easily onto the wall and climb direct over the short black overlap and the smooth wall above to gain ledges shared with Big Apple Crumble and Lost in Paradise. Step right and follow a left-slanting crack to the top (right of Big Apple Crumble's crack).

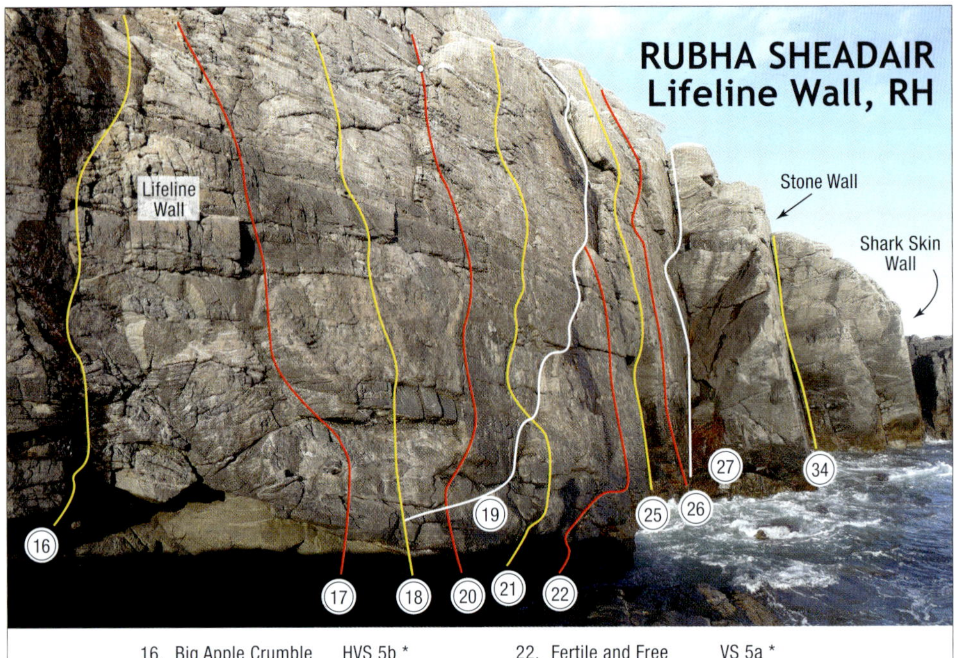

16. Big Apple Crumble	HVS 5b *		22. Fertile and Free	VS 5a *
17. A Pulse is Good	VS 4c **		25. The Future is Now	HVS 5a ***
18. Playing the Cards	VS 4c **		26. Choose Your Destiny	VS 4c **
19. Lifeline	S 4a **		27. Jaw Bone	VS 4c *
20. Lost in Paradise	VS 4c, 4b *		34. No Food for Thought	HVS 5a *
21. Rune the Day	VS 4c *			

19 Lifeline 30m S 4a **

K.Howett, 18 May 2000

An atmospheric wander taking a diagonal line rightwards across the entire face starting at the same place as Playing the Cards. Step onto the wall and traverse right then up into the line of the stepped ledges and grooves.

20 Lost in Paradise 20m VS *

K.Howett, R.K.Howett, N.A.Howett, D.Robinson, 06 Jun 2007

An eliminate but giving good climbing.

1. 15m 4c Start 1m right of Lifeline and pull directly onto the wall and ledge. Climb directly up a steeper wall above and then direct up the brown wall on good holds to gain a big ledge beside a short right-facing corner near the top.

2. 5m 4b Take the vertical crack above to a bold mantle top-out.

21 Rune the Day 25m VS 4c *

K.Howett, 18 May 2000

Start just down and right of the lowest part of the roof. Climb through the roof and up onto the stepped ledge system of Lifeline. Climb direct up the centre of the wall above to finish in a short thin crack in the middle.

22 Fertile and Free 25m VS 5a *

T.Rankin, 18 May 2000

Start just right of the previous route, halfway down the steeper section of the ramp. Use an obvious flake to pull through the lower roof. Step right and climb the wall near the blunt arete onto a small ledge. Follow the shallow right-facing groove above to easy rock. Exit up the left-leaning corner.

23 Lewd and Rude 25m HVS 5a *

T.Rankin, K.Howett, 18 May 2000

From a stance in the sentry box in the middle of the wall above the pool, pull out left and follow a left diagonal crack to the left side of the capping roof. Pull round this and follow easy ground to the easy stepped ledge system. Step left onto the wall, left of the finishing corner of Fertile and Free, and climb the wall to finish in a small diagonal crack.

24 Raging Libido 25m E2 5c *

T.Rankin, K.Howett, 18 May 2000

Climb the awkward slot exiting out of the roof above the sentry box onto a big ledge. Make hard moves up left to undercling the roof and climb the crack above. Finish up and right across the wall.

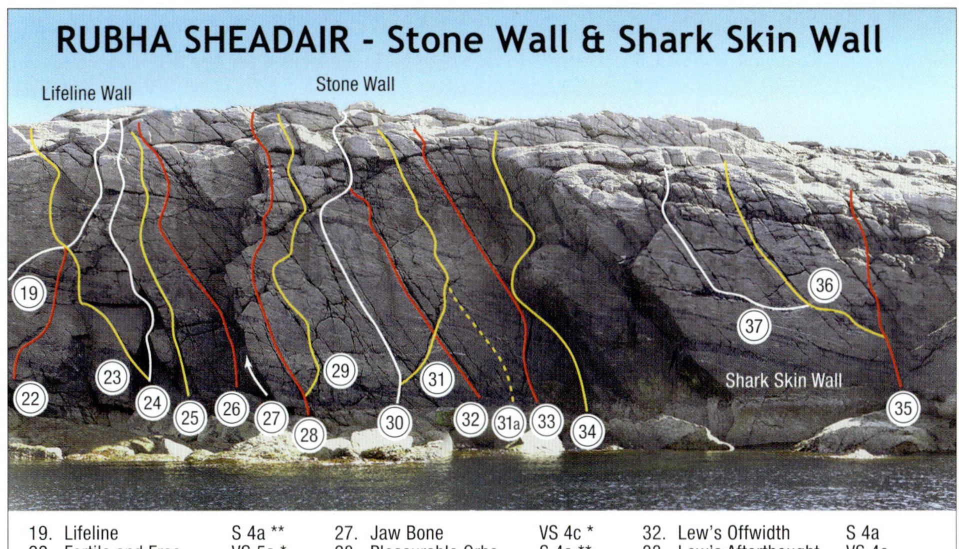

19. Lifeline	S 4a **	27. Jaw Bone	VS 4c *	32. Lew's Offwidth	S 4a
22. Fertile and Free	VS 5a *	28. Pleasurable Orbs	S 4a **	33. Lew's Afterthought	VS 4c
23. Lewd and Rude	HVS 5a *	29. Rolling Stones	S 4a **	34. No Food for Thought	HVS 5a *
24. Raging Libido	E2 5c *	30. Elgin's Envy	VS 4c *	35. Ledge Route	S 4a *
25. The Future is Now	HVS 5a ***	31. Rune-stone Cowboys	VS 4c **	36. Lone Shark	HVS 4c **
26. Choose Your Destiny	VS 4c **	31a. Rune-stone Direct	VS 4c *	37. Cruise Control	VS 4c **

25 The Future is Now 25m HVS 5a ***
K.Howett, 18 May 2000
Start just right of the sentry box on ledges. Pull into the overhanging V-groove and follow it (sustained) with thin moves out the top onto the wall. Direct up the wall to the top.

26 Choose Your Destiny 25m VS 4c **
T.Rankin, 18 May 2000
Climbs a distinctive right to left diagonal crack between the sentry box and the right bounding corner of Lifeline Wall. Start from ledges below the corner.

27 Jaw Bone 25m VS 4c *
R.Mackenzie, P.Calton 23 Apr 2017
Climbs the corner bounding the right side of the wall with some funky gibbon moves.

Stone Wall

The central wall. This is only accessible at mid-tide as the sea fills the rock pool below the base of Lifeline Wall very quickly. Big boulders again litter the base. The wall is distinguished by a series of prominent right to left diagonal cracks, one central crack being bigger than the others.

28 Pleasurable Orbs 25m S 4a **
K.Howett, 27 May 2002
Climbs the left arete of the wall. Step off a boulder leaning against the wall. Step left to a crack near the arete. Climb this and a shallow groove, then the stepped arete itself to the top.

29 Rolling Stones 25m S 4a **
T.Rankin, 18 May 2000
Climbs the left side of the face. Step off the boulder as for the last route and climb a left diagonal crack up the wall on the right to a right diagonal crack that leads into a slot to finish.

30 Elgin's Envy 25m VS 4c *
K.Howett, 27 May 2002
Climbs the next diagonal line comprising a set of twin cracks. Follow the cracks, but just before they enter the finishing slot of Rolling Stones, pull out right onto the wall and climb this direct into another recess at the top of the biggest diagonal crack.

31 Rune-stone Cowboys 25m VS 4c **
K.Howett, T.Rankin, 18 May 2000
Takes a line up the centre of the wall. Pull up from a boulder in the centre of the wall and follow a crack rightwards, bisecting the main crack of Lew's Offwidth. Gain a thinner crack in the wall above which leads to thinner moves to gain good holds near the top.
Variation: **31a Direct VS 4c ***
R.K.Howett, K.Howett 23 Apr 2017
Climb the wall right of Lew's Offwidth to gain the top of the diagonal crack, more sustained than the original.

32 Lew's Offwidth 25m S 4a
L.Creamer, 27 May 2002
The big central, slightly off-width, diagonal crack.

33 Lew's Afterthought 25m VS 4c
L.Creamer, 27 May 2002
The thinner diagonal crack in the right side of the wall.

34 No Food for Thought 25m HVS 5a *
K.Howett, A.Munro, N.A.Howett, 28 Jun 2013
The main right-bounding corner of Stone Wall; possible belay on the large mid-way ledge.

Shark Skin Wall

The most southerly wall. Gain it from the south by descending broken rocks to a large platform overlooking the wall. It is characterised by its lower third being sea-washed and covered in seaweed.

Descent: Down a gully between the platform and the wall, to belay as low as possible, sea permitting.

35 Ledge Route 10m S 4a *
T.Carruthers, S.Tyson, 7 Jun 2007
Gain a small ledge 2m up the wall. Take the short wall above to ledges.

36 Lone Shark 15m HVS 5a **
T.Carruthers, S.Tyson, 7 Jun 2007
Gain the small ledge. Take a traverse line left for 2m to the base of twin diagonal cracks. Gritstone crack aficionados will cruise to the top, others will struggle.

37 Cruise Control 20m VS 4c **
K.Howett T.Carruthers, 7 Jun 2007
The natural traverse line across the whole wall. Start as for Lone Shark. Continue the traverse left across a blank section to gain another set of superb twin gritstone finishing cracks near the left arete.

CNOC NÒIDEAMUIL

(NL 633 913)

This is a small hill on the coast about halfway down the western seaboard, mid-way between the Rune Stones Cliff and The Galleries.

The Goldfish Bowl

(NL 635 910) Non-tidal SW facing Map p271

This craglet lies in an bay just south of the Cnoc, with a large raised block platform. The wall lies at the back of the bay. It is split into two separate walls by a right- facing corner. The right-hand wall has a beautiful square rock pool below it and an elevated ledge running along its base. The left-hand wall is steeper and characterised by vertical cracks. The routes are described from left to right.

Descent: Easily down an eroded dyke line immediately north of the wall.

Finrot 10m HVS 5b
R.Strube, H.Cottam, 30 May 2002
Climb to an undercut block 4m left of the left-facing corner of Small Fish in a Big Pond, and finish directly.

Small Fish in a Big Pond 10m E1 5c
K.Howett, T.Rankin, 20 May 2000
Climb the shallow clean-cut left-facing corner on the left side of the left wall. Thin near the top.

The Man Who Fell to Mirth 10m E3 6a
H.Cottam, R.Strube, 30 May 2002
The cracked wall right of the corner of Small Fish in a Big Pond. Make hard tenuous moves up the thin cracks with hard-won protection to gain better holds above half-height. Finish up the slight left-facing groove. Some suspect holds.

Spherical Views 10m E2 5c
T.Rankin, K.Howett, 20 May 2000
Climbs the bigger central crack-line up the wall. Continually steep but well protected.

Bowl of Contentment 10m HVS 5a
T.Rankin, 20 May 2000
Climb the right-hand crack-line just right of Spherical Views, leading to jugs up the upper wall.

Flip to Freedom 10m S
T.Rankin, 20 May 2000
The V-groove just to the right.

Lennies Route 10m VD
G.Lennox, 20 May 2000
Climb the stepped overhanging arete that borders the corner splitting the two walls.

Bob 10m D
T.Rankin, 20 May 2000
The big corner separating the two walls.

Fishfinger 10m E1 5b
H.Cottam, R.Strube, 30 May 2002
At the right-hand side of the wall are twin cracks; follow the left-hand crack.

Fillet 10m VS 4b
R.Strube, H.Cottam, 30 May 2002
The right-hand crack near the right end of the wall.

Wailing Wall

(NL 635 909) Tidal W facing

This is the geo that lies at the furthest seaward end of the large platform below the Goldfish Bowl.

Great Whitey Wail 10m HVS 5b
H.Cottam, R.Strube, 30 May 2002
Climb a direct line mid-way up the right-hand wall of the geo.

The Galleries

(NL 637 907) Partially Tidal SW facing Map p271

These walls lie further down the west coast of the island parallel with Loch na Cuilce. Three clean walls are separated by projecting buttresses of overhanging rock. The walls, running from north to south, are: The Tate Gallery, The Burrell Gallery and The Louvre Gallery.

Descent: The Tate Gallery is easily walked into at any state of the tide by descending an easy-angled rock ramp from the north.

The Burrell is reached from The Tate Gallery. The ramp drops into a gulch, which is sea-washed at high tides, on the far side of which is a higher platform under a projecting buttress. Gain the platform up a short wall from the gulch where it continues to form a viewing platform for The Burrell Gallery which is undercut by a sea cave.

The Louvre Gallery is accessed from the south down an easy scramble to ledges just above high tide. Traversing the base the Louvre, and into its far side along broken ledges, requires low tides and calm seas.

The Tate Gallery

Diagrams p278 & p279

This is the shortest of the three walls, gaining in height as one approaches down the access ramp. The first part of the wall is too small and broken but, just beyond an undercut section, the wall becomes more continuous, and finishes at an obvious corner where the sea encroaches into the gulch. The routes are steep and the holds extremely sharp. Routes are described from left to right when walking down the ramp, beginning with a series of micro-routes (or highball boulder problems).

1 Smart Attack 8m VD
N.A.Howett, R.K.Howett, 5 Jun 2007
A shallow left-facing groove bounding the left side.

2 Sketch Pad 8m S 4a
T.Rankin, 18 May 2000
The wall at the extreme left end.

3 Cracked Canvas 8m S 4a
K.Howett, 18 May 2000
The disjointed crack-line running the height of the cliff.

4 Unfinished Works 8m S 4a
K.Howett, 18 May 2000
The thinner crack to the right which peters out at half-height.

5 Scribble 8m HS 4b
K.Howett, 18 May 2000
The V-slot to the right and wall above.

6 Perspective 10m VS 4b
T.Rankin, 18 May 2000
The small left-facing groove to the right.

7 Delicate Brush Strokes 12m E1 5c **
K.Howett, 18 May 2000
The steep wall right of the slim corner split by a very thin crack-line.

8 Small Arms 12m VS 5a *
T.Carruthers, M.Howard, 15 Sep 2001
The small flake in the left side of a slight hanging scoop immediately right of the steep wall and the easier wall left of the upper roof.

9 Making a Statement 12m HVS 5b *
K.Howett, 18 May 2000
The centre of the slight hanging scoop leading to the roof which is climbed direct.

10 Look From Within 12m VS 4c
T.Rankin, 18 May 2000
The wall right of the scoop direct into the hanging corner bounding the right side of the roof.

11 Don't See, Feel! 12m HVS 5a
T.Rankin, K.Howett, 18 May 2000
The distinctive clean-cut left-facing corner and the steep wall, direct to the top.

Art Nouveau (E3) Ian Renshaw (photo Gordon Lennox)

1. Smart Attack	VD	9.	Making a Statement	HVS 5b *	14.	Rockart	E4 6a **
4. Unfinished Works	S 4a	10.	Look From Within	VS 4c	15.	Smoothly Sculptured	E4 6a **
5. Scribble	HS 4b	11.	Don't See, Feel	HVS 5a	16.	Rough Cast	E4 6a **
7. Delicate Brush Strokes	E1 5c **	12.	Exhibitionist	E2 6a **			
8. Small Arms	VS 5a *	13.	Eye of The Beholder	E3 5c *			

12 Exhibitionist 12m E2 6a **
T.Rankin, 18 May 2000
The wall just right of the corner to gain a slim shattered groove in the upper wall.

13 Eye of the Beholder 15m E3 5c *
T.Rankin, K.Howett, 17 May 2000
Roughly follows a series of hairline cracks up the wall right of Exhibitionist. Go up the wall rightwards to an obvious big projecting layback hold (crux). Climb direct to the top on good holds.

14 Rockart 15m E4 6a **
L.Creamer, K.Howett, 27 May 2002
Climbs the line of the shallow left-facing groove marking the left end of an overlap that extends rightwards at one-third height. Climb thin cracks diagonally rightwards into the top of the small groove. Pull out direct to a good jug and then climb the wall to the top.

15 Smoothly Sculptured 15m E4 6a **
L.Creamer, K.Howett, 27 May 2002
A slightly eliminate line but providing good climbing. Just right of Rockart, climb a thin vertical crack into the base of the left-facing groove of that route. Pull over on an obvious jug and up right to a big hold shared by Rough Cast. Climb direct up the centre of the wall above.

16 Rough Cast 15m E4 6a **
K.Howett, G.Lennox, 5 May 1999
Climbs the steep wall direct through the overlap at one-third height. Start below a slight niche in the overlap. Climb up to the niche. Pull out left to a big hold, then back right into a short left-facing corner. Go up this, then direct up the black friable wall above, slightly left near the top.

17 Art Nouveau 15m E3 5c **
G.Lennox, G.E.Little, K.Howett, 1 May 1999
Start 5m right of Rough Cast at a series of cracks up the wall leading to a quartz splodge and an area of fired rock. Climb the cracked wall with difficulty to the quartz. Pull up and left on better holds to gain a black hole and exit slightly right.

THE GALLERIES - The Tate Gallery, Right-hand

16. Rough Cast E4 6a **
17. Art Nouveau E3 5c **
18. The Minimalist E3 5c *
19. Art Deco E2 5b **
20. Art Farty HVS 5a **
21. New Wave HVS 4c **
22. Empty Canvas E2 5b *
23. Dada HS 4b **
24. Clean Sheet VS 4c

18 The Minimalist 15m E3 5c *
T.Rankin, K.Howett, 17 May 2000
Takes a direct but eliminate line on Art Nouveau. Start just right of that route and climb cracks to a black overlap. Pull left and up into the quartz holds of Art Nouveau. Pull steeply directly up the wall and step right to bigger holds. Go up the wall just right of Art Deco to black rock, then step left and pull into a scoop at the top.

19 Art Deco 15m E2 5b **
G.Lennox, G.E.Little, K.Howett, 1 May 1999
Just right of Art Nouveau is an open corner leading to a black roof and flake-crack. Climb the corner to a bulge then step out right onto the wall. Move up and into the flake-crack to finish.

20 Arty Farty 15m HVS 5a **
K.Howett, G.Lennox, 5 May 1999
A good route climbing the wall between Art Deco and New Wave. Climb a short arete then over the right end of the low roof. Step left across the lip then up into a scoop in the wall. Climb direct up the steep wall, finishing in a short corner at the top.

21 New Wave 15m HVS 4c **
G.E.Little, G.Lennox, K.Howett, 1 May 1999
Climb an overhanging stepped corner right of Arty Farty.

22 Empty Canvas 20m E2 5b *
T.Rankin, K.Howett, 17 May 2000
Climb the wall between New Wave and Dada. Crux up the steep lower wall and climb direct above the mid-way ledge to the top.

23 Dada 20m HS 4b **
G.E.Little, 30 Apr 1999
The obvious large corner at the right end of the wall just before the rock step leads to the higher platform of The Burrell Gallery.

24 Clean Sheet 20m VS 4c
G.Lennox, K.Howett, 5 May 1999
Climbs the slabby wall which forms part of the rock step onto The Burrell Gallery, right of the big corner at the right end of the wall. Go up the wall passing a large horizontal break to trend right near the arete, then back left into the centre of the slab to finish onto a big ledge. Escape up left.

The Burrell Gallery

Diagrams p280 & p282

The highest, and most spectacular of the three walls. Its main feature is a smooth sheet of perfect overhanging orange rock, which is undercut along its base by a sea cave, the lip being tantalisingly at full reach from the platform for most climbers. This platform dips

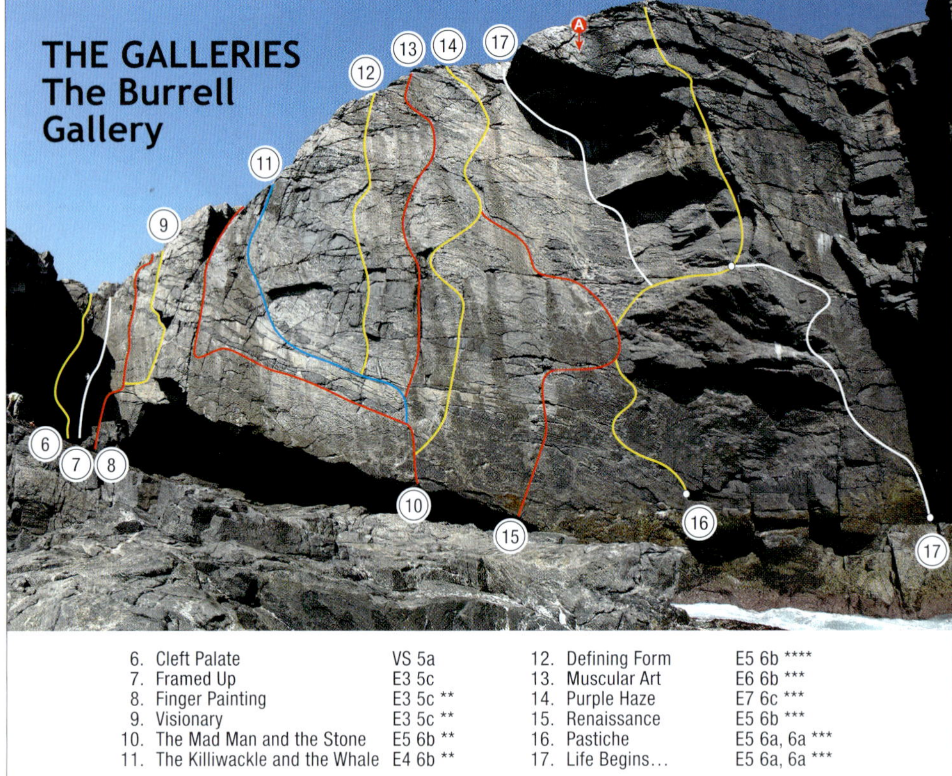

into the back of the cave on the left and to the sea on the right, where the right-hand side of the wall drops into deep water. Above this point the wall merges with the overhanging corners bounding The Louvre Gallery, and a superbly positioned, spectacular ledge lies just above the waves at the base of a scooped corner and roof system marking the right edge of the smooth wall. Routes are described left to right as approached along the platform.

1 Pollock Original 20m VS 4c
T.Carruthers, S.Tyson, 5 Jun 2007
Just onto the platform are twin disjointed corner-lines. This takes the right-hand line. The first corner is the crux, stepping up left onto a ledge. Go up a further corner then right to ledges, leading to a fine headwall crack.

To the right is a short undercut wall off the platform, and forming the left side of the overhanging prow.

2 The Golden Rule 20m E2 6b
K.Howett, 1 May 1999
Climb the centre of the block wall via thin edges onto the ledge. Easily to the top.

3 Cubist 20m VS 5b
G.E.Little, G.Lennox, 2 May 1999
Start just left of the prow at the right end of the block wall. Make a hard move up the wall to gain a ledge. Climb the corner onto a square-cut block, then continue up easier ground.

4 Hung Wrong 20m E2 5c *
K.Howett, G.Lennox, 19 May 2000
Climbs the flying ramp cutting horizontally through the huge prow. Start just left of the raised ledges under the corners of Gouache and Cleft Palette. Climb a jutting slabby arete to the right end of the ramp. Follow it with hard moves at the end onto a ledge in a spectacular position.

5 Gouache 10m E1 5b
G.E.Little, G.Lennox, K.Howett, 2 May 1999
Climbs a Flared-chimney groove and corner-crack-line on the immediate right side of the projecting prow between The Tate and Burrell Galleries. Start left of The Burrell Gallery cave. Go up easy ledges leading leftwards under the prow, and below the flared-chimney. Getting into it provides the enjoyment.

6 Cleft Palette 15m VS 5a
G.E.Little, G.Lennox, 2 May 1999
Immediately right of Gouache is a block recess bounding the left side of The Burrell wall itself. Climb this from easy raised ledges with one hard move.

7 Framed Up 15m E3 5c
L.Creamer, K.Howett, 27 May 2002
The thin vertical crack just right of the arete of Cleft Palette. A little eliminate and poorly protected.

8 Finger Painting 15m E3 5c **
G.Lennox, G.E.Little, K.Howett, 2 May 1999
Climbs the wall just left of the cave. Move up to a higher ledge under the wall to gain the obvious horizontal crack. Follow it up and right, then climb the wall direct on flakes and a layback edge to easy rock.

9 Visionary 20m E3 5c **
T.Rankin, G.Lennox, K.Howett, 19 May 2000
Climbs the hanging slabby corner above the cave roof just right of Finger Paint. Start off the same ledge and traverse right into the groove. Exit it leftwards round the capping roof and up an easy corner to the top.

The immaculate orange wall contains six routes, all starting from a central point where the lip of the cave is closest to the platform below. Desperate moves to get established lead to jugs below a vertical crack, and for the vertically challenged will prove to be the crux for all routes!

10 The Mad Man and the Stone 25m E5 6b **
N.McGeachy, G.Tyldsey, 3 Jul 2013
Pull onto the wall. Hand-traverse left along the lower of two black bands until forced to leave it and climb a pocketed wall below. Finish up an obvious ragged crack on the far left of the wall.

11 The Killiwackle and the Whale 25m E4 6b **
N.McGeachy, G.Tyldsey, 3 Jul 2013
Pull onto the wall. Follow a good horizontal break in the higher black band leftwards to under a conspicuous overlap. Pass this on its left and climb to a large quartz pocket. Finish up the groove on the left.

12 Defining Form 25m E5 6b ****
L.Creamer, K.Howett, 29 May 2002
Takes a direct line up unlikely terrain. Pull onto the wall. Gain the good horizontal break in the higher black band and traverse it leftwards for 2m to a thin groove which leads to a block roof in black rock. Step left and up the black rock, passing the right end of the conspicuous overlap to reach a smaller one above. Hard moves directly up the orange wall above gain a break forming the base of a rightwards-leaning flake. Go up this then direct to finish.

13 Muscular Art 25m E6 6b ***
G.Lennox, K.Howett, 4 May 1999
The original climb on the wall, directly up the centre. Pull onto the wall and climb the obvious crack above to a small ledge in the middle of the wall. Move out left and up to a series of huge pockets. Gain a rounded edge up right which leads to further good holds in the wall above and left leading to the top.

14 Purple Haze 20m E7 6c ***
G.Lennox, 25 Jun 2009
Climbs the wall right of Muscular Art with the crux gaining a thin left-facing edge high on the wall. Pull on as for Muscular Art and traverse up and right until a big span can be made to gain holds leading to the flake on the right side of the ledge in the middle of the wall. From the ledge, move out right and make desperate moves on small scoops and edges to gain the left-facing edge and a jug on the left. Climb up to the top break and then follow a line of holds leading out left to near the top of Muscular Art.

15 Renaissance 20m E5 6b ***
G.Lennox, 27 Jul 2006
Climb the hanging crack reached from the slab sloping into the sea right of Purple Haze (again hard for small climbers) to jugs and a rest in the corner to the right (junction with Pastiche). Move back left and up on fingery holds to a thin left-facing edge and gain a jug on the left (junction with Purple Haze). Follow Purple Haze to the top.

Purple Haze (E7) Gordon Lennox (photo Michael Shorter)

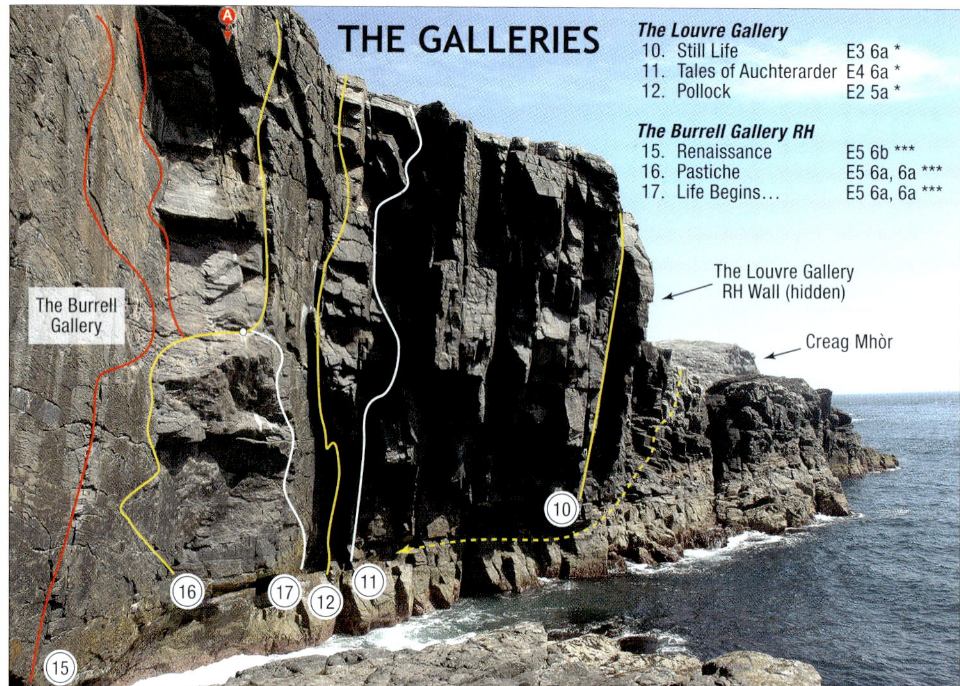

The orange wall of the Burrell Gallery merges with the overhanging corners of The Louvre to its right as a scooped corner-line with two roofs. Under the lower roof lies the spectacular ledge. The following routes are gained by a sea-level traverse from The Louvre (low tide and calm sea only), although the spectacular ledge for Pastiche can be gained direct by an incredibly awkward abseil and lies high enough above high tide level to be safe at any state of the tide.

16 Pastiche 35m E5 ***

K.Howett, G.Lennox, 6 May 1999

A deceptively steep and pumpy route in a great position, starting from the spectacular ledge. Originally climbed during wild seas.

1. 15m 6a Traverse out left from the ledge along the obvious rail and make a hard move up to pockets. Span right to a slight groove then up to under the roof. Pull over and climb up to a big horizontal break.
2. 20m 6a Traverse the big break right above the roof until it is possible to stand up into a slight groove. From the top of the groove, pull out right round the arete to jugs. Climb the arete until under a capping overlap. Pull over with a final steep effort.

17 Life begins... 35m E5 ***

I.Small, T.Fryer, 26 Jul 2006

A counter diagonal to Pastiche starting below the furthest left black groove on The Louvre Wall and finishing up the main hanging corner on the right edge of the Muscular Art wall. Traverse in at high-tide level under The Louvre to the furthest ledge and belay.

1. 15m 6a A series of hard and committing moves up a leftward-diagonal crack and the arete leads to a sloping, overhung ledge. From the right end, a move up gains a good quartz jug. Step right and climb a rib on small holds to a horizontal break. Traverse left to a footledge, and step up the groove above to a horizontal break and belay (junction with Pastiche).
2. 20m 6a Traverse the horizontal break left on big holds to gain the slight corner bounding the right side of The Burrell Wall. Pull over a small roof onto a slab above. Step left onto the wall, then climb this and the corner with interest and wild, steep finishing moves to get through a hanging corner. Magnificent.

The Louvre Gallery

Diagrams above & opposite

This is in two parts. A smooth overhanging wall which finishes on its left as an overhanging arete, from where it turns 90° to form a series of overhanging corners leading left to join The Burrell Gallery. Ledges under here can be traversed in calm seas at low tide. The most striking line on the wall is the line of a faint crack towards the right side. At the top of the wall near the left arete is a roof. Routes are described right to left, as approached.

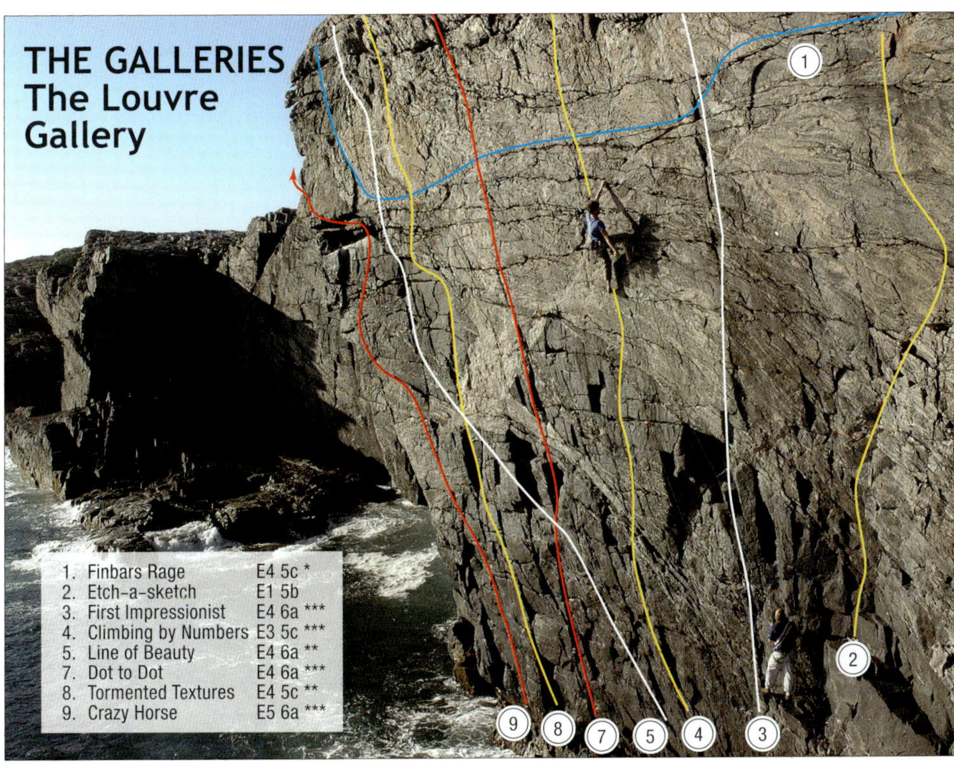

1 Finbar's Rage 25m E4 5c *
N McGeachy, G.Tydesly, 30 Jun 2013
A right to left high-level traverse of the wall for rough sea days. From the highest point of the ledges on the right, hand-traverse a break, stepping down to a lower break at 5m. Continue along this line, climbing upwards just before the ledge on Crazy Horse.

2 Etch-a-sketch 15m E1 5b
I.Small, T.Fryer, 24 Jul 2006
The furthest right-hand side of the wall, following a right-trending ramp system. Follow a black groove on slightly suspect rock to gain and follow a ramp-come-ledge until it is possible to go straight up a small but immaculate headwall near the right edge.

3 First Impressionist 25m E4 6a ***
K.Howett, G.E.Little, 2 May 1999
The hairline crack. Climb the black wall directly below the crack via a flared recess and follow the crack (less blank than it appears). A long reach near the top brings good holds just left of the, now deeper, crack to finish.

4 Climbing by Numbers 25m E3 5c ***
L.Creamer, K.Howett,28 May 2002
An excellent line up the blank looking wall immediately left of the First Impressionist crack. Start up twin black cracks (hard), passing a thread runner in the left crack, to pull onto a small ledge. Go up right to gain an obvious excellent deep horizontal crack in the lighter-coloured rock above, near faint twin cracks. Climb direct up the wall following excellent holds.

5 Line of Beauty 30m E4 6a **
T.Fryer, I.Small, 25 Jul 2006
A rising traverse across the face from right to left, following the obvious breaks below the wavy quartz vein. Start just left of First Impressionist (at the base of Climbing by Numbers), traverse up and left, crossing other lines, past a huge quartz splodge in the centre of the wall into the corner of Tormented Textures. Move up the wall left of this to the right end of a guano ledge-come-cave below a roof; the eye in the Indian's face feature on Crazy Horse. Committing moves gain a camouflaged incut hold. Continue boldly to the top.

6 Art for Art's Sake 25m E4 6a *
I.Small, T.Fryer, 2006
Very squeezed in but offering good climbing. Start 2m right of Dot to Dot, at a thin crack. Follow the crack on good holds to a small triangular niche. Continue to a mini overlap in orangey rock. Make a long move up to a good hold. Continue directly up the wall on hidden holds to the left of a hairline crack.

7 Dot To Dot 25m E4 6a ***
K.Howett, G.Lennox, 4 May 1999
Climbs a line in the centre of the wall between Climbing By Numbers and Tormented Textures, up a faint crack that emanates from the small overlap at half-height. Start directly below the line, up a crack in black rock to a small projecting ledge. Go up the crack above, through the overlap, and direct to the top.

8 Tormented Textures 25m E4 5c **
G.Lennox, K.Howett, 2 May 1999
Towards the left side of the wall is a hanging black corner (left-facing) leading up to a capping overlap. Start at a crack-line leading directly into the corner. The crack proves to be juggy but the corner awkward. Pull through the overlap on jugs and make a hard move up to gain more (hidden) jugs in the orange wall above. Finish direct.

9 Crazy Horse 25m E5 6a ***
J.Clark, A.Robertson, 25 Jul 2006
Follows the left arete, where a feature like an Indian's face is obvious. Start in a groove just right of the arete. Follow the groove and crack up the wall, trending slightly left until able to make committing moves onto the Indian's face. Either pull into a huge guano niche-come-cave (sometimes home to a shag) or, better, hand-traverse at eye level and step onto the mouth. Pull round using good holds on the arete (stepping onto the nose in a wild position) and up to a big break. Finish up the top wall on the left side of the arete, with continued interest. Low in the grade.

Round the arete to the left is a steep wall formed by a series of vertical grooves and corners.

10 Still Life 30m E3 6a *
K.Howett, G.E.Little, 1 May 1999
Climbs the stepped corner immediately around the arete. Belay on a good ledge 2m up the corner. Climb the corner to the roof. An excursion out on the very steep left wall gains the upper corners to finish with further interest.

11 Tales of Auchterarder 30m E4 6a *
T.Emery, M.Gardner, 26 Jun 2009
This takes the bottomless groove a few metres right of the corner bounding The Burrell Gallery. Gain the groove with some difficulty and exit to the right before continuing up the grooves and corners above.

12 Pollock 30m E2 5c *
I.Renshaw, B.Winston, 14 Jun 2008
Climbs the left-facing corner between The Louvre and The Burrell Gallery. Start up the corner to a handrail on the left wall. Mantel this and chimney the off-width above to a ledge. Follow the general line direct to the top. Originally climbed in two pitches, escaping left from the off-width.

Climbing by Numbers (E3) Andy Benson (photo Ben Winston)

ÀIRD PHABACH

Àird Phabach is the peninsula at the extreme south-west tip of the island and is home to the largest cliffs. The whole west side of the peninsula is craggy. The highest point is Creag Mhòr and the cliff of that name, lying below, is the biggest and steepest. The hill steadily diminishes in height south towards the point. The cliff line becomes slabby and vegetated until a distinctive drop in elevation is reached after about 300m, marking the top of a vertical gully dropping into the sea. Beyond here the peninsula gains height again slightly, before descending to the end of the point. This has been christened Creag Beag. The cliff line here extends continuously to end at the point and is composed of excellent quality, clean, solid rock. The cliffs cannot be viewed easily, so individual sections are described based on prominent cliff-top features and differing access points.

CREAG MHÒR

(NL 640 902) Partially Tidal SW facing
Map p271 Diagrams p286 & p288

The main feature is an awesomely steep wall beside a huge sea cave. The cave is accessed by descending a slabby promontory which shelters the cave from the open sea, and which can be descended easily to sea-level. The area of cliff above the lip of the cave is called The Aisle, with the main cliff The Auditorium. Both can be viewed from the slabby promontory. A much smaller wall lies under the viewing promontory and is approached from the north along a lower rock platform at sea-level, called The Stalls. Further south, just beyond the highest point of the hill, lies a further wall consisting of two buttresses essentially joined but separated by different access; Drum Buttress is accessed on foot; Cream Buttress is an extension south of Drum Buttress but only accessible by abseil.

There are colonies of auks and kittiwakes on the south side of Creag Mhòr but they only really affect One Flew Over The Kittiwakes' Nest.

The Aisle

All routes are accessed from the top of the promontory.

1 Standing Room Only 25m E2 5c *
L.Creamer, K.Howett, 29 May 2002
This climbs the obvious horizontal break cutting rightwards across the wall above the cave. Start off the top left side of the platform. Climb a right-facing corner formed by a large block to gain the crack. Follow it rightwards till it widens into a big grin. Pull onto the hanging slab and climb a shallow groove to the top.

2 Nurse Ratchitt 13m E4 6b
C.Adam, G.Lennox, 27 May 2005
Start right of the blocky corner of Standing Room Only to gain the break. Layback up to holds leading left then traverse right to a flake hold (crux). Climb up to a block and gain the ledge above. Finish straight up.

3 Trap Door 15m E6 6a/b
G.Lennox, C.Adam, 27 May 2005
Climbs directly through Standing Room Only, finishing straight up the wall above. Start at a small right-facing corner right of Nurse Ratchet and up on layaways. Move up and right to more layaways and make committing balance moves to gain the break (serious). Pull straight up to obvious jugs and follow the faint groove above with more balance moves to a slight niche. Make a difficult move up and left to a good flat hold and pull through the short V-corner to finish (very run-out).

The Auditorium

The main crag is uniformly steep with the huge sea cave on the left-hand side of the wall. The main features are two hanging walls that lie at a slight angle to the main face, facing south. The right-hand wall is bounded by a big corner, the right wall of which is a large slab covered in splashes of guano. Beneath this the wall overhangs into the sea. Above the corner and the slab (at about two-thirds height) is a large series of roofs.

Descent: The routes are all accessed by abseil and described from left to right, from above the right side of the cave. The first route is reached by abseil down to hanging ledges above the lip of the cave.

4 Crowbar Corner 15m E1 5b
C.Adam, G.Lennox, 31 Jul 2005
Climbs the black corner above the cave, right of the finish of Standing Room Only. From the hanging ledges, traverse left, move diagonally left up a short wall to gain the black corner and finish up this passing some rattling flakes.

Descent: The following routes are reached by an abseil down the very steep central fault (using wires to keep the abseil into the wall) to a birdy ledge at half-height.

5 Central Reservations 20m E1 5b
C.Adam, G.Lennox, 26 Jul 2005
Climbs the central fault between the two hanging walls. Climb the wide crack above the ledge and continue steeply up the fault on huge holds.

6 Tangoed 30m E5 6b *
G.Lennox, C.Adam, 26 Jul 2005
Climbs a line on the left-hand hanging wall. Continue the abseil to a semi-hanging stance above the lower overhangs. Climb up the fault and out to a spike on the left. Move up and left passing cracks through a black band to a shakeout flake in the centre of the wall. Climb up to the overlap and cross it rightwards to below another small overlap (crux). Turn the small overlap on the left and finish straight up.

CREAG MHÒR - The Auditorium & The Aisle

1. Standing Room Only E2 5c *
2. Nurse Ratchitt E4 6b
3. Trap Door E6 6a/b
4. Crowbar Corner E1 5b
5. Central Reservations E1 5b
6. Tangoed E5 6b **
7. Pissin' in the Wind E4 6a **
8. The Don Mac Highway E4 6a, 5c **
9. Orangoutang E6 5b, 6b, 5c ***
10. Mhòr Air E5 6a, 6a, 5a ****
11. The Gift E5 6a ***
12. Between Hell and High Water E3 5c **
13. One Flew the Kittiwake's Nest E5 5b, 5c, 6b *

7 Pissin' in the Wind 30m E4 6a **
G.Lennox, C.Adam, 30 Jul 2005
Follow Tangoed to the black band. Traverse left to juggy ledges at the left arete. Move up and right to gain thin cracks in the leaning headwall (crux). Finish up these.

8 The Don Mac Highway 30m E4 **
C.Adam, G.Lennox, 27 Jul 2005
Start from the semi-hanging stance of Tangoed.
1. 20m 6a Climb the fault swinging out left to a large flake. Sling the flake and traverse horizontally left with difficulty and continue boldly to a good square jug. Step down to foot holds at the lip of the roof. Move left to gain a thin crack and climb this with difficulty to gain better holds. Continue up round the arete to a stance.
2. 10m 5c Climb the bulging crack above.

Descent: The first two routes are gained by abseiling down the corner bounding the guano slab and the overhanging wall below it to land on the only small ledge at sea-level hereabouts. This passes the big ledge belay on Mhòr Air, from where the other three routes start.

9 Orangoutang 55m E6 ***
G.Lennox, C.Adam, 27 Jul 2005
A superb route through the lower roofs direct into Central Reservations.
1. 10m 5b Traverse left along breaks to gain a semi-hanging stance at footledges.
2. 25m 6b Take a rising leftwards fault heading towards an obvious block. Swing round this and continue in the same line to a second block and do the same. Move left and up to the main roof and climb through this rightwards. Pull through on the incredibly formed rock and climb up to the big birdy ledge shared with Central Reservations. A wildly steep pitch.
3. 20m 5c Cut across the steep fault of Central Reservations to a square roof, turn this on the left and continue up a steep groove at the right edge of the left-hand hanging wall.

10 Mhòr Air 50m E5 ****
K.Howett, G.E.Little, 30 Apr 1999
The first climb recorded on the island. It climbs up the centre of the right-hand hanging wall. Low in the grade. Start from the small ledge at sea-level.
1. 10m 6a Climb into a slim hanging groove directly above the ledge and exit with difficulty onto the slab above. Belay on a big ledge in the base of the slabby corner.
2. 25m 6a Traverse horizontally left across the wall until it is possible to make blind moves up to gain the left-hand side of a slight ramp. Follow the ramp back right, and at its right end climb up and left into a small hanging groove. Near its top, step left to gain obvious

holds above and left then make hard moves up to the deep horizontal break under the roofs. Traverse this left for 3m to a lessening in angle and belay.
3. 15m 5a Climb up into a conspicuous hanging flared chimney to finish.

11 The Gift 30m E5 6a ***
G.Lennox, C.Adam, 30 Jul 2005
Start from the big ledge belay on the slab of Mhòr Air. Traverse left to gain a slight ramp. Move up left to a line of edges. Follow these until they peter out. Make a move out right to a quartz hold and climb up to a pocket. Trend left to flakes, and finish more easily to gain the horizontal break leading left to finish.

12 Between Hell and High Water 30m E3 5c **
T.Rankin, G.Lennox, 21 May 2000
Climbs a direct line out through the roofs. Start from the big ledge belay on the slab of Mhòr Air. Climb obvious big flakes in the left wall, just left of the back corner, to gain the break under the big roof. Traverse left along this until it is possible to pull up and traverse back right above the lip of the roof onto an easy black slab (threads and possible belay). Follow the tapering slab leftwards into a final corner and the crux.

13 One Flew Over The Kittiwakes' Nest 55m E5 *
C.Adam, G.Lennox, 2005
An adventurous line weaving through the enormous roofs right of the main corner. Start from the big ledge belay on the slab of Mhòr Air.
1. 20m 5b Scramble up right across the birdy slab to a ledge and climb the break back left across the first roof. Move up to a stance.
2. 20m 5c Traverse the grey wall rightwards to jugs on the arete where the roof above recedes. Climb up steeply to belay at a short corner in the black rock band, below the final capping roof (more belay anchors can be found in the harder yellow rock up right).
3. 15m 6b Traverse left with increasing difficulty along a narrowing corridor in an incredible situation, until the capping roof is passed.

The Stalls

Directly below the viewing promontory for The Auditorium, this 20m wall is partially tidal. It receives a lot of pounding during times of rough seas. The main feature is a huge long roof above an easy-angled slab. Left of this is a large right-angled corner bounding a superb slabby section of smooth rock. The climbs are described from right to left.

Puffin Boots 10m VS 4c
H.Cottam, R.Strube, 30 May 2002
From a platform at the extreme right-hand end of the big roof, climb the awkward corner.

Comedy Tern 15m S
T.Carruthers, S.Tyson, 28 May 2002
The obvious V-groove just left of the left arete bounding the slabby section.

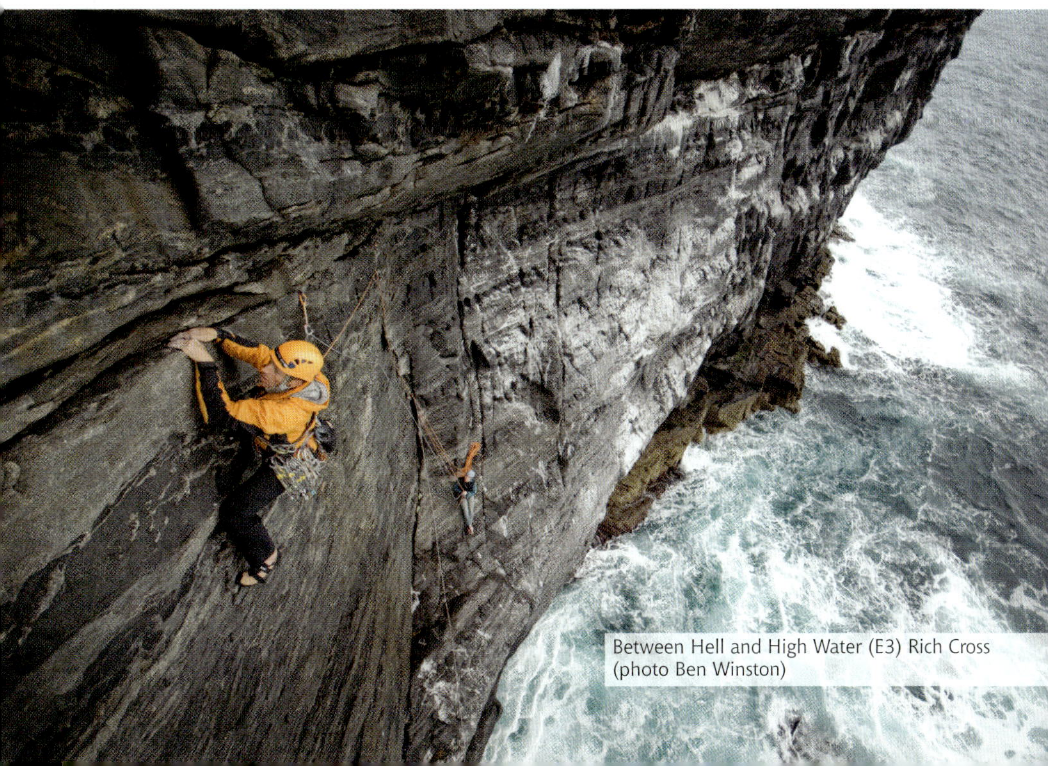

Between Hell and High Water (E3) Rich Cross (photo Ben Winston)

Fit Old Men 15m VD *
T.Rankin, 21 May 2000
Climbs the excellent right-facing corner up the slab 3m left of the arete, left of the area of roofs.

Quiet in the Cheap Seats 15m HVS 5b
T.Carruthers, H.Cottam, 28May 2002
Climbs the bulge and slim ramp immediately left of Fit Old Men.

Racing Day 15m HVS 5b
R.Strube, H.Cottam, 30 May 2002
The right-hand end of the first wall has a slabby corner in the arete. Climb the steep wall to an overlap, climb this and enter the corner that leads to the top.

Sunshine 15m VS 4c
R.Strube, H.Cottam, 30 May 2002
Climb up to the small roof with a wide slot on its right-hand side. Surmount this and then to the top.

Drum Buttress

Diagram above

The main cliff of Creag Mhòr continues for about 300m, slowly diminishing in height from it's highest point. The cliffs become vegetated and slabby and these slabs can be descended to sea-level where the cliff rears up again at an area of brown stained rock called Drum Buttress, containing a big brown corner. The main feature here is a twin crack-line in the back of the corner starting from good ledges 3m above the sloping platform in the base of the corner.

Descent: Easy scrambling down broken ground just to the north of the corner is possible, or alternatively and more easily, by walking along a natural ramp that begins just south of a foul smelling gully which marks the southern extremity of The Auditorium (seabird colonies inhabit the gully and the faces either side). The ramp starts grassy and with rock steps to reach orange-coloured slabs about 20m above the sea. The slabs run into a rock ramp, narrowing and descending to the seaward arete of the corner. Sloping rock ledges at its base are sea-washed, particularly in a swell.

1 Come Uppance 30m HS 4a
R.Illingworth, E.Parker, 13 Jul 2017
Start where the approach traverse narrows and drops down to a slab under the main face. Climb the left side of the arete and follow the indistinct arete to the top.

2 Bongo Fury 40m HVS 5a *
E.Parker, R.Illingworth, 13 Jul 2017
Start 5m right of the arete and climb a black groove with a thin crack out of the top, followed by easy ground.

3 Passing the Baton 40m HVS 5a **
A.Davis, P.Botterill, A.Rutherford, 13 Jun 2017
Start below an obvious light-coloured groove in the left wall of the corner recess.
1. 25m 5a Climb the short black wall and move right into the groove. Climb it steeply to ledges.
2. 15m 4a Climb the open groove above, passing to the right of a nose.

4 Beginnings 40m HVS 5a
C.Fennell, S.Chinnery, 9 Jun 2008
Start on a ledge below the twin cracks. Trend left up cracks and grooves. Go up, then across the base of a pegmatite band, then left. Climb up to a roof in a right-facing corner and go through the roof on good holds, then trend slightly left to finish.

5 Reduced-Fat Bastard 40m HVS 5a
H.Cottam, M.Howard, 5 Jun 2007
The line of the twin cracks. Start below them. Go up and right into an obvious corner leading to a roof. Turn the roof on its left and gain the twin cracks to finish.

6 Guister's Arete 40m HVS 5a **
R.Cross, A.Benson, 9 Jun 2008
Climb Reduced-Fat Bastard to the first ledge. Pull right onto the arete at an obvious pegmatite spike. Follow the wall on huge holds to two left-slanting red grooves. Climb these pulling right to a ledge. A juggy wall finishes.

7 Atlantic Drum 50m HVS ****
K.Howett, T.Rankin, 19. May 2000
An atmospheric route up the steep wall to the right of the twin crack-line. Take a belay on the raised ledges.
1. 25m 4c From the right end of the ledges, traverse hard right under a small roof and across a black slab. Pull up the wall and climb diagonally right up the steep wall until it is possible to climb vertically into a corner. Go up this to belay on a ledge below a roof.
2. 25m 4c Take the crack out of the left side of the roof in a spectacular position, then follow a direct line into another corner to finish.

Cream Buttress

Diagram opposite

Beyond the area of the corner, but inaccessible from it, is an undercut buttress of black rock containing an arching roof at mid-height.

Descent: The climbs are all accessed by abseil. The first climbs the pillar between Drum Buttress and Cream. The central climbs start from a series of small ledges just above the undercut lower section and slightly right of centre. The final two are gained by an abseil just right (looking out) of the deep gully marking the boundary between Creag Mhòr and Creag Beag to footledges in a large right-facing corner capped by roofs at 10m. Possible in most states of the tide.

8 Crock's Rock 30m HVS 5a **
A.Benson, R.Cross, 9 Jun 2008
Climbs the obvious shattered groove to the right of Atlantic Drum. Gain a ledge by abseil above the high tide line on the pillar on the right-hand side of a narrow chimney. Climb the pillar, followed by the steep shattered groove and the wall above.

9 Cream Seas 30m E2 5c **
K.Howett, L.Creamer, 27 May 2002
From the central ledge, climb direct through bulging rock to gain big holds under the roof, about 5m left of the right end. Follow the roof leftwards passing through a slight corner in the roof to beneath an obvious V-slot break in the roof. Pull through this then step up and right to follow a shallow groove and cracks onto easier ground.

10 I Am Legend 30m E1 5b **
I.Renshaw, L.Callaghan, 8 Jun 2008
From the central ledge of Cream Seas, step right and climb up to the big roof with two obvious jam cracks. Pull through the roof on good jams and climb the wall above.

Atlantic Drum (HVS) Kevin Howett (photo Kevin Howett collection)

11 Cream Liberator 45m E1 5b **
L.Callaghan, B.Winston, I.Renshaw, 8 Jun 2008
From the footledges, traverse out left to a sharp arete. Ascend this in a fine position to a niche at the left-hand end of the roof. Make moves left onto the nose and continue straight up the easier upper walls, stepping left into a short steep groove from the ledges at two-thirds height.

12 The Cat Who Got the Cream 45m E2 5b **
L.Callaghan, C.Fennell, 8 Jun 2008
Step 2m right from the belay and go straight up to the roof. Good holds lead round the roof to vertical grey layback flakes. Step left from these and continue more boldly up the slabby wall to easier ground.

CREAG BEAG

(NL 641 902) Partially Tidal SW facing Map p271

A conspicuous gully forms the start of the Creag Beag cliff line of perfect rock, that continues to the end of the headland. Creag Beag has been divided into separate sections, based on access, for ease of information. Some of the cliff sections can be partially viewed from below the big corner of Drum Buttress, and north to south they are The Destiny Walls, separated from Cream Buttress by the deep gash in the top of the cliff and accessed only by abseil. These continue unbroken to the headland where the base of The Sea Creature Walls can be accessed by a sea-level traverse in calm seas.

There are no obvious nesting ledges on Creag Beag and the walls appear to be bird free, but black guillemots have been seen in tiny slots in the junction between Ripple Buttrss and The Arch. These are specially protected and should be avoided if seen.

The Destiny Walls

Lying between Cream Buttress and the Sea Creature Walls there are very few sea-level ledges and abseil is necessary to gain mainly hanging stances at the start of each batch of routes. The cliff is extensive and complex and the routes can be difficult to locate without a brief inspection over the lip on abseil. They are split into separate buttresses based around distinctive features. The routes are described north to south as approaching from Creag Mhòr.

Ripple Buttress

Diagram opposite

To the south of Cream Buttress is a vertical gash or gully which merges into the wall as it drops towards the sea. On the south side of this is a clean, continuous face. When viewed from the platform below the corner of Atlantic Drum, the most distinctive feature is a black, glassy, rippled slab near the skyline, with a big left-facing corner above.

Descent: The following five routes start from a silvery ledge under an overlap about 5m above the barnacles and about 10m left (looking in) of the rippled slab. Abseil from a point 10m left of the top of the gully (looking out).

1 The Unfathomable Disappearance of Howett's Crabs 40m E4 6a **
L.Callahan, I.Renshaw, Jun 2008
Traverse left from the belay ledge bypassing the left end of the overlap, and pull easily upwards into a smooth shallow grey groove. Go up the groove and exit with

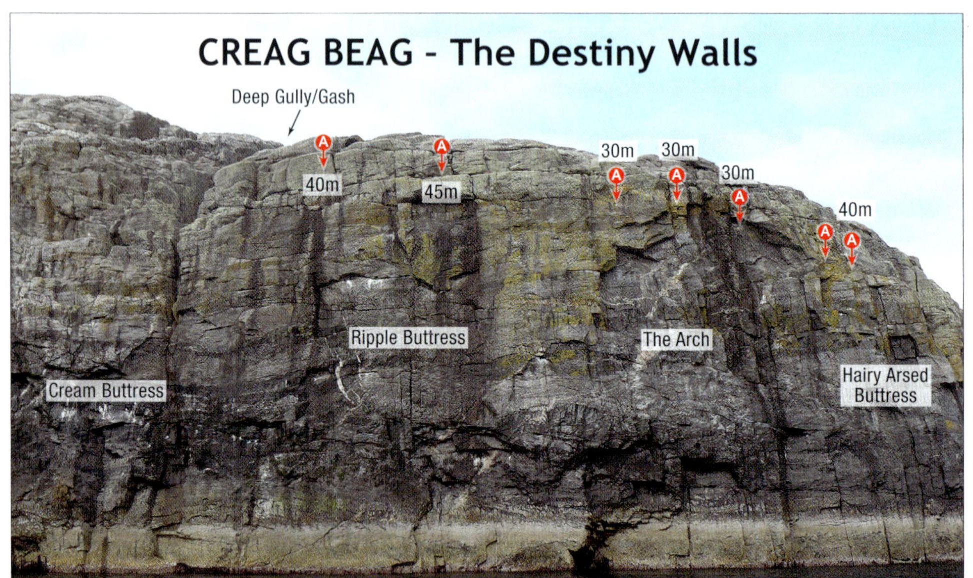

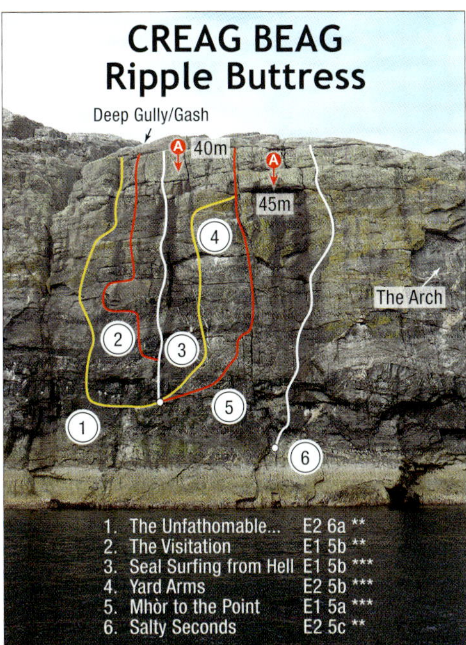

difficulty (5c for tall people). Climb through the gap in the overlaps above and up the wall above, finishing in a corner on the right.

2 The Visitation 40m E1 5b **
R.K.Howett, K.Howett, 26 Apr 2017
Climb into a corner from the right end of the ledge and step immediately out left onto the slab. Go up the slab diagonally left to a steepening and traverse left to an obvious big flake. Climb this to a sloping ledge then, step right and take the steep wall direct. More easily into a steep finish right of the corner of Howett's Crabs.

3 Seal Surfing in the Swell from Hell 40m E1 5b ***
K.Howett, T.Rankin, 20 May 2000
Climb the corner-line from the right end of the ledge to a bulge. Step left onto the wall and climb delicately up to pull onto a projecting ledge. Go up the slight arete above and climb the overhanging wall up and rightwards to pull into a superb flake-crack in a recess. Exit directly up the hairy wall above.

4 Yard Arms 45m E2 5b ***
G.Lennox, T.Rankin, K.Howett, 20 May 2000
Climbs a direct line up the wall between Seal Surfing and the rippled slab on the right. Step right from the ledge and follow a rightwards-diagonal quartz seam. Pull direct up the wall to an overlap. Pull through at its widest point via a jug (long reach). The easier wall leads to the capping overhanging wall. Climb this via a left diagonal crack to gain a horizontal flake. Follow this rightwards into the top of the big left-facing corner to finish.

5 Mhòr to the Point 45m E1 5a ***
T.Rankin, G.Lennox, K.Howett, 20 May 2000
Climbs the rippled slab. From the belay ledge follow smaller ledges rightwards to their end. Pull onto the slab above and take a diagonal line rightwards (bold) into a short slim hanging groove. Go up this into the base of a left-facing corner which passes to the left of a conspicuous horizontal roof near to the top. Excellent climbing.

The next route climbs the wall right of the rippled slab.

Descent: Abseil from the top of the cliff about 15m beyond the previous abseil point. Abseil over the horizontal roof near the top of the crag.

6 Salty Seconds 45m E2 5c **
K.Howett, T.Rankin, G.Lennox, 20 May 2000
Start from a tiny footledge just on the barnacle line, directly below a low roof underneath and right of the rippled slab. Calm seas essential. Pull steeply from the stance rightwards through bulges to the right side of the overlap. Pull through to a small sharp flake. Go up the wall direct into a perfect vertical crack. Follow this to a hole. Bypass the hole on the right and up a clean slab (the horizontal roof lies to the left) finishing in a conspicuous thin vertical crack through the final steep headwall.

The Arch

Diagrams opposite & p292

Just to the south is the largest single feature on the walls: an undercut slab defined on either side by large diagonal corners that meet as an overlap along its top to form a shallow arch.

Descent: locate a large open recess under a raised knoll just back from the top of the cliff, roughly above the centre of the arch. Various abseil lines from this recess over the arch gain the lowest ledges possible.

1 Like Father Like Son 30m HVS 5a *
R.K.Howett, K.Howett, 4 Jun 2015
Takes the general line of the left side of the arch via a stepped corner system. Abseil from 5m north of the recess to a tiny foot stance below the corner, just above the lip of a lower roof 5m above the sea. Climb up into the corner system and follow it all the way to a capping roof. Pull out left onto the wall and take a crack on the right to the top.

2 Sighting Land 30m HVS 5a *
K.Howett, T.Rankin, 17 May 2000
Abseil from the north end of the recess down a slight corner in the roof of the arch to gain small ledges at the base of a slab before it is undercut, 5m above the sea. Go up the slab into a right-facing corner. At the top of the corner exit direct through a bulge, then climb the wall into a final short corner in the roof of the arch.

3 The Grieff Games 35m HVS 5a *
R.K.Howett, C.Bendall, K.Howett, 30 May 2015
Abseil from the centre of the recess and gain a precarious stance on the left arete of a short roofed right-angled corner that drops cleanly into the sea. From the arete, climb up onto a very smooth grey slab on the left and enter a black groove (just right of the corner of Sighting Land). Go up this and exit right via quartz to a ledge. Take the wall above direct to gain the continuation of the diagonal break of Mad Monarch and follow this left-wards to its end and then the black streak into a hanging corner. Climb its left arete and exit the capping overhang direct.

4 The Mad Monarch's Mission of Maceration 30m HVS 5a **
R.K.Howett, C.Bendal, 30 Jun 2013
Abseil from the south side of the recess to gain a belay on a ledge below a short right-facing corner. Go up the corner to good underclings and step left to a ledge. Step back right to quartz blocks, then up to stand on a large diagonal break. Follow this left for a few moves until it is possible to climb direct to the capping overlap. Pull through at a break.

5 The True King of Scotland 30m E2 5c **
K.Howett, A.Munro, 30 Jun 2013
From the Mad Monarch abseil, gain a lower ledge down to the right. Step up right and climb the wall direct to steep rock below a tiny groove. Go up this in a great position to a slab below the diagonal roof of the arch. Follow the slab under the roof (thin and bold) to exit out right.

Hairy Arsed Buttress

The next batch of climbs are located around two corner

systems south of The Arch. Locate an area of slabs at the top of the cliff about 15m south of the recess at the top of The Arch.

Descent: For the first three routes, abseil to the base of the left-hand corner to small ledges at barnacle level (calm seas essential). Hairy Arsed Groove itself is gained by abseiling down the right-hand corner.

6 The Scone Thief 40m HVS 5a *
K.Howett, C.Bendall, 3 Jun 2015
Belay on a good but tiny ledge below the left arete. Climb up the wall via a shallow groove to below an isolated roof. Turn it on the left and gain an immaculate thin crack up the slab above to enter a vertical recess. Exit this on the right and climb to a final steepening.

7 The Stone in the Wall 40m HS **
R.K.Howett, C.Bendal, 30 Jun 2013
Belay on a small ledge right at the base of the left-hand corner. Climb the vertical crack leading into the large right-facing corner which leads to easy slabs above.

8 The Great Seal of Scotland 40m E1 5b *
K.Howett, A.Munro, 30 Jun 2013
Belay as for Stone in the Wall. Climb the wall up and right to gain the rounded arete. Climb cracks in the left side of the arete directly to a small slot in the roof above. Through this and take easy slabs above.

9 Hairy Arsed Groove 40m VS *
K.Howett, R.K.Howett, N.A.Howett, 9 Jun 2008
The right-hand of the two corners is characterised by thick hairy lichen in its upper regions. Abseil down it and the wall below to a small ledge 3m above the barnacles. Alternatively, traverse in below the Sea Creature Walls.
1. 20m 4c Up the easy black wall leftwards to below a bulge and a short corner. The brown flaky wall on the right leads to a gap in the roof, guarding access into the corner. Pull over and belay on a ledge above.
2. 20m 4b The excellent (hairy) corner above to the top.

The Sea Creature Walls

(NL 642 901) Partially Tidal SW facing
Diagram p294

This is the area of crag from the very tip of the peninsula, leading round towards The Destiny Walls. It is defined by the limit of easy traversing along a series of ledges just above high tide level, which allow access between the routes at most states of the tide in calm seas. The routes are described right to left as met traversing along the base.

Descent: Walk toward the tip of the point and find Dolphin Rock. This is a conspicuous raised ridge of rock running slightly downhill toward the point resembling a dolphin surfacing with its head pointing toward the water - use your imagination! Below the end of this ridge are slabs and directly below the head of the dolphin is a flake spike. Abseil 25m from here down a big black diagonal corner to ledges.

The wall extends to the right (looking in) as a black wall on the end of the point above a large platform, and to the left above disjointed ledges below corners passing a deep brown chimney which bounds the right side of a silver slab. The ledges finish left of this slab below a left-facing off-width corner which overlooks Hairy Arsed Groove.

Dolphin Wall

Diagram p295

The area either side of the abseil point with large ledges along the base.

1 Un-named 20m VD
J.Briggs, 25 Apr 2017
There are three distinct crack-lines up the black wall above the ledge. The furthest right is more broken and unclimbed. Climb the central one to a halfway ledge, then the corner above past a small roof.

2 Shag Happy Too 25m HS 4b
T.Carruthers, S.Tyson, D.Robinson, 7 Jun 2007
The main crack in the centre of the black wall. Follow the slim chimney above to finish.

Seal Surfing in the Swell from Hell (E1) Ian Renshaw (photo Ben Winston)

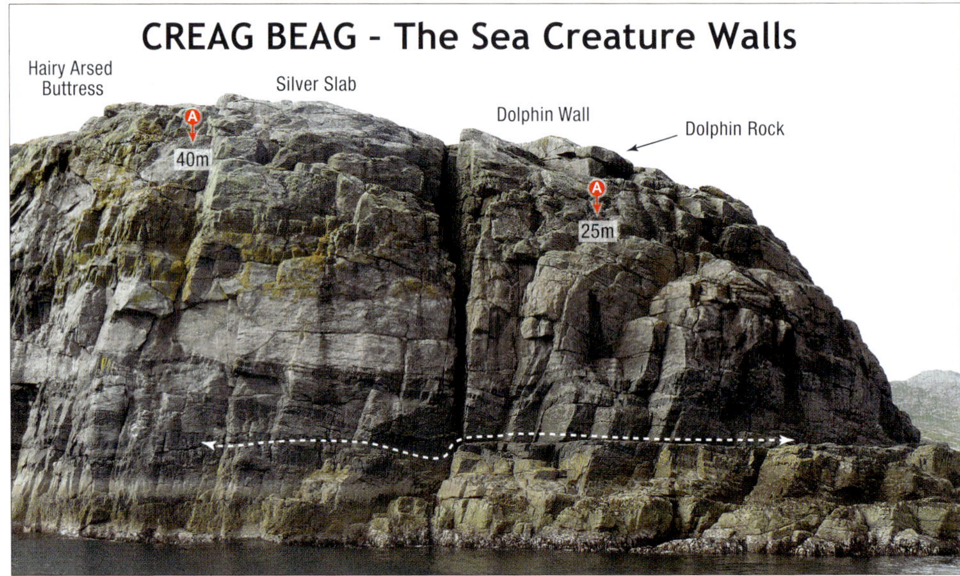

3 Claws for Thought 25m VS 5a
K.Howett, A.Munro, 30 May 2015
The even blacker streak down the wall left of Shag Happy is climbed into a slight corner leading to a steepening above a break. Pull up right into the small roof and gain the slab above. Exit left.

4 Without Good Claws 20m E1 5b *
R.K.Howett, C.Bendall, 30 May 2015
Takes the obvious vertical crack into a left-facing corner. Steep and sustained.

5 Sucking on Crab Claws 20m E2 5c *
K.Howett, R.K.Howett, 25 Apr 2017
The steep crack right again which disappears at half-height. Steeply up the crack to gain jugs in a black biotite band. Climb the blunt rib above boldly to easier ground.

6 Pilot Fish 20m VS 4c *
R.K.Howett, K.Howet,t 25 Apr 2017
The furthest left crack-line is much easier than it looks. A steep start gains a slabby recess leading boldly to a capping bulge. Pull directly over.

7 Dolphinium 20m HS 4a
R.K.Howett, K.Howett, 25 Apr 2017
The left arete, starting up a slight groove in its right side, then on its left before transferring right again. Gain a flake and easy groove to ledges and join the previous routes to finish.

8 Bottle and Nose 10m VS 4b
R.K.Howett, K.Howett, 25 Apr 2017
Eliminate but bold fun up the middle of the wall between the arete and the corner, ignoring the possibilities of using either to gain a big ledge.

9 Dunsonby Dave's Island Art 25m VD
T.Carruthers, S.Tyson, D.Robinson, 7 Jun 2007
From the ledge where the abseil lands you, climb the short right-angled corner to a large ledge and finish up easy corners to the right.

10 Mayday! Mayday! 25m S 4a
A.Dunhill, R.Kenyon, 9 Jun 2017
Start just left of Dunsonby Dave and climb the short wall and the arete directly above (sporting!) to finish up that climb.

11 Escape Pod 25m D
R.K.Howett, 7 Jun 2007
The large stepped black corner that joins Dunsonby Dave's Island Art, through which the abseil line descends.

12 A Senior Moment 25m E1 5b *
P.Botterill, A.Davis, 9 Jun 2017
Climb the right end of the short lower wall to the big ledge below the steep wall of the abseil. Continue up a thin crack in the steep wall to better holds and easy ground.

13. Senility 25m HVS 5a
P.Botterill, A.Davis, A.Rutherford, 13 Jun 2017
Climbs the centre of the short wall right of Rockabilly Groove to the left end of the big ledge. Continue straight up the crimpy wall just left of a black streak to easier ground.

14 Rockabilly Groove 25m HVS 5a **
T.Carruthers, S.Tyson, 7 Jun 2007
The steep groove bounding the left side of the black corner. The next ledge left contains a big corner with a subsidiary corner on its right. Go up the smaller right

1. Un-named	VD	7. Dolphinium	HS 4a	14. Rockabilly Groove	HVS 5a **
2. Shag Happy Too	HS 4b	9. Dunsonby Dave's Island Art	VD	15. Wet Dreams	VS 4c
3. Claws for Thought	VS 5a	10. Mayday! Mayday!	HS 4a	16. Wide Mouthed Monster	HS 4b *
4. Without Good Claws	E1 5b *	11. Escape Pod	D	17. Katching Krabs	S 4a
5. Sucking on Crab Claws	E2 5c *	12. A Senior Moment	E1 5b *	18. The Moist Merman	VS 4c *
6. Pilot Fish	VS 4c *	13. Senility	HVS 5a		

corner to a small roof. Pull right and rock up into the flying groove in the arete. This and other things lead to the abseil point.

15 Wet Dreams 25m VS 4c
R.K.Howett, C.Bendall, 3 Jun 2015
The shallow groove and roofs immediately left of Rockabilly Groove.

16 Wide Mouthed Monster 25m HS 4b *
K.Howett, N.A.Howett, R.K.Howett, 7 Jun 2007
Climb the main corner, by-passing the small roof low down steeply on its left, into a bigger corner above. Go up left under a bigger roof to pull over right onto a ledge and belay. Follow easy slabs rightwards to the abseil point.

17 Katching Krabs 25m S 4a
R.K.Howett, M.Morrison, 3 Jun 2015
The wall immediately left of the main corner. Go up the centre of the wall passing a low roof on the arete via a short corner, then step right over a second smaller overlap. Climb direct left of the big roof at the top and take the upper wall then easy ledges rightwards to the abseil point.

18 The Moist Merman VS 4c *
I.Howie, R.K.Howett, 3 Jun 2015
The left arete of the Dolphin Wall overlooking the deep brown chimney. Climb direct up the right side of the arete to the low roof. Swing left to cracks in the left wall and follow these and the arete as close as possible to easier ground.

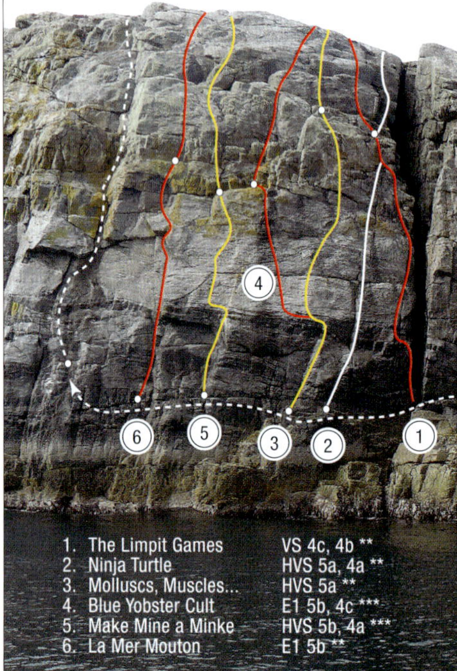

The Silver Slab

To the left, the brown chimney looks interesting for those of a speleological bent. The Silver Slab follows left again. Gain the base of the slab by descending to sea-level below the chimney and traversing a steep wall to gain a small ledge below the centre of the slab. The first route climbs the very edge of the slab, from a belay below the chimney.

1 The Limpit Games 40m VS **
K.Howett, N.A.Howett, R.K.Howett, 8 Jun 2008
1. 25m 4c From the base of the chimney climb the steep left arete of the chimney to jugs out left and follow a short crack up and back right to the arete. Climb a short corner in the arete, exit left onto the slab and join Ninja Turtle just below its belay ledge.
2. 15m 4b Follow the corners above.

2 Ninja Turtle 40m HVS **
K.Howett, N.A.Howett, R.K.Howett, 8 Jun 2007
Climbs a more or less continuous crack-line up the right side of the slab from the right end of the small belay ledge at the faint start of the crack.
1. 25m 5a Steeply up onto the slab and into the crack. Follow this with continuous interest, steepening slightly before exiting to a large ledge overlooking the chimney.
2. 5m 4a Go up slabs above and left to finish.

3 Molluscs, Muscles and Mantelshelves 40m HVS **
K.Howett, M.Morrison, 4 Jun 2015
The centre of the slab. Start below a short ramp from the left side of the small belay ledge.
1. 25m 5a The ramp leads to a black bulge. Make a move horizontally left in the bulge and mantel onto the slab. Mantel your way up a slight rib above to gain a horizontal break. Go up the slightly steeper but easier slab to gain a vertical crack leading to a ledge.
2. 15m Easy stepped rock to finish.

4 Blue Yobster Cult 40m E1 ***
K.Howett, R.K.Howett, N.A.Howett, 7 Jun 2007
A superb line up the blankest part of the slab. Start below the short ramp as for Molluscs.
1. 25m 5b The ramp leads to a black bulge. Traverse horizontally left in the bulge to pull onto the slab on slopers near its left end. Go up the blank looking slab to a horizontal break. Climb the steeper slab above leftwards to gain ledges.
2. 15m 4c A fine slim corner directly above.

5 Make Mine a Minke 45m HVS ***
K.Howett, R.K.Howett, N.A.Howett, 8 Jun 2007
The left side of the slab. Gain a bigger ledge below the next short corner by a sea-level traverse across a steep wall.
1. 25m 5a From the right side of the ledge, go up a steepening corner to the roof. Pull round its right side into a small hanging groove in the slab above. From the top of the little groove, go left along a break for a couple of moves and up the steepening slab past another break. Go diagonally left past a small pocket into a short left-facing corner and so gain the left side of the ledge of the previous route.
2. 20m 4a Take the clean line up the slab above and left of the ledge, then easier ground above.

6 La Mer Mouton 40m E1 5b **
K.Howett, A.Munro, 30 May 2015
The large left-facing corner bounding the left side of the slab. Continue the traverse from The Minke ledge to below the obvious off-width corner (4a and the limit of easy traversing – Hairy Arsed Groove is just to the left). Climb the corner to a capping roof. Exit right onto the edge of the slab and pull up and left into a recess. Exit above to a ledge and clean easy walls lead rightwards and up.

THE SHAG SLOT

On the east side of the Headland, just round from the point itself and on a lower level than Sea Creatures Wall, is a deep slot of a geo only 3m wide inhabited by shags. The back of the geo forms a cave heading into the hillside.

Shag Hole 25m HVGreasy *
I.Renshaw, B.Winston, R.Cross, A.Benson, Jun 2008
A fantastic subterranean adventure. Abseil into the landward end of the geo to sloping ledges (washed at higher tides). Tunnel into the greasy slot, heading for daylight, to emerge through a narrow hole onto the hillside.

CLEITE HEADLAND

On the south side of the island, four promontories project into the sea. The highest of these is the Cleite Headland.

CANAL WALK

(NL 646 902) Tidal W facing Map p271
Diagrams below & p298

This series of walls lies on the west side of the headland. A long wall about 20m in height, is separated from a distinctive long, low island lying just offshore, forming a canal of deep water between them. The island has a gap in it where the water surges into a splash pool. The landside wall above is smooth and streaked black.

The main feature here is a large corner stepped with big ledges, left of the black streaks (Sealap Dancing), forming a natural partition between the right and left walls. Right of this the wall becomes accessible from mid tides. A large open corner bounds the right side of the wall with a shorter steep wall, the final feature, to the right again. The left-hand wall, left of Sealap Dancing, drops into the deep water of the canal itself.

Descent: Make a short abseil from the lower end of a sloping shelf at the top of the right-hand side of the wall (looking in). This gives access at most states of the tide to the routes right of the splash pool. At lower tides or calmer seas it is possible to walk past the splash pool to the corner of Sealap Dancing, and then onwards to small ledges in the centre of the left-hand wall, traversed at about 4b at barnacle level. Routes further left are accessed directly by abseil.

1 Keepers Arete 15m HVS 5a *
T.Stephenson, J.Beveridge, 30 May 2002
The blunt arete on the right side of the big open corner on good holds, to finish on the left side of the nose.

2 Loch and Quay 15m E2 5c
T.Stephenson, J.Beveridge, 30 May 2002
The steep wall forming an overhanging recess just right of the big open corner. Climb up ledges to a left-leaning corner. Follow flakes up and right to a rest, then climb left on flakes for 2m before tackling the bulge direct.

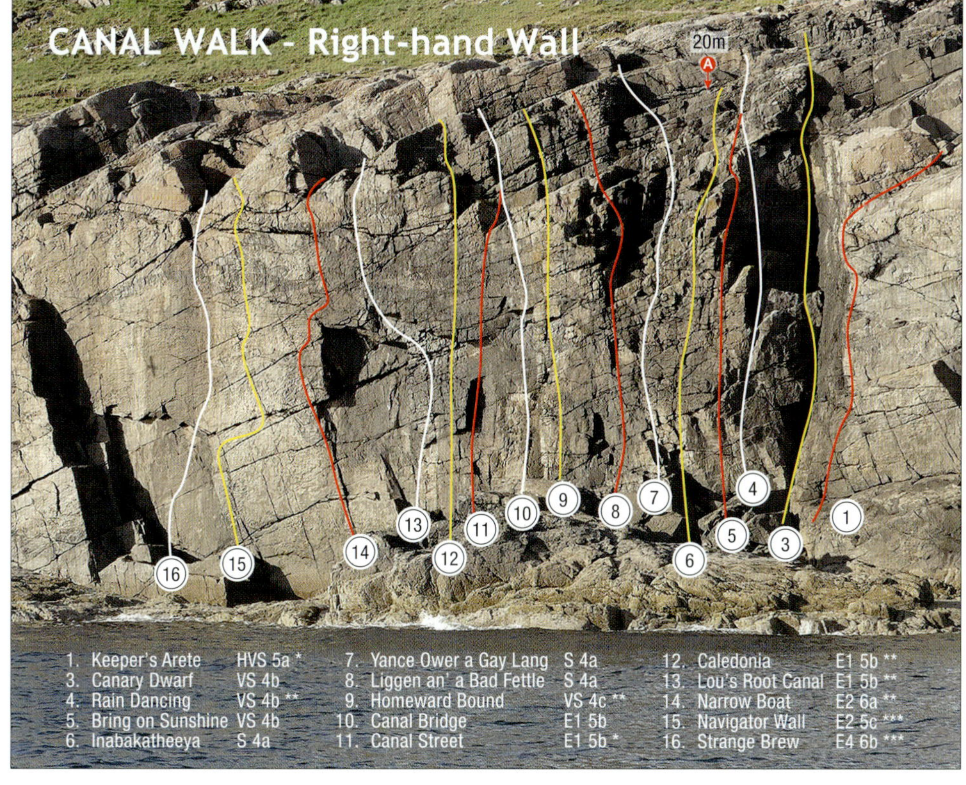

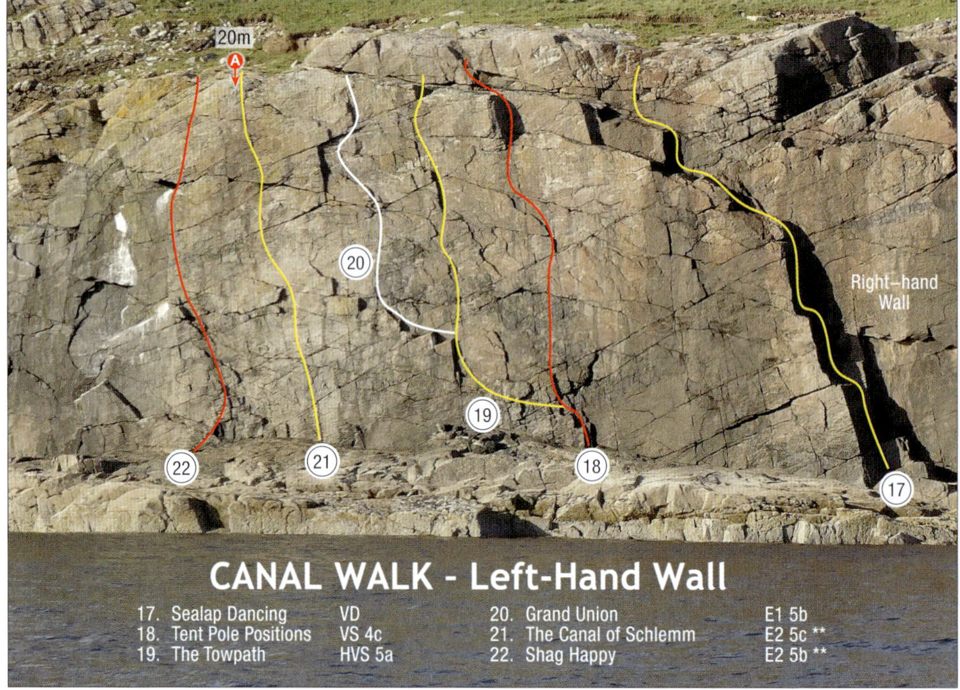

3 Canary Dwarf 20m VS 4b *
J.Beveridge, T.Stephenson, 30 May 2002
This is the big left-facing open corner bounding the right side of the main buttress.

4 Rain Dancing 20m VS 4b **
J.Beveridge, T.Stephenson, 28 May 2002
Climbs the left wall of the big open corner to exit into a notch.

The wall to the left is easy-angled and seamed by several vertical cracks.

5 Bring on the Sunshine 20m VS 4b
R.Kenyon, A.Dunhill, 10 Jun 2017
Climb the straight crack just left of Rain Dancing.

6 Inabakatheeya 20m S 4a
T.Carruthers, S.Tyson, 30 May 2002
The first line to the left again, up the edge of the slabby wall.

7 Yance Ower a Gay Lang Sen 15m S 4a
S.Tyson, T.Carruthers, 30 May 2002
The next line to the left, keeping just right of a crescent overlap.

8 Liggen an' a Bad Fettle 15m S 4a
S.Tyson, T.Carruthers, 30 May 2002
Climb direct to the crescent overlap and pull over to a commodious ledge.

9 Homeward Bound 20m VS 4c **
G.E.Little, K.Howett, 3 May 1999
Climbs a line up the left edge of the wall, just right of the deep-cut left-facing corner starting from the ledges at the base of the wall, which connects it to the island at low tide. Climb the front face to enter and climb a slim hanging groove on its left edge.

10 Canal Bridge 20m E1 5b
T.Stephenson, J.Beveridge, 28 May 2002
Climb the deep-cut corner that forms the left side of Homeward Bound, passing a roof at two-thirds height.

Left of Canal Bridge the ledges drop into the splash pool. The roof of that route continues leftwards, cutting across the top of a conspicuous black pillar hanging below it (with shallow corners either side of it).

11 Canal Street 20m E1 5b *
R.Strube, H.Cottam, 30 May 2002
Climb the shallow corner forming the right side of the pillar, just left of the corner of Canal Bridge and pull direct through the capping roof.

12 Caledonia 20m E1 5b **
J.Berveridge, T.Stephenson, 30 May 2002
Climbs the front of the pillar and roof and wall above.

13 Lou's Root Canal 20m E1 5b **
L.Creamer, K.Howett, 30 May 2002
Climbs the corner forming the left side of the pillar, to pull through the recess at its top formed by a bigger first roof, then slightly left and up past the left end of the diminishing roof above to gain a flake system leading to the top.

14 Narrow Boat 20m E2 6a **
T.Stephenson, J.Beveridge, 30 May 2002
Just left of the pillar the wall becomes smoother, steeper and seamed with diagonal cracks. Climb a vertical crack up the right edge of this wall to gain the left end of the bigger roof on the above route. Follow good cracks above to finish.

15 Navigator Wall 20m E2 5c ***
T.Stephenson, J.Beveridge, K.Howett, 30 May 2002
Climbs a line up the centre of the superb smooth wall above the splash pool. Start off the right end of the lower big ledge below the Sealap Dancing corner. Climb a vertical crack just right of a slight rib right of the black wall with difficulty to a break. Pull up to the next break and traverse it right to a vertical crack direct up the centre of the wall. Superb climbing.

16 Strange Brew 20m E4 6b ***
L.Creamer, K.Howett, 30 May 2002
Climbs the right edge of the black streak above the splash pool. Start off the sea-washed ledge at the base of Sealap Dancing. Climb the lower black wall diagonally right with hard moves to gain the right end of a small overlap. Pull up onto the wall above and gain the horizontal break above. Go up the wall following the right edge of the black streak, passing a further break, and make a very hard move up and left to gain the base of a left-facing corner. Follow this to finish.

17 Sealap Dancing 20m VD
G.E.Little, K.Howett, 3 May 1999
The easy-angled right-facing big corner system above the left side of the splash pool. Ledge belay at the base at low tides.

18 Tent Pole Positions 20m VS 4c
K.Howett, 30 May 2002
From the lowest ledge as for The Towpath, climb onto the next ledge and then take a direct line up the wall past hollow flakes to gain a very slim ramp leading left near the top. Take a thin flake-crack to enter a slabby right-facing corner hanging at the top of the wall.

19 The Towpath 25m HVS 5a
G.E.Little, K.Howett, G.Lennox, 3 May 1999
Climbs the line of least resistance up the left-hand wall above the Canal itself (left of the splash pool). Either traverse to ledges in the centre of the wall from the right at low tide at 4b or abseil to the ledges and belay on the lowest possible ledge. Follow the ledges up left then the wall above direct into a shallow left-trending groove system that leads to near the top. Exit right.

20 Grand Union 20m E1 5b
I.Renshaw, B.Winston, Jun 2008
From the ledges as for The Towpath, climb the wall above trending slightly rightwards.

21 The Canal of Schlemm 25m E2 5c **
L.Callaghan, I.Renshaw, Jun 2008
Climbs a line up the steepest part of the wall between the Towpath and Shag Happy. Abseil to a hanging stance and footledge above the barnacle line at the base of a shallow left-facing corner, about 8m right of the left arete (looking in). Climb up the shallow corner to its top and trend up and left towards a black hole overlap. Pull over this to a break below a large left-facing crescent-shaped finger edge. Use the crescent to make thin technical moves leftwards and up to improving holds and the top.

22 Shag Happy 20m E2 5b **
H.Cottam, R.Strube, 30 May 2002
Takes a line just right of the arete at the extreme left end of the main wall. Abseil down a corner to the left of the arete and belay on a ledge at low tide. Traverse round the arete and continue 3m rightwards, then climb the wall direct.

HIDDEN GEO

(NL 648 902) Tidal W facing Map p271 Diagram p300

This is the deeply indented, double geo (Y-shaped) in the tip of the headland, visible from the very end of the headland beyond Canal Walk. The western geo is more open, with a few good rock features whilst the eastern geo is a narrow, deep affair with a compact little wall. The cliff between them, in the neck of the Y, is large but disappointingly broken. The following climbs are on the west-facing wall of the eastern geo. The main area of interest is a black wall capped by roofs guarding the entrance to the deeper geo beyond. Below the roofs are three short corners, whilst a larger left-facing corner extends from below the right end of the roof. The wall diminishes rightwards thereafter and contains a conspicuous chimney.

Descent: From the hillside above Canal Walk, contour round the headland and cross over the top to find a grassy rake heading down and south to the top of the wall. Abseil from the top of the wall down the left-facing corner to barnacle ledges. Climbs are described left to right.

1 Grauple Corner 20m VD **
P.Calton, R.Mackenzie, 24 Apr 2017
Climbs the left arete of the wall, starting off the left end of the barnacle ledges.

2 Act Natural 20m HVS 5a **
R.Mackenzie, P.Calton, J.Briggs, 24 Apr 2017
Climb the left-hand of the short corners, over a bulge onto the black crozzly wall and up to under a roof. Pull over direct on jugs and into a final short groove.

1. Grauple Corner VD **
2. Act Natural HVS 5a **
3. A Cure For Curiosity HVS 5a *
4. Hole in The Wall Gang E1 5b *
5. Last Supper for Nuts VD
6. Rum Tum D

3 A Cure for Curiosity 20m HVS 5a *
R.K.Howett, K.Howett, 24 Apr 2017
Climb the central short groove and the crozzly wall to under the centre of the upper roof. Traverse left on jugs to enter the final groove of Act Natural.

4 Hole in the Wall Gang 20m E1 5b *
K.Howett, R.K.Howett, S.Paterson, 24 Apr 2017
Climb the right-hand short groove and the crozzly wall to a ledge. Climb the steepening wall above to gain a flake-crack in the right side of the roof to finish.

5 Last Supper for Nuts 10m VD
S.Paterson, J.Briggs, 24 Apr 2017
Climb the right arete of the abseil corner.

6 Rum Tum 10m D
R.Mackenzie, P.Calton, 24 Apr 2017
Climbs the chimney further right.

CREAG NAN FRITHICH

(NL 648 903) Non-tidal S facing

On the east side of Cleite is a smaller geo. This cliff lies at the back of the geo, which forms a small cave. The wall to the left of the cave is clean and blank.

Descent: From the same grassy rake descent for Hidden Geo, turn left across steep grass and rocky slabs to gain the base of the cliff.

Where's Yer man? 20m E3 5c **
R.Mackenzie, P.Calton, 25 Apr 2017
Climb the obvious corner up the centre of the wall.

Block Wall

(NL 649 902) Tidal W facing Map p271
Diagram below

The east wall of the geo extends south from the cave as a continuous wall forming the west face of a small peninsula. The main features are a diagonal roof on the left above stepped ledges and a smaller block wall above a large sea-level platform near the tip of the peninsula.

Descent: Walk over the top of the hill and contour above the back of the geo to make an easy descent down onto the peninsula. An abseil gains the stepped ledges or a scramble down the end gains the platform. Climbs are described left to right.

1 Getting in Yer Slot 15m E1 5a
R.Mackenzie, P.Calton, 25 April 2017
Start from the higher left end of the stepped ledges. Climb up rightwards under the big roof.

2 Right Spikey 15m S 4a
P.Calton, R.Mackenzie, 25 April 2017
Start off the bottom right of the stepped ledges and climb a diagonal crack-line up the wall.

3 Right Spikey Right 15m VS 4c
P.Calton, R.Mackenzie, 25 April 2017
Starting further right along this part of the wall, near

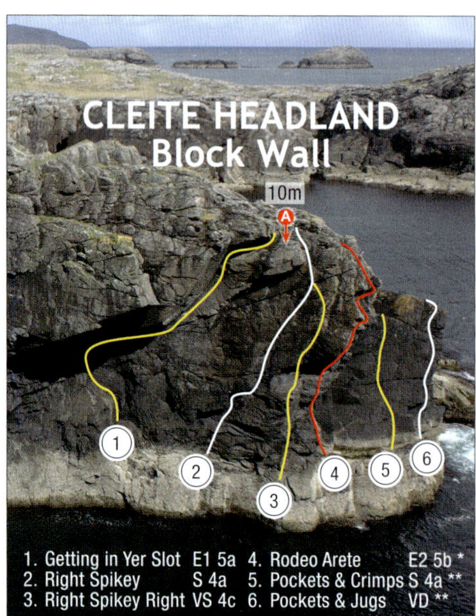

a larger platform on the lip of the peninsular, climb a direct line up the right side of the Right Spikey wall to finish as for that route.

4 Rodeo Arete 15m E2 5b *
R.Mackenzie, P.Calton, 25 April 2017
Start from the large platform and climb the extremely steep arete on its left side; juggy and well protected but an absolute pump-fest.

5 Pockets and Crimps 10m S 4a **
R.Mackenzie, P.Calton, 25 April 2017
Climb directly up the middle of the block wall.

6 Pockets and Jugs 10m VD **
P.Calton, R.Mackenzie, 25 April 2017
Climb the right-hand arete of the block wall.

Creag Bubh

(NL 648 905) Tidal E facing Map p271

The small stream of Allt nam Bodach drains the marshlands of Gleann Mòr from the centre of the island southwards into a deep-cut sandy geo between the peninsulas of Cleite on the west and Lìthinis on the east. The east-facing wall of this geo sports some excellent deep water solo lines. High tide is required and care must be taken, as there are rocks in the water under some parts of the wall. The routes are gained by abseil down each line.

Sprackle Corner 8m F4 (S3)
C.Adam, Jun 2009
This route climbs the chimney and corner in the centre of the crag.

The following three routes are left from the corner.

Stir Crazy 8m F6a+ (S0)
C.Adam, Jun 2009
Climbs the obvious crack left of the corner.

Routes Manoeuvre 8m F6b (S0)
M.Shorter, Jun 2009
Abseil down to a jug and climb out trending slightly left.

Root it Out 8m F6b+ (S1)
M.Shorter, Jun 2009
Abseil down to a manageable hold, traverse left and climb the arete keeping a watchful eye on the landing.

LÌTHINIS PENINSULA

The most southerly point of the island, this is the long peninsula which overlooks the Gleann Mòr geo. Its west face presents a long continuous cliff line of black rock.

Black Slab

(NL 650 902) Non-tidal W facing Map p271

Halfway along the cliff line is an obvious black shield-like slab with an overhanging wall chimney immediately to its left (facing in). Scramble down to the foot of the slab.

Megan's Meander 12m VD
L.Callaghan, Jun 2008
Ascend the slab trending slightly leftwards to follow a shallow depression. Unprotected.

Charlie's Chimney 13m VD
L.Callaghan, Jun 2008
Just left (facing in) of Megan's Meander is a deep chimney. Ascend the slabby right wall to enter the chimney at half-height.

Ginger Geo

(NL 652 903) Non-tidal E facing Map p271

On the east side of the Lìthinis peninsula is a small geo. Scramble down the most southerly tip of the peninsula and traverse at barnacle level (about 4b) to a bay beneath a large roof and rightward-facing groove.

This Would Never Do at Head Charge 15m HVS 5a
I.Renshaw, L.Callaghan, Jun 2008
On the east side of the geo, climb the wall beneath the groove then enter the groove, following it rightwards with continued interest.

MEANAIS PENINSULA

MULDOANICH WALL

(NL 656 909) Non-tidal S facing Map p271

This small undercut wall composed of immaculate and very clean orange gneiss is situated on the eastern side of the Meanais peninsula which defines the eastern side of the big sandy beach at the south-east corner of the island. The cliff itself is very sheltered, but it does have some seepage.

Descent: Easily down a steep ramp below the wall to a single entry point onto the wall at the left side of the sea cave beneath it. It may be wise to abseil down when wet.

Legendary Friend 18m HVS 5a
S.Chinnery, C.Fennell, Jun 2008
Climb the capped corner that defines the left side of the orange wall; turn the roof on the left.

Jellyfish Tour 20m HVS 5a
S.Chinnery, C.Fennell, Jun 2008
Start below the corner of Legendary Friend. Gain the lower undercut wall and traverse right under the orange wall, across two corners, to gain the dark rock defining the right side of the wall. Climb the fractured crack-line on improving holds.

PABBAY (PABAIGH)

This island lies between Sandray and Mingulay, some 12km to the south of Barra, and rises to a height of 171m. The ruins of a small settlement lie above the beach in the sheltered Bàgh Ban in the east.

Although in general offering smaller cliffs than neighbouring Mingulay and Berneray the rock is exceptionally clean and solid, giving excellent climbing. The Great Arch is the most notable natural feature of all the islands, over 90m at it's highest point. The south coast, in particular around the south-west tip, has the best cliffs, contained in a series of geos with large, open walls between.

The routes are described on cliffs clockwise round the island, starting at the bay on the east coast.

Camping: The machair above the beach in the sheltered Bàgh Bàn beside the settlement offers the best campsite with fresh running water from a small stream.

Access: See Bishop's Isles introduction p268.

RUBHA CHÀRNAIN

This is the most southerly peninsula on Pabbay. About 1km south of the campsite in Bàgh Bàn, the furthest point of the peninsula is named Ruadh-phort on the OS 1:25,000 map.

Rubha Chàrnain an Ear

(NL 607 867) Partially Tidal E facing

This cliff is near the south-east tip of the peninsula and can be seen from the campsite in Bàgh Bàn, from where it's an easy 10min stroll. It forms a short wall above a sloping ramp dropping into the sea. A calm sea at low tide is best. Climbs are described left to right.

The Watcher in the Waves 8m E1 5b *
M.Kocsis, Jun 2016
From the bottom of the ramp, an exciting traverse left along an obvious break leads to an obvious foothold in the middle of the face above the sea, and a rest. From here the only way is up.

Minor Miner 8m VS 4c *
M.Kocsis Jun, 2016
Starting at the same point as The Watcher, and climb direct following the orange crystal vein.

The Great Pabbay Rope Theft 8m VS 4b
M.Kocsis, Jun 2016
A slightly bolder line breaking out right from Minor Miner, and climbing the wall direct.

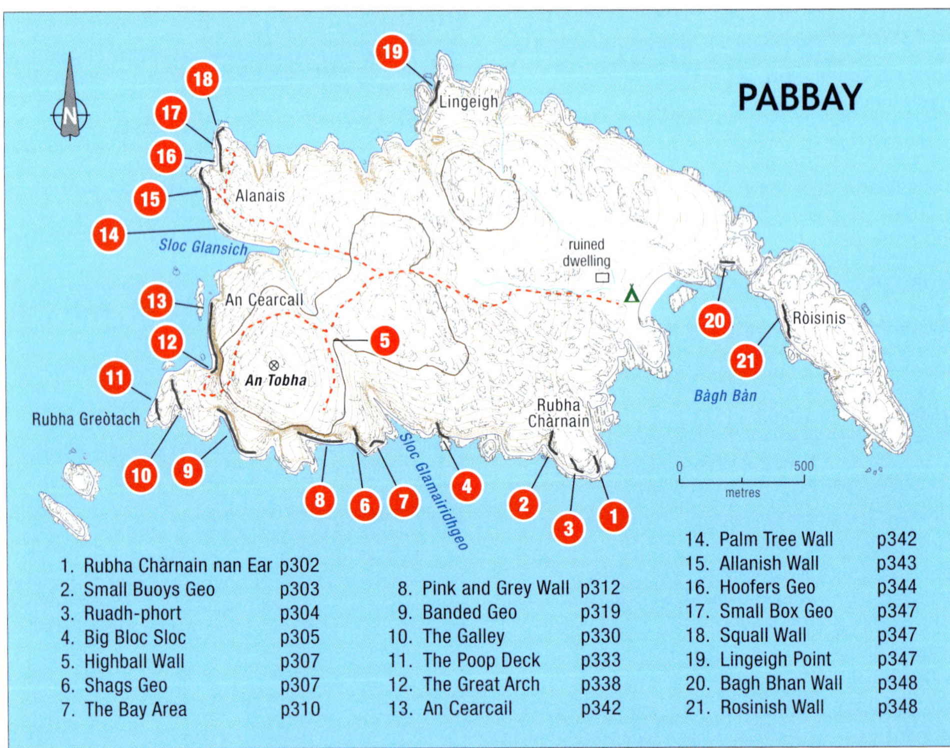

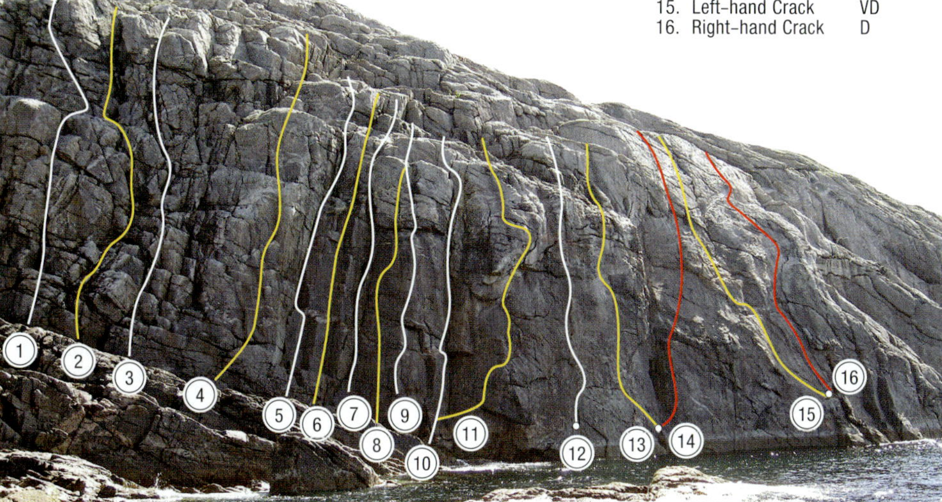

The Wave Jumper 8m VD
M.Kocsis, Jun 2016
There are two corners in the centre of the wall; this is the more agreeable left-hand corner.

The Seal of Approval HVS 5b
M.Kocsis, Jun 2016
The right-hand side of the wall is split by a big horizontal break. Climb a gritstone-like problem through the break.

Slap and Tickle S 4a
M.Kocsis, Jun 2016
The corner leading to the right-hand side of the wall.

SMALL BUOYS GEO

(NL 605 867) Partially Tidal W & S facing
Map opposite Diagram above

This little geo lies on the west side of Rubha Chàrnain. A slabby shelf runs down the east side of the geo below a low wall. Initially this wall is broken, then seamed with grooves and corners, finally becoming slabby as its base becomes sea washed and bends round to face south. The rock is excellent and the climbing is friendly with an outcrop feel to it.

The west side of the geo holds a seriously undercut wall promising sterner action if it ever dries out. The first routes start on the more broken rock to the left of the main recess containing the distinctive corners. A large raised ledge in the base of the recess can be accessed at high tide by abseil.

Descent: Most of the routes can be gained easily via the shelf (low tide required) but those on the slab can only be accessed by abseil.

1 Time for a Cormorant 15m VD
H.Salisbury, V.Hennelly, 3 Jun 2003
Climb the corner left of the crack of Reprieve until an awkward step right into a shallow sentry box. Climb up and left of this to easier ground.

2 Reprieve 20m VD
M.Nicoll, A.Vaughn, 15 May 1998
Start 10m left of Spare Rib. Climb a thin crack in a short steep black wall (crux) to gain a ledge. Continue to the top, finishing up a wide black slot.

3 Re-tyred 15m D
A.Vaughn, M.Nicoll, 15 May 1998
Start 6m to the left of Spare Rib at an undercut black wall. Start up this (awkward) and head for the obvious notch in the skyline, over large steps.

4 Spare Rib 15m S 4a
G.E.Little, 28 May 1997
Climb a shallow hanging groove in the left-bounding rib of the obvious recess holding three grooves.

5 First Groove 15m S 4a
G.E.Little, K.Howett, 28 May 1997
The leftmost of the three grooves in the large recess.

6 Wildlife on Two 15m HS 4a
A.Todd, K.Howett, 14 May 1998
The central, shallow groove.

7 Third Groove 15m VS 4b
G.E.Little, K.Howett, 28 May 1997
The right grooves.

8 Spicy Mayhem 20m E1 5b *
R.Jones, F.Murray, 30 May 1999
Takes the centre of the wall between Third Groove and Designer Rib, keeping away from the crack on the left and the rib on the right. Eliminate.

9 Designer Rib 20m HVS 5a *
K.Howett, G.E.Little, 28 May 1997
This superb little route climbs the right-bounding rib of the large recess.

10 Deceptive Corner 20m S 4a
G.E.Little, K.Howett, 28 May 1997
The corner immediately right of Designer Rib and bounding the slabby south-facing wall. Easier than it looks.

11 Easy Over 20m E1 5b **
K.Howett, A.Todd, 14 May 1998
Climbs the blunt rib right of Deceptive Corner (the rib separating the two walls of the face). Start in the base of Deceptive Corner and traverse out right onto the rib. Climb up the slabby section to the bulges near the top and take the obvious fat flake out right to reach a small horizontal black seam in the bulge. Step left in the seam to pull with difficulty onto the final slab.
Variation: **Fascinating Waves HVS 5b ***
M.Kocsis, Jun 2016
Exit the corner via a hanging groove which leads naturally to the finish of Easy Over.

The following routes climb the slab issuing from the sea and are accessed by abseiling to precarious hanging stances just above the water.

12 What Doing? 20m E1 5b **
K.Howett, G.E.Little, 28 May 1997
Abseil down the left-hand side of the slabby wall to a hanging belay in a crack just above the sea (calm seas essential). Climb above the belay following small cracks up and right, until it is possible to move back left into the centre of the wall. Climb direct up a shallow scoop in the wall to a horizontal break near the top. Follow the runnel above to finish.

13 Friends in Tibet 20m VS 5a **
G.E.Little, K.Howett, 28 May 1997
Abseil down the right-hand side of the wall to a small ledge above the sea, just left of a recess. Climb up and left for 5m then direct up the wall on surprisingly good holds.

14 Lobstered Ross 20m VS 5a **
F.Murray, R.Jones, 1999
From the belay of Friends in Tibet, climb up to the right of the recess to a crack in a small overhang. Follow this to the top.

The following two routes climb the easier-angled right-hand section of the slab. Abseil descent.

15 Left-hand Crack 20m VD
A.Todd, A.Vaughn, 16 May 1998
Start at the obvious large tidal ledge. Follow the left-hand crack to a ledge. Step left and climb the blunt arete to the top.

16 Right-hand Crack 20m D
A.Todd, A.Vaughn, 16 May 1998
Climb the obvious crack.

Ruadh-Phort

(NL 605 867) Non-tidal W facing Map p302

This is a small but perfectly formed wall further out towards the point. From the top of the slab of Small Buoys Geo, continue to a downward sloping ledge system that reaches sea-level. The retaining wall is where it's at! It was previously called Evening Wall, but we have adopted its local name.

The left end is a short pink wall. As the wall increases in height a black band of diorite appears along the base; below a right-facing groove are twin holes in the diorite, the band follows a smooth grey wall to the right. Further right is another large hole in the black band with a slim hanging groove above. A thin flake-crack splits the wall immediately right and a very conspicuous deep chimney-crack is found right again. Further right is a big kinked diagonal crack and then the wall drops into the sea. The routes are described left to right as one approaches.

Nom 8m 4c
R.I.Jones, 7 Jun 2003
Climbs the centre of the pink wall at the right end of the wall, to reach the right end of a ledge and go direct to the top.

The Sandgorgan 8m 5b
R.I.Jones, 7 Jun 2003
About 2m left of Stalking the Corncrake are two small cracks at 1.5m height. Climb these and the wall directly above.

Stalking the Corncrake 10m VS 4c
D.Carr, V.Hennelly, 7 Jun 2003
Left of Beach Bums. Climb the crack to a prominent thread on the left and climb this direct. Continuing up the crack right of the thread lowers the grade to 4b.

Pleasant Rib 10m S 4a
D.Carr, 7 Jun 2003
Climbs the rib immediately left of Beach Bums.

Beach Bums 10m VS 4c
K.Howett, 26 Aug 1999
The right-facing corner above the twin black holes near the left-hand side of the wall, leading to a roof near the top. Take a step right under this then pull through in the centre and take a rounded finish.

Late 10m VS 4c
A.Todd, W.Wright, 16 May 1998
Start slightly left of the twin black holes. Climb the wall direct to the top via a small curved overlap.

The Loneliness of the Long Distance Tokker 10m HVS 5a
K.Howett, 26 Aug 1999
The shallow groove above the black hole right of Late. Go up the groove to an obvious hold, then pass the small isolated roof on the left to a flake in another, smaller black band. Continue direct up the wall through a horizontal break to the top.

Lazybeds 10m S 4a
K.Howett, 26 Aug 1999
Climbs a conspicuous thin flake-crack between Tokker and Early. Go up the flake to ledges. Take the continuation crack directly above and to the right of the isolated roof of Tokker to gain the top.

Far From the Funicular (HVS) Bill Wright (photo Alistair Todd)

Early 10m S 4a
W.Wright, 16 May 1998
Climb the wall to the left of Later. Step right and climb direct to the top.

Later 10m VD
M.Nicoll, W.Wright, 16 May 1998
Climb the obvious deep chimney-crack.

37th Tick 10m S 4a
W.Wright, M.Nicoll, 16 May 1998
Climb the wall to the right of the chimney-crack to gain a recess. Finish up a left-trending ramp.

Far From the Funicular 10m HVS 5a *
W.Wright, M.Nicoll, A.Todd, 16 May 1998
Where the wide access ledges reach the high water mark a diagonal crack rises from right to left. Climb the wall direct to reach the crack where it is horizontal and then go direct up the slab to the top, following the line of a thin blind crack.

Dice Onions or Die 10m HVS 5a
K.Howett, 26 Aug 1999
The prominent diagonal crack in its entirety, through which Far From the Funicular climbs.

Sand Flies 10m HVS 5a *
K.Howett, 26 Aug 1999
Start up the crack of Dice Onions or Die. Climb the vertical start to the crack to a small roof. Pull over via a shallow flake, then go up and left to a thin rounded crack in the slab. Follow this to a break (or step left and up a black scoop, easier), then step left and go up the slab via a sharp flake-crack to a rounded finish.

Serious Mooching 10m VS 4c
K.Howett, 26 Aug 1999
Climbs a final line on the right of the cliff as it drops into the sea. Start right of the crack of Dice Onions or Die and climb the wall to gain a small ledge. Go up a smooth scoop to a horizontal break with a slight overlap. Pull over direct and go up to a diagonal break. Step slightly left and climb an easy-angled slab.

BIG BLOC SLOC

(NL 600 869) Tidal W facing Map p302 Diagram p306

Halfway along the south coast a geo cuts some way into the island. This is Sloc Glamairidhgeo (or more accurately Sloc Glamairi Geodha). To the east of this Sloc is a small (shallow) geo which has a very distinctive triangular wedge of clean black rock forming its east wall. The opposite wall of the geo is almost non-existent, forming a diminishing headland, and the back of the geo is a black and pink slab. The gap between the wedge and the slab is a deep vertical geo only a metre wide at sea-level. The wedge is actually only one of three walls separated by two corners. A bungalow-sized jammed block defies gravity in the upper part of the first corner south of the wedge. There are climbs in three different walls around the geo.

Descent: Abseil from bocks at the top of the triangular wedge. Cormorants sometimes nest just below the top of the cliff off to the side of the routes; take care not to disturb them when abseiling.

The following routes climb the impressive wedge, described from left to right.

1 Let Sleeping Storks Lie 25m E4 6a ***
P.Thorburn, R.Campbell, 27 May 1998
Climbs the left arete of the wall. Abseil down the arete to a foothold at barnacle level, just under a small roof. Calm seas essential. Go up the thin crack of Lifeline to a rest. Step left onto the arete. Climb the right wall of the arete, then step round to a good hold on the left wall under a small overlap. Gain the small groove above (crux) then follow it to a break. Climb the right side of the arete to a ledge and finish on the left side. At low tides it is possible to scramble down the slab in the back of the geo, to start the route by stepping across the watery gap onto the arete.

2 Lifeline 25m E3 5c ***
K.Howett, G.E.Little, 26 May 1997
An immaculate line up the thin central crack in the wall, starting under the left arete as for Sleeping Storks. Pull out right from the belay, by-passing the roof to climb a thin crack with difficulty. Where it peters out step right into a continuation crack which leads directly to the top with continual interest.

3 Immaculate Conception 25m E2 5b ***
G.E.Little, K.Howett, 25 May 1997
Abseil to a small ledge at the base of the outer edge of the wedge. Move left onto the face to gain a thin ledge above. Ascend 3m to reach a layaway hold in a small hole and traverse hard left to gain better holds. Climb direct into a hanging groove which leads to a small overlap. Pull out left round the arete and up to another small overlap, then pull back right into a final corner above.

4 Head-bread Ian 20m E2 5c **
I.Taylor, T.Freyer, May 1999
Follow Immaculate Conception to the layaway hold in the hole. Continue straight up the delicate wall to a roof. Go left 2m and then pull through the roof and trend right to finish.

The left and right walls of the corner below the massive jammed block are generally birdy and of little interest. The next corner south is shorter but clean. The following routes are in this square-cut corner.

Descent: From the top of the triangular wedge, scramble down above the wall (to the left looking out) until the top of the corner is reached; abseil to a small tidal ledge. The routes are described left to right.

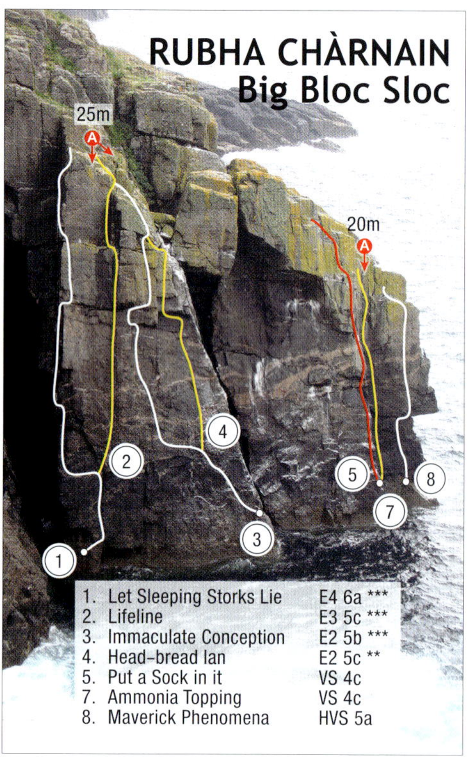

5 Put a Sock in It 20m VS 4c
L.Wright, P.Gibson, May 2002
The left arete of the corner.

6 Wee Bairns 20m VS 4c
M.Kingsley, J.Dale, 6 Jul 2007
Climb the left side of the left wall and continue by easy lichenous rock to the top.

7 Ammonia Topping 20m VS 4c
P.Gibson, L.Wright, May 2002
The main central corner to a triangular roof and flake above.

8 Maverick Phenomena 20m HVS 5a
L.Wright, P.Gibson, May 2002
Just left of the right arete of the wall is a short corner. Climb this and pull right round the overlap, then straight up the wall to finish left of the final arete.

The following routes climb the wall left of the mainland side, opposite the deep geo from the wedge. Approach by scrambling down to a small terrace above the wall and abseil.

Ying 15m VD
R.I.Jones, 5 Jun 2003
The wide crack on the left.

Yang 15m S 4a
R.I.Jones, A.Erskine, 5 Jun 2003
The central crack to a short steep wall and the crack above.

Yo 15m D
R.I.Jones, A.Erskine, 5 Jun 2003
On the right wall via a shallow groove.

AN TOBHA

An Tobha is the hill at the far western side of Pabbay and at 171m is the highest on the island. Its southern and western coasts contain the biggest and the best of the cliffs. They are concentrated in a series of geos into three areas: the south coast area west of Sloc Glamarigeo (containing Shags Geo, The Bay, Pink Wall and Grey Wall Recess), the area around the promontory of Rubha Greòtach at the far west end of the island (containing Banded Geo, The Galley and The Poop Deck) and the Great Arch on the west coast. They are described in this order.

Highball Wall

Map p302

When walking towards the climbs around An Tobha you reach a high col of flat grass just before skirting the hill. Sitting in this flat area is a 10m slab. All possible lines were soloed by K.Howett in 1995 and 1996 to give a range of bold climbs up to 5c.

SHAG'S GEO

(NL 597 869) Tidal W facing Map p302 Diagrams above & p308

This lies on the headland to the west of the deep inlet of Sloc Glamarigeo and east of Pink Wall. Its west facing flank forms an overhanging wall towards the back of a geo above a sea cave and is characterised by a huge wide-mouthed cave at mid-height. It diminishes in height seawards, becoming a wall seamed with corners and grooves towards its end near the tip of the headland. This face can be viewed, in part, from the headland to the west (just east of the Pink Wall). The most conspicuous and biggest corner is about halfway along. This is Cracking Corner. Routes are described from the back of the geo out towards the headland.

Approach: A long sloping grass terrace runs across the top of the wall with a 10m-high broken upper tier above. The upper tier can be descended in places but the terrace is most easily accessed by descending from the distinctive moss cairn at the top of the hill above the face (on its east side), towards the tip of the headland and traversing round to where the upper tier relents.

Descent: All routes are accessed by abseil from this terrace or beyond.

The first two routes are gained by abseil from a point just down from a large bay near the upper end of the grass terrace. Descend (with a little faith) into a small hidden cave a couple of metres above the sea, on an otherwise blank wall dropping into deep water.

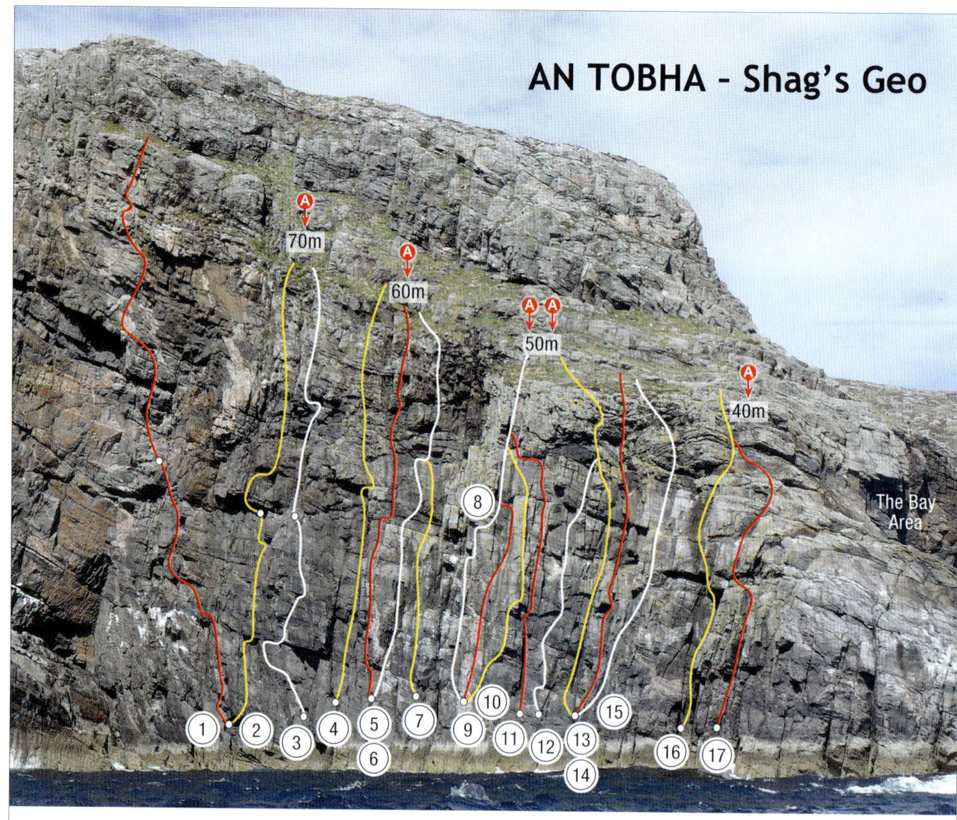

1. Up Before The Beak E3 5b, 5c ***
2. Deflated Flight VS 4c, 4c **
3. Shags with Attitude E3 5c, 4c **
4. Cracking Corner S 4a **
5. Truly Stunning VS 4c **
6. Quartz Waltz VS 4c
7. A Semblance of Reason VS 4c *
8. Butterfly Kisses VS 4c **
9. A Wok on the Wild Side HS 4b
10. Stealing Beauty HVS 5a *
11. Muscle Crack S 4a
12. Sweetness E1 5b **
13. Hunting the Gripper VS 4c *
14. Groovy Attitude VS 4b
15. Splitting The Growler S 4a
16. Barnacle Belay VS 4c *
17. Now It's Freda's Turn VS 4c

1 Up Before The Beak 80m E3 ***

G.E.Little, K.Howett, 24 May 1997

This tackles the highest part of the cliff near the back of the geo. It has a serious feel about it and a sting in the tail.

1. 35m 5b Exit from the left side of the small cave and climb a left-slanting ramp to a wide ledge. Move left along the ledge to gain the base of another ramp. Climb this, crossing an overlap and a juggy wall above to belay at a rounded spike at a band of steeper pink rock.

2. 45m 5c Climb up into a short corner leading to a deep horizontal fault capped by an overlap. Step right and stand on the fault. Pull up the leaning wall above on jugs and traverse 4m left along a hand-traverse line until beneath a hairline crack in the very steep wall above. Climb direct up this into a flared-chimney-corner and then on under a large roof. Exit left.

2 Deflated Flight 65m VS **

K.Howett, G.Nicoll, 16 May 1998

Climbs the line of a shallow left-facing corner system some 10m to the left of Cracking Corner. Again rather exciting.

1. 30m 4c Pull out of the right side of the cave and climb a steep crack to enter the base of the shallow corner. Climb this to a small belay ledge below the capping roof.

2. 30m 4c Climb through the roof into a hanging corner capped by another roof. Exit right and climb steeply on jugs to easy ground. Follow the least messy line slightly rightwards.

Descent: The following routes are gained by an abseil from mid-way along the grass terrace at a triangular block a short distance beyond a semi-detached pinnacle, and directly above a prominent black corner.

3 Shags with Attitude 60m E3 **

K.Howett, G.E.Little, 28 May 1997

Just to the left of Cracking Corner is a large black roof about 10m above the sea. Left again is a short, steep, narrow ramp just above sea-level. Gain the base of the ramp and a hanging belay at the high water mark.

1. 25m 5c Move up the ramp and where it peters out pull up onto an overhanging wall. Follow a thin crack-line up the wall to a horizontal break. Step right into this then up into a short left-facing slot formed by a large flange cutting through small roofs. Pull out right above the slot and follow the wall on good holds direct to a ledge and belay.

2. 35m 4c Climb an open corner to a roof. Traverse left below the roof then climb up on slightly messy ground to reach the grass ledge.

4 Cracking Corner 50m S 4a **

G.E.Little, K.Howett, 25 May 1997

Abseil from the block to just above sea-level at the base of the very obvious black corner. Climb the corner on big holds to its capping roof. Move right and continue in the same general line to the top to belay on the abseil block.

Between Cracking Corner and the next prominent corner (Wok on the Wild Side) is a vertical quartz cracked rib.

Descent: For the following routes, abseil as for Cracking Corner to a ledge just above sea-level and below an overhang directly below the quartz band.

5 Truly Stunning 48m VS 4c **

R.I.Jones, M.Snook, 31 May 1999

From the ledge step left and climb the vertical wall and small overhang on jugs. Go up the centre of the left-hand wall of a corner to a large ledge. Climb through the roof above to the top.

6 Quartz Waltz 48m VS 4c

R.I.Jones, M.Snook, 31 May 1999

From the ledge step up and right. Make a hard move across and up to exit to the right of the overhang to join the quartz crack. Climb this, and as it becomes less distinct step right onto an arete and follow this to a ledge. Climb through the roof above to finish to the right of the abseil point.

7 A Semblance of Reason 50m VS 4c *

R.I.Jones, M.Snook, 31 May 1999

Start 3m right of Quartz Waltz and left of the next prominent corner. Climb the wall and cracks to the large ledge. Climb through the roof on the left above as for Quartz Waltz.

The next routes are concentrated around the conspicuous corner of A Wok on the Wild Side which is mid-way between the unclimbed corner right of A Semblance of Reason and the next corner of Hunting the Gripper. It has a distinctive quartz patch at its base and a large triangle-shaped rock at a quarter height in the corner.

Descent: Approach by abseiling down the corner from a block on the grass terrace that can be threaded.

8 Butterfly Kisses 40m VS 4c **

P.Swainson, J.M.Given, May 1997

Climb the arete left of the grooved corner by cracks to an overhang. Turn this on the right and finish up A Wok on the Wild Side.

9 A Wok on the Wild Side 40m HS 4b

J.M.Given, P.Swainson, May 1997

From the quartz patch, climb the corner for 20m, then take the left wall by an exposed traverse (or the corner direct) and finish by a prominent jutting beak of rock.

10 Stealing Beauty 40m HVS 5a *

P.Swainson, J.M.Given, May 1997

Climb the right side of the corner by fragile holds to a crack, then enter a delicate little undercut groove. Finish as for A Wok on the Wild Side.

Descent: The following routes are again accessed by abseil from the block to ledges below a corner containing a spike, just above the barnacles.

11 Mussel Crack 40m S 4a

P.Swainson, J.M.Given, May 1997

Some 6m left of the spike belay is a stance below a wide crack. Climb the crack to an overhang, turn it on the right, up cracks to the jutting beak of A Wok On The Wild Side.

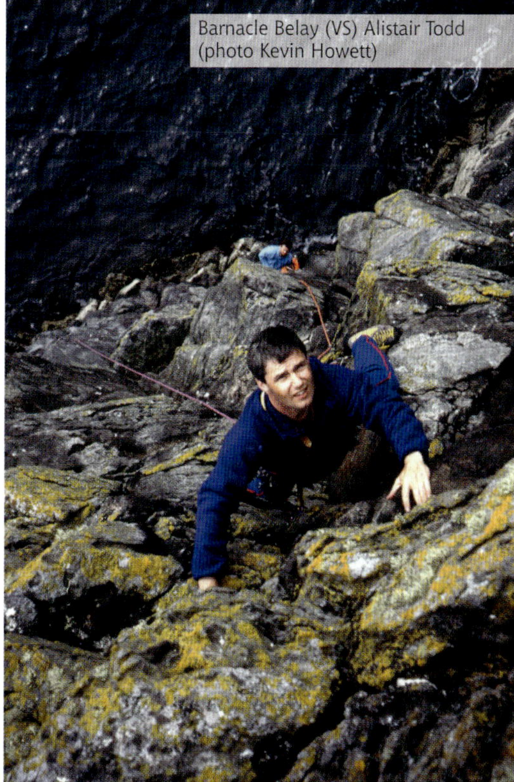

Barnacle Belay (VS) Alistair Todd (photo Kevin Howett)

12 Sweetness 35m E1 5b **
R.I.Jones, J.Wardman, 4 Jun 2003
The rib between Mussel Crack and Hunting the Gripper. Belay at the bottom right of the rib. Step onto the wall and make delicate moves up the wall. Trend slightly rightwards as you gain height, moving to easier ground. Finish direct through the overhanging finishing slot.

13 Hunting the Gripper 40m VS 4c *
J.M.Given, P.Swainson, May 1997
From the spike, trend left via a steep wall to a wide crack, follow this to a ledge. Climb the overhang (thread), then trend left to an overhanging finishing slot.

14 Groovy Attitude 35m VS 4b
J.Wardman, R.I.Jones, 4 Jun 2003
From the spike climb the small right-facing corner to an overhang. Take this on the right to a ledge. Step right and climb the corner above to a steep juggy finish.

15 Splitting the Growler 40m S 4a
P.Swainson, J.M.Given, May 1997
From the spike take a groove and crack to a ledge. Trend right to a steep juggy finish.

The next two routes lie on the farthest section of the west wall of the geo before it degenerates into ledges at the headland.

Descent: Access is by abseil from a small outcrop beside a level rock pavement near the edge of the cliff. The routes start around a little inlet approximately 10m seaward from an obvious arete, with a small stance.

16 Barnacle Belay 30m VS 4c *
A.Todd, W.Wright, 16 May 1998
Start from the small stance at the base of the inlet. Climb a crack direct with brief excursions to the right. Pull through two overhangs and climb a steep wall to the top.

17 Now It's Freda's Turn 30m VS 4c
W.Wright, A.Todd, 16 May 1998
Start at an obvious overhanging recess further seaward. Climb through the initial overhang and go up the groove above. Step left, ascend a little then right and finally direct to the top.

The Bay Area

(NL 597 868) Non-tidal S facing Map p302 Diagram opposite

This is a small bay of rock facing south-east on the very tip of the headland containing Shags Geo. It is essentially on the east side of the section containing Barnacle Belay. The base of the cove is a huge rock slab dipping into the sea at the eastern end. It is a veritable sun trap and ideal on windy or big sea days.

Descent: It is possible to scramble down the far right side of the cove (looking out) at about D standard. Routes are described left to right as approached from the descent.

1 Baywatch 10m E3 6a
W.Moir, M.Atkins, Aug 2003
The obvious roof and rib at the left-hand end of the wall.

2 Stoney Middleton Lip 15m E1 5c **
T.Carruthers, S.Tyson, Jun 2000
Start below a crack in the roofs. Climb quickly through the bulge to undercuts below the main roof. Reach over for a set of Biffo ears above the roof and pull onto the wall below the next roof. Move left into a little groove made of cinder toffee. Digest this at leisure. Steep, but very good gear.

3 Honorary Curbar 15m E1 5c *
T.Carruthers, T.Stevenson, 28 May 1998
Start up Stoney Middleton Lip. Climb over the main roof and take the vertical crack in the roof and wall above direct.
Variation: The original line moved out right after the main roof and climbed a black groove at the same grade.

4 Irish Rover 15m E3 6a *
W.Moir, P.Allen, N.Morrison M.Atkins, Aug 2003
Climb cracks in the wall left of Rum, Sodomy and The Lash. Start up black rock, then make a hard pinch move to better holds.

5 Rum, Sodomy and the Lash 15m E3 5c *
T.Stevenson, T.Carruthers, 26 May 1998
Start below a left-facing bulging groove. Climb the groove into a corner. Finish via the short corner above.

6 Dogs of Law 20m E4 6a *
M.Boyer, K.Howett, 28 Aug 1999
Climbs a shallow, clean-cut corner in the wall between Rum, Sodomy and the Lash and the large corner of The Roaring Forties. Go up the steep entry into the shallow corner. Climb its right wall to bulging rock. Undercling right and gain a ledge on the right arete. Pull up left into a niche below a roof. Make tenuous moves left around the arete into a hanging groove and so to a ledge. Climb the easy wall to the top.

7 The Roaring Forties 25m E4 6a *
T.Stevenson, T.Carruthers, 28 May 1998
Climb the obvious right-facing corner to a long capping roof. Pull out left to the arete (crux) in a fine position and cruise dreamily up the juggy wall.

The centre of the cove is characterised by a continuous band of roofs at half-height and a shallow cave undercutting it. The most conspicuous line is that of a pink vein slicing through the left side of the roof.

8 Rebel without a Porpoise 25m E5 6a ***
P.Craig, N.Craig, 6 May 2004
Start in a black groove just left of a blunt rib left of The Herbrudean. Climb the groove for a few metres, then right on to the rib. Climb this to the slab under a band

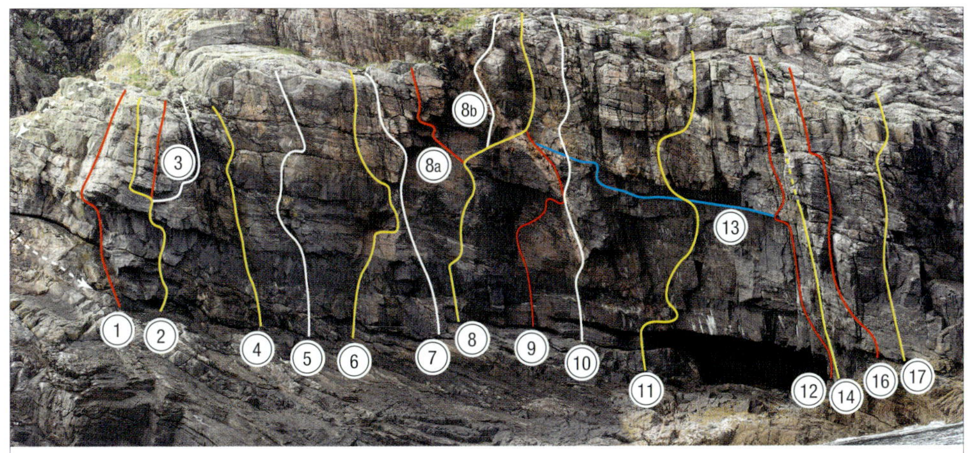

AN TOBHA - The Bay Area

1.	Baywatch	E3 6a	8b.	The Pegmatite Finish	E5 6a
2.	Stoney Middleton Lip	E1 5c **	9.	The Herbrudean	E5 6a ***
3.	Honorary Curbar	E1 5c *	10.	The Herbaloner	E6 6b *
4.	Irish Rover	E3 6a *	11.	Every Cormorant...	E7 6b ***
5.	Rum, Sodomy and the Lash	E3 5c *	12.	B.A.R.T	E5 6a *
6.	Dogs of Law	E4 6a *	13.	Traverse of the Cods	E6 6b **
7.	The Roaring 40's	E4 6a *	14.	Jesus Don't Want...	E1 5b **
8.	Rebel without a Porpoise	E5 6a ***	16.	Starboard Grooves	VS *
8a.	Styloric Nites of Suberbarra	E5 6a	17.	It's Not the Size...	VS 4c

of overhangs. Step right into a bottomless groove, then climb strenuously up and right to a junction with The Herbrudean. Follow this to the top.

Variation: **8a Styloric Nites of Suberbarra 25m E5 6a**
N.McNair, A.Robb, Jun 2005
A spectacular finish directly through the stepped roofs on positive holds.

Variation: **8b The Pegmatite Finish 25m E5 6a**
P.Thorburn, R.Campbell, Jun 2005
A sustained pump up the pink streak left of The Herbrudean.

9 The Herbrudean 20m E5 6a ***
P.Tanton, R.Kirby, 28 Aug 1999
An excellent excursion into steep ground, climbing across the pegmatite vein in the middle of the wall. Start in a short corner right of The Roaring Forties. Go up the corner by difficult bridging to gain a ledge under the roof. Traverse hard right to gain the pink vein and huge threads under the right end of the roof. Climb the vein, really steep, and the easier wall above to the right of a corner to the top.

10 The Herbaloner 20m E6 6b *
N.McNair, A.Robb, Jun 2005
A dangerous direct line into the pink vein of The Herbrudean and a finish out right. Start 5m to the right of that route and gain the hanging crack on the arete. Climb direct to the pink vein, via a very hard and bold move, gaining the threads of The Herbrudean. Step right to a hanging corner and right again to finish up a small wall.

11 Every Cormorant is a Potential Shag 30m E7 6b ***
D.Birkett, 8 Jun 2008
Sustained but well protected climbing taking the main challenge of the wall. Large cams required. Start beneath the obvious stepped right-facing corner. A boulder start into the first hanging corner is followed by a traverse right to good holds. Go back left to a groove. Move up and right into a shallow groove (good holds and gear on the left) to gain a big break under the main roof. Traverse 3m left using a shattered handrail and pull through the roof into a shallow corner. Finish up and right.

12 B.A.R.T 30m E5 6a *
I.Small, J.Clark, 5 Jun 2005
Climb a shallow groove and crack just left of Jesus to below the right end of the huge roof. Pull over the roof to finish boldly up the headwall above.

13 Traverse of the Cods 35m E6 6b **
I.Small, G.Ulrich, 9 Jun 2010
A trip traversing the prominent break across the main section of the face, right to left. Long slings and a confident partner recommended! Start up B.A.R.T to the break below the main roof and traverse left along this

to join Every Cormorant is a Potential Shag. Continue along the now widening break and pull into a niche. Cross a hanging slab to swing onto an arete and make hard moves up to below the roof. Follow the improving finger-rail left to eventually pull into and follow the upper corner of The Herbrudean.

14 Jesus Don't Want Me As a Shelf Stacker 20m E1 5b **

R.Campbell, M.Davies, May 1999

The obvious corner near the right side of the cove. Pull up through a small roof and a bulge to gain a ledge with difficulty. Climb up into the perfect corner above to finish.

15 Sea An-enema 20m E1 5b **

R.Strube, T.Carruthers, 28 Aug 1999

A wild route for the grade and stature. Start as for the corner through the first roof. Climb across the wall rightwards to a downward-pointing flake. Go up and left into a recess under a capping roof and pull direct through, via a flake-crack leading to the top.

16 Starboard Grooves 20m VS *

T.Carruthers, T.Stevenson, 26 May 1998

This takes a series of grooves in the arete at the eastern end of the cove. Scramble rightwards to a ledge above the platform. Move up and step immediately left round the rib. Haul joyously up grooves to the top.

The Herbaloner (E6) Niall McNair (photo Gordon Lennox)

17 It's Not the Size That Matters 10m VS 4c

P.Cunningham, M.Airey, Aug 2007

Scramble round the corner to the right (low tide) to a large sloping platform 4m above the sea. This route takes the obvious crack-groove up the centre of the short steep 10m wall above, finishing up a small niche on the left. Sustained and pleasant despite its lowly size.

THE PINK WALL & GREY WALL RECESS

(NL 594 869) Tidal S facing Diagram p307

This is an amazing big wall between Shags Geo and Banded Geo out near the west side of the island. It presents the highest vertical cliff on the island but has a complex structure of different walls.

The left-hand section presents the most continuous wall, the full height of the cliff, with a lower quarter as yet unclimbed!

The middle section of the cliff is split into two tiers. The lower tier is almost all broken and of poorer quality rock and not currently climbed on, whilst the upper tier, the Pink Wall, gives the cliff its name because of a huge diagonal pink pegmatite band.

The right-hand section of the cliff is The Grey Wall Recess. It is a huge recess with a large platform in the base and is split from top to bottom by distinctive corners with bands of roofs.

The Pink Wall

Map p302 Diagrams p307 & p315

Probably one of the best cliffs for harder climbing on these islands. The stunning Pink Wall offers very steep pitches on great rock in a spectacular setting. The pink pegmatite band cuts left to right across the middle of the wall from the left edge to produce a huge splodge in the centre, before continuing round the right arete and across the Grey Wall Recess. Above the pink band the wall is slabby and easy. Down the wall just left of this pink splodge is a central fault-line (the line of the abseil descent) which peters out into a small messy gully in the broken lower tier at the left side of ledges. These ledges lead up right to a large rock terrace sitting below the steep Pink Wall itself. The left-hand side of the wall is more continuous, but of poorer quality rock, rising steeply from the sea to a black glacis with shattered ledges some 20m lower than the terrace. Above this the wall overhangs all the way to the highest point of the cliff.

Descent: At the top of Pink Wall there are two short rock steps with grass ledges between. The higher ledge holds a small rock pool, the lower a big flat block abutting the wall. Abseil from here. Descend to the lower ledges down the general line of the central vertical fault that splits the wall (100m). For the routes starting on the Terrace, direct the abseil to the left (looking out) and go down the left side of the steep wall. Runners have to be used to keep in to the rock during the abseil.

The following routes start from the lower shattered ledges near the black glacis and climb the left-hand side of the wall.

1 The Tomorrow People 110m E4 *
G.E.Little, K.Howett, 26 May 1997
The first route on the cliff. This climbs the line of least resistance up the left side of the face onto the left arete to finish. An expedition with a serious feel and some strange rock in places, but in a spectacular setting. Start at a cluster of big spikes just above a black glacis about 10m from the left side of the cliff.
1. 25m 5b Trend up and left on weird rock to a large spike where the wall bulges. Climb a shallow chimney through the bulge then immediately hand-traverse out of it to the right into another chimney. Climb this to its top then traverse right across a ledge to a left-facing corner with a strange little pillar in the back. Belay.
2. 25m 5c Step up and left and make a hard move left to gain a thin crack up the steep wall. Go up this to a jug then step right to gain a big flake edge. This leads into the big corner (of the belay) below its capping roof. Traverse hard left below the roof to a hanging belay on fired rock just after blind downwards moves.
3. 20m 5c Move left and enter the strenuous shallow chimney-line to a capping roof. Pull over this via a deep crack into a recess. Trend left 3m to belay by a big semi-detached block.
4. 40m 5b Step right and climb an immaculate crack up the flying edge above to easier slabs leading to the top.
Variation: **What the Eagle? 40m E3 5b ***
D.Toon, R.Toon, 30 May 2008
An alternative start taking a more direct line into the start of pitch 3, which is steep and character building. From the same starting stance, climb a grey groove above the stance to where a traverse right gains a black corner. Climb this to a yellow wall with a down pointing flake. Climb this on its left to the red-fired rock ledge of The Tomorrow People. Finish up this.

2 Night Terrors 100m E4
L.McGinley, T.Leppart, Jul 2003
Start at the belay on the big spikes of The Tomorrow People.
1. 20m 5b Take a line directly up the wall right of The Tomorrow People to gain the belay of Tickled Pink below the central fault.
2. 15m 5b Traverse left and into a chimney breaking through the bulge and onto the ledge in the left-facing corner of The Tomorrow People.
3. 25m 5c Follow the corner to the roof and exit out right with difficulty onto the upper wall. A slanting groove trends left to gain a belay on ledges above.
4. 40m 4c Easily up to top.

The following two routes climb around the central fault, starting near the bottom end of the slight gully in the lower tier.

3 Tickled Pink 100m E2 *
L.McGinley, M.Pointon, T.Leppert, Jun 1999
Climbs the line of the central fault. Start just below the slight gully which leads up to the ledges and cracked block of Raiders of the Lost Auk.
1. 20m 5a Climb steeply up cracks to the right end of a big ledge (above and left of the rock terrace). Walk left for 10m to belay at the right-hand side of the fault-line.
2. 40m 5b Step left and climb a crack for 10m. Step right into the fault-line and follow it over several bulges, skirting the left edge of the pink splodge, to belay by a block.
3. 40m 5a Continue straight up over a huge block to reach a good ledge. Climb the flake-crack off this to the top.

4 Where Seagulls Dare 90m E3 **
L.McGinley, M.Pointon, T.Leppert, Jun 1999
Climbs a line just right of Tickled Pink, attacking the pink splodge directly. Start as for that route.
1. 10m 5a Up the steep cracks of Tickled Pink to the big ledge.
2. 40m 5c Pull over the bulge directly above to gain a soaring flake crack-line which leads to a ledge. A truly magnificent experience!
3. 40m 5b Trend up and left over some overlaps to reach the flake-crack of Tickled Pink. Follow this to the top.

5 Aukward Escape 85m E4 **
J.Morgan, M.Cooper, S.Halstead, 13Jun 2009
Climbs a fine pitch up the wall between Tickled Pink and Where Seagulls Dare to finish up the top pitch of the former route. Start from the far left-hand end of the main terrace, beyond the cracked block.
1. 45m 6a Cross the top of the slight gully and climb up a right-facing corner. Traverse left to the big ledge of Where Seagulls Dare (possible belay). Another line of flakes a few metres left of Where Seagulls Dare are climbed up the wall and where the flakes run out, pull up and leftwards onto a pink slab with two useful finger pockets. Pull up left into a smaller flake system and follow it with increasing difficulty until you can step left into the top of the chimney of the second pitch of Tickled Pink, and block belay as for that route.
2. 40m 5a Tickled Pink top pitch.

The following routes climb the wall to the right of the fault and start from the main terrace below the steep wall.

6 Raiders of the Lost Auk 80m E3 **
P.Thorburn, R.Campbell, 26 May 1998
Start on the top of a conspicuous cracked block at the left-hand side of the main terrace.
1. 20m 5c From the block, climb the tricky wall on the left to gain a hanging right-facing groove. Climb this and the cracks above on the right to belay on the left end of a narrow ledge.
2. 20m 5c Climb the steepening groove above, then make a long traverse left to gain a vertical crack (joining Where Seagulls Dare). Follow this to a ledge.
3. 40m 5a From the right end of the ledge, follow a line to the top.

7 Fondue Macpac 70m E6 **
P.Robins, J.McHaffie, 2 Jul 2003
A gap between In Profundum Lacu and Raiders of the Lost Auk.
1. 20m 6b From the block of Raiders of the Lost Auk, gain the right-hand side of a small overlap above. Move left and up to a good flake and steepening. Strenuous moves gain a crack and then a belay on the left-hand side of the narrow ledge of Raiders.
2. 50m 6a Go up a corner and move right to join In Profundum Lacu below a bulge. Pull over the bulge as for that route, then move up and right to gain protruding flakes and an undercut break. Continue more easily to the top, first right then left.

8 In Profundum Lacu 80m E5 ***
R.Campbell, P.Thorburn, 26 May 1998
Climbs the next crack-line to the right of Raiders. Start off the cracked block.
1. 40m 6a Step right off the block to gain cracks which lead into a hanging V-groove (crux). Climb up and left to a long narrow ledge (junction with Raiders). Make awkward moves up the crack on the right, then gain a left-facing flake. Traverse left and gain a pegmatite flake above a bulge. Continue up left to gain and climb a bottomless groove. Belay on the left.
2. 40m 5b Climb a crack on the right and continue to a steep, blocky left-facing groove. This leads direct to the top.

9 The Bonxie 75m E6 ****
R.Campbell, G.Latter, M.Davies, 15 May 2000
P.Thorburn, R.Campbell (without a hanging belay), Jun 2005
The long continuous crack system up the wall left of the hanging corner of I Suppose. Sustained and very well protected. Start 8m left of that route, beneath a short vertical crack.
1. 35m 6b Climb the crack and traverse left along a rounded break to the main crack system. Make a long reach past a good undercut to a big jug, and continue up the crack, which soon forms twin deep cracks. Continue up these, and a third crack higher up, to an obvious break beneath the pegmatite band. Layback the central of three flared cracks above and pull out left to a jug. Move right up a short diagonal crack tenuously to undercuts. Pull through these to gain good flakes leading up left to a belay
3. 40m 5c Follow I Suppose to finish.

10 Huffin' 'n' Puffin 75m E6 ***
T.Wood, G.Latter, 5 Jun 2005
Another excellent sustained main pitch.
1. 30m 6b Start up a short crack between The Bonxie and I Suppose. Climb the crack to a break, stand on this and reach a small flake. Make hard moves up the wall to reach another flake, then trend left following flakes. Atop the second flake-plinth, make hard moves up a shield to a break. Traverse left into the break beneath the pegmatite band of The Bonxie. Hanging belay.
2. 45m 6b Follow The Bonxie until the jugs after the undercuts, then direct through a black niche and bulges until below an obvious weakness. Pull through this on sloping holds (crux) and continue more easily to top.
Variation: **Direct Start 40m E6 6b**
S.Williams, U.Hawthorn, 15 Jun 2014
Instead of traversing left at the break after the plinth, climb direct into the crack through the roof on I Suppose and follow this to the undercut flake. Jam out right until it is possible to join the flakes on The Ancient Mariner. Follow this to the belay. Finish up this route.

11 I Suppose a Cormorant's Out of the Question Then? 85m E5 ***
R.Campbell, P.Thorburn, 25 May 1998
The most distinctive feature on the right-hand part of the face is a large left-facing, hanging corner. The true classic of the cliff. Start below and right of a series of strange flakes under the corner.
1. 20m 5c Gain and climb the flakes, then follow the diminishing flake-line on the right to a break. Traverse left, gain the large and easy corner, and belay halfway up it.
2. 25m 6a/b From the top of the corner, traverse left to a crack in the roof. Climb this and make hard moves to gain pegmatite flakes. From a vertical flake, undercut left to gain a diagonal line of jugs which lead to a belay in a break.
3. 40m 5c Step left, then climb a steepening to make an awkward pull left onto a shelf. Continue up a groove to another shelf. Traverse left below a steep wall with a loose flake and step left around a lichenous arete; climb direct to the top.
Variation: **Cormorant your Way to the Top 20m E5 6b**
R.Campbell, G.Latter, 14 May 2003
2a. Climb monster flakes up the wall left of the parent route past a hard move to an impasse 3m below the roof. Step right into the parent route and follow this to top.

12 The Ancient Mariners 85m E4 ***
P.Thorburn, R.Campbell, 25 May 1998
Climbs the cracks to the right of the corner. Start as for the previous route.
1. 40m 5c Climb the flakes and make a hard pull right before the break. Climb the cracks above until a flared crack is encountered. Climb the groove on the right, then traverse left to gain the pegmatite flakes of the previous route. Follow these past a pair of spikes to a break, traverse right and belay under a groove with a short wide crack.
2. 45m 5a Climb the groove to a ledge, then continue in the same line joining The Guga to finish.

13 What! More Puffin? 80m E6 ***
S.Crowe, K.Magog, 15 May 2003, 9 Jun 2007
The grooved arete on the right edge of the wall (right of The Ancient Mariners). Originally climbed as What, No Puffin?, but later re-climbed by the same team with a better finish as described.

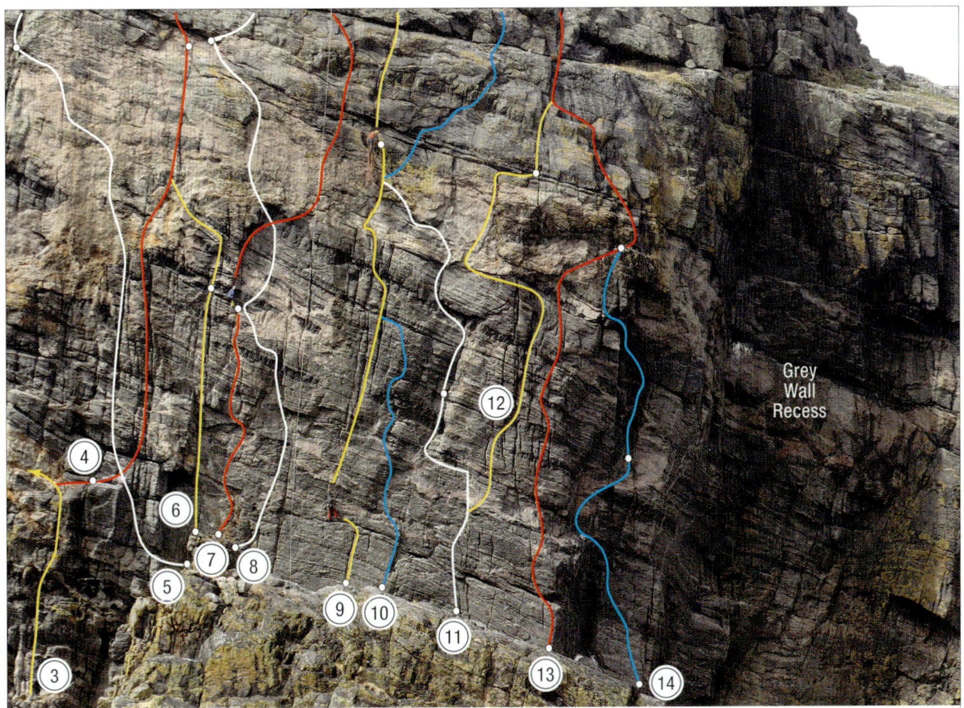

AN TOBHA - Pink Wall

3. Tickled Pink	E2 5a, 5b, 5a *	9. The Bonxie	E6 6b, 5c ****
4. Where Seagulls Dare	E3 5a, 5c, 5b **	10. Huffin 'n' Puffin	E6 6b, 6b ***
5. Awkward Escape	E4 6a, 5a **	11. I Suppose a Cormorant	E5 5c, 6a/b, 5c ***
6. Raiders of the Lost Auk	E3 5c, 5c, 5a **	12. The Ancient Mariners	E4 5c, 5a ***
7. Fondue Macpac	E6 6b, 6a **	13. What! More Puffin?	E6 6b ***
8. In Profundum Lacu	E5 6a, 5b ***	14. The Guga	E5 6a, 6b, 4c ***

1. 40m 6b The initial arete has a crack on both sides. Start by climbing either crack to gain the ledge, then move up to the Y-shaped crack. Move up then left to fingerlock powerfully through a steep bulge (just right of The Ancient Mariners) and gain a good break and awkward knee bar rest. Tip toe rightwards on good crimps to regain the arete and move up steeply to a huge flake. Teeter right to reach easy ground and a good belay (as for The Guga) in a superbly exposed position on the very edge.
2. 40m Follow The Guga or go back left and follow The Ancient Mariner.

14 The Guga 90m E5 ***
P.Thorburn, R.Campbell, 27 May 1997
Climbs a spectacular line up the black overhanging corner on the immediate right side of the arete of The Pink Wall as it turns into The Grey Wall Recess. A bold first ascent from the team that made The Pink Wall their own.
1. 20m 6a From a belay below the corner 10m right of the arete, climb the wall into the corner and follow it with a difficult exit left onto a ledge. Move up the overhanging wall on the right to a ramp and a belay.
2. 25m 6b Climb the corner on the right, then make hard moves through a bulge to gain the left arching pegmatite bulge (capping roof). Follow this to a crack, then move up, then rightwards to gain a ledge.
3. 45m 4c Climb up left from the belay and take a direct line to the top.

The Grey Wall Recess

Map p302 Diagrams p307 & p316

Round the corner from the Pink Wall lies this huge recess of grey rock. The right-hand section of the Pink Wall containing The Guga forms the upper part of the left-hand wall of the recess. Below this is a stunning wall of perfect rock (the Grey Wall). The right-hand wall of the recess is composed of grooves, corners and roofs, with

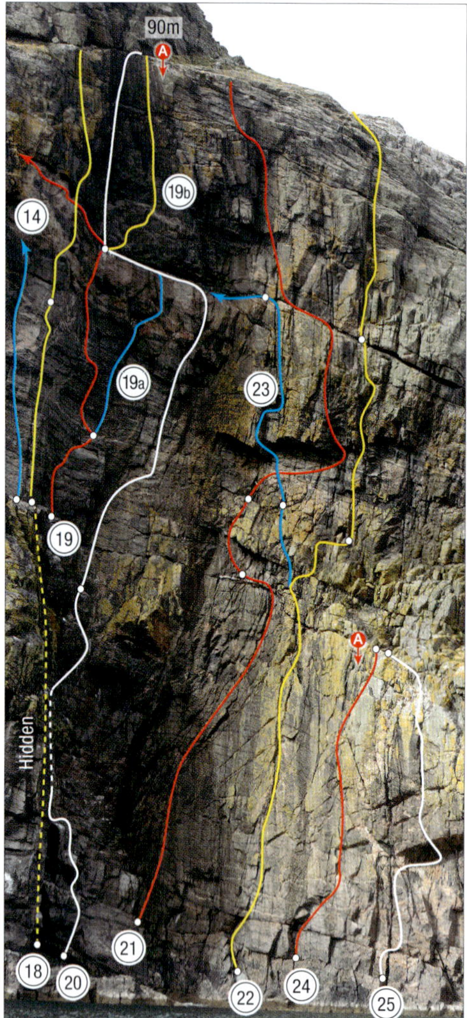

AN TOBHA
Grey Wall Recess

14.	The Guga	E5 6a, 6b, 4c ***
18.	Bravura	E7 6a, 6b, 6b ***
19.	Amber Nectar	E5 5a, 6a, 5c, 5a ***
19a.	Elysium	E4 6a ***
19b.	More Steam McPhail!	E6 6a **
20.	Spit in Paradise	E4 5c, 6b, 6a ***
21.	U-Ei	E2 5b, 5a, 5b ***
22.	Make Mine a Treble	E2 5a, 5b, 5a **
23.	Paradise Regained	E4 5a, 5c 5b, 6a ***
24.	The Three Mantras	E3 6a
25.	Dopes on a Rope	E1 5b

two huge corner-lines dominating. The biggest left-hand corner (Spit in Paradise) contains a huge roof which bisects the back of the recess. There is a large platform in the bay at the base of these corners. The extreme left-hand side of the recess forms a Lower Tier to the Pink Wall with routes finishing on the terrace below it.

Descent: Gain the base of the recess by a 90m abseil down the left-hand corner. From the top of the wall descend to the east (left looking out) a little way and traverse back right on an obvious grass terrace which ends above the large roof. An initially free abseil from boulders above the end of the roof gains the platform.

The following three routes lead to the terrace beneath Pink Wall where the options of escape to freedom are to either continue up one of the Pink Wall routes above, or to take a long traverse right and gain the top two pitches of Spit in Paradise.

15 E-up 50m E2

T.Fryer, I.Taylor, 15 May 2000

Start round the arete from Oi, beneath a right-facing corner on the face.

1. 20m 5c Climb a steep corner and groove above to belay below a roof.
2. 30m 5c Swing right round a small arete and make strenuous moves through a roof to a ledge. Go up a flake leftwards to a vertical crack and climb this, easier, to belay on the large terrace.

16 U 50m E4 6a

T.Rankin, G.Lennox, 2003

The groove between Oi and E-up, finishing up the latter's top pitch.

17 Oi 50m E3

R.Campbell, G.Latter, M.Davies, 14 May 2000

Follow a line of cracks and grooves up the very left edge of the open recess. Start beneath an obvious crack at the left end of the ledge.

1. 30m 5c Climb the crack, stepping right to a good ledge. Continue up the crack-line, pulling out left of a steep jam crack in a short groove higher up with difficulty to take a belay in a small recess.
2. 20m 5b Move out right then up past a flake to gain the right end of the terrace beneath the Pink Wall.

The following routes climb the stunning grey wall forming the left wall of the upper half of The Grey Wall Recess.

18 Bravura 100m E7 ***

G.Latter, R.Campbell, lower pitches, 15 & 17, May 2002; I.Small, R.Campbell, pitch 3, 15 Jun 2008

Stunning very sustained climbing up the twin intermittent cracks up the left side of the grey wall, just right of the arete. Start at the right end of the sea-level platform, beneath a short blunt arete.

1. 55m 6a Arrange a runner or belay in an obvious deep triangular slot up in the right side of the arete. Make hard moves up the left side of the arete, then

pull rightwards and up into a groove. Continue up this, passing an overhung jam slot with interest, leading to easier ground. Go direct up a crack to a platform directly beneath the arete.
2. 25m 6b A stunning pitch. Climb a wide gritty crack up the left side of the arete to the top of a pedestal. Hard moves lead past cams in pockets (Camalot 0.1 crucial) to a good hold in a crack almost on the arete. Move up right and follow the crack system, eventually transferring to a further crack system on the right which eases to a fine finger-crack leading up into an easier short left-facing corner, belay.
3. 20m 6b Make a long move from the top of the corner to a hidden flake-crack. Head right and up to a flake letterbox. Use a small ear in the wall above to gain the traverse break on pitch 3 of Amber Nectar. Go left along this, until awkward moves up and left gain an arching crack coming in from the left. Follow the crack through a bulge with difficulty until an easing when it turns vertical. Go right and up to a belay.

19 Amber Nectar 85m E5 ***
R.Campbell, G.Latter, 15 May 2001
A route of considerable character, climbing the right side of the Grey Wall. Start at the base of the left-facing groove forming the right side of the wall.
1. 10m 5a Climb the groove to belay on the upper of two ledges.
2. 20m 6a Move left and up on flakes into a hanging groove in the wall. Traverse out left and up another flake system leading to a roof in the pegmatite band. Cross this on good holds on the right and step right to the thread belay at the stance below the top pitch of Spit in Paradise.
3. 20m 5c Traverse left along a wide break with interest to swing left round a corner and climb a groove to a ledge on the edge of the wall as for The Guga.
4. 35m 5a Climb a short corner and pull out leftwards at its top and follow a line of stepped corners leftwards to finish at the top of the cliff.
Variation: **19a Elysium 35m E4 6a *****
G.Latter, R.Campbell, 13 May 2001
2a. An excellent pitch following the left-facing groove bounding the right edge of the Grey Wall all the way. From the ledge continue up the orange wall above on large flakes leading into the left-facing groove. Climb this, stepping right at the top past a birdy ledge to the thread belay at the top of pitch 2 of Spit in Paradise.
Variation: **19b More Steam McPhail! 30m E6 6a ****
P.Thorburn, R.Campbell, 6 Jun 2005
3a. A well protected but strenuous pitch that climbs the horribly steep right wall of the upper pitch of Spit in Paradise. From the huge thread belay, undercut out right on huge flakes and climb the strenuous wall past numerous rounded breaks to a sting in the tail.

20 Spit in Paradise 110m E4 ***
R.Witt, J.Fischer, 19 Jun 1995
An audacious ascent, one of the first on the island and accessed by dingy! The left-hand side of the Grey Recess contains two large corner-lines. This is the largest left-hand corner bounding the Grey Wall. Start on the platform at sea-level in the base of the recess, below and right of an overhanging crack.
1. 45m 5c Climb direct over birdy ledges. After about 15m move left to gain the overhanging crack. Climb this (hard) to reach somewhat easier birdy ground. Ascend another 7m to reach a good ledge.
2. 35m 6a Trend left towards a wide overhanging crack. Climb this to reach a ledge. Step right to climb the wall right of an obvious corner system to a huge roof. Trend left via overhanging cracks in the pegmatite band (crux) which crosses the wall, to reach a ledge and good thread belays.
3. 30m 6a Climb straight up, passing small roofs on a slabby wall to gain the final corner. Follow this to the top.

21 U-Ei 110m E2 ***
G.Gantzhorn, S.Wacker, 19 Jun 1995
The companion route to Spit in Paradise climbing the general line of the right-hand corner. The right side of this lower wall is slabby and drops into the sea. Start on a small ledge about 3m above the platform just right of a prominent seepage line.

Spit in Paradise, P2 (E4) Fritz Miller (photo Ralf Gantzhorn)

U-Ei, P3 (E2) Michele Knaup
(photo Ralf Gantzhorn)

1. 50m 5b Climb the wall on perfect holds for 25m, to step left into a short hanging corner. Follow this corner to a roof. Bottle out left to a comfortable ledge.
2. 15m 5a Climb an easy corner to an overhanging block. Pass the block on the right to gain a ledge and a luxurious belay.
3. 45m 5b From the belay, move up to a roof and traverse right under it to gain the base of a fine overhanging corner system. Climb this and finish by a left-slanting ramp.
Variation: **U-th 30m E3 5c ****
T.Fryer, I.Taylor, 12 Jun 2007
2a. Well protected and low in the grade. Left of the corner on pitch 2 is a slightly right-trending crack. Gain and climb the crack from the right, follow it through roofs and bulges to join U-Ei below its final pitch.

The following routes climb the slabby wall right of the huge overhanging corners of Grey Wall Recess starting from good ledges 4m above the high tide level. A couple are single pitch, finishing on a large inescapable terrace with an abseil descent back to the base from an in-situ thread belay (which may need replacing).

Descent: Direct the abseil off the left end of the ledge (looking out) to the good ledges at the base of the wall (100m). Alternatively, scramble out of the recess from U-Ei when the sea is calm.

22 Make Mine a Treble 90m E2 **
D.Turnbull, G.Rimmer, J.Jones, 7 May 2002
An excellent and enjoyable route on great rock. Start at the base of the obvious main crack in the right wall of the recess about 10m right of U-Ei.
1. 35m 5a Climb up and diagonally left to reach a flakey crack which is followed through an overlap to reach good twin cracks above. Follow these keeping left toward the large ledge system. Good belay stance 5m higher, below the third groove from the left edge of the wall.
2. 25m 5b Climb the groove above following the left-leaning flake above the roof steeply to a black groove. Move up 3m and swing left again onto a vertical wall which is followed to the second terrace. Good stance and belay.
3. 30m 5a Move 2m left into an immaculate right-leaning layback groove. Follow this to below a V-groove. Enter this awkwardly and follow it to easier rock and the top.

23 Paradise Regained 115m E4 ***
I.Taylor, T.Fryer, 12 May 2002
This cuts across the face of the two large corner-lines, climbing through some impressive ground. Start as for Make Mine a Minke.
1. 45m 5a Climb a crack-line through a small overlap to a niche.
2. 30m 5c Trend up and leftwards to a hanging corner between two large roofs. Pull left into the corner, then follow cracks to a belay on a ledge below the final corner of U-Ei.
3. 15m 5b Traverse left along a break to belay below the final pitch of Spit in Paradise. Very exposed.
4. 25m 6a The final pitch of Spit in Paradise.
Variation: Finishing up the final pitch of U-Ei gives an excellent E2.

24 The Three Mantras of Hesitation 45m E3 6a
N.McNair, R.Welch, 12 May 2002
Start right of Paradise Regained. Follow a groove to a small overlap and then gain the bow crack above and continue directly to the broken ledges.

25 Dopes on a Rope 45m E1 5b
R.Welch, N.McNair, 12 May 2002
Start beneath the prominent roof at the far right end of the wall. Climb up the obvious groove-crack which leads to the left side of the roof. Tackle the roof via a crack in the centre and head straight up to broken ledges.

RUBHA GREÒTACH

This is the headland at the south-westerly tip of the island. It offers an area of immaculate wave-washed rock and two short walls one behind the other, facing south-west. The first encountered when heading out to the tip is The Galley. Beyond this the headland terminates in a sheer wall, dropping into the sea at its east end. This is called The Poop Deck. Included here is Banded Geo, and although not strictly on the headland, it is accessed by the same way.

BANDED GEO

(NL 592 870) Partially Tidal SW facing
Map p302 Diagram p320

Just to the east of the Rubha Greòtach peninsula that forms the south-west tip of the island, lies a geo holding a long 60m high wall. The wall starts on dry land on the left, developing into a cave as it curves round the back of the geo over easy-angled slabs which dip into the sea in the back of the geo. As the wall continues, now tidal, it gains its maximum height where twin distinctive quartz bands run across it. It continues out to a headland as a diminishing wall.

The extensive wall has been split into sections easily identified from the opposite side and accessed differently: The Back Wall, Fools Wall, Banded Wall (the main section characterised by quartz bands), Spooky Pillar, The Shield (a shorter section of smooth, almost boiler-plate rock), The Black Walls (a series of corners and walls leading to a conspicuous spur) and The South Face forming the headland beyond the spur with a platform below it.

The Back Wall

The cave-like back of the geo. From the point where the easy access slabs dip into the sea in the back of the geo, the wall increases in height with a brown-coloured lower section and corners near the top guarded by overhangs. Large boulders sit in the back of the geo below here.

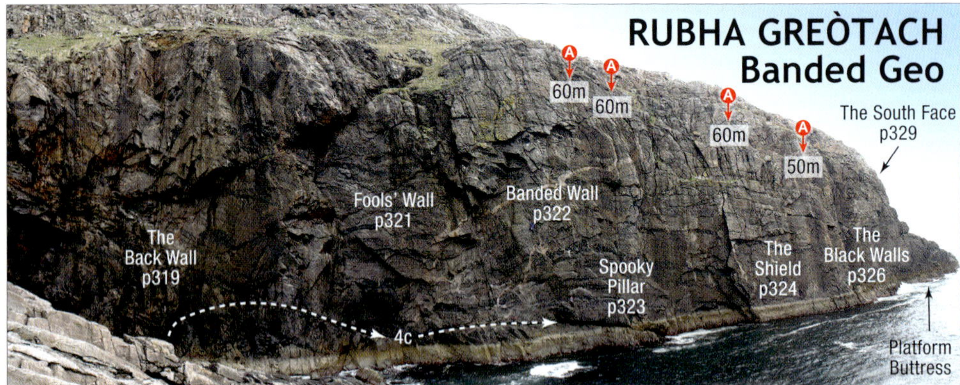

Approach: The routes sitting above the easy slabs are accessible on foot at all states of the tide. A scramble up a very steep wall covered in jugs to the left of the boulders in the back of the geo gains ledges at 5m at most states of the tide. These shattered ledges continue rightwards around the base of the wall into a deep chimney-corner capped by roofs on the left of Fools Wall.

1 My Neighbour 25m HVS 5a
T.Powell, T.Everett, 17 Jun 2009
The first obvious line left of the chossy corner at the left end. A tricky move gains the corner. Climb up on improving rock to a left-trending crack below a roof. Follow this boldly to an exciting steep finish.

2 Never Too Old 20m E2 5b
P.Gibson, L.Wright, 15 May 2002
Climbs the orange wall at the left side of the back wall. The wall ends at a chossy, undercut corner. Start in the short overhanging corner right of this. Climb up and swing left into the chossy corner. Climb up a short way until able to step right onto the fine orange wall and climb the centre of this.

3 Dust My Credenza 25m HVS 5a
P.Gibson, L.Wright, 15 May 2002
Start as above, but traverse right on a slab between two overhanging walls. Move up and right into a V-groove, then straight up to finish just left of The Swabber.

4 The Swabber 25m HVS 5a
G.Nicoll, L.Hughes, 26 May 1997
Start at the left end of the geo, near where the grass meets the slabs. Climb a richly pocketed groove to below a leaning headwall, then move leftwards up the obvious ramp to pull over a bulge.

5 The 36th Chamber 20m E4 6a
L.Hughes, G.Nicoll, 26 May 1997
Start up The Swabber, then launch up the leaning headwall, first to an obvious flake, then rightwards and straight up to finish.

6 No Midges My Arse 20m E5 6b
I.Lewis, P.Drew, 7 Aug 1999
Climbs the overhanging corner 5m right of The 36th Chamber. Exit left under the capping roof. Some friable rock.

7 Redemption Ark 85m E6
N.McNair, D.McManus, Jun 2007
The first route to breach the impressive gothic cave of Banded Geo. The first pitch is superb but the other pitches are loose and often wet. At the bottom of the geo is a boulder-choke and the innermost boulder is the size of a small car; start on top of this.
1. 25m 6b Move hard left for 3m into a wildly overhanging groove-corner system and follow this to a wall and an obvious bow-shaped crack. Take the crack rightwards and up to step out right under the overhang. Hanging belay from good flakes and quartz spikes on the right.
2. 30m 5b Traverse left for 4m to a prominent spike, then climb up and over a bulge to reach an obvious but wet and loose traverse leftwards across pink and orange rock. Continue past a detached block for 6m, step down and belay in the black corner.
3. 30m 5c Step left and climb the middle and slimmest of three corner-crack systems. Continue up this terrifyingly until better rock is reached in a bay. Take the middle groove to grass. Belay anchors another 15m up the hill, sandwiched between two small boulders.

8 Chocarockaholic 65m E2 **
K.Howett, G.Nicoll, 16 May 1998
Climbs a spectacular line through the brown walls above the boulders in the geo, the most striking feature being a left to right diagonal crack in the lower wall. Belay on the traverse ledges at the turn of the wall just past the boulders.
1. 40m 5a Pull steeply up the stepped rib to a horizontal break. Go up a smaller diagonal crack trending right up the wall above to meet the main diagonal crack at its right end. Climb the wall above rightwards to gain a small ledge that leads left to a shattered ledge beside luminous green moss. Poor micro-nut belay.

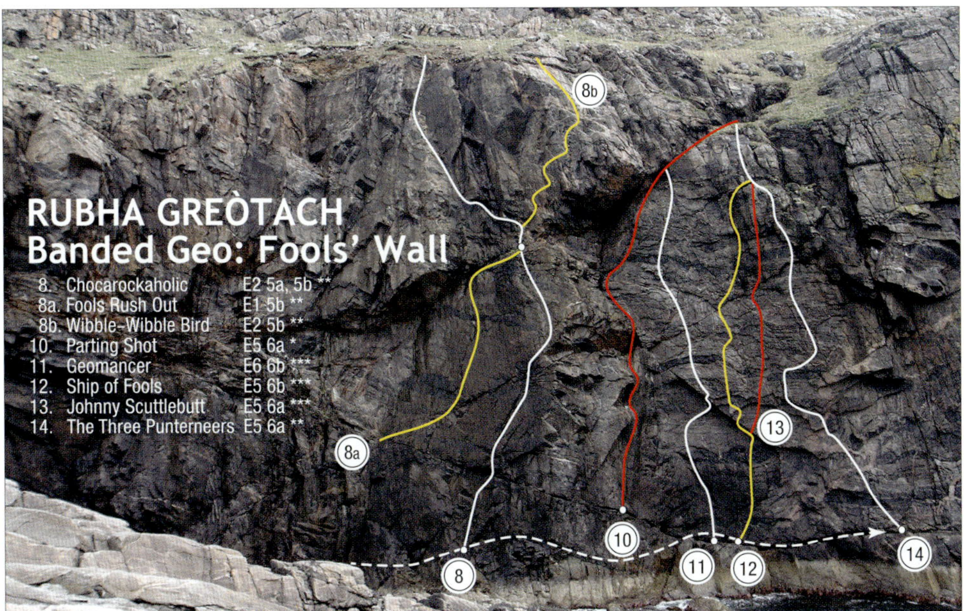

2. 25m 5b Pull up a steep groove containing flakes and blocks directly above the grass to enter a large slabby corner whose right wall is multi-coloured. Trend left across the slab to gain the arete and climb it to under a roof. Directly above hangs a ramp. Gain this and follow it to the top.

Variation: **8a Fools Rush Out 30m E1 5b ****
P.Thorburn, R.Campbell, 27 May 1998
1a. Takes a different line to the first stance at the shattered ledge. Start below the left end of big right diagonal cracks. Follow the cracks across the brown wall to a thin break. Climb the thin flake above and left to below the roofs, then traverse right to gain the belay.

Variation: **8b Flight of the Wibble-Wibble Bird 30m E2 5c ****
S.Chinnery, T.Bridgeland, Jul 1998
2a. From the large slabby corner above the roof on pitch 2, traverse rightwards in an exposed position across several grooves above a huge roof to gain the arete. Finish up a slab above.

9 Copper Got a Pollock 90m E3
R.Pullen, J.Spanken, 2 Jul 2003
A bit of an expedition, a diagonal line running from the Back Wall across Chocarockaholic, Fools Wall and Banded Wall finishing at the top of Spring Squill. Start left of Chockarockaholic on the shattered ledges below the start of the crack.
1. 25m 4c Follow the big diagonal crack across the brown wall to belay in the overhanging chimney-corner left of Fools Wall.
2. 25m 5c Traverse steeply across the continuation break that cuts across Fools' Wall to easier ground.
3. 40m 4c Continue in the same line above the upper band of roofs across the top of Banded Wall to reach and finish up Spring Squill

Fools' Wall

Diagrams opposite & above

The very steep section just to the right of Chocarockaholic and the overhanging chimney-corner topped by roofs. This is a narrow but wickedly overhanging wall, bounded on its right by further corners and smaller roofs, which form the edge of Banded Wall. A small ledge at high water level below Banded Wall ends just right of Fools Wall.

Descent: The base of the left-hand side of the wall is easily reached by the shattered ledges from the back of the geo. However, Vomtanion and the Three Punterneers starts under the right-hand side of the wall off the left end of a long low ledge below the central section of Banded Wall, and can be gained by a sea-level traverse (4c) at low tides and calm seas. Alternatively gain the ledge from the Banded Wall abseil.

10 Parting Shot 50m E5 6a *
S.Crowe, K.Magog, 2008
The deep chimney-corner capped by roofs on the left of Fools Wall was climbed, by persons unknown, to the roofs at E4 5c. This is a logical finish to this line. Climb the corner to gain a large sloping ledge. Continue up the wall rightwards to join Geomancer below its final bulge and finish up this.

11 Geomancer 45m E6 6b ***
N.McNair, P.Newman, May 2003
A stupendous line up the left side of Fools Wall. Start up a black groove until an obvious traverse can be made out to the roof. Tackle the roof via pockets and a small right-facing flange (crux). Once on the headwall climb up trending slightly left to head for a large pod-flake. Attack the bulge directly above this to reach the capping roof. Escape rightwards along this to the best belay in the world and with the biggest pump ever!

12 Ship of Fools 45m E5 6b ***
R.Campbell, P.Thorburn, 27 May 1998
Climb the centre of the acutely overhanging wall. From the easy ramp below the wall, climb boldly up biotitic rock to gain the slanting roof 4m left of its lowest point. Gain the flake above the lip with difficulty, move up left to cross the bulge by some flakes. Continue straight up until the rock becomes noticeably compact (alcite). Move up and right, then back left through a bulge, then up right again to pull through another bulge to gain a flake. Step right past a detached flake into a black niche. Step right and climb direct to belay on a slab. Scramble to the top.
Variation: **12a The Fool of Ships 45m E6 6b ****
N.McNair, May 2002
A straightened out version of Ship of Fools.

13 Jonny Scuttlebutt 45m E5 6a ***
N.McNair, A.Robb, Jun 2007
Climbs the wall right of Ship of Fools. Start as for that route to the roof. At the rib on the lowest point of the roof, gain the wall above. Climb slightly left then follow the line of least resistance to an obvious crack in steep brown rock near the top and go up this, then belay.

14 Vomtanion and the Three Punterneers 50m E5 6a **
J.McHaffie, T.Badcock, P.Robins, 4 Jul 2003
A line up the right edge of Fools Wall. From the good ledge, climb easily up a shallow groove for about 10m to a steepening. Step left beneath the upper of two overlaps; continue awkwardly left for 3m to some larger undercuts and a rest. Move up on small holds (crux) to gain a break. A short traverse right gains a flake. Climb more or less directly past some small ledges and a vague crack to a final bulge and the top.

Banded Wall

Diagrams p320 & opposite

This is the cleanest and biggest section of the wall which has a long overhang at two thirds height. A deep corner sits above a slab on the right of the wall and there is a long ledge below the wall at high water level. The most conspicuous feature here is a left to right diagonal quartz band at about half-height. The routes are described from left to right.

Descent: The routes to Spring Squill all start off the long low ledge below the wall. Access this along the shattered ledges from the back of the geo to Fools' Wall followed by a 4c traverse to gain the ledge; at high tides, an abseil (60m) directly down the wall from a block gains the ledge.

The wall above the left end of the long low ledge is very steep, seamed with cracks and capped by triple roofs. The most prominent feature is an undulating quartz band trending diagonally right under the cracked wall.

15 Strawberry Jellyfish 55m E2 *
S.Chinnery, T.Bridgeland, Jul 1998
This climbs the prominent leftmost forked cracks to gain a groove below a prominent hanging nose in the roof above.
1. 30m 5b Climb the cracks into the groove amongst the roofs. Traverse left above the lip of the first roof for 2m. Move up and pull left under the nose (crux) to gain a groove. Climb this to belay in a large niche below a loose broken groove.
2. 25m 4c Swing out right and climb the wall above on crozzly holds.

16 Endolphin Rush 60m E3 ****
K.Howett, G.E.Little, 27 May 1997
A magnificent and strenuous route on excellent rock following the undulating quartz band.
1. 25m 5c Climb up to and follow a right diagonal, wide band of pink pegmatite across the overhanging wall. As the steepness relents onto a smooth slab, move up and right to gain a crack-line that trends back left slightly with increasing difficulty to reach a small stance and belay beneath the big roofs. A very pumpy pitch.
2. 35m 5c From just above the belay move down and left between the big roof above and another below. Pull through the roof, which is a leaning wall at this point, via a conspicuous fat spike to gain a ledge below another roof. Move left to bypass this and climb direct to the top on huge holds.
Variation: **16a At the Drop of a Hat 30m E3 5c ***
C.Henderson, R.Durran, 11 Aug 2003
2a. Pull directly over the roof above the belay into a small hanging corner. Step left to the arete, finish easily up and left.

17 Blue Archipelago 50m E3 **
T.Bridgeland, S.Chinnery (pitch 1), Jul 1998; S.Chinnery, O.Metherell (Pitch 2), 1998
This is a combination of a direct start and a direct finish to Endolphin Rush that gives a sustained line cutting across that route.
1. 20m 5c Take a line up cracks in a brown streak just right of the cracks of Strawberry Jellyfish above the quartz band. Climb steeply up the crack-lines on big juggy holds until it is possible to pull rightwards onto a small basalt ledge. Continue up the slabby wall slightly leftwards to below the roof and gain the belay of Endolphin on the right.
2. 30m 5c Go up and right into an L-shaped roof, left of a massive downward-pointing flake. Climb direct

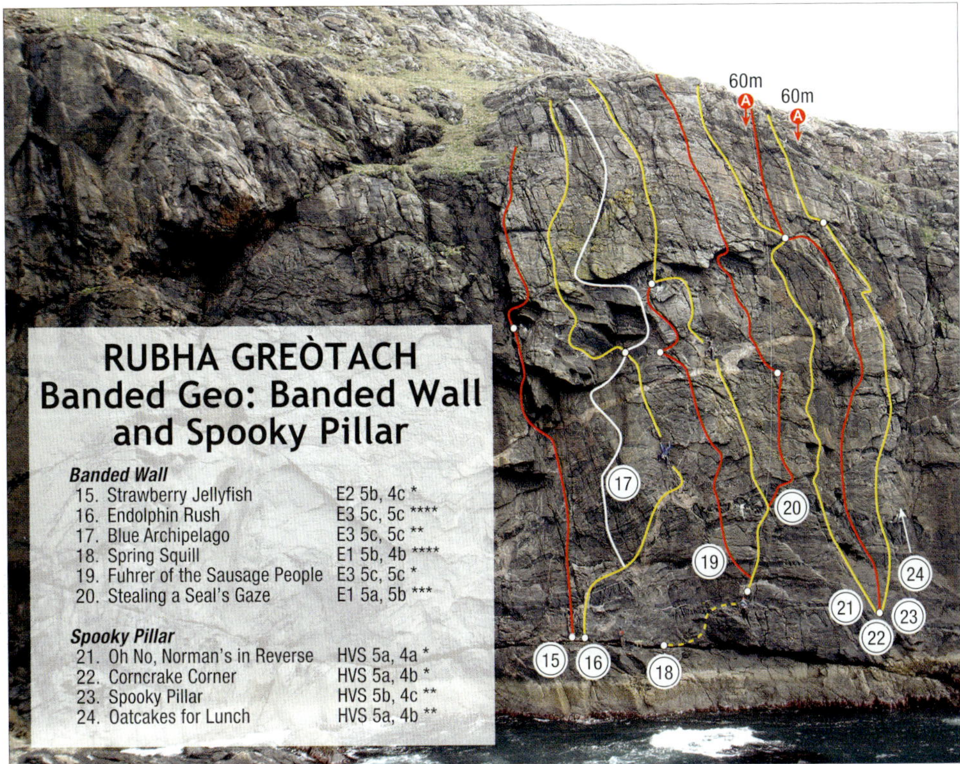

through the corner of the L-shaped roof to large holds under the next roof. Traverse left to the arete and up easy orange lichen covered rock, bearing right near the top.

18 Spring Squill 65m E1 ****
A.Cunningham, G.Nicoll, 30 Jun 1995
One of the best routes on the island. Start from the right end of the long ledge at high tide level.
1. 40m 5b Move up and right to a smaller ledge with a flake thread (rough sea alternative belay). Follow a flake-line rightwards to a ledge and then trend steeply back left and into the right-hand of two short cracks leading to easier climbing. Move into a vague depression, past a huge downward-pointing flake, to climb a crack through a bulge (crux) on the left and then go up to belay on the left under a break in the long overhang.
2. 25m 4b Pull through the narrowing in the overhang and continue directly to the top.

19 Fuhrer of the Sausage People 50m E3 *
I.Taylor, T.Fryer, 14 5 2000
Start as for Spring Squill.
1. 20m 5c Go steeply up and left to easier ground, then follow flakes leftwards to beneath small overlaps. Pull through these and continue up and left to a hanging belay left of the massive downward-pointing flake near Blue Archipelago.
2. 30m 5c Go back right and climb the awkward crack right of the flake to gain a circular depression. Pull through the overhang and finish as for Spring Squill.

20 Stealing A Seal's Gaze 65m E1 ***
K.Howett, A.Todd, 15 May 1998
A good companion to Spring Squill, only a touch harder.
1. 35m 5a Follow Spring Squill up flakes to the steep wall. Move up and right across a black pegmatite band to under a small isolated overlap. Step right under it and pull over. Climb direct then slightly right into the top of a shallow groove.
2. 30m 5b Climb out left to a thin crack leading to a quartz band. Move left and up and left into a depression (above and right of that on Spring Squill) below the widest part of the roofs above. Pull out left through the roof and follow a discontinuous crack to the top.

Spooky Pillar

Diagrams p320, above & p327

The following routes immediately right of Spring Squill are centred around twin corner and chimney-lines with a clean pillar between.

Endolphin Rush, P1 (E3) Ed Shaw & Sue Hazel (photo Kyle Pattinson)

Desent: Abseil from a point about 10m south of Spring Squill, down the line of the prominent chimney-corner (60m). Belay on a tiny ledge at the base of a black slab.

21 Oh No, Norman's in Reverse! 65m HVS *
G.Nicoll, A.Cunningham, 30 Jun 1995
Climbs a line up the edge right of Stealing a Seal's Gaze. Start off the black slab.
1. 40m 5a Climb leftwards up the slab to an obvious break in the left arete of the corner. Swing left onto the wall and climb, passing an awkward little overhang, to a ledge on the right.
2. 25m 4a Move left and climb an orange ramp to easy ground and the top.

22 Corncrake Corner 65m HVS *
G.Nicoll, A.Cunningham, 30 Jun 1995
This route climbs the line of the obvious chimney-corner, the line of the abseil (as for the previous route).
1. 40m 5a Climb up into the deep chimney. Follow this then up the right wall of the corner to pass an overhang. A quartz bulge above is climbed directly to easier ground and a belay ledge (in common with the previous route).
2. 25m 4b Climb directly up the wall above to finish.

23 Spooky Pillar 65m E1 **
A.Cunningham, G.Nicoll, 30 Jun 1995
This route tackles the pillar to the right of Corncrake Corner. Abseil to the tiny ledge.
1. 45m 5b Climb straight up keeping slightly left of the edge through bulges until a move right round the edge at the top bulge leads into a crack. Follow this to a good ledge and belay.
2. 20m 4a Easier climbing straight up to finish.

24 Oatcakes for lunch 70m HVS **
B.Darvill, I.Lovatt, Jun 2004
Start at the base of the easy slab beneath the corner of Chocolate Starfish.
1. 30m 5a Climb the slab, then direct through bulges, keeping just left of the corner. Finish up a satisfying crack to belay on a perfect stance.
2. 40m 4b Step right from the stance onto the slabby wall, and climb straight up, tackling the juggy overhang to finish.

25 Chocolate Starfish 60m HVS
T.Bridgeland, S.Chinnery, Jul 1998
Climbs the prominent right-facing corner, right of Corncrake Corner. Belay on the black slab at the base of the corner. Climb it. Easy in its upper half. Not inspiring.

The Shield

Diagrams p320 & opposite

To the right of Spooky Pillar the wall of the geo diminishes in height a little and is split by a large grass ledge at two-thirds height. The lower tier is composed of a smooth holdless-looking clean shield of rock. An unclimbed flakey corner separates Spooky Pillar from this shield which is split into two walls by an obvious

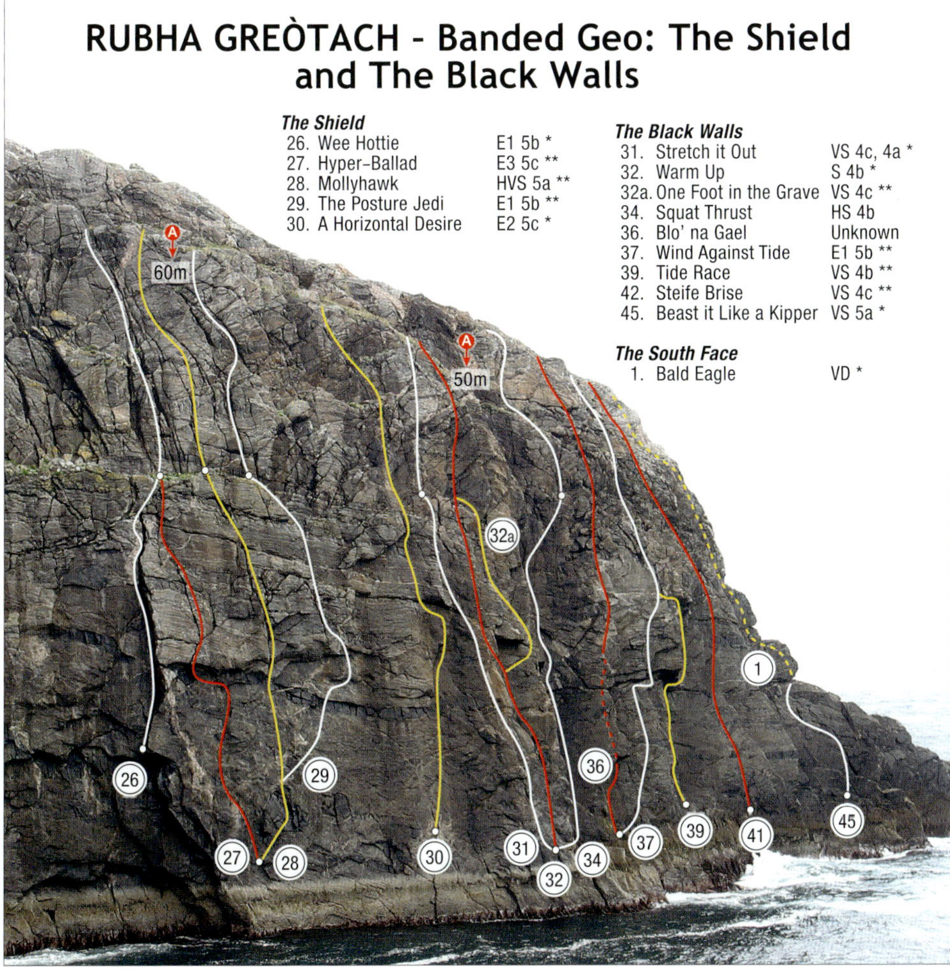

left-facing corner. All the following routes climb the right-hand wall.

Descent: Abseil (60m) from a large boulder to a hanging stance on a footledge 4m right of the base of the central corner; calm seas are pretty much essential.

26 Wee Hottie 20m E1 5b *
G.Latter, A.Lole, 5 Jun 2006
The prominent left-facing corner between the two walls was climbed from the start of the vertical section to join Hyper-Ballad in the upper section. Finish up Hyper-Ballad top pitch.

27 Hyper-Ballad 55m E3 **
L.Hughes, G.Nicoll, 27 May 1997
This takes a line up the wall just right of the left-facing corner separating the walls. Low in the grade.

1. 30m 5c From the footledge climb directly up to an overlap. Traverse 6m left and pull spectacularly through the overlap at a crack (brutal). Continue to a grass ledge.
2. 25m Easy cracks and slabs to the top.

28 Mollyhawk 55m HVS **
G.Nicoll, L.Hughes, 27 May 1997
Starts from the footledge of Hyper-Ballad.
1. 30m 5a Move up and right and climb a right-facing groove. Move left to an obvious break in the overlap, pull through and continue to the grass ledge.
2. 25m Easy cracks and slabs to the top.

29 The Posture Jedi 25m E1 5b **
G.Latter, A.Lole, 5 Jun 2006
Start at the belay of Mollyhawk. Trend up and right following hidden holds to go through the roof at its

right-hand end. Climb more easily up left to gain ledges.

30 A Horizontal Desire 40m E2 5c *
A.Lole, G.Latter, 5 Jun 2006
Start from a belay in a vertical crack at the base of a right-facing groove right of the main roof system. Access down the line by abseil. Go up the groove to the roof. Break out left up a crack and easier to the top.

The Black Walls

Diagrams p320, opposite & p325

This is the area either side of a very prominent brown-stained off-width corner, just before the wall diminishes in height towards the South Face. The right wall of the corner has been the scene of a huge rockfall obliterating the previous classic route, Blo' Na Gael. At the time of going to press, the line has not been re-climbed. The first five routes lie on the wall between The Shield and the off-width corner, based around the smaller corner-line of Warm Up.

Descent: Abseil to the base of Warm Up (50m).

31 Stretch It Out 45m VS *
A.Cunningham, F.Fotheringham, 23 Jun 1996
Climbs a line around the edge between The Shield and the corner of Warm Up.
1. 30m 4c From the base of Warm Up swing left round the edge and up and left into a corner. Follow the corner and continue left onto a large ledge.
2. 15m 4a Climb straight through the bulge above after which easy ground leads to the top.

32 Warm Up 45m S *
R.Gantzhorn, R.Witt, 18 Jun 1995
The most obvious feature on the wall is a corner leading to a roof at half-height.
1. 30m 4b Climb a crack-line to gain the corner. Go up the corner to a smaller overlap below the main roof and step left to climb a slab for 7m to reach a ledge. Gain a flake-corner above the roof and follow it to a large ledge.
2. 15m Climb darker rock to the top.
Variation: **32a One Foot in the Grave 45m VS 4c ****
A.Lole, F.Murray, G.Latter, 6 Jun 2006
Climb the crack and corner all the way to the roof. Exit right below it and finish up an easy groove and wall.

33 Run Daftie Run 45m HVS 5a
A.Lole, G.Latter, 5 Jun 2006
The right arete of Warm Up. Climb easily up the wall on the right to protection in a black plaque. Step right to good holds on the arete and up the right side of the arete and then easily to the top.

To the right of Warm Up is a black chimney leading to a hanging groove. Just right again is an off-width chimney and flake-crack, the next most obvious feature on this part of the cliff.

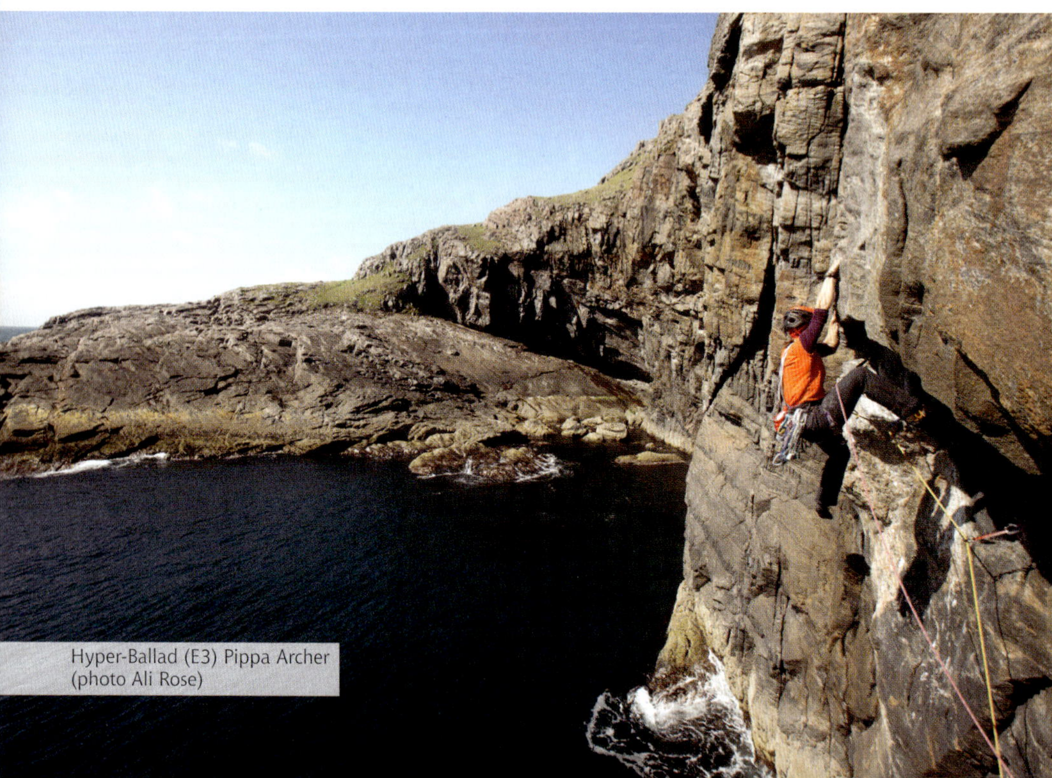

Hyper-Ballad (E3) Pippa Archer (photo Ali Rose)

Spooky Pillar

21.	Oh No, Norman's In Reverse	HVS 5a, 4c *
22.	Corncrake Corner	HVS 5a, 4b *
23.	Spooky Pillar	E1 5b, 4a **
24.	Oatcakes for Lunch	HVS 5a, 4a **
25.	Chocolate Starfish	HVS 5a

The Black Walls

31.	Stretch It Out	VS 4c, 4a *
32.	Warm Up	S 4b *
32a.	One Foot in The Grave	VS 4c **
33.	Run Daftie Run	HVS 5a
34.	Squat Thrust	HS 4b
35.	Prominent Nasty Offwidth	E2 5b
36.	Blo' Na Gael	Unknown
37.	Wind Against Tide	E1 5b **
38.	Wind Against Tide RH	E1 5b ***
39.	Tide Race	VS 4b **
40.	Cup Final	VS 5a *
41.	Stiff Upper Lip	VS 4c *
42.	Steife Brise	VS 4c **
43.	At Last	VS 4c *
44.	Raindance	E1 5b *

34 Squat Thrust 55m HS

F.Fotheringham, A.Cunningham, 23 Jun 1996

1. 40m 4b From the base of Warm Up traverse right over low tide barnacles into the black chimney. Go up this and the groove above to a ledge. Break rightwards across the wall and up to a ledge.

2. 15m Easy to the top.

Variation: **Right Finish 40m HVS 5a**

G.Latter, A.Lole, 5 Jun 2006

Follow the initial chimney stepping up right into a shallow groove in the arete and finish direct.

35 Prominent Nasty Looking Off-width Groove 50m E2 5b

I.Taylor, G.Stanworth, May 2001

The prominent off-width corner between Squat Thrust and Wind Against Tide was not as nasty as the first explorers thought it would be. The recent rockfall may have affected the upper section.

36 Blo' Na Gael 50m

A.Cunningham, F.Fotheringham, 23 Jun 1996

The original (E1) climbed the wall between The Nasty Looking Off-width Groove and a smaller, shorter off-width to the right. It suffered an initial rockfall in 2008 making it substantially harder and an easier variation was climbed. But the whole section including the shorter off-width has now been demolished by a much bigger collapse and the route with it. The line is indicated for anyone wishing to investigate further.

37 Wind Against Tide 50m E1 5b **

A.Cunningham, F.Fotheringham, 23 Jun 1996

Climbs the right wall right of the old line of Blo' na Gael.

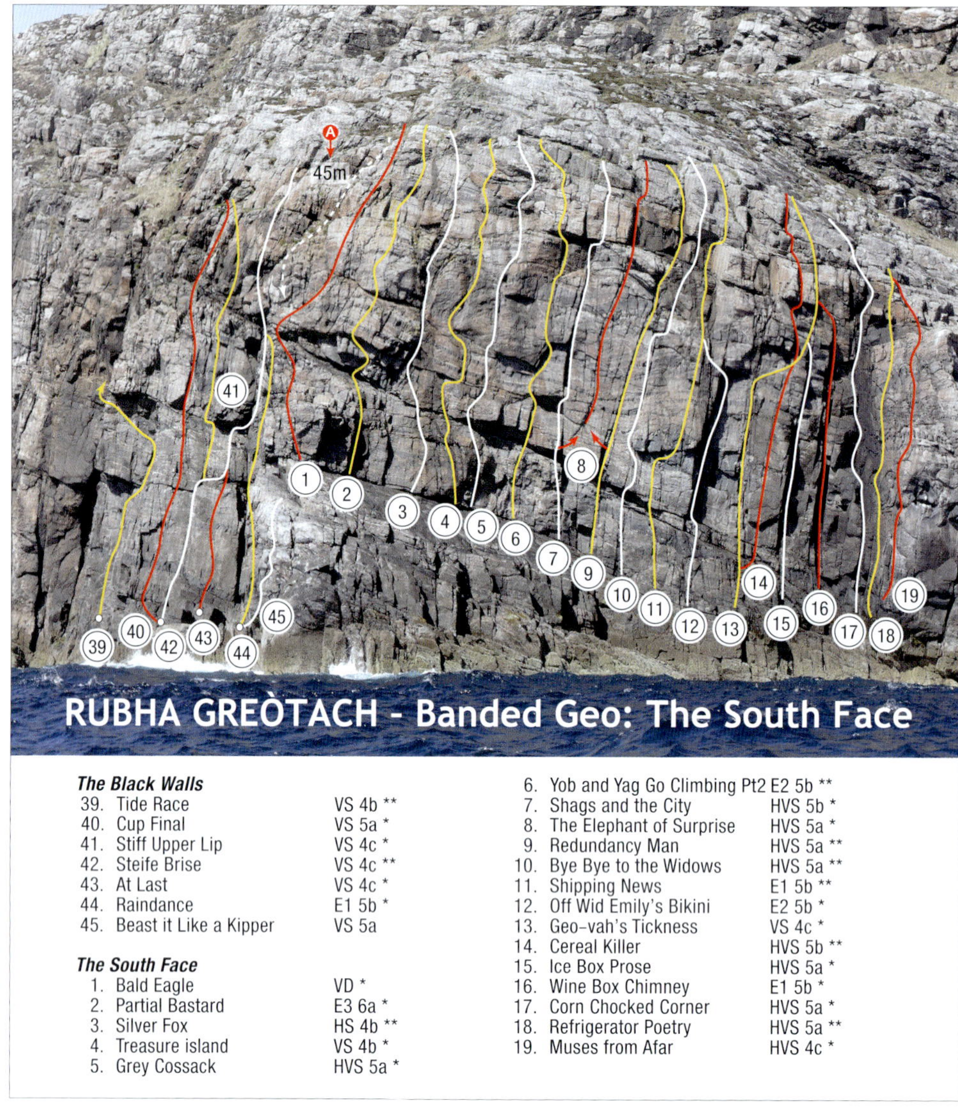

RUBHA GREÒTACH - Banded Geo: The South Face

The Black Walls

39. Tide Race VS 4b **
40. Cup Final VS 5a *
41. Stiff Upper Lip VS 4c *
42. Steife Brise VS 4c **
43. At Last VS 4c *
44. Raindance E1 5b *
45. Beast it Like a Kipper VS 5a

The South Face

1. Bald Eagle VD *
2. Partial Bastard E3 6a *
3. Silver Fox HS 4b **
4. Treasure island VS 4b *
5. Grey Cossack HVS 5a *
6. Yob and Yag Go Climbing Pt2 E2 5b **
7. Shags and the City HVS 5b *
8. The Elephant of Surprise HVS 5a *
9. Redundancy Man HVS 5a **
10. Bye Bye to the Widows HVS 5a **
11. Shipping News E1 5b **
12. Off Wid Emily's Bikini E2 5b *
13. Geo-vah's Tickness VS 4c *
14. Cereal Killer HVS 5b **
15. Ice Box Prose HVS 5a *
16. Wine Box Chimney E1 5b *
17. Corn Chocked Corner HVS 5a *
18. Refrigerator Poetry HVS 5a **
19. Muses from Afar HVS 4c *

It may have escaped the ravishes of the rockfall. Climb the wall towards its right side to gain a large horizontal break. Traverse the break rightwards until level with large roofs and climb a thin crack, then up and right to a good ledge. Finish more or less direct.

Just right of Wind Against Tide is another corner system with a small triangular belay ledge.

38 Wind Against Tide RH Start 30m E1 5b ***
G.Latter, A.Lole, 6 Jun 2006
Starting from the belay at the base of the corner, step left around the arete and follow grooves to gain the large horizontal break and the thin crack.

39 Tide Race 35m VS 4b **
S.Pierson, A.Cain 16, May 1998
Go up the corner to the first roof and turn it on the right. Traverse left below the main roof to the edge of the buttress to join Wind Against Tide at the good ledge.

Right again is a sloping ledge at the bottom of a slab, just above high tide level. Above the sloping ledge is an open corner and to the right is a chimney-corner bounding the prominent spur which marks the end of the west section of the wall as it turns into its south wall.

Descent: By abseil, the same as for the South Face down the spur of Bald Eagle but continuing slightly left (facing in).

40 Cup Final 35m VS 5a *
S.Pierson, A.Cain, 16 May 1998
From the sloping ledge climb up the slab on flakes to a ledge (escapable via a ramp on the right). Finish up easy broken ground.

41 Stiff Upper Lip 40m VS 4c *
P.Swainson, J.M.Given, May 1997
Climb the first corner-crack of Steife Brise to under the roof. Traverse left to turn the roof and finish by an obvious black groove.

42 Steife Brise 40m VS 4c **
J.Fischer, A.Seeger, 18 Jun 1995
Climbs the final corner of the wall. Start on the sloping ledge. Climb the corner and head right to under a large roof. Negotiate this on the right, then climb the corner above, via flakes, to reach easier ground.

43 At Last 35m VS 4c *
S.Pierson, A.Cain, 16 May 1998
A direct entry into Steife Brise. Climb the easy slab into a prominent left-facing corner. Ascend the bulge and continue on easy ground to the top.

Descent: The final section of Banded Geo, before reaching the platform of the South Face, can be gained by abseil from the top of the spur between the two faces (the line of Bald Eagle) to gain a ledge beside a deep man-sized chimney.

44 Raindance 15m E1 5b *
A.Fulton, M.Airey, 22 Jun 2008
Start at the left end of the ledge, right of the deep man-size chimney. Climb a small shallow, right-facing groove-crack, over a slight bulge on small but positive holds. Continue up and slightly left on easier ground, then up the steep juggy headwall above to finish on Bald Eagle.

45 Beast it Like a Kipper 10m VS 5a
M.Airey, A.Fulton, 22 Jun 2008
Start 4m right of the chimney. Climb a steep wide left-slanting crack to where the crack becomes horizontal. Trend right on good holds up the wall above to finish up Bald Eagle.

The South Face

Diagrams p320 & opposite

Left (looking out) of the prominent spur is a large non-tidal platform sloping down from right to left (looking out) below the length of this section of cliff to reach sea-level near the end of the face.

Descent: By abseil down the line of the spur (Bald Eagle) to gain the right end of the platform (45m).

1 Bald Eagle 40m VD *
J.M.Given, P.Swainson, May 1997
The spur separating the west and south faces of Banded Geo includes a few delightfully delicate moves for the grade.

2 Partial Bastard 40m E3 6a *
A.Fulton, August, 2007
The obvious challenge of the roof on the prow at the junction between the west and south faces. Climb easily to the fist-sized crack splitting the roof at its widest point, which is powerful and technical. Finish easily up an S-shaped crack.

3 Silver Fox 40m HS 4b **
P.Swainson, J.M.Given, May 1997
About 5m right of the spur, the left-facing corner and undercut crack will delight any gritstoner.

4 Treasure Island 35m VS 4b *
J.Preston, G.Ettle, 7 Jun 2004
Start mid-way between Silver Fox and Grey Cossack, below a small roof. Climb a black slabby wall to the roof (a ragged crack on the left). Pass the roof on the right and continue up to a superb flake-crack which is followed to the top.

5 Grey Cossack 30m HVS 5a *
J.Lyall, M.Davies, 14 May 2001
Climb the rib just right of Silver Fox, over a roof, up a left-facing corner and up flakes to the top.

6 Yob and Yag Go Climbing Part 2 30m E2 5b **
A.McSherry, M.Howard, May 1998
Climbs through the left edge of three big roofs in the centre of the main wall.
Variation: **30m E1 5c**
M.Sakano, P.Hanlon, 22 Jun 2015
Follow the cracks direct through quadruple roofs finishing at the final off-width crack.

7 Shags and the City 30m HVS 5b *
M.Mortimer, C.Pulley, 5 Jun 2006
The most distinctive main crack on the right side of the three roofs. After the second roof, follow a crack to the right of the final off-width crack.

8 The Elephant of Surprise 30m HVS 5a *
A.Lole, G.Latter, 6 Jun 2006
The thinner hanging crack in the wall. Gain the crack by starting up either of the adjacent routes and traversing in above the lower roof.

9 Redundancy Man 30m HVS 5a **
S.Pierson, A.Cain, 16 May 1998
The crack above a slight recess in the roof at the base.

10 Bye Bye to the Widows 30m HVS 5a **
S.Pierson, A.Cain, 16 May 1998
Climbs through the roof to gain the right-hand crack.

11 Shipping Views 35m E1 5b **
M.Davies, J.Lyall, 14 May 2001
Climb the wall 3m right of Bye Bye to the Widows to break through the right end of the grey roof. Follow a crack up the right edge and corners to the top.

12 Off Wid Emily's Bikini 35m E2 5b *
C.Pulley, M.Mortimer, 5 Jun 2006
Just right of Shipping Views is a recess. Take the right-facing corner in the left side of this into an off-width chimney. Cut loose right and follow an overhanging flakey corner to the upper roof. Go left to join Shipping Views to finish.

13 Geo-vah's Tickness 35m VS 4c *
C.Wiles, D.Ferguson, Jun 1999
Start from the ledge up and right of the previous routes, below the right side of the recess. Climb a shallow corner that forms the recess and take a rising line to the right to finish just right of an overhang.

14 Cereal Killer 35m HVS 5b **
J.Lyall, M.Davies, 13 May 2001
The first line right of the recess. Climb a left-facing quartz corner, then cracks through a roof system.

15 Ice Box Prose 35m HVS 5a *
R.I.Jones, M.Gear, 6 Jun 2003
Some 4m left of the prominent corner-crack of Corn Choked Corner is a right-facing corner. Climb this and the cracks up the wall system above. Shares the last 5m with Wine Box Chimney.

16 Wine Box Chimney 35m E1 5b *
A.Erskine, J.Wardman, 6 May 2003
The chimney 2m left of the corner, and the right-facing corner above (crux). Finish up the steep wall.

17 Corn Choked Corner 30m HVS 5a *
J.Lyall, M.Davies, 13 May 2001
At the right end of the narrowing ledges is a recess. Climb the right-hand corner-crack, with a steep finish through a slot.

18 Refrigerator Poetry 35m HVS 5a **
R.I.Jones, M.Gear, 6 Jun 2003
Takes the wall between the corner and Muses from Afar. From the bottom of the corner step right to the wall and climb the centre to the top.

19 Muses from Afar 35m VS 4c *
R.I.Jones, M.Gear, 6 Jun 2003
From the corner, traverse right to the crack in the centre of the wall and climb this to the top.

The Galley

(NL 589 871) Non-tidal W facing Map p302 Diagram opposite

West of Banded Geo the first cliff encountered is The Galley. The Galley wall increases in height to the right when its base forms a gully descending into the sea. The features are best described from right to left. Above the tidal section on the right is a conspicuous roof at three-quarters height. To its left are two parallel overhanging corners. Left again is a clean wrinkled wall bounded on the left by two larger corners. Routes are described from right to left.

Descent: To gain the base of the Galley it is necessary to descend a choice of two ramp-come-corner-lines near the north side of the headland (the right-hand side looking out). The furthest north is easiest.

1 Wu-Tang Will Survive 30m E1 5b *
L.Hughes, G.Nicoll, 25 May 1997
Start as for Winos and take a diagonal line rightwards across the wall to finish at the right end of the big roof.

2 Winos in a Barren Land 25m E3 5c **
K.Howett, G.E.Little, 23 Jun 1996
This climbs through the big roof at the right-hand side of the wall. Traverse the obvious break along the base of the wall (low tide preferable) to a belay in the base of a small right-facing corner directly below the roof. Go up the corner to below the roof and pull left through the roof with difficulty and up the wall above to the top.

3 Conch Corner 25m VS 4c *
G.Nicoll, L.Hughes, 25 May 1997
Left of Winos are two parallel disjointed corners. This route climbs the right-hand corner. Start by climbing rightwards to gain the steep flakey corner.

4 Wu-Tang Forever 25m E1 5b *
L.Hughes, G.Nicoll, 25 May 1997
Follow Conch Corner for a few metres, then pull left through a bulge to gain and climb the left-hand corner.

The impressive centrepiece of the cliff is a wrinkled, streaked wall with an undercut base. A projecting buttress used to reside below the base of the wall but has collapsed, raising the grade to 5b on suspect rock to gain the ledge from below.

Descent: Abseil in to what remains of the ledge to start. The grades below are for an abseil approach.

5 Wiggly Wall 20m HVS 5a ***
G.Nicoll, M.Crowther, J.Lowther, 23 Jun 1996
Climbs the clean wall in the middle of the cliff. Superb climbing leads first rightwards then direct to finish up a crack forming the left side of a huge block. Excellent and intimidating.

6 Un-named 20m E2 5b **
P.Thorburn, R.Campbell, 2007
Takes the middle of the wall between Wiggly Wall and The Abridged Version. A bold eliminate with good climbing.

7 The Abridged Version 25m S 4a *
G.E.Little, K.Howett, J.Lowther, 23 Jun 1996
This climbs the large corner left of Wiggly Wall. Abseil to a ledge above the now loose lower section.

RUBHA GREÒTACH - The Galley

1. Wu-Tang Will Survive — E1 5b *
2. Winos in a Barren Land — E3 5c **
3. Conch Corner — VS 4c *
4. Wu-Tang Forever — E1 5b *
5. Wiggly wall — HVS 5a ***
6. Un-named — E2 5b **
7. The Abridged Version — S 4a *
8. Anthology Arête — HVS 5a **
9. The Complete Works — S 4a *
10. Jesus Made Me Stumpy — VS 4c **
11. Yob and Yag Go Climbing Part 1 — E1 5b **
12. Retreat Unthinkable! — E1 5a
13. A Cream of White Sauces — HVS 5a

8 Anthology Arete 25m HVS 5a **
G.Nicoll, W.Wright, 14 May 1998
Climb the arete between The Abridged Version and The Complete Works directly, to finish at a beak of rock.

9 The Complete Works 25m S 4a *
G.Nicoll, M.Crowther, J.Lowther, 24 Jun 1996
Start as for The Abridged Version and climb the left-hand corner, finishing up a ramp and an overhang (crux).

10 Jesus Made Me Stumpy 25m VS 4c **
T.Carruthers, P.Trower, Aug 1998
Climbs the arete to the left of The Complete Works. Start up that route following the corner to a black band. Traverse hard left round the arete and climb a slim groove roughly in the arete itself, passing the roof near the top on its right side and following cracks up a slab to the top.

11 Yob and Yag Go Climbing Part 1 25m E1 5b **
A.McSherry, M.Howard, May 1998
Climbs an obvious large undercut corner left of The Complete Works. Start up that route and follow Jesus Made Me Stumpy round the arete and continue along the lip under a grey wall into the corner. Go up this to the roof, then traverse left under this into another corner leading to the top.
Variation: **11a Birthday Balloons 25m HVS 4c**
P.Gibson, L.Wright, 13 May 2000
From the arete climb diagonally up and left across the grey wall into the corner. Climb this, going left past the roof.

12 Retreat Unthinkable! 8m E1 5a
R.Jones, G.Stein, 1 Jun 1999
At the top of the gully is a large boulder under a small corner capped by a roof. Climb off the boulder into the corner and turn the roof on the right (bold).

13 A Cream of White Sauces 60m HVS
J.Cox, D.Haige, 7 Aug 1999
Takes a left to right traverse line just below the top of the wall across the right-hand side of The Galley starting up Retreat Unthinkable.
1. 15m 5a Step off the boulder, pull into the hanging corner, then climb the wall to the roof. Traverse right around the arete to a belay ledge.
2. 15m 4c Continue in the same line across The Complete Works to a belay in the corner of The Abridged Version.
3. 15m 4c Cross Wiggly Wall, taking the upper of the two horizontal breaks to continue around the arete to a ledge (scramble to the top if required).
4. 15m 4c Take a good rising diagonal line on the wall to the right above the large roof of Winos in a Barren Land.
Variation: **13a Dream of White Faeces 40m VS 4c ***
S.Chinnery, S.Littlefair, A.Loftus, O.Metherell, Jul 1998
The original traverse along the obvious horizontal break in the Galley, started by descending The Complete Works to the ledge at the end of pitch 1.

To the left of the boulder is a featured wall with a very large block on the left-hand side, which is detached from the wall. The base of the wall is littered with smaller boulders. The following routes climb this wall.

14 The Hatman 10m VS 4c
R.I.Jones, M.Snook, A.Callum, 4 Jun 1999
Climbs the centre of the wall. From a boulder at the base of the middle of the wall, gain a left-facing flake up and rightwards. Pull up onto a large sloping ledge and climb the short wall to finish.

15 Absolution 10m E1 5b
R.I.Jones, M.Snook, A.Callum, 4 Jun 1999
Start 2m left of The Hatman. Climb the right-facing hanging corner to a horizontal crack. Climb the small crack-line above to finish at the highest point of the wall.

To the left of the very big block is the descent ramp.

16 Squiggle 7m S 4a
R.I.Jones, 4 Jun 1999
At the left corner of the block is a small crack-line on the wall behind. Climb this.

17 Squidge 7m D
R.I.Jones, 4 Jun 1999
Climb the crack-line 2m left of Squiggle.

The Opposite Wall

The wall on the opposite side of the geo, further east from Wiggly Wall as it descends into the sea.

18 The Engine Room 15m VS 4c
R.Spillett, D.Barlow, 3 Jul 2007
Starts from sea-level ledges. Climb a vertical crack which then slants rightwards towards the top of the wall.

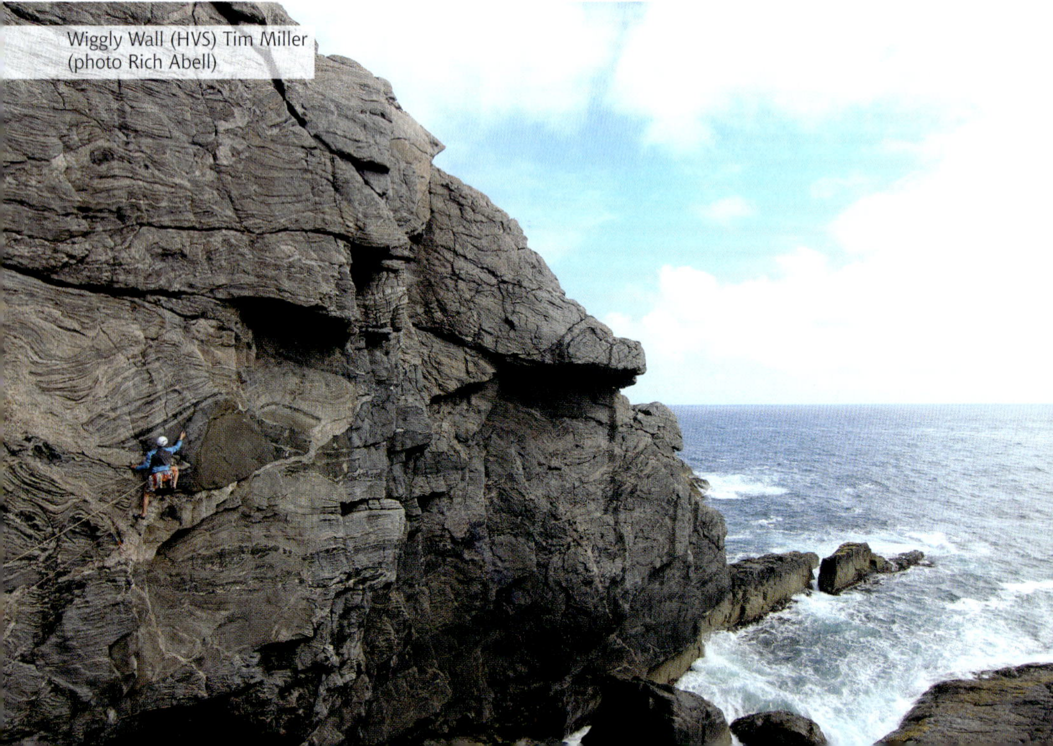
Wiggly Wall (HVS) Tim Miller (photo Rich Abell)

2.	One Last Look	E4 6b **	9.	The Stowaway	S 4a **
3.	101 Damnations	E7 6b ***	10.	Walking with Giants	E3 5c
4.	The Raven	E5 6a ****	11.	Big Al Looks Better	E2 5c *
5.	Thursday's Setting Sunrise	E5 6a ***	12.	Incommunicado	E2 5c **
6.	Don't Fool Yourself Girl	E4 6b *	13.	Pause for Jaws	E2 5c *
7.	Bogus Asylum Seekers	E3 6a **	14.	Human Cargo	HS 4b *
7a.	Soggy Cornflakes	E3 5c **	15.	Geovanie	E1 5b *
8.	Corncrakes for Breakfast	E2 5c **	17.	The Immigrant	VS 4b, 4a *

The Poop Deck

(NL 588 871) Map p302 Diagrams above & p335

A longer, higher, steeper version of The Galley with stunning quality routes. Like The Galley, only the base of the right end is sea-washed at high tide, where there is an immaculate wall seamed by cracks. In the centre of the wall is a steep lower projecting grey buttress which terminates at a series of ledges two-third of the way up the cliff; an easier wall lies above. This buttress has a slabby corner defining its right side and a steep corner its left side. The left side of the Poop is a steeply overhanging wall which develops a long roof further left, terminating in a beak like nose. Below the beak is a colony of guillemots best avoided in the breeding season. The routes are described left to right.

Descent: To gain the base of The Poop Deck it is possible to scramble down the north end of the wall at about VD grade, or simply abseil over anywhere.

The left side of the wall overhangs ferociously and is split by three main vertical crack-lines and several smaller ones. The central one lies above a rock pool whilst the right-hand is a horribly flared off-width.

1 Poop 20m D

G.Nicoll, L.Hughes, 24 May 1997

The left end of the wall is formed by a strange projecting nose. Climb easily up to the crest of the nose then move left and finish in a short flared groove. The short square-cut groove left of the flared groove can be climbed at VD.

2 One Last Look 25m E4 6b **

P.Thorburn, R.Campbell, 29 May 1998

At the left-hand end of the steep wall is a shallow recess with a large pegmatite vein on the right wall. Climb to a man-sized spike, follow cracks up the recess, then hand-traverse right through the roof. Make hard moves into a scoop to gain a hole on the right. Step left, then direct to the top.

3 101 Damnations 25m E7 6b ***

P.Thorburn, R.Campbell, G.Latter, 10 Jun 2004

Stupendous sustained climbing, tackling the twin, thin hanging cracks in the wall right of the pegmatite. Start up the first few moves of The Raven, then pull up and left onto an incut shelf (skyhook in pocket). Make a hard move rocking over to gain a horizontal break above, then move left and gain the cracks. Mainly follow the right one to pull into a large break beneath the roof. Move left to pull rightwards though the roof with very difficult moves to stand on the lip. Continue much more easily directly up the wall above.

4 The Raven 30m E5 6a ****
P.Thorburn, R.Campbell, 25 May 1997
This is the left-hand crack up the centre of the overhanging wall and roof above. Start left of the rock pool and climb up to gain the crack to then gain the roof. Pull through the roof at a hairline crack leading up to a large break. Follow this down left, then move up and follow pockets up the headwall to the top.

5 Thursday's Setting Sunrise 30m E5 6a ***
P.Thorburn, R.Campbell, 28 May 1998
The central crack-line. Make one move up the right-hand crack, then traverse left to a niche (alternatively, step onto the boulder in the pool and climb the crack direct, don't fall off!). Make difficult and committing moves to a jug, then climb the crack direct to the break. A flange on the left gains the lip of the roof above. Pull up right and take parallel cracks on the left to the top.

Corncrakes for Breakfast (E2) Pippa Archer (photo Al Docherty)

6 Don't Fool Yourself Girl 25m E4 6b *
R.Campbell, G.Latter, 13 May 2000
The shorter flared rightmost crack, climbed with increasingly difficult moves to a good ledge. Break left through the roof and finish more easily up the headwall.

7 Bogus Asylum Seekers 30m E3 6a **
G.Nicoll, L.Hughes, 23 Jun 1996
The right side of the steepest wall has black streaks issuing from a diagonal crack at the top into a left trending groove-ramp at the bottom. This is the line of the route. Climb the groove-ramp to a ledge. Gain the diagonal crack on the right and attack the overhanging crack in the headwall. Superb and well protected.
Variation: **7a Soggy Cornflakes 30m E3 5c ****
The diagonal crack out right in the finishing headwall.

To the right is the corner of The Stowaway, defining the left side of the central projecting buttress.

8 Corncrakes for Breakfast 30m E2 5c **
R.Campbell, P.Thorburn, 25 May 1997
Start left of the corner of The Stowaway. Follow a flake to head for a small overlap in the leaning headwall. Pass this on the right.

9 The Stowaway 30m S 4a **
G.Nicoll, L.Hughes, 24 May 1997
This is the deep corner forming the left side of the projecting buttress. Wide bridging leads to easier ground, then a steep finish in another short corner.

10 Walking with Giants 35m E3 5c
E.Nind, G.Latter, 14 May 2014
A traverse across the left-hand side of the Poop. Start up The Stowaway corner to a ledge part way up. Gain the good flake on Corncrakes for Breakfast up and left, then traverse left on jugs to gain the right end of the roof and pull through as for Thursday's Setting Sunrise. Traverse the lip easily left, stepping down to a steeper juggy traverse to exit the cliff.

11 Big Al (looks better on a face than Ray-bans) 30m E2 5c *
A.McSherry, M.Howard, 27 Aug 1999
Climbs the upper wall between The Stowaway corner and Corncrakes for Breakfast. Start up The Stowaway and then up the wall direct to finish just right of an isolated roof near the top.

12 Incommunicado 30m E2 5c **
S.Chinnery, O.Metherell, Jul 1998
Climbs thin cracks up the left-hand side of the projecting grey buttress, 7m right of The Stowaway to go past a small square-cut niche onto the large ledge. Then take the rightward rising ramp-line above to finish in a deep crack.

13 Pause for Jaws 30m E2 5c *
C.Henderson, R.Durran, 27 Jul 2000
The slim left-facing groove 5m right of Incommunicado

RUBHA GREÒTACH - The Poop Deck, Right Hand

12.	Incommunicado	E2 5c **	20.	Who Shot RJ?	E2 5c **
13.	Pause for Jaws	E2 5c *	21.	Tick on my Dick	E1 5b
14.	Human Cargo	HS 4b *	22.	Head and Heart	E3 5c **
15.	Geovanie	E1 5b *	23.	Illegal Alien	E1 5b ***
16.	Pabbarotti	E1 5b *	24.	The Craik	E3 6a ***
17.	The Immigrant	VS 4b, 4a *	25.	In The Pink	E2 5b **
18.	The Notorious B.I.G.	E3 6a **	26.	Castlebay Castaway	VS 4c **
19.	Wetter Than The Beach	E1 5b **	27.	Party Kitchen	E2 5c **

gives surprisingly technical and interesting climbing. Finish easily direct above the mid-height ledge into the final crack of Incommunicado.

14 Human Cargo 30m HS 4b *
G.Nicoll, M.Crowther, L.Hughes, 23 Jun 1996
The line of least resistance up the projecting buttress. Climb steps rightwards up the front face of the projecting grey buttress to gain the right end of the ledges and continue up left to the highest ledge. Step left to join Pause for Jaws up the steep juggy headwall.

15 Geovannie 30m E1 5b *
L.Hughes, S.Muir, 24 Jun 1996
Climb the arete of the slabby corner to the ledge. Follow the crack-line directly above to finish.

16 Pabbarotti 25m E1 5b *
N.Morrison, W.Moir August, 2002
The meat of this route is the flakey wall right of the crack-line on Geovannie. Start right of Geovannie and climb the left side of the slab running into the corner-ramp of The Immigrant. Join that route just below the ledge. From the ledge step out right onto the wall and follow flakes and juggy breaks in a fine position to the top.

17 The Immigrant 35m VS *
G.Nicoll, M.Crowther, 23 Jun 1996
A wander round the projecting buttress. Start up the corner forming the right side of the projecting buttress.
1. 15m 4b Climb the slabby corner-ramp to belay on a ledge at its top.
2. 20m 4a Walk left along to the end of the ledges then climb stepped corners and ledges up and rightwards to the top.

18 The Notorious B.I.G. 30m E3 6a **
L.Hughes, G.Nicoll, 24 May 1997
A fierce route tackling the obvious isolated roof right of The Immigrant. Start just right of that route and climb a diagonal crack-line to the roof. Make hard moves over this, then step right and climb the blunt arete to the top. A long reach helps.

19 Wetter Than a Day At The Beach 30m E1 5b **
L.Hughes, S.Muir, 24 Jun 1996
Climbs the hanging corner which essentially bounds the left side of this wall. Start below the isolated roofs near the top of the cliff. Climb a crack-line leading into the corner which leads to the top.

Illegal Alien (E1) Helen Every (photo Mike Hutton)

20 Who Shot RJ 30m E2 5c **
R.Durran, R.Austin, 20 Aug 2004
The obvious hanging crack. Gain a spike below and left of the crack with difficulty (probably difficult to protect for those of average height or less!). Gain and climb the crack, finishing direct.

21 Tick On My Dick 30m E1 5b
S.Littlefair, D.Long, Jul 1998
The wall just left of Illegal Alien. Somewhat eliminate but good climbing.

22 Head and Heart 25m E3 5c **
G.Latter, E.Nind, 14 May 2014
A direct line crossing Illegal Alien, starting up the left arete of that route to its ledge. Climb the short wide crack directly above and continue up the wall, past a good flakey break just before the top.

23 Illegal Alien 30m E1 5b ***
G.Nicoll, M.Crowther, 23 Jun 1996
Start at the base of a small right-facing corner below the centre of the wall. Climb the corner to a small ledge on the left. Continue up cracks to finish up the twin cracks at the top. Another superb route and low in the grade.

24 The Craik 30m E3 6a ***
K.Howett, G.E.Little, 23 Jun 1996
This climbs the stunning vertical crack in the smooth headwall. Start at the base of the corner of Illegal Alien. Step into the corner then climb steeply up and right through a small hanging niche with difficulty to better holds below a deep crack. Go up this to a footledge and climb the superb thin crack above with further difficulty.

25 In The Pink 30m E2 5b **
G.E.Little, K.Howett, J.Lowther, 24 Jun 1996
The pink quartz corner near the right side of the wall. Start directly above a beautiful rock pool under the overhanging base of the wall. Go up a slight groove through an overlap with difficulty to the base of the quartz. Climb this and the corner above to pull out left at the top.

26 Castlebay Castaway 25m VS 4c **
G.Nicoll, W.Wright, 14 May 1998
The right end of the wall is bounded by a ramp. Start in a chimney at the right side of the ramp and climb easily up to a pink corner. Finish by a strenuous layback up this.

27 Party Kitchen 20m E2 5c **
R.Durran, R.Adie, 18 Aug 2006
Start as for Castlebay Castaway. The prominent slot on the right leads to an overhang. Go over this, gain a small ledge then finish up a crack.

Prophesy of Drowning, P3 (E2) Neil McCallum
(photo Mike Hutton)

RUBHA GREÒTACH - The Great Arch
100m
A
A
100m
Upper Tier
1. Northumbrian Rhapsody E5 6b, 6a, 5b *
2. Child of the Sea E5 6b, 6a, 5a **
3. Full Fathom Five E2 5a, 5c, 5a *
5. Hebridean Overtures E5 5b, 6b, 5c ***
6. Out of the Womb HVS 4a, 5a, 5a
7. The Priest E1 4c, 5b, 5b ***
8. Prophecy of Drowning E2 5b, 5a, 5c, 5a ****
10. The Great Arch E8 5a, 5c, 6b, 6a, 5a, 6c ***
11. Crash Course E6 6b, 6a, 5a

THE GREAT ARCH

(NL 592 873) Tidal W facing Map p302

Just to the north of Rubha Greòtach lies an immense rock arch which has become synonymous with climbing on these islands. A massive horizontal roof guards access at mid-height and the arching roof itself near the top of the cliff gives spectacular architecture even by Hebridean standards. To its left are two slender 100m high pillars separated by an open corner (which is still unclimbed and will probably remain so unless someone of a botanical bent makes a visit). The right-hand pillar is narrow at its base, widening with height and holding twin corners near the top capped by a big roof. The left-hand pillar is generally steeper, but scrappier in its upper half. To the north of this the cliff gradually becomes lower and less steep.

Approach: Routes on the arch are accessed on foot, whilst those on the pillars require two different 100m abseils.

Descent: For the first two routes on the front face of the left-hand pillar, abseil from a short boulder-choked gully at the top of the left-hand pillar, directly down the face just to the right (looking out) of the arete to a hanging stance.

For those on the sidewall of the left-hand pillar (the left wall of the botanical corner) abseil from a small wall overlooking the black slab of Out of the Womb. It's necessary to pendulum leftwards at the bottom to gain these routes.

For those on the right-hand pillar, take the same abseil but gain a small ledge in the extreme right base of the black slab, 5m above sea-level.

1 Northumbrian Rhapsody 100m E5 *

S.Crowe, K.Magog, Jun 2005

Climbs the wall left of the arete.

1. 25m 6b Belay on a small ledge on the arete as for Child of the Sea. Move leftwards across the wall to cross an overlap and gain easier flakes above. Climb rightwards to belay below a notch in the right side of the long roof.

2. 25m 6a Pull through the roof into a groove. Step left out of the top of this to gain the slabby headwall. Continue to a belay ledge.

3. 30m 5b Continue up solid but lichenous rock above.

2 The Child of the Sea 100m E5 **

S.Chinnery, T.Bridgeland, Jul 1998 (1 rest); P.Thorburn, R.Campbell, 6 Jun 2005 (without the rest)

Climb the awesome right arete of the pillar. Take a

hanging stance directly below the overhanging arete (just above barnacle level and 3m left of a large chimney pod).
1. 30m 6b Climb steeply up a groove on the right for 8m until a hard traverse left for 2m gains the base of a hanging flake on the arete (crux). More easily up steep flakes and shallow corners to gain the bottom of an obvious scoop.
2. 35m 6a Follow the right trending overhanging groove above on large rounded holds, passing spikes, to join Sturm und Drang. Follow this rightwards through a roof to gain a bottomless corner and continue up this to a belay.
3. 35m 5a Continue up lichenous covered walls and cracks just right of the arete.

3 Full Fathom Five 100m E2 *

O.Metherel, S.Littlefair, Jul 1998

An amenable way up otherwise difficult rock. Start by abseiling into the bottom of the chimney pod of Sturm und Drang.
1. 30m 5a Climb the pod and then trend leftwards across the wall above to pull into the scoop of Child of the Sea.
2. 35m 5c Step left to enter and climb a chimney-groove left of the arete for 15m until a step right can be made to belay just left of Child of the Sea.
3. 35m 5a Go up lichenous rock above, trending right.

4 Sturm und Drang 115m E5

P.Thorburn, R.Campbell, 25 May 1997

This serious route climbs the left wall and upper left arete of the huge open book corner. Abseil down the corner to the lowest foothold below the lowest black diorite band.
1. 25m 6a Taking a high side runner, traverse left across the wall above the level of the belay to gain the top of a large chimney pod. Follow cracks up the wall, then move left past a loose block to belay on a ramp (the scoop of Child of the Sea) on the left.
2. 45m 6a Climb up to a prominent spike then ascend the twin grooves above, moving left onto jugs below the roof. Move right into a bottomless corner with care (loose block and crux) and gain the groove above. Follow this to belay on a vegetated ramp.
3. 15m 4b Traverse right to belay at the left-hand side of a large ledge.
4. 30m 5b Climb to a large flake on the right, step left, then follow the cleanest crack to the top.

5 Hebridean Overtures 95m E5 ***

R.Campbell, M.Davies, May 1999

Climbs a left to right-slanting crack up the sidewall starting as for Full Fathom Five. Abseil to the black slot 10m above the sea.
1. 30m 5b Follow the slot and the crack to a hanging belay on a flake 3m below the roofs.
2. 20m 6b Pull left, then up right through the roof to a ledge. Continue up the fault-line above to belay on the left on easy ground.
3. 45m 5c Follow clean cracks up the slab to the left, then move right onto a large ledge. Finish up a final central crack-line as for Sturm und Drang.

The huge open botanical corner follows, the right wall of which contains the next route.

6 Out of the Womb 100m HVS

S.Muir, L.Hughes, 23 Jun 1996

Climbs the large black slab forming the right wall of the large corner. Belay at a large ledge approximately 10m above the sea near the centre of the wall.
1. 45m 4a Climb easy ground heading for an obvious square-cut block. Go up and left into a curving groove. Good holds lead out of the groove and up to the left to a belay.
2. 20m 5a Traverse up and right to a large footledge. Make hard and exciting moves up a series of steep flakes to get established above a roof. Traverse right, then left and climb up to belay in the large corner.
3. 35m 5a Climb up the chimney-corner of the main corner to the top.

7 The Priest 110m E1 ***

G.E.Little, K.Howett, 30 Jun 1995

This climbs the pillar between The Great Arch and the big open corner, finishing up the left-hand of the twin roof-capped corners high on the cliff. It has great character and atmosphere with big-route commitment. Start from a belay on the lowest small ledge some 5m above the sea on the right side of the slab.
1. 50m 4c Climb the slabby wall just left of the right edge to gain a small ledge and belay on the very edge.
2. 25m 5b Move up into a groove, step right then enjoy sustained and intricate climbing via cracks and grooves, well right of the edge, leading to a belay on a rusty slab under a roof.
3. 35m 5b Move up to the roof, step right then climb to the base of the left-hand corner. Climb this fine corner to the big roof then make a short, difficult traverse left to finish.

8 Prophecy of Drowning 115m E2 ****

K.Howett, G.E.Little, 24 Jun 1996

One of the finest routes on these islands and a must do for anyone visiting. This climbs a line parallel and to the right of The Priest, up an amazing series of corners overlooking the Great Arch. Start at the Priest belay.
1. 40m 5b Climb the right edge of the slab passing to the right of a larger ledge to reach a small block about 10m above. Swing wildly round the overhanging right arete into the base of a hanging groove with a distinctive projecting ledge in its base. Go up the groove and the larger continuation above in an excellent position to exit right onto shattered ledged rock, level with the lip of the great roof of the arch.
2. 20m 5a From the edge of the roof, climb up and right across an immaculate wall to enter a small right-facing groove. This becomes a ramp. Belay at its top below the main corner-line.
3. 30m 5c Climb the superb corner with hard moves through its steepest section. Go up the easy corner above to a roof and exit left onto a large ledge below the final corner.
4. 25m 5a Climb the excellent final corner to the capping roof. Exit right in a great position.

Variation: **E2 5b ****
C.Forrest, A.N.Other, 2002
4a. A direct finish from the final belay. Climb back into the main corner-line and follow it to easy ground.

9 The Breath of Life E3 **
N.Foster, C.Reading, 29 May 2010
A line of slimmer grooves around Prophecy. Start as for Prophecy.
1. 40m 6a From the belay, follow Prophecy up the arete and rightwards into the hanging groove to a band of soft grey pillows. Step right and climb a thin crack and a continuation groove just right of Prophecy until twin parallel cracks gain the Prophecy stance.
2. 45m 5c Climb a crack left of the Prophecy slab, past a triangular overlap, until it curves right, but continue direct up a thin crack, which eases with the angle. Follow an obvious line up and left, passing a short corner, before a shattered looking bulge gives access to a stance at the base of the arete between Prophecy and The Priest.
3. 20m 5b Pull awkwardly into a narrow groove in the arete above and where it fades, move left to finish up The Priest.

10 The Great Arch 90m E8 ***
D.Cuthbertson, L.Hill (rest points), Jun 1997; S.McLure, L.Creamer (1 rest), 2012; D.MacLeod, Jul 2013
A stupendous line through the centre of the arch, marred by some poor rock in the middle section. Start on huge sea-washed boulders below the centre of the big lower roof.
1. 10m 5a Climb onto the wall and traverse left under the corner leading up to the roof.
2. 15m 5c Traverse left across the undercut and overhung wall heading for the arete where the roof above relents. Pull through here and step left and climb up to a good stance beneath a sloping ramp (usually covered in guano).
3. 20m 6b Climb up and right into an open corner and ascend its right wall onto the right arete which leads to the roof above. Traverse out left on the obvious horizontal break in the roof until a hard pull through the roof rightwards gains a corner. Continue up right then back left over poor rock to belay below the hanging bomb bay chimney splitting the big roof.
4. 10m 6a Climb through the chimney into the huge open corner above the roof.
5. 10m 5a Climb the easy wall diagonally right into the centre of the wall to belay beneath a shield of grey rock below the apex of the arch above.
6. 25m 6c Climb the shield of rock with difficulty to the apex of the arch. Climb out through this passing some peg runners with extreme difficulty, continue to the top.
Variation: **10a Exit Stage Left 120m E6 ****
P.Robins, J.McHaffie, 2003
A very good combination, climbing the first four pitches of The Great Arch to get through the big roof (5a, 5c, 6b, 6a). Continue up the corner to the left-hand end of the arch and go round the arete into Prophecy of Drowning to take the direct finish (5b, 5b, 5b).

11 Crash Course 80m E6
N.Sellars, T.Briggs, 29 May 2007
Follows the furthest left feasible corner in the right-hand side of the Great Arch.
1. 35m 6b A powerful entry into the corner with hard moves and not perfect gear (crux). Easier up the corner above, then step right to place a cam in the corner to the right. Step back left and climb the wall and layback to the roof. Belay on large cams.
2. 10m 6a Cross the arch via a hanging corner. A boulder problem gains a spike and a rockover onto a slab. Pull up and across a hanging shelf to a sit-down belay in a niche.
3. 30m 5a Pull into the bottom of a large chimney-corner and follow it to the top.

12 Memory Loss 35m E2 5b
T.Briggs, N.Sellers, 29 May 2007
The rightmost corner in the black rock to the right of Crash Course.

The Arch Headwall

(NL 592 873) Non-tidal W facing

This 25m high slabby wall of immaculate rock lies above the right side of the Great Arch

Descent: The wall can be accessed by walking in along a grassy ledge from the right.

The routes are described from right to left.

Shortbread Fingers 20m S 4b
Seitze, Bohnacker, 19 Jun 1995
Start at the first obvious groove. Scramble up to a ledge. Starting close to the edge, climb straight up for 8m then move left to reach a ledge. Climb the slabby wall above.

Snipe Corner 25m S 4a
M.Snook, J.Sanders, 1 Jun 1999
Start 2m right of Orang-Utang Klaus and climb a right-facing corner-crack to a ledge. Climb the crack in the wall above.

Orang-Utang Klaus 25m S 4b
A.Seeger, Lotze, 19 Jun 1995
This route starts below two distinctive roofs. Climb a corner for 7m, outflank the roofs on the right to gain another corner. Follow this to a ledge, then climb the slabby wall above on good holds.

Chilly Dick 25m VS 5a
M.Gear, R.Benton, 2 Jun 1999
Start 10m right of the large flake of Geniestreich. The crux is in the initial 3m. Continue straight up the slabby wall, avoiding steeper ground on the left, to join a ramp coming up from the right. Easy to the top. Better holds

The Great Arch, P6 (E8) Steve McClure
(photo Tim Glasby)

and protection than first appearances would suggest. The relationship between this and the other routes already established is uncertain.

Pat and Patachon 25m S 4b
Seitze, Bohnacker, 19 Jun 1995
Start 5m left of Orang-Utang Klaus. Climb the centre of the wall passing a curved horizontal break then straight up to a block belay.

Telephonmann 30m S 4a
A.Seeger, Lotze, 19 Jun 1995
Make a 6m traverse left along a ledge from a short distance up Pat and Patachon to gain a corner. Climb straight up to reach a small roof, cross this, then follow the continuation line above.

Geniestreich 30m S 4b
J.Fischer, A.Seeger, 19 Jun 1995
Start at a large flake. Climb the distinctive fading crack to gain the ledge above.

Katzenklo 30m VS 5a
R.Gantzhorn, 19 Jun 1995
Start at the lowest point of the headwall, 5m left of the large flake. Climb the wall for about 10m (poor protection) to a small darkish corner. Climb this then head for a small overhang. Easier ground leads to the top.

Es gibt Reis Baby 30m HVS 5b
J.Fischer, A.Seeger, 19 Jun 1995
Start 5m left of Katzenklo, close to a block. Follow the black groove to the top on slabby rock.

Das ist doch die Situation Hier 30m S 4b
A.Seeger, Lotze, 19 Jun 1995
Start to the left of the block. Follow a slab for 5m then traverse right to a corner. Follow the corner to the top.

Leftie 30m VS 4c
R.Witt, Seitz, 19 Jun 1995
Start at the left end of the grass ledge. Climb the wall (crux) for 6m then go straight up to a roof. Pass the roof at the right-hand edge then climb easier ground to the top.

An Cearcall

(NL 592 874) Tidal W facing Map p302

The cliff continues north from the area around the arch itself for 200m but is very lichenous. It gradually diminishes in height and angle. However, there is a fine clean slab opposite a long skerrie at the north end of the cliff. The following climbs are found on this.

Descent: Abseil to ledges at high tide level.

Nothing To Declare 45m VD
G.Nicoll, J.Lowther, 24 Jun 1996
Climb to the apex of a triangular slab. Pull leftwards over the overlap and continue easily up the slab above.

Customs and Exercise 45m E1 5b
G.Nicoll, J.Lowther, 24 Jun 1996
Start left of the previous route. Climb a corner leading towards a short steep crack. Go up this then into the niche above. Pull out of this then up the easy slab above.

Prophecy of Paddling 45m E1 5b
I.Taylor, T.Fryer, 16 May 2002
Start 3m left of Customs and Exercise. Climb up the left side of a flake, gain an overhung ledge then pull left round onto a black slab. Climb up the arete above and finish up slabs and blocks.

ALANAIS PENINSULA

This is the large area of land forming the north-west end of the island. Its southern boundary is the deeply incised geo of Sloch Glansich. The western side of the peninsula, between Sloc Glansich and the northern tip of the peninsula, is an almost continuous line of cliffs, of which the long black slabby wall dropping directly into the sea towards the north is the most impressive and is named Allanish Wall. The obvious feature here is a huge open-book corner in the centre of the line of cliff, another slabbier corner near the headland and the headland itself comprising a buttress standing proudly into the worst of the Atlantic swell.

The most northern point of the peninsula (which is east of the Allanish Wall and separated from it by a shallow geo cutting some way south into the peninsula) is less precipitous but holds a couple of walls along its east side. Near the back of this geo (Hoofer's Geo) is an immaculate short wall (JA's Wall) which epitomises the quality of the island's gneiss, whilst further north lie Small Box Geo and Squall Wall.

Sloc Glansich

(NL 594 876) Non-tidal N facing

The stream that drains westwards from the islands central col flows through this impressive boulder-choked sloc. Rumour has it that this was once the site of an illicit still. It is possible to scramble into the east end of the sloc. The north wall overhangs dauntingly while the south wall is slabby and is home to the following route.

The Jaws of Hell 30m E3 5b
T.Fryer, I.Taylor, 12 May 2002
A serious route on very poor rock. Halfway down the slabby south wall are three diagonal cracks; the left two forming the letter A. Climb up the right-hand of the A-cracks, pulling through an overlap at a tottering pinnacle. Stand on the pinnacle, pull rightwards onto the slab above and boldly climb to the top.

Palm Tree Wall

(NL 593 877) Non-tidal S facing Map p302

North of Sloch Glansich, but some 50m south of the start of the Allanish Wall, and visible from the approach to the Great Arch, lies this small wall.

Descent: Scramble down ledges on the left of the wall (facing out) until a sea-level platform can be reached.

One Armed Bandit 15m VS 5a
J.Dale, Y.Sell, 4 Jul 2007
Start at the extreme left end of the wall. Climb up and rightwards to gain the obvious crack leading to the top.

The Missing Arm 10m VS 4c
D.Barlow, R.Spillett, 5 Jul 2007
Follow the first crack-line. Effectively a direct start to One Armed Bandit.

Afternoon Showers 10m E1 5b
D.Chadderton, H.Merritt, 5 Jul 2007
Follow the second crack-line.

Thirty Metre Cheese Course 10m HVS 5a
R.Spillett, D.Barlow, 5 Jul 2007
Follow the third crack-line.

Barra Crack 15m VS 5a
J.Dale, S.Thompson, Y.Sell, 4 Jul 2007
Follow the fourth crack-line.

Ta Mo Chridhe 25m S 4a
S.Thompson, J.Dale, Y.Sell, 4 Jul 2007
The corner-crack followed directly.

Black Guillemot 20m VS 4b
J.Dale, S.Thompson, Y.Sell, 4 Jul 2007
Good climbing up the slab to the right of the corner, following the right-trending crack to the top.

Mr Dressup 20m S 4a
Y.Sell, J.Dale, 4 Jul 2007
Around the corner from the Black Guillemot slab. The route follows two short walls split by a large ledge

Allanish Wall

(NL 591 879) Tidal W facing Map p302

This is the long west wall towards the north end of the peninsula and it forms a continuous cliff of black rock extending towards a distinctive headland. The most obvious features are two open-book corners facing south. The most distinctive one is approximately halfway along the cliff and can be seen from right along the west side of the island, whilst the other is near the north end where the wall projects out to sea as a slight headland. The routes are described in two sections based around these two corners, from south to north.

Descent: For all the routes, access is by abseil in calm seas. Beware, this wall takes the full force of any storm swell and regularly sees waves crashing over the top.

The following routes are found in the area around the huge open-book corner in the centre of the cliff.

Wee Free 25m VD *
G.Ridge, K.Pyke, 23 Jun 1996
This climbs the huge open-book corner. Abseil down the corner to the lowest pedestal at the base of the slab. The cracks in the slab just right of the corner are climbed.

Corncrake Chorus 30m HS 4b *
K.Pyke, G.Ridge, 23 Jun 1996
From the pedestal belay, step out right onto the slab and climb directly up the centre. A lot easier than first impressions would suggest.

Kath's Chorus 25m M
G.Ridge, K.Pyke, 23 Jun 1996
Climbs a line to the right of Corncrake Chorus.

South of the second corner and the headland, the slab is split into two distinct sections, the northerly one being steeper than the southerly one with a prominent gulch between them. Both slabs drop cleanly into the sea and take the biggest sea swells going.

Youth of Today 40m HS 4a *
M.Airey, A.Dell, 16 Aug 2006
The wall to the right of the slabby corner. Start from the lower of two ledges above the sea, on the left wall of the corner. Traverse right for 5m and go up cracks past small left-facing corners and a band of black rock. Trend back left and finish up a fine thin crack just right of the corner.

Un-named 30m VS *
A.Loftus, D.Long, Jul 1998
Climbs the large slabby corner bounding the south side of these slabs.

Ripple Slab 30m S 4a *
K.Howett, A.Todd, 14 May 1998
Climbs the southerly slab starting from the obvious good ledge on the lower lip of the slabs. Climb direct up the slab via a thin crack then small flakes on the right through a steepening and easily to the top.

The Cruel Sea 30m VS 4c *
A.Todd, K.Howett, 14 May 1998
Abseil down the northerly slab about 10m south of the corner of Zen, immediately south of a small deep chimney, to a long slim ledge just above the sea. Climb a thin crack rising from the left end of the ledge into a recess and then onto a horizontal break above. Go up to a flake in the steeper wall above to gain a ledge and climb the cracked wall above to a ledge and so to the top.

The left wall of the corner, jutting out from the cliff-line, is overhanging and sports a conspicuous crack, with several climbs based around it.

Zen and the Art of Corncrake Management 25m E3 5c *
A.Cunningham, F.Fotheringham, 24 Jun 1996
The left wall sports a fine dog-leg crack. Start from a higher ledge in the corner and climb the crack on the left onto a large ledge below the dog-leg. Go up this with difficulty.
Variation: **E3 6a**
I.Taylor, T.Fryer, May 1999
Avoid the dog-leg (often wet) by climbing a thin crack to the right.

Zen Left-Hand 25m E2 5c *
N.Morrison, W.Moir, Aug 2003
Where Zen and the Art of Corncrake Management's dog-leg moves right, climb direct in the line of a crack to a ledge. The crack-line continues up a steep juggy headwall.

Fifteen Minutes of Fun 20m HVS 5a
I.Taylor, J.Horrocks, T.Fryer, May 1999
From the large ledge below the dog-leg, go left along a break to the undercut arete and pull round into a groove. Go up this to a ledge, then continue up the left side of the arete.

HOOFER'S GEO

(NL 592 880) Tidal W facing Map p302 Diagram opposite

Not strictly a geo, more of a wall on the east side with easy-angled slabs forming its west side from where the routes can be conveniently viewed. At the north end of the wall is a recess of easy stepped rock. The south end is bounded by a deep gully in the back of the geo. Left of this deep gully is the most obvious feature of the face, a striking smooth wall with a vertical crack up its centre known affectionately as JA's Wall. Left of this are various buttresses and corners culminating in a distinctive beak-like overhang next to the north end recess.

Descent: Go down the recess at the north end of the wall by an easy scramble onto large ledges (well above high tide level, but not in a big swell) leading south along the base of the cliff. In big seas, abseil in. The first route is left of the descent (looking in), the remainder right of the descent.

Wee Bill 15m S 4a
S.Thompson, P.Drew, 3 Jul 2007
Left of the descent. Start on ledges 15m above the sea. Climb the obvious corner with a steep start.

More Whine and Whiskey 25m HS 4b
P.Drew, S.Thompson, 3 Jul 2007
The wall and pillar to the left of an easy corner-crack. Starts on a good ledge to the left of a deep chimney bounded on the right by the beak-like overhang taken by Harry Hoofter.

Tick, Tack, Toe 28m VS 4c
P.Drew, S.Thompson, 3 Jul 2007
Takes the wall and arete left of the deep chimney to a fine finish up a crack overlooking the chimney. Start as for More Whine and Whiskey.

Beak Buttress

The unmistakable prow jutting over the descent.

1 Harry Hoofter 35m E2 5c *
R.Campbell, G.Latter, 16 May 2000
The first steep wall encountered sits under the beak-like overhang. This finely situated climb tackles the hanging crack in the arete above the drooping beak-like overhang. Easily up to the arete, then pull round right and up the crack to belay on the slab above. Finish more easily.

2 Bint There Dun It 25m E1 5b **
G.Ridge, K.Pyke, 24 Jun 1996
This climbs the wall right of the beak. Belay left of a deep slot just right of Harry Hoofter. Follow a blunt rib to a roof right of the beak. Pull over directly and follow a groove to the top.

3 Hoofer's Route 25m E1 5b ***
K.Pyke, G.Ridge, 23 Jun 1996
Start as for Bint There Dun It and follow the blunt rib to under the roof. Pull over and trend right to link up with a fine rising crack-line. Jugs lead to the top.

The Bay Area

To the right of Beak Buttress is a wide bay with slabby grooves, cracks and chimneys on either side. Right of this is a steep lower wall which abuts the central corner-line on the face, Squeeze Job.

4 Boosh 25m E5 6a
P.Robins, J.McHaffie, N.Dyer, 3 Jul 2003
Climbs a striking left-slanting crack on the right side of the deep chimney in the bay. Gain the crack and go up to a small overlap. Tricky moves over this lead to better holds as the crack approaches a corner. Climb straight up the wall above to the top.

5 The Ramp 40m HS 4b *
F.Fotheringham, A.Cunningham, 24 Jun 1996
This climbs the shallow groove and crack-line in the middle of the bay. Follow this to its end and finish up the headwall on surprising jugs.

6 Skuaed 35m HS 4b *
H.Salisbury, V.Hennelly, 4 Jun 2003
Climb the crack right and parallel to The Ramp. Move slightly right onto the wall at 5m and up to a ledge. Continue up the crack 2m on the right and the chimney above.

7 Cast and Shadow 40m HVS 5a
D.Carr, A.Arnott, 4 Jun 2003
The prominent sharp arete to the right of The Ramp. Climb up to the arete. Climb this first on the right and then up the arete to a large ledge and easier ground above.

8 Right Chimney 35m VD
The open chimney, with a steep finish. A variation leads out right along a fault, avoiding the steep finish (D).

9 Refried Feet 35m HVS 5a
T.Catterall, M.Telfer, 1 Jun 2008
Climbs the front of the buttress right of the bay by the

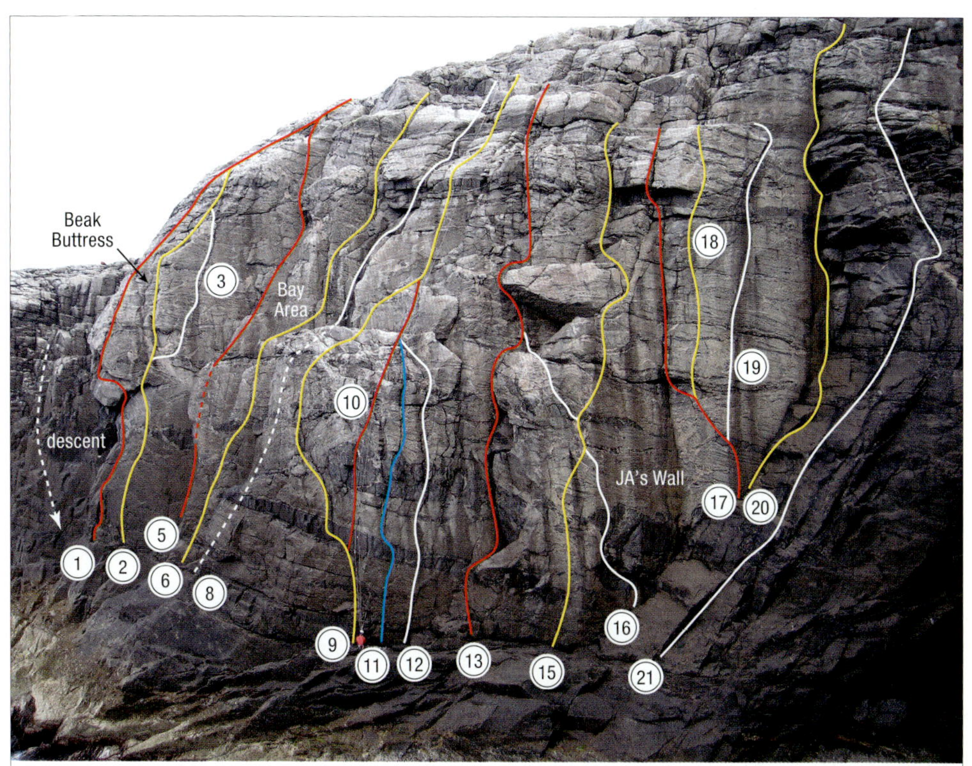

ALANAIS PENINSULA - Hoofer's Geo

1.	Harry Hoofter	E2 5c *	12.	Fracture Clinic	E2 5b **
2.	Bint There Dun It	E1 5b **	13.	Squeeze Job	HVS 5a *
3.	Hoofer's Route	E1 5b ***	15.	Honey Trap	E5 6a **
5.	The Ramp	HS 4b *	16.	More Lads and Molasses	E5 6a **
6.	Skuaed	HS 4b *	17.	As Sound As Mr JA	E2 5b ***
8.	Right Chimney	VD	18.	JA's Maelstrom	E4 5c *
9.	Refried Feet	HVS 5a	19.	Sugar Cane Country	E4 6a ****
10.	Hypnotize	HVS 5a **	20.	Vitrified Cinders	HVS 5b **
11.	Ankle Wrapper	E2 5c	21.	Buckets for Breakfast	HVS 4c **

line of least resistance. Start 4m left of Squeeze Job at a blunt arete. Climb the arete to gain a flake ramp up. From its left until end, continue up the wall and easier ground above.

10 Hypnotize 35m HVS 5a **

L.Hughes, G.Nicoll, 28 May 1997

Climbs the front of the buttress right of the bay direct. Start up Refried Feet and climb the blunt arete all the way to easier ground above.

11 Ankle Wrapper 30m E2 5c

R.Taylor, G.Latter, 23 Jun 2015

Climb the wall, then flakes 2m left of Fracture Clinic.

12 Fracture Clinic 35m E2 5b **

K.Howett, A.Todd, 15 May 1998

In the left wall of Squeeze Job is a fine crack system. Climb directly into the cracks by bold climbing up the steep lower wall. Follow the cracks with decreasing difficulty to a recess. Pull out of this onto easy ground.

13 Squeeze Job 35m HVS 5a *

A.Cunningham, F.Fotheringham, 24 Jun 1996

Bounding JA's Wall is a steep corner-crack leading through a bulge into a chimney, then leading into an off-width above. Climb this line finishing up the left wall after the leaning off-width.

JA's Wall

Although not extensive, this wall of immaculate rock has been criss-crossed with numerous routes, variations and combinations, but all are worthwhile.

14 Rite of Passage 30m E4 6a
S.Crowe, K.Magog, Jun 2005
Follow the steep side of the arete bounding the wall.

15 Honey Trap 20m E5 6a **
N.McNair, A.Robb, May 2005
Superb bold climbing taking the full challenge that More Lads and Molasses avoids. Start up the golden wall to the left of that route, up quartz edges, heading for the pockets and jugs of More Lads. Tackle the headwall direct via a black inset flake to gain a hanging crack, and continue to the top.

16 More Lads and Molasses 35m E5 6a **
R.Campbell, M.Davies, May 1999
A very bold route, the first to take the challenge of the blank looking wall left of Mr JA. Start up black flakes and at a small break move left then up past twin pockets to jugs in another break. Move up left to a hanging black flake and escape leftwards up a scoop to finish as for Squeeze Job. Tricams are useful.

Sugar Cane Country (E4) Roger Newell (photo Mike Hutton)

17 As Sound As Mr JA 25m E2 5b ***
K.Pyke, G.Ridge, 24 Jun 1996
Climbs the obvious hanging groove to the left of Sugar Cane Country. Start as for that route and trend up and left to the base of the groove via steep moves. The groove is straightforward but the direct finish through the off-width above is not.
Variation: **Fear an Bháta 30m E4 6a**
S.Crowe, K.Magog, Jun 2006
An alternative start up the black flakes of More Lads and Molasses; after the initial moves climb boldly up and rightwards to join As Sound as Mr JA.

18 JA's Maelstrom 30m E4 5c *
N.McNair, P.Newman, May 2003
Takes a parallel line to the right of Mr JA, starting as for that route and taking the flakes above the traverse into the groove of Mr JA, finishing up an arete.

19 Sugar Cane Country 35m E4 6a ****
K.Pyke, G.Ridge, 24 Jun 1996
Technical sustained climbing up the centre of the smooth wall, essentially tackling the right-hand and thinner crack. From a belay on the ledge left of a stepped corner, climb on good edges to gain a ledge and the start of the flake-crack. Follow this with difficulty to a ledge. Step left and climb a steep crack to exit.
Variation: **Brother Ray 30m E5 6b ****
R.Campbell, P.Thorburn, 11 Jun 2004
The wall right of Sugar Cane Country. Fine climbing though escapable from below the crux. High in the grade and bold. Climb to the start of the crack, traverse right along a break into the centre of the wall before going up to a pocketed break. Ascend the middle of the wall with difficulty to a good slot and continue to a shake out on Sugar Cane Country. Stroll up the headwall above the right end of the flake with surprising ease.

20 Vitrified Cinders 40m HVS 5b **
G.Nicoll, L.Hughes, 28 May 1997
Romp up the ramp below Sugar Cane Country and climb the fine corner bounding the right side of the smooth wall.

21 Buckets for Breakfast 40m HVS 4c **
P.Gibson, L.Wright, 14 May 2000
Climb the right side of the ramp to a notch and belay on the large ledge above. Overhead is a large curving roof. Cross this at its widest point on big holds, then pull out to finish up a short wall on small holds. Great position.

Right of the right-bounding gully of the face is a triangular wall, accessed by scrambling down a shelf from the right. The shorter wide crack at the right side gives a fine climb at M finishing out left, or D finishing up the short jam crack.

SMALL BOX GEO

(NL 592 881) Non-tidal W facing Map p302

The following routes lie in a square-cut recess about 50m north of the descent into Hoofer's Geo, just south of the tip of the headland.

Descent: Abseil down the overhanging right-hand side-wall of the recess to a commodious ledge in the base. The first route however, is gained by a scramble down easy rocks to the east of the headland and traversing around the headland just above high tide level.

Midget Gem 10m D
P.Drew, I.Lewis, 9 Aug 1999
Climbs the easy corner to the left of the recess.

Just a Tick 20m HS 4b
P.Drew, I.Lewis, 9 Aug 1999
Belay at the left end of the ledge in the base of the recess. Traverse 3m left to the left arete. Climb this to the big capping roof. Turn this on the left with difficulty to reach the top.

Riff-Raff-Roof 20m HVS 5b
P.Drew, I.Lewis, 9 Aug 1999
Start at the left end of the ledge. Climb directly up to the obvious niche in the roof above. Pull over the roof at the niche with difficulty and continue direct up the wall above.

Windy Corner 20m HS 4b
D.Long, A.Loftus, Jul 1998
Climb the open-book corner in the back left corner of the recess.

Tick-tack 20m VS 4c
P.Drew, I.Lewis, 9 Aug 1999
Start at the foot of the obvious corner. Climb the corner to the top.

Another Tick 20m HVS 5a
I.Lewis, P.Drew, 3 Jun 1999
Climb the middle of the wall to the right of Tick-tack.

Headless Duck 20m E1 5b
P.Gibson, L.Wright, 16 May 2002
The right crack.

Sudden Squall 20m E2 5c
D.Long, A.Loftus, Jul 1998
Climbs the imposing right-hand arete of the box geo. Start on the right side of the arete and climb it directly in a fine position. At high water it can be started from the right-hand end of the ledge, beneath an overhanging wall and stepping right onto a ledge at the base of the arete.

Double Tick 20m E1 5c
I.Lewis, P.Drew, 9 Aug 1999
Start just around the arete forming the right end of the recess. Climb the steep wall with an overhanging start.

Squall Wall

(NL 592 882) Non-tidal W facing Map p302

Squall Wall is the wall immediately north of Small Box Geo, providing short climbs on immaculate rock. Routes are described left to right.

Descent: Abseil down the line of Squall Wall to reach a ledge system.

Squall Wall 15m VS 4c
D.Long, A.Loftus, Jul 1998
Takes cracks and a shallow corner on the left side of the north wall of the geo.

Tempest 15m VS 4c
P.Allen, M.Atkins, 8 Aug 2003
The obvious crack-line to the right of Squall Wall.

Eliminator 15m HVS 5a
M.Atkins, P.Allen, 8 Aug 2003
Takes the sheet of rock right of Tempest, starting at a small box corner. Climb straight up to join the stepped ledge system. Good climbing on incuts, but unfortunately escapable leftward.

Zephyr 15m HVS 5a
P.Allen, M.Atkins, 8 Aug 2003
The fault-line to the right of Eliminator provides pleasant technical moves to finish.

LINGEIGH POINT

(NL 603 883) W facing Map p302

This is the most northerly point on Pabbay looking north towards the island of Lingeigh. Its west side forms a series of small buttresses up to 15m high.

Descent: From the northern end of Lingeigh Point, scramble down ledges on the west side until the first rock step into a deep gully is reached.

Seal Wall 15m VD
P.Drew, M.Kingsley, 2007
Climbs the wall left of a deep gully.

Too Hard for the SMC 15m S 4a
P.Drew, M.Kingsley, 2007
Climbs wall right of the deep gully.

RÒISINIS PENINSULA

This is the extensive low headland on the north side of the bay which shelters the beach at Bàgh Bàn and the normal camping area. There is a line of short cliffs overlooking the bay that get any sun going and can be climbed on when the winds or the seas are too rough on the west. The peninsula is actually an island, with an extremely narrow tidal gap separating it from the main island. This gap can be leapt across at any state of the tide.

During the first few years of development on Pabbay, various climbers soloed here during inclement weather and did not report their climbs initially, so there was a bit of confusion about first ascents, although the following climbs have been confirmed.

Bàgh Bàn Wall

(NL 612 875) Non-tidal S facing Map p302

Not strictly on the Ròisinis Peninsula, this is the cliff on the far side of the beach from the campsite just before the tidal gap, where there is a small section of steeper wall surrounded by more broken walls on either side. The slightly leaning flake-crack of Buns in the Oven is the most obvious feature.

Descent: From just before descending to the tidal gap, scramble down by a small cairn heading right (looking out) and then traverse back left (looking out) to a large partially tidal ledge. Routes are described left to right.

Black Slab 10m D
F.Williams, 2008
Ascend the obvious smooth black slab 3m left of the obvious flake-crack and finish up the blocky wall above.

Buns in the Oven 10m VD
F.Williams, 2008
Climb the obvious flake to the right of the thin crack to a break and then climb the wall above. Steeper than it looks!

Family Way 10m D
F.Williams, 2008
Climb the stepped left-trending blocky ramp to the top.

Black Cracks 10m VD
F.Williams, 2008
To the right of a blank looking wall, follow the obvious broken cracks to the top.

Ledge Route 8m D
F.Williams, 2008
To the right of the cracks is a short wall. Start beneath this and make some nice moves between ledges up this to an easier more broken finish. Tidal.

Rosinish Wall

(NL 614 872) Non-tidal SW facing Map p302 Diagram opposite

About halfway out along the line of cliffs is an obvious larger, more continuous section of cliff. In the middle of the cliff is a dark basalt chimney (usually wet), brooded over by an overhanging buttress topped by a massive prow. Left of the chimney is an excellent wall which forms the centrepiece of the cliff. About 6m right of the chimney is a black slab. On the right of this, the wall diminishes in height with the upper section being broken and very easy. Here can be found some good bouldering around an overhanging nose, just before the wall dips into the sea.

1 Hass 10m VD
A.Rutherford, R.Kenyon, 27 May 2015
Climbs the clean corner left of Lottie.

2 Hans 10m VS 4c
A.Rutherford, R.Kenyon, 27 May 2015
Start up Hass, then forsake it for the arete, without using the crack of that route.

3 Lottie 10m HVS 5b
R.Spillett, D.Barlow, 3 Jul 2007
Just to the left of a fetid pool is a deceptively steep series of cracks up a wall, just to the right of an arete. Climb the cracks, trending rightwards.

4 Taxi for Tam 12m E3 6a
W.Moir, N.Morrison, M.Atkins, Aug 2002
The left-slanting groove 8m left of Plan B.

5 Whaler's Wall 12m E2 5b
T.Catterall, M.Telfer, 3 Jun 2008
Climb the central crack in the small broken wall left of Plan B; at half-height move slightly right into the groove and follow this to the top.

6 More Training Required 15m E1 5b
R.Spillett, D.Barlow, 7 Jul 2007
The groove immediately to the left of the Plan B arete, moving onto the arete to avoid the loose yellow exit.

7 Plan B 15m E3 5c ***
T.Carruthers, May 1998
A superb wee climb up the smooth slightly overhanging wall. Move up on slots and then left to gain the arete near the top. Bold in its first half.

8 The Purfect Mur D'Or 15m E4 6a ***
N.McCallum, A.McCallum, M.Hutton, J.Wright, 30 May 2014
Start up Plan B and climb the hairline crack and wall above direct. A good set of RPs are essential. It may be harder for an on-sight.

9 Autoclave 15m HVS 5b *
M.Telfer, T.Catterall, 3 Jun 2008
Climb the dark basalt chimney, until it spits you out.

10 Rising Damp 15m VS 4c *
S.Littlefair, O.Metherell, 10 Jun 1998
Start 5m right of the basalt chimney. Climb a groove right of a sharp arete, stepping right to follow a ramp-line.

11 Squeak 15m E2 5c
D.Toon, 31 May 2008
The wall right of Rising Damp with the crux a move left under the roof at mid-height into that route.

12 Baby Don't Hurt Me 15m E1 5b *
D.Carden, E.Quin, J.Spoor, 29 May 2014
A Y-shaped crack system 2m right of Squeak. Follow the

3. Lottie	HVS 5b	7. Plan B	E3 5c ***	11. Squeak	E2 5c
4. Taxi for Tam	E3 6a	8. The Perfect Mur D'Or	E4 6a ***	12. Baby Don't Hurt Me	E1 5b *
5. Whaler's Wall	E2 5b	9. Autoclave	HVS 5b *	13. Thuggy Crystal	HVS 5a *
6. More Training Required	E1 5b	10. Rising Damp	VS 4c *		

left fork to gain vertical cracks on the right-hand lip of the roof (crux). Finish direct up the blunt, bulging arete above.

13 Thuggy Crystal 15m HVS 5a *
D.Barlow, R.Spillett, 3 Jul 2007
About 6m right of Rising Damp is a black slab, bounded on its right by a V-groove. Climb the groove and the continuation crack to the capping crystal overhang. Pull and hop over it to finish more easily.

The following routes climb on the bouldery area near the right end and were all soloed in May 1998 and later claimed as routes. The names of the claimed routes have been retained.

14 No More Ticks 15m HVS 4c
T.Carruthers, May 1998
On the left of the overhang of The Whoop of the Aviator is a left-facing corner. Pull into this and reach up awkwardly to a flat hold. Pull up and continue more easily to the top of the cliff.

15 The Whoop of the Aviator 15m E1 5c
T.Carruthers, May 1998
Climb the overhang in the centre of the nose in a series of committing moves until easier ground is reached at 3m. Continue up an easier crack above.

16 Ticks Too 15m VS 5a
T.Carruthers, May 1998
Climb the right-facing corner 2m right of The Whoop of the Aviator.

17 The Trouser's Last Stand 15m VD
T.Carruthers, May 1998
Climb the right-facing corner 3m right of Ticks Too and to the left of a clean wall. Continue up the crack and the wall above.

18 Oh No Not Another Tick 15m VS 4c
T.Carruthers, May 1998
The wall capped by a small overhang 4m right of The Trouser's Last Stand. Climb the centre of the wall and then through the overhang on the left-hand side. Poorly protected.

There is a small 10m wall to the right (looking out) from the Rosinish Wall; it has three cracks.

Wing n' Prayer 10m E2 5c
D.Toon, 31 May 2008
Climb the right-hand of the three cracks, stepping left at the top.

What is Love? 10m HVS 5a
D.Carden, J.Spoor, 29 May 2014
The square-cut corner between two aretes 5m left of Wing n' Prayer is capped by a roof. Boldly climb the corner and swing past the roof via a spike on the right.

MINGULAY (MIÙGHLAIGH)

This, the biggest of the Bishop's Isles measures 4km by 3km, with Càrnan (its highest point) rising to 273m; a Marilyn summit. The island contains the highest cliffs, but the biggest prove most disappointing with grotty rock and nesting sea bird colonies. The western seaboard presents a continuous line of cliffs to the Atlantic, reaching a maximum height of 210m at the Biulacraig (Bual na Creige). Mingulay offers some impressive sea stacks including the formidable Lianamul and Arnamul. Both are probably unclimbed by modern climbers although it is said that the Mingulayan men climbed onto the top of Lianamul by subterranean clambering through the huge caves that are a feature of this stack. There are also a couple of smaller stacks to the north-west, which require a boat rather than a swim as the currents here are strong.

The cliffs are conveniently concentrated into three areas with three different approaches: a southern area, a north-western area and a north-eastern area. With the removal of sheep the underfoot vegetation has grown dramatically, making for tough walking in places, but climbers and NTS staff have trodden down a few paths which make life a little easier and are the described approaches.

Basecamp: Mingulay Bay (Bàgh Mhiùghlaigh) in the east is the safest anchorage and landing point although this is obviously weather dependent. The best campsite may appear to be adjacent to the ruined village at Bàgh Mhiùghlaigh, but the National Trust for Scotland would prefer visitors to camp near the school house. This also has clean running water nearby. The school house itself is used by work parties and staff of the NTS.

Access: See Bishop's Isles introduction p268.

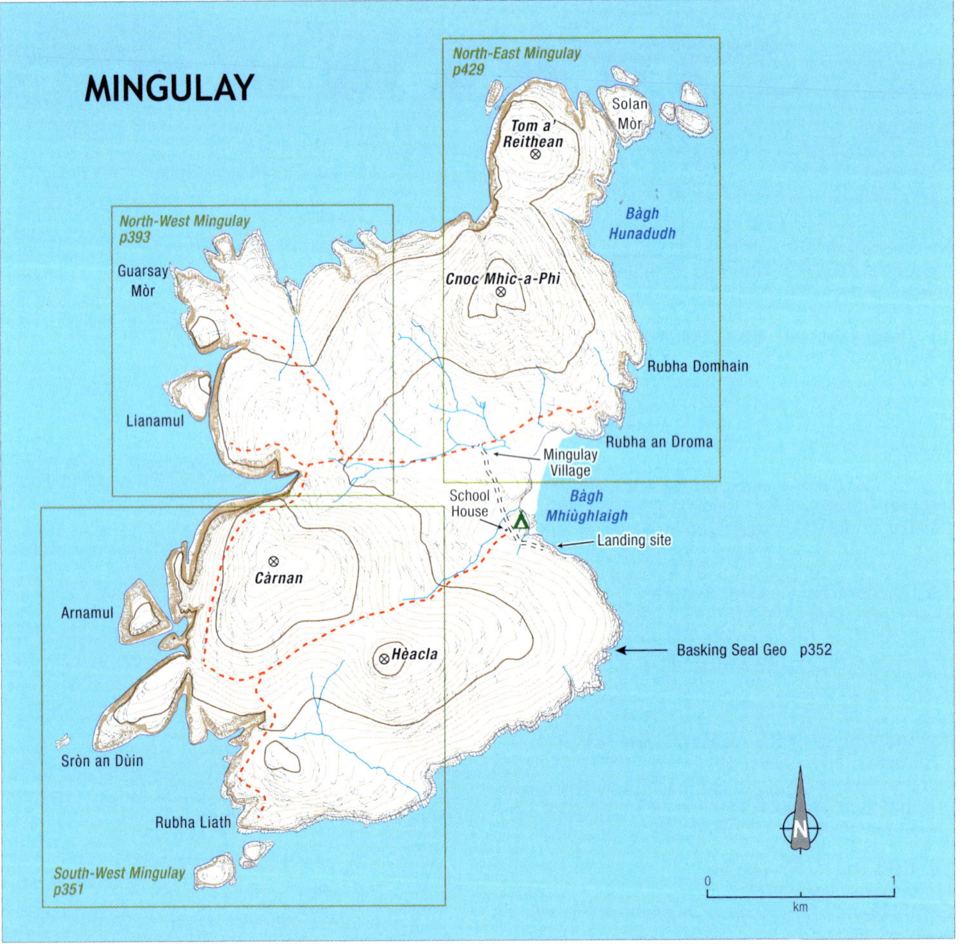

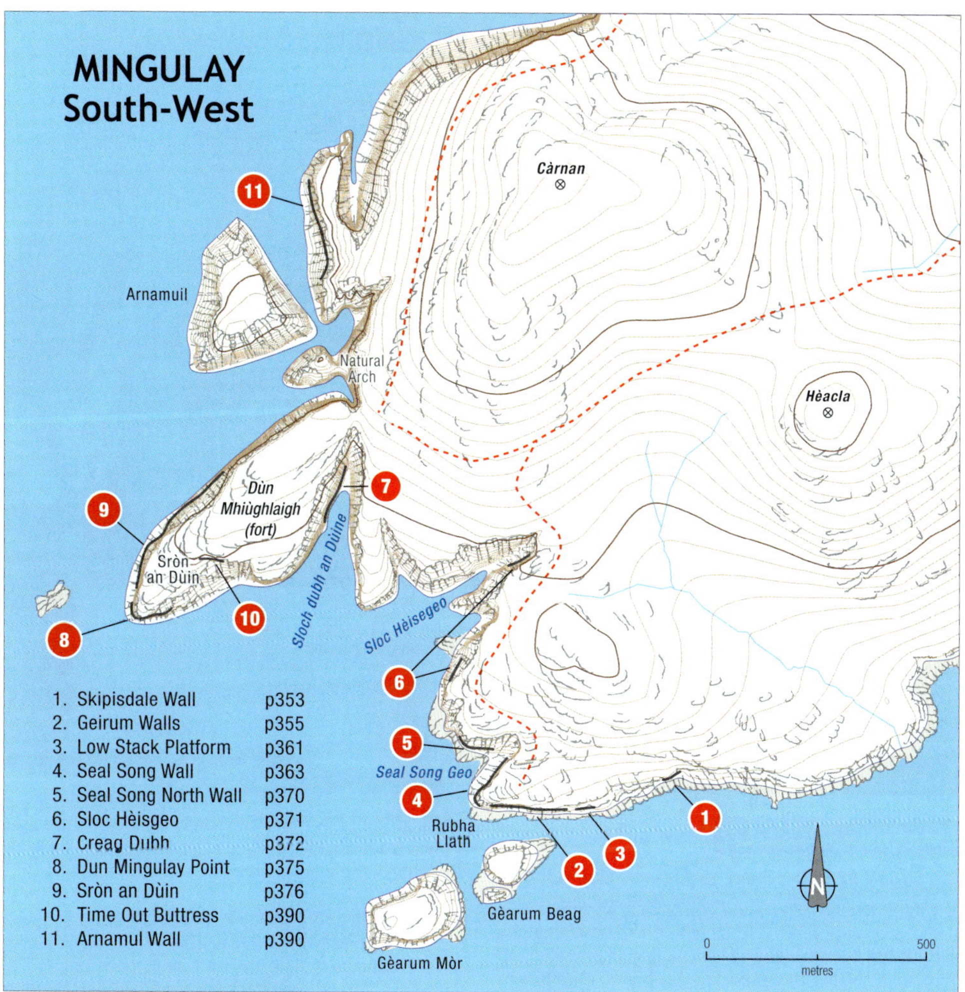

THE SOUTHERN CLIFFS

There is a diverse mix of cliffs here from small non-tidal outcrops above the sea (some with easy descents) to larger more serious cliffs requiring calm seas and competent abseiling, and including the best cliff of all the islands; Sròn an Dùin on Dun Mingulay. Most of the southern cliffs are concentrated in the far south-west corner. The cliffs are described clockwise starting at Basking Seal Geo not far south of Bàgh Mhiùghlaigh, to the furthest south outcrops of the Gèirum Walls, Rubha Liath and Seal Song Wall, to the south west tip of Dun Mingulay and finishing at Arnamul, part way up the west coast.

Approach: From the school house beside the camp-ground, take a path up a small stream heading for the col between the two hills of Càrnan and Hèacla. On the other side, the path contours round Càrnan towards the tiny neck of land connecting to Dun Mingulay. Arnamul is an easy walk north from here. To gain the cliffs around Rubha Liath, strike off the path early and head left towards the back of the obvious huge Sloc Hèisegeo, which cuts deeply into the hillside, and follow the cliff-top south (avoiding the small hill which is a Bonxie colony).

School House Boulder

There is a single large boulder not far from the school house which has been climbed on, probably first by Gordon Lennox in 2004.

BASKING SEAL GEO

(NL 57039 82200) Tidal S facing Map p350

A very sheltered east coast geo giving an alternative option when the winds and the seas are too awful on the west. It lies between Rubha Hèacla (the main headland 1km south of the bay) and the open Sloc Chremisgeo marked on the map. It is wedge shaped, getting lower towards the sea, and can be viewed easily from a large expanse of flat rock to the south. The rock is of very good quality and devoid of all bird life except for the easy stepped corner in the centre of the cliff. This should be avoided in the nesting season as a shag normally nests here. Some of the routes have been soloed, and DWS grades are given for when the most elegant way in is to take the sea-level traverse in from the right. The routes are described from left to right.

Approach: From the path just before the jetty in the bay, follow the line of the drystane dyke up the hill on the right and then the general line of dykes till they descend. Branch off left and down towards Sloc Chremisgeo.

Descent: The first route starts at the head of the geo, just to the right of the obvious easy-angled seep line. Abseil in from the bay immediately right of the seep, to a small ledge above the high water mark, from where all the routes can be accessed by an easy traverse.

1 Tormentil 20m E1 5b (S0, 5+) *

T.Catterall, W.Renshaw, 20 May 2001

Use the arete and climb the wall on its right side to the large flake; moves lead back left from here to the arete which is followed to the top.

2 The Minging Gardens of Babylon 20m E2 5c *

T.Catterall, W.Renshaw, 20 May 2001

Start directly below the narrow chimney which cuts through the left-hand end of the obvious overhang. Climb the wall on hidden holds to the large hanging flake at the left end of the roof. Use this to gain access to the narrow, pleasantly vegetated bottomless chimney and follow this to the top.

3 The Shag Who Spied Me 20m E4 5c

S.Crowe, K.Magog, 26 May 2001

The steep wall, starting just left of the prominent groove, and then crossing the lightning shaped feature at the roof. Pull through the roof and go up the final headwall on jugs.

4 Pyrites Pleasure 22m E2 5c **
T.Catterall, S.Porteus, W.Renshaw, 26 May 2000
Climb the steep ramp to the roof. Move right onto the wall and continue up, trending right via the obvious fault-line. Superb.

5 L'Arete d'Amour 20m E2 5c (S0, 6a+) **
S.Ponsford, 22 Jun 2009
The neat rightwards-slanting arete bounding the right-hand side of the roof to join Pyrites Pleasure on good holds to the top.

6 Slave to the Rhythm 20m E5 6b (S0, 6c+) ***
T.Catterall, 2008
On the left-hand side of the steep immaculate wall are parallel cracks. Climb these with increasing difficulty and the small arete above. The route was originally climbed with a deviation onto and up the left arete for a section in the middle before re-joining the main line; an easier alternative.

7 The Night of the Storytellers 20m E1 5b ***
B.Roberts, W.Renshaw, 26 May 2001
Start at the left end of the large ledge in the centre of the cliff. Pull up by the hand-jamming crack and continue steeply up the cracked wall above to the break. Continue direct to the top.

8 Captain John Allan 20m E3 5c ***
T.Catterall, S.Wells, 2008
From the left end of the big ledge, climb the blunt rib.

9 Cracking Shag 20m HS 4b (S3,4+) *
T.Catterall, 2000
Climb the corner-crack from the large ledge.

10 Pete's Route 20m E2 5b (S0, 6a+) *
P.Graham, 22.06.09
The wall right of the corner, finishing up a shallow groove in the arete above a small roof.

11 Puffin Fly Past 20m S 4a
K.Summers, F.Williams, 2008
The wall right of the corner but at the small roof, traverse right and climb the groove above.

12 Puffin Rafters 22m VS 4c *
T.Catterall, S.Porteus, W.Renshaw, 26 May 2000
From a small ledge in the base of the corner to the right, climb to where it steepens and move right onto a ledge. Easily to the top.

13 Whiskey Galor 22m E2 5c
T.Catterall, J.Harrington, 1 Jun 2013
From the stance of Puffin Rafters, step right onto the bottomless wall and climb diagonally right to under a small roof. Turn this on the left and move up right to a smooth leaning groove. Cross this rightwards to the top.

14 Tidy Like 20m (S0, 6b+) *
T.Luddington, 22 Jun 2009
Climb the left side of the square slot and go right over the overhang.

15 Piffle 10m VS 4c (S1, 4+) *
A.Moles, 22 Jun 2009
The short pillar to the right of a deep corner recess containing a ledge, near the right-hand side of the cliff.

16 Imminent Assignment Crisis 120m 6a (S0, 6a)
T.Catterall, 26 May 2000
A sea-level traverse of the whole cliff from left to right. Start just above high water mark. Stay at this level until a large right-facing corner, below overhangs, is reached. This forces a higher line. The crux is gaining the slab below the roofs. Continue right until the cliff peters out or the swim seems more inviting.

Skipisdale Wall

(NL 55423 81465) Partially Tidal S facing
Map p351 Diagram p355

Continuing along the south coast towards the most southern extremity at Rubha Liath, but before you reach the Gèirum Walls, lies this smaller wall which is set back into the coastline. It has been variously called Gèirum Far Eastern Walls and The Pink Wall by different groups, but its original name was a reference to the second settlement on the island whose ruins are passed whilst walking from the bay.

Skipisdale Wall is about 300m east of the Gèirum Wall, with two large wave-washed platforms split by a narrow sloc. The main wall lies directly behind the eastern platform, the principal features are a large left-facing corner and a series of walls with a large capping roof at the eastern end. This then turns into a pink buttress, which disappears into a small sloc where the platform ends. Just to the west of Skipisdale Wall is some good bouldering on two walls, one above the other, accessed from the platform or the large ledge breaking the face. The routes are described from left to right.

Descent: From the west end of the platform, cross over a boulder in a small channel that is under water at high tide, or simply abseil (15m).

1 Devilsbit Scabbious 10m E3 6a
T.Catterall, T.Wood, 2001
Climbs the left-hand slanting crack on the undercut left wall of the corner. Climb the crack from an undercut start until the arete is reached; use this to gain the top.

2 T.N.T. 10m E2 5b
T.Wood, T.Catterall, 2001
Climb the right-hand slanting crack and small sharp corner. An explosive little route.

3 Murphy's Law 10m S 4a
M.Telfer, T.Catterall, 5 Jun 2008
Climb the crack in the black right-angled corner.

4 Sealed with a Kiss (2) 10m S 4a
T.Catterall, 2000
Climb the crack 1m right of the corner.

High and Dry (VS) Joe Spoor (photo Tim Catterall)

5 Down Mingulay Way 10m S 4a
T.Catterall, 2000
Climb the broken wall and vertical overlapping wall.

6 Viking Burial 15m HS 4a
T.Catterall, 2000
The basalt dyke.

7 Lost Souls 15m VD
T.Catterall, 2000
The broken wall right of the basalt vein.

8 Fin Slab 15m VS 4b
J.Carter, M.Glanville, 25 May 2014
Climb the left side of the obvious arete and continue up a small left-facing corner.

9 Plundered and Pillaged 15m D
T.Catterall, 2000
The blocky overlap.

The next routes are on the wall with overlaps at half-height.

10 The Barra Time Warp 15m S 4a
T.Catterall, 2000
Climb the slabby corner on the left side of the wall.

11 Be Careful With That Paddle Eugene 15m E3 5c
M.Telfer, T.Catterall, 5 Jun 2008
Climb the wall directly below the left-hand, left-facing corner. Climb the corner and wall above.

12 Never Mind The Pollocks 15m E1 5b
M.Telfer, T.Catterall, 5 Jun 2008
Climb the overlapping wall to the lower left-facing corner. Ascend the corner and crack above.

13 Down To Mingulay With a Bump 15m VS 4c
M.Telfer, T.Catterall, 5 Jun 2008
Climb the wall 2m to the right and the stepped overhang above.

14 Mingulay Blazers 15m S 4a
R.Jones, 7 Jun 2001
The obvious left-slanting crack-line left of the roof.

15 Otter Man's Empire 15m E4 6a
M.Telfer, T.Catterall, 5 Jun 2008
Climb the steep ramp up to the widest part of the roof. Powerful moves lead to the lip and easier ground above.

16 High and Dry 15m VS 5a *
R.Benton, R.Jones, 5 Jun 2001
Takes the line on the left of the final buttress and the right arete of the corner. Move onto the arete from the left and climb to the top.

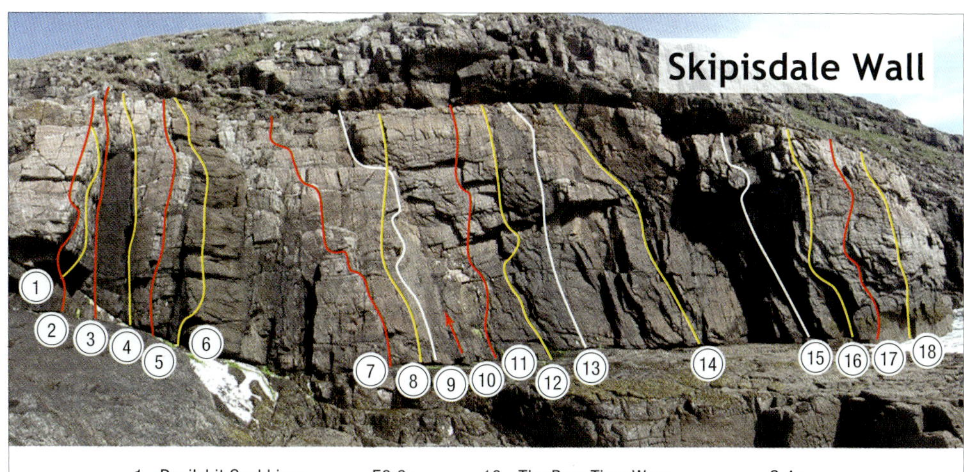

1.	Devilsbit Scabbious	E3 6a	10.	The Bara Time Warp	S 4a
2.	T.N.T.	E2 5b	11.	Be Careful With That Paddle	E3 5c
3.	Murphy's Law	S 4a	12.	Never Mind The Pollocks	E1 5b
4.	Sealed with a Kiss (2)	S 4a	13.	Down To Mingulay With a Bump	VS 4c
5.	Down Mingulay Way	S 4a	14.	Mingulay Blazers	S 4a
6.	Viking Burial	HS 4a	15.	Otter Man's Empire	E4 6a
7.	Lost Souls	VD	16.	High and Dry	VS 5a *
8.	Fin Slab	VS 4b	17.	Frodo's Frenzy	E1 5a **
9.	Plundered and Pillaged	D	18.	The Tide Waits for No Man	E2 5b *

17 Frodo's Frenzy 15m E1 5a **
R.Jones, R.Benton, 5 Jun 2001
Start 2m right of High and Dry. Step onto the undercut wall and climb to a small bulge, passing this on its left. Straight to the top to finish just left of a block forming a small, left-facing right-angled corner.

18 The Tide Waits for No Man 15m E2 5b *
R.Jones, A.Dow (1 rest), 7 Jun 2001
The undercut crack-line 4m right of Frodo's Frenzy. Great climbing marred by a wet start. The rest was taken as the tide came in.

Skipisdale Buttress

Tidal S Facing

The following routes are west of Skipisdale Wall on an attractive buttress. The first route climbs the left arete. Low tide required.

My Gull's Mad at Me 15m VS 4c
J.Dale, P.Curtis, 30 May 2001
Climb the arete, pulling leftward through the bulges, and finish direct.

Happy Landings 15m HVS 5a
J.Dale, N.Murphy, 30 May 2001
Start immediately right of My Gull. Bridge up the groove for a few moves, then swing right into a shallow scoop. Climb directly up the front face of the buttress, finishing in a short corner. Not overly well protected.

RUBHA LIATH

(NL 5512 8140)

This Is the headland near the southern extremity of the island, overlooking two small off-shore islands, Gèirum Mòr and Gèirum Beag, beyond which lies Berneray. There are climbs either side of the headland and they are described as three distinct walls. Firstly, The Gèirum Walls on the south side are between 8m and 15m in height and are composed of three distinct sections. Secondly, The Point itself which increases in height to about 30m. Thirdly, the west side of the Point forms an excellent north-west facing wall known as Seal Song Wall (Seal Song being the name given to the geo that forms in the back of the wall). Also included in this section is the smaller North Wall of Seal Song on the opposite side of the geo facing south.

The Gèirum Walls

(NL 5514 814) Non-tidal S facing Map p351

These offer short but immaculate walls on the south coast, extending eastwards from near the headland for about 200m. The routes lie on a series of separate sections and are described from west to east:

The Platform Wall is about 50m east of The Point; a large platform cuts down the cliff eastwards. Little

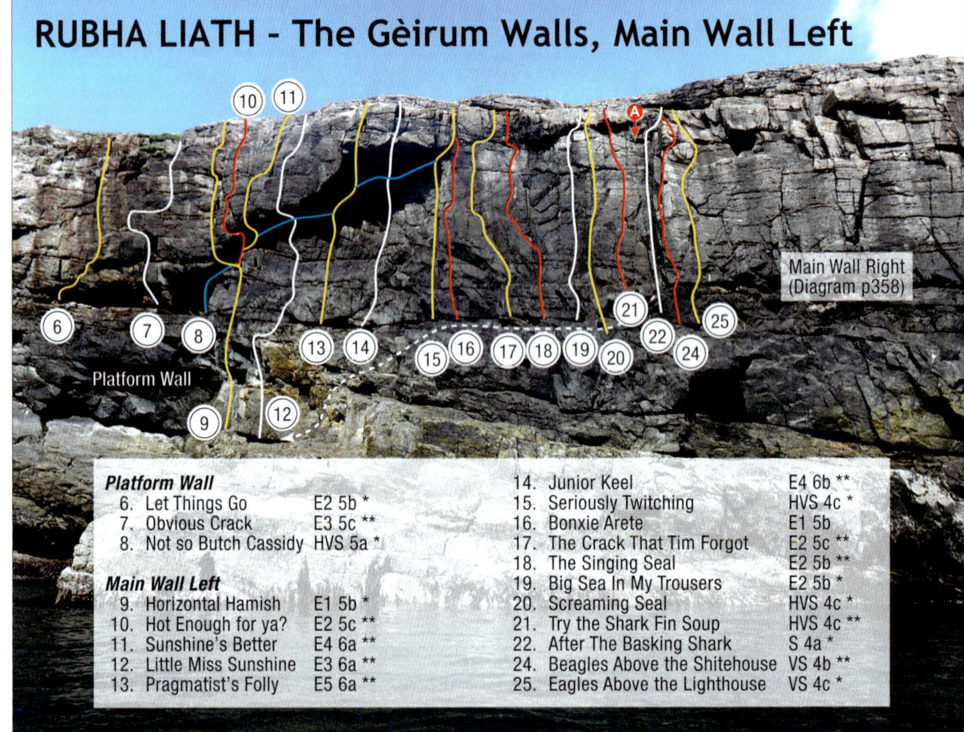

of note exists under the platform but the orange wall above is excellent and steep. This is the Platform Wall and runs into an area of roofs, where the platform itself disappears.

RUBHA LIATH - The Gèirum Walls, Main Wall Left
Main Wall Right
(Diagram p358)
Platform Wall
Platform Wall
6. Let Things Go E2 5b *
7. Obvious Crack E3 5c **
8. Not so Butch Cassidy HVS 5a *
Main Wall Left
9. Horizontal Hamish E1 5b *
10. Hot Enough for ya? E2 5c **
11. Sunshine's Better E4 6a **
12. Little Miss Sunshine E3 6a **
13. Pragmatist's Folly E5 6a **
14. Junior Keel E4 6b **
15. Seriously Twitching HVS 4c *
16. Bonxie Arete E1 5b
17. The Crack That Tim Forgot E2 5c **
18. The Singing Seal E2 5b **
19. Big Sea In My Trousers E2 5b *
20. Screaming Seal HVS 4c *
21. Try the Shark Fin Soup HVS 4c **
22. After The Basking Shark S 4a *
24. Beagles Above the Shitehouse VS 4b **
25. Eagles Above the Lighthouse VS 4c *

East of The Platform Wall a very conspicuous 45° roof split by deep cracks sits above a slab and a resurgence of the platform. This is the Main Wall and it lies directly opposite the cliff end on Gèirum Beag. It is possible to traverse under the roofs to link the Platform Wall with the Main Wall but it is steep 4b, subject to wave wash, and scary. The platform continues underneath the main section of the Gèirum Wall, continually dropping towards sea level, until it runs out into a series of three small caves, the lower of which is tidal.

A further platform east of the caves can be accessed by scrambling, and leads to the wall above the third cave; Low Stack Platform.

The Platform Wall

As the platform descends it is topped by an increasingly steep orange wall, which merges with a series of roofs at the far end where the platform disappears. Initially the walls are broken but they become more continuous where they are undercut by small roofs and particularly so around an obvious hanging left-facing corner and arete.

Descent: Follow the top of the Gèirum Walls towards The Point until the cliff becomes more broken and can easily be scrambled down to the start of a large platform heading back east.

1 Crooked Thumb 10m VS 5a
K.Tighe, H.Roberton, 24 Apr 2000
Start under an isolated roof at 4m. Climb the fierce roof and the wall above via a crack.

2 Corner and Slab 10m VS 4c
M.Tighe, E.Knudson, 24 Apr 2000
Climb the steep lower wall below and left of the hanging corner to gain the easier slab above.

3 Lunar Pull 10m VS 5a *
M.Robson, F.Bennet, D.Godfrey, 18 Sep 1998
The excellent left-facing hanging corner climbed direct through the steep lower wall and roof.

4 Pocket Wall 10m E1 5b
M.Tighe, E.Knudson, 24 Apr 2000
To the right of the hanging corner. Climb the lower wall on big holds to the horizontal break, then pockets up the wall to the top.

5 The Abyss of Numbers 10m E2 5c *
D.Godfrey, M.Robson, F.Bennet, 18 Sep 1998
Just right of the arete is an obvious vertical crack. Gain the crack through the guarding roof and follow it to its

end. Finish direct onto a sloping ledge

Variation: **5a Hopalong Howett E2 5c**
K.Howett, D.Turnbull, 26 May 2000
Move up and left from the end of the crack to an obvious jug near the arete and once on the ledge, lob off!

6 Let Things Go 10m E2 5b *
F.Bennet, D.Godfrey, M.Robson, 18 Sep 1998
Start where the platform narrows. Follow the large flake rightwards to a crack through the overlap. Continue up the crack to the top.

7 Obvious Crack 10m E3 5c **
D.Turnbull, K.Howett, 22 May 2000
A meaty route near the west end of the platform; just as it merges into the roofs, take a belay under a hanging ledge in the guarding roof. Pull over the roof onto the ledge and into a hanging right-facing groove-flake. Go up this then traverse left and up to holds leading back right to gain a phallic looking downward-pointing projection. Pass this to gain a big break. Pull out direct into a scoop (hidden jug) to finish. There is no crack climbing involved anywhere on this route!

8 Not so Butch Cassidy and the Stanley Kid 20m HVS 5a *
C.McMahone, A.Cassidy, 30 May 2010
Starts off the platform next to the roof of Horizontal Hamish. Climb direct to a spike beneath the left end of the roof. Traverse rightwards under it to finish up Seriously Twitching.

Gèirum Main Wall

Diagrams opposite & p358

This extends from the platform as it re-emerges below the 45° roof eastwards for about 100m. It is possible to view the roof easily from the top of the cliff to its east, above a clean-cut, black, west facing corner (After the Basking Shark). East of the corner the wall juts out to form a long wall with a smaller platform along its base, about 5m above the sea. There are two bad steps along this platform, which are useful markers, before the wall turns an arete and cuts back into a clean-cut east facing corner. It then continues above a bigger platform which slopes down into a double cave. The left-hand cave is tidal and the platform disappears into the sea under the right-hand cave.

Descent: Abseil down the black corner of After the Basking Shark onto the platform, from where all the routes can be gained. They are described from left to right (west to east). The start of the first few routes is gained by a scramble down left from the main platform to a lower ledge system directly beneath the 45° roof. Hand-traverse left to gain a large ledge (calm seas only, it may be better to abseil).

9 Horizontal Hamish 10m E1 5b *
M.Tighe, H.Roberton, Y.Colwell, 25 Apr 2000
Climbs a line just left of the roof. Climb direct by grooves and through a small roof on good holds to gain the left end of a long tapering ledge below the main roofs. Take a horizontal flake below and left of the roof to gain an upright position with difficulty into a left-facing groove. Climb the groove to the top.

10 Hot Enough For Ya? 30m E2 5c **
G.Latter, M.Harding, 16 Aug 2011
Start as for Horizontal Hamish. Climb direct by grooves and through a small roof on good holds to gain the left end of a long tapering ledge below the main roofs. Continue to a large flake at the left side (up and right of a similar smaller feature on Horizontal Hamish). Pull through the roof leftwards in a fine position, then climb direct up the wall, pulling out right at a horizontal crack to finish up the crack on the right.

11 Sunshine's Better 15m E4 6a **
G.Latter, M.Harding, 16 Aug 2011
Climb the easy wall to the main roof (as for Hot Enough For Ya?), then go directly through this on good holds to finish up the crack above.

12 Little Miss Sunshine 15m E3 6a **
M.Harding, G.Latter, 16 Aug 2011
Climb straight up from near the right end of the ledge to gain a juggy break beneath the main roof. Using a good hold, launch up to a flat jug on the lip and pull over into the hanging crack which leads to the top.

13 Pragmatist's Folly 15m E5 6a **
G.Latter, M.Harding, 15 Aug 2011
The impressive looking off-width crack through the 45° roof, climbed on surprisingly good holds, mainly on its right side. Large cams useful.

The following routes now start off the main platform.

14 Junior Keel 10m E4 6b **
E.Brown, 29 Jun 2007
Breaches the right side of the 45° roof. Climb the deceptively steep, juggy wall to the left of Seriously Twitching to below the right-hand of the two cracks breaching the roof. Make wild moves out to and over the lip of the roof.

15 Seriously Twitching 10m HVS 4c *
J.Horrocks, C.Birmelin, 13 May 1999
Below the right end of the 45° roof is a chimney in a left-facing corner. Climb the chimney, pulling out right in an exciting and strenuous position on big holds.

16 Bonxie Arete 10m E1 5b
P.Johnson, P.Drew, 7 Jun 2015
The right arete of Seriously Twitching climbed direct and finishing as for that route. Very close to the next route.

17 The Crack That Tim Forgot 10m E2 5c **
T.Carruthers, C.Boulton, 31 May 1999
Immediately round the right arete of Seriously Twitching is a tapering slab. Climb this and the thin crack above to the top horizontal break. Step right and finish in a shallow V-groove. Surprisingly strenuous.

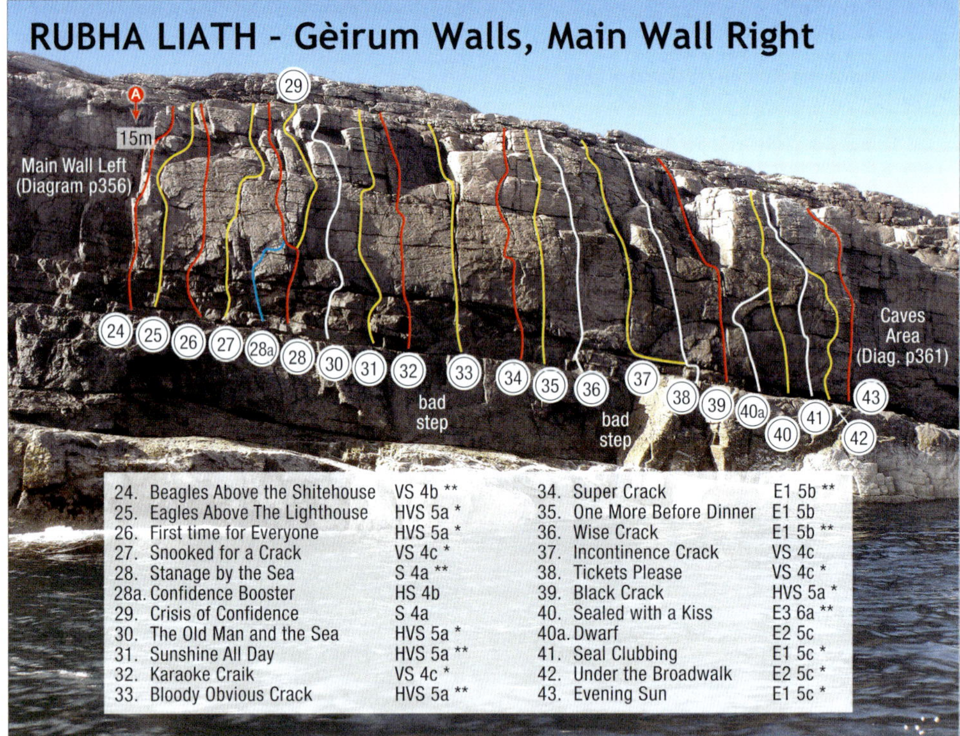

24.	Beagles Above the Shitehouse	VS 4b **	34.	Super Crack	E1 5b **
25.	Eagles Above The Lighthouse	HVS 5a *	35.	One More Before Dinner	E1 5b
26.	First time for Everyone	HVS 5a *	36.	Wise Crack	E1 5b **
27.	Snooked for a Crack	VS 4c *	37.	Incontinence Crack	VS 4c
28.	Stanage by the Sea	S 4a **	38.	Tickets Please	VS 4c *
28a.	Confidence Booster	HS 4b	39.	Black Crack	HVS 5a *
29.	Crisis of Confidence	S 4a	40.	Sealed with a Kiss	E3 6a **
30.	The Old Man and the Sea	HVS 5a *	40a.	Dwarf	E2 5c
31.	Sunshine All Day	HVS 5a **	41.	Seal Clubbing	E1 5c *
32.	Karaoke Craik	VS 4c *	42.	Under the Broadwalk	E2 5c *
33.	Bloody Obvious Crack	HVS 5a **	43.	Evening Sun	E1 5c *

18 The Singing Seal 10m E2 5b **

J.Horrocks, C.Birmelin, 13 May 1999

Start at a smaller tapering slab to the right of The Crack That Tim Forgot. Climb the slab to gain a vertical crack. Climb the wall on its left to a good ledge (bold). Step left 2m and pull over the steep headwall.

19 Big Sea in My Trousers 10m E2 5b *

T.Catterall, 23 May 2000

Climb the crozzly cracks in the wall immediately right of The Singing Seal. A fingery start with only adequate small protection.

20 Screaming Seal 10m HVS 4c *

T.Catterall, S.Porteus, W.Renshaw, 22 May 2000

In the middle of the wall is a crack emerging from a short left-facing niche at foot level. Climb the crack direct to the top.

21 Try the Shark Fin Soup 10m HVS 4c **

H.Harris, L.Beck, 22 May 2000

Climbs the smooth wall between Screaming Seal and the corner of After The Basking Shark. Climb directly up the wall and awkwardly past a shield-like feature to the break under the roof (bold). Finish over the capping roof on good holds.

22 After The Basking Shark 8m S 4a *

F.Murray, M.Snook, 4 Jun 1998

The large left-facing corner of the abseil descent. Start at the bottom of the corner. Go up the corner and take the right-hand corner exit for the last 2m.

23 The Curious Grey 10m VS 4b

S.Crowe, 22 May 2000

Climb the centre of the right wall of the corner. Hard start and easier to finish.

24 Beagles Above the Shitehouse 10m VS 4b **

T.Carruthers, C.Boulton, 31 May 1999

Climb the arete from its lowest point, staying committed to the upper slabby section.

25 Eagles Above The Lighthouse 10m VS 4c *

F.Murray, M.Snook, 4 Jun 1998

To the right of the arete, surmount overhangs then climb an obvious crack to nearly join the arete. Take the ramp out right and the wall above.

26 First time for Everyone 10m HVS 5a *

H.Harris, L.Beck, 22 May 2000

Climb the wall between the cracks of Eagles and Snooked.

27 Snooked for a Crack 10m VS 4c *
F.Murray, M.Snook, 4 Jun 1998
Follows the next obvious large crack to the right.

28 Stanage by the Sea 10m S 4a **
T.Carruthers, C.Boulton, 31 May 1999
Climb the lower steep bulges of Crisis of Confidence for 3m. Step left onto the face and climb a crack to the top.
Variation: **28a Confidence Booster 10m HS 4b**
Climb the bulge just left of Crisis of Confidence to gain the crack.

29 Crisis of Confidence 10m S 4a
M.Snook, F.Murray, 4 Jun 1998
Start below a right-facing corner. Climb the lower steep bulges into the corner and finish up an easy slabby corner.

30 The Old Man and the Sea 10m HVS 5a *
C.Boulton, T.Carruthers, Jun 1999
Climb the wall immediately right of the corner direct via two horizontal breaks.

31 Sunshine All Day 10m HVS 5a **
F.Murray, M.Snook, 4 Jun 1998
Start 3m right of Crisis of Confidence. Surmount an overhang and follow a crack with some delicate moves.

32 Karaoke Craik 10m VS 4c *
T.Catterall, S.Porteus, W.Renshaw, 22 May 2000
Starts just before the first Bad Step in the platform. Climb onto a pedestal and climb the right-hand crack. When it disappears climb the slab above by the left-hand rounded arete.

33 Bloody Obvious Crack 10m HVS 5a **
H.Harris, L.Beck, 20 May 2001
Immediately after the first Bad Step, climb the bloody obvious crack.

34 Super Crack 10m E1 5b **
D.Turnbull, K.Howett, 22 May 2000
Start mid-way between the two bad steps in the platform. Climb up the lower bulges to a short, fat, left-facing flake. Pull out on the top to a good horizontal break. Step slightly left and go up a good crack onto a ledge, then up the final wall.

35 One More Before Dinner 10m E1 5b
N.Stabbs, M.Holt, 20 May 2001
Start 1m right of Super Crack, climb the wall direct to finish up a thin crack. Requires blinkers!

36 Wise Crack 10m E1 5b **
K.Howett, D.Turnbull, 22 May 2000
Start immediately before the second bad step. Pull up onto an overhung ledge and gain a fat flake in the wall above. Gain a further flake up and right, then exit onto the ledge above via a short vertical crack.

37 Incontinence Crack 10m VS 4c
T.Catterall, S.Porteus, 22 May 2001
Start below Black Crack just past the second bad step. Traverse left until directly over the bad step and climb the crack above to gain the smaller, left-hand of the two recesses where easy climbing leads to the top.

38 Tickets Please 10m VS 4c *
H.Harris, L.Beck, 20 May 2001
Start below Black Crack. Traverse left 2m and climb the wall to gain a left-trending stepped flake. Instead of going left, climb directly up the wall above on good holds to finish up the small pillar between two recesses.

39 Black Crack 10m HVS 5a *
B.Kerr, A.Smith, 5 Jul 1999
The crack-line just right of the second bad step. Finish in the larger, right-hand recess.

40 Sealed with a Kiss 10m E3 6a **
R.Durran, M.Somerville, B.Kerr, 6 Jul 1999
Start right of Black Crack below the centre of an arched overlap. Climb the wall to a good break. Make a long reach for the obvious hold on the lip of the overlap. Pull over with difficulty and climb direct to the top.
Variation: **40a Dwarf 10m E2 5c**
An alternative start for normal-height people! Climb the slim corner leading to the left end of the overlap. Step up left, then traverse right to gain the hold over the lip.

41 Seal Clubbing 10m E1 5c *
G.Latter, 19 Aug 2004
Start just right of Sealed with a Kiss. Climb up to the right end of the small overlap. Then go direct up the wall to finish up the final section of the flake-crack of Under the Broadwalk.

42 Under the Broadwalk 10m E2 5c *
C.Fowler, K.Tighe, 3 May 1997
Start between the slim corner and the arete at the right-hand end of the wall. Hard moves lead to good horizontal breaks and a ledge. Finish easily up the left-slanting flake-crack.

43 Evening Sun 15m E1 5c *
G.Lennox, T.Rankin, 8 May 1999
Excellent moves up the right arete of the front wall with a bold, bouldery start.

44 On the Beach 15m E1 5c
C.Fowler, K.Tighe, 3 May 1997
Around the arete to the right. Climb the wall by a thin crack and then a wide crack.

45 Hawaiian Tropic 15m VS 4c **
C.Fowler, K.Tighe, 3 May 1997
Climbs the big right-facing corner.

The wall right of the corner is a steep slab.

46 Mesajanier 10m E3 6a **
M.Tweedly, M.Somerville, 6 Jul 1999
Climbs the wall immediately right of the corner of Hawaiian Tropic. Start below a slim right-facing corner-groove and move up and left onto the wall. Climb this direct to breaks below an overlap. Finish up the left-hand of two cracks on the right or the niche through the overlap on the left.

47 Water Babies 15m E2 5c **
C.Fowler, K.Tighe, 3 May 1997
Right of the corner, climb a slim right-facing corner-groove. Go left onto jugs on the left rib. Climb direct by breaks to a sensational finish through the roof above by the left and most obvious crack-line.

48 Land Baby 15m E2 5c *
M.Sakano, P.Hanlon, 17 Jun 2015
Instead of going left onto the face, go direct up the corner and surmount the roof via the corner-crack. The crack between Water Babies and Mary Doune is followed with difficulty.

49 Mary Doune 15m E1 5b **
C.Fowler, K.Tighe, 3 May 1997
The vertical rounded crack and roof above. Very pumpy finale.

To the right is a distinctive diagonal crack issuing from the left lip of a roof and joining the roof of Mary Doune.

50 Double Walrus 15m HVS 5a *
G.Lennox, T.Rankin, 8 May 1999
Climb breaks direct to gain the middle of the diagonal crack, just left of a short (unclimbed) right-facing corner. Climb the diagonal crack rightwards then the wall to a ledge. Cracks above lead to the top.

51 Alan's Route 15m E1 5b
A.Taylor, B.Kerr, 1999
Climb direct passing the left side of the low roof to gain the diagonal crack. Climb awkward twin cracks past a niche to gain the ledge. Finish up the steep wall above.

There follows two caves separated by a pillar in the centre. The platform disappears into the sea beyond the second pillar and forms a third cave beyond that.

52 The Sirens of Mingulay 12m E2 5c
C.Fowler, K.Tighe, 3 May 1997
Just left of the deep cave, climb over a bulge and up to the roof. Gain a steep hanging groove in the wall above to gain a ledge. Short thin cracks up the face above lead to the top.

53 Underseal 10m E2 6a
R.Durran, R.Adie, 13 Aug 2006
Gain and climb a short hanging groove sandwiched between two overlaps (crux) and finish up a short diagonal crack.

54 Calling Seal 12m E3 6a **
T.Rankin, G.Lennox, 8 May 1999
Start in the centre of the small arch and using an obvious flat jug, gain a break above. Move out right to good holds over the lip. Climb up and right on good holds to a hard finish up a short hanging corner above an overlap.

Mary Doune (E1) Andy Hyslop (photo Colin Moody)

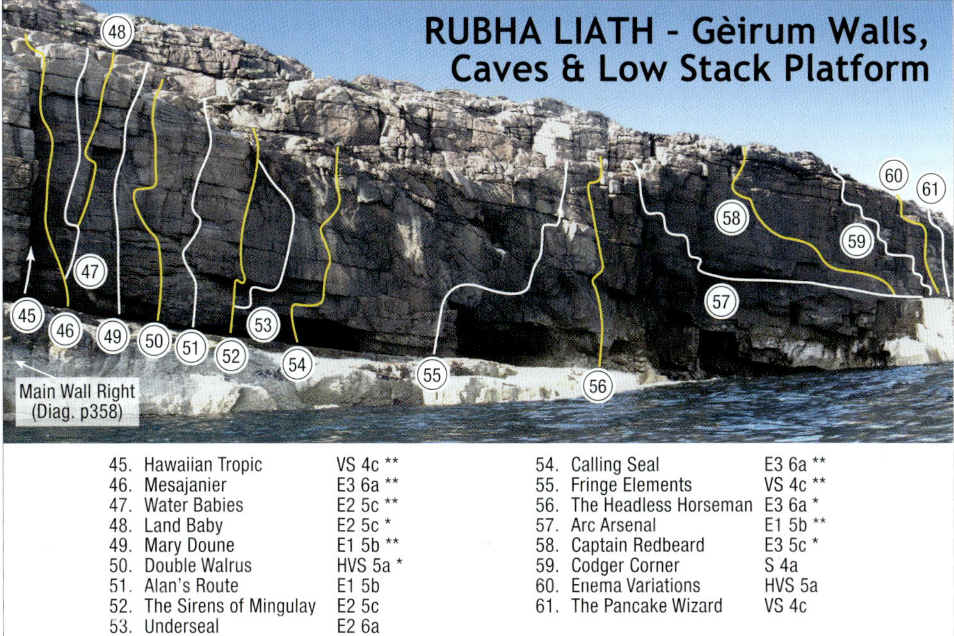

45.	Hawaiian Tropic	VS 4c **	54.	Calling Seal	E3 6a **
46.	Mesajanier	E3 6a **	55.	Fringe Elements	VS 4c **
47.	Water Babies	E2 5c **	56.	The Headless Horseman	E3 6a *
48.	Land Baby	E2 5c *	57.	Arc Arsenal	E1 5b **
49.	Mary Doune	E1 5b **	58.	Captain Redbeard	E3 5c *
50.	Double Walrus	HVS 5a *	59.	Codger Corner	S 4a
51.	Alan's Route	E1 5b	60.	Enema Variations	HVS 5a
52.	The Sirens of Mingulay	E2 5c	61.	The Pancake Wizard	VS 4c
53.	Underseal	E2 6a			

55 Fringe Elements 20m VS 4c **
M.Tighe, H.Roberton, Y.Colwell, 25 Apr 2000
A line traversing the lip of the cave to the right of Calling Seal. Start off the pillar and climb up the wall, then right across the lip of the roof until an easy wall leads to the top.

56 The Headless Horseman 12m E3 6a *
T.Catterall, 22 May 2001
Start from the platform at the base of the pillar at low tide or from the ledge just above. Climb the vague blunt crack to the roof, surmount this using the clue in the name to gain the top.

Low Stack Platform

(NL 5525 8140) Non-tidal S facing Map p361

A low sea-filled cave now cuts into the cliff and marks the end of the Gèirum Wall. The next routes lie to the east of this and these start from another flat platform.

Descent: A scramble decent is possible at the left-hand end, which gains the widest end of this platform just before another small cave. There is also a small low-level flat topped stack adjoining the platform. The routes are described from the extreme left-hand end of the platform when looking in.

57 Arc Arsenal 25m E1 5b **
D.Carden, N.Morbey, 31 May 2013
A striking horizontal fist-width crack allows a leftward traverse to be made over the entire cave that separates this from Gèirum Main Wall, firstly along ledges then sandwiched between the lip and a roof above. The crux comes near the end; leaving the crack to gain the large right-facing corner which leads to the top.

58 Captain Redbeard 15m E3 5c *
N.Morbey, D.Carden, 27 May 2013
Start on the pedestal at the start of Arc Arsenal. From the start of the horizontal line, begin to work up and leftwards on fairly rounded holds with small gear protection and the possibility of a swim. Continue until completely pumped or you reach better holds on the upper left of the slab. Seconds will appreciate a secondary gear placement from the top.

59 Codger Corner 12m S 4a
S.Porteus, T.Catterall, 22 May 2001
From the end of the platform, climb a stepped staircase to the top.

60 Enema Variations 12m HVS 5a
T.Catterall, S.Porteus, 22 May 2001
Climb the crack 1m right of the stepped corner.

61 The Pancake Wizard 12m VS 4c
T.Catterall, S.Porteus, 22 May 2001
Climb the second crack right of the stepped corner.

62 Tidal Rush 10m VS 4c
T.Catterall, S.Porteus, 22 May 2001
Climb the steep right-angled corner-crack to the top.

The Point

(NL 5500 8145) Tidal SW facing Diagram opposite

This is the very end of Rubha Liath between the Gèirum Walls and Seal Song Wall, which can only be viewed from a boat. The front tip of the point itself is a steep barrel-shaped wall capped by a horizontal roof. A deeply inset chimney leading to a corner defines its right side. A conspicuous hole lies just left of the base of this chimney. Right of the chimney is a slim pillar, to the right of which are two partially hidden, right-facing corners. Further right again, before the point starts to decrease in height and the rocks break up, is a steep compact wall called Hidden Wall (for reasons that became obvious when trying to find it!).

The Gull Who Shagged Me (E3) Dave Towse (photo Kevin Howett)

Descent: For routes on The Point, abseil directly from the end of the point down the line of the chimney to the ledges below the headland tip. Access Hidden Wall from the immediate east side of The Point (see below). Calm seas are essential.

1 Rubha Soul 30m E1 5a **
K.Pyke, G.E.Little, 26 Jun 1996
From directly below the barrel feature of the point, move up a little on black rock, then traverse left on jugs across an overhanging wall to pull up into a hanging groove in the left side of the barrel. Follow this to below a roof then pull up into the final groove to finish.

2 Soul Sister 35m E4 *
K.Howett, J.Horrocks, 15 May 1999
A line up the very edge of the point (the junction between The Point and Seal Song Wall). In the very edge is a short hanging groove. Start from the ledges at the base below the arete.
1. 25m 6a Climb the easy lower wall to a ledge. Pull into the hanging groove and struggle up it and out the top before exiting leftwards above the abyss to gain a ledge and corner. Go up the corner to a big ledge below the capping roof.
2. 10m 5a Climb into the hanging groove in the left side of the roof above to finish.

3 Eaglesea 35m VS 4c *
M.Tighe, K.Tighe, J.McClenaghan, G.Leckie, J.Cargill, 3 May 2000
Climb the inset chimney and the easier corner of the last route above to the top.

4 Crack nan Euan 35m VS 4c ***
M.Tighe, K.Tighe, J.McClenaghan, G.Leckie, J.Cargill, 3 May 2000
From the big hole, traverse right past the chimney and climb into the superb clean crack and corner forming the right side of the pillar, finishing in a wide-open, easy corner.

5 Flyaway 35m VS 4c *
M.Tighe, K.Tighe, J.McClenaghan, G.Leckie, J.Cargill, 3 May 2000
From the big hole, traverse right past the chimney along the steeper sea-level rocks to the base of the second, more slabby, corner. Climb this and easy rocks above to the top.

Hidden Wall

Tidal S facing Diagram opposite

A superb pink wall emanating from the sea. It forms the east side of The Point.

Descent: From the top of The Point by taking an easy scramble descent eastwards down to a large platform as for Platform Wall on Gèirum Wall. Partway along the platform descend a series of short corners back westwards to a ledge about 5m above the sea and overlooking the wall. Abseil onto wave-washed ledges.

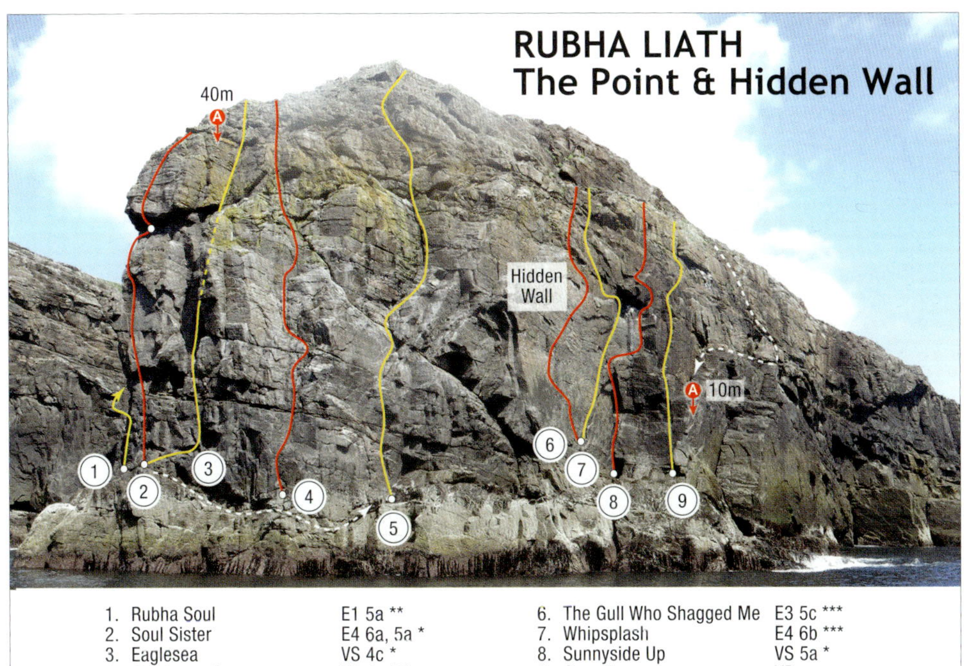

1. Rubha Soul	E1 5a **	6. The Gull Who Shagged Me	E3 5c ***
2. Soul Sister	E4 6a, 5a *	7. Whipsplash	E4 6b ***
3. Eaglesea	VS 4c *	8. Sunnyside Up	VS 5a *
4. Crack nan Euan	VS 4c ***	9. Over Easy	VD
5. Flyaway	VS 4c *		

6 The Gull Who Shagged Me 25m E3 5c ***
D.Towse, G.Huxter, D.Turnbull, 26 May 2000
From the base of the abseil, rush across to a small elevated ledge under the wall. From this, take a rising traverse left on flakes until it is possible to climb back right. A short wall provides the crux to gain a down-pointing spike and a ledge. Finish direct above. Excellent position.

7 Whipsplash 25m E4 6b ***
G.Huxter, D.Towse, D.Turnbull, 26 May 2000
From the small elevated ledge, take the gently overhanging crack directly above and the corner above it to a ledge. Move leftwards and finish up a final steep wall.

8 Sunnyside Up 25m VS 5a *
C.Stein, A.Sanders, I.Hall, 6 Jun 2008
The corner bounding the smooth wall of Whipsplash. Start at a big hole beneath the obvious left-facing corner. Climb up the hole, either on its right or by bridging, to gain the bottom of the main corner-crack and twin cracks on the right. Climb the strenuous corner and mantelshelf onto a square ledge. Follow the series of short continuation corners to gain the right-hand end of a ledge under a roof. Step right and reach the top by an easy rightwards traverse on a ledge.

9 Over Easy 25m VD
C.Stein, A.Sanders, I.Hall, 6 Jun 2008
The vague arete to the right of Sunnyside Up. Start at the right-hand end of the wave-washed ledges. Follow a groove to a ledge on the arete and climb a series of short walls and ledges to belay as for Sunnyside Up.

SEAL SONG WALL

(NL 551 815) Tidal N facing Map p351 Diagram p364

This is the west face of Rubha Liath which forms the east wall of Seal Song Geo. The wall is composed of a succession of corner-lines stretching from the back of the geo to the point. They can all be easily viewed from the other side of the geo.

The higher left (north) section of the geo is split by a large, sometimes broken ledge system at two-third height forming an Upper Tier, which contains some single pitch routes. Extending rightwards from the back of the geo, the lower wall drops overhanging into the sea with only occasional small sea-level ledges. The most obvious is a luminous green ledge about 10m above the sea from which several shallow corners spring. The wall turns outwards a little beyond here to form The Projecting Buttress which constricts the geo to give the impression of an Inner Sanctum. Above this Projecting Buttress, the Upper Tier forms an impressive steep prow. There follows an area of intimidatingly blank, steep, roofed walls with no visible ledges from which to start.

The main features of the right-hand section are a series of distinctive large left-facing corners which all extend

RUBHA LIATH - Seal Song Wall

the full height of the cliff. The walls between these contain smaller corners, aretes and grooves. Some 20m right of the blank section is The First Corner extending the full height of the cliff. Between this and The Second Corner is a huge, roofed recess at sea-level. The Third Corner, immediately to its right, has two roofs in its left wall and a distinctive deep crack in its right wall and a small ledge at sea-level. A smaller corner 10m right again has a distinctive wriggly crack up its right arete. Ledges lie at the base of this extending right to finish under a deep off-width chimney. The Fourth Corner is some 10m right again bounding the left side of a slabby looking wall above an area of ledges above high tide level. The Fifth Corner separates this from The Point and is a large tapering affair emanating from ledges.

Descent: Abseil down to the lowest ledges possible. Several routes can usually be climbed from each abseil.

(i) For routes in The Inner Sanctum, abseil to the luminous green ledge down Power of the Sea, from a cairn at the top of a very obvious square-cut black corner in the upper tier (easily seen when looking out). To gain the lower ledge at the base, either abseil down a large open upper corner system further left (looking out), or abseil as for Ocean Wrath but aim slightly left (facing in).

(ii) For routes around The Projecting Buttress (Ocean Wrath), abseil down the steeper part of the Upper Tier (left of the large open upper corner system, looking out) to gain small ledges 10m above the sea in a spectacular position.

(iii) For routes between The Second Corner and The Fifth Corner, abseil from near an obvious slab in the top of the cliff-line, down the line of the third corner or further left (looking out) down a deep off-width chimney.

(iv) For routes near the point, abseil from outcrops 10m right of the point (looking out), down The Sixth Corner.

The Upper Tier

Diagrams above & p366

The routes all start from the large ledges at two-third height. It is possible to walk along the ledges but some sections are awkward and exposed and may require a rope. They are all easily accessed by short abseils down the routes themselves. Worth a visit in wild seas in order to get some climbing done.

1 The Extraordinary Relief Map of Iceland 25m E2 5b

R.Durran, H.Lawrenson, 13 Aug 2003

Start from the extreme left end of the ledge beneath an obvious hanging groove capped by a small roof which lies in the upper wall to the right of the top diagonal corner of Party Later Alligator. Climb very steeply up, move left, then up and back right to the base of the groove. Climb the groove and turn the capping roof on the right.

2 Un-named 15m VS 4c

S.Gardiner, R.Benton, 3 Jun 1998

The diagonal left to right fault to the right of Relief Map of Iceland at the left end of the ledge.

3 The Boat 15m HVS 5a *

R.Durran, A.Taylor, 9 Jul 1999

The striking left to right slanting groove left of the top corner of The Power of the Sea. Good jamming and bridging to a steep finish.

4 Flying Hex 15m VS 4c *
A.Callum, J.Sanders, 4 Jun 1998
Takes the cracks immediately on the left of the upper corner of The Power of the Sea. From the ledges climb to a horizontal flake and move up into an open corner. Climb this to obvious twin cracks which lead to the top.

The big black corner to the right is pitch 2 of The Power of the Sea (VS 4c).

5 The Girl in the Boat 15m E4 6a **
R.Durran, A.Taylor, 4 Jul 1999
The thin flake-crack in the right wall of the top corner of The Power of the Sea. Climb the wall to a good sidepull at the base of the flake. Make hard moves with improving protection to a good flake below the top. Finish more easily.

The arete to the right is pitch 3 of Seventh Heaven (E2 5b).

Right again is a more open corner of a slab leading to steeper cracked bulges and a steep right-hand wall. The following routes climb around this area.

6 Solid Dude 18m HVS 5a
J.Sanders, A.Callum, 4 Jun 1998
Start below the obvious right-slanting crack-line cutting through Seventh Heaven's arete. Gain and follow it to a position beneath an overhang. Fist jam the overhang and pull strenuously to the top.

7 The Mooring 15m E1 5c *
R.Durran, A.Taylor, 1999
The steep crack in the right wall of the open corner. Well protected.

8 The Wake 15m E4 6a *
R.Durran, A.Taylor, 1999
An eliminate pitch up the wall immediately right of The Mooring but with some excellent moves. Climb a steep broken crack right of that route's crack and then make harder moves between thin breaks above to the top.

The arete between The Wake and the easy corner of Propaganda to the right is pitch 3 of Its Not My Fault (VS 4c).

The easy corner right again (on the left side of the overhanging projecting buttress) is pitch 3 of Propaganda and Far From the Dogging Crowd (VS 4c). The top pitches of Ocean Wrath (pitch 2: E2 5c), Walking on Waves (pitch 2: E1 5a) and Spitting Fury (pitch 2: E3 5c) are on this wildly steep, projecting buttress. An airy but easy 20m traverse right leads under the projecting buttress into a large bay, with triple diagonal crack-faults in the back and defined on the right by a left-facing corner and a smaller projecting buttress.

9 Not Ali's Crack 15m E1 5b
F.Murray, J.Sanders, 4 Jun 1998
In the centre of the bay is an overhanging right-slanting crack starting at half-height. Start directly below it and climb the lower wall via ledges, then attack the crack.

10 Pumping Up 15m VS 4c
J.Sanders, A.Callum, 4 Jun 1998
Start as for Not Ali's Crack and move into the corner on the right. Climb it direct, exiting left at the top.

The following routes lie on the steep buttress on the right side of the bay.

11 Doppelkratzer 15m HVS 5a
A.Callum, J.Sanders, 4 Jun 1998
Start in the centre of the right-hand steep bulging wall at a thin crack-line. Ascend the delicate crack (poorly protected) and make an awkward balance move (crux) up and left to mantelshelf onto a ledge. Step right to finish.

12 The Monster Waves 15m HVS 5a *
N.Morbey, P.Bamberski, 27 May 201
Starting 2m right of Flying Hex. Climb up to a small overhang, surmount this via small jugs heading for a rightwards diagonal line, which tops out on the arete for a lovely belay position.

13 The Trusted Scallop 15m E2 5c *
D.Carden, W.Quinn, 27 May 2013
Starts just round to the left of the front of the buttress. Climb a right-facing corner for 5m to a hard, well protected move off slopping scalloped crimps up a steep wall to a rail beneath a prominent grey roof. Lurch up and left through the roof to better holds and a finish onto the large square ledge.

The Inner Sanctum

Diagrams opposite & p366

The area from the back of the geo to the Projecting Buttress has several large corner-lines starting from sea-level. The most distinctive near the left end is the upper pitch of The Power of the Sea.

The first route climbs a line in the back of the geo and can be accessed without abseiling. Start by descending steep slabs on the opposite side of the geo (above and left, looking out, of the North Wall) until it is possible to traverse into the back of the geo about 20m above water level.

14 Party Later Alligator 15m E1
D.Towse, G.Huxter, 8 May 1999
Climbs the junction between the main wall and the diamond-shaped back wall.
1. 5m 4c Traverse a big bird infested ledge. From its end climb up a flake to a niche in the corner.
2. 10m 5b Climb the groove rightwards then back left up a diagonal corner.

The next route starts on the luminous green ledge gained by abseil down the black corner.

The Inner Sanctum

15.	The Power of the Sea	E2 5b, 4c **
16.	It's Not My Fault	E1 5a, 5b, 4c *
17.	Seventh Heaven	E3 5b, 6a, 5b **
18.	Far From the Dogging Crowd	E2 5b, 5b, 4c **
19.	Propaganda	E2 5c, 4c *

Projecting Buttress

20.	Ocean Wrath	E2 5a, 5c **
21.	Walking on Waves	E1 5b, 5a ***
22.	Spitting Fury	E6 6b, 5c ***

15 The Power of the Sea 40m E2 **

K.Pyke, G.E.Little, 26 Jun 1996

1. 25m 5b From the left end of the ledge, climb a sustained flake-crack. From its top step right to enter a narrow slot breaking through overhanging rock. Climb this to reach a horizontal fault-line and the ledges.
2. 15m 4c Enter and climb the fine black corner above.

The following four routes start from a small sea-level ledge in the base of a corner between the luminous green ledges and the projecting buttress.

16 It's Not My Fault 55m E1 *

C.Waddy p1, Jun 1998; G.Farquar, N.Craine p2 and p3, Jun 1998

Start in the base of the corner.

1. 10m 5a Climb cracks in the left arete to gain the luminous green ledge.
2. 30m 5b Climb an overhanging groove characterised by sharp-angled flake-cracks, from near the right end of the green ledge. Belay on the large ledges below the open slabby corner.
3. 15m 4c Climb more easily up right then up an arete right of the corner above to the top.

17 Seventh Heaven 55m E3 **
K.Howett, J.Horrocks, 15 May 1999
An excellent route with a technical crux in a space walking position. Start from the small ledge in the base of the corner.
1. 10m 5b From the ledge, climb the corner which arches leftwards for 9m to a large horizontal break, which leads to the right end of the luminous green ledges
2. 30m 6a From the extreme right end of the ledges, climb a slim tapering corner to reach a good undercut in an overlap. Swing immediately out right around the arete into another overhanging corner. Go up this more easily to the large ledges to belay below the slabby corner. The initial corner can be climbed direct to the same point at E3 5c when dry.
3. 15m 5b From the ledge, climb diagonally left towards the arete overlooking the corner of The Power of the Sea. Climb the arete via a tapering shallow groove in an excellent position to a rounded finish.

18 Far From the Dogging Crowd 55m E2 5b **
C.Waddy, Jun 1998
1. 10m 5b As for Seventh Heaven; from the ledge climb the corner which arches leftwards to the large horizontal break. Traverse right under the steep slim groove of Seventh Heaven to gain a ledge below a larger and easier looking groove to its right.
2. 30m 5b Climb this groove for 1m or so, then move left onto a flake on the arete that leads to another groove. Go up this to the large ledges. A big easy corner lies above; belay below it.
3. 15m 4c Finish more easily above up the easy open corner containing a big ledge halfway.

19 Propaganda 55m E2 5c *
C.Waddy, Jun 1998
1. 40m 5c From the right end of the ledge, layback up the precarious arete 3m to the right to gain an easier slabby corner leading to the ledge on Far From the Dogging Crowd. Climb straight up the juggy overhanging arete above and then step right to gain a short green walled groove. Follow this, then step left and up a short wall to gain the large ledges.
2. 15m 4c Finish up the large easy corner of Far From the Dogging Crowd.

The Projecting Buttress

Diagrams opposite & page p364

The right boundary of the Inner Sanctum is The Projecting Buttress. The following routes climb up this buttress and start from small ledges about 10m above the sea.

A small colony of razorbills nest on an obvious horizontal ledge in the overhanging prow taken by the second pitch of Walking on Waves and Spitting Fury; this should be avoided during nesting.

20 Ocean Wrath 40m E2 **
T.Rankin, G.Lennox, 10 May 1999
A good climb with two contrasting pitches. Abseil slightly right (looking down) of the prow of the buttress to gain a good triangular ledge at about 10m above the sea.
1. 25m 5a Climb the left edge of the corner above into an open groove. Follow the easiest line above to the mid-way ledges and belay below Far From the Dogging Crowd in the steep upper tier.
2. 15m 5c Climb the right wall of the corner by a short open groove and crack directly above.

21 Walking on Waves 40m E1 ***
T.Rankin, G.Lennox, 10 May 1999
An outstanding and intimidating climb for the grade. Abseil as for Ocean Wrath but take a more direct line to a very small ledge in the blunt arete of the projecting buttress 10m above the sea.
1. 25m 5b Move up left on good holds to a ledge below a blunt bulging rib. Climb this on surprisingly good holds, then continue up the wall to belay on a good ledge.
2. 15m 5a Climb the sensational overhanging groove in the left side of the overhanging prow in the upper tier.

22 Spitting Fury 45m E6 ***
G.Lennox, T.Rankin, 10 May 1999
An excellent route requiring a certain amount of aggression. Start as for Walking on Waves.
1. 25m 6b Traverse hard right from the small stance to an obvious spike. Make committing moves up and right into a hanging corner. More hard moves lead to below the roof. Squirm out right round the roof to climb a corner. Move left at its top and continue up easier ground to belay below the upper prow.
2. 20m 5c Move up to climb the impressive steep shallow groove in the prow, right of the groove of Walking on Waves.

The Corners Area

Diagrams p364 & p369

There is a concentration of routes between The Second Corner and an off-width chimney between The Fourth and Fifth Corners. The first routes all start from a sea-washed ledge at the bottom of The Third Corner (Durdle Huxter start). Calm seas are essential.

23 The Wet Look 50m E1 **
K.Howett, L.Creamer, 21 May 2001
Climbs The Second Corner (to the left of Durdle Huxter). Start on the sea-level ledge at the base of The Third Corner.
1. 30m 5b Climb the rounded rib on the left to enter a thin corner with a small ledge. Go up this to a footledge at its top. Climb past the left edge of the lower roof of Durdle Huxter and into the bigger corner above. Follow it more easily to ledges above a second roof.
2. 20m 4c Climb the continuation corner through a small roof and onto a higher ledge system below the final section of the Upper Tier. Climb the hanging groove in the arete above to the top.

Spitting Fury, P1 (E6) Gordon Lennox & Tim Rankin (photo Kevin Howett)

The Corners Area				***Sixth Corner Area***	
23. The Wet Look	E1 5b, 4c **	26. Surfs-Up	E2 5a, 5b **	30. Horroxed	VS 4c *
24. Durdle Huxter	E2 4c, 5b **	27. Smurfs-Up	E2 5b **	31. Provoked	E1 5b *
25. Mingin' in the Rain	E3 5a, 5c ****	28. Swell-Time	E3 5c **	32. Un-named	VS 4c
		29. Sun-Dew	E1 5b **		

24 Durdle Huxter 45m E2 **
D.Towse, G.Huxter, 9 May 1999
Climb The Third Corner.
1. 15m 4c From the small ledge, climb the tapering corner direct to then step out right to bypass the roof and gain the main corner-line. Belay on a good ledge just over the roof.
2. 30m 5b Climb the corner with the deep crack in the right wall to a roof. Traverse right into a groove and go up this to finish.

25 Mingin' in the Rain 50m E3 ****
H.Harris, K.Howett, 9 May 1999
Climbs a line just right of The Third Corner. Start as for Durdle Huxter.
1. 15m 5a Take the obvious traverse line out right to the base of a hanging corner. Pull into this and exit it out left under a roof to an airy ledge on the arete of the Third Corner.
2. 35m 5c Pull into the slim groove directly above and follow it past a small ledge (sparsely protected) to easier ground. Trend up and right, then back left to the abseil point.

26 Surfs-Up 50m E2 **
H.Harris, K.Howett, 10 May 1999
Start as for Mingin' in the Rain.
1. 15m 5a Traverse right to the hanging corner of Mingin' in the Rain. At its top, exit out right to a small ledge.
2. 35m 5b Pull through the roof directly above via a shallow corner to gain a horizontal break. Step right and go up a flake until it is possible to gain a slim hanging groove on the left. Go up this to easier ground leading to the abseil point.

The next series of climbs are concentrated around the deep off-width chimney. They are gained by abseiling down the line of the chimney to a large ledge 5m above the sea. If the swell is too great to access the Durdle Huxter ledge, this offers a good option.

27 Smurfs-Up 45m E2 5b **
L.Creamer, K.Howett, 21 May 2001
Begin from a flat ledge projecting from a small but deep cave just left of ledges below the chimney. From the ledge, climb the left rib and through the roof via a large flake-crack to join the second pitch of Surfs-Up at its flake.

28 Swell-Time 45m E3 5c **
K.Howett, H.Harris, 10 May 1999
Climbs the smooth looking wall immediately left of the off-width chimney. From the base of the chimney, yard out leftwards across the small roof barring access to the wall to pull over on jugs. Climb direct through two horizontal breaks to easier ground, then climb direct through a slight, roofed prow and onto the top.

29 Sun-Dew 45m E1 5b **
G.Huxter, D.Towse, 10 May 1999
Climb the line of the right arete of the off-width chimney with continual interest. Climb the upper wall slightly right, then direct.

The Sixth Corner Area

Diagrams p364 & p369

Running left from the base of The Fifth Corner is a good ledge along the base of a steep slab which is capped by a roof. The ledge remains above high tides.

30 Horroxed 30m VS 4c *
J.Horrocks, K.Howett, 15 May 1999
Climb the slim right-facing corner off the left end of the ledge to the upper roof. Pull round left to escape.
Variation: **30a Direct Finish 30m E1 5a**
K.Howett, J Horrocks, 15 May 1999
Climb direct through the roof on good holds but without protection.

31 Provoked 30m E1 5b *
S.Gardiner, R.Benton, 3 Jun 1998
Climbs the crack-line in the steep slab immediately left of The Sixth Corner and directly through the capping roof.

32 Un-named 30m VS 4c
Climbs The Sixth Corner direct.

The North Wall of Seal Song Geo

(NL 551 816) Tidal S facing Map p351

This short wall lies opposite the back part of Rubha Liath's Seal Song Wall, directly opposite The Inner Sanctum. It is characterised by a black slab emanating from sea-washed slabs leading up to a steep upper wall forming a sizeable roof near the top. Routes are described from right to left.

Descent: A huge block sits on a flat rock shelf at the top of the wall. Gain this by a scramble from the west. Abseil from the block down a left-facing corner to ledges near the base of the slab. Calm seas preferable.

The Girl with Extraordinary Eyes 25m E3 6a *
R.Durran, C.Henderson, 23 Jul 2000
Down and right of the wall taken by Fergus Sings the Blues is a clean wall, undercut on its right-hand side by a low cave. Surmount the left edge of the cave and move right to a prominent line of rightward trending flakes. Climb these to a rest below a capping roof and surmount this with difficulty in a fine position to finish.

Fresh Out the Box 30m E4 6a
H.Harris, H.Hall, 25 May 2003
Climbs the wall to the right of the sharp arete, right of the corner of Delayed Reaction.
1. 20m 6a Start about 5m right of the arete below a rightward-leaning groove. Climb to the bottom of the groove and move up and left to flat holds. Hard moves horizontally leftwards gain a better hold (bold). Climb straight up to a ledge (bolder!), then continue up trending rightwards to reach a large platform and belay.
2. 10m Scramble to the top of the ramp.

Delayed Reaction 30m E1 5c
L.Thomas, T.Turner, 3 Jun 1998
The prominent hanging crack below the right side of the upper roofs, gained via the lower corner. Climb the corner on good holds to a huge platform on the right. Traverse left on good holds to gain the crack. Follow it, the crux being saved for the final moves to gain good holds just short of the top.

Fergus Sings the Blues 35m E4 6a *
G.Latter, F.Murray, 3 Jun 1998
Excellent sustained climbing breaking through the roof at the top of the cliff, just left of Delayed Reaction's crack. Start at the base of the corner of Delayed Reaction. Move up and leftwards along a good flake handrail. Climb the wall above past some good horizontal slots to the roof. Pull out right to two good undercut flakes, then make a long reach to a good break. Pull up the wall above on jugs, then left and follow slabby twin cracks. Finish quite boldly up the steadily impending wall above.

Gneiss Helmet 40m E3
H.Harris, K.Howett, 13 May 1999
Climbs a natural diagonal line from right to left under the roofs starting from the base of the corner of Delayed Reaction. Take a belay just down and left of the corner on the base of the black slab.
1. 30m 4b Take a diagonal line leftwards across the slab to the blunt arete under the left side of the biggest part of the roof; belay in a small alcove 2m below the level of the roofs.
2. 10m 6a Step up and take a diagonal, pink quartz ramp leftwards under the capping overhanging wall to an impasse just before a bottomless groove. Pull steeply

through a small roof into a hanging niche under a bigger capping roof. Skitter left to escape.

Descent: For the following routes, abseil from near the west end of the shelf to further good ledges that lead round the base of the now barrel-like cliff to the west. There is a prominent horizontal overlap at 25m, usually with nesting Guillemots in season.

Castlebay Hen Party 35m E1
C.Pulley, P.Hemming, 13 Aug 2006
Start below a left-facing corner in the centre of the wall to the left of the black slab.
1. 20m 5b Gain the corner via blocks and a short chimney and its continuation to a ledge on the right.
2. 15m 4c Break through the overlap above to gain the left end of the pink quartz of Gneiss Helmet. Traverse airily left above the overlap and the birds but beneath a triangular roof to gain and finish up a corner.

Mistaken Identity 30m VS 4c
P.Hemming, C.Pulley, 13 Aug 2006
Takes a direct line to the left edge of the overlap and the finishing corner of Castlebay Hen Party. Start below a vertical chimney-slot. Climb rightwards to the base of a steep crack. Climb this and the broken corner above to the birdy ledge. Break through the overlap to finish up the corner in a great position.

Guano no dae that? 45m S 4a
N.Wilson, J.Walker, S.Campbell, Aug 2000
Climbs the wall near the right-hand side to gain guano rich ledges (guillemots permitting). Finish easily up the wall to the top (fulmars permitting).

Dancing with Hens 30m VS 4c
P.Hemming, C.Pulley, 13 Aug 2006
Climbs the wall around the buttress to the left. Start left of a sea-level niche beside a prominent orange band of rock. Climb a blocky corner to a steep orange wall where jugs lead through the continuation corner. Pull through an overlap and step out right above the void. Spacewalk rightwards and gain a slab to easy ground.

SLOC HÈISEGEO

(NL 550 817) Non-tidal W facing Map p351

This is the huge sloc immediately to the west of Seal Song Geo, which cuts almost 400m deeply into the hillside of the island. The main wall of the sloc can be viewed from an easily descended rib to the west and whilst it is very extensive, there are large areas of poor rock and ledges.

The topography of the wall, from left to right is as follows: At the termination of the sloc, deep inland, is a black, north facing 50m overhanging wall sitting high above the now deep sloc. Below, the rock is less inviting. To the right (as viewed from afar) there is firstly a large area of poor broken ground, then a prominent long projecting fin. To the right again is a massive area of brown coloured rock with impressive roofs, but which unfortunately is of poor quality rock. Right of this a grass ramp runs down rightwards to stacked blocks about 70m above the sea. Right again the wall reduces both in quality and in height as it turns through 90 degrees into two large broken corners to meet the North Wall of Seal Song Geo.

Descent: The first routes are on the clean wall in the termination of the geo. Abseil down the line of the wall to grass ledges.

Eagle Gravy 60m E1
P.Graham, F.Cookson, 25 Jun 2010
An adventurous route taking the obvious ramp-line up the right side of wall but starting on the left side. Loose snappy rock. Start at the lowest point of the wall.
1. 25m 4c Climb straight up the wall (no gear) to reach a ledge and gear behind a large dubious flake. Traverse right into a short corner, which is climbed to the big brown ledge in the centre of the wall.
2. 35m 4c Move across right and slightly downwards into the bottom of the obvious ramp-line, which is climbed to the top.

Un-named 30m E5 6b
G.Huxter, D.Towse, 1999
Climbs a hard and sustained line up the middle of the wall from the brown ledge. Its relationship to Shooting Straight (pitch 2) is not certain.

Shooting Straight 30m E4
F.Coxwell, T.Green, 2 Sep 2009
1. 20m 5c (HXS!) Climb direct onto the obvious brown ledge, 20m up below the centre of the wall (not recommended by the first ascensionists).
2. 30m 6a Climb up via a large flakey nose past a small overhang to the main left-facing flake. Blast up the flake and at its end traverse left to the pink crack and climb this to the top.

Descent: The next route is gained by abseil from the stacked blocks at the far end of the grass ramp. Abseil down a corner to ledges at 30m, then a further 40m abseil slightly right (looking out) to ledges 5m above the sea.

Don't Layback in Anger 70m E1 **
N.Stabbs, H.Harris, 22 May 2001
A superb route and a classic at the grade.
1. 35m 5b Trend rightwards aiming for a large leftward projecting, stripey flake at 20m. Avoid it on the right via an obvious corner, before traversing rightwards to a belay ledge below the main corner.
2. 35m 5b Follow the huge flake on the left wall of the corner, heading for a projecting flake close to the arete. Finish directly above on slightly loose rock.

DUN MINGULAY

Dun Mingulay (Dùn Mhiùghlaigh) is the almost isolated headland in the south-west corner of Mingulay, joined to the parent island by a narrow neck of land. There are three separate cliffs on the headland currently containing climbs. By far the most important is the west facing section of the headland called Sròn an Dùin towards the tip (overlooking two tidal skerries), which forms a superb 90m high wall of clean, vertical to overhanging rock providing climbing of exceptional quality. Secondly there is a huge distinctive roof at the end of the point itself and thirdly the east face of the promontory forms an 80m wall of black rock easily seen inside the deep and foreboding Sloc dubh an Dùine, when approaching the promontory to cross the narrow neck of land. The cliffs are described clockwise round the headland. Gaining the base of the cliffs is by abseil, and dependent upon calm seas due to the swell and near sea-level belays.

Creag Dubh

(NL 547 821) Non-tidal E Facing Map p351

This huge wall lies in Sloc dubh an Dùine and forms part of the East Face of Dun Mingulay. With its heavily featured, coal black rock it seems less than inviting, but the routes are steep and exciting and often sheltered when Sròn an Dùin is being battered by the elements.

The wall of the sloc is 80m in height and over 300m in length, extending from the back of the sloc round to a huge open grass bay just east of Dun Mingulay Point.

There are nesting auks on some of the horizontal ledges, particularly in the back of the sloc and out

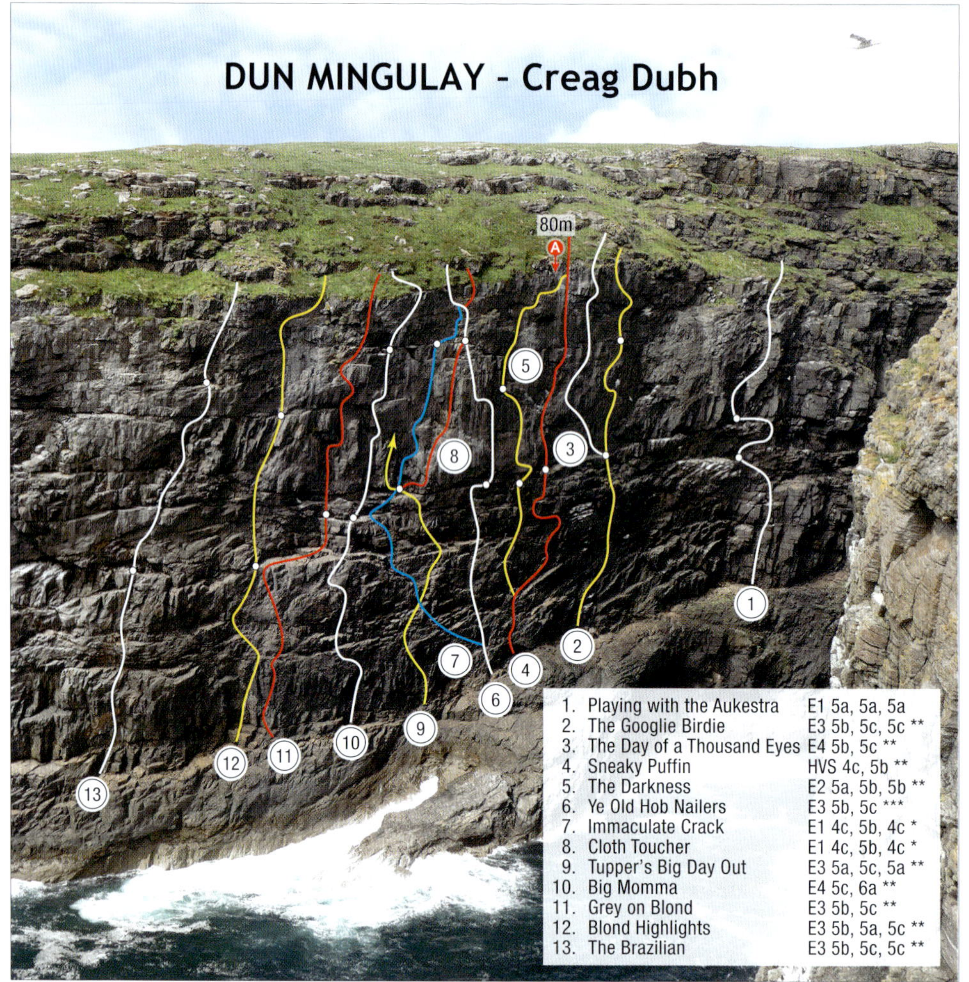

1.	Playing with the Aukestra	E1 5a, 5a, 5a
2.	The Googlie Birdie	E3 5b, 5c, 5c **
3.	The Day of a Thousand Eyes	E4 5b, 5c **
4.	Sneaky Puffin	HVS 4c, 5b **
5.	The Darkness	E2 5a, 5b, 5b **
6.	Ye Old Hob Nailers	E3 5b, 5c ***
7.	Immaculate Crack	E1 4c, 5b, 4c *
8.	Cloth Toucher	E1 4c, 5b, 4c *
9.	Tupper's Big Day Out	E3 5a, 5c, 5a **
10.	Big Momma	E4 5c, 6a **
11.	Grey on Blond	E3 5b, 5c **
12.	Blond Highlights	E3 5b, 5a, 5c **
13.	The Brazilian	E3 5b, 5c, 5c **

towards the bay. There is however one section where there are few birds. This lies above a huge rock platform at sea-level about a third of the way out from the back of the sloc. This wall can be viewed easily from the opposite peninsula of Ban-nish.

The main features of the wall above this platform are described from right to left. First a silvery-coloured slab in the upper half, sitting above steeper rock (diagonal corners bound the right side of the slab). Left of this the lower wall seems to be split by many horizontal ledges, but is actually overhanging. At mid-height there is a horizontal ledge, above which is a smooth wall characterised by a prominent hole in its right side. This section is capped by a roof. Left again is a big right-facing corner in the upper half with big flake-lines leading up to it from the right. This corner bounds a steeper (overhanging) pillar to the left (only in the upper half), which has a curving right-facing groove in its right side. Small disjointed corners define the upper left side of the pillar. Below these corners the platform disappears into a gulch of frothing sea. To the left of the gulch the wall is steep and characterised by two large corner-lines containing large roofs in the upper half. Left again is a vertical scoop-like corner extending the full height of the cliff. Routes are described right to left.

Descent: Gain the platform below the wall by abseil from above the centre of the wall, there being a very good block belay in the steep grass.

1 Playing with the Aukestra 85m E1

H.Harris, L.Beck, 24 May 2000

Climbs a line up corners to the right of the silvery slab. Start in the open corner in the right end of the platform, just before a narrowing (the corner contains some vegetation at its base).

1. 30m 5a Climb the right side of the corner for 20m where ledges run out right. Climb direct for 10m to a belay in a small bay.

2. 15m 5a Traverse horizontally right for 8m to a slim black pillar. Climb this for 2m and move up left to a traverse line back left into another small bay.

3. 40m 5a Climb the groove above the belay to reach a hanging slab. Go up this and then grooves above and slightly left to finish

2 The Googlie Birdie 80m E3 **

K.Howett, D.Towse, 24 May 2000

Climbs the upper wall near the conspicuous hole. Start as for The Day of a Thousand Eyes.

1. 35m 5b Climb the first pitch of The Day of a Thousand Eyes to the halfway ledge. Belay just to the right of that route, directly below the hole and a hanging corner below it.

2. 30m 5c Pull up onto a hanging flake and then enter a short corner. Step right into the excellent corner-crack leading towards the hole. At its top pull out horizontally left using a series of big pockets to reach jugs in the base of a slight groove. Follow the groove diagonally right to a shallow corner. Step right above the hole into another corner and up this to a small ledge below a hanging flake.

3. 15m 5c Pass the hanging flake and go up to under the roof. Step right and pull through leftwards past a projecting block under the lip. Pull leftwards into an easy deep finishing corner.

3 The Day of a Thousand Eyes 80m E4 **

K.Magog, S.Crowe, 23 May 2000

Just below and to the left of the mid-way ledge is a horizontal slot with nesting birds. Start directly below the slot at a rightward trending staircase. A bold lead.

1. 35m 5b Follow the staircase to a narrow ledge. Step right 2m and pull through the bulge via a groove, to gain a small ledge. Follow a right-trending corner to gain the mid-way ledge. Belay below a left-trending flake groove.

2. 45m 5c Climb the steep flake leftwards for about 5m. Step first left then back right and up across a smooth wall. Climb back left to gain and follow a right-facing groove that leads to the left end of the upper roof. Pull over the roof on jugs and finish in a groove in the headwall.

4 Sneaky Puffin 80m HVS **

R.Mackenzie, T.Sweeney, 23 May 2000

Start in the centre of the wall, roughly 5m left of the left end of the capping roofs and directly below a small right-facing corner formed by a yardarm (a huge jutting block) about 20m up.

1. 35m 4c Climb up easy ledges diagonally right to under a roof. Pass the left side of the roof and climb up and right onto the left end of the mid-way ledge.

2. 45m 5b Climb flakes out left and gain a precarious block. Move right and climb a hanging groove to ledges (just left of the right-facing groove on the second pitch of The Day of a Thousand Eyes). Finish out left of the roof (crux).

5 The Darkness 80m E2 **

G.Lennox, K.Howett, 4 May 2004

Climbs the smooth wall between Sneaky Puffin and Ye Old Hob Nailers. Start in the same place as Sneaky Puffin, below the yardarm.

1. 30m 5a Climb ledges direct to steep rock. Gain a hidden flake in the wall above and go left and up to the yardarm. Go up the right side of this and exit left to a belay below a shallow roof (right of the belay of Hob Nailers).

2. 20m 5b Climb direct through the roof by the obvious breach. Traverse the lip rightwards for 3m and gain a left-trending groove. Follow this then the same general line across the wall into the base of the large right-facing corner.

3. 30m 5b Go up the corner and out right round its capping roof to a ledge. Climb to a thin overlap in the headwall. Undercling right until it is possible to gain a handrail in the wall above. This can be climbed direct, but the first ascent escaped right into Sneaky Puffin due to pouring water.

6 Ye Old Hob Nailers 80m E3 ***

K.Howett, D.Towse, 23 May 2000

Climbs a line up the pillar, taking the striking flake-corner in the right edge. Start just before the gulch in the platform, directly under the flake-corner. The first pitch is serious and the second spectacular.

1. 30m 5b Climb up steep ledge covered rock just left of a low roof until under the centre of a noticeably smoother area of grey rock. Climb this boldly up and right to a left-pointing spike. Continue direct, then through a weakness in the bulge above to a ledge under the base of the pillar. Step right to a good belay under a roof beneath the line of the flake-corner.
2. 50m 5c Go up through the bulging wall into the flake-corner. Follow this to jugs at its top. Above are two hanging corners. Climb with difficulty into the smaller left-hand one. Exit this direct and take the easiest line diagonally leftwards onto a big ledge below a final steep wall. Climb this leftwards passing under an unstable looking block on the lip of the cliff.

7 Immaculate Crack 80m E1 *
D.Turnbull, G.Huxter, 23 May 2000
Climbs a line up the disjointed corners defining the left side of the pillar. Start near the left end of the platform, just before the gulch, as for Ye Old Hob Nailers.
1. 40m 4c Climb diagonally left up the lower wall, via multiple ledges, heading for a huge block on the mid-way ledges. From the block move up and right to a large ledge in a bay.
2. 30m 5b Move up and right to climb a series of immaculate slim grooves, then make a tricky move right and climb a left-facing corner to a ledge.
3. 15m 4c Move right and up ledges to the top out left of the unstable looking block.

8 Cloth Toucher 85m E1 *
R.Mackenzie, T.Sweeney, 24 May 2000
Climbs a line up the left side of the pillar close to Immaculate Crack. Start as for that route.
1. 40m 4c Climb Immaculate Crack to the belay on a large ledge in a bay.
2. 30m 5b Take a rising right traverse past the first corner, over an area of quartz feldspar, to gain entry to a hanging corner. Climb this to a ledge shared with Ye Old Hob Nailers.
3. 15m 4c Go directly up the wall to exit by the unstable looking block.

9 Tuppers Big Day Out 80m E3 **
H.Harris, L.Beck, 21 May 2001
This weaves a line around Immaculate Crack. Starts 10m left of Immaculate Crack at the start of the traverse leading left past the gulch.
1. 35m 5a Climb flakes and then a slim corner to a ledge (junction with Immaculate Crack). Move up to a right-trending ramp and climb it, and the wall above to another ledge (level with the block belay on Immaculate Crack). Climb slightly left and then straight up to belay in a bay as for Cloth Toucher.
2. 25m 5c Climb up and left to a block and then back right to a flake that turns into an undercut. Go up this, and the wall above (long reach) to left trending-flakes that lead to the right end of a ledge. Pull up and then left into a groove. Climb the groove to a traverse right and pull up to a flange. Good hanging belay.
3. 20m 5a Traverse horizontally right along the ledge to join and finish up the blunt rib of Immaculate Crack.

10 Big Momma 85m E4 **
K.Howett, L.Creamer, 21 May 2001
Climbs a line up the right-hand of the two large corner systems left of Immaculate Crack. Start at an obvious triangular corner-come-niche mid-way along the ledge from the gulch.
1. 40m 5c Go up the overhanging niche and exit left with difficulty. Climb a flake up to a ledge. Climb the broken overhanging groove just on the left, leading into a conspicuous curving right-facing corner. Exit this rightwards and climb to the big block on Immaculate Crack.
2. 45m 6a Enter the large corner above. Follow it on good holds steeply to just below a capping roof. Take the slim corner on the right of the roof and at its top make desperate moves up a slim left-facing groove. Easier but steep rocks lead up and right to a ledge under the headwall and large roof (possible belay). Pull directly through the centre of the roof and up the wall slightly right into a very shallow groove. Exit right.

11 Grey on Blond 85m E3 **
L.Creamer, K.Howett, 22 May 2001
Climbs a line around the left-hand of the two large corner systems. Start below an obvious undercling flake 5m left of Big Momma and just right of the white streaked corner of Blond Highlights.
1. 40m 5b Climb to the undercling. Pull through directly and up a shallow groove to step right at its top onto a small ledge (serious). Go up slabby rock to the base of a shallow left-facing groove. Climb this and exit right. Traverse right and up the easy wall to the left side of the big block on the ledge.
2. 45m 5c Go up the large corner to the big roof. By-pass it on the right and continue to a glacis under a black roof. Pull over into a slim silver grey ramp. From its top gain a slim hanging groove above the bulge on the left which leads to a ledge. Climb up right to another ledge below the headwall, just left of Big Momma. From a small horizontal flake in the wall, pull steeply direct into an obvious finishing corner.

12 Blond Highlights 85m E3 **
L.Creamer, K.Howett, 20 May 2001
Climbs the prominent vertical scooped recess that extends the height of the cliff about 30m left of Immaculate Crack. From the gulch in the large platform at the base of the cliff, traverse left to gain smaller ledges leading to the recess.
1. 35m 5b Climb the white streaked corner in the right side of the recess and at its top step right round the arete into a smaller groove and a ledge. Continue directly up the steep bulge onto slabby rock. Trend left a little to a small break with a tiny overlap. Pull out rightwards across the smooth wall into a small shallow groove to gain a large ledge.
2. 35m 5a Climb directly up the wall and through bulges to gain a corner-ramp leading rightwards to a ledge. Consecutive small shallow corners lead up grey rock, to a step right and a belay under an obvious block forming a small roof.
3. 15m 5c Gain the block above. Stand on it and exit the bulge above rightwards with difficulty. Traverse right and finish next to a large pointed block.

13 The Brazilian 80m E3 **
K.Howett, G.Lennox, 7 May 2004
A line up the wall left of Blond Highlights. Start 5m left at a groove containing twin crack-lines.
1. 35m 5b Climb the steep groove and exit left to a ledge. Go up the wall and enter the right-hand of two corners, climb this with difficulty to exit right. Move up and left 3m to a small ledge and belay below the centre of the wall above (larger ledges to the left and right have poor belays).
2. 30m 5c Take the wall above diagonally right through the steepening, then take broken ground direct heading to a flake in the steeper band above. Using the flake, gain the slab above and belay near its right end.
3. 15m 5c Take the tapering overhanging scoop and flake above direct through the headwall.

Dun Mingulay Point

(NL 542 819) Tidal SE facing Map p351

On the tip of the promontory is a huge roof, clearly seen in profile from along the rest of the south coast of Mingulay. The following route climbs a line to its left.

Descent: Abseil down left (looking out) from huge blocks just to the east of the very tip to gain a niche at the base of a huge corner which leads up to the 12m roof.

The Scottish Play 50m E3
C.Waddy, A.Cave, Jun 1998
1. 25m 6a Pull left out of the niche with difficulty and climb up onto a slab. Pull left round the capping roof above, and continue up a crack to gain ledges level with but 12m to the right of the huge roof.
2. 25m 5a Traverse right, then climb easily direct to the top.

Descent: The very tip of the point itself can be down-climbed to near sea-level, but it is easier to abseil. The first route starts from a large ledge part way down the point. The second climbs the wall just round to the west, towards the start of Sròn an Dùin.

Western Exposure 40m VD
H.Harris, L.Beck, 22 May 2001
From the large ledge, pull over a bulge at its left side, and up a wall to a guano covered ledge and then a square recess behind leading to another wall and the final bulge. Huge holds!

Big Calm 65m HS
N.Stabbs, M.Holt, 22 May 2001
Abseil to the big ledge of Western Exposure, then a further 30m off the right side (looking out) of the ledge to a small ledge at the high tide line.
1. 50m Climb up and leftwards, following a line of flakes and recesses towards a large corner at 45m. This is avoided by climbing flakes and walls to the right. Belay on a large ledge.
2. 15m Climb the slim corner on the right to reach the abseil point.

Golden Eagle on Mingulay (photo Ron Kenyon)

SRÒN AN DÙIN

(NL 543 820) Tidal W facing Map p351

Considered by some as quite simply the best cliff in the UK for quality, exposure and adventure. The wall's topography cannot be seen from any vantage point except that of a boat, so find an abseil point and commit! The north end of the Dun Mingulay cliff-line is distinguished by a pronounced buttress seen in profile from right down the western side of the island and which holds the route Children of Tempest. To the north of this the rock is broken and vegetated but merges into one of Mingulay's hidden secrets; a narrow rock arch through the 150m high promontory of Gunamul. A small boat can squeeze through when conditions are suitable and the even more foreboding cave almost cutting under the neck of Dun Mingulay can be entered and reversed back out. This is an area dubbed Roraimer. Immediately south of Children of Tempest the quality of the rock increases and forms an unbroken steep cliff to the end of the point. The cliff is described in three sections Northern, Central and Southern, from north to south.

The Northern Section

Diagrams below & opposite

Slabby, undistinguished rock to the north rears up into the steeper pillar of Children of Tempest. South of this is a shallow but very impressive sea cave which is formed by two main roof systems, one at about 30m and the other across the top of the wall. This is home to Perfect Monsters. It is not possible to walk round the back of the cave onto the central area.

Descent: Make a 90m abseil from beside a collection of large blocks near the northern end to gain small ledges below the shallow pillar of Children of Tempest that run into the back of the shallow cave.

1 Pain au Chocolate 100m E3 5c **

M.Shorter, N.Guillotine, Jun 2008

A line up the left side of the pillar of Children of Tempest. Start from the far left end of the lowest ledges.

1. 50m 5a Traverse out left on good holds for about 10m, then start to trend upwards via ramps until below a small roof. Take the roof on its right and continue upwards 20m until below another larger roof.
2. 50m 5c Take the roof on its left side via cracks. Climb straight up on easier ground and belay with the birds at the top.

2 Children of Tempest 95m E2 **

G.E.Little, K.Howett, 1 Jun 1995

This climbs the centre of the pillar. The main feature of the route is the thin crack in the otherwise blank wall on pitch 2. Start at a flake at the left end of the highest ledge.

1. 25m 5a Trend left up a black slabby wall to enter a short slim groove with a cracked left wall. Climb this to a horizontal break. Pull up the wall above, step left then climb another short groove to reach a small triangular rock ledge. A fine, intricate pitch.
2. 40m 5c Ascend the diagonal crack in the wall above rightwards, with a thin move at its end, to gain ledges. Climb easily to below the base of a deep flake-crack in the steep, clean pillar above. Follow this on grand holds to reach a large ledge.
3. 30m 4a Climb trending right up rock steps to belay at the abseil point.

3 The Great Shark Hunt 100m E3 **

G.Farquhar, N.Craine, Jun 1998

This finds a way through the huge roof at an almost unbelievably low grade. Start about 5m right of Children of Tempest at a groove line directly below the hanging corner issuing from the left side of the roof.

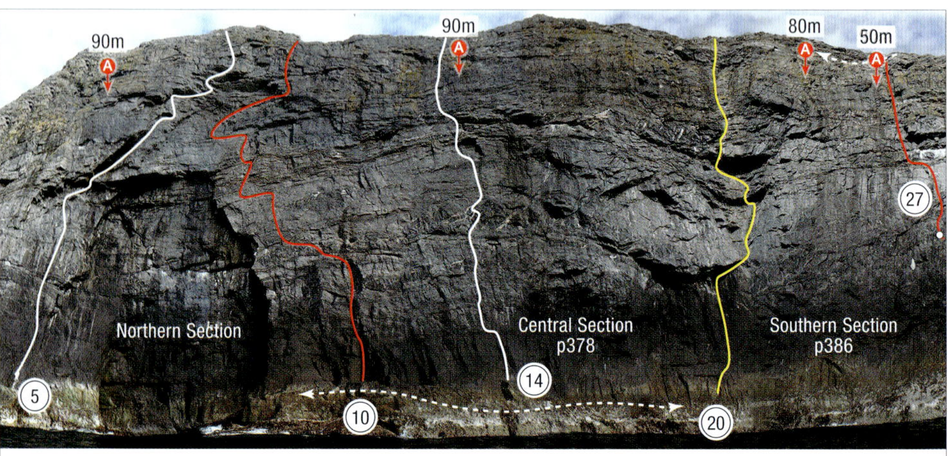

DUN MINGULAY
Sròn an Dùin

5. Perfect Monsters	E7 6b ***	20. Big Kenneth	E5 6a ****
10. Voyage of Faith	E3 5c ****	27. Fifteen Fathoms	S 4a ****
14. The Silkie	E3 6a ***		

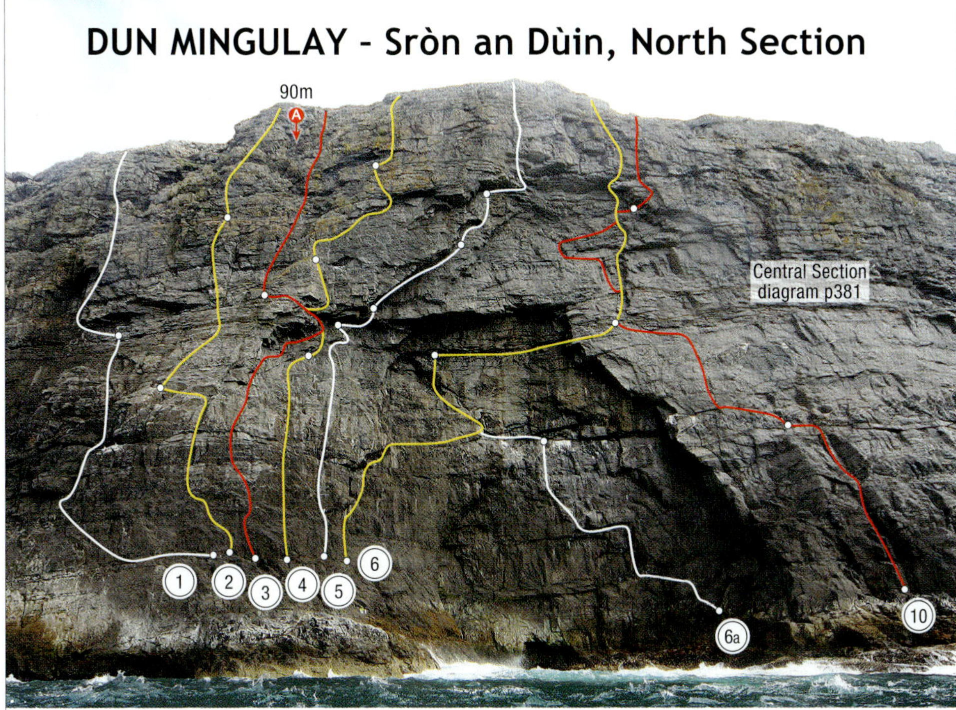

1. Pain au Chocolate E3 5a, 5c **
2. Children of Tempest E2 5a, 5c, 4a **
3. The Great Shark Hunt E3 5c, 5a **
4. Ride the Monster E4 5a, 6a, 5c, 4c ***
5. Perfect Monsters E7 5c, 6b, 6b, 6a, 6a ***
6. Ray of Light E4 5c, 5c, 5c ***
6a. Searching in the Sun E4 6a
10. Voyage of Faith E3 5b, 5b, 5b, 5c ****

1. 55m 5c Climb the wall direct past several ledges (bold) then bear right in a diagonal overhanging groove to a rest below the roof. Climb leftwards through this (impressive) and take a belay.
2. 45m 5a Finish direct up walls above.

4 Ride the Monster 110m E4 ***

K.Howett, L.Creamer, 22 May 2001

Climbs a spectacular and exposed line through the huge roof right of The Great Shark Hunt then up the headwall above the roof and the flying groove of Perfect Monsters. Start about 3m left of Perfect Monsters at a slightly left-trending line of flakes and grooves.

1. 30m 5a Climb the flakes and discontinuous shallow grooves to a small ledge below the left end of the small diagonal overlap about 6m below the break in the big roof.
2. 25m 6a Climb up to join The Great Shark Hunt below the big roof and climb through the roof leftwards to below a secondary roof. The Great Shark Hunt continues left. Instead, make hard moves right along the lip of the big roof to gain an open book corner. Follow this to a small stance on its left arete.
3. 30m 5c Continue up the slimmer corner above for 5m, until a thin traverse line right can be taken to step onto an obvious small loose block. Step up and right again into the underclings below the roof. Follow these rightwards under the roof into a slight recess, then pull directly over to a good flake-crack. Take this and the easy wall to a ledge.
4. 25m 4c Climb the wall directly to take a belay on a block back from the edge.

5 Perfect Monsters 110m E7 ***

T.Turner, G.Latter, L.Thomas (1 rest), P1&2 4 Jun 1998; P3&4 5 Jun 1998; C.Simes, N.Guillotine, 5 Jun 2008

An outrageously exposed route following a diagonal line rightwards through the impressive roofed arch, but marred by the use of pegs, most of which will now be severely corroded. Start from the commodious ledge to the right of Children of Tempest, just left of Ray of Light.

1. 30m 5c Follow a line of shallow grooves and cracks to undercut right at a diagonal line of smaller overlaps, 5m below the main roof system. Belay on a flat spike in the leftmost of two grooves, directly beneath the big roof.

2. 10m 6b Move up to the main roof. Undercut right to a jammed block jug, then launch over the roof to a good jug over the lip. Then step out right to a cramped belay (pegs) on the lip of the horizontal roof. A spectacular pitch.
3. 20m 6b The awesome overhanging flying groove. Undercut, bridge or whatever seems right (some peg runners) to reach a good nut belay at a small footledge where it becomes a vertical corner.
4. 15m 6a Climb the short black corner to the roof, then undercut this rightwards to pull round into a slim cracked groove. Climb this, pulling leftwards over a bulge on good holds. Step left and up to belay under the roof above.
5. 35m 6a Another truly spacewalking pitch. Traverse right along the obvious juggy handrail for 8m, then pull up through the roof to gain a good knee-bar rest on a horizontal spike. Psyche up and launch straight up on perfect monsters to finish up an immaculate vertical wall on good holds.

Ray of Light, P3 (E4) Howard Lawledge (photo Tom Powell)

6 Ray of Light 130m E4 ***
C.Waddy, A.Cave, Jun1998
An impressive route that climbs under the arch right of Perfect Monsters. Start from the end of the commodious ledge beneath the left side of the arch.
1. 45m 5c Climb a large rightward-facing groove for 15m to a point where a horizontal traverse right can be made across the wall. Make hard moves up and then right to a belay at a thin horizontal fault below the big roof.
2. 40m 5c Traverse spectacularly right under the arch to a corner. Move right and belay on a small ledge in a great position; junction with Voyage of Faith belay.
3. 45m 5c Climb directly up the wall to a humungous tusk in the roof. Move up onto it and then climb more easily direct to the top.

Variation: **6a Searching in the Sun E4 6a**
D.O'Sullivan, R.Cowie, T.Marsh, 6 Jun 2008
An alternative start which breaches the area of rock under the huge arch, starting from below the right-hand side of the arch left of Les Voyageurs. Abseil access as for the Central Area. Belay on the far left of small ledges below a wet off-width chimney.
1. 40m 6a Climb easily up and left to the bottom of a short black left-facing corner. Climb this and then traverse horizontally left along the lip of a small overhang for 5m. Now launch up the bulging arete to a good rest. Continue up and left to belay among the birds at the prominent horizontal break.
2. 15m 5c Traverse left to gain the upper section of Ray of Light pitch 1. Follow this to belay at the big roof.

The Central Section

Diagrams p376 & p381

The Central Section covers Les Voyageurs to Big Kenneth. In the centre of the face is a flat sheet of rock with tidal ledges and slabs across its entire base. These are exposed at most states of the tide but are often washed during a heavy swell. This wall contains Voyage of Faith on the left and The Silkie to the right. The southern edge of this section of the wall is roughly indicated at the top of the cliff by a prominent raised clump of thrift right on the cliff edge. To the south again is another shallow sea cave formed by a series of roofs arching southwards from The Silkie. Perfectly Normal Paranoia traverses up rightwards through these roofs. The base of the cliff here can be easily traversed at low tides and calm seas into the shallow cave where Big Kenneth starts and further, bigger, roofs cut across the upper part of the wall.

Descent: A 90m abseil from the edge of the cliff just north of the raised clump of Thrift (there may be a cairn), down the line of The Silkie. This gains ledges at the base that lead left towards the right-hand side of the northern section. The most obvious feature here is a short square-cut corner, the start of Voyage of Faith. If the seas are washing the lower ledges, Voyage of Faith can be gained by abseil from a point between the north cairn and this abseil to gain a small ledge at the base of a short square-cut corner 3m above tidal ledges.

7 Les Voyageurs 110m E3 ***
T.Turner, G.Latter, L.Thomas, 2 Jun 1998
A fine line up the wall just right of the arch and crossing Voyage of Faith. Start beneath easy open grooves 5m left of Voyage and 5m right of the end of the ledges.
1. 10m 4b Climb the easy open grooves leftwards to a large ledge at the base of a flake-crack.
2. 30m 5b Follow the obvious flake-crack (shared with Voyage in its upper half) to its top to take a belay on small footledges where Voyage of Faith goes left along the horizontal fault.
3. 25m 5c Climb the wall above, moving rightwards to a groove. Climb the groove to a corner under a horizontal roof. Traverse right to break through the roof on huge holds, then follow a big crack back left to a belay.
4. 30m 5b Step left and round some huge flakes to pull out right at 10m onto the wall at prominent spiky flakes. Continue up the wall to beneath a slim smooth groove (Voyage of Faith crux). Traverse left 5m and climb the wall to the top.

8 The Lobster Man 100m E3 **
A.Cave, C.Waddy, Jun 1998
Climbs a line starting left of Voyage of Faith, crossing it and finishing up a huge flake corner-crack. Start as for Les Voyageurs.
1. 10m 4b Climb up easy grooves leftwards to the large ledge.
2. 40m 5c Climb the wall above the right side of the ledge, right of the obvious flake of Les Voyageurs and cross Voyage of Faith just above its pitch 1 belay. Move right and up after a few metres to pass a conspicuous small shield of quartz to make technical moves up to a belay in the base of a gigantic flake that forms a corner below the headwall (this curves left to form the roofs on Voyage top pitch).
3. 50m 5b Climb the huge flake-corner leftwards to a good rest in a niche. Pull out right on jugs and climb easy ground to the top.

9 Lemmings 95m E3 6a *
S.Crowe, K.Magog, May 2001
A wandering line following parts of The Lobster Man and Voyage of Faith before following close by Les Voyageurs then towards The Hurried Path and pulling through the left side of its roof. Start as for The Lobster Man.
1. 25m 5b Go up the easy groove until a pull right gains the groove of Voyage: follow this to its first belay.
2. 45m 6a Pull out right then trend back left to climb a smooth wall directly above the initial groove. Trend right to gain and follow a groove, then step right to a small ledge below the left end of the large roof. Powerful moves lead through the left edge of the roof. Step right and up to a belay.
3. 30m 5a Directly to the top.

10 Voyage of Faith 120m E3 ****
G.E.Little, K.Howett, 31 May 1993
This outstanding and committing voyage, with stunning exposure, offers intricate and sustained climbing through ground normally associated with much harder grades. Start about 10m right of the left end of the ledges, below a short square-cut corner.
1. 25m 5b Ascend the short square-cut corner to a small ledge at the base of an open groove. Climb the groove then pull out left to belay on a small ledge.
2. 30m 5b Move out left from the ledge then follow a line of flakes trending left until a vertical flake-crack leads to an obvious horizontal fault. Hand-traverse left along the fault then move up to a very exposed belay on a small nose of rock at the base of a slight corner (this whole area is undercut by a sea cave).
3. 30m 5b Climb the corner to a small ledge, then traverse a 2m left to a short parallel groove. Ascend this then step left and slightly down to a very narrow ledge. Follow this leftwards until the overlap can be bypassed giving access to a traverse line back right above the overlap. Belay at blunt rock spikes adjacent to an obvious break in the main band of overhangs.
4. 35m 5c Traverse out right through the overhangs (lower line) then climb directly up on steep rock via a groove to the base of a short hanging corner. Climb this with difficulty and thence to the top.

11 The Hurried Path 115m E3 ***
K.Howett, H.Harris, 29 May 1998
A fairly direct line up the wall right of Voyage of Faith, taking the steepest part of the central wall and the biggest section of the capping roof. Start at the left edge of an open-book bay in the centre of the wall between Voyage of Faith and Sula.
1. 45m 5b Gain, then follow, the easy left-trending shallow groove and where it fades climb a crack in a rib to below an overlap. Step left under the overlap and enter a quartz niche on its immediate left. Exit right and climb up to gain an obvious fat flake in the steeper wall above. Belay on small footledges at its top.
2. 20m 5b Climb up and slightly right into a small groove leading to horizontal breaks under roofs. These lead rightwards until a step up can be made into a shallow cave under the large overhang. Belay in the right side of the cave.
3. 50m 5c Pull directly through the biggest part of the roof via an obvious quartz flake. Step right and surmount another big bulge above to easier ground. Follow the steep but juggy wall diagonally left to the top.

12 The Silk Route 110m E3 ***
H.Harris, K.Howett, 11 May 1999
Takes a direct line up the blankest looking part of the centre of the wall. Start in the open-book bay.
1. 20m 5b Climb the slim groove in the right wall of the bay and pull onto the wall above. Climb up into a small left-facing groove and exit right to gain the base of an obvious short fat flake and belay.
2. 35m 5c Go up the flake then step right into the base of a short corner containing a square block-spike. Pull out the top to a horizontal break and climb up left into a hanging quartz groove (the leftmost of two) and exit this left to gain a small jutting prow with a sloping ledge on top. Climb the wall above the ledge up and right via

small flakes to step left at a small horizontal break. Go up and left to attain a horizontal band of quartz and black diorite under bulges. Belay on a big flake to the left. A superb pitch.

3. 55m 5b Traverse horizontally right along the black band to an obvious big hold (the nose of rock on Sula pitch 2 lies just to the right). Pull up to an undercling flake then up to the big roofs. Pull through direct via a weakness of big flakes (just left of Sula) to the excellent juggy upper overhanging wall leading to the top.

13 Sula 100m E2 ***

T.Turner, G.Latter, L.Thomas, 3 Jun 1998

A great route and the easiest line up the main face, although bold in places. Start just right of the open-book bay of The Silk Route, directly below a distinctive triangular roof at 30m.

1. 30m 5b Climb the slabby wall to the right of the bay diagonally up leftwards towards a short fat flake and junction with The Silk Route. Follow Silk Route into the shallow groove and spike on the right. Exit the horizontal break above rightwards for 1m until it is possible to pull up and right to a good nut belay in a small niche above the apex of the triangular roof.

2. 40m 5b Climb direct out of the niche to small ledges. Climb boldly via small flakes to the left end of an overlap. Pull over and gain an obvious jug in a further larger overlap above. Pull over this to under a distinctive jutting prow of rock and climb round its right side to gain a small ledge on its top. Surmount the roofs above on obvious huge flakes in a wild position to gain the vertical wall above (the flakes to the left are on the Silk Route and the quartz groove of The Silkie is 8m to the right). Climb the wall to a yellow ledge and belay.

3. 30m 5a Climb the steep juggy wall to the top.

Variation: **13a Direct Start 30m E3 5c ****

J.Thacker, G.Stein, Jun 2004

Start at a left-facing groove line between Sula and The Silkie directly below the right end of the triangular roof. Climb up towards the bottom of an open groove, move out right and climb directly to enter a shallow scoop. Move up under the crescent shaped roof (good runners) before moving left and up to the first stance on Sula.

Sula, P1 (E2) Anna Gilyeat (photo Viv Scott)

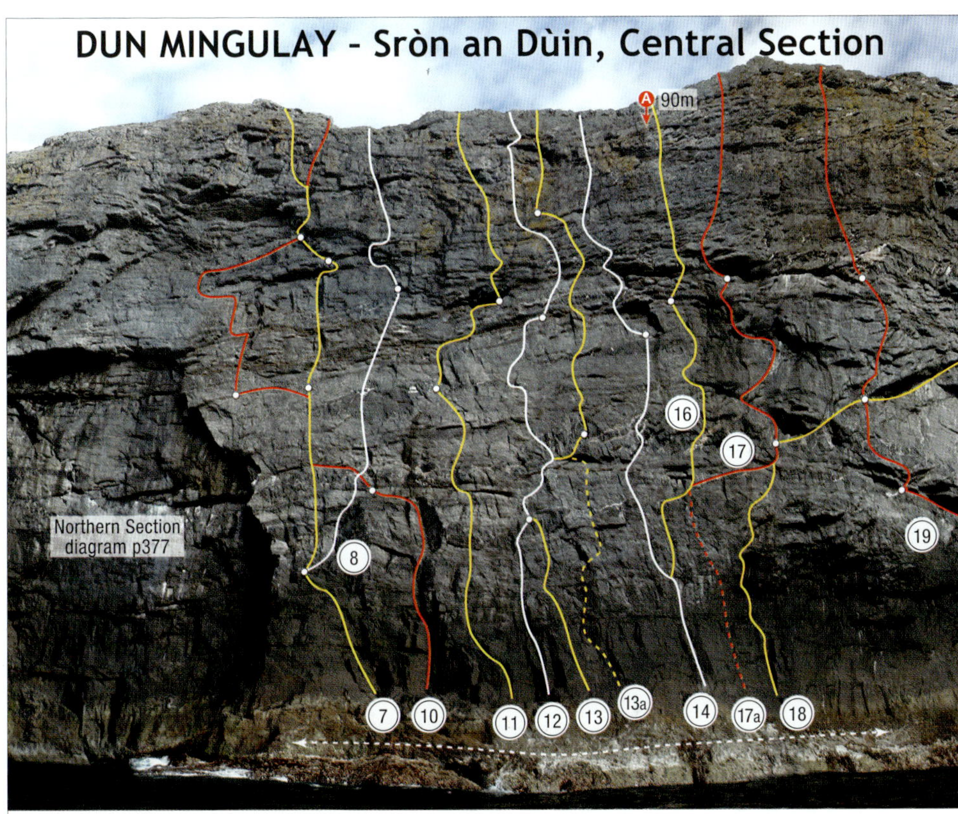

7.	Les Voyageurs	E3 4b, 5b, 5c, 5b ***	14.	The Silkie	E3 6a, 5b, 4a ***
8.	The Lobster Man	E3 4b, 5c, 5b **	16.	Call of the Sea	E3 5c, 5b ****
10.	Voyage of Faith	E3 5b, 5b, 5b, 5c ****	17.	Sirens	E4 5c, 6a, 5b ***
11.	The Hurried Path	E3 5b, 5b, 5c ***	17a.	Last Call	E4 6a
12.	The Silk Route	E3 5b, 5c, 5b ***	18.	Perfectly Normal Paranoia	E6 6b, 5c, 6a, 5b ***
13.	Sula	E2 5b, 5b, 5a ***	19.	Subterranean Exposure	E5 6a, 6b, 5c, 5b **
13a.	Direct Start	E3 5c **			

14 The Silkie 100m E3 ***

G.E.Little, K.Howett, 31 May 1993

The inaugural modern route on the wall (and the Island). Start below a prominent slim groove (containing a small rock plinth a couple of metres above the tidal ledges) in the right side of the central face. An impressive, direct line with intricate climbing on perfect rock.

1. 45m 6a Climb the groove to distinctive red bands. Traverse left along these to a small ledge (possible big sea belay). Climb straight up to below a black diagonal arching overlap and follow it rightwards to below its widest point. Move up then pull through into a small scoop on the left (crux). Step back right across the lip then climb flakes trending left up a wall of compact rock to belay on the right below a square roof. A magnificent pitch!

2. 45m 5b Turn the square roof on the left then take a quartz corner breaking out right through a second roof. Step left onto the lip then go directly up a juggy wall to another small roof. Cross this to gain a cracked block ledge. Ascend slightly rightwards to reach a better ledge and belay.

3. 10m 4a Climb steep but easier ground to the top.

15 Ribbed For Her Pleasure 100m E3

G.Farquhar, N.Craine, 1998

A line based around The Silkie. Start as for that route.

1. 20m 5a Climb the first part of Call of the Sea to the recess under the isolated roof.

2. 25m 6a Climb up and left until under The Silkie's crux roof and follow this route to the break and belay under the big roof.

3. 55m 5b The Silkie goes left around the roof, finish right through the roof and the wall above to the top.

16 Call of the Sea 100m E3 ****

K.Howett, H.Harris, 14 May 1999

One of the Top 10 routes to do before you die! A direct line between The Silkie and Sirens gives superb and surprising climbing up apparently desperate ground. One of the best single pitches here. Start as for The Silkie.

1. 50m 5c Climb the groove of The Silkie until it fades then step right and climb up to gain an obvious recess under an isolated roof. Move 2m right along a traverse line to below a small but obvious flake in the lip of the bulge above. Pull over and reach quartz underclings under further bulges above. Climb directly over this bulge to gain more underclings under another bulge. Make an undercling move right then go up the middle of the wall above to gain a jug rail under the extreme left end of a large diagonal roof (the extension of Sirens pitch 2 roof). Where the roof recedes, pull over onto the slab above. Climb up into a slight shallow corner then up and left to a belay in a big horizontal break, 3m below roofs.
2. 50m 5b Climb direct through the roofs above via the left end of the block roof of Sirens (which climbs through via the obvious flake to the right) then continue direct to the top.

Call of the Sea, P2 (E3) Charlie Woodburn
(photo Dave Pickford)

17 Sirens 115m E4 ***
H.Harris, K.Howett, 28 May 1998
An impressive line weaving between the roofs above Perfectly Normal Paranoia. Start as for The Silkie and Call of the Sea.
1. 40m 5c Follow Call of the Sea to the recess under the isolated roof. Take the traverse line rightwards with continual interest to gain a distinctive projecting block. Belay just above, below a roof (junction with Paranoia).
2. 25m 6a Follow the crack below the roof leftwards to pull rightwards through the slight break with difficulty. Follow flakes up and right to beneath a further roof and traverse left under it into a small corner which leads to a good ledge under another bigger roof on the right.
3. 50m 5b Pull through the left side of the roof via a spectacular flake. Follow the jug rich wall to the top.
Variation: **17a Last Call 35m E4 6a**
D.Towse, G.Huxter, May 1999
A logical alternative start which climbs a vertical crack to the left of the first pitch of Perfectly Normal Paranoia to gain the traverse line on the original route.

Descent: The following climbs are accessed from the central abseil down The Silkie and walking southwards into a shallow sea cave where Big Kenneth starts.

18 Perfectly Normal Paranoia 105m E6 ***
P.Thorburn, R.Campbell, 30 May 1997
This route takes a diagonal line across the roofed wall above the shallow sea cave, with a worrying first pitch. Start 10m right of The Silkie to belay below a left-facing blocky groove.
1. 25m 6b Climb the groove through the square recess in the left-hand side of the lower roof, then make increasingly difficult moves right until a shallow groove can be followed to reach a projecting block ledge. Belay under the roof above. A very serious pitch.
2. 15m 5c Traverse right under the roof, rising slightly, to a semi-hanging stance at the start of a left to right diagonal roof with undercuts.
3. 25m 6a Follow the undercuts to the obvious fault in the roof, pull through this and continue to a shake out. Climb rightwards up the wall then left under the roof to an uncomfortable belay in slanting breaks under the main weakness.
4. 40m 5b Pull through the weakness then climb directly to the top; sustained.

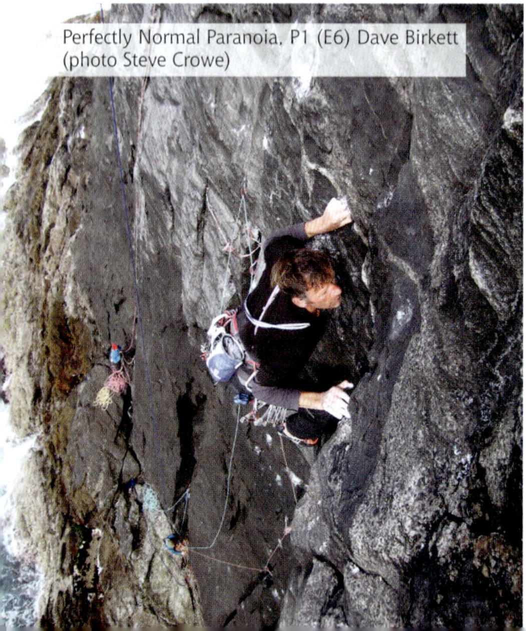

Perfectly Normal Paranoia, P1 (E6) Dave Birkett (photo Steve Crowe)

19 Subterranean Exposure 115m E5 **
G.Lennox, R.Campbell, 14 May 1999
Climbs out the left side of the shallow cave of Big Kenneth as a counter diagonal through the roofed area of Perfectly Normal Paranoia, employing some traditional Victorian climbing techniques. Start from the extreme right end of the ledges about 10m right of Paranoia at the base of a pillar in the left side of the shallow cave.
1. 30m 6a Climb a flake in an open corner on the left side of the pillar to undercuts leading rightwards under bulging rock. Step round the pillar and climb up to a break. Follow the break right past a belly-crawl ledge until it is possible to climb through the roof and follow a groove-flake to belay in a chimney.
2. 15m 6b Wriggle up through the chimney and follow the continuation break leftwards past a hard section to ledges.
3. 25m 5c Pull up rightwards through the roof above and move back up left to gain the base of a line of right-trending undercut flakes above the diagonal roof of Perfectly Normal Paranoia. Follow these to a ledge up on the left. A spectacular pitch.
4. 45m 5b Climb direct through a huge flake-roof and follow the hardest line to the top.

20 Big Kenneth 90m E5 ****
C.Waddy, A.Cave, Jun 1998
One of the best routes on the wall. Climbs a line out of the back right side of the shallow cave, joining and crossing Rory Rum to finish up a hanging crack in the huge upper roof. Start by climbing easily round the back of the cave to a belay at the base of a rightward-facing corner.
1. 25m 6a Climb the corner for a few metres to the base of a roof. Undercut rightwards, initially on big holds (often wet). At the end swing out strenuously right to a big jug, then trend up and slightly right to belay below the second roof.
2. 20m 6a Move up right and then back left to a horizontal break below the roof (junction with Rory Rum). Pull over the roof, then make interesting moves left and then climb up to belay below the crack in the biggest roof.
3. 45m 6a Layback and jam the overhanging crack on big holds until forced out right, making a long reach in a stunning position to a positive pocket. Easier to the top.
Variation: **20a Little K E5 6a ****
S.Crowe, K.Magog
Miss out the wet underclings in the lower roof by stepping down, traversing right and down until it is possible to pull round into a groove leading back to the roof.

Big Kenneth, P2 (E5) Blair Fyffe & Rick Campbell (photo Neil Carnegie)

The Southern Section

Diagrams opposite & p388

Beyond the Big Kenneth cave the wall drops steeply into the sea and there are no ledges below the routes. It is usually impossible to traverse below this area except in low spring tides and calm seas. Rory Rum climbs into the upper roofs from the south, starting 8m above sea-level. Dun Moaning and A Few Fathoms More lie on the vertical wall to the south again.

Descent: A wide ledge runs just below the top of the cliff here. This can be gained by a short scramble from the south. An 80m abseil from the ledge gains hanging stances. A couple of different abseil points gain different groups of climbs. For the next routes, abseil from a recess near the northern termination of the ledge, about 10m north of a cairn marking Fifteen Fathoms of Fear.

21 Rory Rum the Story Man 100m E5 ***
K.Howett, G.Ridge (2 rests), 26 Jun 1996; R.Campbell, G.Lennox, May 1999
This winds an impressive line with a high angle of dangle through the centre of the wall to the left of Dun Moaning. Start by abseiling into the wall to gain a small quartz ledge just above the lip of the lower water-washed bulge left of Dun Moaning. Belay at the furthest left end of this ledge.
1. 25m 6a Climb a slim leftward diagonal overlap (issuing from the ledge) to its end. Hard moves up a slight rib gain a small ledge above. Follow the thin flake above to below a bulge. Teeter left under it to gain an obvious ledge in the base of a small groove.
2. 30m 6a Climb the groove. Make a hard move up and left to gain good holds under the first roof. Traverse left under the roof with increasing difficulty past a deep horizontal slot when sloping holds lead to a jug. Pull directly through the roof above by a large projecting hold and take a hanging stance just over the lip.
3. 15m 6a Climb directly through the roof above into a curious hole. This is near the left-hand side of the second and biggest roof on this section of the wall. Take a belay on the big ledge above. (Pitches 2 and 3 can be led in one, but beware of rope drag).
4. 30m 5a Traverse right for 5m and follow easy ground to the top.

22 Dun Moaning 75m E2 **
K.Howett, G.E.Little, 1 Jun 1995
The first route to breach this impressive area climbs a line skirting the right side of the huge roofs of Rory Rum and Big Kenneth starting from a belay on a ledge in an alcove at seaweed level about 5m right of Rory Rum; low tide desirable!
1. 25m 5b Climb up and rightwards on the initial black wall then trend leftwards into a triangular niche. Exit this and climb to a ledge on the left under a bulge.
2. 25m 5b Climb the short corner on the left of the bulge with difficulty then step back right above it to gain a groove line heading up leftwards to the right side of the huge upper roofs. Belay below the roof at a tiny ledge.
3. 25m 5b Move up to the roof, pull left over it to gain a hanging corner which leads up to the upper larger roof. Traverse right below it to pull over its right edge at an obvious hanging groove. Ascend a black wall on the left to finish at the abseil ledge.
Variation: **22a Direct 30m E4 6a ****
K.Howett, G.E.Little, 1997
Follow pitch 3 to the upper roof. Traverse left under the roof until it fades and climb the wall to the top.

23 Where's Rory? 75m E3 5c **
P.Thorburn, R.Campbell, May 1997
A variation on Dun Moaning, climbed when mistaken for Rory Rum.
1. 30m 5b Follow Dun Moaning pitch 1 to a belay a little higher.
2. 20m 5b Climb direct instead of going right, to gain the normal stance on a tiny ledge beside the big roof.
3. 25m 5c Gain the hanging corner as for Dun Moaning to below the huge roof. Pull direct over it going slightly left and right over the lip. Easily to the top.

24 Dunne Slimmin' 70m E2 ***
R.Kirby, P.Tanton, 7 Jun 2000
Climbs through smaller upper roofs right of those of Dun Moaning. Start as for Dun Moaning in the alcove.
1. 25m 5b Follow Dun Moaning over the bulge and left until about 5m from the first belay of Dun Moaning. Move up and right to a ledge and belay.
2. 45m 5b Move left up an obvious right-facing groove to a very obvious break about 5m below roofs. Traverse right for 8m until below the right-hand side of the roofs. Climb steeply up a crack to a large thread and pull left over the roof (Dun Moaning's upper roof is about 7m up and left). Climb direct to the abseil point.

25 Done Mingulay 70m E2 **
A.Cunningham, G.Nicoll, 1 Jun 1995
Belay on the ledge in an alcove at seaweed level; low tide desirable!
1. 50m 5b Climb up and rightwards on the initial black wall then trend leftwards into an obvious groove line heading for a small prominent roof (well right of the bigger ones). From the top of the groove climb right into a flake-crack leading to the roof. Pull rightwards through the right end of the roof and into a corner leading to belay ledges.
2. 20m 4a Climb straight up a right-facing flake-crack to the top.

Descent: The following routes are accessed by an abseil from about the centre point of the wide cliff-top ledge, at a cairn 5m north of some boulders.

26 Yob and Yag Go Climbing Part 3 50m E1 **
A.McSherry, M.Howard, Aug 1998
Start on tidal ledges at the undercut base of the wall below the starting ledge of Fifteen Fathoms of Fear.
1. 25m 5a Climb through the bulging wall by the obvious break to join Fifteen Fathoms belay. Climb to a good flake up left then traverse left 3m to enter a groove. Climb this to a belay.

18.	Perfectly Normal Paranoia	E6 6b, 5c, 6a 5b ***	22.	Dun Moaning	E2 5b, 5b, 5b **
19.	Subterranean Exposure	E5 6a, 6b, 5c, 5b **	22a.	Dun Moaning Direct	E4 6a **
20.	Big Kenneth	E5 6a, 6a, 6a ****	23.	Where's Rory?	E3 5b, 5b, 5c **
20a.	Little K	E5 6a **	24.	Dunne Slimmin'	E2 5b, 5b ***
21.	Rory Rum the Story Man	E5 6a, 6a, 6a, 5a ***	25.	Done Mingulay	E2 5b, 4a **

2. 25m 5b Traverse left for 3m to a wide crack in a slim corner and finish up this.

Variation: **26a Direct 25m E1 5b ****
H.Bonner, T.Cottam, Aug 1998
Keep traversing left from the wide crack on the final pitch to a crack in a slight arete and finish up this.

27 Fifteen Fathoms of Fear 50m S 4a ****
G.Nicoll, A.Cunningham, 1 Jun 1995
An awesome excursion for the grade; the abseil in is probably harder than the route! Belay on a small ledge above the undercut base of the wall. Climb up leftwards into a vague corner-crack, the rightmost of several, then continue straight up keeping well left of a large horizontal break (holding a colony of guillemots) and the long roof above it. An open depression in the wall above leads to a steeper finish at the abseil point.

28 Storm Warning 60m E2 *
R.Austin, R.Durran, G.Latter, 17 Aug 2004
Start on tidal ledges at the undercut base of the wall at the base of an obvious flake-crack in a black bulge, to the right of Yob and Yag...
1. 30m 5c Climb the black flake to the ledge of Fifteen Fathoms, move up to another curving flake and climb it to gain short twin cracks leading with difficulty to a good ledge.
2. 30m 4c Trend leftwards to finish as for Fifteen Fathoms of Fear.

Variation: **28a Direct Finish 40m VS 4b**
M.Edmonds, G.Stein, J.Thacker, 3 Jun 2008
Follow a direct line, trending rightwards through steep but steady terrain to the top.

29 A Few Fathoms More 50m VS **
G.E.Little, K.Pyke, 27 Jun 1996
Some very impressive situations for a VS! Abseil to the belay ledge of Fifteen Fathoms of Fear above the undercut base of the wall.
1. 30m 4c Climb up and slightly right to another ledge. Ascend a flake-crack on the right then go straight up until a few metres below a wide slot rising above the horizontal break (colony of guillemots). Make a short left traverse (crux) then up to belay on the horizontal fault (just left of the birds).
2. 20m 4c Climb a groove immediately left of the wide slot, step right then climb directly through bulges to finish.

Girdle Traverses of Sròn an Dùin:

30 Oceanside Expedition 200m E4 **
S.Crowe, K.Magog, 21 May 2001
A diagonal expedition across the left-hand side of Sròn an Dùin, which perversely starts by trending up and right, by starting up Sirens.
1. 40m 5c Climb Sirens to belay in the niche.
2. 50m 5b Follow the handrail of jugs leftwards underneath the diagonal roof into Call of the Sea and pull over at the left end onto the slab. Climb up and left to reach the prominent left-facing corner of the Silkie.

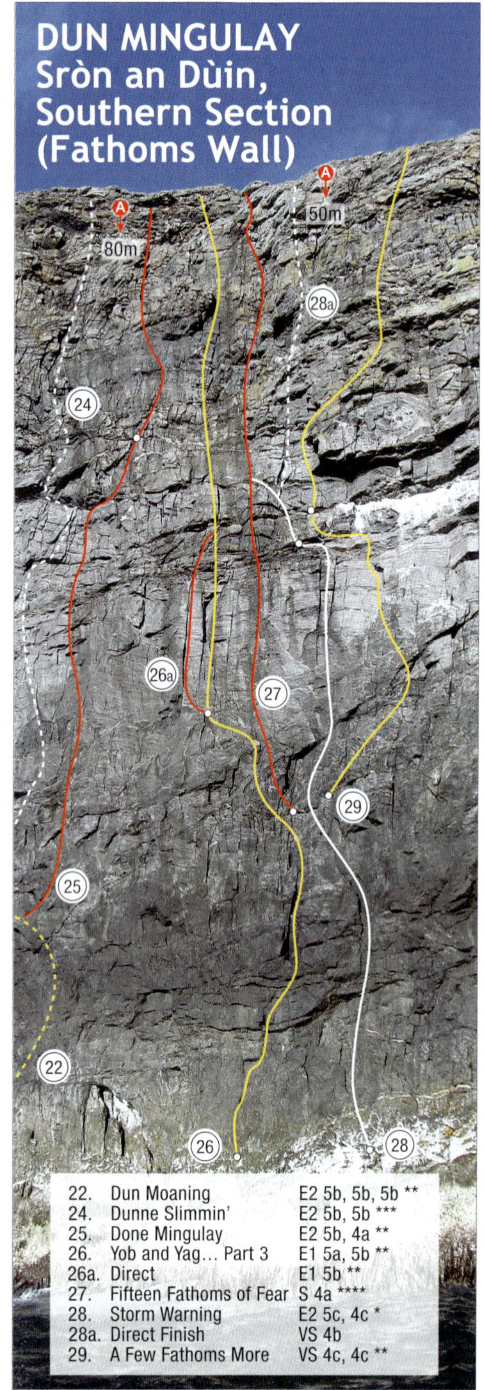

Fifteen Fathoms of Fear (S) Steve Bowker
(photo Mike Hutton)

Follow good holds left to move up as for Sula to gain a traverse line of good holds about 2m below the roof system. Follow these left to belay below the roof as for Hurried Path.
3. 50m 5c Continue left for about 5m until it is possible to step down 3m to a lower break. This eventually leads to Voyage of Faith. Follow this up and left to belay on a small ledge at the point where Voyage of Faith leads back right
4. 30m 5c Step right then climb up to beneath the top roof where a good break leads leftwards through the hanging roofs in a spectacular position to join Perfect Monsters. Belay in a small niche above the roof.
5. 20m 5a The upper wall as for Perfect Monsters.

31 The Swell 210m E4 *
D.O'Sullivan, R.Cowie, T.Marsh, 5 Jun 2008
A right to left girdle of Sròn An Dùin. For the most part it follows the obvious fault-line across the whole cliff which marks the boundary between the smooth lower wall and the more broken upper wall. An amazing adventure!
1. 40m 5c Start up Dun Moaning and follow this until level with the big roof of Big Kenneth. Traverse left around an arete then traverse under the roof to belay at a slot just beyond where Big Ken breaches the roof.
2. 30m 6a Follow the fault strenuously left (passing Rory Rum) to an arete and then easily for another 20m.
3. 30m 4c Cruise the juggy fault-line to belay above the plinth of Silkie.
4. 40m 5b Continue easily left for 20m and then descend a few metres to a lower break. This leads left past an orange shield to a comfortable belay on the edge of the huge arch (the Ray of Light belay below the tusk).
5. 40m 5c Take a diagonal line up and left to gain the break under the huge roof. Traverse easily left for 7m and belay on Perfect Monsters.
6. 30m 5c An exposed traverse left on the lip of the roof gains a small ledge. Finish direct.

Time Out Buttress

(NL 543 819) Non-tidal E facing Map p351

Located on the top of Dun Mingulay, 200m east of the abseil point for Fifteen Fathoms of Fear are two large and rather precarious buttresses, both split by left-facing corners. They provide an alternative when wind prevents climbing on the main cliff. Time Out Buttress is the lower of the two.

De-institutionalisation 25m HVS 5a
R.Jones, A.Dow, 2001
Surprisingly solid climbing. Climb the left-facing corner which ends at mid-height with a roof. Step right and after 2m, traverse left above the roofed corner. Pull through on large jugs. Step right and climb the right-facing corner to the top.

Roraimer

(NL 548 824) Tidal W facing

The area of rock in the back of the area between Dun Mingulay and the natural arch of Gunamul. The walls are black and can be seen easily from the neck of land attaching Dun Mingulay to the mainland. The single climb lies on the large cliff just north of this neck and south of the arch. Abseil 90m down walls and corners starting 40m north of the neck to gain a damp niche well above the sea.

The Dark Half 90m E1
D.Barlow, P.Donnithorn, 4 Aug 2000
An atmospheric route!
1. 35m 5a Climb the corner to a ledge of the right.
2. 30m 5a Move left and follow another corner to a ledge on the right.
3. 25m 5a From the top of the ledge, climb directly to a grass terrace. Finish up a short overhung corner.

ARNAMUL WALL

(NL 548 827) Non-tidal W facing Map p351 Diagram opposite

This, the long wall opposite the Arnamul Stack **(NL 545 826)**, is only really visible from near Dun Mingulay. A huge platform runs below the cliff about 15m above the water which rarely gets washed, although in big seas a spectacular waterspout forms. The wall is generally vertical, has a ledge system cutting the entire length at mid-height and with the better rock towards the point, to the left of the abseil line.

The first feature left of the abseil is a slight pillar with a large left-facing corner, curving left to form a roof in the lower half of the wall. Left again, the most obvious feature lies above this halfway ledge, a clean-cut corner containing a roof. To the left of this, towards the left end a prominent overhanging buttress is formed by groove-corner systems on either side, the main buttress, the right-hand corner being Lament to the Abyss. Most of the routes are concentrated around this section of the cliff and the main buttress, but the first batch are located around the abseil line and to its right.

Descent: Abseil off the promontory from a large block about mid-way along the wall.

1 Friends with the Arnamuls 85m VS *
E.Quinn, D.Carden, 28 May 2013
Climbs a conspicuous crack system 5m right of a narrowing of the platform at the right end of the wall.
1. 25m 4c Climb a left-leaning crack to a roof, just to the right of a large hanging shield of rock at 15m. Swing up and left onto the shield and take a belay above and slightly right on a ledge beside a prominent hole.
2. 25m 4b Climb the steep juggy wall above and trend slightly leftwards to a belay beneath a square-cut corner.
3. 35m 4b Near the foot of the corner, step right and finish direct up broken ground.

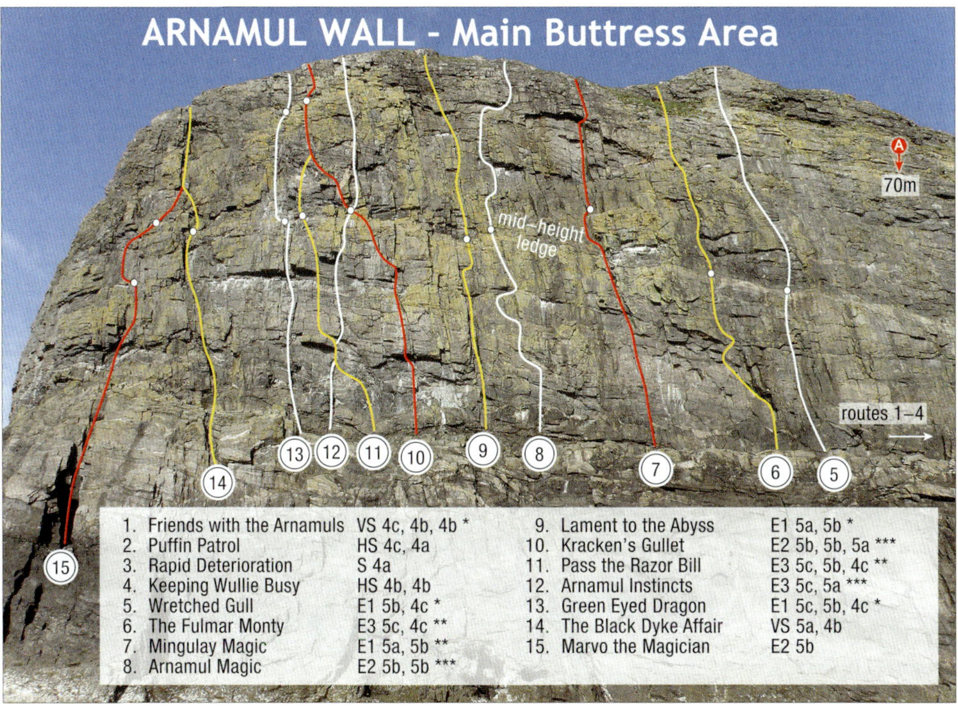

2 Puffin Patrol 75m HS
I.Hall, M.Snook, 4 Jun 2001
Start 10m right of the abseil line at a shallow quartz groove.
1. 25m 4c Ascend the groove, moving left to gain a crack and small chockstone. Move past the chockstone (crux) and continue easily to belay at the top of a right-slanting ledge.
2. 35m 4a Turn a small overhang above on the left and step back right to a ledge. Climb the steep wall above on superb holds to belay on a large ledge.
3. 15m Traverse left along this ledge until a rib of good rock can be followed to the abseil block.

3 Rapid Deterioration 75m S 4a
C.Mortimer, A.Dow, 3 Jun 2001
Climb the nice crack about 4m right of Keeping Wullie Busy. After 20m the crack deteriorates. Follow the most solid line to the top.

4 Keeping Wullie Busy 75m HS
A.Callum, I.Hall, 3 Jun 2001
Start 10m left of the abseil line, just right of a twin crack system.
1. 25m 4b Climb up and left on good jugs to reach the right-hand of the twin cracks. Follow this for 20m to belay on a large ledge.
2. 25m 4b Move up right of a downward-pointing flake. Step delicately right on a slabby wall to gain a groove and good holds. Continue for 20m to belay in a recess on a large ledge.
3. 25m Climb directly out of the recess. Traverse right on a vegetated ledge to avoid a fulmar colony before moving up to belay at the abseil block.

The following climbs start 20m left of the abseil towards the main buttress.

5 The Wretched Gull 75m E1 *
K.Magog, S.Crowe, 27 May 2000
Start just right of the left-facing corner on the right edge of a slight pillar.
1. 30m 5b Follow cracks over roofs up the face of the pillar to belay on a good ledge.
2. 45m 4c Continue directly above to a large ledge just below the top. Escape left into a grass bay, or continue direct to the top.

6 The Fulmar Monty 75m E3 **
M.Davies, G.E.Little, 28 May 1998
Climbs the curving corner system bounding the left side of the slight pillar.
1. 30m 5c Climb up the corner towards stepped roofs and a small ledge. Move up and right, then break back left, then straight up to belay on a good ledge.
2. 45m 4c Take a direct line up the slightly vegetated wall on good holds to belay well back.

7 Mingulay Magic 75m E1 **
M.Davies, G.E.Little, 27 May 1998
This climbs up to and through the conspicuous clean-cut

corner in the upper wall. Start below a break in bulging rock about 15m left of The Fulmar Monty.
1. 45m 5a Climb the lower wall into a short corner and through the mid-way break, then go directly up to a large ledge below roofs.
2. 30m 5b Climb the big corner to below the main roof then move right to an exposed edge. Climb straight up to finish. A brilliant pitch!

8 Arnamul Magic 80m E2 ***
H.Harris, L.Beck, 26 May 2000
This tackles the wall immediately right of the corner-line of Lament to the Abyss. Start 6m right of that route, just right of a quartz patch at ledge level and below a porthole at 4m. An excellent sustained route.
1. 35m 5b Climb past the porthole to reach good holds trending up and left. Follow them to a position well below, but in line with, a left-facing corner-slot. Head straight up to this feature, then left and back right to pass it, to gain a good ledge. Pull directly over the bulge, entering a groove that leads to roomy ledges.
2. 45m 5b Climb the short corner behind the belay. At its end, move right to a crack leading to the left end of the roof. Pull leftwards round the roof to enter a steep crack-line which is followed straight up on jugs and then slightly rightwards to the right end of the thin roof above. Turn this to the right and follow the groove and wall to the top.

9 Lament to the Abyss 75m E1 *
S.Muir, A.Cunningham, F.Fotheringham, 27 Jun 1996
This route roughly follows the groove-corner systems forming the right side of the main buttress.
1. 35m 5a Climb steeply into the right-facing corner and follow this line to the base of a detached pillar. Move right and up cracks to reach the middle ledge.
2. 40m 5b Climb the crack directly above the belay into a right-facing corner, over overlaps, to the top in a fine exposed position.

10 Kraken's Gullet 85m E2 ***
K.Howett, T.Catterall, 25 May 2000
Climbs the right-hand groove line through the roofs in the centre of the Main Buttress. Easier than it looks and spectacular on the second pitch.
1. 40m 5b Climb an overhanging arete to the roof. Pull left into the hanging left-facing corner above the roof and follow it and a short wall to a small ledge. Climb the steep wall above by a thin vertical crack just on the left to a belay on the mid-way ledge.
2. 35m 5b Step left round a nose of rock and climb diagonally left across the steep, sensational upper wall to the left edge. Enter a final easy corner leading to a big ledge.
3. 10m 5a Climb direct up the wall off the left end of the ledge (5m left of the central corner) to finish up a clean grey buttress via a vertical slot.

11 Pass the Razor Bill 85m E3 **
K.Magog, S.Crowe, 27 May 2000
Climbs a line across the lower roofs around Arnamul Instincts. Start just left of Kraken's Gullet.
1. 40m 5c Follow the left-trending break under the roofs to join Arnamul Instincts. Pull through as for that route, then step left onto the lip of the roof. Moves up lead to a corner-flake above. Continue past a small ledge to the big mid-way ledge.
2. 35m 5b Continue more or less direct to a large ledge below the top.
3. 10m 4c Finish direct.

12 Arnamul Instincts 85m E3 ***
K.Howett, H.Harris 28.05.98
Climbs the main left-hand line in the centre of the Main Buttress below a prominent double roof, just left of Kraken's Gullet.
1. 40m 5c Climb a steep lower wall to a ledge, then a thin crack running vertically to the roof. Pull over into the short right-facing corner below the larger roof. Pull out directly on jugs. Easier climbing leads into a large left-facing corner capped by another roof. Pull out strenuously right and climb more easily to the mid-way ledge.
2. 45m 5a Climb the steep shallow corner above to reach broken ground (care with large poised blocks).

13 The Green Eyed Dragon Slayers 80m E1 *
G.E.Little, M.Davies, 1998
Climbs the fault defining the left side of the Main Buttress with a distinctive wide slot through the roof at 25m. The route name derives from two eye like holes full of stagnant green slime at its base.
1. 40m 5c Gain and climb the fault with strenuous moves through a bulge and surprisingly less demanding climbing through the slot to belay on a good ledge just left of a guano covered ledge.
2. 30m 5b Ascend the green corner above for a few metres until a swing out right gives access to a hanging rib. Climb this, in an exposed situation, to reach a wide ledge.
3. 10m 4c Climb straight up to finish.

14 The Black Dyke Affair 70m VS
G.E.Little, M.Davies, 28 May 1998
This obvious left-trending diagonal fault lies to the left of the Main Buttress where the ledge along the base begins to fade.
1. 45m 5a Climb the fault with interest until a section of black dyke gives awkward moves and access onto a wide sloping ledge on the right.
2. 25m 4b The flared chimney above holds some dubious blocks so step across to the left side and ascend a steep wall on good jugs to finish.

15 Marvo the Magician 90m E2
D.Godfrey, K.Clarke, 17 Sep 1998
Start at an obvious black niche at a lower level, beyond the end of the ledge.
1. 35m Climb the groove until it bends left, and then break out right onto the steep slab. Trend rightwards to a niche, climb this to a stance.
2. 15m 5b Traverse left and climb a crack with a hard move low down. Trend rightwards to a good stance.
3. 40m Climb the superb crack-corner system on positive holds and good jams to finish over a shattered band above.

THE NORTH-WESTERN CLIFFS

These are the cliffs concentrated around the headlands to the extreme north-west from the gap, where the geo of Bàgh na h-Aoineig cuts deeply into the west side of the island, directly over from Bàgh Mhiùghlaigh on the east. The top of the mighty Biulacraig (Bual na Creige), sitting above Bàgh na h-Aoineig, can just be glimpsed from Bàgh Mhiùghlaigh. The cliffs are on the west side of the small hill of Tom a'Mhaide overlooking Lianamul Stack and on the Guarsay Mòr and Guarsay Beag promontories. The cliffs are consistently higher than those to the south and they include some of the best middle grade climbs on the island.

Approach: From the flat grass behind the old village in Bàgh Mhiùghlaigh a path follows the stream, initially on its left bank then on its right, to reach the gap overlooking The Biulacraig. The summit of Tom a' Mhaide is just to the north and is a bonxie nesting site, and is best avoided. To gain the Lianamul Slabs contour round the south side. To gain Guarsay Mòr and Guarsay Beag, break off the main path just after crossing the stream and head for a slight col on the right skyline. A path descends around the side of Tom a' Mhaide.

The south side of Bàgh na h-Aoineig contains the highest cliff on Mingulay **(NL 542 832)**, the 210m high Biulacraig. This remains unclimbed, probably due to apparent loose rock and grass and it never seeing the sun, feeling very intimidating.

SLOC CHIASIGEO

This is the name for the geo that cuts into the back of the gap between Guarsay Mòr and the stack of Lianamul.

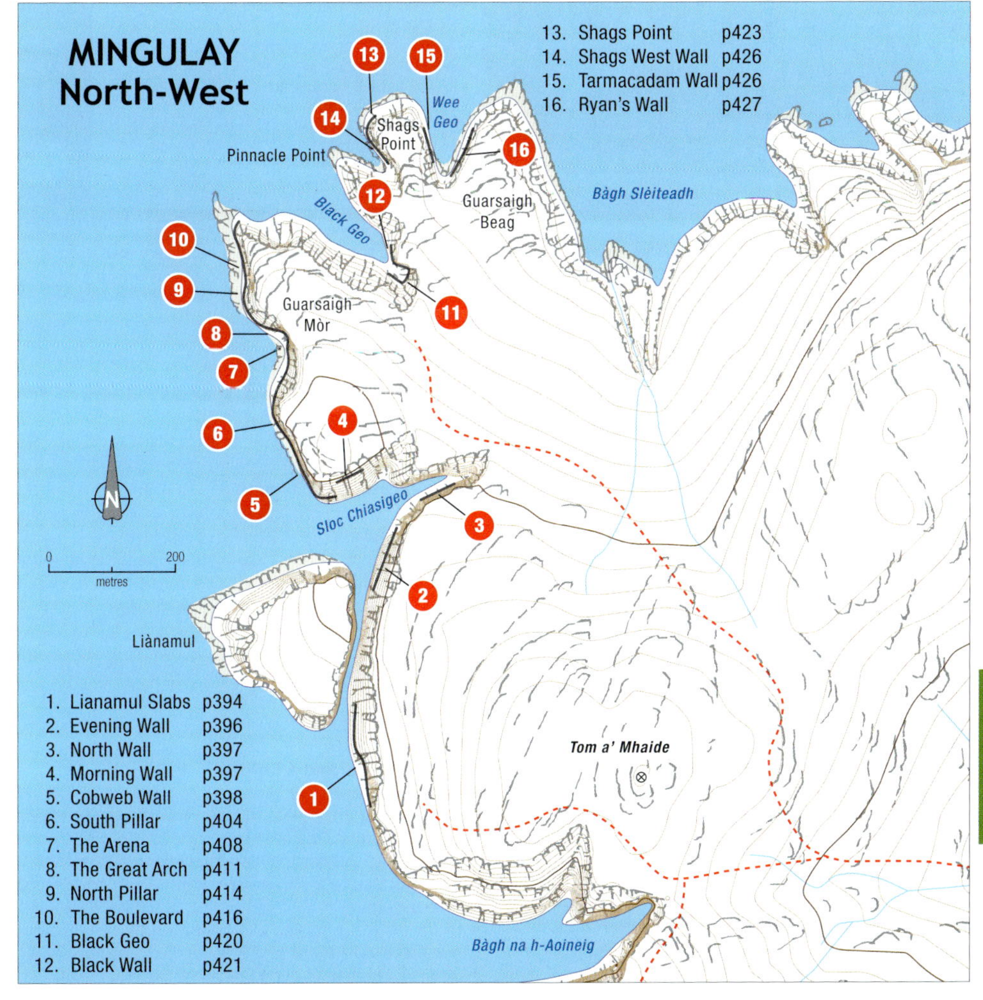

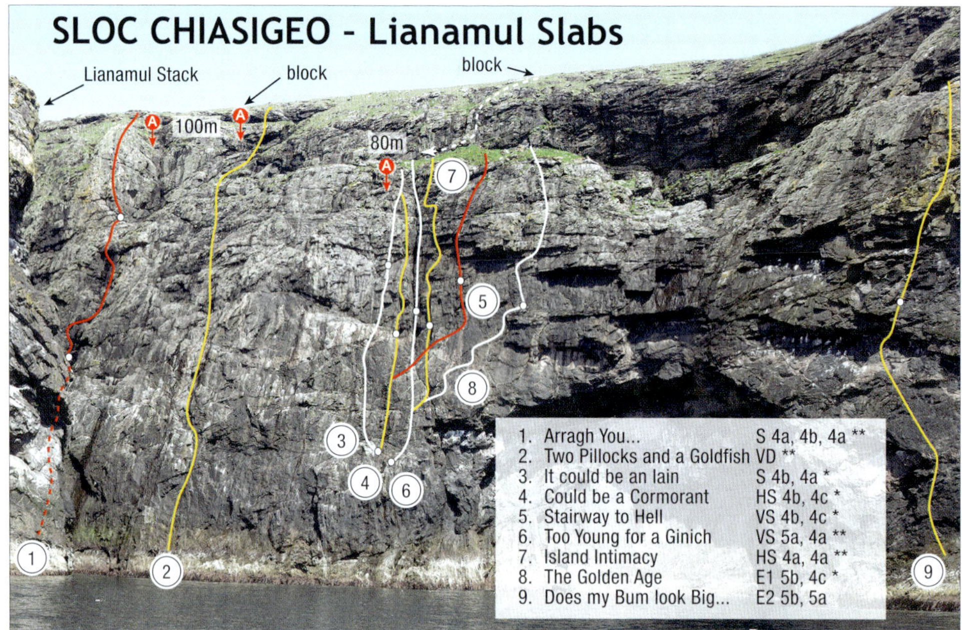

The west-facing wall is a long affair, composed of black rock with many vertical groove lines. It faces the stack and as it goes north it narrows and cuts into the back of the geo. For ease of identification it is split into four sections. Firstly Lianamul Slabs, opposite and nearest to the stack, then Evening Wall, the area of grooves based around a small sea-level cave roughly mid-way between the north end of the stack and the more constricted part of the sloc. Next is the North Wall, right in the back of the sloc facing north and finally Morning Wall, on the south facing wall of the geo, approximately halfway out from the back in a very small indented sub geo.

Lianamul Slabs

(NL 5505 8355) Partially Tidal W facing
Map p393 Diagram above

The west facing slabby wall that faces Lianamul Stack and includes an area dominated by huge roofs forming a multiple arch around a large square-cut cave at the south end. It gives atmospheric routes at surprisingly amenable grades. However, be aware that at some states of the tide and big seas, huge surges rush through the channel, the narrowness of the gap increasing the waves to incredible heights. The routes are spread at intervals along the cliff with different abseil access points. The main concentration is currently just north of the cave around a huge corner and chimney-line (Too Young for a Ginich). This corner lies roughly opposite the southern tip of the stack. To the north lies a large expanse of slabs leading into the gap.

Descent: Abseil from various large blocks that are scattered along the grass slopes above the cliff. It is useful to reference the block opposite the south edge of Lianamul Stack first (indicating the way into Too Young for a Ginich). See individual route descriptions. Routes are described left to right.

1 Arrgh You the Real Jack Sparrow! 110m S **

T.Catterall, K.Summers, 2 Jun 2016

A superb route at the grade. It takes the slabs deep into the constriction. Locate a large broken gully at the top of the cliff about 100m north of Too Young for a Ginich. Abseil to large sloping ledges and traverse left to gain a small triangular ledge 10m above sea-level.

1. 35m 4a Climb a ramp issuing from the left end of the ledge to a bulge. Pull through this in its centre to gain a huge ledge. Belay to the left of a small cave.
2. 30m 4b Climb the bulge above, heading left to follow an obvious crack. Continue over the overhang above and belay at the base of a right-facing corner system.
3. 40m 4a Climb the final corner until it eases. Follow broken ground to the top.

2 Two Pillocks and a Goldfish 110m VD **

G.E.Little, M.Davies, 1998

Climbs a line up the slabs almost opposite the southern tip of Lianamul. Find a large block in the grass slope about 50m to the north of Too Young for a Ginich. Abseil from here to a ledge in a little right-facing corner just above the sea.

1. 45m Move right and climb smooth black rock until moves left can be made to a ledge at the top of the corner. Follow a crack-line above to belay on a small ledge.

2. 45m Climb up to an overhung bay and ascend the steep juggy face above (easier alternatives available) then on up easier-angled rock to a belay.
3. 20m Walk up and right to a grass terrace, then climb a short wall above to finish.

The following batch of routes climb around the corner of Ginich.

Descent: From the block in the grass slope opposite the south end of the stack, descend grass then easy rock (Diff) and a rock ramp leading down an upper tier to a terrace. A large block sits on the terrace below a roof to the right. Abseil from here down slabs to extensive sloping ledges below the chimney-line about 8m above sea-level.

3 It could be an Iain 75m VS *
R.K.Howett, J.Young, 12 Jun 2016
Climbs a series of intermittent roofed corners left of the corner of Cormorant.
1. 45m 4b Gain a right-facing corner above the left end of the ledge, leading to a small ledge. Follow the quartz corner above to another ledge. Step right, enter the clean-cut corner with small roofs in the steeper upper wall and follow this to exit slightly right to ledges.
2. 30m 4a Go up the steep corner above, then easier to gain the terrace by the abseil.

4 Could be a Cormorant 70m HS *
D.Ostler, T.Sweeny, P.Freudenthal, 4 May 2004
Climbs the hanging corner with a big roof just left of the central corner. Start from a belay at the left end of the ledges to the left of Too Young for a Ginich.
1. 30m 4b Off the left end of the ledge about 8m left of the above route, climb the wall up and right easily to a belay below a right-facing corner with a roof.
2. 40m 4c Climb out left of the roof and continue on easy ground to belay at the terrace near the top.

5 Stairway to Hell 75m VS *
R.K.Howett, J.Young, 12 Jun 2016
Takes a natural diagonal line across the base of the central corner with the meat of the route being the impressive inverted staircase corner through the upper roof, right of the corner. Start from a belay at the left end of the ledges, as for Cormorant.
1. 45m 4b Climb the wall as for Could be a Cormorant, to gain a diagonal right-trending break crossing beneath the big chimney, then Too Young for a Ginich and Island Intimacy. Just beyond these, gain and climb a bulging cracked groove above leading to beneath the inverted staircase.
2. 30m 4c Climb into the inverted staircase corner and exit through the roof. Easy slabs to finish.

6 Too Young for a Ginich 70m VS **
R.D.Mackenzie, R.Mackenzie, D.Ostler, 5 May 2004
Climbs the main central corner. Take a belay at the lowest right ledge close to the edge of the wall and below the base of the corner-line.
1. 30m 5a Climb the vertical wall to a large ledge with a roof above, guarding entry to the corner. Take the roof direct into the base of the corner.
2. 30m 4a Climb the corner to the grass terrace.

7 Island Intimacy 70m HS **
P.Calton, K.Howett, M.Morrison, 12 Jun 2016
Climbs a small subsidiary left-facing corner just right of the central corner.
1. 30m 4a From the belay shared with Too Young for a Ginich, climb up into the small corner. Follow it to where it fades into easy ledges. Gain the small continuation corner above and belay.
2. 40m 4a Go up the corner and exit direct to under the upper roofs. Climb past their left end until just below a square ledge on the right. Hand-traverse left along a rail and pull over bulges to easier ground leading to the terrace.

Island Intimacy, P1 (HS) Paul Calton (photo Kevin Howett)

8 The Golden Age 75m E1 *
K.Howett, P.Calton, 12 Jun 2016
An intricate line across blank looking ground. Start from the belay shared with Too Young for a Ginich.
1. 45m 5a Climb up slightly right to the arete overlooking the sea cave under the big roof. Climb up right across the wall to gain a huge golden quartz streak. Find a line across it diagonally rightwards heading to the right arete of the wall just shy of a second roof. Go up the arete and bypass the roof to gain ledges.
2. 30m 4c Climb direct to the upper roof, step right and break through the gap. Easy rock leads more or less direct to the terrace.

The following route is on the south side of the square roofed sea cave and can be viewed from the summit of Biulacraig.

Descent: Find a large triangular block on the lowest grass terrace above the wall. Abseil past roofs to gain a large flake on very sloping ledges 6m above the sea.

9 Does my Bum look Big in this Roof 60m E2 5b
R.D.Mackenzie, R.Mackenzie, T.Sweeny, 7 May 2004
A pleasant route in a stunning situation on the edge of Bagh na h-Aoineig and the towering wall of the Biulacraig, climbing a line just right of the huge square roofed sea cave.
1. 35m 5b Climb up and left to the widest part of the roof and go for it! Easy ground follows to a large ledge and belays.
2. 35m 5a Pad up slabs to the roof above, step over, and continue up the orange slab near an arete to the grass terrace.

Evening Wall

(NL 5510 8380) Tidal NW facing Map p393

This north-west facing wall lies mid-way between the north end of Lianamul stack and the head of the narrow geo. The features of the wall can best be viewed from the top of Guarsay Mòr. The main feature is a sea-level cave containing a flat platform in its right side, which itself contains a rock pool. Above here, the biggest features are two diverging crack and groove systems extending the full height of the wall to form a Y-shape cutting through much steeper rock near the top. Routes are described right to left.

Descent: The least scary descent is to abseil to the south of the area, gaining the slabs overlooking the narrow channel between Mingulay and Lianamul. A scramble northwards leads to the platform with a small pool just above high water. Alternatively, and taking in more big air, abseil from a large block down the line of the right-hand groove system to gain the platform.

Into the Light 135m E1 *
H.Harris, L.Beck, 24 May 2001
Climbs a line parallel to the right branch of the Y-groove systems, right of Liverbird. Start from the foot of the ramp on the first pitch of Liverbird.

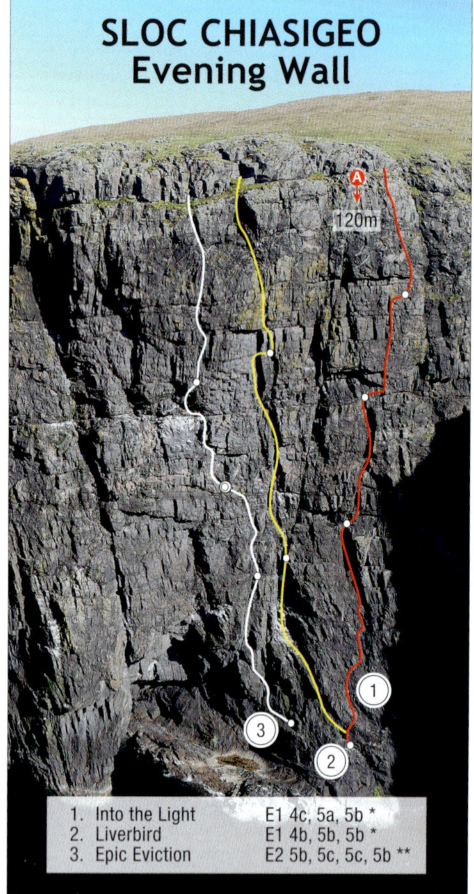

1. 50m 4c From the ramp, move straight up to a flake. Go up this then trend up and right to gain a left-trending groove. Climb this to ledges at its top.
2. 25m 5a Pull out right and go up to a short square-cut groove. Climb it and then go up rightwards to gain a longer groove. This leads to ledges.
3. 30m 5b From the right side of the ledges, climb up to and through the roof above. Climb the wall into a groove and follow this to a slot. Traverse right, avoiding the roofs above, to belay in a large bay.
4. 30m Climb easily up the right side of the bay to the top.

Liverbird 125m E1 *
C.Bonington, M.Fowler, 1 Jun 1993
From the right-hand end of the large platform, it follows a fairly obvious left branch of the Y-groove system.
1. 50m 4b Climb easily up to a ramp then diagonally up the ramp into a steep corner. Climb this to a small ledge.

2. 35m 5b Continue straight up the crack system and at about 20m enter a black overhanging groove. Climb this to a point about 6m below capping overhangs. Step up and pull rightwards round an arete to gain a small stance in a corner.
3. 40m 5b Climb through the overhang above using the left-hand crack and then pull across and round a rib to the right-hand crack, to reach a horizontal break. Move slightly left into a steep, deep-cut groove and follow this on excellent holds to the top.

Epic Eviction 125m E2 **
R.Mackenzie, T.Sweeney, 23 May 2001
Climbs a line to the left of Liverbird. Start as for Liverbird and scramble easily to ledges above the pool cave, belaying in a slot.
1. 40m 5b Rising leftwards, cross the foot of a guano-covered groove. Follow flakes and cracks to a sloping corner belay with a large block.
2. 20m 5c Climb the groove to the left of the pointed block and continue to the foot of a large left-facing corner.
3. 20m 5c Take a committing rising left traverse to gain a feldspar jug and pull through the roof to a good belay on an exposed ledge directly over the cave.
4. 45m 5b Climb the corner directly above and continue on a direct line to the top. Care required for loose rock.

North Wall

(NL 5520 8390) Tidal N facing Map p393

The following routes lie further left into the back of the geo in the left wall, looking out from the back of the geo.

Pot of Gold 55m E1 5b **
A.Cave, C.Waddy, Jun 1998
The most obvious crack system, well seen from opposite. Well protected steep climbing up cracks all the way; awesome!

Freddie Fulmar's Funky Food Franchise 60m HVS
T.Wood, K.Martin, 22 May 2001
Start 50m left of an obvious chimney-groove at the back of the geo, directly opposite a chimney high up on the other side of the geo. Abseil down to a ledge 2m below a square-cut roof.
1. 25m 5a Climb direct back up the corner and over the roof to a large belay ledge.
2. 35m 5a Climb the steep crack at the back of the ledge into a groove which leads to the top.

Morning Wall

(NL 5505 8395) Non-tidal SE facing Map p393

Actually part of Guarsay Mòr, the south facing wall of the geo, approximately halfway out from the back, contains a very small indented sub-geo. To its left (west) is a clean orange wall sitting above some huge ledges about 50m above the sea. The orange wall is bounded on the left by a distinctive black right-facing corner, from where routes are described left to right.

Descent: Abseil to the base of the black corner in the centre of the wall.

Morning Glory 70m E1 *
G.E.Little, K.Howett, K.Pyke, 26 Jun 1996
This route climbs the centre of the wall.
1. 30m 5a Climb up the wall on the right of the black corner via an obvious short but steep crack, then a black wall through bulges heading leftwards to a ledge below the orange wall.
2. 40m 5b Climb the superb orange wall diagonally rightwards to a bulge. Pull through direct and climb the wall above, again slightly rightwards, to the top.

Mourning After 85m E1
H.Hunt, K.Howett, 13 Sep 2001
Climbs the wall directly right of Morning Glory. Start 5m down and right of that route, just left of a shattered raised ledge.
1. 30m 5b Climb to level with the top of the shattered ledge. Step right and up a black cracked wall to gain the centre of a horizontal cave. Struggle up the pure jam crack issuing from the centre of the cave's roof to gain another smaller cave. Pull directly over this to a big ledge and block belay.
2. 55m 5a Climb past the block to a blackened wall. Climb this slightly rightwards into a left-facing groove. At its top, step left through a bulge to gain a ledge. Climb the groove and ramp then step out left and up to gain the base of a curving overlap. Pull out right onto the wall and follow a direct line to the top.

The Knight Before 80m E1
N.Stabbs, H.Harris, 13 Sep 2001
Climbs a direct line up the wall following the distinctive features of a right-facing corner in the centre of the face, then a rightward-leaning arching groove near the top of the wall. Start 10m down and right of Mourning After at an orange patch of rock and a projecting block at 5m.
1. 40m 5a Climb the wall direct, passing between two caves at 35m. Follow a steeper section to a good ledge below the right-facing corner.
2. 40m 5b Climb the corner and then go direct up the wall, passing a pegmatite band to a steep pull into the leaning groove. Go up this, then easy rock to a belay on blocks on a broken ramp.

Treading on Eggshells 25m VS 4c
K.Martin, T.Wood, 24 May 2001
Start at the base of an obvious right-slanting corner at the right-hand end of Morning Wall, gained by descending the obvious block filled gully. Climb the corner.

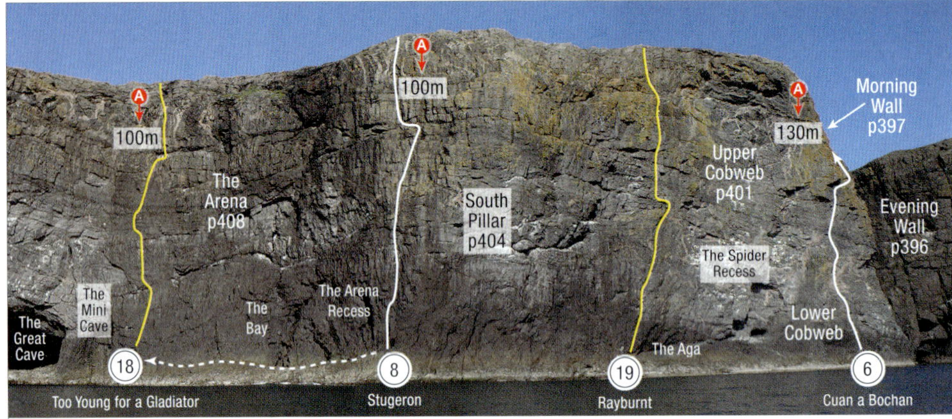

GUARSAY MÒR - The Arena, South Pillar & Cobweb Walls

GUARSAY MÒR

The most north-westerly headland on Mingulay comprises two headlands. Guarsay Mòr (Guarsaigh Mòr) is the highest whilst Guarsay Beag (Guarsaigh Beag), to its north, is lower. From its north-east coastline overlooking Guarsay Beag, Guarsay Mòr rises gently from sea-level to reach its highest point overlooking Lianamul. This south side of Guarsay Mòr forms the north wall of Sloc Chiasigeo. As the wall turns a corner westwards it forms a continuous, awe inspiring 500m long west- facing line of cliff reaching a height of 120m leading to the point of Guarsay Mòr itself. This complex wall has been divided into separate walls based on access, to allow for easier reoute identification. The walls are described from south to north as follows.

Cobweb Wall. The south-east tip of Guarsay Mòr overlooks Lianumul Stack. As the wall turns north from the shelter of Sloc Chiasigeo (and Morning Wall) there is a conspicuous wall with two areas laced with cobwebbed veins of pink rock. They are considered as two parts because of different access, Lower Cobweb Wall is the area of pink veins at sea-level under a couple of big roofs at two-thirds height, and Upper Cobweb Wall is the area full of pink veins much higher up and left beneath large capping roofs at the highest point of the wall. The separation between the two walls is a tall recess (The Spider Recess) formed by a slabby left-facing corner facing a steep roofed corner with a cave in the base. A non-tidal ledge runs leftwards from The Spider Recess and has been nick-named The Aga. The roofs above Lower Cobweb Wall continue towards the upper cobwebs and form the top of the recess.

The South Pillar. Continuing north the wall forms a huge rounded pillar, The South Pillar, before it turns into the next section.

The Arena. This is an almost perfect semi-circular cliff-girt bay.

The Great Arch. In the northern side of The Arena is a square-cut sea cave with a series of huge roofs in the wall above it.

North Pillar. The north end of the bay begins to diminish in height and terminates in The North Pillar whose north side is a deeply incised corner capped by a huge curving roof.

The Boulevard. The curving roof forms the south end of the final section leading to the point itself. Here the nature of the rock becomes more featureless and compact forming a clean 70m high wall.

There are several areas of large bird nesting colonies. Disturbance to these should be avoided in the breeding season. In any case these areas would give unpleasant climbing due to the amounts of guano on all the ledges. Most of the routes described keep a safe distance from these colonies and those that don't are indicated.

Lower Cobweb Wall

(NL 5495 8395) Tidal SW facing Map p393 Diagrams above & p400

The lower of the two Cobweb Walls. It forms a triangular wall at the extreme south-east tip of Guarsay Mòr, as the wall turns into Sloc Chiasigeo and diminishes in height rightwards to under the left section of Morning Wall. The upper left point of the wall is capped by roofs. Further right the wall becomes less steep and lower down its right edge is a further roof. Routes are described right to left.

Descent: Getting to the base is difficult due to the upper roofs, as abseiling directly over the middle of the wall leaves you 10m out to sea. For Salvaged, take an abseil from corners at the top of the cliff, next to a deep horizontal slot, and gain a pink-streaked ledge about 10m above the sea; 120m rope required.

The easiest access to the main left-hand side is by an abseil from large twin blocks, at the extreme south-west tip of the headland (directly opposite a cave on the north side of Lianamul stack). Abseil 50m down easy-angled rock onto a large ledge system. Redirect a further 80m abseil off to the left slightly over the edge of overhangs (mostly free) to gain a belay on a good ledge system at sea-level beneath the bulging pink wall (Cuan a' Bochan belay). Further to the left (north) are The Aga ledges. Traversing in from there is also possible but only with low tide and calm seas.

1 Salvaged 100m VS
R.Mackenzie, T.Sweeney, 15 Sep 2001
From the pink-streaked ledge this climbs a line just round the right side of the edge of the wall, overlooking Sloc Chiasigeo.
1. 45m 5a Climb a steep left-facing corner. Trend left when the angle eases, for about 15m. Then go direct over the lip of a roof and onto a flat black wall. Continue to a grass terrace and belay at the foot of the left corner of a giant yellow flake.
2. 45m 5a Climb direct up the corner to the top of the flake, then continue direct up feldspar to the top.

2 Bill's Yellow Edge 110m HVS **
R.Mackenzie, T.Sweeney, 22 May 2001
Follows the right edge of the wall, right of the cobweb section. From the first abseil ledge, redirect the abseil down the edge of the wall all the way to a large ledge below the lower roof.
1. 35m 5b Climb rounded jugs heading to the roof above and to the left. Exit the roof on the right and follow a rising left traverse above it to gain the foot of the yellow corners.
2. 35m 4c Go up the corners and then trend left to gain a left-rising crack. Follow the shoulder up to the large ledge of the abseil.
3. 40m 5a Keeping to the fine edge above, follow rounded rock past a yellow scoop to the top.

3 Pieces of Eight 135m E1 **
S.Ohly, J.Morgan, 30 May 2003
Start from the same ledge as Cuan a Bochan, below a small overhang.
1. 35m 5b Traverse right for 15m until a good ledge is reached below a distinctive groove with a hand jamming crack going diagonally up and right. Follow this crack to reach a good ledge and belay.
2. 20m 5b From the ledge, follow the groove above to reach a wall, follow this moving slightly right to an obvious spiky hold feature. Continue up to belay under the lower roof.
3. 35m 5b Move diagonally rightwards and clamber through the roof at the right-hand edge (crossing Bill's Yellow Edge). Continue straight up the wall above to a good belay ledge.
4. 35m 5a Continue upwards following yellow rock until reaching the huge ledge system.
5. 30m 4a Climb a groove from the top left of the ledges all the way to the top.

4 Jugs to Blow your Mind 110m E1 **
S.Ohly, J.Morgan, 29 May 2003
Start fas for the previous route, below the small overhang.
1. 30m 5b Traverse right into a groove-come-ramp below a roof, and then go up steeply and over the left-hand side of the lower roof. Move right along the pegmatite band to belay on a ledge below another big roof.
2. 50m 5b Climb through the big roof above and slightly to the right of the belay for 10m. Once the roof is breached, continue more easily for 40m until the huge ledge system is reached.
3. 30m 4a Climb the groove from the top left of the ledges, all the way to the top.

5 Itsy Bitsy Spider 105m HVS ***
G.Latter, C.Pulley, 15 Aug 2004
This tackles a right-trending grey ramp system high up in the right side of the pink-veined wall. Start as for Cuan a Bochan, from a small ledge below a small overhang.
1. 50m 5a Move up to the small overhang, take it on its right-hand side and follow jugs up to a pink bay. Follow bulging rock and a crack on the right-hand side of the pink bay, to an obvious right-rising grey ramp-line. Follow jugs up this to its top.
2. 55m 4c Follow a series of short corner systems and a broken slab to reach the first abseil ledge. Pleasant easy climbing on fragile rock leads to the top.

6 Cuan a Bochan 130m E1 ****
M.Tighe, K.Tighe, J.Cargill, J.McClenaghan, G.Leckie, 2 May 2000
A fantastic route which tackles the pink veined wall and the upper overhangs.
1. 35m 5a From a small ledge below a small overhang, go left for 8m into a recessed groove. Climb this to reach another shallow groove in wonderful pink rock. Go up and slightly left over gently bulging pink and black rock on fabulous jugs and pockets to belay below a small overhang 20m below the main line of roofs.
2. 45m 5b Go up and right under the small overhang, then bulging rock above leading to a break in the large roofs above. Pull through these and climb a pleasant ramp back to the first abseil ledge.
3. 50m 4a Pleasant easy, though fragile, rocks up a slight arete lead to the top.

The next two routes climb Lower Cobweb Wall but are accessed from The Aga ledge. See the Upper Cobweb Wall descent on p401.

7 Bikini Dreams 120m E3 5c **
A.Lole, G.Latter, 10 Jun 2006
Takes a diagonal left to right line across the lower cobwebs. Gain a good ledge in the lower left side of the wall, beneath a short V-slot in a low roof, by a traverse at barnacle level from the The Aga.
1. 40m 5c Climb easily up to good flakes and cross the initial roof on these. Continue directly, then up a fine right-trending pegmatite ramp to a recess.
2. 30m 5c Climb directly up the wall, then trend right on good flakes to an awkward step right into a shallow groove. Step up right onto an exposed ledge, then pull directly through a roof to better holds. Continue more easily up a right-slanting ramp to the abseil ledge.
3. 50m 4a Climb easily up and slightly right, then back left and direct to finish.

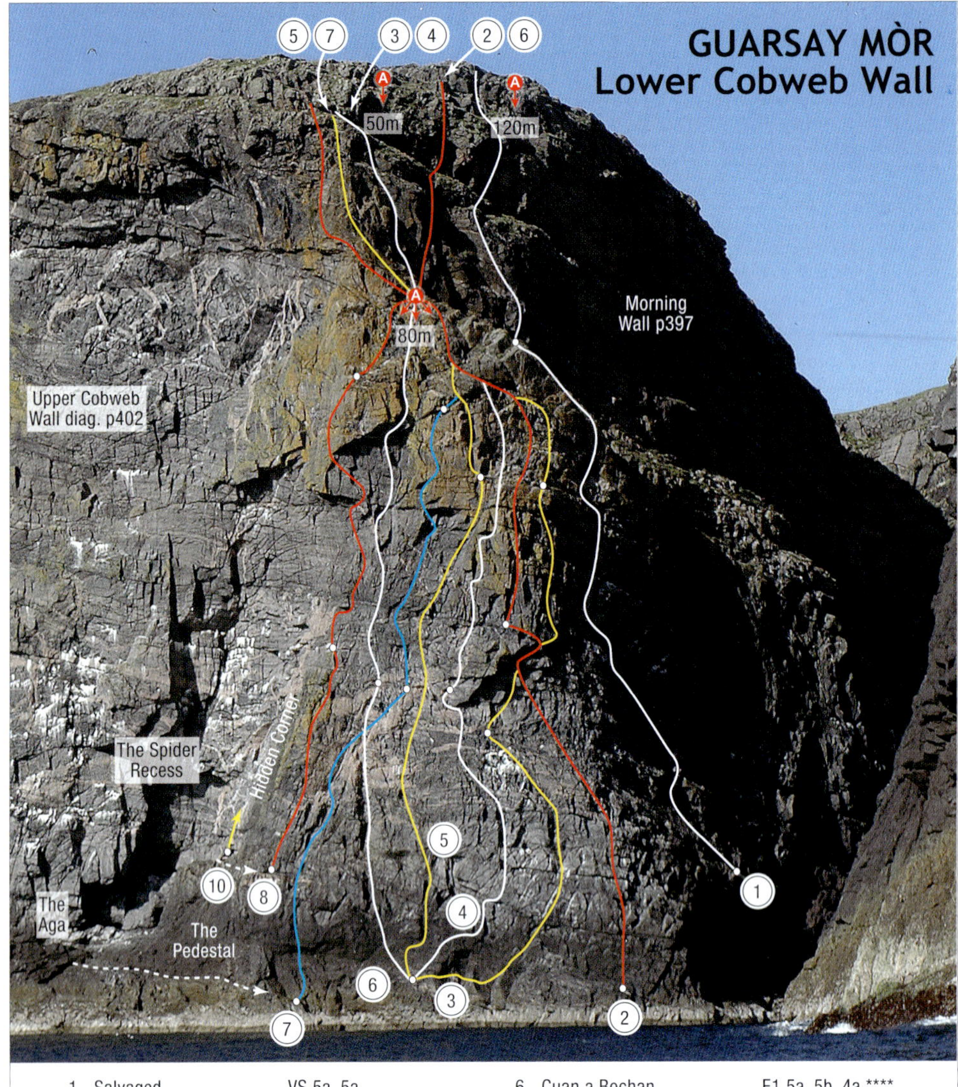

1. Salvaged VS 5a, 5a
2. Bill's Yellow Edge HVS 5b, 4c, 5a **
3. Pieces of Eight E1 5b, 5b, 5b, 5a, 4a **
4. Jugs to Blow your Mind E1 5b, 5b, 4a **
5. Itsy Bitsy Spider HVS 5a, 4c ***
6. Cuan a Bochan E1 5a, 5b, 4a ****
7. Bikini Dreams E3 5c, 5c, 4a **
8. The Adventures of Ray Chup E3 5c, 5c, 5a ***
10. Digging a Watery Grave E4 5b, 6a, 5b **

8 The Adventures of Ray Chup, the Brummie Midget 110m E3 5c ***

H.Hall, H.Harris, 29 May 2003

Takes a fantastic line up the junction arete between the two Cobweb Walls and weaves between the larger roofs near the top of the lower wall, before finishing more easily. Immaculate rock in a great position. Start from the top of the pedestal and traverse easily 10m right round the arete to a belay on a good ledge at the foot of a huge rightwards leaning groove.

1. 30m 5c From the ledge, climb steep rock directly above, staying left of the pegmatite, to a stiff pull onto a ledge. Awkward moves right lead to better holds leading straight up to a belay ledge which is down and left of a small diamond-shaped roof, and 20m below the larger roofs.

2. 30m 5c Climb up to the diamond-shaped roof. Pass it on its right and climb directly up to the first of the big overhangs. Step right and pull through, then move up left into a corner to contemplate the second big overhang. Go out of the corner leftwards and then up to the roof before swinging leftwards to pass the roof at its left end. The wall above is climbed trending rightwards over a bulge, passing a weird pocket to reach a good ledge.
3. 50m 5a The walls and ledges behind the belay are climbed directly to the top.

Upper Cobweb Wall

(NL 5495 8497) Non-tidal SW facing Diagram 402

This is the area of cliff with a similarly cobweb-like area of rock at the top of the cliff under the large capping roofs. The Spider Recess is a huge vertical recess in the bottom right corner, and large non-tidal ledges extend left from it under the wall; The Aga. To the right of The Spider Recess is The Pedestal, a large pedestal some 8m above sea-level slabs. Below this, there is a long narrow pool tucked under the base of the cliff. The Aga peters out on the left-hand side below a prominent black corner.

Descent: Abseil as for Cobweb Wall to the first ledge system (50m), but then direct the abseil off the extreme left end of the ledge (facing in), down a corner to gain the pedestal and ledges below the recess (80m).

An area in the centre of The Aga, left of the recess, contains nesting auks and kittiwakes and should be avoided in the nesting season, when it is quite disgustingly guano-laden anyway.

9 Burning Sensation 120m E1 **

H.Harris, L.Beck, 23 May 2001

Climbs the extreme right-hand side of the wall, to pull round rightwards onto the upper section of Lower Cobweb Wall and follows a line under the upper roofs. Start on The Pedestal.
1. 50m 5a Move up rightwards to follow a rising flake and groove system in the green slab to a recess at a pink patch of pegmatite. Move up right, to follow a line just below the conspicuous pink streak for 8m to a pull through a bulge at flakes. Go up these to a pedestal and then traverse right to a hanging belay on the edge of the wall.
2. 20m 5b Move up above the belay, then traverse right to an awkward pull into a groove. Move up and right to the narrowest point in the roof above (junction with Cuan a Bochan). Pull through and climb the ramp under the large roof to belay on ledges.
3. 40m Climb the easy arete on fragile rock as for Cuan a Bochan.

10 Digging a Watery Grave 120m E4 **

N.Stabbs, M.Holt, 23 May 2001

Takes the line of the corner of the abseil above the right side of the recess and finishes up Cuan a Bochan's top pitch. Start from The Pedestal.
1. 35m 5b From The Pedestal climb the centre of the pink slab above, 3m left of the green slab of Burning Sensation. Trend slightly rightwards to join that route at the recess at the pink pegmatite patch and belay below a large hanging flake.
2. 40m 6a Climb through bulging rock via the hanging flake to a small ledge. Attack the overhanging wall above, trending right to meet the top of flakes. Continue to under the break in the roofs. Move right and enter the corner above. Climb this to a belay on the left.
3. 45m 5b Climb flakes just right of the belay, crossing a bulge leftwards. Follow the crack above towards the arete (abseil point and optional belay) and continue up rightwards to join Cuan a Bochan at a ledge. Easily to the top.

11 Burning Desire 120m E5 ***

K.Howett, L.Creamer, 26 May 2001

An awesome line up the right side of The Aga, through the upper cobweb section and through the right break in the capping roofs. Start on The Pedestal.
1. 50m 5c Gain the centre of the pink slab above then head up left into a groove issuing from a small roof on the left. Continue up the wall, weaving around small overlaps keeping just on the left side of the pink pegmatite streaks to an isolated roof. Exit onto the wall above and climb to a niche with an obvious protruding spike on its left side (perfect for a no hands, bum rest). Leaving this, head up and left to undercuts below a left to right undercut flake. Tricky moves up and right gain a belay ledge under a large horizontal roof.
2. 25m 6b Climb directly to the roof and launch leftwards (slightly harder for the short) to flake holds and an obvious jam in the lip to pull powerfully round onto the wall above. Climb the still steep wall to a big ledge.
3. 30m 5c Climb sculptured rock features to reach a steepening, soaring, pink pegmatite arete. Climb it on slightly unnerving rock to bridge the slight groove above to under an overlap. Step steeply left and pull over into a short clean-cut right-facing corner. From its top step right to a black sloping ledge.
4. 20m 6a Climb to loose-looking blocks above. Use these (with care) to gain height on the left, then make bold moves up to the roof. Undercut your way leftwards into a wild position at the top of the cliff. Finish into the final groove.

12 Bird is the Word 120m E4 **

D.Russell, A.Swinton, 17 Jun 2015

Start on The Pedestal.
1. 50m 5c Climb a corner on the left into The Spider Recess until below an overlap that cuts back right, and surmount this on the right joining Burning Desire. Continue on jugs upwards keeping right of the birdy ledges to join Burning Desire with a hard move to gain the ledge under the roof.
2. 55m 5c Traverse 6m left along a break, pulling through a roof on the left-hand side. Continue up the wall until a left-rising traverse is reached. Make a hard move to gain the traverse and follow this into the cave on the lip below the big roof.
3. 15m 5c Move left round a bulge, then pull up and right to below the final hanging corner. Commit to pulling into the corner and continue up this to the top. A good exposed pitch.

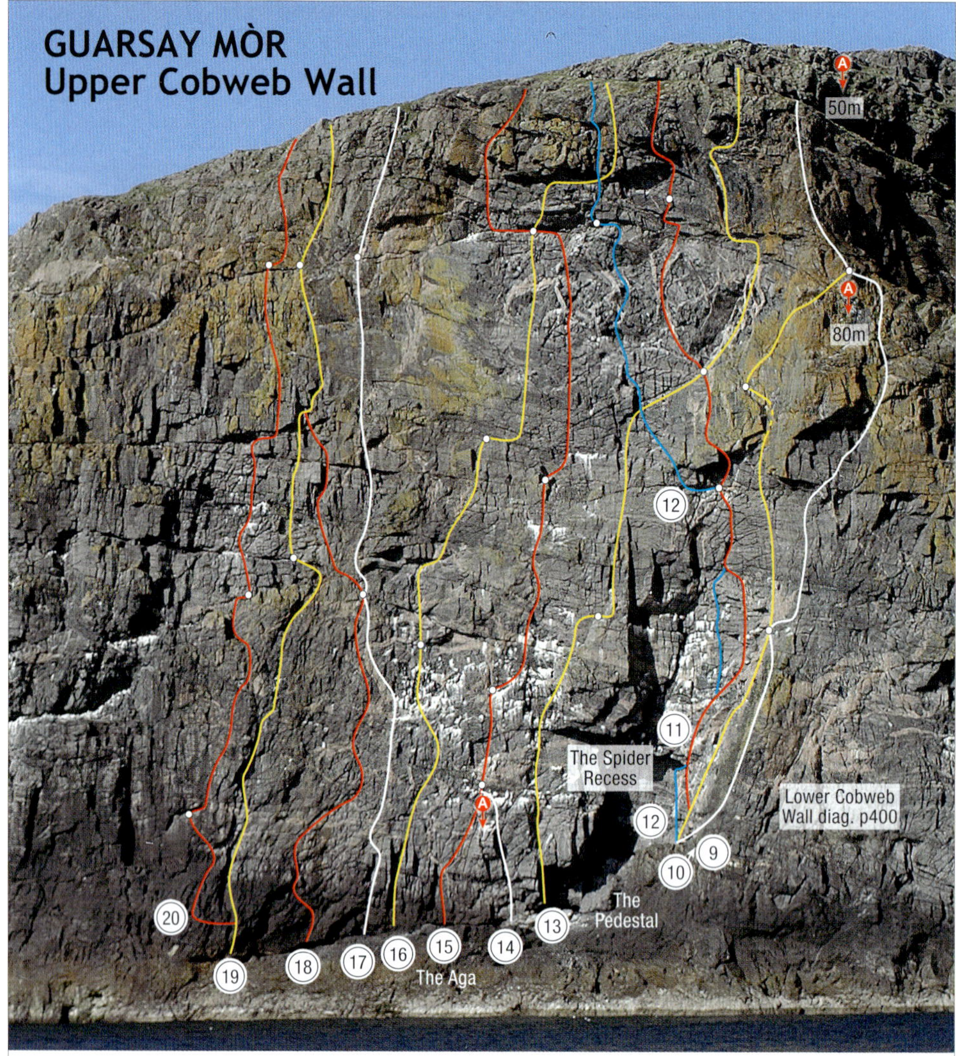

9.	Burning Sensation	E1 5a,5b **	15.	The Aga Sanction	E4 6a, 5b, 5c, 5c ***
10.	Digging a Watery Grave	E4 5b, 6a, 5b **	16.	Taking the Hump	E5 6a, 5c, 5b, 6a **
11.	Burning Desire	E5 5c, 6b, 5c 6a ***	17.	The Ocean of Time	E5 6a, 5c ***
12.	Bird is the Word	E4 5c, 5c, 5c **	18.	The Secret's Out	E5 6a, 5c ***
13.	Hot White Spider	E4 6a, 5b, 5c ***	19.	Rayburnt	E4 6a, 5c, 4a ****
14.	Fine Lines	E5 6b ***	20.	Kelvin and Hobbs	E3 5c, 5a, 5b ***

13 Hot White Spider 120m E4 ***

H.Tyce, G.Latter, J.Crook, 18 Aug 2011

Another superb varied route up the wall. Start beneath the short hanging arete, just left of the large low roof and the leftmost of two caves (The Spider Recess).

1. 40m 6a Climb the twin hanging cracks in the arete with difficulty to good jams leading more easily to the large open groove. Continue fairly directly, steeply on big holds to guano covered ledges. Traverse right and up to belay on a perfect clean triangular ledge.

2. 40m 5b Move out right, then directly up the wall on incut holds, trending rightwards on easier ground, heading for a prominent leaning pegmatite band breaking through right side of second last roof system.

Belay on large guano ledges, just left of a large (possibly suspect) spike.
3. 40m 5c Climb initially gritty rock up to the roof, move left then up through an overlap on good holds. Continue up the fine sustained overhanging groove with good gear to a small roof. Cross this slightly leftwards on surprisingly good holds, then directly, then move out right to follow a crack up the wall in a superb position to the top.

14 Fine Lines 23m E5 6b ***
G.Latter, E.Nind, 10 Jun 2014
A short single pitch climbing the good rock below the kittiwakes nesting colony. Start a few metres left of Hot White Spider. Climb an undercut crack with difficulty to good holds at the base of a hanging right-facing corner, then go up this. Trend leftwards more easily to belay on a small bollard shared with The Aga Sanction. Abseil off, probably leaving a sling to do so.

15 The Aga Sanction 125m E4 ***
H.Tyce, J.Crook, G.Latter, 17 Aug 2011
Superb climbing up the centre of the wall. Start just right of the long narrow pool.
1. 35m 6a Climb the vertical pegmatite band, with difficult reachy moves to gain good holds beneath a prominent right-slanting flake system. Continue up this, then go direct to belay on a sloping ledge below a small roof.
2. 25m 5b Traverse right 4m, then go straight up the corner above to a comfy ledge.
3. 30m 5c From the right end of the ledge, climb the steep wall on rounded holds, then go straight up to belay beneath the upper roof.
4. 35m 5c Traverse left, then climb straight up to gain and climb the hanging roof-capped corner. Climb this, then step right onto small slab, pull out rightwards on superb holds in a stunning position and finish directly on good holds.

16 Taking the Hump 135m E5 6a **
T.Wood, G.Latter, 10 Jun 2005
Another line breaching the wall, spectacularly breaking through the capping roofs. Start left of the Aga Sanction at a prominent right-facing grey groove, at the left end of the narrow pool along the base of the wall.
1. 35m 6a Climb the prominent right-facing capped groove. Break out right at a roof and continue up to a prominent horizontal break. Move up left through bulges and continue to a good ledge.
2. 35m 5c Continue straight up to the first small roof, move right and follow a rising right-trending line to a commodious ledge.
3. 30m 5b Continue right along the ledge to a weakness in the bulging wall. Climb this then move right to a block belay on a ledge below roofs.
4. 35m 6a Pull through the roof using a quartz rail clump, then follow crazy runnels to a second roof. A long stretch reaches good holds. Continue to a third roof which is surmounted via a diagonal left-trending crack. Traverse right along an easy break (birdy!) under final large capping roofs past a lichenous yellow hanging corner. Climb a groove right of this on good holds to the top.

17 The Ocean of Time 120m E5 6a ***
S.Williams, U.Hawthorn, 10 Jun 2014
Start 3m left of Taking the Hump.
1. 45m 6a Use black jugs and make a long move to a good spike (good gear). Move up to obvious corner above. Step left, gain a sloping rising handrail, and lunge to a pocket. Continue straight up more steadily. Follow the quartz tongue to belay under the left end of the large roof.
2. 50m 5c Step left, and continue straight up, taking a hanging corner with interest.
3. 25m Scramble to glory.

18 The Secret's Out 120m E5 6a ***
G.Boswell, M.Shorter, 11 Jun 2014
A superb route on stunning quality rock, bypassing the broken nesting ledges in the centre of the wall. Start just right of a short arching groove left of The Ocean of Time, just right of a quartz smile.
1. 50m 6a Make a hard pull from a jug to reach a short crack. Step left and make powerful moves to reach then follow the rising rightwards crack-line. Belay at a ledge.
2. 50m 5c Move up directly from the ledge, weaving through some large roofs to belay at an obvious ledge.
3. 20m Scramble to the top.

19 Rayburnt 120m E4 ****
L.Creamer, K.Howett, 23 May 2001
A stunning route, one of the best on the island at the grade. It takes a corner system at the left end of the wall. Start at the extreme left end of the ledges below the obvious black leaning corner.
1. 50m 6a Pull steeply into the corner. Climb it with a hard section near its top to gain better holds above. Step right to small ledges and climb a slimmer quartz groove to gain a commodious ledge (just!). Belay by a slight prow just left of the right end of the ledge.
2. 50m 5c Climb the prow and go direct up the wall towards a prominent large triangular roof. Step right under the roof into a corner, which leads past the roof for a couple of moves, then traverse right onto small ledges. Go up a black groove to its finish in a steep wall. Take sharp flakes up and left to gain a quartz wall leading into the base of a final steep corner. Climb this with a hard final pull onto the ledge above.
3. 20m 4a Take the easy final corner to the top.

20 Kelvin and Hobs 120m E3 5c ***
H.Hall, H.Harris, 30 May 2003
Another superlative route. It starts as for Rayburnt and takes a line up the fine wall to its left.
1. 20m 5c From one move up Rayburnt, strenuously traverse out leftwards above the roof for 5m, and then move up to a projecting flake. Climb up rightwards to the blunt arete. Then make some awkward moves back leftwards across a flat, smooth section of rock to gain

holds leading up and right to a semi-hanging stance below the roof.
2. 25m 5a Step right and pull through the roof at a groove and follow a line of buckets straight up to ledges. Step up right to belay on a 2m square ledge in a rightward-facing corner. This is 8m left of, and 5m below, the first belay on Rayburnt.
3. 50m 5b Climb straight up to the large ledge and then follow huge holds and cracks through steep guano-covered rock, aiming slightly rightwards to a huge ledge below a groove. Pull into this groove and follow it for 10m to below a projecting block that forms a small roof. Move out right, then up and then back left to stand on the block. Climb up rightwards to a ledge and then up leftwards to a steep pull onto a big ledge (a fulmar shooting gallery!).
4. 20m Step right and climb up an easy ramp-line leftwards and finish up steeper rock to gain the top.

Variation: **Direct Variation 120m E3 5c ****
G.Latter, E.Nind, 10 Jun 2014
1. 55m 5c Follow the original line to the projecting flake, but then continue slightly left, then direct on beautiful rock to gain the belay at the end of the original second pitch (45m). Move out right and climb the wall to belay on a large clean ledge beneath a groove.
2. 50m 5b Continue directly up the fine groove, passing just right of a prominent large triangular roof. This avoids the numerous birdy ledges encountered on the original third pitch.
3. 15m Scramble up rightwards.

Rayburnt (E4) Lucy Creamer (photo Kevin Howett)

The South Pillar

(NL 5495 8405) Tidal W facing Map p393 Diagrams p398 & opposite

The wall to the north of Cobweb Wall continues for some way before turning into the circular bay of The Arena. The South Pillar is a huge barrel of a wall and is separated from Cobweb Wall by the fact that it is not possible to sea-level traverse easily from one to the other. The main distinctive features, seen from a distance are large break lines (sometimes with ledges) at one-third and two-third height. These undulating breaks start just beyond The Aga area of Cobweb Wall, cross The South Pillar and continue right across The Arena.

In the centre of the lower break line is a highly conspicuous nesting colony covered in guano, above which is a large horizontal seam of pink quartz in the centre of the pillar. The main features below the line of this break line are a vertical right-facing corner below the right-hand end (Conspiracy Theory) and a large, stepped left-facing corner below the left-hand end, above some sloping ledges at sea-level (Fisherman's Blues).

Further north, as the pillar turns into The Arena, there is a small cave just above high tide level marking the start of Stugeron (the first route to be established on the wall) and a larger tall, square-topped recess just to the left. The South Pillar merges with The Arena beyond this point and for identification the boundary is defined as the tall recess.

Descent: There are limited tidal ledges below the wall, accessed by abseil. Calm seas are essential. For the first two routes abseil 100m directly down the routes.

1 Conspiracy Theory 100m E1
N.Adams, A.Fulton, 21 May 2009
Take a direct abseil from a point beyond the north edge of the Upper Cobweb Wall to gain a small ledge in the base of a large square-cut corner well above high water. Best avoided in the breeding season.
1. 50m 5a Climb the square-cut corner and move rightwards up ledges until you reach the wide, guano covered ledge. Ascend the steep crack 4m from the left edge of the ledge to a wide ledge above (low headroom).
2. 50m 5b Climb the steep groove above, trending leftwards at the top. Climb up left through an overhang into a short corner (crux). Finish up easy ground.

2 Bill Oddie Eat your Heart Out 100m E1 *
P.Hemmings, C.Stein, 8 Jun 2004
Climbs the wall through the large guano-covered ledges. Abseil down the wall about 15m south of the Mayday abseil, trending rightwards (facing in) to an isolated section of projecting rock, under which lies a hidden ledge at high water level. Best avoided in the breeding season.
1. 20m 5b Climb the crack on the immediate right to arrive on the top of the projecting rock feature. Climb corners trending rightwards and upwards to gain a ledge below a steep wall.
2. 20m 5b Climb the wall immediately behind the belay starting from the left and then pulling into the centre, climbing flakes and flutes. Follow the natural

GUARSAY MÒR - The South Pillar
100m
6a
100m
100m
100m
Kevin and Jobbs
The Arena
diag. p408 & p410
The Aga
1. Conspiracy Theory E1 5a, 5b
2. Bill Oddie... E1 5b, 5b, 4c, 5b *
3. Shady Intentions E1 5b, 5a, 5b **
4. Fisherman's Blues E1 4c, 5b, 5a ***
5. The Gangplank E1 5b, 4c, 5a *
6. Mayday E1 5b, 4c, 4c ***
6a. Mayday Alt. Finish E1 5a *
7. Mer Malade E1 5a, 4c, 5b **
8. Stugeron HVS 5a, 4b, 4c **
9. Pressure Band HVS 5a, 4a, 4c **

Fisherman's Blues, P2 (E1) Rory Howett (photo Kevin Howett)

weakness moving first rightwards, until forced into a series of broken corners to arrive on Guillemot ledge. Move across rightwards to small ledges and belay below a wall.

3. 15m 4c Climb the face above the belay trending leftwards, then back right up an obvious corner to gain a platform. An excellent pitch.

4. 45m 5b Climb the corner above. Move left when it runs out (tricky) and pull onto a ledge. Ascend a small wall to another ledge, then climb pink feldspar to the top.

Descent: The next batch of routes can all be accessed from the same abseil point. Find a flake-crack in a small recessed corner some 3m back from the edge, 5m left (looking out) of the junction of the top of the South Pillar and The Arena (small cairn). Abseil direct onto a large ledge 15m down from which you can redirect the abseil line depending on the climb you wish to do.

3 Shady Intentions 105m E1 **

R.Mackenzie, T.Sweeney, 22 May 2001

Abseil direct off the ledge, free hanging, to pass to the left (facing in) of the guano ledge and gain a small ledge 5m above the barnacles at the base of a right-facing off-width corner-crack.

1. 30m 5b Climb the off-width corner, over a roof and exit left and go up the wall and slabby corners to gain the large ledge at one-third height shared with Fisher-

man's Blues, below a large isolated roof.
2. 45m 5a Continue to the roof. Exit left onto the wall. Carry on to a large terrace directly above. Traverse 6m to the left and belay below a corner with two triangular roofs.
3. 30m 5b Climb directly up the corner above, then up the headwall on a bristly jugfest.

4 Fisherman's Blues 110m E1 ***
M.Tighe, H.Roberton, M.Horlick, 27 Apr 2000
A superb route tracing a diagonal line rightwards up the big wall to the left of the guano ledges, and cutting through the pink band. Start on the sloping ledges below the stepped corner.
1. 35m 4c Follow a series of shallow grooves trending rightwards to a ledge below stepped corners. Follow these diagonally rightwards passing a couple of large ledges before climbing straight up to gain the left end of the big ledge at one-third height with an isolated roof above. Belay beyond the right end of the roof.
2. 35m 5b Climb diagonally right up rounded cracks to gain a small horizontal break below the area of bulging pink rock. Climb through this on brilliant but very thin flakes, to pull out slightly left to a lessening in angle. Go diagonally right and climb a shallow groove to belay on a guano-covered ledge on the right. A stunning and exposed meander.
3. 45m 5a A vertical 4m crack leads boldly to ledges, followed by an 8m left-facing corner. More cracks in the gently overhanging wall directly above lead to easier ground and the top.

5 The Gangplank 105m E1 *
C.Pulley, M.Mortimer, 10 Jun 2006
Start on the larger of the ledges 15m up the stepped corners of Fisherman's Blues.
1. 25m 5b Follow flakes and grooves in the left wall to gain a sloping ramp (the gangplank). Follow this boldly rightwards to step into a corner above the belay. Move up to a small roof and swing rightwards and follow jugs to the left-hand end of the ledge of Fisherman's Blues and belay below the isolated roof.
2. 35m 4c Follow rounded cracks bypassing the right end of the isolated roof. Traverse leftwards across the wall above the roof and climb directly up the steep wall to a large ledge below a prominent chimney.
3. 45m 5a Follow the exposed chimney, steeply, and then a small left-facing corner to the top.

6 Mayday 100m E1 ***
M.Tighe. K.Tighe, J.McClenaghan, J.Cargill, G.Lackie, 1 May 2000
Another stunning route. Start from the sloping ledges of Fisherman's Blues.
1. 20m 5b Go left to below a beautiful, smooth grey wall. Climb the wall via small flakes to reach a fine grooved belay ledge on the left in an airy position.
2. 45m 4c Go up and right from the belay and into a groove for a few metres, before moving slightly back left to follow a system of grooves and bulges trending left to a big ledge below an impressive open corner with a grey left wall.
3. 35m 4c Climb the final impressive corner and a small overhang direct to the top.
Variation: **6a Alternative Finish 30m E1 ***
R.K.Howett, K.Howett 28 May 2018
3. 30m 5a From near the top of pitch 2 trend direct to take a belay under the groove of Shady Intentions. Climb the steep V-groove to the right of that groove, guarded by a prominent rock spike, exiting left through a capping roof.

7 Mer Malade 100m E1 **
A.Nelson, B.Bathirst, 27 May 2018
A quality line up the edge between Mayday and Stugeron. Start at the apex of the high water mark below a black slab.
1. 25m 5a Go up the intricate slab working toward the left arête. Continue up a hanging groove and cracks to belay as for Mayday.
2. 40m 4c Climb up and left through the bulges above. Continue direct passing an open yellow corner to gain the large ledge below the impressive open corner of Stugeron.
3. 35m 5b Climb the centre of the impending left wall of the corner. Finish up a smaller quartz corner.

Descent: The following two routes start from the small cave just above high tide level some 15m left of Mayday. This can still be accessed from the same abseil point, but head down a little further left (facing in). It is possible to traverse left from Mayday. Alternatively an abseil from the absolute junction of the pillar and Arena heading slightly right (facing in) gains the cave.

8 Stugeron 105m HVS **
C.Bonington, M.Fowler, 31 May 1993
This route climbs the groove line to the immediate left of the crest of the pillar on the south edge of The Arena. Start from the cave immediately above high water at the foot of the groove line.
1. 30m 5a Hand-traverse out left from the cave and climb the subsidiary groove (crux) until it is possible to step right at 10m into the main groove line. At a roof move right onto a ledge and a belay at its right end shared with Mayday
2. 45m 4b Move up and right through a bulge above and then carry straight on up to reach a ledge system below the headwall.
3. 30m 4c Move left to a deep V-groove, pull over a small roof then continue to the top.

9 Pressure Band 100m HVS **
M.Fowler, C.Bonington, 31 May 1993
Starts as for Stugeron and initially climbs the right edge of the tall recess.
1. 45m 5a Follow the initial groove of Stugeron for 5m (crux) then pull left out of the groove and round a rib to follow the obvious steep crack-line to a good ledge.
2. 25m 4a Step up and right then go back left to reach the ledge below the headwall. Traverse left for 5m to the foot of a steep groove.
3. 30m 4c Climb the groove to the top.

The Arena

(NL 5595 8415) Tidal SW facing Map p393 Diagrams p398, above, p410 & p412

The wall has complex features. Its right boundary is a tall square-topped recess in the base; The Arena Recess. Running across wall are undulating breaks which become more defined before petering out further left; the lower one forms a large ledge system with the section in the middle being particularly guano covered.

In the back of The Arena, above the guano, is a left-facing corner that arches leftwards into a large horizontal roof which what appears to be a huge block hanging from it.

Below this is The Bay, an open bay at sea level containing a distinctive raised plinth. Left of this is a fine, smooth grey wall extending the full height of the cliff, just before a 30m high sea cave; The Mini Cave. Beyond this are sloping ledges, and halfway up the cliff above these is a hugh arching roof that extends out over The Great Cave; this is the Great Arch of Guarsay Mòr.

Descent: Several routes start from a single belay point, gained direct by abseil. However, in calm seas at low tides, it is possible to sea-level traverse from the base of The South Pillar abseil all the way along the base of The Arena, nearly to the cave.

The first three routes share a start, and climb lines in the sidewall of The Arena. They can be gained by a traverse in from Stugeron, under The Recess, to gain the base of slabs. In a swell, a circle-shaped ledge 15m above high tide level can be gained by abseil. From the top of the junction of the South Pillar with The Arena, a grass rake cuts down and right. From a point 5m down this, abseil straight down aiming just left of The Arena Recess (facing in).

10 Shooting Star 110m E1 **

M.Airey, J.McCulloch, Aug 2007

Takes a long soaring groove up and right from the right-hand guano ledge, extending nearly the full height of the cliff.

1. 15m Up the easy slab to a circle-shaped ledge.
2. 30m 4b From the right edge of the ledge, follow a left-facing cracked corner up an easy-angled wall up to the large guano-infested ledge below a steep grey wall.
3. 10m 5b Ascend the grey wall above via interesting layback flakes and pull right with difficulty at the top onto a narrow ledge.
4. 30m 5a Climb the big corner-groove system issuing from the right end of the ledge, weaving left into a small cave, then back right at 20m, to a big 3m ledge at its top.
5. 25m 5b At the back of the ledge is a big right-facing corner. Climb it to exit left via some detached blocks at its top on to a ledge.

11 Guantastic 110m E1 *

R.Barnes, A.Fulton, 28 Aug 2007

A good route spoiled by a poor final pitch but well worth the effort for the exposure.

1. & 2. 45m Climb the first two pitches of Shooting Star to the guano ledge.
3. 40m 5b Follow that route up the grey wall via layback flakes for 8m, then traverse left via jutting blocks onto the frontal face. Gain another guano-covered ledge and move left until under a blocky overhang. Ascend this and follow stepped corners and cracks to below an overhanging right-facing corner-crack.
4. 25m 5a Ascend the steep corner and step left onto a small ledge. Make a rightward rising traverse onto a juggy wall, climbed straight up to a ledge. Follow the line of least resistance to the top of the cliff.

12 Wake up and Smell the Guano 115m HVS

P.Cunningham, A.Goodridge, Aug 2007

Despite a revolting first pitch, good climbing is to be had above. Start as for Guantastic.

1. 15m Climb to the circle-shaped ledge.
2. 45m 4b From the ledge, climb the left-facing cracked corner of the above routes to the large guano-infested ledge. Traverse this ledge left for 15m (yuck) until you can climb onto a large clean platform with a right-slanting corner-groove system above.
3. 20m 5b Climb the groove above until it is possible to climb directly up a huge flake to a roof. Step right with difficulty to gain a small sloping ledge.
4. 20m 4c Continue right for 6m until a groove leads directly up. Boldly climb up to reach good holds. Continue up to a second guano ledge, and step right to under a chimney.
5. 30m 4b Climb direct up the chimney, step left to climb a dark left-facing corner and continue direct to the top on easier ground

13 Sidewalk Slot 100m E2

S.White, G.Saxelby, 28 May 2018

This takes a direct line out of The Bay to go up the left-facing corner below the right end of the central roof. Start on a good ledge, above the high water mark, with a large right-facing corner and chimney at its left hand end.

1. 45m 5b Follow the corner and chimney and its continuation crack over steep ground until a headwall impedes progress. At this point step airily left to a rib. Head more easily upwards, via a short layback crack, to the large ledge and belay.
2. 55m 5b Climb the wall and groove direct to under the roof to join Wake Up and Smell the Guano. Follow this out rightwards and continue direct into the final diagonal easy line leading left.

The following collection of routes is centred around the fine grey wall.

Descent: On a grassy ledge just under the top of the cliff at the back of the bay, is a large boulder. Abseil from here down the grey wall, slightly re-directing the abseil to reach the base of the chosen route.

14 Ken, The Fire 65m HVS *

K.Martin, T.Wood, 22 May 2001

Starts from the guano ledge in the centre of the wall below a peapod-shaped groove 25m below the large horizontal roof. This is on the same horizontal break as the top of pitch 1 of The Breach, but about 15m right.

1. 35m 5b Climb out of the groove and go up the wall to the roof. Turn it on the left into a deep groove. Follow this to a hanging stance on a ramp 5m right of the big triangular ledge on The Breach.
2. 30m 5a Exit through the roof above and trend right to a groove. Climb this and continue up the wall to finish.

15 The Breach 100m HVS *

M.Tighe, K.Tighe, J.McClenaghan, J.Cargill, 4 May 2000

Climbs the diagonal, left to right, series of ledges and grooves bordering the right side of the fine grey wall.

1. 30m 4a From the lowest ledges follow the easy stepped grooves trending rightwards to the big guano-covered ledge system at one-third height.
2. 30m 5a Pull through the overhang and bulging wall above on the jugs. Follow a continuing right-trending fault to reach the right side of the big triangular ledge below the final wall.

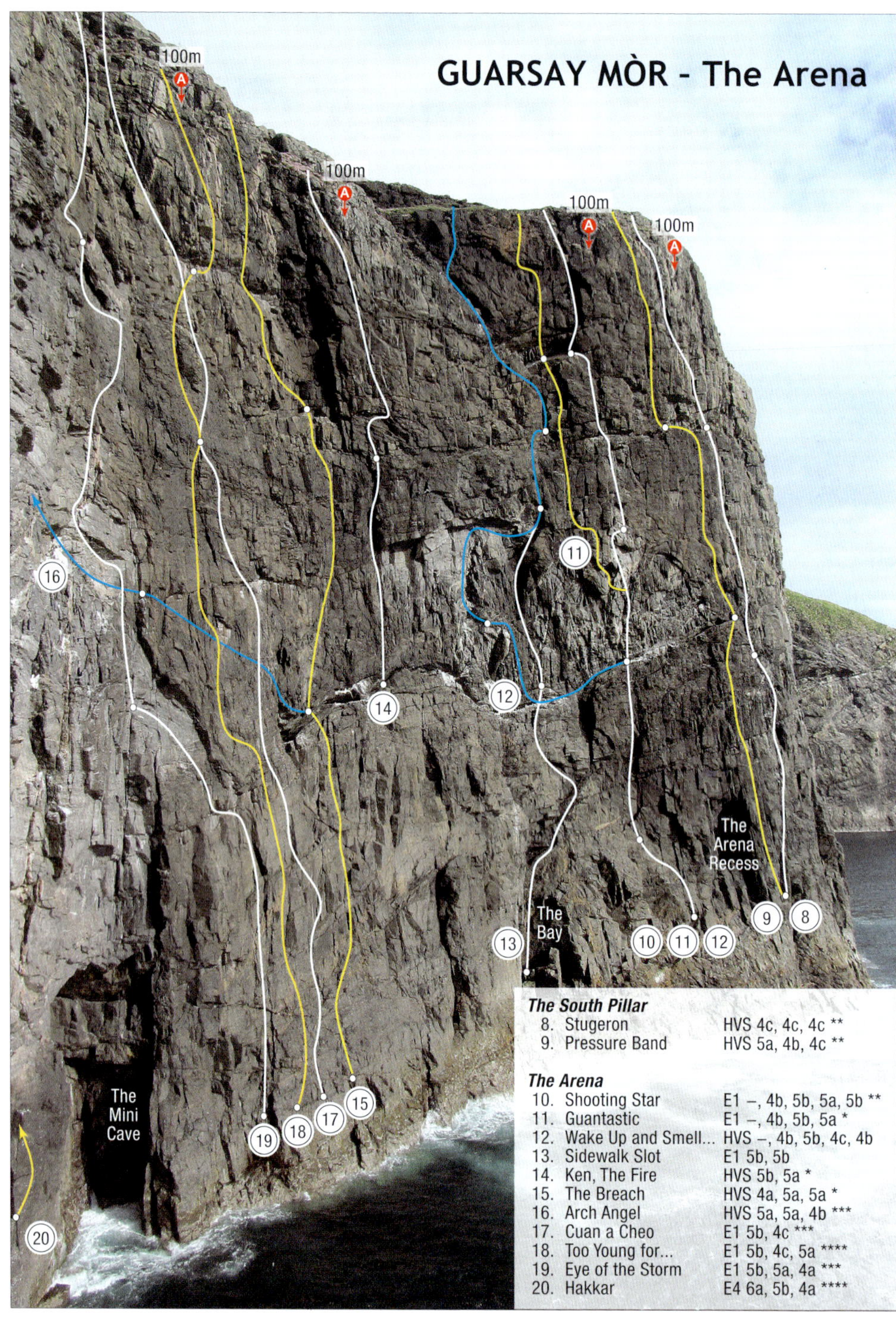
GUARSAY MÒR - The Arena
100m
100m
100m
100m
The Arena Recess
The Bay
The Mini Cave
The South Pillar
8. Stugeron HVS 4c, 4c, 4c **
9. Pressure Band HVS 5a, 4b, 4c **
The Arena
10. Shooting Star E1 –, 4b, 5b, 5a, 5b **
11. Guantastic E1 –, 4b, 5b, 5a *
12. Wake Up and Smell... HVS –, 4b, 5b, 4c, 4b
13. Sidewalk Slot E1 5b, 5b
14. Ken, The Fire HVS 5b, 5a *
15. The Breach HVS 4a, 5a, 5a *
16. Arch Angel HVS 5a, 5a, 4b ***
17. Cuan a Cheo E1 5b, 4c ***
18. Too Young for... E1 5b, 4c, 5a ****
19. Eye of the Storm E1 5b, 5a, 4a ***
20. Hakkar E4 6a, 5b, 4a ****

3. 40m 5a The fault-line continues vertically above, but is overhanging and wet, so climb pleasantly up a wall on the left, and pull into a grey groove and climb sculptured rock above leading to the top.

16 Arch Angel 100m HVS ***
M.Tighe, K.Tighe, J.McClenaghan, J.Cargill, G.Leckie, 6 Jun 2000
This takes a huge traverse line leftwards across the upper section of The Arena, crossing Cuan a Cheo, towards the right-hand side of the big roofs of The Arch Deacon. Start from the guano ledge at one-third height.
1. 30m 5a Trace a slight fault-line going diagonally up and leftwards from the ledge, crossing Cuan a Cheo and Too Young to belay on an upper horizontal break.
2. 30m 5a A walk on the wild side leftwards leads to a fantastic ledge in space below a vertical fault-line.
3. 40m 4b Follow the fault-line and pink and black wall above directly to the top.

On the left, the slabby base of the grey wall drops into the sea and is often washed in a big swell. Belays 8m higher are possible on two very small ledges 1m apart.

17 Cuan a Cheo 100m E1 ***
M.Tighe, K.Tighe, G.Leckie, J.Cargill, J.McClanaghan, 5 May 2000
Climbs a wandering line up the fine grey wall. Start on the right-hand small ledge.
1. 50m 5b Climb the short shallow groove above, pull out left onto the blank wall and climb diagonally left to the right end of the overlap on Too Young. Climb diagonally out right and follow easier ground on black flakes to below a band of roofs. Traverse left and escape through the roofs, then ascend direct to a perched ledge below a rib and a right-facing corner.
2. 50m 4c Climb the slabby pale corner, then up to ledges and follow the broken fault on the left to the top.

18 Too Young for a Gladiator 100m E1 ****
R.D.Mackenzie, D.Ostler, R.Mackenzie, 6 May 2004
An immaculate first pitch, climbs the left side of the grey wall. Start on the left-hand small ledge.
1. 50m 5b Climb the left-facing corner to an overlap. Pull over on its right side and head diagonally left above it to climb the stunning wall to the perched ledge of Cuan a Cheo.
2. 25m 4c Climb the wall left of the Cuan a Cheo corner to ledges. Belay on the right under the roof.
3. 25m 5a Pull through the roof at its narrowest point and follow a jugfest up the pink streaked headwall to complete one of the best E1s on the island.

19 Eye of the Storm 110m E1 ***
G Lennox, K Howett, 5 May 2004
Takes a line of stepped left-facing corners bounding the left side of the fine grey wall. Start from sea-level ledges just left of Cuan a Cheo.
1. 35m 5b Climb up into a left-facing recess below a short left-slanting green groove. Go into the groove, then traverse left then diagonally leftwards under a roof to reach a small ledge and belay in the centre of a silver-grey area under the roof-line.
2. 40m 5a From under the left end of the roof, exit left into cracks and follow the corner all the way to pull out right at the top. Easy up the wall rightwards into a flake leading to an isolated pink quartz roof. Traverse hard left and belay at the end of the roof.
3. 35m 4a Move out left into a large right-facing corner. Follow this to its top. Quartzy and wrinkled rock to finish.

To the left is the 30m high Mini Cave with a depression and a left-facing corner above it. Beyond and out of reach is a pillar bounding the right side of The Great Cave and the start of the next route. Access is only possible by direct abseil, placing gear on the way so as not to miss the ledge.

20 Hakkar 110m E4 ****
G.Lennox, K.Howett, 6 May 2004
An awesome line out leftwards across the very lip of the cave and up the overhanging wall above. Left of the grey wall is an isolated pillar at sea-level which forms the absolute edge of the cave. Start from a good ledge at its base. Avoid during the nesting season.
1. 20m 6a Pull directly through the bulge with difficulty into the base of a pink, quartz-studded corner (small wires in a slot were pre-placed on abseil due to greasy wet rock). Traverse left along the lip of the cave to gain a ledge.
2. 55m 5b Climb directly above the belay via a groove to pull out right onto ledges (possible kittiwakes). Go diagonally up right to a guano-covered bower, then up the steep wall direct to enter a hanging, right-facing corner. Climb this to a roof. Turn it on the left, then back right on its lip and up the wall into a final large hanging corner. Belay near its top on a ledge on the left.
3. 35m 4a Continue up the continuation corner (shared with Eye of the Storm) and on to the top.

The Great Arch of Guarsay Mòr

(NL 5495 8420) Non-tidal W facing Map p393 Diagram p412 & p414

Above and left of The Mini Cave is a big arching roof coming in from the north. There are large kittiwake and auk colonies inhabiting ledges beneath the arch but the routes climbed so far do not go through these.

The following routes are located around this arch. To the north of the arch a broad broken gully separates it from The North Pillar. This gully runs down into a steep ramp, containing sloping ledges opposite the lower end of the arch, before culminating in a ledge near sea-level. A narrow geo separates the ramp from the cave under the arch. Routes are described right to left from the base of the descent ramp.

Descent: Gain a recess just over the lip at the top of the broken gully, and abseil from here (70m, several rope protectors required). It is possible to down-climb the route Two Men and a Boat with care, there being only one short section of steep wall at VD standard.

1 McCall of the Wild 95m HVS 5a **

M.Tighe, K.Tighe, 2 May 1997

Start on a ledge at the very base of the ramp.

1. 25 4c Step across the deep slot geo and climb a short wall to The Dance Floor which is a big open cave. Belay on its left side.

2. 30m 5a Exit left around a rib onto a tricky wall (crux) and climb to a break in the overlap of The Arch Deacon pitch 1. Continue and belay on ledges above.

3. 40m 4a Easier to the top.

2 Razorbill Roofs 65m E1 **

R.Mackenzie, T.Sweeney, 25 May 2000

Descend the ramp to take a belay at the top of the deep slot geo that lies at the base of the sloping ledges part way down the ramp.

1. 30m 5b Step across the top of the deep slot geo and climb a groove (just right of that of The Arch Deacon) heading rightwards towards the right end of the roof above. Traverse on undercuts 2m rightwards and surmount the roof. Trend easily rightwards and up to another roof and take a wonderfully exposed hanging stance under it.

2. 35m 4b Exciting moves directly over the roof on jugs are followed by an easy but wild looking wall to the next roof. Tackle this directly, again on jugs, to reach a ledge near the top.

The Arch Deacon, P2 (HVS) Rory Howett (photo Kevin Howett)

3 The Arch Deacon 140m HVS 5a ****
M.Tighe, K.Tighe, 2 May 1997

Another real adventure that is a must do. It describes a wonderful arc across the roof of the arch, initially above the serried ranks of a guillemot colony, and then above space. Starts from part way down the ramp at a sloping ledge and to the left of the start of the huge arch. Take care during nesting season to avoid disturbing birds.

1. 30m 4c Step across the top of the deep slot geo and climb the centre of the wall towards an overlap via a shallow groove. Move right under the overlap until it is possible to climb through it, pulling leftwards on jugs. Traverse the obvious line up and right to a brown coloured perch between overhangs.
2. 45m 5a Go right around the back of an undercut recess and gain an immaculate band of pink rock, which gives a spacewalk along the lip of the huge arch, with an overhang above and a yawning abyss below. Once past the overhang gain a horizontal rail and take a hanging stance. Take care with rope drag.
3. 10m 4c Traverse the rail 3m right and enter a small hanging groove. Climb this to a good ledge.
4. 35m 4a Climb more or less direct to an overhanging exit.

Variation: **3a Five Star Finish 50m HVS 5a *****
M.McKenna, R.Lovell, 25 May 2018
A spectacular finish on the headwall above the arch.
2. 50m 5a At the end of the overhangs, instead of belaying, go up a flake groove for 3m to belay on a good ledge.
3. 45m 5a Traverse left to an obvious nose in the hanging corner-groove, and use this to pull onto the wall above. Finish direct.

4 The Arch Bishop of Mingulay 85m HVS
T.Catterall, J.Harrington, 31 May 2013
Climbs a line on the very left edge of the wall.
1. 40m 5a Climb just left of the first pitch of The Arch Deacon and belay on an arete before a recess.
2. 45m 4c Climb to the left end of the roof and the wall above to another roof, pull through this on very featured jugs and belay where the angle eases.

5 Two Men and a Boat 75m VD
C.Fowler, S.McNeil, 2 May 1997
From the sloping ledge head up left and out towards the arete, and then straight up the easiest line. Belay where appropriate.

The North Pillar

(NL 5490 8420) Tidal W facing Map p393

This is the buttress standing slightly proud on the north side of The Arena, beyond The Great Arch. The pillar is composed of nice grey, generally less steep rock. Further round the pillar to the north, it ends as a large left-facing corner-recess, capped by a roof overlooking The Boulevard. There is large guillemot colony here, so the buttress should be avoided during the nesting season. The routes are described right to left looking in.

Descent: The first three routes are situated on The North Pillar, but access to them is from the same abseil

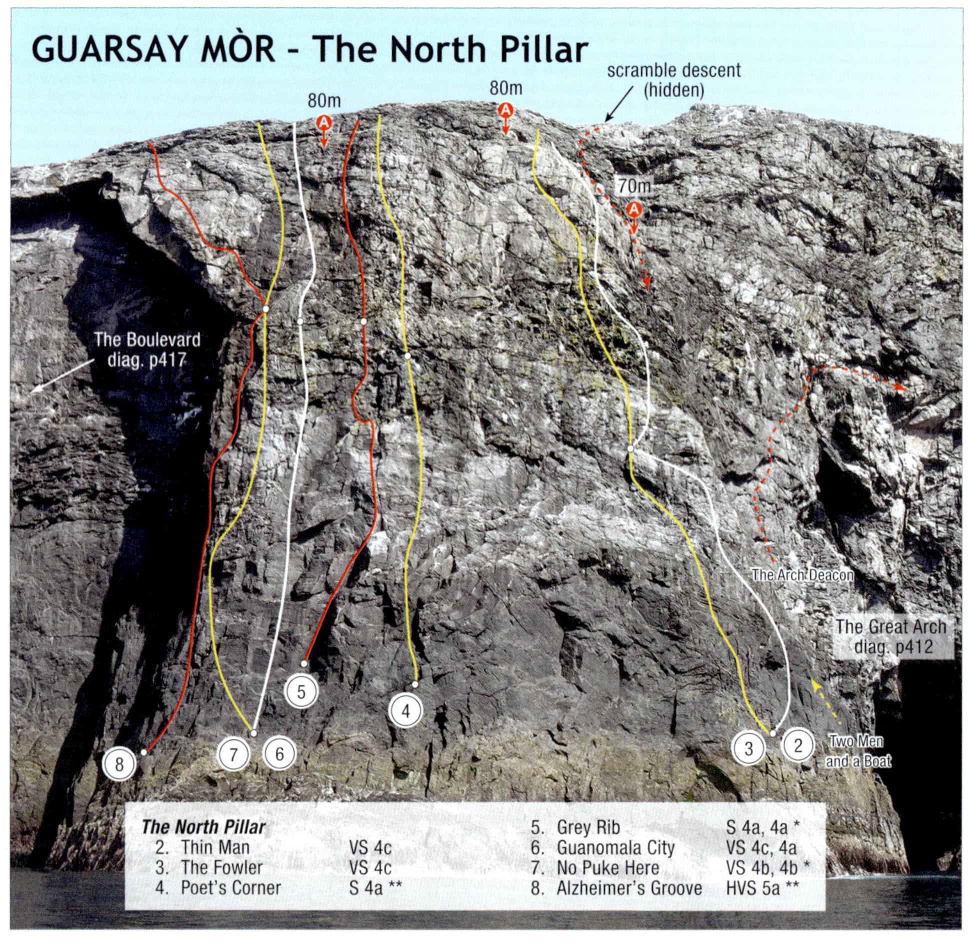

point as for The Great Arch (70m). They climb the wall just left of the descent ramp of Two Men and a Boat.

1 Blood on the Rocks 50m S 4a
K.Tighe, Y.Colwell, 25 Apr 2000
From the sloping ledges at the start of Two Men and a Boat, move left to below the edge of the grey wall and climb a line up the wall just left of the ramp.

Start the following routes from a good stance at the base of a right-facing corner further left (looking in) below a nice wall of grey rock. Approach by a slight redirect of the abseil.

2 Thin Man 75m VS 4c
C.Fowler, S.McNeil, K.Tighe, 2 May 1997
1. 35m 4c From the stance, move down and right to gain a crack system. Climb this and the face above, just left of a conspicuous arete, to gain the same ledge as the previous route.
2. 50m Easy climbing on good rock with big holds leads back to the abseil point.

3 The Fowler 75m S
C.Fowler, S.McNeil, K.Tighe, 2. May 1997
1. 35m 4c Move up and right to a seam. Go up this and over a bulge to easy ground. Follow a crack up to a good ledge.
2. 50m Easy rocks parallel with the Thin Man lead to the top.

Descent: For the next routes, which are further left on the front face of the pillar, either abseil approximately 15m right of The Arch Deacon abseil (looking out), or further along towards Grey Rib; 80m abseil

4 Poet's Corner 50m S 4a **
J.M.Given, P.Swainson, D.Craig, W.Skidmore, May 1997
Start from ledges 10m above the sea.
1. 25m From the left-hand end of the ledge climb up and left to gain a short left-facing corner. Climb this trending right up Grey Rib and over an overlap to a stance.
2. 25m 4a Wander up the superb juggy wall above.

5 Grey Rib 70m S 4a *
C.Bonington, M.Fowler, 30 May 1993
Start from the highest point of ledges, just above the high water mark, at the foot of the front of the buttress and below a hanging corner.
1. 35m 4a Climb 3m leftwards to gain a ramp leading up into a short corner. Move up and left out of the corner onto the crest of the buttress and continue up for 12m to a stance.
2. 35m 4a Climb straight up, steeply on superb holds.

6 Guanomala City 60m VS
J.Dale, M.Coleman, 3 Aug 2000
Takes a line between No Puke Here and Grey Rib. Start as for No Puke Here.
1. 35m 4c Climb rightwards via a groove and an awkward scoop to a right trending flake. Follow this for a few metres, then step left and climb directly up the smooth wall via thin flakes and through a bulge to gain narrow ledges.
2. 20m 4a Climb directly to the top on large holds, passing through the centre of the bulge above.

7 No Puke Here 65m VS *
M.Fowler, C.Bonington, 30 May 1993
Start on the lower left end of the ledges.
1. 45m 4c Climb a shallow groove, up the absolute edge of the wall, to a small roof. Pull over and climb up a wall, then use a thin flake in the left edge of the wall to gain a good ledge shared with Alzheimer's Groove.
2. 35m 4a Direct up black rock to the top.

8 Alzheimer's Groove 70m HVS **
F.Fotheringham, A.Cunningham, 1996
This climbs a line starting from the lowest ledge left of the start of No Puke Here.
1. 40m 5a Move left into grooves running up to the right end of the roofed recess. Switch from the right to the left-hand groove, then trend right and up to belay above the right end of the roof.
2. 30m Step left and climb trending left and up above the roof to the top.

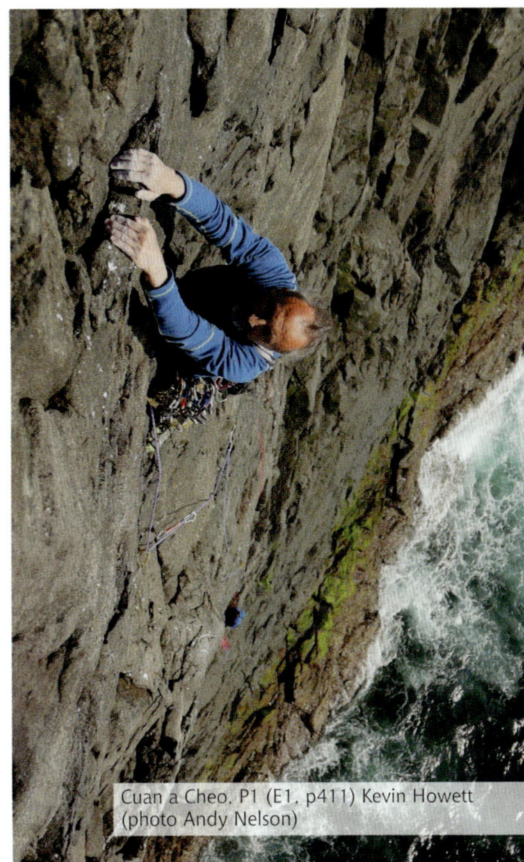

Cuan a Cheo, P1 (E1, p411) Kevin Howett (photo Andy Nelson)

The Boulevard

(NL 5490 8425) Non-tidal W facing Map p393

The northern extremity of the Guarsay Mòr headland, north of the roofed corner-recess, presents an immaculate wall of clean, vertical rock skirted by a big rock ledge at a comfortable height above the sea. The routes are described from right to left and are all of very high quality.

Descent: The big ledge just above high tide level is accessed by abseil, the best starting point being a huge semi-detached block near the cliff edge (50m).

1 Save our Souls 60m E5 **
T.Turner, G.Latter, I.Thomas, 1 Jun 1998
Good climbing up the right side of the wall. Start on small ledges down and right of the right end of the big rock ledge.
1. 40m 5c Step down right into a groove and follow it and cracks directly to a prominent quartz niche with a crack in the back. Pull out right and head up to a small flake, then direct on perfect juggy rock to belay on a good ledge beneath the capping roof.
2. 20m 6b Move easily up right to a break near the right end of the roof. Reach out to a good flat hold halfway out, then make hard moves to reach and pull over the lip. Easy to the top.

2 Sruth na Fear Gorm 55m E5 **
R.Campbell, P.Craig, 13 May 2003
A wandering line whose main interest is a leftwards crossing of Lost Souls, breaking through the first weakness in the bulge left of that route. Start from the right end of the ledge.
1. 10m 4c Follow the intermittent ledge rightwards under the smooth bulging wall into Save our Souls and thus up into its quartz recess and belay.
2. 40m 6b Move left round a rib and climb up the wall to the flake hold on Lost Souls. Move up left to a position under the centre of the overlap, move left again before making a hard move up into a groove. Continue steeply to easier ground and finish as for Lost Souls.

3 Lost Souls 55m E4 ***
K.Howett, G.E.Little, 2 Jun 1995
From the right end of the big ledge, traverse a few metres rightwards and up to a small ledge which is the start. Bold, blind, poorly protected, yet superb!
1. 30m 6a Climb rightwards off the ledge then move up to a higher ledge. From near its right end, make thin moves up right to a small flake. Step right and further thin moves on small quartz holds lead up a narrow wall between two small roofs. Step left to the edge of the second roof then pull through the break between the two to gain thank-god jugs. Move up to a small roof, step right under it then climb to reach a horizontal crack. Follow it leftwards to belay in a niche.
2. 25m 5b Climb the slabby wall above trending slightly right to reach the right-hand end of a horizontal breach in the capping roof. Gain and follow the hand-traverse line out left, in a spectacular position, then at its end climb straight up to finish.
Variation: **3a Direct Start 25m E2 5b**
N.Craig, P.Craig, 12 Jun 2004
Climb up and left round the rib to the left of the belay at the top of the first pitch of Save our Souls, into a shallow groove right of Lost Souls. Climb this and the wall above direct to a belay below the roof of Swimming to America.
Variation: **3b Swimming to America 20m E4 6b ****
P.Thorburn, R.Campbell, 29 May 1997
From the beginning of the hand-traverse line on pitch 2 make a long reach out over the roof to jugs in the lip and pull over.

4 Taxing Macphee 55m E3 ***
K.Howett, G.E.Little, 31 May 1995
Start at the right-hand end of the big ledge at a dark flake-crack.
1. 30m 5c Climb the flake-crack to its top, pull up then move left across the wall into a slight scoop. Climb up through the cleavage in the roof above to a ledge.
2. 25m 5a Follow a rightward-rising line to reach a sloping ledge. Move up to a distinctive quartz flake. Pull over this, step left then climb straight up to finish.

5 Precious Days 50m E6 6a *
S.Crowe, K.Magog, May 2003
A bold eliminate around Crystal Daze and Taxing MacPhee. Start between them and climb to the large pocket of Crystal Daze. Climb boldly in a direct line with small wire protection to reach better holds on Taxing MacPhee. Continue more easily to finish just left of the capping roof.

6 Crystal Daze 50m E4 ***
K.Howett, G.E.Little, 2 Jun 1995
Start at a thin crack below a wide, vertical pink crystal band.
1. 25m 6a Sustained climbing up the thin crack leads to a pull out right to gain a big pocket. Climb the wall above trending left to belay on a small ledge below a bulge (as for Ossian Boulevard).
2. 25m 5b Move right under the bulge then climb up to gain a short dark quartz corner. Ascend this, then follow the curving arch continuation until a big pocket over the lip on the left allows a pull out and the wall above to be climbed.

7 Longships 50m E4 6a **
P.Thorburn, R.Campbell, 29 May 1997
An exciting route taking the wall to the left of Crystal Daze. Start at a small ramp below a small roof at 5m. Climb to the roof and make hard moves up right to gain better holds at the base of a short flared crack. Move up then right to a deep slot below a bulge. Pull over the bulge and climb the wall to belay on Ossian Boulevard. Finish up this.

8 The Mushroom Of My Fear 50m E3 **
R.Durran, C.Henderson, 21 Jul 2000
Somewhat squeezed in but good climbing. Some 5m

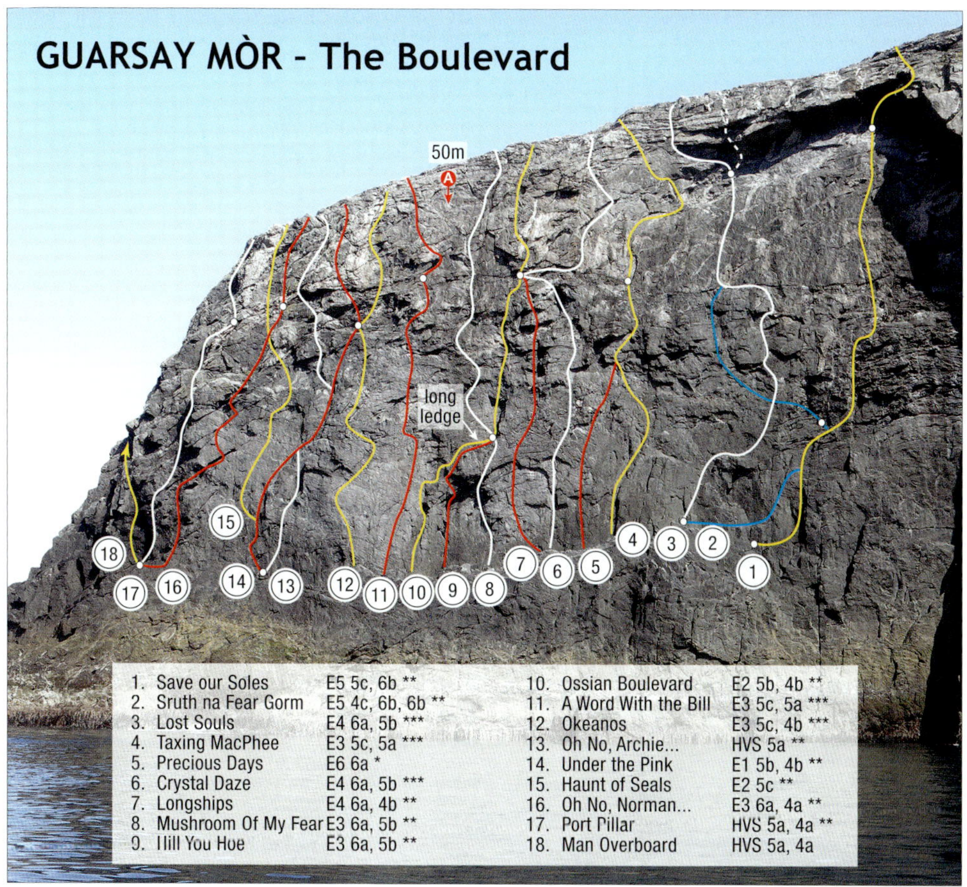

right of Hill You Hoe is a left-facing corner capped by a small roof at 10m.

1. 15m 6a Climb the corner and the roof and short wall above with difficulty to gain the right end of the Ossian Boulevard ledge.

2. 35m 5b Climb up and slightly leftwards for a few metres, then slightly rightwards before continuing directly through some entertaining bulges to reach easier ground. Sustained.

9 Hill You Hoe 50m E3 6a **

G.Latter, T.Turner, L.Thomas, 1 Jun 1998

A route crossing Ossian Boulevard. Start beneath the right-facing groove on the right side of the pillar of Ossian Boulevard. Climb the groove, pulling slightly leftwards to large sloping holds on a ledge (crux). Pull right and up the crack to the long ledge on Ossian Boulevard. Finish up the second pitch of The Mushroom of my Fear.

10 Ossian Boulevard 60m E2 **

A.Cunningham, G.Nicoll, R.Reid, 31 May 1995

The central line up the cliff with a hard start into a natural line of easier corners. Start about 5m right of the left end of the big ledge at a slightly rightwards-slanting left-facing groove.

1. 35m 5b Climb the groove until moves right above an overhang lead to a long ledge. Follow a series of corners off the right end to belay on a small ledge under a bulge at the top corner (shared with Crystal Daze).

2. 25m 4b Climb left through the bulge then directly to the top with one move left to cross a patch of quartz.

11 A Word With the Bill 50m E3 ***

A.Cunningham, G.Nicoll, 2 Jun 1995

More good climbing with an excellent first pitch.

1. 30m 5c Climb the thin crack just to the left of Ossian Boulevard with a hard pull up into an easier-angled scoop. Step left and climb another crack for a few moves then head rightwards and up to an overlap. Traverse right under the overlap then climb straight up to a ledge.

2. 20m 5a Follow the right-curving crack above and pull left through a quartz bulge to finish straight up.

12 Okeanos 50m E3 ***
G.Nicoll, A.Cunningham, 2 Jun 1995
Start at the left end of the big ledge.
1. 25m 5c Gain a good spike then make hard moves up and left to holds leading back right into a steep crack. Climb the crack then move left along a juggy break to twin diagonal cracks leading to a ledge and belay (shared with Under the Pink).
2. 25m 4b Climb slightly rightwards passing to the right of a blotch of pink quartz then go up a left-facing corner.

The next routes start at a small stance about 8m left of the big ledge. Gain it by one of two traverse lines from the left end of the big ledge (4a). Limited belay.

13 Oh No, Archie's Going Around In Circles 50m HVS 5a **
A.Cunningham, F.Fotheringham, 26 Jun 1996
Climb straight up the bulging wall to enter a right-hand groove with difficulty. Go up this to join Under The Pink in a continuation flake-groove. From a little way up this, climb leftwards into the middle of the wall. Climb more or less direct up the middle of the wall through a small quartz recess to easier ground above.

14 Under the Pink 50m E1 **
G.E.Little, R.Reid, 2 Jun 1995
One hard move but decidedly poorly protected.
1. 25m 5b Move up and left to enter the base of a smooth scalloped groove heading rightwards. Balance up this (crux) then follow the flake-groove line diagonally rightwards to belay at a small ledge at its end (shared with Okeanos).
2. 25m 4b Climb directly upwards to pass a big blotch of pink quartz on its left.

15 Haunt of Seals 50m E2 5c **
L.Thomas, T.Turner, G.Latter, 1 Jun 1998
An excellent route up the distinctive thin crack in the middle of the wall. Follow Under the Pink left off the belay and climb the wall diagonally left to a niche below the thin crack (the slanting corner of Oh No, Norman's Due Back Tomorrow is just to the left). Climb the crack to a slanting break and follow this rightwards, then climb directly up the wall to a big break. Finish up the black wall just left of a corner.

Descent: The next routes cannot easily be gained from the large ledge. Either climb down the ridge leading to the very point of Guarsay Mòr (D) and follow seaweed-covered platforms back south to reach a slabby ramp, or abseil 45m to reach the ramp from above.

16 Oh No, Norman's Due Back Tomorrow! 50m E3 **
A.Cunningham, G.Nicoll, R.Reid, 2 Jun 1995
Start from the top right end of the ramp.
1. 30m 6a Descend a little and move right onto a slabby wall. Move up into a layback corner-crack and climb this to a good ledge on the left. Climb up then right into a diagonal crack under an overlap. After a few moves pull onto the wall above and make hard moves left into another diagonal crack. Follow this into a right-trending corner leading to the right end of a belay ledge.
2. 20m 4a A corner and easier ground leads to the top.

Variation: **16a Oh No Norman's Gone Off Route Again 40m E1**
J.Roulleau, P.McCarthy, 8 Jun 2015
A variation finish.
1. 15m 5b Climb the normal route to belay on a good thread, standing on top of the layback corner.
2. 25m 5a Follow a rising diagonal crack to the right for 3m then pull onto the wall above and continue straight to the top.

17 Port Pillar 45m HVS **
G.Nicoll, A.Cunningham, R.Reid, 2 Jun 1995
Start below the base of an obvious large corner above the ramp.
1. 25m 5a Climb the diagonal trending crack rightwards then the fine pillar. Belay on a ledge at the top of the pillar at the base of another large corner.
2. 20m 4a Climb the corner directly to the top.

18 Man Overboard 45m HVS 5a
S.Campbell, N.Wilson, J.Walker, Aug 2000
Start as for Port Pillar.
1. 25m 5a Climb the diagonal trending crack rightwards for 3m and then left to make a difficult move to a sloping ledge on the left. Continue up, trending right to a large ledge. Go up the wall above to belay in the corner left of Port Pillar.
2. 20m 4a Easily direct to top.

19 One Luxury Item 130m E1 *
D.Ferguson, A.Ekins, 9 Jun 2000
A fine outing, particularly when a big sea is running. The route traverses The Boulevard from left to right at half-height to break through the capping roof on the right-hand side. Start by scrambling down the ridge to ledges about 25m above the sea.
1. 20m 4c Move down over ledges to the arete. Swing round on good holds and make a short hand-traverse to take a belay in a small niche.
2. 25m 5a Continue traversing at the same level until an awkward move leads across to a ledge. Climb up and right to the next ledge and belay.
3. 25m 5a Move up right and follow the hand-traverse line right in a fine position to a stance in a square recess.
4. 50m 4b Take a rising traverse line right through some pink quartz to a ledge under the left-hand side of the big overhang. Traverse easily rightwards to a stance in the far right-hand corner.
5. 10m 5b Fierce jamming rightwards under the roof leads all too quickly to the top.

Descent: The following two routes are to be found right on the tip of the headland. Abseil off the north west tip of Guarsay Mòr to a large tidal ledge.

Aqualung 45m S
D.Wilby, R.Wilby, 24 May 2001
Slightly right of the abseil are two crack-lines. Climb the left-hand crack.

Soggy Chalk 45m S
R.Wilby, D.Wilby, 24 May 2001
This climbs the crack and chimney left of Aqualung and then direct up the wall to the top.

Okeanos, P1 (E3) Matt Harding
(photo Crispin Cooper)

GUARSAY BEAG

This is the name given to the headland to the east and north of Guarsay Mòr, although it is composed of three separate promontories separated by two smaller geos. The whole headland is separated from Guarsay Mòr on the west by the impressive deep and constricted Black Geo, which contains an impressive small cave. On the east side it is open to a large bay (Bàigh Slèiteadh). The westerly promontory (Pinnacle Point) is a small affair that can be scrambled down to gain a view of the central promontory of Shags Point and its West Wall. Shags Point is bounded on its east by the larger and more open geo Wee Geo.

Black Geo

(NL 5515 8425) Tidal SW facing Map p393

This is the complex geo between Guarsay Mòr and Guarsay Beag which ends in a cave with a black slabby sidewall. To the left of the cave (easily viewed from the other side of the geo) are two large impressive hanging corners before the wall turns a 90° arete to form the black wall for which it is named. This is home to the only routes on these islands employing direct aid, due mainly to damp conditions encountered on the first ascent. They remain unrepeated for the jackals to have a go at in more amenable conditions. The routes are described right to left.

Descent: Abseil down the lines of the routes where indicated in the descriptions, which is not easy due to the steepness of the cliff.

1 Black Slab 50m VS 4c
G.Nicoll, F.Fotheringham, 26 Jun 1996
Abseil the slab to the ledges at the mouth of the cave. Climb up the slab to a left-facing corner, then easy ground to finish up a corner formed by the headwall above the cave.

2 Pilgrims of Aeolus 50m E4/A0
H.Harris, H.Hall, 28 May 2003
An atmospheric and intimidating climb out of the cave. Care is needed with some brittle rock, and an affinity for soap helps on the first pitch. The route starts from a poor belay on a brown-striped ledge under the roof of the cave and directly below the right-hand corner on the left side of the cave. Gain this ledge by abseiling 45m diagonally rightwards, don't go straight downwards or you'll end up in the sea!

1. 20m 6a/A0 From the left end of the ledges, step up left and then back right to the flake-crack. Climb this until it is possible to move left into the obvious left-trending crack. Climb this (aid point used on first ascent due to slimy rock) to better holds leading leftwards to the arete, and a worrying hanging belay (junction with Journey).

2. 30m 5b Move up and left to the corner-crack. Climb this to a line of leftward trending flakes. Climb these and step left when possible, moving up to better rock below the overhang 1m right of the arete. Pull through the overhang and move left onto a large ledge in a recess. Climb the steep crack above to finish.

3 Journey to Ixtlan 40m E5 6a **
G.Farquhar, N.Craine June 1998
Climbs a spectacular line up the right-hand hanging corner forming the left arete of the cave. Abseil to just reach a small ledge at the base of the corner. Follow the corner to finish on the natural line rightwards over the top of the cave.

4 The Ebony Slipper 60m E3/A0
P.Donnithorn, D.Barlow, May 2001
An atmospheric route left of Journey to Ixtlan. Abseil down the overhanging arete to a pink knobbly nose, 15m above the sea.

1. 20m 5c Traverse right on rounded lumps to gain a corner-crack. Move up for a few metres to a resting place. Swing wildly up and right to a stance on a slab, by a niche below the left-hand hanging corner.

2. 40m 5c/A0 Follow the exposed ramp up left to a crack leading up to below the left end of the roof guarding access to the corner. Go up with difficulty (aid) into the slim hanging groove in the left arete of the larger corner. Climb this to the top.

Black Wall

(NL 5515 8430) Non-tidal W facing Map p393

The following routes all climb a black wall to the north and west of the hanging grooves in the edge of the large cave. Stunning first pitches on immaculate rock, unfortunately followed by broken and sometimes loose upper pitches. Small non-tidal ledges near the base of the cliff allow easy access to the routes, although there is gap in the ledges below a blank-looking black wall toward the left side. The most obvious features are an open recess in the centre of the ledge system and a prominent vertical crack in the wall to the right. The routes are described from left to right.

Descent: Abseil from a prominent pink-coloured feldspar boulder to the left (looking out) of an easy-angled

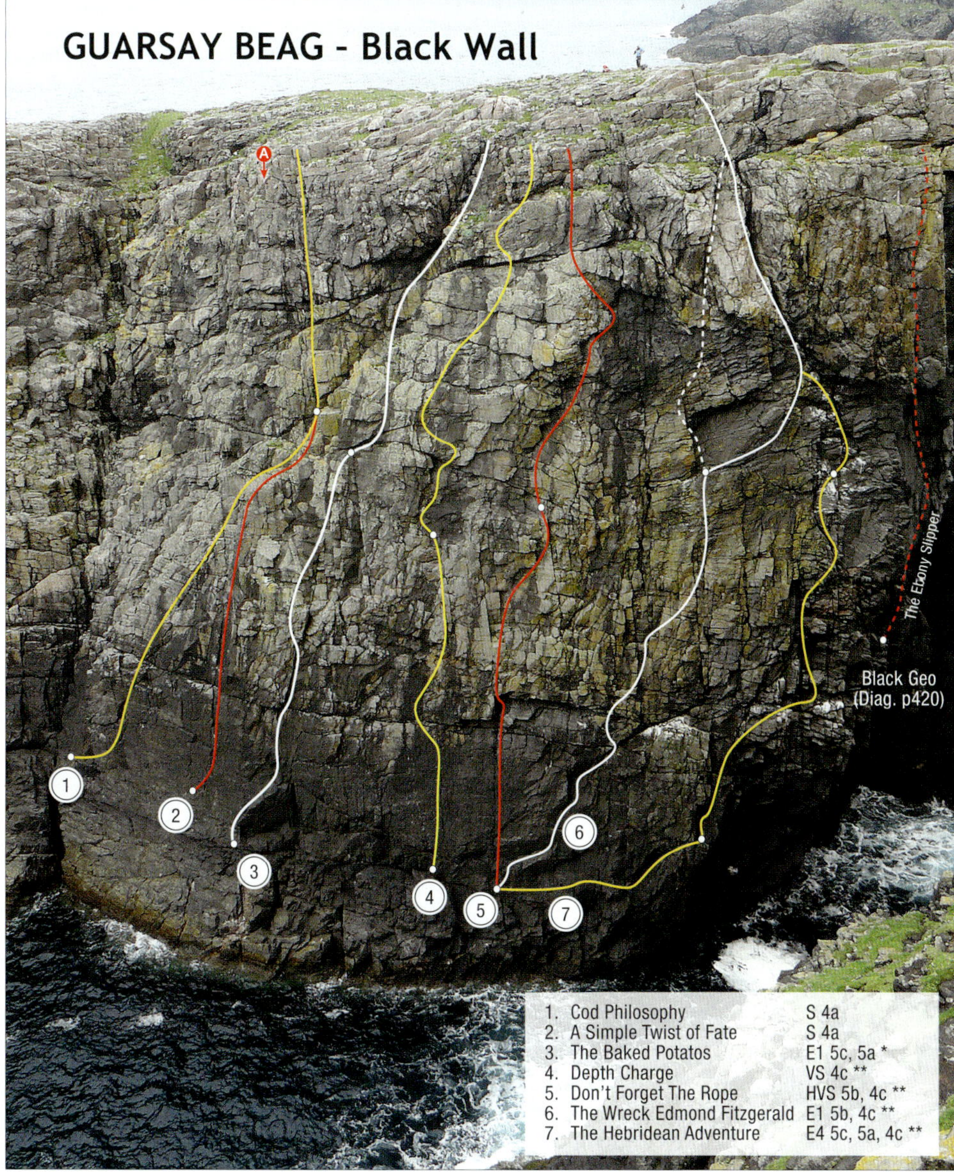

chimney bounding the right side of the wall, to gain the ledge system.

1 Cod Philosophy 55m S 4a
F.Bennet, T.Ward, M.Robson, 15 Sep 1998
Start on a small ledge 3m right of the easy-angled chimney bounding the left-hand side of the wall.
1. 35m Climb a system of superb flakes and corners to a large ledge in the obvious rake that splits the left side of the face.
2. 20m Continue direct to the top.

There follows a blank black wall where the ledge narrows almost to nothing but the wall is easily traversed. Right of this bad step the ledge opens out again with its widest point in a recess. A deep vertical chimney sits in the back of the recess (unclimbed).

2 A Simple Twist of Fate 55m S 4a
D.Godfrey, K.Clark, 15 Sep 1998
Start at the left end of the main ledge, to the right of the blank wall of Cod Philosophy. Climb a superb flake-line in a series of grooves to join the rake of that route and continue direct to the top.

3 The Baked Potatos 55m E1 *
S.Archer, M.Dabjen 28 May 2018
Start on the large ledge just left of the recess.
1. 30m 5c Make strenuous moves up a crack before pulling over rightwards into a scoop. Continue direct up a vertical crack towards a roof. Climb through the roof to the left on good holds and climb easily to a ledge below a further large roof.
2. 25m 5a Go over the roof using a vertical crack in the right side then scramble to the top.

4 Depth Charge 50m HVS **
S.Muir, J.Lowther, 26 Jun 1996
Start 5m left of the right end of the ledges, at a prominent crack that issues directly from the ledge.
1. 25m 5a Climb the immaculate crack to where it ends beneath a small overlap. Go left 1m then up and right through a small bulge and groove to belay on a prominent ledge.
2. 25m Go directly up on flakes right of a small roof to a point where a swing left above the roofs then leads directly to the top.

5 Don't Forget The Rope 55m HVS **
A.Cunningham, F.Fotheringham, 26 Jun 1996
Start below a thinner crack up the immaculate wall to the right, directly below a right-facing step in the roof.
1. 30m 5b Climb the gnarly crack to the roof. Pull out left to gain an airy position and continue direct to a ledge system below the upper wall.
2. 25m 4c Climb a slabby scoop just before a large flake system leads up and diagonally right. Continue directly above up a broken crack and groove system to the top.

6 The Wreck of the Edmund Fitzgerald 55m E1 **
L.Hughes, G.Nicoll, 26 Jun 1996
A sensational first pitch on immaculate rock through ground that looks decidedly more difficult, but with a worrying finale. Belay as for Don't Forget the Rope near the right end of the ledge.
1. 35m 5b From the extreme right end of the ledge climb diagonally rightwards up scooped walls (all undercut) until it is possible to climb direct to a rightward-curving overlap (guano ledges to the right). Step left through the overlap then head diagonally right to belay in a large alcove.
2. 20m 4c Continue more easily rightwards to finish up a wide overhanging and somewhat loose quartz groove (very traditional) out on the right.
Variation: **6a Alternative Finish**
Avoid the loose groove by climbing out the left side of the alcove roof and following the wall above.

7 The Hebridian Adventure 65m E4 **
S.Ohly, J.Morgan, 27 May 2003
Stupendous sea-cliff climbing! Climbs a line between the junctions of the black wall and the roofs in the back of the geo, close to Ebony Slipper in Black Geo. Start from the right end of the ledges on the black wall beyond the start of The Wreck of the Edmond Fitzgerald.
1. 15m 5c Traverse to the far right side of the sea ledges. Drop down 2m and traverse wildly rightwards to grab a prominent block. Move up and right into a rightwards diagonal groove for 10m until a good hold and flakes allow a move right onto a hidden belay ledge.
2. 30m 5a Continue up the corner above the belay ledge for 5m before stepping right for 2m and continuing up the wall above moving slightly left to enter the steep corner leading to a large ledge.
3. 20m 4c Climb straight up to enter a leftward diagonal crack that leads into the final quartz groove of Edmund Fitzgerald and the top.

Pinnacle Point

(NL 5506 8443) Non-tidal W facing

A small cliff on the headland between Black Geo and Shags Point.

Descent: Scramble down the nose (M) and traverse along a ledge at about high tide mark for approximately 50m towards a large tidal ledge just before a blunt pinnacle.

Cesealia 40m VD *
J.Carter, M.Glanville, 2014
Start just before the blunt pinnacle from the large tidal ledge. Head straight up to a black triangular tooth-like feature. Go up the right side of this and continue in same line.

I Am A Rock, I Am An Island 40m VD *
H.Jones, C.Watkins, 2014
Start at chimney on the left of the large tidal ledge before the blunt pinnacle. Climb the chimney to a shallow corner, then follow short corners and ledges above.

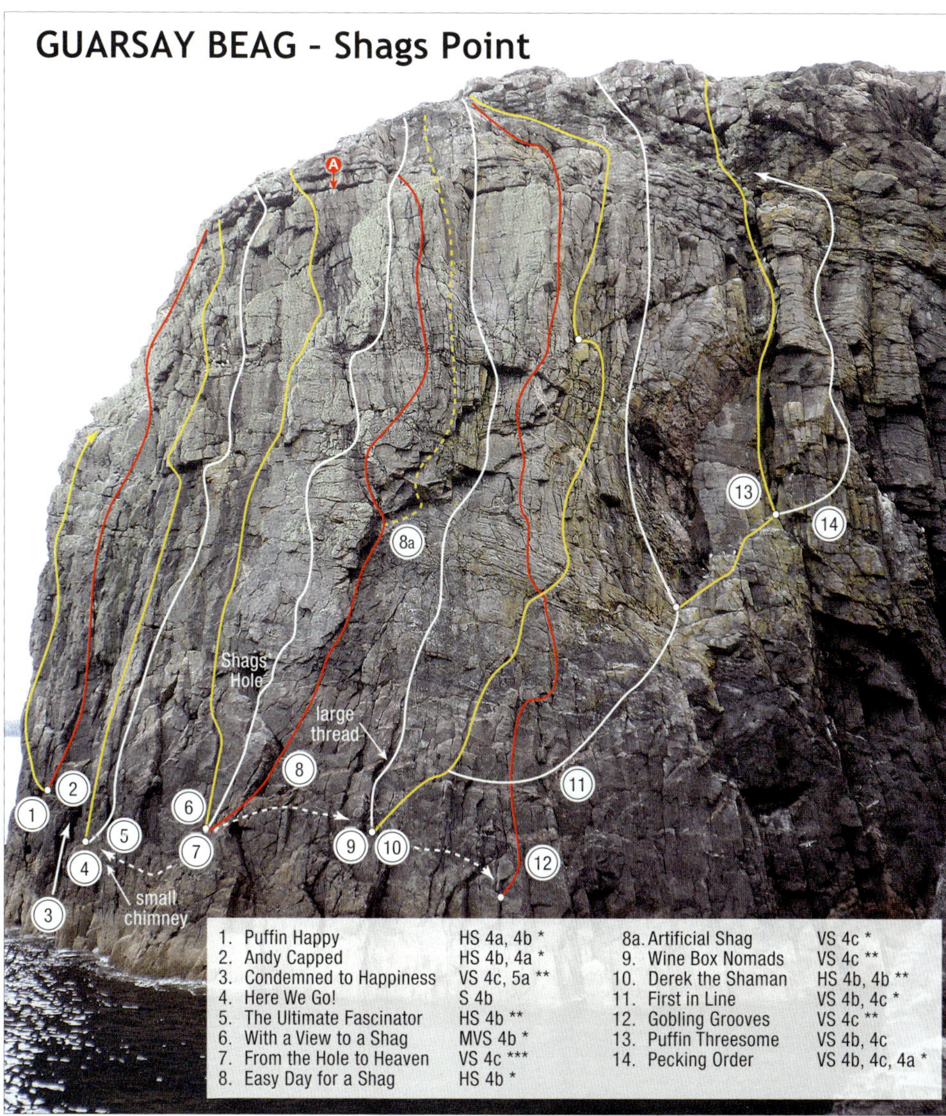

SHAGS POINT

This, the central promontory on Guarsay Beag, is defined by an unanamed geo on its west (separating it from Pinnacle Point) and Wee Geo on its east. It is surrounded by continuous cliffs; described clockwise from the deep cave in the back of the unnamed geo these are The West Wall, Shags Point, then turning into Wee Geo, a more sombre affair of black rock known as Tarmacadam Wall. Wee Geo's east wall is smaller but of light-coloured rock and is known as Ryan's Wall.

Shags Point

(NL 5514 8445) Tidal W facing Map p393

At the north-western extremity lies an obvious face of clean rock directly below an obvious cairn. The face is characterised by a shield-like section of rock, lichened in its upper part and defined by corners on either flank. At the base of the shield, about 5m above the sea, is a curious hole in the rock favoured by sea birds (guano cascades from the hole with an attendant pungent odour). To the right is a clean wall leading to upper corners and grooves. The right side of the wall is essentially a huge circular niche. The routes are described from left to right and reference Shags Hole.

Descent: Accessed by abseil from near the cairn, the start of all the routes is on a ledge about 5m below Shags Hole (the start of With a View to a Shag). Traverses left and right from here between intermittent ledges gain the starts of the routes. The traverse left of Shags Hole is just above sea-level around corners and aretes at D. The traverse right is harder and higher and a rope might be advisable.

1 Puffin Happy 40m HS 4b *
Start from the cave at the base of Condemned to Happiness.
1. 20m 4a Traverse left for 5m and climb the left side of the pillar to a notch. Go rightwards up to a large triangular stance under an overhang.
2. 20m 4b Go straight up through an overhang and up a lichenous wall then a short slab on the left.

2 Andy Capped 40m HS 4b *
A.Munro, A.McNaughton, 2014
Climbs a distinctive crack in the left wall of the corner of Condemned to Happiness. Belay on the left side of the cave at the base.
1. 20m 4b Go up the wall and into a vertical crack. This leads to easier-angled ground and a belay just in the left side of the steep sidewall.
2. 20m 4a Climb the steeper wall above.

Gobling Grooves (VS) Rory Howett (photo Kevin Howett)

3 Condemned to Happiness 45m VS **
J.Sanders, M.Snook, 1 Jun 1998
Climbs a line through a large open but broken corner which is the major feature of the front of the point. Take the traverse just above sea-level around corners, crossing a chimney and around a distinctive arete to belay beneath a cave that lies beneath the large corner (10m D).
1. 25m 4c Bridge up the right side of the cave until established in a crack.
2. 20m 5a Go up the clean black corner before quickly traversing right to pull strenuously into the rightmost groove in the right wall (crux) and continue up the steep groove above.
Variation: **3a C2H2 HS ***
J.Sanders, A.Sanders, 2 Jun 2008
2a. 20m 4b From the belay, move left to an open-book corner; climb this and then move awkwardly onto the right wall (crux). Climb this direct to the top.

4 Here We Go! 45m S 4b
A.Cunningham, F.Fotheringham, J.Lowther, 26 Jun 1996
From the base of With a View to a Shag, follow the traverse left for 9m to just past the chimney to a ledge. Climb the centre of the vague pillar above, over an overlap at half-height.
Variation: **4a Choctaw Bingo 40m S 4b**
J.Sanders, A.Sanders, 2 Jun 2008
Belay in the small chimney. Move up and left in a rising traverse to join Here We Go beneath the small overlap.

5 The Ultimate Fascinator 40m HS 4b **
J.Sanders, A.Sanders, 5 Jun 2008
From the same belay as Choctaw Bingo, climb straight up the short chimney and the wall above on excellent holds to a corner (poorly protected). From the corner move right, around the overlap, to climb the delicate wall above, and then jugs to the top, superb and sustained throughout.

6 With a View to a Shag 35m VS 4b *
G.E.Little, K.Howett, 1 Jun 1993
The left-facing corner bounding the left-hand side of the shield. Pass Shags Hole on the left to gain a ledge below the corner. Climb the corner. Sparsely protected.

7 From the Hole to Heaven 35m VS 4c ***
G.E.Little, K.Howett, 1 Jun 1993
Climbs the centre of the shield on excellent holds in an impressive situation. From the ledge, climb a vertical crack to the base of the hole. Bypass the hole on the right-hand wall, then the steepening shield, first on the right, moving left, then back right and up the centre on excellent holds in a great position. Step right under an overlap and take a groove to finish.

8 Easy Day for a Shag 35m S 4b *
K.Howett, G.E.Little, 1 Jun 1993
Climbs the right-facing corner bounding the right-hand side of the shield and follow it to a roof. Step left through this onto the shield and climb the easiest line

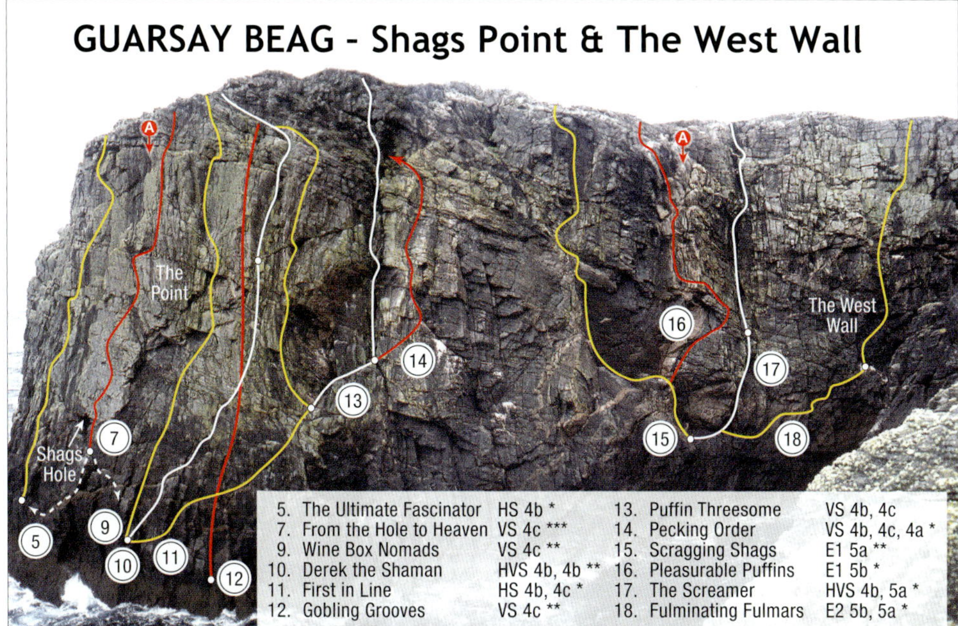

up the right side to the top.

Variation: **8a Artificial Shag 35m VS 4c ***
J.Thacker, M.Edmonds, 1 Jun 2008
Ascend the corner of Easy Day for a Shag to the roof. Pull through the roof on jugs at its widest point a little to the right. Step left then climb an arete in a pleasant situation.

The following routes start from a square ledge just above high water mark, about 4m down and right from Shags Hole. It overlooks a right-facing corner that drops clean into the sea. There is a large quartz thread in a shallow groove about 4m above (optional hanging stance in rougher seas).

9 The Wine Box Nomads 40m VS 4c **

I.Cooksey, M.Radtke, 29 May 2001
The main feature is the most prominent open-book corner high up to the right of Easy Day for a Shag. From the stance, climb direct up a shallow right-facing groove (past the huge thread) then more or less direct on perfect clean juggy rock to the right side of the roofs guarding entrance to the corner. Climb through the double roofs on jugs and bridge up the open-book corner.

10 Derek the Shaman 50m HS 4b **

M.Radtke, I.Cooksey, 29 May 2001
This route appears as a line of thin flakes from the opposite promontory. It climbs the centre of the clean lower wall and skirts the large circular niche to gain a hanging corner above.

1. 30m 4b From the ledge, climb up and right into a groove. Follow the intermittent curving groove line diagonally right across the quartz-veined wall and then more direct on perfect juggy rock to enter the yellow lichen-coloured grooves immediately right of the open-book corner. Belay overlooking the bird filled niche.
2. 20m 4b Climb up steep juggy rock into a corner and follow this to the top.

11 First in Line 55m VS *

M.Edmonds, J.Thacker, 1 Jun 2008
Climbs a line out of the circular niche. Start as for Derek the Shaman.
1. 20m 4b Follow Derek the Shaman up and right into the groove. Traverse out right to gain a large diagonal quartz seam leading rightwards, then the line of least resistance into the base of the niche. Belay on the left-hand side of the niche at an obvious pink thread.
2. 35m 4c Step left to follow the left edge of the pink overhang pulling through on excellent black juggy rock (very steep) finishing up a faint groove system.

12 Gobling Grooves 40m VS 4c **

P.Donnithorn, D.Barlow, May 2001: Direct Start R.K.Howett, K.Howett, May 2017
Takes a more or less direct line up the wall into a hanging groove in the rib between the upper corners of The Wine Box Nomads and Derek the Shaman. Belay on smaller twin ledges 5m right and down from Wine Box Nomads (S). Follow the groove on the right until forced to step right into a crack-line. Climb to an overlap in

the curving groove of Derek the Shaman and pull over leftwards on slopers. Climb direct to a blocky roof, pull over and up to the hanging groove above the right end of the Wine Box Nomads roof. The groove in the arete above is superb.

13 Puffin Threesome 45m VS
A.Callum, S.Gardiner, H.Thorburn, 1 Jun 1998
The prominent corner on the right of the niche.
1. 35m 4b Follow first pitch of First in Line to the niche, and continue across ledges to below the big corner.
2. 35m 4c Climb up the corner.

14 Pecking Order 80m VS *
J.Sanders, M.Snook, 1 Jun 1998
Climbs the steep pillar right of Puffin Threesome.
1. 35m 4b Follow the first pitch of Puffin Threesome.
2. 20m 4c Attack the prominent overhanging prow to the right direct (crux), taking care with the multitude of birds, and continue straight up until just below the cliff-top.
3. 25m 4a Traverse back left below the cliff-top to the abseil point.

The West Wall

Map p393 Diagram p425

The wall from the back of Black Geo (beside Black Wall) forms the small westerly promontory which can be descended easily to view the west face of Shags Point. Viewing from here, the cairn and the grooves below the point are clearly seen. Equally obvious is a huge right to left diagonal crack and a vertical fault starting together near the right side of the west wall. The height of the cliff decreases towards the point. Routes are described left to right.

Descent: The following routes all start from a large ledge 10m above the sea near the base of the cracks (50m abseil).

15 Scragging Shags 50m E1 5a **
D.Barlow, P.Donnithorn, May 2001
Fine climbing on a strong line up the diagonal crack. From the ledge, climb the diagonal crack leftwards to a large ledge with a pink vein crossing it. Continue in the same line to gain an exposed rib. Launch up and right into a hanging corner to finish over a small capping roof.

16 Pleasurable Puffins 50m E1 5b *
P.Donnithorn, D.Barlow, May 2001
Follow Scragging Shags to the pink-veined ledge. Take the steep crack up right to the roof. Swing round it on the right and traverse left above it and then up the rib to finish over large flakes.

17 The Screamer 50m HVS *
E.Alsford, N.Doust, May 2001
Start at the ledge.
1. 20m 4b Step right into the vertical fault-line and follow it for 15m to a ledge on the right.
2. 30m 5a Climb up above the belay, through a bulge and then to the top.

18 Fulminating Fulmars 65m E2 *
P.Donnithorn, E.Alsford, D.Barlow, May 2001
A fine, varied route out right of the cracks. Start from the ledge.
1. 25m 5b Step right across the fault-line and traverse right along a faint break to a hidden crack-groove. Go up this, then steeply up rightwards to a ledge. Belay in the centre.
2. 40m 5a From the right end of the ledge, climb steeply on huge holds to an exposed groove. Trend rightwards over blocks to finish up an obvious slabby wall.

Tarmacadam Wall

(NL 552844) Tidal E facing Map p393

The west wall of Wee Geo. The wall drops direct into deep water with few ledges at the base. It is easily viewed from the opposite side. The main features are an obvious S-shaped crack towards the left side, a roof sitting at half-height just to its right and a right-facing corner-line the full height of the cliff towards the right side (containing a protruding block in its upper section). Routes are described left to right.

Descent: Abseil down the routes.

Bird in the Nest 45m VS
R.Benton, F.Murray, 1 Jun 1998
The S-shaped crack. Start from a small sea-washed ledge uncovered at low tide.
1. 25m 4c The right-curving crack, leading to a ledge going into a niche.
2. 20m 4c Ascend the roof crack system above and continue to the top.

Lord of the Isles 20m E4 6a *
M.Somerville, B.Kerr, Jul 1999
Starts from a halfway ledge. A superb route which tackles the overhang on the black slab. Surmount the overhang at the slight left-facing groove and make an extremely dynamic move (fly) rightwards for a jug. Finish easily.

Ron the Seal's Quick Drying Wall Climb 35m HVS
N.Stabbs, H.Harris, 11 Sep 2001
Abseil from a large block well back on top of the promontory, down the wall to the left of the large corner, to gain a sloping ledge about 3m above high tide level. It does exactly what it says on the tin!
1. 15m 4c From the left end of the sloping ledge, climb the left wall of the corner to a ledge and follow the arete and corners directly to the halfway ledge.
2. 20m 5a Follow the central crack for 2m then gain a small ledge out left. Climb the striated wall direct to the top.
Variation: **Don't Look Back in Anger 45m HVS 5a**
M.Airey, S.Goodridge, Aug 2007
Walk to the end of the halfway ledge and climb an overhanging flakey crack which leads to the right end of a right-curving groove. Pull through the bulge with difficulty.

All Weather Seal 'unt 35m HVS
K.Howett, H.Hall, 11 Sep 2001
Start off the sloping ledge.

1. 15m 5a Climb into the hanging corner in the top of the sloping ledge past one ledge and onto another and an impasse. Gain flakes out on the steep wall on the right. Follow them to their end and pull onto the wall above. Go up to a big ledge. Large block belay.
2. 20m 5a Stand on a raised ledge above the block. Gain the vertical fault in the wall above (junction with Ron the Seal) and follow it direct with a tricky pull onto a sloping ledge below a final overlap. Pull over direct and gain slabs to finish.

Ryan's Wall

(NL 553 844) Non-tidal W facing Map p393

The most prominent features are a series of left-facing corners, the rightmost being the longest and extending from sea-level to the top of the cliff. Left of this (north) is a stepped corner with a ramp at the base and then three further corners. The routes are described from right to left as approaching from the back of the geo.

Descent: Gain the southern end down a rock stairway from the back of the geo, whilst the northern end can be accessed by abseil.

End Play 25m S 4a
G.E.Little, 29 May 1998
Near the base of the rock staircase is a short slim right-facing groove (below and to the left of the obvious roofs). Ascend the groove and wall above to finish up an easier groove.

The biggest and most distinctive black, stepped diagonal corner has a clean cracked face to the left of it. The next two routes start on a good ledge near its base.

Wurst 20m D
K.Hannavy, R.McCaffrey, 27 Apr 1998
Go straight up discontinuous cracks up the right side of the face to the left of the corner for about 10m to a ledge. Move to the left end of the ledge and straight up the wall above.

First in Hand 25m D
G.E.Little, 29 May 1998
A more direct version of Wurst. Climb the discontinuous cracks up the right side of the face all the way to the top.

Second in Hand 25m VD
G.E.Little, 29 May 1998
Climb the discontinuous cracks up the left side of the face.

Auk-kestrel Manoeuvres in the Park 22m S 4a
T.Catterall, S.Porteus, W.Renshaw, 25 May 2000
Climb the arete, starting on its right side (close to Second in Hand).

Next is the discontinuous corner with the ramp at its base. Above the ramp is a slabby black wall with a pegmatite roof above.

Tiggers Don't Like Honey 20m E3 5c
T.Catterall, 25 May 2000
Climb the wall immediately right of the roof to the overlap above. Surmount this with difficulty, moving right to a series of flakes that lead to the top.

Squeeze Out Another One 20m E1 5b
A.Fulton, R.Barnes, Aug 2007
Positioned between Turd Compressor and Tiggers Don't Like Honey. Climb straight up the slab to the roof, climb steeply through the roof, trending slightly right and finish up a short capped corner forming the right side of the roof.

Turd Compressor 20m HVS 5a
T.Catterall, S.Porteus, W.Renshaw, 25 May 2000
Climb up to the left-hand side of the roof. Move up and rightwards following a natural line to the right arete. Climb this passing to the left of a large block at the top.

To the left are three corners. First a diagonal and diminishing corner finishing at the top of the central corner, then in the middle, a shorter curving corner. On the left is the best defined vertical corner with a deep crack (Razorbill Corner, which remains unclimbed and unpleasant).

Pre-empt 25m VD
G.E.Little, 29 May 1998
Climb the centre of the black left wall of the first corner, pull over a pegmatite roof, then continue up on easier ground.

The Schnook 20m VD
K.Hannavy, R.McCaffrey, 27 May 1998
The S-crack in the back of the central curving corner.

Forcing Bid 30m S 4a
G.E.Little, 29 May 1998
Climb the narrow wall to the left of The Schnook, right of Razorbill Corner, by a central line in an exposed position.

Razorbill Arete 25m D
A.Philipson, F.L.Catterall, 21 May 2001
The obvious arete between Forcing Bid and Razorbill Corner. Easier than it looks from below.

Limit Bid 25m D
G.E.Little, 29 May 1998
The left wall of Razorbill Corner is formed by a juggy wall. Climb it by a central line.

Easuspeasuslemonsqueezuz 20m D
K.Hannavy, R.McCaffrey, 27 Apr 1998
A left to right slanting crack in the wall to the left of the Razorbill Corner.

Alpine Squill 20m D
F.L.Catterall, A.Philipson, 21 May 2001
Start 1m left of Easuspeasuslemonsqueezuz and climb straight up the wall.

THE NORTH-EAST CLIFFS

These are concentrated along the east and north coast and although they are generally smaller they are spared the extremes of weather and big seas of the west coast cliffs. Many also offer excellent deep water soloing. They are described from just north of Bàgh Mhiùghlaigh, only minutes' walk from the campsite, and continuing up the east coast to the north-east point opposite the mini-island of Solon Mòr.

Approach: From the back of the burial ground in the old village, cross the north end of the beach to gain a slight path through the dunes and up through the puffin colony onto the Rubha an Droma headland. Beyond here there are no paths, and it is easiest to simply contour above the steepest part of the coastline to gain all the other cliffs.

RUBHA AN DROMA & RUBHA DOMHAIN

North of Bàgh Mhiùghlaigh, between the headlands of Rubha an Droma and Rubha Domhain, is a series of three distinct geos offering respite from the horrors on the west coast. The climbable walls in these geos generally face south and their sheltered position offers an alternative when the west winds howl. They are described in order as one would approach from the bay.

Geo An Droma

(NL 571 834) E & S facing Map opposite

This is the first major geo north of Bàgh Mhiùghlaigh itself. The headland to the north of Bàgh Mhiùghlaigh is Rubha an Droma (which is home to a huge puffin colony). The geo is actually a complex of three inlets between this and a further headland which forms a series of low skerries that jut further seawards. Separating the inlets are two ridges and the climbing is found on both sides of the larger southern one.

This ridge is narrow but is easily descended, finishing on slabs at sea-level. Its steep South Wall contains a huge pink quartz streak running diagonally left to right. This contains some excellent hard routes. The wall turns 90° to form a smaller East Wall, which contains a good selection of middle grade climbs, again above deep water. The North Wall of the ridge is more broken but some longer slabby walls with easy access overlook the impressive deep water in the back of the central inlet.

The second (northerly) ridge is more broken and the third inlet beyond it is a deeply incised slot. A waterfall flows into the back and its south-facing wall is very steep but contains nesting shags and no routes.

South Wall (The Pink Streaked Wall)

Tidal Diagram p430

A beautiful little overhanging wall of immaculate rock that drops into deep water (deep water solos!). Most routes are started from a tidal ledge requiring low tide and calm seas, otherwise a higher, red-coloured ledge can be used for some. Climbs are described from left to right.

Descent: From the ridge, by abseil onto small ledges at the base of the wall.

1 Audience in the Wings 15m E2 5b **
M.Dixon, P.Evans, 11 Jun 1996
Climbs the left-slanting crack system issuing from the low tidal ledge, passing through the higher red-coloured ledge; excellent.

2 The Nematocyst 10m E5 6b **
P.Evans, M.Dixon, 13 Jun 1996
Climbs the crack up the centre of the wall. Start from the red ledge and climb up the pink streak in a scoop to jugs. Follow the thin crack up the wall with difficulty.

3 The Waiting Game 10m E1 5b *
M.Dixon, A.Burgess, 13 Jun 1996
Climb the corner off the left side of the small tidal ledge towards the pink ledge. Follow a large flake rightwards under the roof, passing its right side to enter a corner and a ledge above. Finish up the vegetated groove.

4 Raining Puffins 10m E2 5b **
R.Mackenzie, T.Sweeney, 26 May 2000
Start from the small tidal ledge. Climb the right wall of the corner via a flake to a small roof. Exit out right and gain the corner to join The Waiting Game. Exit right.

5 The Mad Professor 18m E2 6a **
J.Walker, N.Wilson, S.Cambell, Aug 2000
Start from the low ledge. From the right end, traverse hard right to gain a prominent quartz hold on an undercut wall. Hard moves up gain good underclings. Climb a left-trending groove above to a small roof and exit awkwardly right onto a sloping ledge. Finish up the short groove above. Excellent technical climbing.
Variation: **5a Direct Start E2 5c**
From the starting ledge, move up and right via a groove to gain the quartz hold as a foothold.

The East Face

Tidal Diagram p430

The main slab (also with a spectacular pink streak) is defined by the left arete bordering The Pink Streaked Wall, and a chimney and a corner on the right. The base of the wall drops into deep water and most of the routes are accessed by traversing from the chimney.

Descent: Gain the corner by a scramble down the ridge and then descending easy slabs leading back rightwards to a ramp-line under a barrel slab to reach ledges under the corner. All the routes are started by descending from these ledges into the base of the chimney to make a tricky step left at barnacle level to gain a recess in the centre of the wall. Possible belay. The climbs are described left to right.

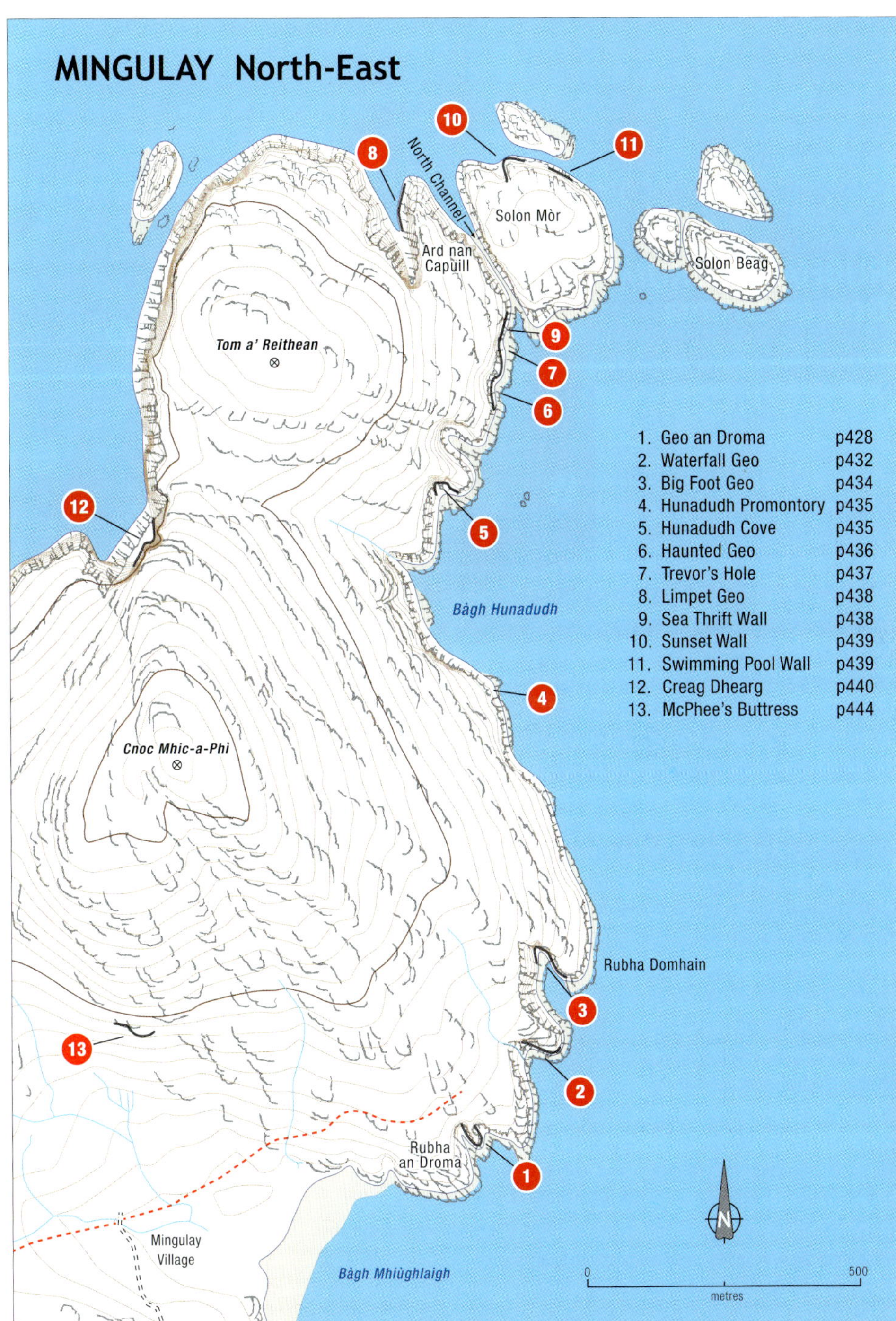
MINGULAY North-East
North Channel
Solon Mòr
Solon Beag
Ard nan Capuill
Tom a' Reithean
Bàgh Hunadudh
Cnoc Mhic-a-Phi
Rubha Domhain
Rubha an Droma
Mingulay Village
Bàgh Mhiùghlaigh
0
500
metres
N
1. Geo an Droma p428
2. Waterfall Geo p432
3. Big Foot Geo p434
4. Hunadudh Promontory p435
5. Hunadudh Cove p435
6. Haunted Geo p436
7. Trevor's Hole p437
8. Limpet Geo p438
9. Sea Thrift Wall p438
10. Sunset Wall p439
11. Swimming Pool Wall p439
12. Creag Dhearg p440
13. McPhee's Buttress p444

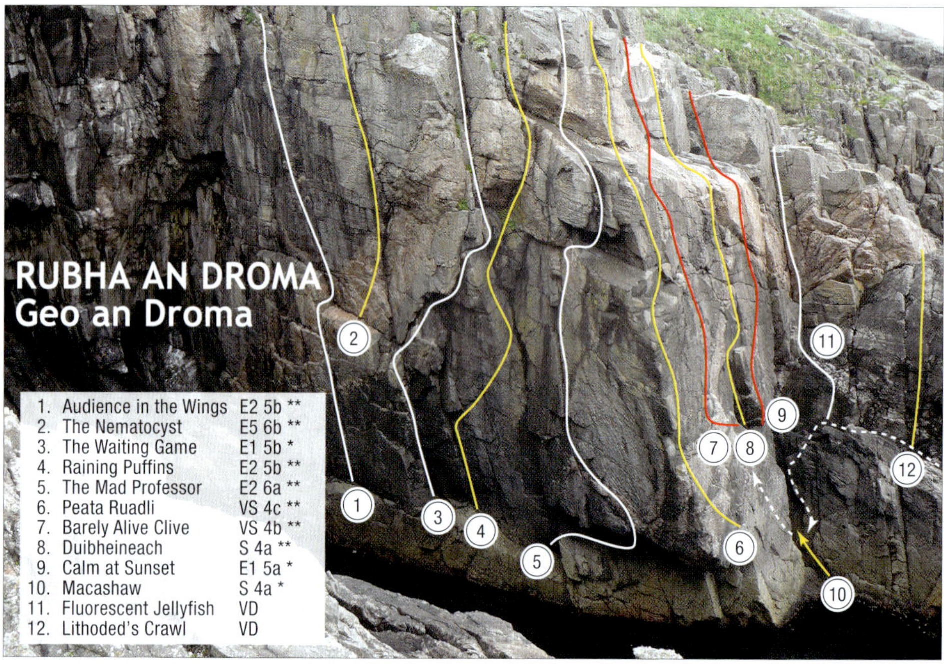

6 Peata Ruadli 10m VS 4c **
P.Evans, 13 Jun 1996
The arete between the south and the east walls. Originally started from a tiny ledge 2m above the water gained by abseil but more usually gained by traversing in. Climb the right side of the arete to an awkward finish.

7 Barely Alive Clive 10m VS 4b **
D.Godfrey, K.Clarke, 16 Sep 1998
Step left out of the recess in the middle of the wall to a sloping ledge and climb direct up the wall between Duibheineach and Peata Ruadli finishing in a thin crack.

8 Duibheineach 15m S 4a **
C.Essery, Z.Brownlie, 13 Jun 1996
The central line of a sort of groove thing. From the recess in the middle of the wall, exit to a ledge on the left then immediately back right to gain a block ledge. The shallow groove gains the top.

9 Calm at Sunset, Calm at Dawn 15m E1 5a *
S.Cambell, J.Walker, N.Wilson, Aug 2000
The wall between the chimney and the groove of Duibheaneach. Cross the base of the chimney and surmount a diagonal overlap rightwards to gain a left-slanting crack-line in a thin curving quartz seam. Move slightly up and traverse right to a good foothold on the right arete. Climb cracks to a slight overlap and finish directly through a quartzy vein above, just left of the arete.

10 Machashaw 15m S 4a *
R.Mackenzie, 26 May 2000
The undercut chimney left of the corner. Descend into the base and udge your way up it.

11 Fluorescent Jellyfish 15m VD
Z.Brownlie, C.Essery, 13 Jun 1996
The corner right of the chimney.

The following two short routes are on the barrel slab above the ramp access.

12 Lithoded's Crawl 8m VD
P.Snow, A.Morris, 8 Aug 2007
The left-hand crack.

13 Pleasure in a Jug 8m D
A.Morris, P.Snow, 8 Aug 2007
The right-hand crack.

Jellyfish Wall (North Wall)

Non-tidal

The slabs in the back of the inlet are very easy-angled but much higher. There is a large rock pool with a large white algae-covered rock under the base of the slabs.

Descent: Scramble down to near the seaward end of the ridge and then double back to the left.

Dubheineach (S) Gary Baum & Jane Meeks
(photo Ron Kenyon)

The Chap 15m VD
P.Snow, A.Morris, 8 Aug 2007
From the algae-covered rock in the rock pool, climb a crack in the lower wall and continue in the same line to finish up the corner left of Desperately Clinging On.

Un-named 15m VS 4c
9 Aug 2007
Start up a tiny inset groove left of Desperately Clinging On and finish up the left wall of the final corner of that route.

Desperately Clinging On 28m VS 5a
P.Snow, A.Morris, 8 Aug 2007
The larger central corner-line above the right-hand side of the rock pool. Climb the corner with increasing difficulty to a thin crux at the top.

End of the Line 18m S 4a
B.Davison, 12 Jun 2015
Climb the wall and groove up the black wall right of Desperately Clinging On to a left-facing groove left of the finish of The Piano.

The Piano 18m S 4a
A.Morris, P.Snow, 8 Aug 2007
There is an obvious pink bulging nose towards the right-hand side of the cliff. This route follows the groove bounding its left side to finish up a prominent pair of flakes.

Whisky Drinkers Destiny 18m HS 4b *
A.Morris, P.Snow, 8 Aug 2007
Climbs the bulbous pink nose itself. Start at the groove of The Piano, and traverse right a few feet before a step up into a small groove allows access to the base of the bulge. Heave over on glorious holds and amble up the pleasant flake-crack to the top.

Sniffing the Breeze (VS) Kevin Howett (photo Mike Webster)

Waterfall Geo

(NL 573 835) N & S facing Map p429

This is the next geo north of Geo an Droma, presenting a superb DWS venue in the easier grades.

South Wall

Non-tidal N facing

The south wall is composed of a short steep wall sitting above extensive easy slabs offering a full view of the north wall opposite. There are four routes on the obvious black wall.

Descent: Easily down the headland.

Route 1 10m VD
B.Davison, 12 Jun 2015
Climb up the wall and right-facing corner at the left end of the wall.

Route 2 13m S 4a
B.Davison, 12 Jun 2015
Start at the right end of the bottom overlap and climb diagonally left to the centre of the wall, stepping left on a ledge at half-height. Finish up on good holds.

Route 3 15m HS 4b
B.Davison, 12 Jun 2015
Start 3m right up the wall and go into a left-facing groove. Go up this to the left of an orange patch of rock.

Route 4 12m S 4a
B.Davison, 12 Jun 2015
At the right side of the wall, climb a left-facing corner to a ledge and continue up the wall passing a short corner.

North Wall

Tidal S Facing Diagram opposite

The main features are a well defined left-facing corner on the right, a vertical chimney in the middle and a steep pink quartz wall with twin cracks left again before the wall steepens up further into the back of the geo. There are no ledges at the base and it drops into deep water.

Descent: Descend the easy slabs almost to the point and traverse back right and down to gain the base of a deep chimney. An obvious traverse line crosses the chimney just above sea-level, leading round an arete into the main corner. The sea-level traverse beyond is at barnacle level at first, then forced to rise slightly.

1 Riding the Boy James 15m VD (S0)
M.Morrison, 10 Jun 2016
The left arete of the deep chimney at the start of the traverse, then into the chimney to finish.

2 Another V Diff! 15m VD (S0)
R.Jones, 3 Jun 2001
The wall just left of the chimney.

3 Retinal Irrigation 15m VD (S0)
M.Morrison, 10 Jun 2016
The arete.

4 Dressed to the Right 18m S 4a (S0)
K.Howett, 11 May 1999
The cracks in the right wall of the corner.

5 Wandering Soul 18m VD (S0)
K.Howett, 11 May 1999
The big left-facing corner.

6 Painted Whyte 18m VS 5a (S0, 5+)
S.White 27 May 2018
Climbs the wall just left of Wandering Soul with the crux through the upper bulge on sloping holds.

7 Dressed to the Left 18m VS 5a (S0, 5+)
K.Howett, 11 May 1999
The wall to the left of the corner is easier than it looks but the exit through a slight bulge is harder.

8 Sniffing the Breeze 20m VS 4c (S0, 4+)
K.Howett, 13 Jun 2016
Some 3m left of the corner the traverse climbs into a niche formed by a glacis below an overhang. A vertical crack exits its right side through a left-facing groove, then a right-facing groove gains bulging quartz. Climb out left and back right through the quartz to easy ground.

9 Swimming Chimp 18m VS 5b (S0, 6a)
S.White 27 May 2018
From the niche, climb the vertical crack line on small pockets and marginal feet leading to jugs. The arête to finish.

10 Snorting Midge Repellent 20m VS 4c (S0, 4+)
K.Howett, 13 Jun 2016
From the niche, climb the corner out the left-hand side of the overhang and a vertical crack using holds on its left. Bear right on quartz, then the steep wall above.

11 Gneiss Slot 20m VD (S0)
R.Mackenzie, 13 Sep 2001
The chimney to the left.

12 Flysheet Minch Crossing 22m VS 5a (S1, 5+)
R.Mackenzie, 13 Sep 2001
Round the arete to the left of the chimney, climb up over bulges heading into an off-width V-slot. Struggle up this and continue direct.

13 Live Camera Action 22m VS 4c (S1, 4+)
K.Howett, 11 May 1999
The traverse ascends to a quartz ledge. Climb into the square recess above and exit right into a steep vertical crack which leads to a large quartz ledge.

14 Island Madness 25m HVS 5a (S1, 5+)
R.Mackenzie, 13 Sep 2001
Follow the quartz ledge rising diagonally left to gain twin cracks. Climb the steep cracks to gain further juggy cracks through the bulging quartz.

Bigfoot Geo

(NL 573 837) Partially Tidal E & S facing
Map p429 Diagram opposite

This is the third geo on the north-east coast, beside Rubha Domhain. This is a much larger and more open geo because of easy slabs on the south side. The main wall is south-facing. The outer part of the wall toward the sea is broken. A ledge system about 10m above the sea can be traversed to an impasse towards the back of the geo, finishing on a guano-covered ledge. In the back of the geo is a cave split in two by a superb pillar. Ledges at the base of the pillar are uncovered at lower tides to form a foot, giving the geo its name. Routes are described right to left as approached along the access ledges.

The ledges in the geo are home to a colony of shags and should be avoided until after the breeding season.

Descent: Descend Rubha Domhain towards the point and gain the ledge system. In calm seas at low tides the 10m wall below the guano ledge can be down-climbed at various points to gain a small ledge at sea-level, under the right side of the base of the wall. The foot at the base of the pillar can be approached by an abseil or a short splash across deep water from either side of the geo.

No Time To Burn, P1 (E5) Neil Stabbs & Hugh Harris (photo Kevin Howett)

1 Wind Stops Play 6m S 4a
R.Jones, 3 Jun 2001
The obvious crack on easier rock, on the short wall towards the east side of the geo when viewed from a distance.

2 A Shag in the Dark 40m E1 5b *
K.Howett, H.Hall, H.Harris, 14 Sep 2001
Climbs the excellent orange wall defining the right side of the main wall. Access along the ledges to a belay directly under the right side of the orange wall beside a large rock boss. Go up the right side of the wall on flakes to under a small roof. Traverse left into the centre of the wall and up this slightly leftwards to a ledge. Climb strange black rock into the base of a very steep left-facing groove. Go up this to its very top then exit out right on jugs on the top of the cliff.

3 Lock, Stock and two Smoking Cuans 40m E1 **
T.Catterall, T.Wood, 15 Sep 2001
Climbs the excellent groove in the immediate left side of the orange wall. Start at a ledge below the groove.
1. 20m 5b Climb the groove to a ledge.
2. 20m 5a Step right and climb the bulging overhangs direct by a series of breaks leading to a good flake and the first roof. Large holds lead over this to the top.

4 No Time To Burn 65m E5 ***
N.Stabbs, H.Harris, 15 Sep 2001
An audacious route climbing the line up the back wall of the geo. Start from the lowest ledges under the end of the access ledges.
1. 15m 6a Climb the flake at the end of the ledge. Make hard moves rightwards through overlaps and continue right along a traverse line to regain the guano-covered ledge.
2. 30m 6a Climb flakes directly up the wall at the end of the guano ledge, passing calcite patches, into a short layback leading to a big hanging flake on the left wall (the large corner above is streaked with green slime). Hand-traverse this leftwards to enter a steep crack which is climbed with difficulty to a belay above the steepest section. Quite outrageous ground.
3. 20m 4c Climb the corner above and easier ground out right at the top.

5 Two Ewoks and A Wookie Up a Scout Walker's Trouser Leg 60m E3 ***
K.Howett, H.Hall, 15 Sep 2001
A superb line climbing the front of the pillar (the foot and leg) in the centre of the cave. Start from the foot.
1. 25m 6a Climb into a recess in the left arete. Exit out right onto the front face, under the roof to pull over onto the cracked wall above and gain a small ledge. Climb directly up the centre of the wall over another bulge to jugs in a final bulge. Exit steeply up right to a small ledge at the lower end of a shattered rake.
2. 35m 5b Climb up into a chimney slot. Exit this and step out right into a subsidiary crack system. Follow it and trend right to stay on better rock into the large

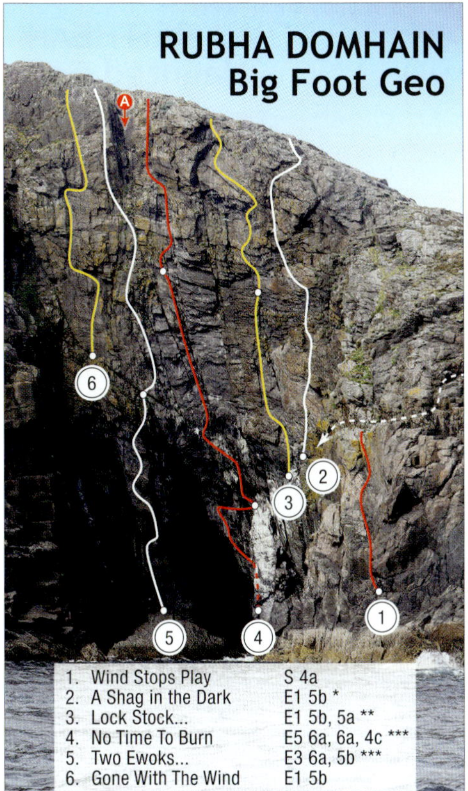

corner. At its top step left and climb the blunt arete on good holds to finish.

6 Gone With The Wind 25m E1 5b
S.Knott, D.Toon, 29 May 2015
Starts from a ledge to the left of and near the second pitch of Two Ewoks. Gain the ledge by a 25m abseil. From the right end of the ledge, climb boldly up the slab on the right (gear on the right drops the grade to HVS) to below the overhang. Step left to a corner and continue pleasantly to below another corner. Step right and finish direct.

HUNADUDH PROMONTORY

(NL 572 841) Non-tidal Map p429

This is the slight headland on the coast south of the Bàgh Shuna Dubh. Potential for other short routes exists at amenable grades further to the left of the recorded routes. Routes are described left to right.

Descent: Scramble down to the left of the rocks (looking out) initially on grass before squeezing through a gap between some boulders and heading back round onto ledges at the base of the cliff.

Puffin Away 18m D
F.Williams, E.Williams, 2008
From the lowest point of the rocks at an obvious black slab, starting at a small black wall just to the right of the toe of the slab. Climb the wall, continue up the slab before climbing directly up a lovely delicate orange slab to a steeper finish left of the big flake.

Pollocks, No Puffins 12m VD
F.Williams, E.Williams, 2008
Start at an overhung niche 10m right of the slab of Puffin Away. Climb the niche to an area of easy slabs. Head up directly to the steep headwall to the right of the big flake and then climb the crack to finish, avoiding the temptation to step left onto the flake. Some nice moves but a bit disjointed.

TOM A' REITHEAN

This is the name given to the hill that forms the north-east part of the island. It is formed by a constriction between Bàgh Hunadudh, the bay north of Bigfoot Geo on the east, and Bay Anelep in the west. This constriction separates Tom a' Reithean from Cnoc Mhic a Phi (McPhee's Hill) the much larger hill lying to the north of Bàgh Mhiùghlaigh. As the area does not possess cliffs of the stature of the rest of the island, its potential was somewhat overlooked in the early '80s and '90s, except for a few tentative forays. There are now a series of good, though small, developed venues that are well worth the trek. The cliffs are described anti-clockwise from Bàgh Hunadudh.

Hunadudh Cove

Map p429

This open, south facing geo lies in the northern extremity of Bàgh Hunadubh. Not to be mistaken for the more deeply indented geo immediately to its north, it is clearly seen across the bay from the Hunadudh Promontory. The rock is not as good as elsewhere on the east side, but it is sheltered and sunny and there are more lines to be done.

Descent: Scramble down to make a 30m abseil from a thread runner and block.

Gently Does It 25m E3 5c
D.Toon, S.Knott, 29 May 2015
Climb the third corner from the bottom of the abseil point to a roof. Step left to below another roof; be gentle as the holds creak. Excellent gear allows you to surmount the next overhang onto the slab above. Boldly finish directly on creaking holds.

Punch in the Face 25m HVS 5a
S.Knott, D.Toon, 29 May 2015
Start below the second corner from the bottom of the abseil. Climb to below the blocky overhang that guards the corner then traverse right on the slab to below the first corner. Finish gingerly up the corner on teetering blocks.

Haunted Geo

(NL 572 846) Map p429 Diagram above

The geo lies just north of Bàgh Hunadudh and is easily identified as it forms an almost perfect U-shape with walls facing all directions, a complex collection of walls on two levels. An expansive rock terrace lies above the main sea-level walls of the geo and in the back of the geo is a very prominent high level cave sitting above the terrace. The terraces on the top of the north side then descend northwards to sea-level and join with Sea Thrift Wall (see later). To the south of the geo, below the approach, is a rocky bay and further walls. There are many more lines unclimbed.

Approach: All the walls are approached initially from the rock terraces above the South Wall. Locate a large grassy rake to the south of the geo that leads north between a small line of crags on the hillside and the lower cliffs around the rocky bay, to gain the terrace above the South Wall.

The first route lies to the south of the geo on an east-facing wall beyond the rocky bay. Follow the rock terraces down into the bay. An excellent sea-level traverse on large holds south from here gains a deep-cut narrow geo. Some 4m back along the traverse is a prominent rib.

Marie Celeste 40m D
S.Porteus, T.Catterall, 23 May 2001
Climb the prominent rib past a light coloured rock band at half-height to easy ground in a superb situation.

The South Wall

Tidal N facing

The south wall contains a shallow low-level sea cave near its seaward end. There are prominent vertical grooves and corners either side of it, with one larger corner on its right side. The wall becomes less featured as it leads into the back of the geo. Routes are described left to right.

Descent: There are sea-level ledges on either side of the cave that cannot be easily traversed, so access to the routes is different on either side. Gaining the left side of the cave is made by descending the rock terrace into the rocky bay and traversing round the corner to the left. The routes to the right of the cave are accessed from above by abseil down an obvious corner onto a small ledge above high water mark to the right side of the cave.

The Exorcist 30m E4 6a
T.Catterall, S.Porteus, 23 May 2001
Climbs from the left-hand side of the cave and above the roof. Start from the right-hand end of the ledge. Make an airy traverse around the corner towards the cave. Climb the corner and crack above to a small square-topped pillar. Hard moves lead right across the wall to the right-hand end of the roof; easier climbing above leads to the top.

Ghost Ship 25m HVS 5a
T.Catterall, S.Porteus, 23 May 2001
Climbs from the ledge at the right-hand side of the cave. From the left end of this ledge, climb the undercut corner immediately right of the cave and follow small grooves to a quartz band. Follow the crack above and gain a slab. Follow the crack to the top.

Spectre Grooves 20m VD
S.Porteus, T.Catterall, 23 May 2001
Start at the large left-facing corner at the right end of the ledge. Climb a series of grooves passing a roof by its

right-hand side at half-height. Continue up the groove to the top. An excellent route.

The High Level Cave

Non-tidal E facing Diagram opposite

This strange and haunted cave presents its open mouth near the top of the cliff. The rock terrace above the South Wall narrows as it continues across the mouth of the cave to further large terraces above the North Wall.

Hell Bound 25m E6 6c
T.Wood, T.Catterall (1 rest), 2001
The cave has had one attempt on the obvious line out across the lip of the roof.

Siren Wall

Non-tidal E facing Diagram opposite

This is the vertical wall to the right of and at the same upper level as the High Level Cave. The main feature is a light-coloured slab capped by a small roof with a prominent edge (the Phantom Pinnacle) between this and the cave.

Descent: From the terrace above the South Wall, cross the top of the geo (beneath the high cave) and scramble up to a higher ledge system below the wall. Above the ledge at the top of the climbs is steep broken ground. There is a convenient large boulder above Funeral For a Friend from which to abseil back down.

Phanton Pinnacle Direct 20m HS 4b
S.Jones, A.Stewart, 27 May 2014
Start at the bulge immediately below a crack. Pull over the bulge (crux), then follow a crack to a small roof, step left and go up left of a fin. Scramble left and finish up the wall left of an obvious corner.

Fiddle's First Siren Song 10m S 4a
S.White, S.Archer, R.K.Howett, 10 May 2017
The hanging groove on the left of the light coloured slab. Climb the crack into the groove and exit over the roof at its top.

The Manatee Of Mingulay 10m S 4a
S.Archer, S.White, R.K.Howett, 10 May 2017
The hanging arete between the groove and the slab. Climb a tiny groove in the left side of the arete to swing round right into a crack leading to the capping roof. Pull directly over.

Caspar 10m S 4a
A.Stewart, S.Jones, 27 May 2014
Start at an obvious light-coloured slab. Go up the cracks, then trend rightwards under the capping roof to finish up a groove on the right.

The Ghost of Pinnacle Presidents Past 10m D
P.Clay, A.Reynolds, 27 May 2014
Start as for Caspar but immediately climb rightwards to follow a crack-line up the edge of the slab, to finish in the groove of Caspar.

Harpies 10m VD
P.Clay, A.Reynolds, 27 May 2014
Pull onto the centre of the slab and climb direct to cross Caspar and finish through the steep wall just left of its final groove.

Funeral For a Friend 10m D
P.Clay, A.Reynolds, 27 May 2014
At the right-hand side of the wall, climb up a wide crack, finishing steeply.

The North Wall

Tidal S facing Diagram opposite

The main feature is a square-cut corner on the right and a V-groove in the centre. There is a colony of nesting shags which should be avoided during the nesting season.

Approach: Scramble down the terraces heading slightly north to gain easy rocks leading back right to near sea-level and the seaward end of the wall. Traverse round into the geo just above sea-level.

Davy Jones' Locker 20m HS 4b
T.Catterall, S.Porteus, 2001
Traverse until directly below the fine square corner just before the wall steps back. Climb the corner, passing a large quartz band at two-thirds height.

Buffy the Vampire Slayer 20m VS 4c
T.Catterall, T.Wood, 2001
Climbs the V-groove halfway along the wall. Traverse in and belay on the last good ledge. Traverse left into the groove, which is followed to a roof. Climb direct through this and onto the top.

Dance with the Devil 20m HVS 5b
T.Catterall, T.Wood, 2001
Traverse in and take a hanging stance at the bottom of an overhanging crack system where there is a vertical quartz band. Climb up this to the roof, pull through the roof using a sharp hold on the lip.

Trevor's Hole

(NL 573 848) Non-tidal S facing Map p429

A small sheltered cave that is a real suntrap. Continue north along the coast past Haunted Geo to scramble down the left end of a small band of cliffs (containing Siren Wall) to gain a terrace leading north to the base.

Liposuction 20m E5 6a *
T.Wood, G.Latter, 11 Jun 2005
The prominent left-rising crack along the lip of the cave. Move in from the right using a dubious pegmatite lump to gain good flakes. Continue into the niche and some gear. You should have shed a few pounds by now! Continue traversing to gain easier ground, then

step left round the arete and finish direct on good holds. Descend by traversing off left.

ARD NAN CAPUILL

(NL 572 849)

This small subsidiary headland of Tom a' Reithean lies at the north-east tip of Mingulay and faces the small offshore island of Solon Mòr. The climbs are dispersed around the headland from the Limpet Geo on the west, the north to south running North Channel (the gap separating it from Solon Mòr) round to Sea Thrift Wall on the east side which continues south to join Trevor's Hole. The climbing area are described from west to east.

Limpet Geo

(NL 571 849) W facing Map p429

The only deeply incised geo on the north coast lies just west of the offshore island of Solon Mòr. It has a good west-facing wall but the rock is not quite as good as other cliffs.

Descent: Scramble down the spur (M) to sea-level ledges that run back into the geo. Follow these ledges to a slim rightward-slanting groove system in the middle of the black wall. A larger slanting groove with green slime at its base is a little further on.

Like it or Limpet 70m E2
A.Ekins, D.Ferguson, 5 Jun 2000
An atmospheric route which follows the groove and then climbs a steep crack to finish more easily. Some friable rock.
1. 30m 5a Make an awkward move up the wall to get established in the groove. Climb this with interest to a ledge and belay.
2. 20m 5b Climb up and make a hard move right into a shallow groove. Climb this to the overhang and take the steep crack to belay on the ledge above.
3. 20m 4b Climb the ramp rightwards until a crack on the left can be followed, on worsening rock to the top.

Pois'n Aliens 50m E4 *
H.Harris, H.Hall, 26 May 2003
Climbs the wall directly above the start of Like it or Limpet and pulls through a dark groove in the roof above. Sustained climbing.
1. 30m 5c Start under the left end of the horizontal ledge at 3m. Climb up to gain this ledge below a leftward-trending crack-line. Climb this, then move awkwardly up and right for about 8m (bold), parallel to Like it or Limpet, to reach good jugs. Follow the line of holds that rise diagonally to the left to the top of the groove. Move up to the traverse line and follow this 3m left to a ledge belay.
2. 20m 5b From the right end of the ledge, move directly upwards to a horizontal break. Move up and right to below the narrowest point of the roof where it forms a groove. Pull steeply through and then climb straight up with some tricky moves to big jugs before the final crack. This is climbed awkwardly to finish.

The North Channel

(NL 56969 85163) Non-tidal NE facing

The following routes lie on the black slabby wall near the north end of the channel separating Mingulay from Solon Mòr.

Descent: Abseil down the black corner demarcating the south side of the slab to belay on a sloping ledge tucked away in a corner.

Loose Living 30m HVS 5a
G.E.Little, K.Pyke, J.Lowther, 27 Jun 1996
Move out right from the corner and climb the black slabby wall by the line of least resistance, finishing just left of a short corner-crack. Some dubious rock!

Slob and Slag Go Climbing Part 1 30m VS 4c
D.Ferguson, A.Ekins, 7 Jun 2000
Takes a line to the left of Loose Living, based on the main corner system. Abseil approach down the corner. Climb easy slabs and then follow the corner to where it steepens. Move right into a subsidiary corner and climb this on deteriorating rock.

The following route is in the constriction between the main island and Solon Mòr.

Descent: Scramble easily down the point at the north-eastern tip, opposite the south end of Solon Mòr and traverse north into the channel to a small ledge on a black wall.

Blue Dolphin 20m VS 4c
T.Catterall, N.Morbey, 2 Jun 2010
Climb the black wall.

Sea Thrift Wall

(NL 57279 84802) E facing Map p429

Sea Thrift Wall lies south of the north eastern tip on Mingulay, extending south until it terminates with Trevor's Hole. Initially it is broken with ledges, then beyond a large left-facing corner the wall rears up, impressively overhanging.

Descent: Scramble down to the point at the north-eastern tip of the island, at the south end of Solon Mòr (as for Blue Dolphin), then turn rightwards for a sea-level traverse.

Pinky and Brain 22m VD
N.Morbey, T.Catterall, 2 Jun 2010
The first square-shaped bay. Climb the centre of the black slab to gain a hanging flake above and then an arete.

Clink and Clank Go Climbing (Part 1) 42m HS 4a
T.Catterall, N.Morbey, 2 Jun 2010
Traverse past the square-cut bay and drop down to a small fin. Climb up the open groove and the arete above to a ledge. Move across to the upper arete that has some small roofs above it, climb the twin cracks up to the roofs and continue up the arete to the top.

I Like Big Nuts and I Cannot Lie 40m S 4a
N.Morbey, T.Catterall, 2 Jun 2010
Traverse past the square-cut bay and drop down to a small fin, pass this until you get to a square blank wall with small ledges at its base. At the left-hand side, climb up the broken stepped ground until you get to a triangular overhanging niche. Use cracks to ascend this and carry on up an easy angle broken ridge above to the top.

Purple Haze 26m E3 5c
T.Catterall, N.Morbey, 2 Jun 2010
From the descent, traverse easily south for about 30m to a large triangular left-facing corner with some small roofs and an arete above. Climb the excellent corner-crack until you are forced right, continue up a small overhang. Hard moves lead to a small ledge. Continue up the arete to easier ground.

SOLON MÒR

(NL 574 850)

Solon Mòr is the largest of five small islands just off the north-east tip of Mingulay. There is a deep though narrow channel between the mainland and Solon Mòr making access to the island feasible. Most of the cliffs around the island are of poor quality, covered in ledges or guano, except for one lurking in a shallow open geo on the north-west side of the island, out of sight from the mainland. This is The Sunset Walls, offering perfect overhanging rock hovering above the ocean, making for a truly inspiring venue, despite their diminutive size.

Approach: The island is accessed via a 8m swim or dingy crossing from the base of the scramble at the north-eastern tip of Mingulay as for Sea Thrift Wall. A tyrolean can be set up. Calm sea conditions are vital as it will be extremely risky if there is a swell, and strong currents running through the channel.

Sunset Wall

(NL 57301 85102) Non-tidal NW facing Map p429

Cross the island until overlooking the smaller, furthest west, island of Creag a'Bharnaich (Barnacle Rock) where there is an obvious right-angled bay.

Descent: An easy scramble leads down the seaward arete of the bay, where turning a corner into the bay by going through a gap between the wall and a large free-standing block gains a small belay platform above high tide level.

Persephone's Revenge 18m HS 4b
Daniels, T.Catterall, N.Morbey, 3 Jun 2010
Climbs the overlapping staircase from the left-hand side of the wall just after the gap, leftwards to the arete.

Solon No Mòr 25m E4 6a
T.Catterall, N.Morbey, 3 Jun 2010
From 3m right of the free-standing block, take the vertical crack up the steep wall through an overlap and onto the roof above. Climb direct through this to a final steep finish.

Sunset Boulevard 30m E3 5c **
N.Morbey, T.Catterall, May 2010
Start up the crack of Solon No Mòr to gain the left end of a striking rising horizontal crack. Using a combination of pumpy hand jams and good holds, follow this right to its end. A set of obvious jugs leads up and slightly right under a stepped roof. Pass the right end of this and launch up the thin headwall above on crimps for an exciting finish.

Swimming Pool Wall

(NL 5735 8507) Non-tidal N facing Map p429

Descend the seaward arete of the bay as for Sunset Wall, but turn right (eastwards) along good ledges to reach a clean wall with a square-cut overhang at half-height.

Barrister's Bottle 15m VD
P.Daniels, T.Catterall, N.Morbey, 4 Jun 2010
Climb the right-hand side of the wall.

The Mingulay Kelp Monster 15m E2 5b
T.Catterall, N.Morbey, 4 Jun 2010
Start just right of a small cave, ascend a crack up to the roof, gain and follow the crack above to the top.

NA GILLEACHÀ RUADH

(NL 566 850) Tidal

Just off the north-west of Tom a' Reithean lies a large sea stack (The Red Bouy). Just to its east is a smaller and more defined stack of more interest to climbers. Access is by swimming, or more sensibly by boat.

Sea Horse 10m VS 4c
M.Tighe, K.Tighe, K.Colewell, Y.Colewell, H.Roberton, E.Knudson, 28 Apr 2000
From a reasonable ledge on the south side of the stack, climb the wall into two short right-facing corners.

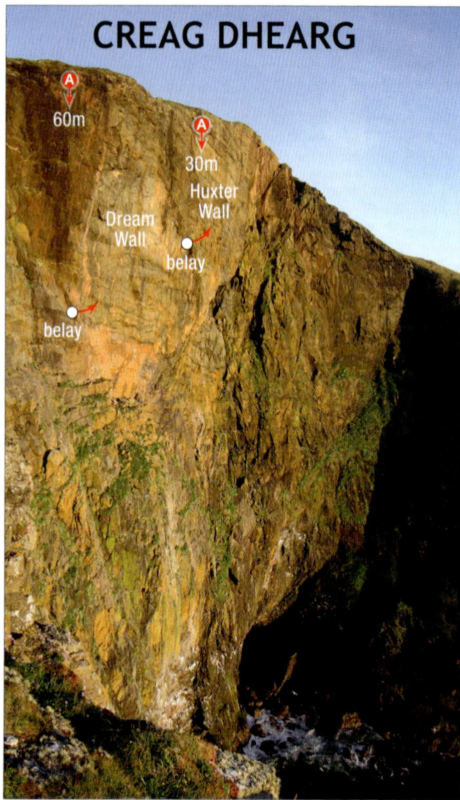

CREAG DHEARG

(NL 5660 8448) Non-tidal NW facing
Map p429 Diagrams p442 & p443

Climbing here feels like flying! The cliff forms the back wall of Bay Analepp in the north-west of the island. The top of the cliff lies at 150m above sea-level; the lower sections are steep but grotty and bird infested, however, the upper 60m wall offers excellent quality gneiss, hanging spectacularly above the sea. The wall can be viewed from spurs of land to either the north or south. There are two facets to the wall, a steep and impressive left-hand wall (Dream Wall) and a smaller right-hand wall (Huxter Wall). The left-hand wall's main feature is a central yellow streak and pink streaks either side of it. Routes are described from left to right across both walls.

Dream Wall

All routes start from a ledge below the left arete.

Descent: Abseil down the north edge of the wall, down a gully with a brown retaining wall, to reach the good ledge below the left arete of the wall (5m above the bigger grass ledges below).

1 The Scream 55m E7 6b **
S.Crowe, K.Magog (1 Rest), 25 May 2000
Climbs the first half of the pink quartz streak just right of the left arete of the wall. Follow Dream the Dhearg Goch to the obvious ledge directly below the stepped roof. From here, thin moves lead up to good undercuts below the roof. Layback into the shallow groove above on improving holds to gain jugs and good protection at the top of some flakes. A powerful move up gains a downward traverse line leading left to the arete. Continue up the brown wall more easily to the top, taking care with some loose holds.

2 K&S Special 60m E6 6a ****
K.Magog, S.Crowe, Jun 2006
The logical direct line on The Scream offering superb sustained climbing, immaculate rock and good protection. Follow The Scream to the good undercuts below the roof. Follow the right side of a flake, then pull leftwards and up to gain a quartz band. Climb direct through the bulges to the wide ledge below the top (junction with Dream and possible belay). Climb direct above with a final hard move.

3 Dream the Dhearg Goch 60m E6 ****
G.Huxter, D.Towse, 13 May 1999
Probably the route of the cliff. It climbs the superb shield of rock via a tenuous line up a pink streak just left of the yellow streak.
1. 20m 6a Pull out right from the belay and climb to an obvious wide pink slot. Traverse right 2m, then back up left to the obvious ledge. Traverse this delicately right to a flake and hanging belay.
2. 25m 6b Climb the pink, cracked vein above the belay, trending rightwards as it steepens and pull out onto a wide ledge. Block belay 3m to the left.
3. 15m 6a Climb the steep wall above just right of the belay towards another pink vein in the roof at the top. Traverse left 2m to an interesting exit.

4 Ocean Voyeur 65m E5 ***
K.Howett, H.Harris, 12 May 1999
Another excellent route climbing a line of least resistance up the centre of the pale sheet, just right of the yellow streak.
1. 20m 5b Pull out right from the belay ledge onto the wall and follow the obvious line traversing rightwards across the lip of the undercut wall, passing a short left-facing corner to climb a flake beyond to a ledge. Awkward belay near the left end.
2. 25m 6a Go up left off the ledge to gain a smaller ledge above bulging rock. Climb excellent flakes direct up the pale wall to gain a diagonal crack leading right. Follow this into a short black open groove. Struggle all the way up this with a hard exit onto sloping ledges above.
3. 20m 5b Follow the left-facing groove to a small ledge. Pull up left onto another ledge and exit in a wild position out left in space to finish.

Dream the Dhearg Goch, P2 (E6) Dave Towse & Glenda Huxter (photo Kevin Howett)

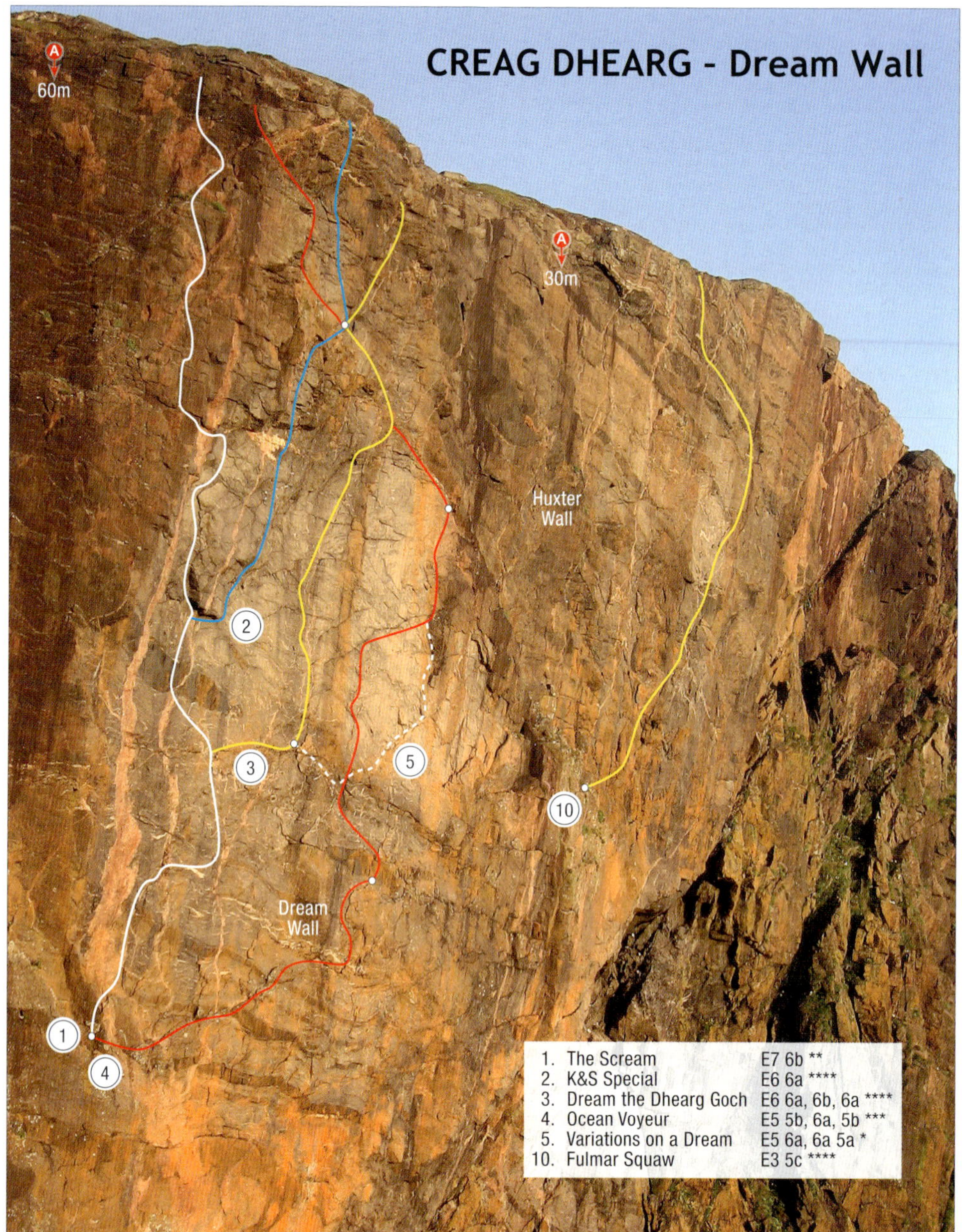

5 Variations on a Dream 55m E5 *

S.Crowe, K.Magog 24, May 2000

Good climbing but a boomerang of a line based around both Dream the Dhearg Goch and Ocean Voyeur.

1. 20m 6a Climb the first pitch of Dream the Dhearg Goch to the hanging belay.

2. 25m 6a Traverse right along the ledge, crossing Ocean Voyeur, until directly beneath the black groove of Ocean Voyeur. Tricky moves gain the base of this groove direct to join Ocean Voyeur, which is followed to gain the sloping ledges.

3. 10m 5a Follow Ocean Voyeur leftwards to the top.

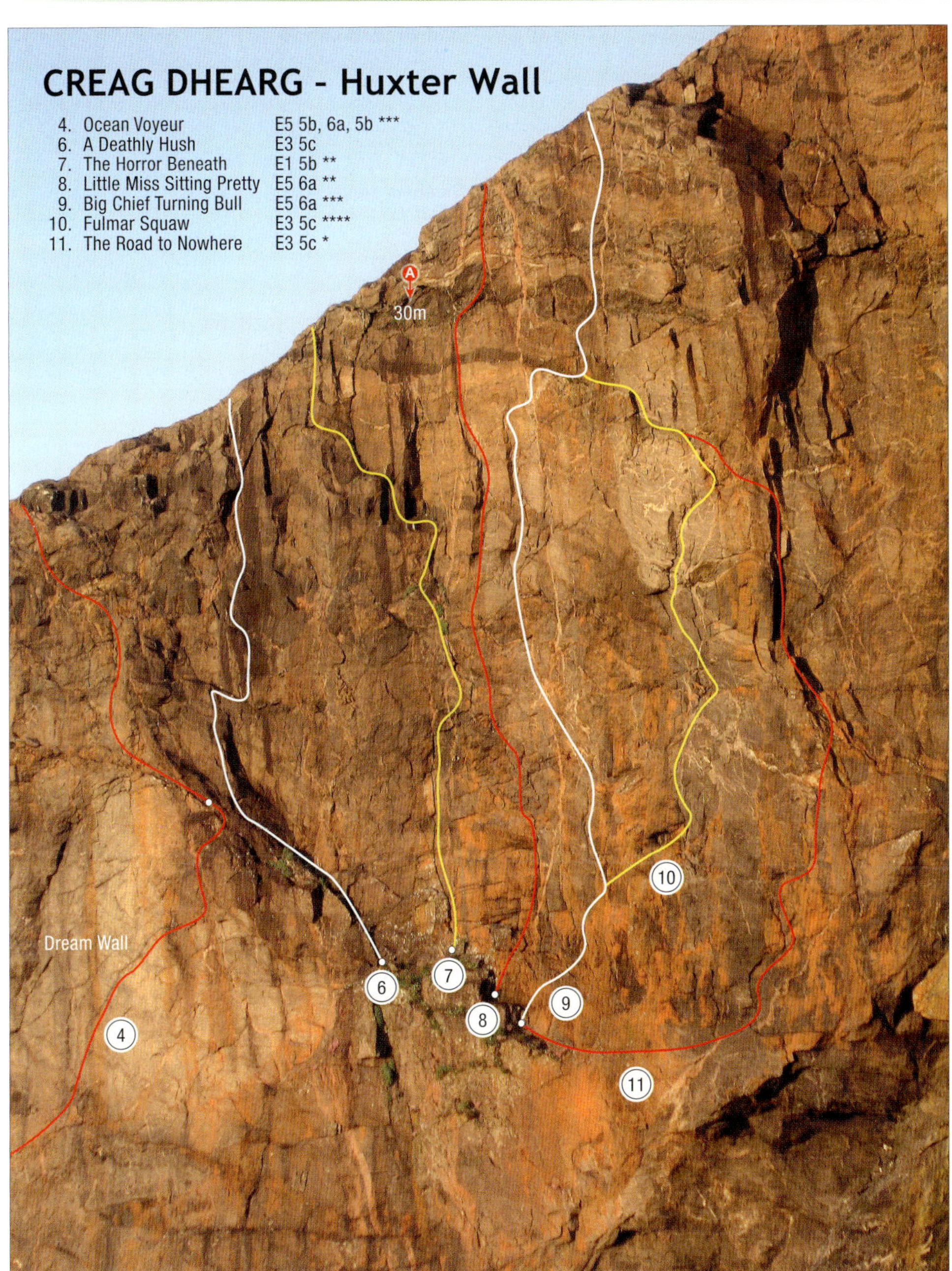

The Huxter Wall

All the routes start from a good ledge which sits central at the base of the wall. Beneath the ledge the wall is undercut and rotten, and only masochists need go lower.

Descent: Gain the base by a 30m abseil to the good ledge near the base of the ramp-line that separates the two walls. It is important to keep swinging during the abseil in order not to miss the ledge.

6 A Deathly Hush 40m E3 5c
K.Magog, S.Crowe, 25 May 2001
From the far left end of the ledge, follow the ramp to reach a prominent V-shaped groove. Climb the left arete of this to reach a ledge. Pull onto the ledge and tentatively traverse right along the detached flake for about 4m to pull into the base of a slim right-facing corner. Bold. Follow the corner to the top. A direct start is possible at 6b but the rock is dubious.

7 The Horror Beneath 40m E1 5b **
D.Turnbull, G.Huxter, 24 May 2000
From the left end of the ledge, climb a perfect right-facing flake, then move right and back left to finish up twin ledges.

8 Little Miss Sitting Pretty 40m E5 6a **
S.Crowe, K.Magog, 21 May 2001
From the centre of the ledge, take a leftward rising line to gain the left side of a ledge below the pair of right-facing grooves. Follow the left-hand groove and continue directly with increasing difficult above the groove until below the left extremity of the final roofs. Ignoring the possibility to escape left, step right and pull over the roof and up the final headwall on jugs.

9 Big Chief Turning Bull 40m E5 6a ***
D.Turnbull, G.Huxter, 25 May 2000
Climb from the right edge of the ledge to a wide flake. From this, go up and left to a ledge in the centre of the wall. Go up a slim right-facing groove and swing right into a slim left-facing groove at a small ledge (crux). Traverse 5m right and finish direct on jugs.

10 Fulmar Squaw 45m E3 5c ****
G.Huxter, D.Turnbull, 25 May 2000
From the right edge of the ledge, climb to the wide flake. Continue up to beneath a hanging right-facing flake. Move up and left, then direct to the top. Jugs and overhanging all the way!

11 The Road to Nowhere 40m E3 5c *
K.Magog, S.Crowe, 21 May 2001
Climb rightwards from the ledge for about 4m to gain a vaguely scooped grey shield of rock. Follow the faint scoop to the ledge. From here, climb the black scoop above to a good break. Traverse right slightly to gain a slim right-facing ramp-line. Follow this up and left until it reaches Fulmar Squaw. and finish as for this on increasingly good holds.

MACPHEE'S BUTTRESS

(NL 5650 8375) Alt 140m S facing Map p429

This crag lies on the south-east side of MacPhee's Hill (Cnoc Mhic-a-Phì), above the old chapel. It is the biggest section of crag on the hillside and the only inland crag on the island big enough to offer routes. The routes are best identified by finding Kingdom of Corpses in the centre, but are described from left to right.

Wall of Wisdom 10m D
L.Catterall, 22 May 2001
At the left-hand side of the crag is a prominent low square-sided roof with a grassy open bay to its left. Start 2m right of the left-hand side the roof, climb the broken wall and slab above.

Sleeping Souls 10m S 4a
T.Catterall, 2008
Climb the wall 2m left of Honeysuckle Wall to a small nose at the base of the undercut slab, surmount this and climb the slab above via the horizontal breaks.

Honeysuckle Wall 10m D
A.Philipson, 22 May 2001
Climb the scoop and broken slab immediately left of the honeysuckle, which grows out of the large grassy central recess.

Leaving MacPhee 10m S 4a
T.Catterall, 2008
Start below the right-hand side of the grassy bay in the centre of the crag. Climb the broken wall going rightwards and climb the centre of the slab above.

Invasion of the Body Snatchers 12m S 4b
T.Catterall, 24 May 2000
Climb the crack from an overhung start 3m left of the left-facing corner of Kingdom of Corpses. Surmount the small roof and move up and climb the left-hand crack above.

Kingdom of Corpses 12m S 4b
T.Catterall, 23 May 2000
Climbs the right-hand of the twin cracks in the centre of the face. Start by a small left-facing corner that forms a roof at head height. Surmount this and flow up the crack on the slab above.

Alles Tote Hose 12m VD
F.Williams, 2008
Takes a direct line up slabs and small walls 2m left of Cracking MacPhee after a steep bouldery start.

Cracking MacPhee 12m D
A.Philipson, 22 May 2001
Climb the thin discontinuous crack 6m right of the left-facing corner of Kingdom of Corpses.

Dawn of the Dead 12m VD
F.Williams, 2008
Start right of Cracking MacPhee just before the crag degenerates into a vegetated broken mess. Make a hard start over the roof, continue directly up slabs and finish over a steep cracked headwall.

Rodent on the Rampage 45m 5c
T.Catterall, 2008
Starting at the extreme left, this is a rising traverse to the right-hand end at head height, following the lip of the roofs.

BERNERAY (BEÀRNARAIGH)

Also known as Barra Head, this is the most southerly point in the Outer Hebrides chain. Covered in verdant grass, the island has a different character from the other Bishop Isles. It rises gently from sea-level along its north coast to gain its highest point along its south coast, where all the current batch of climbs can be found. A lighthouse sits on the highest point near the west end and a good road runs down to a jetty on the north side of the island.

Unlike the other islands, midges can be a problem. There is also a lot of poor rock and more nesting birds spread across a greater area of the island. There are a couple of stunning walls that are amongst the best in the archipelago. Creag na Beiste, at nearly 200m, offers the highest single cliff of perfect quality rock of all the islands, whilst The Giant's Pipes is probably the most unique cliff in all of Scotland. The cliffs are described anti-clockwise from the lighthouse.

Camping: There is no natural shelter from storms, and if caught out refuge could be taken in the area around the lighthouse. There are two old wells next to the road but they appear to be polluted and there are few streams of any size, which means there could be a shortage of water in dry times. Bring sufficient fresh water for any stay on the island.

CREAG NA BEISTE

(NL 545 802) Tidal S facing Map below Diagram p446

The huge geo of Sloc na Beiste lies immediately west of the lighthouse. It is formed by the promontories of Sròn an Dùin to its south and Rubha Sgait (Skate Point) to its north. The south wall of the geo (the south facing wall of Rubha Sgait) forms a massive wall dropping cleanly into the sea. The area towards the back of the geo is broken and home to many nesting birds. However, towards the west end, almost directly opposite the headland of Sròn an Dùin, is a magnificent section of perfect grey rock, 100m wide and nearly 200m high; probably the most stunning sheet of rock on the islands and a great place to observe the aerial acrobatics of the birds flying out of the back of the geo.

The lower half forms a massive clean shield of rock, above which the cliff is composed of two horizontal terrace systems; First and Second Terraces with two overhanging tiers of rock between. The left-hand side of the shield is defined by the most prominent feature of the entire cliff, a deep off-width, right-facing corner formed by a huge, partly detached pillar. A slim, stepped corner system facing left is found on the right side of the shield and a large rectangular roof at about 60m which forms the base of a large pillar. The routes are concentrated on this section of cliff and described left to right.

Descent: Gain the base of the shield by a 200m abseil from a threaded flat boulder that lies against a small outcrop (just west of a prominent rocky knoll), about three-quarters of the way down Rubha Sgait. For the first two routes, abseil in a direct line to go down the lower wall (about 10m left of the partly detached pillar bounding the left side) to belay in a green recess about 10m above sea-level, near the left side of the shield.

1 Atlantic Affront 175m E3 **

G.E.Little, M.Davies, 26 May 1998

Start in the green recess as for Alien Slayer. An adventure.

1. 25m 4c Climb out left from the recess and take a slightly left-trending line to belay on top of a semi detached pillar (down and right from the huge off-width corner).

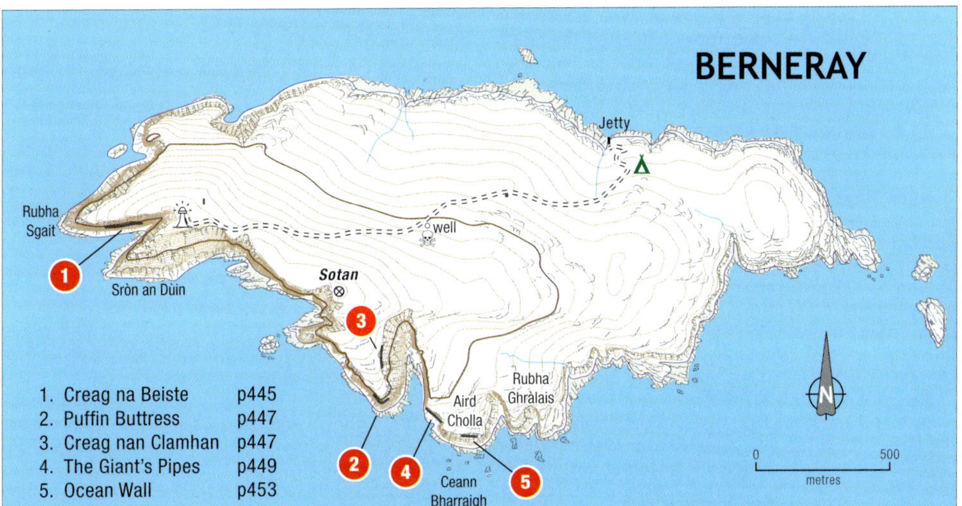

BERNERAY

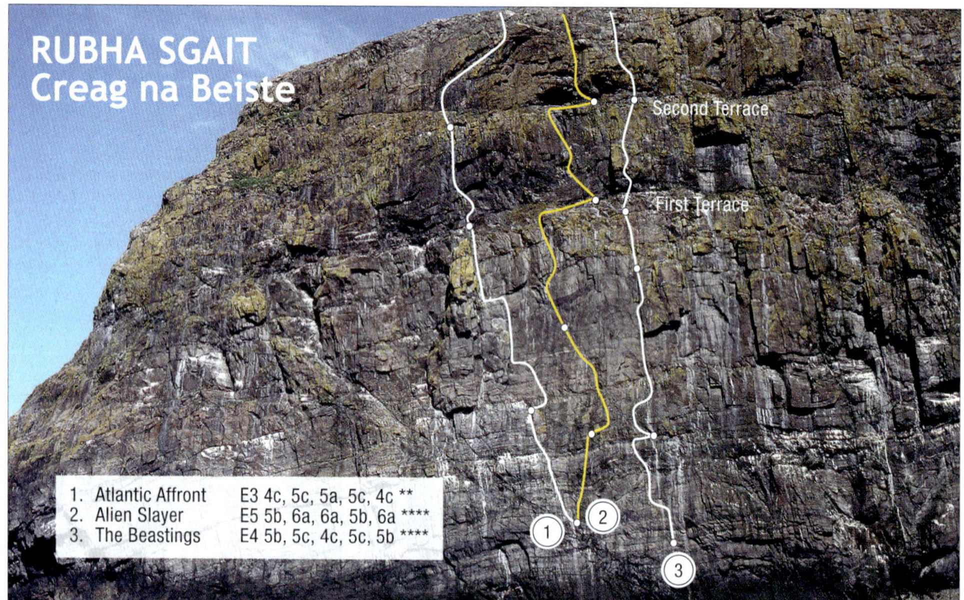

2. 40m 5c Mantelshelf from the top of the pillar, traverse right for 5m to the base of thin vertical cracks. Climb these with increasing difficulty until a horizontal traverse left leads to the distinctive (side on) W-shaped flake. Ascend this and then the slabby wall above until it is possible to traverse up and left to belay at ledges by the large corner formed by the huge semi-detached pillar.
3. 25m 5a Ascend a groove to the right of the corner, step back into the corner and climb it to exit onto the First Terrace.
4. 40m 5c Pull up directly by the belay at a nose then step right to avoid a bulge. Move left above the bulge, then climb, trending leftwards up a series of steep walls with continuous interest to gain the Second Terrace.
5. 45m 4c Follow the obvious diagonal fault up right to an exciting exit over big wedged blocks. Finish over easy ground.

2 Alien Slayer 170m E5 ****
H.Harris, K.Howett, 26 May 1998
Climbs a magnificent natural line up the face left of centre. Start from the green recess.
1. 20m 5b Follow a rising ramp out right from the recess and climb the cracked overhanging rib just before the ramp fades. Follow the rib slightly on its right to a large block belay.
2. 40m 6a Traverse out right below the level of the top of the block, across the blank-looking wall to easy ground leading back left to the base of a slim green corner. Climb the corner to its top and make hard moves left into a ramp-line that leads diagonally up left across the face to gain a hanging belay in a slight depression about 3m below a prominent horizontal band of black biotite.
3. 35m 6a Climb up and left across the biotite into a conspicuous short corner capped by a projecting roof. Make a move up into a traverse line leading right until it is possible to pull into a very shallow groove. Climb this with continuous difficulty to gain the First Terrace. Belay to the right, below a large corner.
4. 40m 5b Climb a flake into a recess below and left of the corner. Exit strenuously out right into the slabby corner which leads to the Second Terrace. Traverse the sloping black ledge rightwards under the overhanging upper tier to belay below a hanging corner.
5. 35m 6a Climb onto a block just right of the corner and make awkward moves left into the corner. Follow it more easily to its capping roof and exit left to finish.

The next route climbs up the right-hand side.

Descent: Take the normal abseil to the First Terrace. Traverse right (facing in) until below a jutting buttress with a roof. Redirect the abseil from here over the rectangular roof below and go down to a small footledge just above the black-green band.

3 The Beastings 175m E4 ****
M.Boyer, K.Howett, 23 Aug 1999
Climbs a direct line up the wall to the left side of the rectangular roof and then up the jutting buttress above. Continuously good climbing in a superb position.
1. 35m 5b Climb a short groove to a ledge. Traverse hard left to a slight arete and go up this to good cracks. Go up and right to gain a good handrail flake leading up and left into a vertical crack. This leads into an obvious shallow corner. At its top traverse hard right, initially difficult, to gain ledges and a belay.

2. 50m 5c Follow the natural curving slab up and left until moves up the wall from its end gain an undercling flake. This leads up right to a small ledge below vertical cracks leading to the left end of the roof. Up these to the roof and climb into and follow the shallow corner above for about 8m until good holds round the right arete allow an escape up the wall to a ledge in the base of a left-facing corner.
3. 15m 4c Climb up the corner, then the ochre-coloured wall via a thin crack to a good ledge and belay about 3m below the jutting buttress (the First Terrace abseil belay).
4. 25m 5c Climb up to guano ledges under the buttress. Pull through the lower bulge via the obvious crack into a short corner under the roof. Pull out left and go up into another corner under another roof. Traverse right around the arete to gain a slab. Climb the wall above to a good ledge; the Second Terrace. Very strenuous.
5. 50m 5b Climb up to a big ledge, then go up a corner and exit out right to a further ledge below the head-wall. Move up to below the base of a right-facing corner with a deep crack in the back. Step right steeply into a subsidiary groove. Follow this (steep) and the general line of the corner to the top.

CEAN SOTAN

Sotan is the name given to an area near the highest hill situated approximately halfway along the length of the island. Cean Sotan (Sotan Head) is the big cliff-girt headland south of here and to the west of Barra Head (Ceann Bharraigh). It is defined on the east by Sloc Veacligeo, a huge geo cutting north into the island. To the west and almost below the highest point is Sloc na Sealbheag with the large promontories of Cirein Beaga and Cirein Mora forming the headlands west side. To the west of here, towards the lighthouse, is a continuous, 180m high line of cliffs (Creag Mhòr), unfortunately broken and vegetated and full of birds.

Puffin Buttress

(NL 555 795) Non-tidal E facing Map p445

The most southerly tip of the headland of Sotan, as it turns into the entrance of Sloc Veacligeo, presents a buttress of excellent unbroken rock in its upper half, whilst below lies darker, shattered rock with ledges emanating from the sea. The buttress itself has a front face (south) and a slender right face (east) containing a prominent corner system. Below this corner, at the junction with the shattered rock below is a small ledge.

Descent: Above the buttress is a wide vegetated ledge, easily accessed and riddled with puffin burrows. The abseil descent starts here and leads to the small ledge.

Huffin and Puffin 65m E2 *
G.E.Little, K.Howett, 29 May 1997
Start from the small ledge below a triangular roof guarding access to the corner system above.
1. 25m 5c Move left to vertical twin cracks which lead to the left end of the roof (crux). Step left onto the front face, then hand-traverse left to gain a short corner-groove. Ascend this then climb diagonally left to belay on a good ledge.
2. 40m 5a Traverse horizontally right along the obvious break, and move up into a short right-facing groove. Climb this, then direct over its capping roof to move right across the lip and climb a slabby section to a bulge. Climb into the bulge to gain a horizontal break. Step left and up to a roof which is passed on the right to gain a ledge. Move out left and take a line of least resistance to the top. An excellent sustained pitch.

Puffin Pantry 55m E3 *
H.Harris, K.Howett, 24 May 1998
Start as for Huffin and Puffin.
1. 20m 5c Follow Huffin and Puffin to the twin cracks to the left end of the roof. Pull directly into the corner above then immediately pull out right to gain a short slabby groove left of the arete. Belay at its top.
2. 35m 5c Climb up slightly leftwards to gain a sloping ledge. Climb the prominent crack-line up the over-hanging wall into a corner. This leads to a roof which is climbed direct to finish.

Creag Nan Clamhan

(NL 556 796) Alt 130m E facing Map p445

This distinctive, heavily roofed crag lies on the east flank of the headland, just above and behind Puffin Buttress. It is more akin to an inland crag, being high above the sea and easy of access.

Descent: Descend by a wide grassy (puffin packed) shelf from near the top of the descent to the ledges above Puffin Buttress on the headland. The most obvious feature at the bottom of the crag is a slipped pillar supporting a big roof. The routes are described from left to right as approached.

1 The Frotteur 30m E5 6a ***
L.Hughes, G.Nicoll, 31 May 1997
A strenuous but well protected route with the crux just when you thought it was all over. Start 4m left of the detached pillar. Climb a crack to the roof. Traverse the break rightwards to the arete and lip of the roof. Pull round the arete and over the roof onto the slab above. Climb up to the next smaller roof and make hard moves onto the slab above. Follow the slab out left round the bigger roof above and escape right above this.

2 The Mauking Bird 30m E1 5b ***
G.Nicoll, L.Hughes, 30 May 1997
Climb the left side of the pillar then a crack 2m left of the big corner. Make a long reach over a bulge onto the slab below the big roof. Traverse the fine slab leftwards until past the big roof above, joining The Frotteur and finishing out right as for that route.

3 Auksiliary Force 30m HVS 5a ***
G.Nicoll, L.Hughes, 30 May 1997
This superb route tackles the big corner below the biggest roof on the crag. Start by climbing the right side

The Frotteur (E5) Laurence Hughes
(photo Kevin Howett)

of the detached pillar then go up the corner, moving onto the right wall to pass the roof. Step right above onto an arete and climb a small overhang at an obvious break. Traverse left then right to finish.

4 Exit Stage Right 30m HVS 5b *
G.E.Little, K.Howett, 30 May 1997
This is the slim, roofed corner about 6m right of the slipped pillar. Climb the corner to twin stepped roofs high up. The first is turned on the right and, more improbably, the second is also turned on the right, by stepping onto a vertical edge. Climb the short wall above (crux).

5 Millennium Man 35m E1 5b **
G.E.Little, K.Howett, 30 May 1997
Start about 9m up from the lowest corner at a slim right-facing corner. Climb this and straight up the wall above to a big ledge. Move left onto a clean rusty wall and climb it direct on good holds.

6 Not So Aukward 35m VS 4c *
G.E.Little, K.Howett, 30 May 1997
This is the lowest corner. Climb it directly to exit right below the capping roof.

BARRA HEAD (CEANN BHARRAIGH)

The most southerly point of the Outer Hebrides and the headland immediately east of Sloc Veacligeo. The highest point is marked on the maps as Àird Cholla. The south face, virtually at the most southern point, holds a smooth vertical wall sitting above sea-level slabs, Ocean Wall, which gives a good collection of easier routes. To the west and the junction with Sloc Veacligeo is a sea cave cutting west to east into Aird Cholla, and an impressive wall overlooks its entrance, The Giant's Pipes, offering sterner stuff.

The Giant's Pipes

(NL 557 795) Tidal S facing Map p445 Diagram p450

One of the most striking cliffs in these islands, it is composed of a series of huge open corners, many of which contain roofs. The whole cliff resembles the organ pipes of a church and the atmosphere of climbing in here can be almost religious. The sea cave itself is a small affair with no climbs around or above it at present. The main wall drops directly into the sea and there is only one small ledge, at the base of Barra Head Games. The wall can be viewed from the small headland on the other side of the cave to the south. The cliff turns 90° into Sloc Veacligeo, and although containing a very enticing huge roof, the slabs below harbour a huge nesting bird colony and the area is covered in guano.

Starting on the right the first feature is an impressive leaning arete bounding the sea cave; the wall to its left being composed of slim grooves with the most distinctive features being an upper horizontal roof and a big right-facing slabby corner. To the left is a deep vertical recess with an off-width crack in its right side. Left again is an area of more defined corners, the big central one starting from a vertical roof-capped slot near

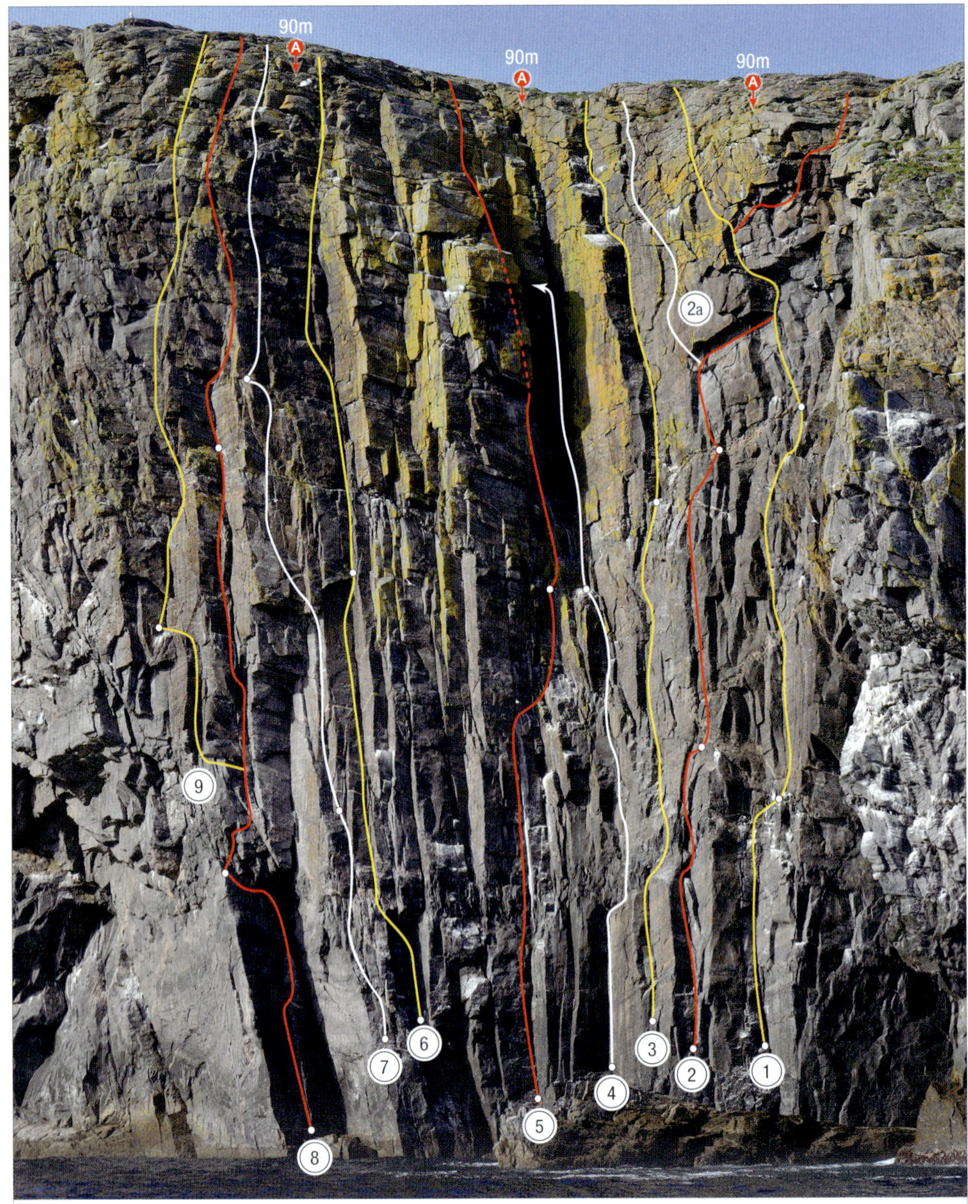

CEANN BHARRAIGH - The Giant's Pipes

1. Piping Up	E1 5a, 5b, 4c ***	5. Victims of Circumstance	E1 5b, 5a *
2. Wavering World	E2 5c, 5b,5a ***	6. The Great Auk	E1 5b, 5a ***
2a. Imagine This	E2 5b ***	7. The Eye of the Eagle	E3 4c, 5c, 6a ***
3. Barra Sounds	E2 5b, 4b ***	8. Barra Head Games	E3 5b, 5c, 5b ****
4. The Book Before The Trial	E3 6a, 5b ***	9. Stolen Moments	E3 5b, 5c, 5b ***

sea-level. Left of this is an immaculate corner that tapers towards the top of the crag and holds the only obvious ledge at sea-level. Left again the wall becomes grossly undercut as it turns the arete into Sloc Veacligeo.

Descent: Gaining the base of the routes is via 90m abseils from different points, and several routes can be climbed from each abseil. For the first routes around the arete near the back of the cave, abseil from the rounded top of the arete itself, down the wall to the base of the small corner at the bottom of the arete. Routes are described right to left.

1 Piping Up 80m E1 ***

M.Boyer, K.Howett, 22 Aug 1999

Climbs a corner-line just left of the arete.

1. 20m 5a Climb the corner until it is possible to traverse out right to gain small ledges near the arete.
2. 35m 5b Climb the immaculate corner to a small ledge at a horizontal quartz band. Climb directly up into a bomb bay groove and exit above to a ledge. Follow cracks above to gain a ledge on top of a pedestal. Step right and gain a better ledge in a corner some 5m below the roofs.
3. 25m 4c Climb up left to under the roof. Traverse left on the fault through it to an arete. Go up to the left end of another roof and pass it to gain cracks up the headwall.

2 Wavering Worlds 90m E2 ***

J.Fisher, R.Gantzhorn, 12 Jun 1998

Takes a pleasing natural line of grooves in the slight arete left of Piping Up and leading to the left end of the upper roofs before escaping right. From the base of the previous route, either pendulum left to a belay below the groove or climb easily to the same spot.

1. 30m 5c Climb the groove to a small ledge. Climb the continuation groove until level with huge flakes in the right wall. Traverse these right to the arete and take a semi-hanging belay.
2. 30m 5b Step back left into the continuation groove and climb it until it fades. Head up and right, passing beneath a grey recess to gain a further short corner. Go up this and exit out left onto a small black ledge 5m below the roof.
3. 30m 5a Climb the groove above the belay to the roof. Traverse right under the roof into Piping Up and follow this through the break in the roof. Traverse right under the upper roof, exiting out right at the top.

Variation: **2a Imagine This E2 *****

K.Howett, M.Boyer, 24 Aug 1999

3. 25m 5b From the small black ledge 5m below the roof, climb up to the roof. Step left round it into a left-diagonal crack in the headwall leading into a hanging right-facing slim corner. Climb this, then go direct to the top.

3 Barra Sounds 90m E2 ***

K.Howett, M.Boyer, 24 Aug 1999

Climbs the next corner system to the left, leading into the large right-facing corner in the upper half. Abseil as for Piping Up to the base of the wall. Traverse across the slabby wall beneath Wavering Worlds and climb cracks up to a small projecting ledge below the well-defined groove.

1. 50m 5b Climb the deep groove until a black biotite band is reached. Exit out right to a small ledge near the arete. Go up the wall to enter a further, more defined groove. Follow this to its end as the rock steepens and exit out right to guano ledges 3m below the upper corner.
2. 40m 4b Climb into and up the big open corner to the top.

Descent: The following routes climb either side of the deep vertical recess. Gain the corners leading into the recess by abseiling from huge blocks at the top.

4 The Book Before The Trial 90m E3 ***

A.McSherry, M.Howard, 24 Aug 1999

Climbs the right side of the deep recess. Start at a large ledge at the base of a perfect square-cut corner below the line.

1. 50m 6a Climb the stunning corner with difficulty to a bulge of biotite. Traverse out right to the arete and continue up left into an open groove, passing a couple of small ledges to belay on a pink quartz ledge.
2. 40m 5b The horrendous looking corner-crack above succumbs to aggressive laybacking to reach a roof where it all goes pear-shaped. Traverse the wall leftwards into the left-hand side of the recess and follow this through a cave behind a huge detached block and easy ground leading to the top.

5 Victims of Circumstance 90m E1 *

M.Howard, A.McSherry, 25 Aug 1999

Climbs the left-hand side of the vertical recess. Start from small ledges in the base of the corner directly below the line.

1. 40m 5b Climb the corner and a slight chimney through a roof to exit right onto commodious ledges.
2. 50m 5a Climb the main left-hand corner of the recess, joining The Book Before the Trial through the cave and finish up easy ground to the top.

Descent: The following routes start around the deep vertical roof-capped slot, a safe distance above the sea, below the large central corner in the upper part of the cliff. Abseil from a big square block just back from the edge of the cliff, down the west sidewall of the main corner.

6 The Great Auk 90m E1 ***

G.E.Little, M.Davies, 24 May 1998

This takes the longest corner system in the centre of the face. Belay in the roof-capped slot.

1. 45m 5b Ascend the left edge of the slot to reach the base of an obvious immaculate slim corner. Climb this to its capping roof then pull out and step right to belay at a big flat-topped flake. Excellent.
2. 45m 5a Climb straight up, then move left into the base of the main corner. Climb this in its entirety, crossing a bulge, to the capping roofs. Ascend the right wall strenuously and continue to the top.

7 Eye of the Eagle 95m E3 ***

G.E.Little, M.Davies, 25 May 1998

This excellent route climbs the wall to the left of The Great Auk. Belay at the lowest feasible point on the pillar immediately left of the roof-capped slot.

Barra Head Games (E3) Grahame Little & Kevin Howett
(photo Grahame Nicoll)

1. 20m 4c Ascend the crack-line on the left edge of the pillar (overlooking the deep recess taken by Barra Head Games pitch 1) to reach a good stance and belay above.
2. 35m 5c Climb a short corner to a slim vertical rib between two crack-lines. Climb the rib to its capping roof. Pull right then strenuously back left and follow the continuation rib and wall to belay on a small ledge by a large shaky flake. Sustained pitch.
3. 40m 6a Move up, step left onto fragile looking flakes, and from their top make a thin move (crux) to a break. Continue over a series of bulges to the top.

Descent: Access to the following routes is by abseil to the conspicuous small ledge at the base of a corner-line, left of the corner of The Great Auk. Taking a line down the upper part of Eye of the Eagle lands on the ledge.

8 Barra Head Games 110m E3 ****
G.E.Little, K.Howett, 31 May 1997
A fantastic route. Start from the sea-washed ledge.
1. 25m 5b Enter and boldly climb the off-width slot (left and parallel to the chimney in the back of the corner) to reach a ledge. Make difficult moves into a V-recess. Move out to the right edge of the recess (effectively into the chimney) and traverse left under the huge roof to a belay on the left arete.
2. 40m 5c Pull up into a hanging groove above the arete, step right immediately into a short corner (crux) then out right again onto a projecting ledge above the roof. Move up and left to go back into the corner, and climb it over a series of bulges to enter a red open-book left-facing corner. Climb it and belay a few metres below its capping roof. Stunning!
3. 45m 5b Continue up the corner to the roof. Traverse right to near the arete, then climb the diminishing corner above to the point where it merges with the arete. Pull up left and climb a left-trending diagonal crack. Step left again onto another arete, then back right through a bulge to continue by the easiest line to reach the abseil point. Another stunning pitch.

9 Stolen Moments 100m E3 ***
H.Harris, K.Howett, 25 May 1998
Climbs a groove line to the left of Barra Head Games, on the very left edge of the wall after climbing the first pitch of that route from the small ledge at the base of the wall. Space walking! Retreat would be problematical.
1. 25m 5b Climb the first pitch of Barra Head Games to the belay on the arete.
2. 25m 5c Climb the crux of Barra Head Games into the short corner. At the first small roof, traverse left across an overhanging wall to enter the base of a hanging corner in a spectacular position. Climb this above thin air until it fades and pull up and left onto a sloping ledge in the base of a larger corner.
3. 50m 5b Climb the corner and pull round the roof on the right. Move back left above this then up into the continuation corner above. Climb this past a thin section to climb out rightwards into another groove above, then the wall leading to the top. Yet another amazing pitch.

Ocean Wall

(NL 559 794) Non-tidal S facing Map p445

Almost at the very tip of the headland. The main interest centres on a lower wall of excellent one-pitch grooves and crack-lines. These all finish on a large ledge system below an upper tier of more broken and vegetated rock and it is best to exit from here by a simple walk off to the right (facing in). Routes are described from left to right with the first route starting from a lower ledge reached by an easy scramble down and left.

Approach: A large terrace at the base can be reached by a scramble from the east at any state of the tide.

Giant McAskill 45m VS 4c
C.Fowler, S.McNeil, K.Tighe, 1 May 1997
Starts in the second left-facing corner down and left from the main terrace. Climb the corner over a bulge directly to the big ledge at the top.

Big Jamie 30m HVS 5a
M.Tighe, C.Fowler, K.Tighe, 1 May 1997
Starting from the centre of the main terrace, climb the conspicuous left-facing corner (which gets wide!). The crux involves a pull over a small roof.

All the way from America 30m HVS 5a
C.Fowler, M.Tighe, K.Tighe, 1 May 1997
The most prominent left-facing corner system.

A Rotting Sea 30m VS 4c
C.Fowler, K.Tighe, M.Tighe, 1 May 1997
Just right of the most prominent corner system, climb another, smaller corner and the face above to reach a finger-crack in a small left-facing corner.

Sea Children 30m VS 4c
M.Tighe, C.Fowler, K.Tighe, 1 May 1997
Climb small corners and walls towards the right side of the face.

Rubha Ghràlais

(NL 562 794)

There is a big arch on the headland of Rubha Ghràlais, just east of Àird Cholla. An unspecified number of routes were climbed here by Charlie Fowler, Kathy Tighe and Sandy McNeil in May 1997.

Keromadal

(NL 568 798)

A small (10 to 15m) crag contains 6 routes graded around VS and a sea-level traverse of the crag (K.Tighe, 1997).

Tresivick Bay

(NL 569 799)

The short but excellent wall on the east side of the bay contains an excellent little crack (M.Tighe, 1997) accessed by traversing in from the south at low tide.

ST KILDA

Maps: OS 1:50,000 Landranger 17; 1:25,000 Explorer 400, below & p462

The St Kilda Archipelago of four islands and several sea stacks is the remotest part of Scotland, lying over 66km (40 miles) west of the Outer Hebrides. They are the remnants of a ring volcano and the rocks are granites and gabbro. Hirta is the largest island and the only one ever fully inhabited, and Dun, Soay and Boreray are scattered varying distances from Hirta. The highest sea-cliff in the UK is Conachair on Hirta reaching 426m (1,400ft) and is classed as a Marilyn (a peak with 150m of re-ascent on all sides) as are the other hills of Mullach an Eilein on Boreray, Cnoc Glas on Soay and Bioda Mor on Dun. Also scattered across the archipelago are a number of very impressive sea stacks some of which are the highest in Britain in particular, Stac an Armin (191m) and Stac Lee (165m) can lay claim to be the most remote stacks, and the most difficult, Marilyns in the UK!

The islands have been inhabited for some 2000 years, and were home to a crofting community for hundreds of years with a substantial village on the main island of Hirta. The islanders were evacuated to mainland Scotland in 1930 and the islands are now owned by the National Trust for Scotland (NTS) and managed by NTS with Scottish Natural Heritage (SNH) and the Ministry of Defence, who have a missile tracking station based on Hirta. Hirta is now a base for NTS work parties, MOD staff and scientists and archaeologist undertaking research.

St Kilda has many important designations including being a Scheduled Ancient Monument, a National Nature Reserve, a Biosphere Reserve, a National Scenic Area, a Site of Special Scientific Interest (SSSI), a European Community Special Protection Area (Wild Birds Directive) and a Special Area of Conservation under the European Habitats Directive. The islands are also a UNESCO World Heritage Site and this is one of the few places in the world which gained this recognition for both natural and cultural significance.

St Kilda's natural abundance of birds makes it one of the most important sea bird breeding venues in North-West Europe with the world's largest colony of gannets. The surrounding marine environment is unique and one of the best diving venues in Britain with its caves, arches and tunnel. The cultural recognition concerns the extraordinary human history of a crofting way of life lost when the islands were evacuated.

Access: Private day trip charters go from Skye, Harris and Uist. For longer visits for climbing a private yacht is useful or there are several boat charters which have berths to choose from, sailing out of Troon in Ayrshire, Achnacraig in Argyll, from Mallaig and from the Isle of Lewis. Because of its oceanic climate, regular strong winds and sea swells of 5m or more, access is only realistically possible in the calmer summer months.

Staying on the island: There is limited camping for 6 people in Village Bay on Hirta, and stay is limited to 5 nights, so prior booking is essential. Contact the NTS at **stkildainfo@nts.org.uk**. The alternative is to stay on board a charter boat during your visit.

Climbing: In the past climbing was essentially prohibited through a bylaw, only being allowed by permission which was rarely granted. But this changed with the Land Reform Act of 2003. Access for climbing is now lawful but because of the importance of the islands for birdlife, climbers must concentrate on the areas of cliff not inhabited by birds. Climbers should contact the warden on arrival and discuss their plans. For further Information see **www.kilda.org.uk**.

HIRTA (HIORT)

(NA 090 995)

RUABHAL, SOUTH-WEST FACE

(NF 095 978) Non-tidal S facing Diagram p456

This is a gabbro crag of excellent rock, usually running to a profusion of good holds and protection. It is largely unaffected by nesting birds and is perhaps the finest climbing crag in the St Kilda archipelago. It is located on the south-west tip of Ruabhal, almost opposite the island of Dun, and is only visible from out at sea. It drops steeply into the sea but fortunately a convenient ledge system runs along the base just above high tide level. There is a less appealing Upper Tier which is descended to a grassy dyke separating the two walls to abseil into the base. The crag is characterised by a central cave with roofed corners to the left and a very conspicuous clean-cut slab in its upper right corner. The climbs on either side of the cave are accessed by different abseils to ledges at the base. These can be accessed in all but very high tides and big Atlantic swells.

Approach: Walk round the bay from the village to the col to the west of Ruabhal and follow the ridge up to the Mistress Stone (sometimes referred to as The Maiden Stone). Go through the arch formed by the stone and drop down a grassy gully in the Upper Tier to gain a grassy bay. A dyke descends leftwards across the top of the cliff.

The Left-Hand Side

Routes on the left-hand side of the face include the main central corner line and are described from left to right.

Descent: There is a good block anchor on the arete to the right (looking out) of the grassy bay from which to abseil (80m) to ledges at the bottom of the crag.

1 Brief Encounter 110m HVS *
M.Mortimer, M.Allen, 31 Aug 1987
A rising leftwards traverse to the arete overlooking the geo which bounds the left-hand side of the cliff.
1. 20m 5a From the foot of the abseil, move left onto slabs which go straight to the sea and take a rising leftward diagonal line under a roof to belay under a corner.
2. 20m 4c Continue leftwards in more or less the same line to reach a fine ledge overlooking the geo on the left.
3. 20m 4c Move left and climb the arete to a ledge.
4. 20m 4c Continue up the arete to a large grass ledge below the final headwall.
5. 20m Move right and climb up to and through a small roof to another ledge.
6. 10m Climb a short crack and either continue up another crack or traverse easily right to reach the top of the abseil.

2 Sideline 90m E2 *
P.Whillance, I.McMullen, 1 Sep 1987
Start below the second groove to the left of Maiden's Corner.
1. 35m 5b Up steeply to enter the groove above the overhang. Climb the groove to a junction with Maiden's Corner. Move up about a metre and take the crack-line leftwards (loose) to a ledge.
2. 30m 5b/c Move up into a groove on the slab above, then go rightwards to a ledge (junction with the top of Maiden's Corner). Up a short wall above, then over an awkward roof and step out left to a grass ledge.
3. 25m Climb rightwards to the final crack of The First Route. Up this and continue leftwards to the top.

3 Maiden's Corner 95m E1 **
C.Bonington, B.Hall, 31 Aug 1987
Follows the main conspicuous corner that bounds the left-hand side of the steep main crag.
1. 35m 4c Climb the hanging chimney to reach the base of the corner and follow it more easily to a ledge on the slabby glacis in the middle of the crag.
2. 20m 5b Climb the steep corner, trending right then left to a ledge.

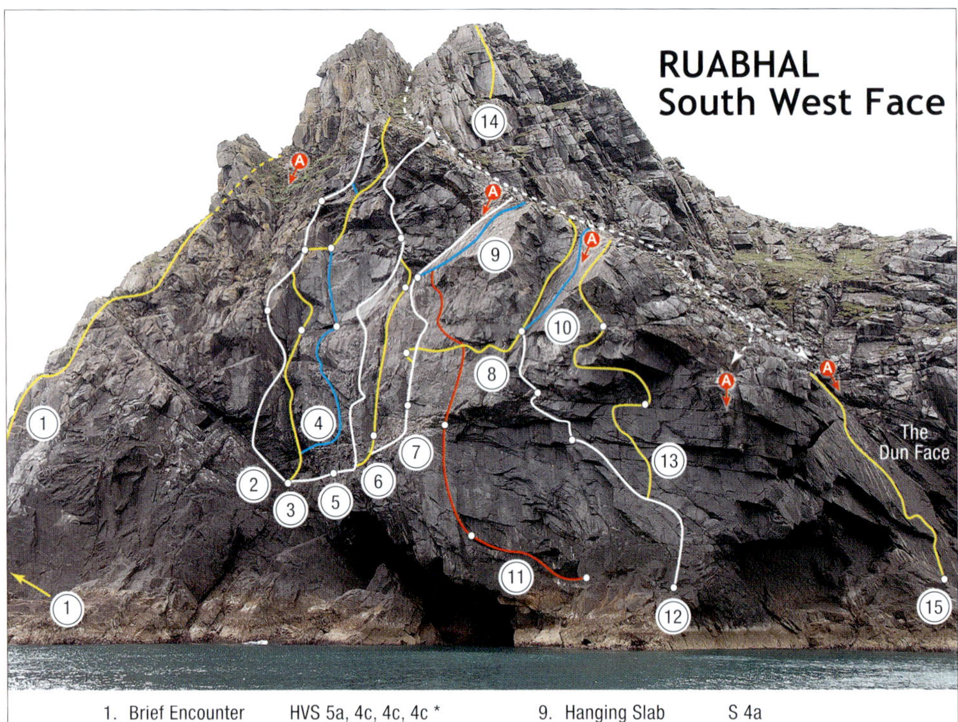

1. Brief Encounter	HVS 5a, 4c, 4c, 4c *	9. Hanging Slab	S 4a
2. Sideline	E2 5b, 5c *	10. Lichen Slab	HS 4b
3. Maiden's Corner	E1 4c, 5b, 5a **	11. Boat Race	E6 5c, 6a,6a ****
4. The First Route	E3 5b, 6a, 5a ***	12. Old Boy Racer	E8 5c, 7a, 6b **
5. Easy Virtue	E1 5a, 5a, 5b **	13. Making a Splash	E7 5b, 6c, 5c ***
6. A Perfect Brief	E1 4c, 5a/b, 5a, 5a **	14. Rehab	E3 6a **
7. A Bit On The Side	E2 4b, 5c, 5b *	15. Blackface	HVS 5a **
8. Continental Drift	E2 4b, 5c, 5b, 4c *		

3. 40m 5a Move right along the ledge into the back of a corner. Move right again, pull over the overhangs, and keep trending right along the overhanging wall on huge holds to a right-facing corner. Ascend this and the corners and grooves above.

4 The First Route 95m E3 ****

I.McMullen, P.Whillance, 18 Aug 1987

Start in the groove line of Maiden's Corner.

1. 35m 5b Climb the chimney's initial overhanging section for 8m and move right to a ledge below an overhanging crack-line. Start this on the right and follow it to a bulge. Climb the flake-crack on the left to a ledge and continue up to a large glacis.

2. 20m 6a The obvious groove come corner above. Climb up into the groove and pass an awkward bulge to a resting place. Bridge up the corner above to better holds and a large ledge.

3. 40m 5a Move up right to a slab below overhangs. Pull over and move rightwards on good holds to a ledge. Climb the obvious grooved crack-line above until it is possible to step up rightwards to the top.

5 Easy Virtue 90m E1 **

C.Bonington, B.Hall, 31 Aug 1987; Direct Finish: M.Mortimer, M.Allen, 1 Sep 1987

Start at the foot of Maiden's Corner. The route weaves its way up the face on the right, heading towards the conspicuous flake-crack in the upper wall.

1. 5m Pull up right on to the ledge system crossing the face. Belay about 3m along this.

2. 35m 5a Move a further 5m right to the foot of an obvious crack. Climb this steeply to another ledge. Traverse right, then back left (to a point above the crack-line) and climb upwards to the left-facing corner on the smooth slab. Belay on a small ledge on the glacis below the obvious flake-crack.

3. 20m 5a Trend left towards undercut holds and then go back right towards the foot of the flake-crack. Climb this until it is possible to exit right to a ledge.

4. 35m 5b Step right to the obvious roof crack, where the roof is at its smallest. Pull over it into a right-facing corner. Exit left onto the arete, climb directly to a loose dyke, then break slightly right over the dyke (5b) to the top.

6 A Perfect Brief 115m E1 **
D.Cuthbertson, B.Hall, 3 Jun 2010
Start on the right side of the wall. The meaty pitch of the route looks unlikely for the grade as it weaves through overlaps, with holds appearing just where needed.
1. 25m 4c Start up slabby rock left of the cave and, via a recess, traverse rightwards above the lip of the cave to a stance and belay.
2. 35m 5a/b Climb the groove above (sometimes wet) with a tricky move to gain a crack. Follow the crack to belay at the bottom left-hand corner of a slab.
3. 25m 5a Move leftwards and negotiate a couple of steeper sections to a stance and belay beneath a breach in the final overhangs.
4. 25m 5a Gain and climb a steep crack and pillar (a bit lichenous but doesn't affect the climbing too much) to an exciting finish.
Variation: **Backshall's Variant E1 5b**
D.Cuthbertson, S.Backshall
2a. From the stance, pull out rightwards in an impressive position and follow well protected overhanging rock on good almost flattering holds to join the original route above the groove.

7 A Bit on the Side 75m E2 *
S.Boyden, H.Lancashire, 31 Aug 1987
Start at the foot of Maiden's Corner.
1. 30m 4b Climb up rightwards a short distance and traverse the obvious ledge 25m to the foot of a prominent V-groove.
2. 20m 5c Climb the groove and crack on the left to gain slabs. Trend slightly right up a shallow groove.
3. 25m 5b Move left 2m, then up and diagonally right into the base of a corner. Climb this onto easy slabs. Go up and slightly left to a block belay.

8 Continental Drift 90m E2 *
P.Whillance, I.McMullen, 1 Sep 1987
Start as for A Bit on the Side.
1. 30m 4b Same as A Bit on the Side.
2. 10m 5c As for A Bit on the Side but exit left at 10m to a small ledge.
3. 30m 5b Move right onto a ledge system and follow this to where it ends. Step down and continue along a horizontal crack to a good ledge. Move down, across and up into the huge corner.
4. 20m 4c Follow the corner-crack to the top.

9 Hanging Slab 35m S 4a
B.Hall, C.Bonington, 1987
Climb the centre of the slab; also the last pitch of Boat Race. Access it by abseil.

10 Lichen Slab 25m HS 4b
B.Hall, C.Bonington, 1987
Climb the centre of a smaller slab further down the access ramp, right of Hanging Slab. Access it by abseil.

The Right-Hand Side

To the right of the central cave is an impressive vertical wall below the conspicuous clean-cut slab which forms a huge slabby hanging corner. The right edge of the wall forms an arete above a further shallow sea cave as the wall turns into a shallow geo.

Descent: From the grassy bay, follow the rake down and left passing the top of the conspicuous easy-angled slab until near the base and abseil close to the right arete of the crag to small platforms just above the sea.

11 Boat Race 90m E6 ****
D.MacLeod, T.Emmett, 3 Jun 2010
Starts near the left side of the wall at a large horizontal break running leftwards into the heart of the cliff below the impressive vertical wall.
1. 20m 5c Traverse the break leftwards past a hard section to gain a ledge. Belay at the left end.
2. 25m 6a Pull steeply onto the immaculate vertical wall and follow a crack-line and continuation line moving left on perfect gabbro to big ledges and a belay at a basalt dyke.
3. 45m 6a Work up and rightwards following the line of a thin seam in a steep slab above (poorly protected). Committing moves lead to a good ledge. Move left on this and climb an easier big groove through bulges to eventually gain the easy slab; finish up this.

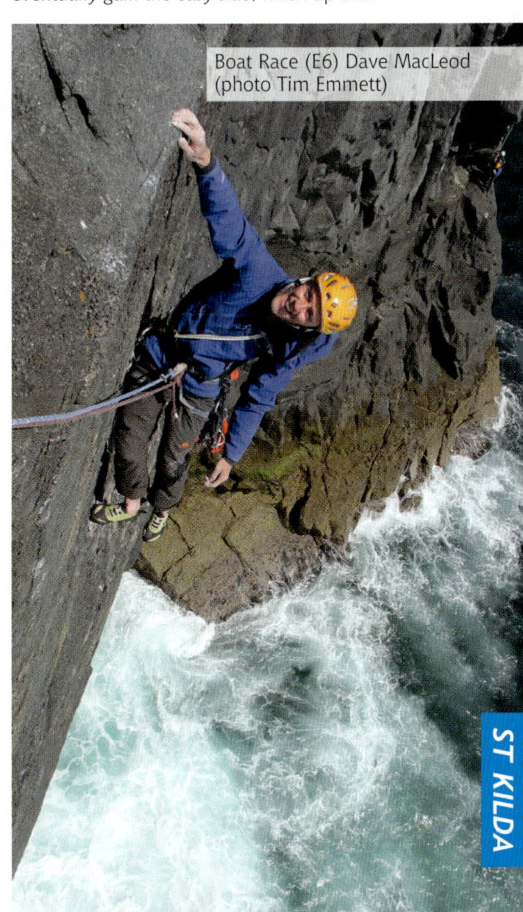
Boat Race (E6) Dave MacLeod (photo Tim Emmett)

12 Old Boy Racer 80m E8 **
D.MacLeod, N.Berry, June 2017
An excellent route on great rock, with a fingery crux roof. Descend by abseil from the lowest ledge on the access ramp, as for Boat Race.
1. 30m 5c Climb good cracks trending leftwards for 20m, before traversing leftwards and stepping slightly down to a hidden ledge below the right end of a long roof system in the wall.
2. 15m 7a Climb up to the roof and traverse left along the break for 5m. Pull through the roof on tiny crimps and make a desperate move left to a large flat sidepull. Gain better holds and gear and move steeply up and back right slightly to a break and a hanging belay (to avoid rope drag).
3. 35m 6b Step up and left into a triangular niche. Climb steeply rightwards out of this to gain a standing position above the overhang. Move back left on slopers to gain good holds and a corner which leads to the easier corner leading up the left edge of the large slab to the top.

13 Making a Splash 75m E7 6c ***
D.MacLeod, N.Berry, June 2017
Superb rock and climbing, snaking a line through the steep, black roofed walls on the right side of the main wall. Descend by abseil from the lowest ledge on the access ramp, as for Boat Race.
1. 30m 5b Start from ledges above the sea and climb the lovely black wall on excellent rock, trending leftwards, before traversing 3m hard right to a belay in a short corner, underneath the huge roof.
2. 20m 6c Step up to the roof and follow the large break left, around the corner to where it dissipates. Arrange gear and continue traversing left with difficulty on edges and poor undercuts in the roof to gain a good undercut (crucial small cam on lip on the left). Reach sidepulls over the lip and make a hard rockover (crux) to gain a distant finger lock in the slab above. Step right to a block and climb the short steep wall directly above this to the large belay ledge.
3. 25m 5c Climb the recess above the ledge and steep flakes above (taking care with a couple of holds) to gain the easier finishing slab.

The Upper Tier

This is the crag to the right of the grassy gully, looking up.

14 Rehab 25m E3 6a **
D.Cuthbertson, S.Backshall, 2010
A worthwhile climb; possibly harder for the vertically challenged. Start beneath an overhang close to the right arete. Awkwardly gain the groove above and, not without some boldness, climb it to better holds and protection where a change in angle is noticeable. Continue via the horizontal breaks above and move slightly right then back left to finish.

RUABHAL THE DUN FACE

Map p454

Round to the right of the main South-West Face opposite Dun is a large sea cave with a clean-cut black slab on its right-hand side.

Descent: From the abseil point for the routes on the right-hand side of the South-West Face, continue down to the foot of the large grass terrace. Scramble or abseil down from its right-hand edge to sea-washed platforms.

15 Blackface 35m HVS 5a **
P.Whillance, 10 Aug 1987
Start 6m right of the huge roof. Climb the slab to a ledge at the right-hand end of the overlap. Pull over leftwards and up the slab via a thin crack to reach a break. Move left and up bubbly rock to where the angle eases. Traverse left below an overhang to regain the terrace.

Further right in the Dun passage is a large grey slab which tapers to become a prominent ridge higher up. The base is best reached by an easy traverse from the right at low tide.

Soay 45m HS 4b *
P.Whillance, 10 Aug 1987
Start below the narrowest point in the overlap. Move up and pull over the overlap on large jugs to gain the slab proper. Follow thin cracks in the slab to join the ridge at the top (several variations possible at Severe to VS).

The Upper Tier

Above Blackface and the large area of grass slope is a black gritstone like buttress seamed with deep cracks.

Old Mens' Dreams 40m S
J.Curran, P.Frost, D.Miller, 5 Sep 1987
Start at the toe of the buttress.
1. 20m 4a Climb the cracks trending left to an obvious stance below overhangs.
2. 20m Exit easily right and climb the upper slab direct to finish.

Two other routes of a similar standard were climbed on this buttress by the same party (6 Sep 1987). A number of short crack-lines on the left-hand side of the Upper Tier were also climbed but do not warrant detailed description.

OISEBHAL, SOUTH FACE

(NF 108 990) Alt 150m S facing Map p454

This is a granite cliff of excellent rock, with well defined groove-lines and good protection. It is located on the hill to the east of the village, set well above the sea and is easily approached by contouring around the hillside. Routes are described from left to right.

The Amazon 40m E2 5b *
M.Mortimer, M.Allen, 14 Sep 1987
This strenuous route takes the groove system on the left-hand side of the crag. Left of the central steep section of the crag, the grass slope steepens to join a gully. Start at the foot of the gully. Climb the gully until it is possible to step right onto the wall to reach a steep groove with a jammed flake. Climb the groove until the angle eases. Step right again to climb the hanging groove strenuously to easy ground. Scrambling remains.

The Harp 40m E3 *
C.Bonington, B.Hall, 5 Sep.1987
To the immediate left of Central Route is another groove-line that peters out about half-way up the crag. The Harp climbs the groove and then breaks out to the left up the line of the arete. Start part way up the grassy gully on the left, below the groove itself.
1. 25m 5c Climb a steep 5m wall to a grass ledge at the foot of the groove. Then climb the left groove which steepens into a bulge near the top. Step right below a small overhang into the continuation of the overhanging crack just to the right of this pitch. Stance on large foothold in the crack.
2. 20m 6a Step back left below the bulge and pull awkwardly round the arete, up for 2m to a line of good holds leading 3m to the left. Move back right with a long reach for a spike to the crest of the arete. Step round to the right, then up and back left pulling back round the arete and up delicately until it is possible to move left to better finishing holds.

Lady Grange 45m E2 *
M.Mortimer, M.Allen, 14 Sep 1987
Interesting and varied with an exciting finish. Start as for The Harp.
1. 30m 5b Go up the steep wall to the foot of the groove. Climb the overhanging crack on the right and the groove above to reach the stance on Central Route.
2. 15m 5c Climb up to the roof, traverse left and climb through the roof on big holds when a metre or so of more delicate climbing leads left to join the finish of The Amazon.

Note: The prominent arete in the centre of the crag was climbed by M.Mortimer, except for the final 3m, and should give an excellent route.

Central Route 45m E2 **
I.McMullen, P.Whillance, 24 Aug 1987
Takes the left-hand of two prominent corner-lines in the centre of the crag.
1. 15m 5c Climb the steep corner past a small overlap and continue to a stance.
2. 30m 5c Continue up the corner-crack to the roof and climb the widening crack with difficulty to reach easier ground. Scramble up to a belay.

Rehab (E3) Dave Cuthbertson (photo Brian Hall)

Making a Splash (E7, p458) Dave MacLeod (photo Chris Prescott / Dark Sky Media)

Right-Hand Corner 45m E1 **
P.Whillance, I.McMullen, 31 Aug 1987
Takes the obvious right-hand corner-line.
1. 25m 5a Bridge up the groove to the start of the crack and climb this to a ledge on the right.
2. 20m 5b Climb the corner-crack to the roof and jam leftwards around this to a sloping ledge. Traverse right and up to a ledge and belay on easy ground.

Botany Bay 45m E1 *
B.Hall, C.Bonington, 8 Sep 1987
Takes a groove line starting from the right-hand side of the bay in the lower part of the face.
1. 30m 5a Climb the groove and two obvious cracked corners until it is possible to pull out left onto a sloping ledge.
2. 15m 5b Step back right into the groove, up to the small triangular overhang and step left, treating a semi-detached flake with great respect. Climb the wall above diagonally right to the bottom of the groove. Up this to the top.

MULLACH BI

SUMMIT CLIFF

(NF 079 994) Alt 250m SW facing Map p454

This is the cliff facing westwards from near the summit. It is reached by traversing grass slopes above the sea from the col near the Lover's Stone.

Rainbow Warrior 90m E1/2 **
S.Boyden, H.Lancashire, 6 Sep 1987
A steep diagonal crack starts just right of centre of the cliff. Start by scrambling right across grass ledges to the crack.
1. 25m 5b Reach the crack by dubious grass tufts and follow it, awkward in its middle section to a ledge.
2. 10m 5b Climb the groove on the left to a crevassed stance.
3. 25m 5b Above on the right is a black-streaked wall. Attain a ledge up on the right, pull into a bottomless right-leaning groove, then go direct up the blank wall, moving left at the top. Easier climbing leads to the large ledge below the final headwall.
4. 30m 5a A crack-line crosses the headwall diagonally up leftwards from the right side of the large ledge. Follow the crack, strenuously at first, to some prominent grass tufts. Pass these carefully and follow the crack more easily to the top.

Nuclear Arms 35m E5
H.Lancashire, S.Boyden, (2 rest points) 7 Sep 1987
An extremely strenuous route; continuously overhanging on its first pitch. Start by abseiling to the big ledge system below the final headwall. Traverse left to the end of the ledge and belay below the shorter left-hand crack splitting the overhanging headwall.
1. 15m 6a Jam the crack, good Friend protection, past the niche and over jammed blocks to a small ledge (one rest below the niche and one above).

2. 20m 5c Step out on to the right arete. Pull up with difficulty on to the slab, then out left on to a ledge and climb an easier slab to finish.

CONACHAIR

NORTH-EAST FACE

(NA 104 005) NE facing Map p454

The grassy hillside to the north of the village rises steeply to the summit of Conachair, the highest hill on Hirta. A promontory extends north-east from the summit and ends in a 1,400ft high vertical wall described by Jim Curran as "strangely reminiscent of the North Face of the Eiger".

Descent: From The Edge of the World cleit, descend the obvious long ridge on the right-hand side of the main face for about 300m, keeping to its grassy northern flank (hand line recommended). From a prominent col in the ridge, an 80m abseil leads down to the slopes at the foot of the face. Alternatively, an inflatable boat is needed.

The Edge of the World 330m E6
P.Whillance, I.McMullen, 15 Sep 1987
Start from shelving slabs about 15m right of the large sea cave.
1. 45m 5b Follow a groove come crack-line in the slab for 20m to a triangular ledge. Traverse left to another groove, then up this past a loose flake to a narrow ledge on the right (3 peg runners, removed).
2. 30m 5c Step back down to the flake and traverse left into a V-groove. Up this and the prominent dyke system above to reach a small ledge in a corner (bolt belay, 3 peg runners, removed).
3. 55m 6b Climb the slab diagonally leftwards for 20m to a rib. Move left for 3m and up a short wall to a peg runner. Step down and go left below a small overhang, then up into a niche below a roof. Move right and climb a short groove, then go steeply leftwards to gain a rib and easier angled rock. Climb the slab to a good ledge and bolt belay (7 peg runners in place).
4. 40m 5b Traverse left into the big corner line and climb this to a large grassy ledge on the right. (Bolt belay, 3 peg runners in place).
5. 30m 6a Climb flakes on the left wall to where they end. Move up the steep wall to a bolt runner and make a long traverse left to reach a big ledge below a prominent groove in the centre of the pink wall. Bolt belay.
6. 40m 5c Climb the slim groove to a break and traverse the ledge leftwards to a good stance and bolt belay (3 peg runners in place).
7. 45m 5b Move up the groove above for a metre or so, then swing left and climb a crack in the left wall to a grass terrace. Go left for 5m, then follow cracks and broken rock to a corner. Up this and exit left to a large ledge.
8. 45m 5c Climb the short overhanging crack above and move up to the corner system which leads to the top.

SOAY (SOAIGH)

(NA 065 015) Map p454

This small island sits 500m off the north-west tip of Hirta and reaches a height of 176m at Cnoc Glas.

NORTH-WEST FACE

This is defined as the stretch of coast between Creagan and Gob a' Ghaill. Mid-way between the two is a smooth 150m wall which drops directly into the sea. The rock is superb and immaculately clean. The large grass platform at the top of this wall is still only halfway up the face itself but the upper section is of little interest to climbers.

Approach: A landing is made on the shelving slabs on the southern side of the Gob a' Ghaill promontory. Scramble up rocks to reach grass slopes, then ascend rightwards and up to a prominent col on the ridge.

Descent: Climb down the opposite side or abseil for 45m to gain a wide ledge system. Follow this for about 200m to the grass platform above the wall. Abseil down close to the left arete to ensure finding belays.

Shipwrecked 105m E2 **
I.McMullen, P.Whillance, 25 Aug 1987
This route takes the left-hand of two obvious crack-lines on the wall, although it was actually started at a good ledge system some 60m above the sea. The missing bottom pitches and the escape line taken on the top pitch were the result of a desperate need to evacuate before an approaching storm!
1. 45m 5c Follow the crack to where it meets the left arete.
2. 15m 5c Step back down and cross the wall on the right, then up leftwards to sloping ledges. Follow the ledges leftwards to below a corner.
3. 45m 5a Take a diagonal line of weakness rightwards until a crack leads to the top.

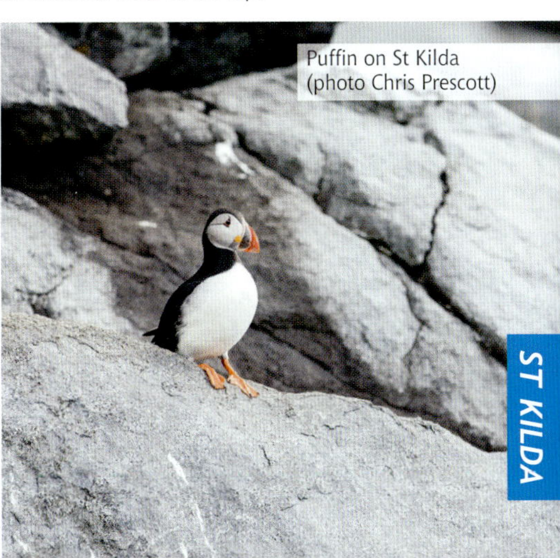
Puffin on St Kilda (photo Chris Prescott)

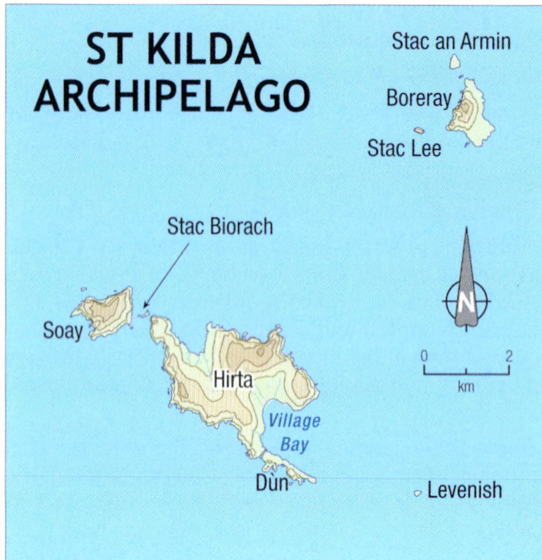

STAC BIORACH

(NA 071 013) Alt 73m Grade unknown

Although this is one of the smaller stacks sitting in the sound between Hirta and Soay it was said to be the hardest of the stacks climbed by the St Kildans. An ascent was first described by Martin Martin in 1697 from accounts told to him by the St Kildans. It requires the use of a thumb for purchase on the crux move and so was described as The Thumb. The first non-native to climb it was Richard Barrington who was guided on it by Donald MacDonald in 1890. The crux is some 20m up.

STAC LEVENISH

(NF 133 966) Alt 62m Grade unknown

A solitary stack about 2.5km south and east of Dun and Hirta. Relatively easy with a harder route up a narrow chimney on the east side. The north face is steeper and more attractive for harder climbs.

The Boreray Group (Boraraigh)

(NA 153 053)

About 7km north-east of Hirta is another island (Boreray) with a collection of satellite stacks which are amongst the most impressive of the archipelago. Boreray (384m) itself is essentially a steep-sided jagged ridge with stunningly precipitous cliffs facing west, and the steepest grass slopes imaginable facing east. There are no recorded climbs. However, its two satellite stacks require some climbing to gain their summits.

STAC LEE

(NA 142 049) Alt 172m S 4a Diagram below

Probably the most impressive of these stacs, jutting from the sea like a shark's fin. It has a vertical wall on the north, an overhanging prow on the east and a slightly less steep south face. The ascent is on the south

STAC LEE
South Face

Landing

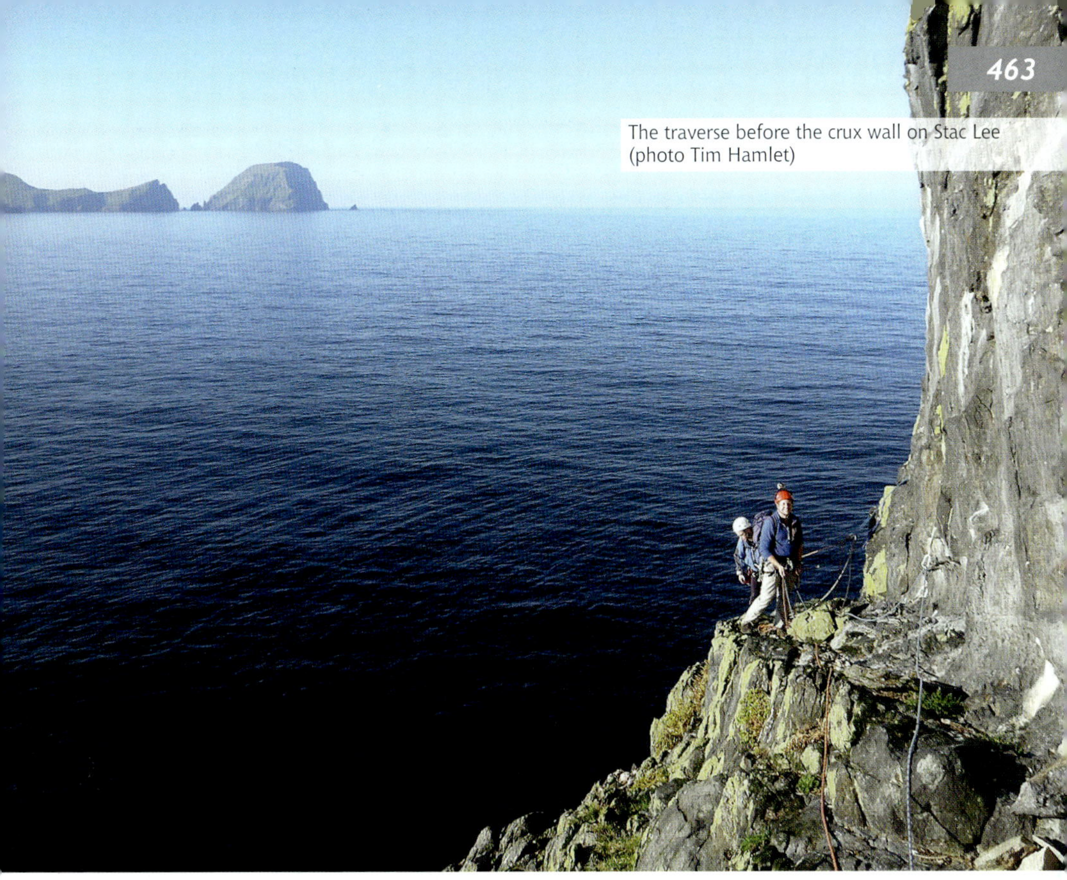

The traverse before the crux wall on Stac Lee (photo Tim Hamlet)

face, where landing is possible onto seaweed-covered slabs at low tide, or alternatively just left (west) of a small shallow geo (Geo Lee) at sea level. The St Kildans lassoed an iron spike and pulled up on the rope to land; this was considered the hardest part of the climb.

1. 20m Once on the stac, negotiate the seaweed (spiked shoes might be helpful) and traverse to the left.
2. 10m A wall blocks access to a friendly ledge that runs up and left. This is essentially a scramble, and leads to the start of the first zigzag ledge.
3. 40m The 'Dyke Pitch'. Follow the ledge up leftwards to its end, at an exposed wall.
4. 4m There is a continuation ledge zigzagging up to the right; gaining it involves an easy but exposed wall.
5. 30m The ledge finishes below another vertical, blank looking wall.
6. 8m 4a This is the crux under normal circumstances: a vertical wall with little in the way of protection. Climb the wall to gain a larger ledge above. There was an in-situ peg below the hardest moves in 2014.
7. 35m The 2m wide Upper Ledge follows, cutting diagonally leftwards across the face. This is easily walked until under a massive overhang, where the ledge reduces to 1m and becomes very exposed. Beyond is a wide platform, where the old 'bothy' can be found.
8. 35m A rubble slope leads to the summit.

Descent: Reverse the ascent as far as the lower end of the Upper ledge; from here abseil down the crux wall. Continue reversing down the lower ledge and the Dyke Pitch with a final abseil to the sea-washed slabs.

STAC AN ARMIN

(NA 151 064) Alt 191m Moderate

Although this is the highest sea stack in the British Isles it is relatively easy. The usual landing place is the south-east corner near a small geo (Am Biran) onto a vertical wall; landing is dependent on sea conditions. An alternative is via the slabs on the south-west corner (Rubha Bhriste) followed by an ascent up easy rock and a traverse across the face to above Am Biran. Either way, the classic route follows the south-east edge of the stack and up a few steep rock bands, to gain a mud and grass slope. This area has a large fulmar colony. At about 100m there is a ruined bothy on a flat terrace. Above this, the easiest ascent is on the south side, leading to a short wall with a large gannet colony mainly on the east face. More short walls follow, before the final section to the summit.

C

Q

U

V

SCOTTISH MOUNTAINEERING CLUB

SCOTTISH MOUNTAINEERING TRUST

Prices were correct at time of publication, but are subject to change

Hillwalkers' Guides

The Munros	£23.00
The Corbetts and Other Scottish Hills	£23.00
The Grahams & The Donalds	£25.00
North-West Highlands	£22.00
Islands of Scotland Including Skye	£20.00
The Cairngorms	£18.00
Central Highlands	£18.00
Southern Highlands	£17.00

Scramblers' Guides

Skye Scrambles	£25.00
Highland Scrambles North	£19.00
Highland Scrambles South	£25.00

Climbers' Guides

The Outer Hebrides	£29.95
Highland Outcrops South	£28.00
Inner Hebrides & Arran	£25.00
Northern Highlands North	£22.00
Northern Highlands Central	£25.00
Northern Highlands South	£25.00
Skye The Cuillin	£25.00
Skye Sea-cliffs & Outcrops	£25.00
The Cairngorms	£25.00
Ben Nevis	£22.00
Glen Coe	£22.00
North-East Outcrops	£22.00
Lowland Outcrops	£22.00
Scottish Winter Climbs	£25.00
Scottish Rock Climbs	£25.00
Scottish Sport Climbs	£28.00

Other Publications

Ben Nevis – Britain's Highest Mountain	£27.50
The Cairngorms – 100 Years of Mountaineering	£27.50
Rising to the Challenge – 100 Years of the LSCC	£24.00
Hostile Habitats – Scotland's Mountain Environment	£17.00
Munro's Tables	£16.00
A Chance in a Million? Avalanches in Scotland	£18.95
The Munroist's Companion	£16.00
Scottish Hill Tracks	£18.00
Scottish Hill Names	£16.00
Mountaineering in Scotland (The Early Years)	£24.00
Mountaineering in Scotland (Years of Change)	£25.00
Ski Mountaineering in Scotland	£18.00

Visit our website for more details and to purchase:
www.smc.org.uk/publications